FOUCAULT LIVE

FOUCAULT LIVE

(INTERVIEWS, 1961–1984)

MICHEL FOUCAULT

Edited by Sylvère Lotringer

Translated by Lysa Hochroth and John Johnston

SEMIOTEXT(E)

Special thanks to Anya Bernstein, Sande Cohen, Jacqueline Desrez,
Mari Fujita, Mari Kelly, Benjamin Meyers, Patricia Moisan,
Daniel Rothman, Dominique Seglard and Thomas Zimmer.

Translation and reprint acknowledgements begin on p. 474.

Semiotext(e) Offices

522 Philosophy Hall
Columbia University
New York, New York 10027 USA

55 South Eleventh Street
POB 568 Williamsburgh Station
Brooklyn, New York 11211 USA

Phone & Fax: 718-963-2603

Printed in the United States of America

CONTENTS

1

MADNESS ONLY EXISTS IN SOCIETY

Q: You have published little up to now besides your remarkable introduction to Binswanger's *Dream and Existence*,[1] where you attempt to show that the dream is as much knowledge as it is an object of knowledge. Suddenly, because of your thesis—*Madness and Civilization*—here you are promoted to the status of a well-known and even famous philosopher.

MF: I was born in 1926 in Poitiers. When I graduated from the Ecole Normale in 1946, I worked with philosophers and also with Jean Delay, who introduced me to the world of the insane.

He has a dialectical smile; he speaks in a tone that apparently aims at instructing, that is, disturbing and reassuring at the same time. His look is a bit distracted, a bit hazy, a bit lost, the archetypal case of the absolute young intellectual: timeless.

MF: But I do not practice psychiatry. What counts for me is the investigation of the very origins of madness. The good conscience of psychiatrists disappointed me.

Q: And how did you get the idea for your thesis?

MF: Colette Duhamel, then an editor at La Table ronde, had asked me for a history of psychiatry. I suggested a book on the relationship between doctors and the insane. The eternal debate between reason and madness.

Q: Any influences?

MF: Most of all, literary works...Maurice Blanchot, Raymond Roussel. What interested me and guided me was a certain presence of madness in literature.

Q: What about psychoanalysis?

MF: You agree that Freud is psychology itself. But in France, psychoanalysis, initially strictly orthodox, has more recently taken on a second and more prestigious life, due, as you know, to Lacan.. .

Q: And it's the second style of psychoanalysis that has most affected you?

MF: Yes. But also, and mainly, Dumézil...

Q: Dumezil? How could a historian of religions inspire work on the history of madness?

MF: Through his idea of structure. Just as Dumézil does with myths, I attempted to discover the structured forms of experience whose pattern can be found, again and again, with modifications, at different levels.

Q: And... what is this structure?

MF: One of social segregation, exclusion. In the Middle Ages, exclusion hit the leper, the heretic. Classical culture excluded by means of the General Hospital, the *Zuchthaus,* the Workhouse, all institutions which were derived from the leper colony. I wanted to describe the modification of a structure of exclusion.

Q: Is it not then a history of confinement that you have written, rather than a history of madness?

MF: In part, yes. Certainly. But I have tried above all to see if there is a relationship between this new form of exclusion and the experience of madness in a world dominated by science and rationalist philosophy.

Q: And does this relationship exist?

MF: Between Racine treating Orestes' delirium, at the end of *Andromache,* and the way a 17th century police lieutenant incarcerating a lunatic or violent person, it's not that there's unity, surely not, but structural coherence.

Q: Is there, then, a philosophy of the history of madness?

MF: Madness can not be found in its raw state. Madness only exists in society, it does not exist outside of the forms of sensibility that isolate it and the forms of repulsion that exclude or capture it. Thus, one can say that in the Middle Ages, then in the Renaissance, madness was present on the social horizon as an aesthetic or daily fact; then in the 17th century—starting with confinement—madness experienced a period of silence, exclusion. It lost its function of manifestation, of revelation, that it had had during the time of Shakespeare and Cervantes (for example, Lady Macbeth begins to tell the truth when she goes mad), it becomes an object of derision, deceitful. Finally, the 20th century gets a handle on madness, reduces it to a natural phenomenon, linked to the truth of the world. From this positivist repossession, there derived on one hand, condescending philanthropy, which all psychiatry manifests with regard to the insane person and on the other, a great lyrical protest that can be found in poetry from Nerval to Artaud, which is an effort to give back a depth and power of revelation to the experience of madness which had been annhilated through confinement.

Q: Is madness then worth more than reason?

Michel Foucault smiles, ever so indulgently.

MF: One of the objections of my dissertation jury was that I had tried to do a remake of *In Praise of Madness.* No, I meant, however, that madness has only become an object of science to the extent that it has been robbed of its ancient powers...But as far as making an apology for madness, in and of itself, no. Each culture, after all, has the madness it deserves. And if Artaud is crazy, and the psychiatrists allowed him to be confined, it is already a beautiful thing, and the most beautiful praise that one could give...

Q: Surely not to madness?

MF: No, to psychiatrists.

Translated by Lysa Hochroth

------

[1] Foucault and Binswager, *Dream and Existence.* Seattle, Washington: Review of Existential Philosophy and Psychiatry (V. 19, No. 1)

2

ANDRÉ BRETON:
A LITERATURE OF KNOWLEDGE

Q: For a philosopher in 1966 who investigates language and knowledge, what do André Breton and surrealism represent?

MF: It seems to me that there are two great families of founders. There are those who build, who lay the first stone, and there are those who dig and hollow out. Perhaps, in our uncertain space, we are closer to those who hollow out, closer to Nietzsche rather than Husserl, to Klee rather than Picasso. Breton belongs to this family. To be sure, the "institution" of surrealism has masked these great silent gestures that opened the space in front of them. Perhaps the surrealist "game," the surrealist mystification, was only this: to open by rites that appeared to exclude, to make the desert grow by imposing apparently imperious limits. In any case, we are now in the hollowed space left behind by Breton.

Q: It would already be old?

MF: A long time ago I saw Breton's image, like that of a dead person's: not that it had ceased to be living or to concern us, but rather his admirable existence created around his image and starting from it an immense emptiness in which we are today lost. It seems to me that we have lived, walked, run, dansed, made signs and gestures without response in the sacred space surrounding the shrine of a Breton stretched out and immobile, dressed in gold. That's not to say that he was far from us, but that we were close to him, under the power of his black scepter. Breton's death, today, is like the doubling of our own birth. His is an all-powerful death, very close to us, like Agamemnon's death was for the House of Atreus (that is, for every Greek). There you have Breton's silhouette, as I see it.

Q: Breton's quasi-sacred presence and this hollow left by surrealism don't stem from magic or the imagination but assume an essential contribution to contemporary thought. What does the latter owe to Breton?

MF: The most important thing for me is that Breton made the two figures of writing and knowledge —for a long time strangers to one another— fully communicate. French literature, before Breton, could easily be woven with observations, analyses, and ideas, but it was never —except in the work of Diderot— a literature of knowledge. That's the great difference, I believe, between German and French culture. In accomodating knowledge to expression (with psychoanalysis, anthropology, the history of art, etc.), Breton is a little like our Goethe. There is one image, I believe, that ought to be effaced: that of Breton as the poet of unreason. We ought not to oppose it, but superimpose upon it the image of Breton as the writer of knowledge.

But this leave given to literature as a savorous ignorance (in the manner of Gide) is affirmed in a very singular way in Breton. For the Germans (Goethe, Thomas Mann, Herman Broch) literature is knowledge when it is an undertaking of interiorization and memory. It's a question of making a calm and exhaustive recollection of knowledge [*connaissance*], of appropriating the world and taking its measure in relation to humanity. For Breton, writing made into knowledge (and knowledge made into writing) is on the contrary a way of pushing it outside of its limits, of forcing it to the brink, of putting it in the closest proximity to what is most distant from it. This accounts for Breton's interest in the unconscious, madness, and dreams.

Q: Like the German Romantics?

MF: Yes, but the German Romantics' dream is the night clarified by the light of awakening, whereas the dream for Breton is the unshatterable kernel of night at the heart of the day. It seems to me that this beautiful abolition of the division between knowledge and writing has been very important for contemporary expression. We are living precisely at a time when writing and knowledge are entangled, as the work of Michel Leiris, Pierre Klossowski, Michel Butor and Jean-Pierre Faye bear witness.

Q: Isn't there, for Breton, the power of writing?

MF: For Breton, I believe, writing in itself, the book in its white flesh, have the power to change the world. Until the end of the nineteenth century language and writing were transparent instruments in which the world came to be reflected, decomposed and recomposed; but in any case language and discourse were part of the world. But perhaps there is a writing so radical and sovereign that it faces the world, equilibrates it, compensates for it, even destroys it absolutely and scintillates outside it. In fact, this experience begins to appear rather clearly in *Ecce Homo* and in Mallarmé. One finds in Breton this experience of the book as anti-world, and it contributes strongly to changing the status of writing. And in two ways: first, Breton somehow re-moralizes writing by demoralizing it completely. The ethic of writing no longer comes from what one has to say, from ideas that one expresses, but from the very act of writing. In this raw and exposed act, the whole liberty of the writer finds itself engaged at the same time that a counter-universe of words is born.

Moreover, at the same time that writing is re-moralized it begins to exist in a sort of rock-like solidity. It imposes itself from outside of all that can be said through it. Hence, no doubt, Breton's rediscovery of the whole dynasty of the imagination that French literature had gotten rid of: the imagination, it's less what is born in the obscure heart of man than what surges up in the luminous thickness of discourse. And Breton, swimmer among words, traverses an imaginary space that had never been discovered before him.

Q: But how do you explain the fact that for certain periods Breton was preoccupied with political engagements?

MF: I have always been struck by the fact that what is in question in his work is not history but the revolution; not politics, but the absolute power to change one's life. The profound incompatibility between Marxists and existentialists of the Sartrian type on the one hand and Breton on the other comes no doubt from the fact that for Marx or Sartre writing is part of the world, whereas for Breton a book, a sentence, a word—those things alone constitute the anti-matter of the world and can compensate for the whole universe.

Q: But doesn't Breton give as much importance to life as to writing? In *Nadja*, *Mad Love*, and *The Communicating Vases*, isn't there a kind of permanent osmosis between writing and life, between life and writing?

MF: Whereas Breton's other discoveries were already at least announced in Goethe, Nietzsche, Mallarmé and others, what one really owes to him in particular is the discovery of a space which is not that of philosophy, nor that of literature, nor that of art, but which would be that of "experience." Today we live in an age in which experience —and the thought that it is inextricably part of— develops with an unheard of richness, at once in a unity and a dispersion that cancels the frontiers of outer regions established in the past.

The whole network that traverses the works of Breton, Bataille, Leiris, and Blanchot, that traverses the domains of anthropology, the history of art, the history of religion, linguistics, and psychoanalysis, cleanly wipes away the old rubrics in which our culture classified itself and made relationships, associations and unforseen connections appear before our eyes. It is highly probable that we owe this new dispersal and this new unity of our culture to the person and work of André Breton. He has simultaneously dispersed and shepherded the whole flecked surface of modern experience.

This discovery of the domain of experience permitted Breton to be completely outside of "literature," and to be able to contest not only all literary works already in existence but also the very existence of literature. But it also permitted him to open to possible languages domains that had heretofore remained silent and marginal.

Translated by John Johnston

3

THE ORDER OF THINGS

Q: How is *The Order of Things* related to *Madness and Civilization?*

MF: *Madness and Civilization,* roughly speaking, was the history of a division, the history above all of a certain break that every society found itself obliged to make. On the other hand, in this book I wanted to write a history of order, to state how a society reflects upon resemblances among things and how differences between things can be mastered, organized into networks, sketched out according to rational schemes. *Madness and Civilization* is the history of difference, *The Order of Things* the history of resemblance, sameness, and identity.

Q: The book's sub-title once again includes this word "archeology." It appeared in the sub-title of *The Birth of the Clinic* and again in the Preface to *Madness and Civilization.*

MF: By archeology I would like to designate not exactly a discipline, but a domain of research, which would be the following: In a society, different bodies of learning, philosophical ideas, everyday opinions, but also institutions, commercial practices and police activities, mores—all refer to a certain implicit knowledge (*savoir*) special to this society.[1] This knowledge is profoundly different from the bodies of learning that one can find in scientific books, philosophical theories, and religious justifications, but it is what makes possible at a given moment the appearance of a theory, an opinion, a practice. Thus, in order for the big centers of internment to be opened at the end of the 17th century, it was necessary that a certain knowledge of madness be opposed to non-madness, of order to disorder, and it's this knowledge that I wanted to investigate, as the condition of possibility of knowledge (*connaissance*), of institutions, of practices.

This style of research has for me the following interest: it allows me to avoid every problem concerning the anteriority of theory in relation to practice, and the reverse. In fact, I deal with practices, institutions and theories on the same plane and according to the same isomorphisms, and I look for the underlying knowledge (*savoir*) that makes them possible, the stratum of knowledge that constitutes them historically. Rather than try to explain this knowledge from the point of view of the practico-inert, I try to formulate an analysis from the position of what one could call the "theoretico-active."[2]

Q: You find yourself therefore confronting a double problem: of history and formalization.

MF: All these practices, then, these institutions and theories, I take at the level of traces, that is, almost always at the level of verbal traces. The ensemble of these traces constitutes a sort of domain considered to be homogeneous: one doesn't establish any differences *a priori*. The problem is to find common traits between these traces of orders different enough to constitute what logicians call classes, aestheticians call forms, men of science call structures, and which are the invariants common to a certain number of traces.

Q: How have you raised the problem of choice and non-choice?

MF: I will say that in fact there should not be any privileged choice. One should be able to read everything, to know all the institutions and all the practices. None of the values traditionally recognized in the history of ideas and philosophy should be accepted as such. One is dealing with a field that will ignore the differences and traditionally important things. Which means that one will take up *Don Quixote,* Descartes, and a decree by Pomponne de Belierre about houses of internment in the same stroke. One will perceive that the grammarians of the 18th century have as much importance as the recognized philosophers of the same period.

Q: It is in this sense that you say, for example, that Cuvier and Ricardo have taught you as much or more than Kant and Hegel. But then the question of information becomes the pressing one: how do you read everything?

MF: One can read all the grammarians, and all the economists. For *The Birth of the Clinic* I read every medical work of importance for the methodology of the period 1780–1820. The choices that one could make are inadmissable, and shouldn't exist. One ought to read everything, study everything. In other words, one must have at one's disposal the general archive of a period at a given moment. And archeology is, in a strict sense, the science of this archive.

Q: What determines the choice of historic period (here, as in *Madness and Civilization,* you go from the Renaissance to the present), and its relationship with the "archeological" perspective that you adopt?

MF: This kind of research is only possible as the analysis of our own sub-soil. It's not a defect of these retrospective disciplines to find their point of departure in our own actuality. There can be no doubt that the problem of the division between reason and unreason became possible only with Nietzsche and Artaud. And it's the sub-soil of our modern consciousness of madness that I have wanted to investigate. If there were not something like a fault line in this soil archeology would not have been possible or necessary. In the same way, if the question of meaning and of the relation between meaning and the sign had not appeared in European culture with Freud, Saussure[3] and Husserl, it is obvious that it would not have been necessary to investigate the sub-soil of our consciousness of meaning. In the two cases these are the critical analyses of our own condition.

Q: What has brought you to adopt the three axes that orient your whole analysis?

MF: Roughly this. The human sciences that have appeared since the end of the 19th century are caught as it were in a double obligation, a double and simultaneous postulation: that of hermeneutics, interpretation, or exegesis: one must understand a hidden meaning; and the other: one must formalize, discover the system, the structural invariant, the network of simultaneities. Yet these two questions seemed to confront each other in a privileged fashion in the human sciences, to the point that one has the impression that it is necessary that they be one or the other, interpretation or formalization. What I understood was precisely the archeological research of what had made this ambiguity possible. I wanted to find the branch that bore this fork. Thus I had to respond to a double question concerning the classic period: that of the theory of signs, and that of the empirical order, of the constitution of empirical orders.

It appeared to me that in fact the classical age, usually considered as the age of the radical mechanization of nature, of the mathematization of the living, was in reality something entirely different, that there existed a very important domain that included general grammar, natural history and the analysis of wealth; and that this empirical domain is based on the project of an ordering of things, and this thanks not to mathematics and geometry but to a systematics of signs, a sort of general and systematic taxonomy of things.

Q: It's thus a return to the classical age that has determined the three axes. How then is the passage in these three domains from the classical age to the 19th century effected?

MF: It revealed one thing that came to me as a complete surprise: that man didn't exist within classical knowledge (*savoir*). What existed in the place where we now discover man was the power special to discourse, to the verbal order, to represent the order of things. In order to study the grammar or the system of wealth, there was no need to pass through a human science, but through discourse.

Q: Yet, apparently, if ever a literature seemed to speak of man, it was our literature of the 17th century.

MF: Insofar as what existed in classical knowledge were representations ordered in a discourse, all the notions that are fundamental for our conception of man, like those of life, work, and language, had no basis in that period, and no place.

At the end of the 17th century, discourse ceased to play the organizing role that it had in classical knowledge. There was no longer any transparence between the order of things and the representations that one could have of them; things were folded somehow onto their own thickness and onto a demand exterior to representation, and it's for this reason that languages with their history, life with its organization and its autonomy, and work with its own capacity for production appeared. In the face of that, in the lacuna left by discourse, man constituted himself, a man who is as much one who lives, who speaks and who works, as one who experiences life, language and work, as one finally who can be known to the extent that he lives, speaks and works.

Q: Against this background how does our situation today present itself?

MF: At the moment we find ourselves in a very ambiguous situation. Man has existed since the beginning of the 19th century only because discourse ceased to have the force of law over the empirical world. Man has existed where discourse was silenced. Yet with Saussure, Freud and Hegel, at the heart of what is most fundamental in the knowledge of man, the problem of meaning and the sign reappeared. Now one can wonder if this return of the great problem of the sign and meaning, of the order of signs, constitutes a kind of superimposition in our culture over what had constituted the classical age and modernity, or rather if it's a question of omens announcing that man is disappearing, since until the present the order of man and that of signs have in our culture been incompatible with each other. Man would die from the signs that were born in him—that's what Nietzsche, the first one to see this, meant.

Q: It seems to me that this idea of an incompatability between the order of signs and the order of man must have a certain number of consequences.

MF: Yes. For example: 1. It makes an idle fancy of the idea of a science of man that would be at the same time an analysis of signs. 2. It announces the first deterioration in European history of the anthropological and humanist episode that we experienced in the 19th century, when one thought that the sciences of man would be at the same time the liberation of man, of the human being in his plenitude. Experience has shown that in their development the human sciences lead to the disappearance of man rather than to his apotheosis. 3. Literature, whose status changed in the 19th century when it ceased to belong to the order of discourse and became the manifestation of language in its thickness, must no doubt now assume another status, is assuming another status, and the hesitation that it manifests between the vague humanisms and the pure formalism of language is no doubt only one of the manifestations of this phenomenon that is fundamental for us and which makes us oscillate between interpretation and formalization, man and signs.

Q: Thus one sees clearly the great determinations of French literature since the classical age take form; in particular, the scheme that leads from a first humanism, that of Romanticism, to Flaubert, then to this literature of the subject embodied in the generation of the *Nouvelle Revue Française,* to the new humanism of before and after the war, and today to the formation of the *nouveau roman.* Yet German literature holds this kind of evolutionary scheme in check, however one envisages it.

MF: Perhaps insofar as German classicism was contemporary with this age of history and interpretation, German literature found itself from its origins in this confrontation that we are experiencing today. That would explain why Nietzsche didn't do anything but become aware of this situation, and now he's the one who serves as a light for us.

Q: That would explain why he can appear throughout your book as the exemplary figure, the non-archeologizable subject (or not yet), since it is starting from what he opened that the question is raised in all its violence.

MF: Yes, he is the one who through German culture understood that the rediscovery of the dimension proper to language is incompatible with man. From that point Nietzsche has taken a prophetic value for us. And then, on the other hand, it is necessary to condemn with the most complete severity all the attempts to dull the problem. For example, the use of the most familiar notions of the 18th century, the schemes of resemblance and contiguity, all of that which is used to build the human sciences, to found them, all that appears to me to be a form of intellectual cowardice that serves to confirm what Nietzsche signified to us for almost a century, that where there is a sign, there man cannot be, and that where one makes signs speak, there man must fall silent.

What appears to me to be deceiving and naive in reflections on and analyses of signs is that one supposes them to be always already there, deposited on the figure of the world, or constituted by men, and that one never investigates their being. What does it mean, the fact that there are signs and marks of language? One must pose the problem of the being of language as a task, in order not to fall back to a level of reflection which would be that of the 18th century, to the level of empiricism.

Q: One thing in your book struck me very sharply: the perfect singularity of its position towards philosophy, the philosophical tradition and history on the one hand, and on the other towards the history of ideas, methods and concepts.

MF: I was shocked by the fact that there existed on one side a history of philosophy which gave itself as a privileged object the philosophical edifices that the tradition signaled as important (at the very most it meant accepting, since it was a little trendy, that it had to do with the birth of industrial capitalism), and on the other side a history of ideas, that is to say sub-philosophies, which took for their privileged object the texts of Montesquieu, Diderot or Fontenelle.

If one adds to that the histories of the sciences, one cannot fail to be struck by the impossibility for our culture to raise the problem of the history of its own thought. It's why I have tried to make, obviously in a rather particular style, the history not of thought in general but of all that "contains thought" in a culture, of all in which there is thought. For there is thought in philosophy, but also in a novel, in jurisprudence, in law, in an administrative system, in a prison.

Translated by John Johnston

----

[1] In the case of Foucault's use of the terms *savoir* and *connaissance,* I have retained the French in parentheses in order to preserve a distinction not available in English. (Trans.)

[2] The "practico-inert" is a historical category developed by Jean-Paul Sartre in *Critique of Dialectical Reason* (Atlantic Highlands, New Jersey, Humanities Press: 1976). The practico-inert field is a structure that unifies individuals from without (e.g., common interest).[Ed.]

[3] Ferdinand de Saussure's *Course in General Linguistics* (New York: McGraw-Hill, 1966), first published in 1916, is at the origin of the modern science of signs, or semiotics.[Ed.]

4

THE DISCOURSE OF HISTORY

Q: The double reception given to your book—critical and public, enthusiastic and reticent—prompts a follow-up interview to the one you gave more than a year ago, where you laid out the nature and the scope of your research. Which appears to you to be the most striking reaction to *The Order of Things?*

MF: I was struck by the following fact: professional historians recognized it as a work of history, and many others, who think of history as an old idea and no doubt feel it to be very outmoded today, cried out at the murder of history.

Q: Does it not seem to you that the form of the book—I mean by that as much the absence of detailed notes and bibliographies, accumulated and acknowledged references, customary for this kind of work, as the mirror play constituted by *Las Meninas* and your style itself—has not this form helped to mask its nature?

MF: No doubt the presentation of the book is not indifferent to these things, but above all I believe that certain people are ignorant of the very important mutation in historical knowledge (*savoir*) already more than twenty years old. One knows that the books of Dumézil,[1] Lévi-Strauss and Lacan count among the major books of our time, but is it similarly known that, among the works that assure a new adventure in knowledge today, one must put the books of Braudel, Furet and Denis Richet, Leroy-Ladurie, the research of the Cambridge historical school and of the Soviet school?[2]

Q: You thus situate yourself deliberately as an historian. To what do you attribute this ignorance?

MF: History, I believe, has become the object of a curious sacralization. For many intellectuals, a distant respect for history, uninformed and traditionalist,

19

was the simplest way of reconciling their political conscience and their activity as researchers or writers. Under the sign of the cross of history, every discourse became a prayer to the God of just causes. There is a more technical reason. One must recognize that in domains like linguistics, anthropology, history of religion and sociology, the concepts, formed in the 19th century and of a dialectical order, one can say, have been for the most part abandoned. Yet, in the eyes of certain people, history as a discipline constituted the last refuge of the dialectical order: in it one could save the reign of rational contradiction. Thus, for these two reasons and against all likelihood, a conception of history was organized on the narrative model as a great sequence of events caught up in a hierarchy of determinations: individuals are grasped at the interior of this totality which transcends them and plays with them but of which they are perhaps at the same time the badly conscious authors. To the point that this history, simultaneously an individual project and a totality, has for some become untouchable: to refuse such a form of historical statement would be to attack the great cause of the revolution.

Q: The novelty of the historical works you allude to consists in what exactly?

MF: One can characterize them a little schematically as follows:

1. These historians are posing the very difficult problem of periodization. They have perceived that the manifest periodization highlighted by political revolutions was not always methodologically the best way possible to mark things out.

2. Each periodization marks out in history a certain level of events, and, inversely, each layer of events calls for its own periodization. There lies a delicate set of problems, since, according to the level one chooses, one will have to delimit different periodizations, and according to the periodization that one is given, one will attain different levels. Thus one accedes to a complex methodology of discontinuity.

3. The old traditional opposition between the human sciences and history (the first studying the synchronic and the non-evolutionary, the second analyzing the dimension of ceaseless great changes) disappears; change can be the object of analysis in terms of structure, and historical discourse is populated with analyses borrowed from ethnology, sociology, and the human sciences.

4. One introduces into historical analysis many more types of relationship and modes of linkage than the universal relation of causality through which one had formerly wanted to define historical method.

Thus, for the first time perhaps, one has the possibility of analyzing as an object a set of materials which have been deposited in the course of time in the form of signs, traces, institutions, practices and works, etc. In all these changes there are two essential manifestations:

(a) On the historians' side, the works of Braudel, the Cambridge school, the Russian school, etc.

(b) The very remarkable critique and analysis of the notion of history developed by Althusser at the beginning of *Reading Capital*.[3]

Q: Thus you mark a direct kinship between your works and those of Louis Althusser?

MF: Having been his student and owing him much, perhaps I tend to place under his sign an effort that he might challenge, so much that I can't respond to what concerns him. But all the same, I would say: open Althusser's books. There remains, however, between Althusser and myself, an obvious difference: he employs the word epistemological break in relation to Marx, while I affirm that Marx does not represent such a break.[4]

Q: Is not this difference over Marx precisely the most manifest sign of what has appeared to be arguable in your analysis of the structural mutations of knowledge (*savoir*) in the course of the 19th century?

MF: What I said *a propos* of Marx concerns the precise epistemological domain of political economy. Whatever the importance of the modifications Marx brings to Ricardo's analysis, I do not believe that his economic analyses escape the epistemological space inaugurated by Ricardo. On the other hand, one can suppose that Marx introduced into the historical and political consciousness of men a radical break and that the Marxist theory of society inaugurated an entirely new epistemological field.

My book bears the sub-title "An archeology of the human sciences": that itself supposes another, which would be precisely the analysis of knowledge (*savoir*) and of historical consciousness in the West since the 16th century. And even before having advanced very far in this work, it seemed to me that the great break has to be situated at the level of Marx. Here we are led back to what I was saying earlier: the periodization of domains of knowledge (*connaissance*) cannot be made in the same way according to the levels where one is positioned. One finds oneself before a kind of superimposition of bricks and the interesting thing, the strange and curious thing, will be to know precisely how and why the epistemological break for the life sciences, economy and language is situated at the beginning of the 19th century, and at the middle of the 19th century for the theory of history and politics.

Q: But that means breaking deliberately with the tendency to privilege history as the harmonic science of the totality as the Marxist tradition transmits it to us.

MF: In my opinion this widespread idea is not really to be found in Marx. But I will respond, since in this domain where one is still only broaching possible principles, it is still way too early to pose the problem of the reciprocal determinations of these layers. It is not at all impossible that one can discover forms of determination such that all the levels line up and move together in a great regimented step on the bridge of historical progress. But that's only an hypothesis.

Q: In the articles that attack your book the words "to freeze history" return like a *leitmotif* and seem to formulate the more fundamental accusation, which puts into question as much your conceptual scheme as the narrative technique it implies, in fact the very possibility, as you intend to do it, of formulating a logic of mutation. What do you think of this objection?

MF: In what is called the history of ideas one describes change in general by making things easy in two ways:

(1) One uses concepts which appear to me to be a little magical, like influence, crisis, the realizationof something (*la prise de conscience*), the interest taken in a problem, etc. All utilitarian, they do not appear to me to be operating.

(2) When one encounters a difficulty, one goes from the level of analysis which is that of the statements themselves to another which is exterior to it. Thus, when confronted with a change, a contradiction or an incoherence, one resorts to an explanation in terms of social conditions, mentality, vision of the world, etc.

I wanted, through a methodological move, to do without all that; consequently, I have tried to describe statements, entire groups of statements, by making the relations of implication, of opposition and exclusion which could link them appear.

I am told for example that I have admitted or invented an absolute break between the end of the 18th century and the beginning of the 19th. In fact, when one carefully examines the scientific discourse of the end of the 18th century, one notices a very rapid and in truth a very enigmatic change. I wanted to describe this change very precisely, in other words to establish the transformations necessary and sufficient for passing from the initial form of scientific discourse, that of the 18th century, to its final form, that of the 19th. The set for transformations that I have defined maintains a certain number of theoretical elements, displaces others, sees old ones disappear and new ones arise; all that allows me to define the rule of passage in the domains I have focused upon. What I have wanted to establish is the very contrary of a discontinuity, since I have made manifest the very form of passage from one state to another.

Q: I wonder if the equivocation doesn't derive from the difficulty of thinking side by side the terms of the change and passage on the one hand, and the picture and the description on the other.

MF: All the same, it's been more than fifty years since we perceived that the task of description was essential in domains like those of history, ethnology and language. After all, mathematical language since Galileo and Newton doesn't function as an explanation of nature but as a description of a process. I don't see why one should contest the attempt of non-formalized disciplines like history to undertake for themselves the first task of description.

Q: How do you conceive the methodological orientation of this first task?

MF: (1) One must be able, if what I have said is true, to account for and analyze exactly the texts I've discussed according to the same schemes by bringing to them several supplementary transformations.

(2) One can very well reconsider these texts, and the material itself that I have treated, in a description that would have another periodization and would be situated at another level. When one makes an archeology of historical knowledge (*savoir*) for example, it will be necessary to utilize again the texts on language and to relate them to exegetical techniques, the criticism of sources, and to all knowledge concerning the holy scriptures and the historic tradition; their description will then be different. But these descriptions, if they are exact, must be such that one can define the transformations that permit one to pass from one to the other.

In one sense description is infinite, in another it is closed, to the extent that it tends to establish a theoretical model capable of accounting for relations that exist between the discourse studied.

Q: It would seem that it is this double character of description that creates the reticence or the bewilderment, since history finds itself at once directly grafted onto the infinity of its archives, therefore onto the non-sense proper to every infinity, and mastered in the models whose formal character challenges inherent to the non-sense every closure. And the effect is all the more powerful as your book observes an absolute distance towards what one could call "living history," where the practice, turns the non-sense into a sort of familiarity in a "natural" world of actions and institutions. How do you understand this break on which *The Order of Things* is established?

MF: I wanted to engage in a rigorous description of the statements themselves, and it appeared to me that the domain of statements very much obeyed certain formal laws, that one could for example discover a single theoretical model for different epistemological domains and, in this sense, infer an autonomy of discouse. But there is no reason for describing this autonomous layer of discourse except to the extent that one can relate it to other layers, practices, institutions, social and political relations, etc. It is this relationship that has always haunted me. Both in *Madness and Civilization* and *The Birth of the Clinic* I precisely wanted to define the different relationships between these various domains. For example, I took the epistemological domain of medicine but also of the institutions of repression, of hospitalization, of aid to the unemployed, of administrative control over public health, etc. I perceived that things were more complicated than I had believed in the first two works, that the discursive domains didn't always obey the structures that had common practical domains and associated institutions; on the other hand, they obeyed structures common to other epistemological domains, there was something like an isomorphism of discourses for a given period. One finds oneself before two axes of perpendicular description: theoretical models common to several discourses, and relationships between a discursive domain and a non-discursive domain. In *The*

Order of Things I traversed the horizontal axis; in *Madness and Civilization* and *The Birth of the Clinic* the vertical dimension of the figure.

For the first, let someone show me, using texts as a basis, that such a theoretical coherence among discourses doesn't exist and a real discussion could begin. As for minimizing the domain of practice, my preceding books are there to show that I am far from doing that; for their relationship I'll refer to an illustrative example. When Dumézil demonstrates that the Roman religion has an isomorphic relationship with Scandinavian or Celtic legends or some Iranian rite, he doesn't mean that Roman religion doesn't have its place within Roman history, that the history of Rome doesn't exist, but that one cannot describe the history of Roman religion, its relationships with institutions, social classes and economic conditions except by taking into account its internal morphology. In the same way, to demonstrate that the scientific discourses of a period stem from a common theoretical model does not mean that they escape history and float in the air as if disembodied and isolated, but that one cannot write the history and analyze the functioning of the role of this knowledge (*savoir*), the conditions that give rise to it, and the manner in which it is rooted in the society without taking into account the force and consistency of these isomorphisms.

Q: This objectivity that you grant theoretical models in view of extensively analyzing history as a science and, for the constitution of these models, the descriptive logic as such, obliges us to investigate the point of departure of this description, its source in some sense. In the case of a book as personal as yours this amounts to trying to understand the relationship of the author and his text, exactly what place it can, wants to, and must occupy.

MF: I can't respond to that without plunging into the book itself. If the style of analysis that I tried to formulate in it is admissible, one should be able to define the theoretical model to which not only my book, but those which belong to the same configuration of knowledge (*savoir*) also belong. No doubt it is one that permits us today to treat history as a set of statements actually articulated, to treat language as an object of description and as a set of relationships in reference to discourse and to statements which make up the object of interpretation. It is our period and it alone that makes possible the appearance of this set of texts that treat grammar, natural history and political economy as so many objects.

So much so in fact that the author, in that and only in that, constitutes that of which he speaks. My book is a pure and simple "fiction": it's a novel, but it's not I who invented it; it is the relationship between our period and its epistemological configuration and this mass of statements. The subject is indeed present in the totality of the book, but he is the anonymous "one" who speaks today in all that is said.

Q: How do you understand the status of this anonymous "one"?

MF: Perhaps we are undoing little by little, and not without great difficulty, the great distrust in allegory. By that I mean the simple idea of demanding from a text nothing but what the text *truly* says beneath what it *really* says. No doubt that's the heritage of an ancient exegetical tradition: underneath everything said, we suspect that another thing is being said. The lay version of this allegorical mistrust has had the effect of assigning to every commentator the task of discovering everywhere the true thought of the author, what he said without saying it, meant without succeeding to say it, wanted to hide and yet allowed to appear. One perceives that today there are many other possibilities for dealing with language. Thus the contemporary critic—and this is what distinguishes him from what was done still very recently—is formulating, according to the diverse texts that he studies, his object-texts, a sort of new combinatory. Instead of reconstituting its immanent secret, he grasps the text as a set of elements (words, metaphors, literary forms, a set of narratives) among which one can make absolutely new relations appear insofar as they have not been mastered by the writer's project and are made possible only through the work as such. The formal relations that one thus discovers were not present in the mind of anyone, they do not constitute the latent content of statements, their indiscreet secret; they are a construction, but an exact construction as long as the relations thus described can actually be assigned to the materials treated. We have learned to put the words of men into yet unformulated relationships stated by us for the first time, and yet objectively exact.

Thus contemporary critics are abandoning the great myth of interiority: *intimior intimio ejus.* They find themselves totally displaced from the old themes of locked enclosures, of the treasure in the box that he habitually sought in the depth of the work's container. Placing themseles outside the text, they constitute a new exterior for it, writing texts out of texts.

Q: In terms of that description it seems to me that modern literary criticism, in its very richness and multiple contributions, is guilty of a curious regression in relation to one in whom it found the essential of its demands: I mean Maurice Blanchot. For if Blanchot, under the name of "Literature," actually won for the space of modern thought the imperious exteriority of the text, in no way did he attribute to himself this facility that tends to avoid the violence of the work as place of the name and of a biography whose secret, precisely, is to be diversely traversed by the irreducible and abstract force of literature. Its vigorous itinerary Blanchot retraces, in each case, without caring to describe it as such in the logic of its forms, as a more learned critic would want to.

MF: It's true that it is Blanchot who has made all discourse on literature possible. First of all because he's the one who has shown above all that works are linked to one another through this exterior face of their language where "literature" appears. Literature is thus what constitutes the outside of every work, what ploughs up every written language and leaves on every text an empty claw mark. It is not a mode of language, but a hollow that traverses like a great movement all literary languages. By making this instance of literature appear as a "common place," an empty space where works come to lodge themselves, I believe that he has assigned to the contemporary critic what must be his object, what makes his work both of exactitude and invention possible.

One can affirm, on the other hand, that Blanchot has made it possible by instituting between the author and the work a mode of relationship that had remained unsuspected. We now know that the work does not belong to the author's project, nor even to the one of his existence. It maintains with him relationships of negation and destruction, it is for him the flowing of an eternal outside, and yet there exists beween them this primordial function of the name. It is through the name that in a work a modality irreducible to the anonymous murmur of all other languages is marked. It is certain that the contemporary literary critic has not yet really investigated this existence of the name that Blanchot has proposed for him. He really ought to deal with it, since the name marks for the work its relations of opposition, of difference with other works, and since it characterizes absolutely the mode of being of the literary work in a culture and in institutions like ours. After all, it's now been five or six centuries since the anonymous, apart from exceptional cases, has disappeared completely from literary language.

Q: It's for that reason, I think, that the lesson of Blanchot, compared with the technical critiques towards which he maintains an equal distance, finds a more accurate echo in an interpretation of the psychoanalytic type, which maintains itself by definition in the space of the subject, than in the linguistic type of interpretation, where often the risk of mechanical abstraction arises. What is precisely important and problematic in certain research of the "scientific" type like yours is a somewhat new relationship of familiarity that they appear to maintain with the more explicitly "subjective" works of literature.

MF: It would be very interesting to know of what the designatable, "nameable" individuality of a scientific work consists; those of Abel or Lagrange for example are marked by characteristics of writing that individualize them as surely as a painting by Titian or page of Chateaubriand. And similarly for the philosophic or descriptive writings of Linnaeus or Buffon. They are caught up however in the network of all those who speak of "the same thing," who are contemporary to them or follow them: this network that envelopes them outlines these great figures without a social identity that one calls "mathematics," "history," or "biology."

The problem of the singularity or the relation between the name and the network is an old problem, but in former times there existed certain kinds of channels and marked paths that separated literary works, works on physics or mathematics and historical works from one another; each one evolved on its own level and in some way in the territory where it was assigned, in spite of a whole set of overlappings, borrowings and resemblances. One can note today that all this dividing up, this separation, is being effaced or being reconstituted in another mode altogether. Thus the relations between linguistics and literary works, between music and mathematics, the discourse of historians and economists are no longer simply of an order of borrowing, imitation or involuntary analogy, nor even of structural isomorphism; these works and progressions are formed in relation to one another and exist for one another. There is a literature of linguistics and not an influence of grammarians on the grammar and the vocabulary of novelists. In the same way, mathematics is not applicable to the construction of musical language, as at the end of the 17th century and the beginning of the 19th; it actually constitutes the formal universe of the musical work itself. In such a way that one is witness to a general and vertiginous effacement of the old distribution of languages.

One says gladly that nothing else today interests us but language and that it has become the universal object. We must not make a mistake there: this sovereignty is the provisional, equivocal, precarious sovereignty of a tribe in migration. Of course we are interested in language; yet it's not that we have finally entered into its possession, but rather that it escapes us more than ever before. Its boundaries have collapsed and its calm universe has entered into fusion; and if we are submerged, it is not so much through its intemporal vigor as through the movement today of its wave.

Q: How do you situate yourself personally in this mutation that pulls the most demanding works of knowledge (*savoir*) into a sort of novelistic adventure?

MF: In contrast to those whom one calls structuralists, I am not so interested in the formal possibilities offered by a system like language. Personally I am rather haunted by the existence of discourse, by the fact that particular words have been spoken; these events have functioned in relation to their original situation, they have left traces behind them; they subsist and exercise, in this subsistence even within history, a certain number of manifest or secret functions.

Q: Thus you yield to the passion proper to the historian who wants to respond to the infinite rumor of the archives.

MF: Yes, for my object is not language but the archive, that is to say the accumulated existence of discourse. Archeology, such as I intend it, is kin neither to geology (as analysis of the sub-soil), nor to genealogy (as descriptions of beginnings and sequences); it's the analysis of discourse in its modality of *archive*.

A nightmare has pursued me since childhood: I have under my eyes a text that I can't read, or of which only a tiny part can be deciphered; I pretend to read it, but I know that I'm inventing; then the text suddenly blurs completely, I can no longer read anything or even invent, my throat constricts and I wake up.

I don't know what there can be of the personal in this obsession with language, which exists everywhere and escapes us in its very survival. It survives by turning its look away from us, its face inclined toward a night of which we know nothing.

How justify these discourses on discourse that I undertake? What status do we give them? One begins to perceive, above all on the side of logicians and the students of Russell and Wittgenstein, that language can be analyzed in terms of its formal properties only on the condition of taking account of its concrete functioning. Language is very much a set of structures, but discourses are unities of function, and the analysis of language in its totality cannot fail to confront this essential demand. To this extent what I do is located in the general anonymity of all the research which today turns around language, that is to say not only the language that permits us to speak, but the discourses that have been spoken.

Q: More precisely, what do you mean by this idea of the anonymous?

MF: I wonder if we're not discovering again today, in the relationship of the name to the anonymous, a certain transposition of the old classic problem of the individual and the truth, or of the individual and beauty. How is it that an individual born at a given moment, having such a history and such a face, can discover, by himself and for the first time, some truth, perhaps even the truth? That's the question to which Descartes responds in the *Meditations*: how could I discover the truth? And many years later we find it again in the romantic theme of the genius: How can an individual lodged in a fold of history discover the forms of beauty in which the whole truth of a period or of a civilization is expressed? The problem today is no longer posed in these terms: we are no longer in the truth but in the coherence of discourse, no longer in beauty, but in the complex relations of forms. It's a question now of knowing how an individual, a name, can be the support of an element or group of elements that, in being integrated into the coherence of discourses or the indefinite network of forms, comes to efface or at least to render empty and useless this name, this individuality of which he bears however to a certain point, for a certain time and in certain respects, the mark. We have to conquer the anonymous, to justify for ourselves the enormous presumption of one day finally becoming anonymous, a little like the classics had to justify for themselves the enormous presumption of having found the truth, and of attaching their names to it. The problem in the past for the one who wrote was to tear himself out of the anonymity of everything; nowadays, it's to succeed in effacing one's own name and of coming to lodge one's voice in this great anonymous murmur of discourses held today.

Q: Does it not seem to you however that it's there, as soon as the movement is pushed to the extreme, that we enter into the double game of affirmation and effacement of the word and silence, of which Blanchot makes the essence of the literary act, when he assigns to the work the chosen function of a rich abode of silence facing the unbearable immensity of speech without which, however, it would not exist? When Lévi-Strauss says of *The Raw and the Cooked:*[5] "Thus this book on myths, in my own way, is a myth," he has seen the sovereign impersonality of myth, and yet few books, from this very fact, are as personal as his *Mythologies*. You are, in a very different way, in a similar situation in relation to history.

MF: What gives books like those which have no other pretension than to be anonymous so many marks of singularity and individuality are not the privileged signs of a style, nor the mark of a singular or individual interpretation, but the rage to apply the eraser by which one meticulously effaces all that could refer to a written individuality. Between writers and people who write (*écrivants*) there are the effacers.6

Bourbaki is at bottom the model. The dream for all of us would be, each in his own domain, to make something like this Bourbaki, where mathematics is elaborated under the anonymity of a fantastic name. Perhaps the irreducible difference between research in mathematics and our activities is that the eraser marks intended to attain the anonymous indicate more surely the signature of a name than the ostentatious penholder. And yet one could say that Bourbaki has his style and very much his own way of being anonymous.

Q: Like your reference to the classic relation of the individual, this leads me to think that the author's position in this kind of research seems like a doubling of that of the philosopher, always ambiguous, between science and literature. In this sense, what do you think is the modern status of philosophy?

MF: It seems to me that philosophy no longer exists; not that it has disappeared, but it has been disseminated into a great number of diverse activities. Thus the activities of the axiomatician, the linguist, the anthropologist, the historian, the revolutionary, the man of politics can be forms of philosophical activity. In the 19th century the reflection that investigated the condition of possibility of objects was philosophical; today philosophy is every activity that makes a new object appear for knowledge or practice—whether this activity stems from mathematics, linguistics, anthropology or history.

Q: Nevertheless, in the last chapter of *The Order of Things,* where you deal with the human sciences today, you privilege history over all other disciplines. Would it therefore be a new way of rediscovering this power of synthetic legislation that used to be the proper privilege of philosophic thought, and that Heidegger already recognized not as that of traditional philosophy, but as "history of philosophy"?

MF: Indeed, history does retain, in relation to my investigation, a privileged position. It's because in our culture, at least for several centuries, discourse has been linked together through history as a mode: we receive things which have been spoken as if they come from a past where they succeeded one another, were opposed, influenced, replaced, engendered and accumulated. The cultures "without history" are obviously not those where there was neither event, nor evolution, nor revolution, but where discourses were not added together according history as a mode; they are juxtaposed; they replace one another; they are forgotten; they are transformed. On the other hand, in a culture like ours, every discourse appears against the background of the disappearance of every event.

That's why in studying a set of theoretical discourses concerning language, economy and living beings I did not want to establish *a priori* the possibilities or impossibilities of such knowledges—this is an element of birth, that of survival, etc. I wanted to do an historian's work by showing the simultaneous functioning of these discourses and the transformations which accounted for their visible changes.

But history for all that does not have to play the role of a philosophy of philosophy, to pride itself in being the language of languages, as the historicism which tended to pass to the account of history the legislative and critical power of philosophy wanted it in the 19th century. If history possesses a privilege, it would rather be to the extent to which it would play the role of an internal ethnology of our culture and of our rationality, and would consequently incarnate the very possibility of every ethnology.

Q: After this long detour, I would like to return to the book, and to ask you the reason for this gap that one senses in your position when one passes from the analysis of the 17th and 18th centuries to that of the 19th and 20th centuries, a gap which has been the object of some of the most lively reservations formulated towards your work.

MF: Yes, something seems to change with the 19th century in the arrangement of the book. The same thing occurred in *Madness and Civilization:* people assumed that I wanted to attack modern psychiatry and in *The Order of Things* that I was being polemical towards the thought of the 19th century. In fact there is a very big difference in the two analyses. I can indeed define the classical age in its own configuration through the double difference that opposes it to the 16th and to the 19th centuries. I can only define the modern age in its singularity by opposing it to the 17th century on one hand and to us on the other; it is necessary, therefore, in order to be able to continuously establish the division, to make the difference that separates us from them surge up under each one of our sentences. From this modern age which begins around 1790–1810 and goes to around 1950, it's a matter of detaching onself, whereas for the classical age it's only a matter of describing it.

The apparently polemical character stems from the fact that it's a question of hollowing out the whole mass of discourse that's accumulated under our feet. One can discover from a gradual movement the old latent configurations; but as soon as it's a matter of determining the system of discourse within which we are still living, at the moment we are obliged to put into question the words that still resonate in our ears and which are indistinguishable from those we are trying to speak, then the archeologist, like the Nietzschean philosopher, is forced to resort to the blows of the hammer.

Q: The unique and enthusiastic status that you accord to Nietzsche—is it not the most manifest sign of this irremediable gap?

MF: If I had to begin again this book that I finished two years ago, I would try not to give Nietzsche this ambiguous status, absolutely privileged and meta-historical, that I gave him out of weakness. It is due to the fact that no doubt my archeology owes more to the Nietzschean genealogy than to structuralism properly called.

Q: But how, in this case, can you return Nietzsche to the archeologist without the risk of being as false towards the one as towards the other? It seems that there is in the very fact an insurmountable contradiction. I see it, in your book, in the figured form of a conflict in principle between Nietzsche and *Las Meninas*. For, without resorting to a facile play on your predilection for spatial metaphors, it is clear that the painting proves to be the privileged place, as it is, in one sense, for all structuralism: it is there, I think, that you compare the anonymity of the present with that of the 17th century, in the name of an idea of reading that can arrange history in a painting as well as in the Borges text on the Chinese encyclopedia where your book has its "place of birth," in the very movement of historical evolution. That's why the 19th century, where history is invented in the form of a gap between signs and humans, is the object of debate, and our period the hope of a new resolution through an attempt to re-integrate the historical subject into the space of the painting in a new anonymity.
Is not Nietzsche precisely the place where all the signs converge in the irreducible dimension of a subject, anonymous by dint of being himself, anonymous by dint of incorporating the totality of voices in the form of a fragmentary discourse; and is it not in that the extreme and exemplary form of thought and of all expression as autobiography without remainder, which is always lacking in the space of the painting just as in the time of history, where it is and is not, for one cannot say it but in the sense of its own madness and not through recourse to an exterior law? Thus the fact that Nietzsche, and with him a certain truth of literature, escapes your book—which owes him so much and brings so much to him—doesn't this fact bear witness of the impossibility of all discourse at the same level? And even that, in the form of your presence in the book, is it not to the exact measure of the impossible anonymity you don, which to be total, can only signify today a world without the written word or, to the point of madness, the circular literalness of Nietzsche?

MF: It is difficult to answer this question; for it is from it, at bottom, that all your questions come, and as a consequence our whole dialogue; it is what supports the passionate interest, a little aloof, that you bring to all that is happening around you, and to the generations that precede you; from this question comes your desire to write and to ask questions. Here then begins the interview with Raymond Bellour conducted by Michel Foucault, an interview that has gone on for several years and from which perhaps one day *Les Lettres françaises*[7] will publish a fragment.

Translated by John Johnston

---

1 Georges Dumézil inaugurated a new era in the study of Indo-European mythologies and religions. [Ed.]

2 Fernand Braudel, François Furet, Denis Richet and Emmanuel Leroy-Ladurie belong to the *Annales* school of French historians, founded by Marc Bloch and Lucien Fèbvre in 1929, which champions the study of "total history." See Braudel's *The Mediterranean and the Mediterranean World in the Age of Philip II* (New York: Harper & Row, 1976), and Leroy-Ladurie's *The Mind and Method of the Historian* (Chicago: University of Chicago Press, 1981). [Ed.]

3 Louis Althusser, *Reading Capital* (London: New Left Books, 1979). [Ed.]

4 The epistemological break is a concept introduced into the philosophy of science by Gaston Bachelard, and employed by Althusser in his reading of Marx. [Ed.]

5 Claude Lévi-Strauss, *The Raw and the Cooked* (New York: Octagon, 1979). [Ed.]

6 The distinction between *écrivains* and *écrivants* (people who use writing for other purposes) was introduced by Roland Barthes in *Critical Essays* (Chicago: Northwestern University Press, 1972). [Ed.]

7 "Les Lettres françaises," directed by Louis Aragon, was the literary (and rather liberal) organ of the French CP. [Ed.]

5

HISTORY, DISCOURSE AND
DISCONTINUITY

Q: Doesn't a thought which introduces constraint of the system and discontinuity in the history of the mind remove all basis for a progressive political intervention? Does it not lead to the following dilemma:
—either the acceptance of the system,
—or the appeal to an uncontrolled event, to the irruption of exterior violence which alone is capable of upsetting the system?

MF: I have chosen the last of the questions put to me (not without regret for abandoning the others): 1) because at first glance it surprised me, and because I became quickly convinced that it concerned the very core of my work; 2) because it allowed me to offer at least a few of the answers which I would have liked to give for the others; 3) because it gave expression to questioning which no theoretical work today can eschew.

I must admit that you have characterized with extreme accuracy what I have undertaken to do, and that you have at the same time singled out the point of inevitable discord: "to introduce constraint of the system and discontinuity in the history of the mind." Yes, I recognize that this is an almost unjustifiable statement. With diabolical pertinency you have succeeded in giving a definition of my work to which I cannot avoid subscribing, but for which no one would, reasonably, ever wish to assume responsibility. I suddenly sense how bizarre my position is, how strange and hardly justifiable. And I now perceive how much this work, which was no doubt somewhat solitary, but always patient, with no other law but its own and sufficiently carried out, I thought, to be able to stand by itself, has deviated in relation to the best-established norms, how discordant it was.

However, two or three details in the very accurate definition which you propose bother me, preventing me from (perhaps allowing me to avoid) agreeing completely with it.

First of all you use the word *system* in the singular. Now, I am a pluralist. Here's what I mean. (You will allow me, I think, to speak not only of my last book, but also of those which preceded it; this is because together they form a cluster of research whose themes and chronological reference points are quite adjacent; also because each one constitutes a descriptive experiment which is opposed to and therefore relates to the other two by a certain number of traits.) I am a pluralist: the problem which I have set myself is that of the *individualization* of discourses. There exist for individualizing the discourses criteria which are known and reliable (or almost): the linguistic system to which they belong, the identity of the subject which has articulated them. But other criteria, which are not less familiar, are much more enigmatic. When one speaks of *psychiatry,* or of *medicine,* or of *grammar,* or of *biology,* or of *economics,* what is one speaking of? What are these curious entities which we believes we can recognize at first glance, but whose limits we would be at a loss to define? Some of these units seem to go back to the dawn of human history (medicine as well as mathematics), whereas others have appeared recently (economics, psychiatry), and still others have perhaps disappeared (casuistry). To these units new terms are endlessly added and they are constantly modified by them (the strange units of sociology and psychology which since their appearance have not ceased to start afresh). There are units which are obstinately maintained after so many errors, neglect, so much innovation, so many metamorphoses and which sometimes undergo such radical mutations that one would have difficulty in considering them as identical to themselves (how can one affirm that economics remains the same, uninterrupted, from the physiocrats to Keynes?).

Perhaps there are discourses which can at each moment redefine their own individuality (for example, mathematics can reinterpret at each point in time the totality of its history); but in each of the cases that I have cited, the discourse cannot restore the totality of its history within the unity of a strict framework. There remain two traditional recourses. The historical-transcendental recourse: an attempt to find, beyond all historical manifestation and historical origin, a primary formation, the opening of an inexhaustible horizon, a plan which would move backward in time in relation to every event, and which would maintain throughout history the constantly unwinding plan of an unending unity. The empirical or psychological recourse: seeking out the founder, interpreting what he meant, detecting the implicit meanings which were lying silent and dormant in his discourse, following the thread or the destiny of these meanings, describing the traditions and the influences, fixing the moment of awakenings, of lapses, of awareness, of crises, of changes in the mind, the sensitivity or the interest of men. Now it seems to me that the first of these recourses is tautological, the second extrinsic and unessential. It is by marking out and by systematizing their very character that I would like to attempt to individualize the large units which scan simultaneously or successively the world of our discourses.

I have retained three groups of criteria:

1) The criteria of *formation.* What permits us to individualize a discourse such as political economy or general grammar, is not the unity of an object; it is not a formal structure; not is it a conceptual coherent architecture; it is not a fundamental philosophical choice; it is rather the existence of rules of

formation for all its objects (however scattered they may be), for all its operations (which often can neither be superimposed nor linked together in succession), for all its concepts (which may very well be incompatible), for all its theoretical options (which are often mutually exclusive). There is an individualized
discursive formation every time one can define a similar set of rules.

2) The criteria of *transformation* or of *threshold*. I shall say that natural
history (or psycho-pathology) are units of discourse, if I can define the conditions which must have been brought together at a very precise moment of time,
in order that its objects, its operations, its concepts and its theoretical options
could be formed; if I can define what internal modifications it was capable of;
finally if I can define from what threshold of transformation new rules have been
brought into play.

3) The criteria of *correlation*. I will say that clinical medicine is an
autonomous discursive formation if I can define the whole of the relations which
define it and situate it among the other types of discourse (as biology, chemistry,
political theory or the analysis of society) and in the nondiscursive context in which
it functions (institutions, social relations, economic and political circumstances).

These criteria allow us to substitute differentiated analyses for the
broad themes of general history (whether it concern "the progress of reason" or
"the spirit of a century"). They allow us to describe, as *epistemic* of a period, not
the sum of its knowledge, nor the general style of its research, but the deviation,
the distances, the oppositions, the differences, the relations of its multiple scientific discourses: the *epistemic* is not *a sort of grand unifying theory*, it is a space
of *dispersion,* it is an *open field of relationships and no doubt indefinitely
describable.* They allow us furthermore to describe not broad history which
would carry off all the sciences in a single swoop, but the types of history—that
is to say, what was retained and transformed—which characterize the different
discourses (the history of mathematics does not follow the same model as the
history of biology, which does not follow the same model of psycho-pathology
either): *the epistemic is not a slice of history* common to all the sciences: it is *a
simultaneous play of specific remanences.* Finally they allow us to situate the
different thresholds in their respective place: for nothing proves in advance (and
nothing demonstrates after examination either) that their chronology is the same
for all types of discourse; the threshold which one can describe for the analysis
of language at the beginning of the nineteenth century has doubtless no counterpart in the history of mathematics; and, what is more paradoxical, the threshold
of formation for political economy (noted by Ricardo) does not coincide with
the constitution—by Marx—of an analysis of society and of history.[1] *The
Epistemic is not a general stage of reason; it is a complex relationship of successive displacement in time.*

Nothing, you see, is more foreign to me than the quest for a constraining sovereign and unique form. I do not seek to detect, starting from various
signs, the unitary spirit of an epoch, the general form of its conscience: something like a *Weltanschauung.* Nor have I described either the emergence and
eclipse of a formal structure which might reign for a time over all the manifesta-

tions of thought: I have not written the history of a transcendental eclipse. Nor, finally, have I described thoughts or century-old sensitivities coming to life, stuttering, struggling and dying out like great phantoms—like souls playing out their shadow theater against the backdrop of history. I have studied, one after another, whole sets of discourses; I have characterized them; I have defined the play of rules, of transformations, of thresholds, of remanences. I have compounded them, I have described clusters of relationships. Wherever I have deemed it necessary I have allowed the *systems* to proliferate.

* * * * *

You say, a thought which "emphasizes discontinuity." This, indeed, is a notion whose importance today—amongst historians as with linguists—cannot be underestimated. But the use of the singular does not appear to me to be entirely suitable. Here again, I am a pluralist. My problem is to substitute the analysis of *different types of transformation* for the abstract general and wearisome form of "change" in which one so willingly thinks in terms of succession. This implies two things: setting aside the old forms of weak continuity through which one ordinarily attenuates the raw fact of change (tradition, influence, habits of thought, broad mental forms, constraints of the human mind), and stubbornly stressing instead the lively intensity of the difference: establishing meticulously the deviation. Next, discarding all the psychological explanations of change (the genius of the great inventors, crises of conscience, the appearance of a new form of mind); and defining with the greatest care the transformations which have—I don't say provoked—but constituted the change. Replacing, in short, the theme of becoming (general form, abstract element, primary cause and universal effect, a confused mixture of the identical and the new) by the analysis of the transformations in their specificity.

(1) *Within* a given discursive formation, detecting the changes which affect the objects, the operations, the concepts, the theoretical options. Thus, one can distinguish (I limit myself to the example of *general grammar*): the changes by deduction or implication (the theory of verb-copula implied the distinction between a substantive root and a verbal inflexion); the changes by generalization (extension to the verb of the theory of word designation, and consequent disappearance of the verb-copula theory); the changes by limitation (the concept of attribute is specified by the notion of complement); the changes by passing to the complementary (from the project of constructing a universal and readily understood language is derived the search for the hidden secrets of the most primitive of languages); the changes by passing to the other term of an alternative (primacy of vowels or primacy of consonants in the constitution of roots); the changes through permutation of dependencies (one can establish the theory of the verb on the theory of the noun or inversely); the changes by exclusion or inclusion (the analysis of languages as systems of representative signs renders obsolete the search for their relationship which is reintroduced, on the other

hand, by the quest of a primitive language).

These different types of change constitute in themselves altogether the whole of the characteristic *derivations* of a discursive formation.

(2) Detecting the changes which affect discursive formations *themselves:*

—displacement of boundaries which define the field of possible objects (the medical object at the beginning of the 19th century ceases to be taken in a surface of classification; it is marked out in the three dimensional space of the body);

—new position and new role of the speaking subject in the discourse (the subject in the discourse of the naturalists of the 18th century becomes exclusively a *looking* subject following a grid, and *noting* according to a code; it ceases to be listening, interpreting, deciphering);

—new functions of language with respect to objects (beginning with Tournefort the role of the discourse of the naturalist is not to penetrate into things, to capture from them the language which they secretly enclose, nor to bring it to light; but to extend a surface of transcription where the form, the number, the size and the disposition of elements can be translated in a univocal manner);

—new form of localization and of circulation of the discourse in society (the clinical discourse is not formulated in the same places, it does not have the same recording procedures, it is not diffused, it is not cumulative, it is not conserved nor is it contested in the same way as the medical discourse of the 18th century.).

All these changes of a type superior to the preceding ones define the transformations which affect the discursive areas themselves: *mutations.*

(3) Finally, the third type of changes, those which affect simultaneously several discursive formations:

—reversal in the hierarchical order (the analysis of language had, during the classical period, a directing role which it has lost, in the first years of the 19th century, to the benefit of biology);

—change in the nature of the directing role (classical grammar, as a general theory of signs, guaranteed in other areas the transposition of an instrument of analysis; in the 19th century, biology assures the "metaphorical" importation of a number of concepts: organisms-organization; function-social function; life-life of words or of languages);

—functional displacements: the theory of the continuity of beings which, in the 18th century depended upon the philosophical discourse, is taken over in the 19th century by the scientific discourse.

All these transformations of a type superior to the two others characterize the changes peculiar to epistemic itself.

Redistributions.

There you have a small number (about fifteen, perhaps) of different changes which one can assign to discourses. You see why I would prefer that one say that I have stressed not discontinuity, but *the discontinuities* (that is to say, the different transformations which it is possible to describe concerning two states of discourse). But the important thing for me, now, is not to establish an exhaustive typology of these transformations.

1) The important thing is to offer as the content of the wearisome and empty concept of "change" a play of specified modifications. The history of "ideas" or of "sciences" must not be the list of innovations, but the descriptive analysis of the different transformations that take place.[2]

2) What is important to me is not to confuse such an analysis with a psychological diagnosis. It is legitimate to ask oneself whether the person whose work bears such an ensemble of modifications had genius or what had been the experiences of his early infancy. But it is another thing to describe the field of possibilities, the form of operations, the types of transformations which characterize his discursive practice.

3) What is important to me is to show that there are not on the one hand inert discourses, already more than half dead, and then, on the other hand, an all-powerful subject which manipulates them, upsets them, renews them; but that the discoursing subjects belong to the discursive field—they have their place there (and possibilities of their displacements), their function (and possibilities of their functional mutation). The discourse is not the place where pure subjectivity irrupts; it is a space of positions and of differentiated functionings for the subjects.

4) What is important to me above all is to define amongst all these transformations the play of dependencies.

—*intradiscursive* dependencies (between the objects, the operations, the concepts of the same formation).

—*interdiscursive* dependencies (between different discursive formations, such as the correlations which I have started in *The Order of Things* between natural history, economics, grammar and the theory of representation).

—*extradiscursive* dependencies (between discursive transformations and others which have been produced elsewhere than in the discourse: such as the correlations studied in *Madness and Civilization* and in *The Birth of the Clinic* between the medical discourse and a whole play of economic, political and social changes).

I would like to substitute this whole play of dependencies for the uniform, simple notion of assigning causality; and by eliminating the prerogative of the endlessly accompanying cause, bring out the bundle of polymorphous correlations.

As you see, there is absolutely no question of substituting a "discontinuous" category for the no less abstract and general one of the "continuous." I am attempting, on the contrary, to show that discontinuity is not a monotonous and unthinkable void between events, a void which one must hasten to fill (two perfectly symmetrical solutions) with the dismal plentitude of the cause or by the suppleness and agility of the mind; but that it is a play of specific transformations different from one another (each having its conditions, its rules, its level) and linked among themselves according to schemes of dependence. History is the descriptive analysis and the theory of these transformations.

* * * * *

A last point on which I hope to be able to be more brief. You use the expression: "history of the mind." In fact, I intended rather to write a history of discourse. You may ask: What's the difference? "You do not study the texts which you take as raw material according to their grammatical structure: you do not describe the semantic field which they cover: it is not language which is your object. And so? What do you seek if not to discover the thought which animates them and to reconstitute the representations of which they have given a durable translation, perhaps, but undoubtedly an unfaithful one? What do you seek if not to rediscover behind them the intention of the men who have formulated them, the meanings which, voluntarily or unbeknownst to them, they have deposited therein, this imperceptible supplement to the linguistic system which is something like the beginning of liberty or the history of the mind?"

Therein lies, perhaps, the essential point. You are right: what I am analyzing in the discourse is not the system of its language, nor, in a general way, the formal rules of its construction: for I do not care about knowing what renders it legitimate or gives it its intelligibility and allows it to serve in communication. The question which I ask is not that of codes but of events: the law of existence of the terms, that which has rendered them possible—they and no other in their place: the conditions of their particular emergence; their correlation with other previous or simultaneous events, discursive or not. This question, however, I try to answer without referring to the awareness, obscure or explicit, of the speaking subjects; without relating the facts or discourse to the will—perhaps involuntary—of their authors; without invoking that intention of saying which is always excessive in relation to what is said; without trying to seize hold of the inaudible when a word doesn't occur in the text.

So that what I am doing is neither a formalization nor an exegesis. But an *archaeology:* that is to say, as its name indicates only too obviously, the description of the *record.* By this word, I do not mean the mass of texts which have been collected at a given period, or chanced to have survived oblivion from this period. I mean all the rules which at a given period and for a definite society defined:

1) the limits and the forms of *expressibility:* what is it possible to speak of? What has been constituted as the field of discourse? What type of discursivity has been appropriated to such and such a domain (what has been designated as the subject; what has one wished to make a descriptive science of; to what has one given a literary formulation, etc.)?

2) the limits and the forms of *conservation:* what are the terms destined to disappear without any trace? Which ones are destined, on the other hand, to enter into the memory of men through ritualistic recitation, pedagogy and teaching, entertainment or holiday, publicity? Which ones are noted for being capable of re-use, and toward what ends? Which ones are put in circulation and in what groups? Which are those which are repressed and censured?

3) the limits and the forms of *memory* such as it appears in the different discursive formations: which are the terms which everyone recognizes as valid or

questionable, or definitely invalid? Which ones have been abandoned as negligible and which ones have been excluded as foreign? What types of relationships are established between the system of present terms and the body of past terms?

4) the limits and the forms of *reactivation:* amongst the discourses of previous epochs or of foreign cultures, which are the ones that are retained, which are valued, which are imported, which one tries to reconstitute? And what does one do with them, what transformations does one impose upon them (commentary, exegesis, analysis), what system of appreciation does one apply to them, what role does one give them to play?

5) the limits and the forms of *appropriation:* what individuals, what groups, what classes have access to such a kind of discourse? In what way is the relationship between the discourse and whoever gives it, and whoever receives it institutionalized? In what way is the relationship of the discourse to its author shown and defined? How does the struggle for taking over the discourse take place between classes, nations, linguistic, cultural or ethnic collectivities?

It is against this background that the analyses which I have begun are set; it is towards it that they are directed. I am writing, therefore, not a history of the mind, according to the succession of its forms or according to the thickness of its deposited meanings. I do not question the discourses concerning what silently they mean, but on the fact and the conditions of their manifest appearance; not on the contents which they may conceal, but on the field where they coexist, remain and disappear. It is a question of an analysis of the discourses in their exterior dimensions. From whence arise three consequences:

1) Treat the past discourse not as a theme for a *commentary* which would revive it, but as a *monument*3 to be described in its characteristic disposition.

2) Seek in the discourse not its laws of construction, as do the structural methods, but its conditions of existence.

3) Refer the discourse not to the thought, to the mind or to the subject which might have given rise to it, but to the practical field in which it is deployed.

* * * * *

Forgive me for being so lengthy, so laborious, just to propose three slight changes in your definition and to ask your agreement, so that we may speak about my work as an attempt to introduce "diversity *of the systems* and the play of discontinuities in the history of the *discourses.*" Do not imagine that I want to distort the issue; or that I seek to avoid the point of your question by discussing its terms *ad infinitum.* But prior agreement was necessary. Now I have my back to the wall. I must answer.

Certainly not the question of whether *I* am a reactionary; nor whether my texts *are* (in themselves, intrinsically, through a certain number of well-coded signs). You ask me a much more serious question, the only one, I believe, which can legitimately be raised. You question me on the *relationships* between what I say and a certain political practice.

It seems to me that two answers can be offered to this question. One concerns the critical operations which my discourse carries out in its own domain (the history of ideas, of sciences, of thought, of knowledge...): was what it puts out of circulation indispensable to a progressive politics? The other concerns the field of analysis and the realm of objects which my discourse attempts to bring out: how can they be articulated in the exercise of a progressive politics?

I shall sum up as follows the critical operations which I have undertaken:

1) *To establish limits* where the history of thought, in its traditional form, gave itself a limitless space. In particular:

a) to challenge again the great interpretive postulate according to which the reign of the discourse would have no designated boundaries; mute things and silence itself would be able still to hear the deeply varied murmur of the meaning; in what men do not say they would continue to speak; a world of slumbering texts would await us in the blank pages of our history. In opposition to this theme I would like to substitute the notion that the discourses are limited practical domains which have their boundaries, their rules of formation, their conditions of existence: the historical base of the discourse is not a more profound discourse—at once identical and different;

b) to challenge again the theme of a sovereign subject which would come from the outside to animate the inertia of the linguistic codes, and which would deposit in the discourse the indelible trace of its liberty; to challenge again the theme of a subjectivity which would constitute the meanings and then would transcribe them into the discourse. In opposition to these themes I would like to substitute pin-pointing the origin of the roles and of the operations exercised by the different "discoursing" subjects.

c) to challenge again the theme of the indefinitely receding origin, and the idea that in the realm of thought, the role of history is to awaken what has been forgotten, to eliminate the occultations, to erase—or to obstruct again—the barriers. In opposition to this theme I would like to substitute the analysis of discursive systems, historically defined, to which one can affix thresholds, and assign conditions of birth and disappearance.

In a word, to establish these limits, to question again these three themes of the origin, the subject and the implicit meaning, is to undertake—a difficult task, very strong resistance indeed proves it—to liberate the discursive field from the historical-transcendental structure which the philosophy of the nineteenth century has imposed on it.

2) *To eliminate ill-considered oppositions.* Here are a few of them in their order of increasing importance: the opposition between the liveliness of innovations and the dead weight of tradition, the inertia of acquired knowledge or the old tracings of thought; the opposition between the average forms of knowledge (which would represent its everyday mediocrity) and its deviating forms (which would manifest the singularity or the solitude characteristic of genius); the opposition between periods of stability or of universal convergence and moments of effervescence when consciences enter into crisis, when sensibil-

ities are metamorphosed, when all notions are revised, overturned, revivified, or for an indefinite time, fall into disuse. For all these dichotomies I would like to substitute the analysis of the field of simultaneous differences (which define at a given period the possible dispersal of knowledge) and of successive differences (which define the whole of the transformations, their hierarchy, their dependence, their level). Whereas one used to relate the history of tradition and of invention, of the old and the new, of the dead and the living, of the closed and the open, of the static and of the dynamic, I undertake to relate the history of ideas as the sum total of the specified and descriptive forms of the non-identity. And thus I would like to free it of the triple metaphor which has encumbered it for more than a century (the evolutionist, which imposes upon it the division between the regressive and the adaptive; the biological which separates the inert from the living; the dynamic which opposes movement and immobility).

3) *To lift the restriction* which has been directed at the discourse in its very existence (and therein lies, for me, the most important of the critical operations that I have undertaken). This restriction consists of several aspects:

a) never treating the discourse except as an unimportant element without its own consistency nor inherent laws (a pure translation surface for mute things; a simple place of expression for thought, imagination, knowledge, unconscious themes);

b) recognizing in the discourse only the patterns of a psychological and individualizing model (the work of an author, and—why not?—his juvenilia or his mature work), the patterns of a linguistic or rhetorical model (a genre, a style), the patterns of a semantic model (an idea, a theme);

c) admitting that all the operations are made before the discourse and outside of it (in the ideality of thought or in the serious realm of mute practices); that the discourse, consequently, is but a slight addition which adds an almost impalpable fringe to things and to the mind; a surplus which *goes without saying,* since it does nothing else except to say what has been said.

To this restriction, I would object that the discourse is not nothing or almost nothing. And what it is—what defines its own consistency, what allows one to make an historical analysis of it—is not what one "meant" to say (that obscure and heavy weight of intentions which supposedly weighs, in the shadow, with a much greater heaviness than the things said); it is not what has remained silent (those imposing things which do not speak, but which leave their traceable marks, their black profile against the light surface of what is said): the discourse is constituted by the difference between what one could say correctly at one period (according to the rules of grammar and those of logic) and what is actually said. The discursive field is, at a specific moment, the law of this difference. It thus defines a number of operations which do not belong to the order of linguistic construction or of formal deduction. It deploys a "neutral" domain in which speech and writing can cause the system of their opposition and the difference of their functioning to vary. It appears as a whole group of practical rules which do not consist simply in giving a visible and exterior body to the inner agility of thought, nor in offering to the solidity of things the reflecting surface which will duplicate them. At the bottom of this restriction which has weighed upon the discourse (to the advantage of the thought-language, history-truth, word-writing, words-things opposition), there was the refusal to recognize that in the discourse something is formed (according to well-definable rules); that this something exists, subsists, changes, disappears (according to rules equally definable); in short, that, side by side with all which a society can produce ("side by side": that is to say, in a relationship which can be assigned to all that), there is formation and transformation of "things said." It is the history of these "things said" that I have undertaken.

4) Finally, the last critical task (which sums up and embraces all the others): *freeing from their uncertain status* this ensemble of disciplines which one calls history of ideas, history of sciences, history of thought, history of knowledge, of concepts or of conscience. This certainly manifests itself in several ways:

—difficulties in limiting the domains: where does the history of sciences end, where does the history of opinions and beliefs begin? How are the history of concepts and the history of notions or themes to be separated? Where lies the boundary between the history of knowledge and that of the imagination?

—difficulty in defining the nature of the object: does one write the history of what has been known, acquired, forgotten, or the history of mental forms, or the history of their interference? Does one write the history of characteristic features which are held in common by men of one period or of one culture? Does one describe a collective spirit? Does one analyze the (teleological or genetic) history of reason?

—difficulty in assigning the relationship between these facts of thought or of knowledge and the other areas of historical analysis: must one treat them as signs of something else (of a social relationship, or a political situation, of an economic determination)? Or as their result? Or as their refraction through a consciousness? Or as the symbolic expression of their total form?

For so many uncertainties I would like to substitute the analysis of the discourse itself in its conditions of formation, in the series of its modifications, and in the play of its dependencies and of its modifications, and in the play of its dependencies and of its correlations. The discourse would thus appear in a describable relationship with the whole of other practices. Instead of having to deal with an economic, social, political history embracing a history of thought (which would be its expression and something like its duplicate), instead of having to deal with a history of ideas which would be referred (either through a play of signs and of expressions, or by relations of causality) to extrinsic conditions, one would be dealing with a history of discursive practices in the specific relationships which link them to the other practices. There is no question of composing a *global history*—which would regroup all its elements around one principle or one unique form—but rather of opening up the field of a *general history* in which one could describe the peculiarity of practices, the play of their relations, the form of their dependencies. And it is in the area of this general history that the historical analysis of discursive practices could be circumscribed as a discipline.

These, then, are more or less the critical operations that I have under-taken. Now allow me to call you to witness the question that I ask of those who might become alarmed: "Is a progressive politics linked (in its theoretical think-ing) to the themes of meaning, of origin, of the constituent subject, in short, to all the themes which guarantee to history the inexhaustible presence of the Logos, the sovereignty of a pure subject, and the profound teleology of an original destina-tion? Is a progressive politics bound to such a form of analysis—or with its being challenged? And is such a politics bound to all the dynamic, biological, evolution-ary metaphors through which one masks the difficult problem of historical change—or, on the contrary, to their meticulous destruction? And further: is there some necessary relationship between a progressive politics and the refusal to rec-ognize in the discourse anything else except a thin transparency which flickers for a moment at the limit of things and of thoughts, then disappears immediately? Can one believe that this politics has any interest in rehashing one more time the theme—I would have thought that the existence and the practice of the revolution-ary discourse in Europe for more than 200 years might have been able to free us from it—that words are just air, an exterior whispering, a sound of wings which one hears with difficulty in the seriousness of history and the silence of thought? Finally must one think that a progressive politics is linked to the devaluation of discursive practices, so that a history of the mind, of conscience, of reason, of knowledge, of ideas or opinions might triumph in its certain ideality?"

It seems to me that I perceive, on the other hand—and quite clearly—the perilous ease which the politics you speak of would assume, if it gave itself the guarantee of a primitive foundation or of a transcendental teleology, if it per-sistently transformed time into metaphors through the images of life or the mod-els of movement, if it renounced the difficult task of a general analysis of prac-tices, of their relations, of their transformations, to take refuge in a global history of totalities, of expressive relationships, of symbolic values and of all those secret meanings in which thoughts and things are enveloped.

* * * * *

You have a right to say to me: "This is all very well: the critical opera-tions which you are making are not as blameworthy as they might appear at first glance. But, after all, how can this work of a termite on the origin of philology, of economics, or of pathological anatomy concern politics, and be included among the problems which pertain to it today? There was a time when philoso-phers did not devote themselves with so great a zeal for to the dust of archives..." To which I will answer, more or less: "There exists today a problem which is not without importance for political practice: the problem of the laws, of the conditions of exercise, of functioning, of the institutionalizing of scientific discourses. That's what I have undertaken to analyze historically—by choosing the discourses which have, not the strongest epistemological structure (mathe-matics or physics), but the densest and most complex field of positivity (medicine, economics, social sciences)."

Take a simple example: the formation of the clinical discourse which has characterized medicine from the beginning of the 19th century until the present, approximately. I have chosen it because we are dealing with a very definite, historical fact, and because one cannot refer its establishment back to some remote origin; because it would be very irresponsible to denounce it as a "pseudo-science"; and above all because it is easy to grasp "intuitively" the relationship between this scientific mutation and a number of precise political events: those which one groups—even on the European scale—under the title of the French Revolution. The problem is to give to this still vague relationship an analytical content.

First hypothesis: it is the conscience of men which has become modified (under the influence of economic, social, political changes); and their view of illness has, by this very fact, been altered: they have recognized its political consequences (uneasiness, discontent, revolts in populations whose health is deficient); they have perceived its economic implications (the desire of employers to have at their disposal a healthy work force; the wish of the bourgeoisie in power to transfer to the State the expenses of assistance); they have therein transposed their conception of society (a single medicine with a universal value, with two distinct fields of application: the hospital for the poor classes; the free and competitive practice for the rich); they have therein transcribed their new conception of the world: desacralization of the corpse, which has permitted autopsies; a greater importance accorded the living body as an instrument of work; the concern for health replacing the preoccupation with salvation. In all this, there are many things which are true; but, on the one hand, they do not account for the formation of a scientific discourse; and on the other hand, they could only have come into existence, and with the effects that one has been able to establish, to the extent that the medical discourse had received a new standard.

Second hypothesis: the fundamental notions of clinical medicine would be derived, by transposition, from a political practice or at least from the theoretical forms in which it is reflected. The ideas of organic solidarity, of functional cohesion, of tissulary communication, the abandonment of the principle of classification in favor of an analysis of the whole body corresponded to a political practice which revealed, beneath stratifications which were still feudal, social relationships of the functional and economic type. Or else, do not the refusal to see in sickness a large family of almost botanical species, and the effort to find the pathological juncture, its mechanism of development, its cause and, in the final analysis, its therapeutic, correspond to the project, in the ruling social class, of no longer controlling the world by theoretical knowledge alone, but by a mass of applicable knowledge, its decision to accept no longer as nature that which would be imposed upon her as a limit and as an evil? Such analyses do not appear to me to be pertinent either, because they avoid the essential problem: what should be, in the midst of the other discourses, and in a general way, of the other practices, the mode of existence and function of the medical discourse in order that such transpositions or such correspondences are produced?

That is why I would change the point of attack in relation to the traditional analyses. If indeed there is a link between political practice and the medical discourse, it is not, it seems to me, because this practice changed, initially, the conscience of men, the way they perceive things or conceive of the world, and then finally the form of their knowledge and its content; nor is it because this was reflected at first, in a more or less clear and systematic way, in concepts, notions or themes which have been subsequently imported into medicine. It is in a much more direct manner: political practice has transformed not the meaning or the form of the discourse, but the conditions of its emergence, insertion and functioning; it has transformed the mode of existence of the medical discourse. And this has come about through a number of operations described elsewhere and which I sum up here: new criteria to designate those who receive by law the right to hold a medical discourse; new division of the medical object through the application of another scale of observation which is superimposed on the first without erasing it (sickness observed statistically on the level of a population); new law of assistance which creates a hospital space for observation and surgery (space which is organized, furthermore, according to an economic principle, since the sick person benefiting from the care must compensate through the medical lesson which he gives; he pays for the right of being cared for by the obligation of being examined, and this goes up to, and includes, death); a new mode of registering, of preserving, of accumulating, of diffusing and of teaching the medical discourse (which must no longer express the experience of the physician but constitute, first of all, a document on illness); new functioning of the medical discourse in the system of administrative and political control of the population (society as society is considered and "treated" according to the categories of health and pathology.).

Now—and here's where the analysis becomes complex—these transformations in the conditions of existence and functioning of the discourse are neither "reflected" nor "translated" nor "expressed" in the concepts, the methods or the data of medicine: they modify its rules of formation. What is transformed by political practice is not the medical "objects" (political practice does not change, this is quite evident, the "morbid species" into "lesional infections"), but the system which offers to the medical discourse a possible object (whether it be a population surveyed and indexed, whether it be a total pathological evolution in an individual whose antecedents have been established and whose disturbances or their abatement are daily observed, whether it be an anatomical autopsied area); what is transformed by political practice is not the methods of analysis but the system of their formation (administrative recording of illnesses, of deaths, of their causes, of admissions and dismissals from hospital, setting up of archives, relations between medical personnel and patients in the hospital field); what has been transformed by political practice is not the concepts but their system of formation; the substitution of the concept of "tissue" for that of "solid" is obviously not the result of a political change; but what political practice has modified is the system of formation of the concepts: for the intermittent mutation of the effects of illness, and for the hypothetical designation of a functional cause, it has allowed the substitution of a tight, almost continual, anatomical graph supported in depth, and local points of reference of anomalies, of their field of dispersion and of their eventual routes of diffusion. The haste with which one ordinarily relates the contents of a scientific discourse to a political practice hides, in my mind, the level where the articulation can be described in precise terms.

It seems to me, that starting from such an analysis, one can understand:

1) how to describe a whole group of relations between a scientific discourse and a political practice, the details of which it is possible to follow and whose subordination one can grasp. Very direct relations since they no longer have to pass through the conscience of the speaking subjects nor through the efficacity of thought. Yet, indirect relations since the data of a scientific discourse can no longer be considered as the immediate expression of a social rapport or of an economic situation.

2) how to assign the proper role of political practice in relation to a scientific discourse. It does not have a thaumaturgic role of creation: it does not bring forth sciences out of nothing; it transforms the conditions of existence and the systems of functioning of the discourse. These changes are not arbitrary nor "free": they operate in a realm which has its own configuration and which consequently does not offer limitless possibilities of modification. The political practice does not reduce to nothing the consistency of the discursive field in which it operates.

Nor does it have a universal, critical role. It is not in the name of a political practice that one can judge the scientific quality of a science (unless the latter claims to be, in one way or another, a theory of politics). But in the name of a political practice one can question the mode of existence and the functioning of a science.

3) how the relations between a political practice and a discursive field can be articulated in turn on relations of another order. Thus medicine, at the beginning of the 19th century, is at once linked to a political practice (on a mode which I analyzed in *The Birth of the Clinic*, and to a whole group of "interdiscursive" changes which were simultaneously produced in several disciplines (substitutions for an analysis of the order and of taxonomical characters, of an analysis of solidarities, of functionings, of successive series, which I have described in *The Order of Things*.

4) how phenomena which one is in the habit of placing in the foreground (influence, communication of models, transfer and metaphorization of concepts) find their historical condition of possibility in these first modifications: for example, the importation, in the analysis of society, of biological concepts such as those of organism, of function, of evolution, even of sickness, played, in the 19th century, the role which one recognizes (much more important, much more ideologically loaded than the "naturalist" comparisons of preceding periods) only in proportion to the regulation given to the medical discourse by political practice.

Through this very long example I am anxious to show you but one thing: how what I am attempting to bring out through my analysis—the *positivity* of discourses, their conditions of existence, the systems which regulate their emergence, their functioning and their transformations—can concern political practice; to show you what this practice can do with it; to convince you that by outlining this theory of the scientific discourse, by making it appear as an ensemble of regulated practices, being articulated in an analyzable fashion upon other practices, I am not just enjoying myself by making the game more complicated for certain spirited souls. I am trying to define in what way, to what extent, to what level the discourse, and particularly the scientific discourses, can be objects of a political practice, and in what system of dependency they can be in relation to it.

Allow me once more to call you to witness the question I ask: Isn't this politics well known which answers in terms of thought or conscience, in terms of pure ideality or psychological traits, when one speaks to it of a practice, of its conditions, of its rules, of its historical changes? Isn't this politics well known which, since the beginning of the 19th century, stubbornly persists in seeing in the immense domain of practice only the epiphany of a triumphant reason, or in deciphering in it only the historic-transcendental destination of the West? And more precisely: does the refusal to analyze the conditions of existence and the rules of the scientific discourses, in what they possess both specific and dependent, not condemn all politics to a perilous choice: either to place upon a mode which one can, indeed, call, if one wishes, "technocratic," the validity and efficacity of a scientific discourse, whatever may be the real conditions of its exercise and the whole of the practices upon which it is articulated (thus establishing the scientific discourse as a universal rule for all the other practices, without taking into account the fact that it is itself a regulated and conditioned practice); or else, to intervene directly in the discursive field, as if it didn't have its own consistency, making of it the raw material of a psychological inquisition (judging what is said by the who says it), or practicing the symbolic valorization of the notions (by discerning in a science the concepts which are "reactionary" and those which are "progressive").

* * * * *

I should like to conclude by submitting several hypotheses to you:
—A progressive politics is one which recognizes the historical conditions and the specified rules of a practice, whereas other politics recognize only ideal necessities, univocal determinations, or the free play of individual initiatives.
—A progressive politics is one which defines in a practice the possibilities of transformations and the play of dependencies between these transformations, whereas other politics rely on the uniform abstraction of change or the thaumaturgical presence of genius.
—A progressive politics does not make of man or of conscience or of the subject in general the universal operator of all the transformations: it defines the levels and the different functions which the subjects can occupy in a domain which has its rules of formation.
—A progressive politics does not consider that the discourses are the

result of mute processes or the expression of a silent conscience; but rather that—science, or literature or religious statements, or political discourses—they form a practice which is articulated upon the other practices.

—A progressive politics, with respect to the scientific discourse, does not find itself in a position of "perpetual demand" or of "sovereign criticism," but it must know the manner in which the diverse scientific discourses, in their positivity (that is to say, as practices linked to certain conditions, obedient to certain rules, and susceptible to certain transformation) are part of a system of correlations with other practices.

This is the point where what I have been trying to do for about ten years now encounters the question which you are asking me. I ought to say: that's the point where your question—which is so legitimate and pertinent—reaches the heart of my own undertaking. If I were to reformulate this undertaking—under the pressure of your questioning which has not ceased to occupy me for almost two months—here is, more or less, what I would say: "To determine, in its diverse dimensions, what must have been in Europe, since the seventeenth century, the mode of existence of discourses and particularly of the scientific discourses (their rules of formation, with their conditions, their dependencies, their transformations), in order that the knowledge which is ours today could come to exist, and, in a more precise manner, that knowledge which has taken as its domain this curious object which is man."

I know, almost as much as any other person, how "thankless" such research can be—in the strict sense of the term—how irritating it is to approach the discourses not from the sweet, mute and intimate conscience which is expressed in them, but from an obscure ensemble of anonymous rules. I know how unpleasant it is to bring out the limits and the necessities of a practice, whereas one was in the habit of seeing unfold in a pure transparency the play of genius and liberty. I know how provoking it is to treat as a cluster of transformations this history of discourses which, until now, was animated by the reassuring metamorphoses of life and the intentional continuity of the past. Finally I know how unbearable it is to cut up, analyze, combine, recompose all these texts which have now returned to silence, without the transfigured face of the author being even discernible in it, inasmuch as each person wants to put, thinks he is putting of "himself" in his own discourse, when he undertakes to speak: what! so many words piled up, so many marks made on so much paper and offered to innumerable eyes, such a great zeal to preserve them beyond the gesture which articulates them, such a profound reverence determined to preserve them and inscribe them in the memory of men—all this, so that nothing will remain of this poor hand which has traced them, of this anxiety which sought to appease itself in them, and of this completed life which has nothing left but them for survival? Discourse, in its deepest determination, would not be a "trace"? And its murmur would not be the place of unsubstantial immortality? Would one have to admit that the time of the discourse is not the time of the conscience carried to the dimensions of history, or the time of present history in the form of conscience? Would I have to suppose that, in my discourse, my survival is not at stake? And that, by speaking, I do not exorcise my death, but that I establish it; or rather, that I abolish all inwardness in this outside which is so unconcerned with my life, and so neutral, that it does not distinguish between my life and my death?

I indeed understand all this and people's uneasiness. They undoubtedly have had enough difficulty in recognizing that their history, their economics, their social practices, the language which they speak, the mythology of their ancestors, even the fables which were told them in their childhood, obey rules which they are not aware of; they hardly wish to be dispossessed, in addition, of this discourse in which they wish to be able to say immediately, directly, what they are thinking, what they believe or imagine; they will prefer to deny that the discourse is a complex and differentiated practice obeying rules and analyzable transformations, rather than be deprived of this tender certainty, so consoling, of being able to change, if not the world, if not life, at least their "meaning" only through the freshness of a word which would come only from themselves and would remain indefinitely so very close to the source. So many things, in their language, have already escaped them; they do not want to lose, in addition, what they say, this little fragment of discourse—word or writing, it matters little—whose frail and uncertain existence is to extend their life further in time and space. They cannot bear—and one can understand them somewhat—being told: discourse is not life; its time is not yours; in it you will not reconcile yourself with death; it is quite possible that you have killed God under the weight of all that you have said; but don't think that you will make, from everything that you say, a man who will live longer than he. In each sentence that you pronounce—and very precisely in this one that you are busy writing at this moment, you have been answering a question so intently, for so many pages, through which you have felt personally concerned and who are going to sign this text with your name—in every sentence there reigns the nameless law, the white indifference: "What does it matter who is speaking; someone has said: what does it matter who is speaking."

Translated by Anthony M. Nazzaro

------

[1] This fact, already pointed out by Oscar Lange, explains at once the limited and so perfectly circumscribed place which the concepts of Marx occupy in the epistemological field which extends from Petty to contemporary econometrics, and the founding character of these same concepts for a theory of history.

[2] In which I follow the examples of the method given on several occasions by M. Canguilhem.

[3] I borrow this word from M. Canguilhem. He describes, better than I have done myself, what I have wished to do.

6

FOUCAULT RESPONDS TO SARTRE

Q: Michel Foucault, it is said, perhaps against your will, that you are a philosopher. What is philosophy for you?

MF: There was the great period of contemporary philosophy, that of Sartre and Merleau-Ponty, in which a philosophical text, a theoretical text, finally had to tell you what life, death, and sexuality were, if God existed or not, what liberty consisted of, what one had to do in political life, how to behave in regard to others, and so forth. One has the impression that this kind of philosophy is now obsolete, that philosophy if you like has if not vanished has at least been dispersed, and that there is a theoretical work that somehow joins together in the plural. Theory, the philosophic activity, is being produced in different domains that are separate from one other. There is a theoretical activity produced in the field of mathematics, a theoretical activity that manifests itself in the domain of linguistics or mythology or the history of religion, or simply in the domain of history itself. Finally, it is in this kind of plurality of theoretical work that a philosophy is being carried out which has not yet found its unique thinker and its unity of discourse.

Q: When did this rupture between the two moments occur?

MF: It was around 1950–55, at a time moreover exactly when Sartre himself renounced, I believe, what one could call philosophical speculation properly speaking, and when finally he invested his own philosophical activity in behavior that was political.

Q: You wrote in the conclusion of your work *The Order of Things* that man is neither the oldest nor the most constant problem that has been raised to human knowledge (*savoir*). Man, you say, is an invention of which the archeology of our thought shows the recent date and perhaps the coming end. It's one of the sentences that has stirred up readers the most. In your opinion what is man's date of birth in the space of knowledge?

MF: The 19th century was the century when a certain number of very important things were invented, microbiology and electromagnetism for example; it's also the century when the human sciences were invented. To invent the human sciences apparently meant to make of man the object of a possible knowledge (*savoir*). It was to constitute man as an object of knowledge (*connaissance*). Yet, in this same 19th century one hoped, one dreamed the great eschatological myth of the 19th century, which was somehow to make this knowledge (*connaissance*) of man exist so that man could be liberated by it from his alienations, liberated from all the determinations of which he was not the master, so that he could, thanks to this knowledge of himself, become again or for the first time master of himself, self-possessed. In other words, one made of man an object of knowledge so that man could become subject of his own liberty and of his own existence.

Yet what happened—and for this reason one can say that man was born in the 19th century—was that insofar as these investigations into man as a possible object of knowledge (*savoir*) were deployed, something very serious was discovered: that this famous man, this human nature, this human essence or this essential human feature was never discovered. When one analyzed for example the phenomena of madness or neurosis, what was discovered was an unconscious, an unconscious completely traversed by impulses and instincts, an unconscious that functioned according to mechanisms and according to a topological space which had absolutely nothing to do with what one could expect of the human essence, of freedom or human existence, an unconscious that functioned like a language, as has been said recently. And consequently, insofar as man was sought out in his depths, to that extent he disappeared. The further one went, the less one found. And similarly for language. From the beginning of the 19th century the human languages had been investigated in order to try and discover some of the great constants of the human mind. It was hoped that, by studying the life of words, the evolution of grammars, by comparing languages to one another, somehow man himself would be revealed, either in the unity of his face or in his different profiles. Yet, by penetrating into language, what did one find? One found structures, correlations, a system that is in some way quasi-logical, and man, in his liberty, in his existence, there again had disappeared.

Q: Nietzsche announced the death of God. You foresee, it would seem, the death of his murderer, man. It's a just turn of things. Isn't the disappearance of man contained in the disappearance of god?

MF: This disappearance of man at the very moment that we sought him in his roots doesn't mean that the human sciences will disappear. I never said that, but rather that the human sciences will now be deployed within a space whose horizon is no longer closed or defined by this humanism. Man disappears in philosophy, not as object of knowledge (*savoir*) but as subject of freedom and existence. Yet, man as subject of his own consciousness and of his own liberty is really a sort of correlative image of god. Man of the 19th century is god incarnated in humanity. There was a kind of theologizing of man, a re-descent of god to earth in which god became 19th century man theologized. When Feuerbach said that "we must recuperate on earth the treasures that have been spent in the heavens," he placed in the heart of man the treasures that man had formerly attributed to god. And Nietzsche was the one who by denouncing the death of god at the same time denounced this divinized man that the 19th century never ceased to dream. And when Nietzsche announced the coming of the superman, what he announced was not the coming of a man who would resemble a god more than a man, but rather the coming of a man who would no longer have any relation with this god whose image he continued to bear.

Q: Is this the reason that when you speak of the end of this recent invention, you say "perhaps"?

MF: Of course. I am sure of all this only insofar as it's a matter of doing (of my doing) a diagnosis of the present.

You were asking me a while ago how and in what way philosophy had changed. Well, perhaps one could say this: philosophy from Hegel to Sartre has essentially been a totalizing enterprise, if not of the world or of knowledge (*savoir*), at least of human experience. I would say that perhaps if there is now an autonomous philosophical activity, if there can be a philosophy that is not simply a sort of theoretical activity within mathematics or linguistics or ethnology or political economy, if there is a philosophy free or independent of all these domains, then one could define it as a diagnostic activity. To diagnose the present is to say what the present is, and how our present is absolutely different from all that is not it, that is to say, from our past. Perhaps this is the task for philosophy now.

Q: How do you define structuralism today?

MF: When you ask those who are classified under the rubric of "structuralism"—like Lévi-Strauss, Lacan, Althusser and the linguists, etc.—they answer that they have nothing in common with one another, or very little in common. Structuralism is a category that exists for others, for those who are not structuralists. It's from the outside that one can say that so and so are structuralists. You must ask Sartre who the structuralists are, since he thinks that Lévi-Strauss, Althusser, Dumézil, Lacan and me constitute a coherent group, a group constituting some kind of unity that we ourselves don't perceive.

Q: Well then, how would you define your work?

MF: My own work? As you know, it's very limited. Very schematically, it consists of trying to discover in the history of science and of human knowledge something that would be like its unconscious. My working hypothesis is roughly this: the history of science and of knowledge doesn't simply obey the general law of reason's progress; it's not human consciousness or human reason that somehow possesses the laws of its history. Underneath what science itself knows there is something it does not know; and its history, its becoming, its periods and accidents obey a number of laws and determinations. These laws and determinations are what I have tried to bring to light. I have tried to unearth an autonomous domain that would be the unconscious of science, the unconscious of knowledge, that would have its own laws, just as the individual human unconscious has its own laws and determinations.

Q: You just alluded to Sartre. You have saluted his magnificent efforts, efforts which you have said are those of a man of the 19th century trying to think in the 20th. He was even, you have said, the last Marxist. Since then Sartre has responded to you. He reproaches the structuralists for constituting a new ideology, which he calls the last barrier the bourgeoisie can still erect against Marx. What do you think of this?

MF: I would say two things in response. First, Sartre is a man with too much important work to do—literary, philosophical, political—to have the time to read my book. In fact, he hasn't read it. Consequently, what he says about it can't seem very pertinent to me. Secondly, I'll confess something to you. I was in the Communist Party some time ago for a few months, or a little more than several months, and at that time Sartre was defined for us as the last rampart of bourgeois imperialism, the last stone of the edifice, etc. So it's with amused astonishment that I find this phrase coming from Sartre's pen now, fifteen years later. Let's say that he and I have turned around the same axis.

Q: You don't find any originality there?

MF: No, it's a phrase that's been around for twenty years; he uses it, that's his right. He's giving back change for money we once passed to him... .

Q: Sartre reproaches you, and other philosophers as well, for neglecting and showing contempt for history. Is it true?

MF: No historian has ever reproached me for this. There is a sort of myth of History for philosophers. Philosophers are generally very ignorant of all other disciplines outside their own. There is a mathematics for philosophers, a biology for philosophers, and also a History. For philosophers, History is a kind of grand and extensive continuity where the liberty of individuals and economic and social determinations come to be intertwined. If you touch one of these great themes—continuity, the effective exercise of human freedom, the articulation of individual liberty with social determinations—then right away these grave gentlemen begin to cry rape, and that history has been assassinated. In fact, it was some time ago that people as important as Marc Bloch, Lucien Fèbvre and the English historians put an end to this myth of History. They write history in a completely different mode. The philosophical myth of History, this philosophical myth that I am accused of having murdered, well, I would be delighted if I have killed it, since that was exactly what I wanted to do. But not at all history in general. One doesn't murder history, but history for philosophy. That's what I wanted to kill.

Q: Who are the thinkers, scholars and philosophers who have marked or influenced your intellectual formation?

MF: I belong to a generation of people for whom the horizon of reflection was defined by Husserl in a general way, Sartre more precisely and Merleau-Ponty even more precisely. It's clear that around 1950–55, for reasons that are equally political, ideological and scientific, and very difficult to straighten out, this horizon toppled for us. Suddenly it vanished and we found ourselves before a sort of great empty space inside which developments became much less ambitious, much more limited and regional. It's clear that linguistics in the manner of Jakobson, the history of religions and mythologies in the manner of Dumézil, were for us invaluable points of support.

Q: How could your position in regard to action and politics be defined?

MF: The French left has lived on a myth of sacred ignorance. What has changed is the idea that political thought can be politically correct only if it is scientifically rigorous. And in this sense, I think that the whole effort made today by a group of communist intellectuals to re-evaluate Marx's concepts, to finally grasp them at their roots in order to analyze them and to define the use that one can and must make of them, I think this whole effort is both political and scientific. And the idea that to devote oneself as we are doing now to properly theoretical and speculative activities is to turn away from politics strikes me as completely false. It's not because we are turning away from politics that we are occupied with such strictly and meticulously defined theoretical problems, but rather because we realize that every form of political action can only be articulated in the strictest way with a rigorous theoretical reflection.

Q: A philosophy like existentialism encouraged people to action and engagement. You are reproached for having the opposite attitude.

MF: Well, that is a reproach. It's normal. But once again, the difference is not that we have now separated politics from theory, but rather to the contrary: insofar as we bring theory and politics more closely together, we refuse this politics of learned ignorance that I believe characterizes the one that is called engagement.

Q: Is it a language or vocabulary that today separates the philoso-phers and scholars from the great public and the people with whom they live as contemporaries?

MF: It seems to me, on the contrary, that today more than ever the transmission of knowledge (*savoir*) is extensive and efficacious. Knowledge in the 14th and 15th centuries, for example, was defined in a social space that was circular and restricted. Knowledge was a secret, and the authenticity of knowl-edge was at the same time guaranteed and protected by the fact that this knowl-edge didn't circulate or circulated only among a strictly defined number of peo-ple; as soon as knowledge was made public, it ceased to be knowledge and con-sequently ceased to be true.

Today we are at a very developed stage of a mutation that began in the 17th and 18th centuries when knowledge finally became a kind of public thing. To know was to see clearly what every individual placed in the same conditions could see and verify. To that extent the structure of knowledge became public. Everyone possessed knowledge; it's simply not always the same knowledge, with the same degree of formation or precision, etc. But there weren't ignorant people on one side and scholars on the other. What happens at one point in knowledge is very quickly reflected at another point. And to this extent, I believe, knowledge has never been more specialized, yet never has it communi-cated with itself more quickly.

Translated by John Johnston

7

THE ARCHEOLOGY OF KNOWLEDGE

Q: You have entitled your book *The Archeology of Knowledge*. Why "archeology"?

MF: For two reasons. I first used the word somewhat blindly, in order to designate a form of analysis that wouldn't at all be a history (in the sense that one recounts the history of inventions or of ideas) and that wouldn't be an epistemology either, that is to say, the internal analysis of the structure of a science. This other thing I have called therefore "archeology." And then, retrospectively, it seemed to me that chance has not been too bad a guide: after all, this word "archeology" can almost mean—and I hope I will be forgiven for this—description of the *archive*. I mean by archive the set of discourses actually pronounced; and this set of discourses is envisaged not only as a set of events which would have taken place once and for all and which would remain in abeyance, in the limbo or purgatory of history, but also as a set that continues to function, to be transformed through history, and to provide the possibility of appearing in other discourses.

Q: Isn't there also in archeology the idea of excavation, of a search into the past?

MF: No doubt. The word "archeology" bothers me a little, because it recovers two themes that are not exactly mine. First, the theme of a beginning, as *arché* in Greek signifies. Yet I try not to study the beginning in the sense of the first origin, of a foundation starting from which the rest would be possible. I am not searching for the first solemn moment after which all of Western mathematics becomes possible, for example. I don't go back to Euclid or Pythagoras. It's always the relative beginnings that I am searching for, more the institutionalizations or the transformations than the foundings or foundations. And then I'm equally bothered by the idea of excavations. What I'm looking for are not relations that are secret, hidden, more silent or deeper than the consciousness of men. I try

57

on the contrary to define the relations on the very surface of discourse; I attempt to make visible what is invisible only because it's too much on the surface of things.

Q: You are interested, that is, in the phenomena, and refuse interpretation.

MF: I'm not looking underneath discourse for the thought of men, but try to grasp discourse in its manifest existence, as a practice that obeys certain rules—of formation, existence, co-existence—and systems of functioning. It is this practice, in its consistency and almost in its materiality, that I describe.

Q: So you refuse psychology.

MF: Absolutely. One must be able to make an historical analysis of the transformation of discourse without having recourse to the thought of men, to their mode of perception, their habits and the influences to which they have submitted, etc.

Q: You begin your book with the observation that history and the human sciences have been inversely transformed. Instead of searching for the events that would constitute the ruptures, history now searches for continuities, whereas the human sciences search for discontinuities.

MF: Indeed, historians today—and I am thinking of course of the *Annales* school, Marc Bloch, Lucien Fèbvre, Ferdinand Braudel—have tried to enlarge the periodizations that historians usually make. Braudel, for example, has succeeded in defining a notion of material civilization that would have an extremely slow evolution: the material universe of European peasants from the end of the Middle Ages to the 18th century—the landscape, techniques, tools and crafted objects, their customs—has been modified in an extremely slow manner; one might say that it has developed on a very gradual incline. These great blocks, much more massive than the events one ordinarily isolates, have now become part of the objects that historians can describe. Thus one sees large continuities appearing that until this work had never been isolated. On the other hand, the historians of ideas and of the sciences, who used to speak above all in terms of the continuous progress of reason, of the progressive advent of rationalism, etc., now insist on discontinuities and ruptures. For example, the break between Aristotelian and Galilean physics, the absolute eruption represented by the birth of chemistry at the end of the 18th century. It's from this paradox that I started: the regular historians were revealing continuities, while the historians of ideas were liberating discontinuities. But I believe that they are two symmetrical and inverse effects of the same methodological renewal of history in general.

Q: Which is to say that when you attack those who mythologize history, by showing that they are attaching themselves again to the traditional philosophy of transcendental consciousness, of man as sovereign, you attack them on their own ground, which is that of history. Whereas the structuralists, who attack them equally, do it on another terrain.

MF: I don't believe that the structuralists have ever attacked the historians, but a certain historicism, a certain reaction and historicist mistrust with which their work collided. A number of traditional thinkers have been frightened by structural analysis. Not, to be sure, because one began to analyze the formal relations among indifferent elements; that was done a long time ago, and there was no cause for alarm. But these traditional thinkers felt very strongly that what was in question was the status of the subject. If it is true that language and the unconscious can be analyzed in structural terms, then what is there of this famous speaking subject, this man reputed to put language to work, to speak it, to transform it, to make it live! What is there of this man, reputed to have an unconscious, capable of becoming conscious of this unconscious, of assuming its burden and making a history of his fate! I believe that the belligerence or in any case the bad feelings that structuralism raised among the traditionalists was linked to the fact that they felt that the status of the subject had been put back into question.

And they sought refuge on a terrain that appeared for their cause, infinitely more solid, that of history. And they said: let's admit that a language, considered outside its historical evolution, outside of its development, consists in effect of a set of relations; let's admit that the unconscious in an individual functions like a structure or set of structures, that the unconscious can be located starting from structural facts; there is at least one thing on which the structure will never catch: that's history. For there is a becoming that structural analysis will never account for, a progression which on the one hand is made of a continuity, whereas the structure by definition is discontinuous, and on the other hand is made by a subject: man himself, or humanity, or consciousness, or reason, it matters little. For them, there is an absolute subject of history that makes history, that assures its continuity, that is the author and guarantor of this continuity. As for the structural analyses, they can never take place but in the synchronic cross section cut out from this continuity of history subject to man's sovereignty.

When one tries to challenge the primacy of the subject in the very domain of history, then there is a new panic amongst all the old faithful, for that was their line of defense, the point from which they could limit structural analysis—stop the "cancer"—by restricting the power of its disturbance. If, in regard to history, and precisely in regard to the history of knowledge or of reason, one manages to show that it doesn't at all obey the same model as consciousness; if one succeeds in showing that the time of knowledge or of discourse is not at all organized or laid out like the time of lived experience, that it presents discontinuities and specific transformations; if finally, one shows that there is no need to pass through the subject, through man as subject, in order to analyze the history of knowledge, one raises great difficulties, but one touches perhaps on an important problem.

Q: As a result, you were led to challenge the philosophy of the last two hundred years, or, what is worse for it, to leave it aside.

MF: Indeed, at present this whole philosophy, which since Descartes has given primacy to the subject, is falling apart before our eyes.

Q: And do you date the onset of this decline from Nietzsche?

MF: It seems to me that one could fix this moment starting from Marx, Nietzsche and Freud.

Q: In addition, in your book, you denounce the anthropologizing interpretation of Marx and the interpretation of Nietzsche in terms of a transcendental consciousness as a refusal to take into consideration what is new in their contributions.

MF: Exactly.

Q: I quote the following passage from your introduction: "To make of historical analysis the discourse of continuity and to make of human consciousness the originary subject of all progress and of every practice are two phases of the same system of thought, where time is conceived in terms of totalization and revolutions are never but the assumptions of consciousness." Aren't you directly attacking Sartre there, all the more as the assumption of consciousness and totalization belong especially to his vocabulary?

MF: In using those words Sartre only takes up a general style of analysis that one can find in the work of Lucien Goldman, Georg Lukács, Dilthey and the Hegelians of the 19th century. The words are certainly not specific to Sartre.

Q: Sartre would simply be one of the end points of this transcendental philosphy that is falling apart?

MF: That's right.

Q: But apart from the structuralists, who find themselves in a position analogous to your own, there are few philosophers who are conscious of the end of transcendental philosophy.

MF: On the contrary, I believe there are many, among whom I would put Gilles Deleuze in the first rank.[1]

Q: When, in *The Order of Things,* you wrote that man is to be cast aside, you unleashed "diverse movements." Yet, in *The Archeology of Knowledge,* you say that not only things but even words are to be cast aside.

MF: That's what I meant. My title *The Order of Things* [*Les Mots et les choses*, i.e. words and things] was perfectly ironic. No one saw it clearly;

doubtlessly because there wasn't enough play in my text for the irony to be sufficiently visible. There is a problem: how can it happen that real things, things that are perceived, can come to be articulated by words within a discourse. Is it that words impose on us the outline of things, or is it that things, through some operation of the subject, come to be transcribed on the surface of words. That's not at all the old problem that I wanted to treat in *The Order of Things*. I wanted to displace it: to analyze the discourses themselves, that is, these discursive practices that are intermediary between words and things; these discursive practices starting from which one can define what are the things and mark out the usage of words. Let's take a very simple example. In the 17th century the naturalists multiplied the descriptions of plants and animals. One can write a history of these descriptions in two ways. Either by starting with things and saying: the animals being what they are, the plants being such as we see them, how is it that the people of the 17th and 18th centuries saw them and described them? What did they observe? What did they omit? What have they seen, what have they not seen? Or one can do the analysis in the inverse direction, by establishing the semantic field of the 17th and 18th centuries, by seeing what words and consequently what concepts they then had available, what the rules of usage for these words were, and starting from there, determining what grid or pattern was placed over the whole set of plants and animals. These are the two traditional analyses.

I have tried to do something else, to show that in a discourse, as in natural history, there were rules of formation for objects (which are not the rules of utilization for words), rules of formation for concepts (which are not the laws of syntax), rules of formation for theories (which are neither deductive nor rhetorical rules). These are the rules put into operation through a discursive practice at a given moment that explain why a certain thing is seen (or omitted); why it is envisaged under such an aspect and analyzed at such a level; why such a word is employed with such a meaning and in such a sentence. Consequently, the analysis starting from things and the analysis starting from words appear at this moment as secondary in relation to a prior analysis, which would be the discursive analysis.

In my book there are no analyses of words and no analyses of things. And a number of people—the oafs and hedgehoppers—have said it's scandalous, that in a book called *The Order of Things* there are no "things." And the more subtle ones have said that there is no semantic analysis. Well, to be sure: I didn't want to do either.

Q: Since your scientific trajectory begins with a sort of empirical groping, how did you arrive—by what itinerary—at this completely theoretical book which is *The Archeology of Knowledge*?

MF: Yes, of course, it started with empirical research on madness, sickness and mental illness, on medicine in the 18th and 19th centuries, and on the set of disciplines (natural history, general grammar, and the exchange of money) that I treated in *The Order of Things*. Why has this research led me to construct the theoretical machinery of *The Archeology of Knowledge,* which seems to me to be a rather difficult book for the reader? I encountered several problems: when one did a history of the sciences one treated in a privileged, almost exclusive fashion the beautiful, very formal sciences like mathematics and theoretical physics. But when one broached disciplines like the empirical sciences, one was very constricted, most often being content with a sort of inventory of discoveries; it was said that these disciplines were only in sum a mix of truths and errors; in these knowledges that are so imprecise, the minds of men, their prejudices, mental habits and the influences to which they submit, the images in their heads, their dreams—all that prevents them from acceding to the truth; and the history of these sciences was finally only the history of the mixture of these massive and numerous errors with some nuggets of truth, the problem being to know how one day someone had discovered a nugget.

Such a description bothers me for several reasons. First because, in the real historical life of men, these famous empirical sciences that the historians or the epistemologists neglect have a colossal importance. The progress of medicine has had consequences for human life, for the human species, for the eonomy of societies, and for the social organization certainly as great as those that the discoveries of theoretical physics have had. I regretted that these empirical sciences had not been studied.

On the other hand, it seemed interesting to me to study these empirical sciences insofar as they are more closely linked to social practices than the theoretical sciences are. For example, medicine or political economy are disciplines perhaps lacking a high degree of scientificity, compared to mathematics; but their articulations onto social practices are very numerous and that's precisely what interested me. The Archeology that I just described is a kind of theory for a history of empirical knowledge (*savoir*).

Q: Hence your choice, for example, of a history of madness (*Madness and Civilization*).

MF: Exactly.

Q: The advantage of your method, among others, is thus to function in two dimensions: diachronically and synchronically. For example, for *Madness and Civilization* you go back in time and study the modifications, whereas in the case of natural history in the 17th and 18th centuries, in *The Order of Things,* you study this science in a state that is not completely static, but more immobile.

MF: Not exactly immobile. I tried to define the transformations: to show the discoveries, inventions, changes of perspective and theoretical upheavals that could occur starting from a certain system of regularities. One can show for example what makes possible the appearance of the idea of evolution in the 18th century in the discursive practice of natural history; or what makes possible the emergence of a theory of the organism, which was unknown to the first naturalists. Thus when certain people, happily very few in number, accused me of only describing states of knowledge and not the transformations, it was simply because they hadn't read the book. If they had, if only leafing through it in a cursory fashion, they would have seen that it deals only with transformations and with the order in which these transformations occur.

Q: Your method studies the practice of discourse, a method that you base, in *The Archeology of Knowledge,* on the statement, which you distinguish radically from the grammatical sentence and the logical proposition. What do you mean by the statement (*énoncé*)?

MF: The sentence is a grammatical unity of elements linked together by linguistic rules. What the logicians call a proposition is a set of symbols constructed such that one can say if it is true or false, correct or not. What I call a statement is a set of signs that can be a sentence or a proposition, but envisaged at the level of its existence.

Q: You deny being a structuralist even if for the common consciousness you are part of the group. But your methodology has two points in common with the structural method: the refusal of an anthropological discourse and the absence of a speaking subject. Insofar as what is in question is the place and status of man, that is, of the subject, don't you align yourself automatically on the side of the structuralists?

MF: I think that structuralism is inscribed today within a great transformation of knowledge (*savoir*) in the human sciences, and that this transformation has less to do with the analysis of structures than with a challenge of the anthropological status, the status of the subject, and the privileges of man. And my method is inscribed within the framework of this transformation in the same way that structuralism is—along side of the latter but not in it.

Q: You speak of structuralism's "legitimate limits." Yet, one has the impression that structuralism tends to absorb everything: myths with Lévi-Strauss, the unconscious with Lacan, then literary criticism—all the human sciences pass through it.

MF: I don't have to speak for the structuralists. But it seems to me that one could say this in response to your question: structuralism is a method whose field of application is not defined *a priori*. What is defined at the start are the rules of the method and the level at which one inserts oneself in order to apply them. It may very well be that one can do structural analyses in domains that are absolutely unforeseen at this point. I don't believe that one can set *a priori* limits to the expanse of this research.

Translated by John Johnston

---

1 In 1969, at the time of this interview, Gilles Deleuze had published, among others: *Nietzsche and Philosophy.* [French, 1962] (New York: University of Columbia Press, 1983); *Bergsonism.* [1966] (New York: Zone Books, 1988); *Spinoza: Expressionism in Philosophy.* [1968] (New York: Zone Books, 1990); *Logic of Sense.* [1969] (New York: Columbia University Press, 1990) [Ed.]

8

THE BIRTH OF A WORLD

Q: Michel Foucault, you are known today as one of the great theorists of the immense field of investigation constituted by epistemology, and above all as the author of two books enthusiastically received by a vast public: *Madness and Civilization* and *The Order of Things*. You just recently published *The Archeology of Knowledge*. Would you mind trying to specify what unites them?

MF: The three books that precede this last one—*Madness and Civilization, The Order of Things* and *The Birth of the Clinic*—I wrote in a state of happy semi-consciousness, with a great deal of naiveté and a bit of innocence. At the last moment, while editing *The Order of Things,* I realized that these three series of studies were not unrelated and that, moreover, they raised a large number of problems and difficulties, so much so in fact that even before finishing *The Order of Things* I felt obliged to write another book which would clarify the unity of the preceding ones and which would attempt to resolve the problems they had raised. I was very disappointed when I became aware of this. When writing one always thinks that it's the last time, but in fact it's not true. The questions raised and the objections made have forced me to go back to work, reasonably stimulated, either out of amusement or interest, and sometimes out of irritation. This book, *The Archeology of Knowledge,* is at once a resumption of what I have already attempted, motivated by the desire to correct the inaccuracies and carelessness contained in the precedent books, and an attempt to trace in advance the path of a later work that I really hope never to write, owing to unforeseen circumstances!

Q: Could you clarify this concept of archeology which is essential to your undertaking?

MF: I have used it as a play on words to designate something that would be the description of the *archive* and not at all the discovery of a beginning or the bringing to light of the bones of the past.

By the archives, I mean first the mass of things spoken in a culture, presented, valorized, re-used, repeated and transformed. In brief, this whole verbal mass that has been fashioned by men, invested in their techniques and in their institutions and woven into their existence and their history. I envisage this mass of things that were said not on the side of language and of the linguistic system that they elicited, but on the side of the operations which give it birth. My problem could be stated as follows: How does it happen that at a given period something could be said and something else has never been said? It is, in a word, the analysis of the historical conditions that account for what one says or of what one rejects, or of what one transforms in the mass of spoken things.

The "archive" appears then as a kind of great practice of discourse, a practice which has its rules, its conditions, its functioning and its effects.

The problems raised by the analysis of this practice are the following: What are the different particular types of discursive practice that one can find in a given period? What are the relationships that one can establish between these different practices? What relationships do they have with non-discursive practices, such as political, social or economic practices? What are the transformations of which these practices are susceptible?

Q: You have been reproached—I am thinking of Jean-Paul Sartre in particular—for wanting to substitute archeology for history, for replacing "the cinema with the magic lantern" (Sartre). Is your vision the opposite of a historical and dialectical thought like Sartre's? How does it contradict the latter's?

MF: I am completely opposed to a certain conception of history which takes for its model a kind of great continuous and homogenous evolution, a sort of great mythic life. Historians now know very well that the mass of historical documents can be combined according to different modes which have neither the same traits nor the same kind of evolution. The history of material civilization (farming techniques, habitat, domestic tools, means of transportation) doesn't unfold in the same way as the history of political institutions or as the history of monetary flows. What Marc Bloch, Febvre and Braudel have shown for history *tout court* can be shown, I think, for the history of ideas, of knowledge and of thought in general. Thus it is possible to write a history of general paralysis, the history of Pasteur's thought; but one can also, at a level that has been rather neglected until now, undertake the analysis of medical discourse in the 19th century or in the modern era. This history will not be one of discoveries and of errors, it will not be one of influences and originalities, but the history of conditions that make possible the appearance, the functioning and the transformation of medical discourse.

I am also opposed to a form of history which assumes change as a given and which gives itself the task of discovering its cause. I believe that there is a preliminary task for the historian, more modest if you like, or more radical, which consists in raising the question of what this change constitutes exactly. This means: Are there not between several levels of change certain modifications that are immediately visible, that leap to the eye as highly individualized events, and others, however exact, that are buried and appear much less evident? In other words, the first task is to distinguish different types of events. The second is to define the transformations that have actually been produced, the system according to which certain variables have remained constant while others have been modified. For the great mythology of change, evolution and the *perpetuum mobile* we must substitute a serious description of types of events and systems of transformation, and the establishment of series, and series of series. Obviously this is not cinema.

Q: Your work has often been brought together with that of Claude Lévi-Strauss and Jacques Lacan under the label of "structuralism." To what extent do you accept this grouping? Is there a real convergence in your different researches?

MF: It's for those who use the label to designate very diverse works to say what makes us "structuralists." You know the joke: what's the difference between Bernard Shaw and Charlie Chaplin? There is no difference, since they both have a beard, with the exception of Chaplin of course.

Q: In *The Order of Things* you speak of the "death of man," which has provoked vivid emotional reactions and innumerable controversies among our good humanists. What do you think of all this?

MF: The death of man is nothing to get particularly excited about. It's one of the visible forms of a much more general decease, if you like. I don't mean by it the death of god but the death of the subject, of the Subject in capital letters, of the subject as origin and foundation of Knowledge (*savoir*), of Freedom, of Language and History.

One can say that all of Western civilization has been subjugated, and philosophers have only certified the fact by referring all thought and all truth to consciousness, to the Self, to the Subject. In the rumbling that shakes us today, perhaps we have to recognize the birth of a world where the subject is not one but split, not sovereign but dependent, not an absolute origin but a function ceaselessly modified.

Translated by John Johnston

9

Rituals of Exclusion

Q: Mr. Foucault, it's been said that you've given us a new way of studying events. You've formulated an archeology of knowledge, the sciences of man, objectifying literary, or non-literary, documents of a period, and treating them as "archives." And you're also interested in current politics. How do you live out your science; how do you apply it to what's going on today? In other words, how do you uncover today's discourse? How do you perceive changes taking place at this moment?

MF: In the first place, I am not at all sure that I have invented a new method, as you were so kind to assert; what I am doing is not so different from many other contemporary endeavors, American, English, French, German. I claim no originality. It is true, though, that I have dealt especially with phenomena of the past: the system of exclusion and the confinement of the insane in European civilization from the sixteenth to the nineteenth century, the establishment of medical science and practice at the beginning of the nineteenth century, the organization of sciences of man in the eighteenth and nineteenth centuries. But I was interested in them—in fact, profoundly interested—because I saw in them ways of thinking and behaving that are still with us. I try to show, based upon their historical establishment and formation, those systems which are still ours today and within which we are trapped. It is a question of presenting a critique of our own time, based upon retrospective analyses.

Q: In terms of what's been happening in higher education around the world, do you see us, yourself, all of us, imprisoned in some kind of system?

MF: The form in which societies pass on knowledge is determined by a complex system: it hasn't yet been fully analyzed, but it seems to me that the system is being shattered; more under the influence of a revolutionary movement, in fact, than of mere theoretical or speculative criticism. There's a significant difference between the insane and the sick on the one hand, and students on the other, in this respect: in our society it is difficult for the insane who are confined or the sick who are hospitalized to make their own revolution; so we have to question these systems of exclusion of the sick and the insane from the outside, through a technique of critical demolition. The university system, however, can be put into question by the students themselves. At that point criticism coming from the outside, from theoreticians, historians or archivists, is no longer enough. And the students become their own archivists.

Q: Several years ago, a document appeared here called *The Student as Nigger*. Are there parallels aside from the master-slave relationship between the student as an excluded figure and the madman? And are there other "pariahs" defined and set by society in order to maintain its own rationality and cohesion?

MF: Your question is far-reaching and difficult to answer. At any rate, it concerns me greatly because it points essentially in the same direction as my work. Until now, it seems to me that historians of our own society, of our own civilization, have especially sought to get at the inner secret of our civilization, its spirit, the way it establishes its identity, the things it values. On the other hand, there has been much less study of what has been rejected from our civilization. It seemed to me interesting to try to understand our society and civilization in terms of its systems of exclusion, of rejection, of refusal, in terms of what it does not want, its limits, the way it is obliged to suppress a number of things, people, processes, what it must let fall into oblivion, its repression-suppression system. I know very well that many thinkers—though if only since Freud—have already tackled the problem. But I think there are exclusions other than the suppression of sexuality that have not been analyzed. There's the exclusion of the insane. There is, up to a certain point, the exclusion whereby we short-circuit those who are sick and reintegrate them in a sort of marginal circuit, the medical circuit. And there is the student: to a certain extent he is similarly caught inside a circuit which possesses a dual function. First, a function of exclusion. The student is put outside of society, on a campus. Furthermore, he is excluded while being transmitted a knowledge which is traditional in nature, obsolete, "academic" and not directly tied to the needs and problems of today. This exclusion is underscored by the organization around the student of social mechanisms which are fictitious, artificial and quasi-theatrical (hierarchical relationships, academic exercises, the "court" of examination, evaluation). Finally, the student is given a gamelike way of life; he is offered a kind of distraction, amusement, freedom which, again, has nothing to do with real life: it is this kind of artificial, theatrical society, a society of cardboard, that is being built around him; and thanks to this, young people from 18 to 25 are thus, as it were, neutralized by and for society, rendered safe, ineffective, socially and politically castrated. There is the first function of the university: to put students out of circulation. Its second function, however, is one of integration. Once a student has spent six or seven years of his life within this artificial society, he becomes "absorbable": society can consume him. Insidiously, he will have received the values of this society. He will have been given socially desirable models of behavior, so that this ritual of exclusion will finally take on the value of inclusion and recuperation or reabsorption. In this sense, the university is no doubt little different from those systems in so-called primitive societies in which the young men are kept outside the village during their adolescence, undergoing rituals of initiation which separate them and sever all contact between them and real, active society. At the end of the specified time, they can be entirely recuperated or reabsorbed.

Q: Could you then study the university the way you studied hospitals? Hasn't the system of the university changed somewhat? For example, are there not in recent history, and for various reasons, exclusions that were initiated by the excluded themselves?

MF: What I have just said is obviously only a very rough outline; it needs to be tightened up, for the mode of exclusion of students was certainly different in the 19th from that in the 20th century. In the nineteenth century, higher education was only for the children of the bourgeoisie, or that fringe of the petite-bourgeoisie which the higher echelon needed for its industry, its scientific development, its technical skills, etc. Universities now have a greater number of students from poorer groups of the petite-bourgeoisie. Thus we have, inside the university, explosive conflicts between, on the one hand, a lower-middle class which finds itself politically and socially more and more proletarianized by the very development of this higher bourgeoisie, for its development depends upon technology and science, that is, upon those contributions to it that are made by students and scientists sought from the ranks of the lower-middle class. This end result is that the upper-middle class, in its universities, recruits and enrolls, in order to turn them into scientists or technicians, people already undergoing a proletarian conversion and who consequently arrive at the university bearing a revolutionary potential: the enemy is within the gates.

So the status of the university becomes problematical. The upper-middle class must see to it that universities remain environments of exclusion where students are cut off from their real milieu, that is, from one which is undergoing a proletarian change. Concomitantly, universities must increasingly provide rituals of inclusion inside a system of capitalistic norms. Thus we have the strengthening of the old traditional university, with its character of both theatricality and initiation. However, as soon as they enter the system, students understand that they are being played with, that someone is trying to turn them against their true origins and surroundings. There follows a political awareness, and the revolutionary explosion.

Q: Aesthetics aside, do you see in what's happening in the university a parallel with Peter Weiss's play *Marat-Sade*[1]—there also is a director-producer seeking to put on a play acted out by mental patients who try to turn the play against the spectators?

MF: That's a very interesting reference. I believe that play tells what is happening now better than many theoretical essays. When Sade was an inmate at Charenton, he wanted to have plays acted by the inmates. In Sade's mind, his plays were to question his own confinement; in fact, what happened was that the inmates acting out his plays questioned not only the system of confinement, but the system of oppression, the values which Sade enforced upon them as he made them act out his plays. To a certain extent, Sade plays today's professor, the liberal professor who says to his students, "Well, why don't you just question all the bourgeois values they want to impose upon you," and the students, acting out this theater of academic liberalism, end up questioning the professor himself.

Q: This is just what I wanted to ask you about the relation between faculty and students: are not professors in a way themselves excluded? After all, professors and administrators live in the university community as well as students. Of course, one could say that administrators are only representatives of society, but in most cases, they are professors who have become administrators, and often temporarily. Are there differences between faculty and students?

MF: I don't know the American university system well enough to give you even the beginning of an answer. In France, a professor is a public official and therefore is a part of the state apparatus. Whatever personal opinions he may hold, the professor, as a public official, maintains the system of transmission of knowledge required by the government, that is, by the bourgeois class whose interests are represented by the government. In the United States, it is probably different because of the open market for professors. I don't know whether the American academic is more threatened, more exploited, or more ready to accept the values imposed upon him. The position of professor is almost untenable at the present, as is perhaps that of the lower-middle class: are not professors the most striking manifestation of this class which, in the nineteenth century, at least in France, managed to obtain from the upper-middle class delegate the right to exercise power? There existed what has been called a Republic of Professors and the political framework of the Third Republic was borrowed directly from the teaching profession, or from professions of the same type, physicians, lawyers, etc. Now that the Republic is functioning in a quite different framework, the lower-middle class in France is losing all control of the state apparatus. Therein lies its sense of misfortune, and its simultaneous wavering between the temptation to join the students and their revolutionary struggle, and the temptation to regain power, to seduce once more that upper-middle class which is no longer willing to accept it except as a technician.

Q: Before coming to Buffalo, you were teaching at Vincennes, an avant-garde university, which some consider in complete chaos, seeking to adapt itself to the process you just described. You were saying that the position of professor is becoming untenable—coming as you are from Vincennes to Buffalo, did you find yourself in a strange, exotic land?

MF: When I arrived in Buffalo, I thought that I still was in Vincennes; in spite of relatively superficial differences in behavior, dress, gestures and speech, it seemed to me that the same struggle was being waged in France and the United States. However, I believe that, as far as tactics and political strategy are concerned, American students are in a much different position from their French counterparts. French students, in fact, have to deal with a large, organized working class which, through its unions and political organizations, clamors its allegiance to Marxism: French workers are perhaps ready to listen to students and understand their struggle, but at the same time, French students have to fight the conservative influence of the Communist Party and the C.G.T.[2] The situation of American students appears very different: it seems to me that the working class in America relates less easily to the students' cause. It must be more difficult for an American student to militate together with workers. On the other hand, the advantage in America is that there are no great conservative forces like the Communist Party and the C.G.T. In prohibiting and prosecuting the Communist Party for so many years, I think that the American government worked, in a sense, for the revolutionary cause; it kept open the possibility of ties between the students and the workers. Obviously, there is also in America a specific stress point, the racial problem that we also have in France, but on a much smaller scale (one must not forget that there is in France a rather sizable group of African, Algerian or black workers, which constitute a numerically important subproletariat).

Q: Has there been an intensified chauvinism in France in the last few years, a growing refusal of anything that comes from the outside? It's true that America is a melting pot; does it make a difference?

MF: Well, it seems to me that, at least in intellectual circles, one does not encounter in America the unbearable chauvinism one finds in France. One must not forget that we are a small country caught between the two great models, the United States on the one hand and the Soviet Union on the other. We had to struggle for a long time against these two models. It was the Communist Party which suggested and imposed the Russian one, and the struggle against the Party's conservative influence brought a somewhat systematic refusal of the Soviet model; on the other hand, a certain liberal bourgeoisie tied up with American interests never stopped putting forward the American model, against which it was also necessary to struggle. At that point, I think, the mechanisms of chauvinism appeared inside the French Left. These are mechanisms that are not always conscious; they manifest themselves by a game of exclusion, of refusal and oversight. American literature, for instance, is very little read in France. One does not read American philosophy, history and criticism at all. American books are translated after an enormous delay. One must not allow the struggle against American economic influence and relations to affect relations with American intellectuals. We must have a selective nationalism. I believe that a small country like France is necessarily bound to be somewhat nationalistic in its politics and economy if it wants to preserve some degree of independence; on the other hand, we must understand that a struggle which today is ideological, but will become some day openly revolutionary, is turning up in every corner of the world. Cultural chauvinism must be abandoned.

Q: This has been your first trip to America, your first teaching assignment in an American university. In relation to the cultural change which you just spoke about, how will these two months affect you?

MF: My problem is essentially the definition of the implicit systems in which we find ourselves prisoners; what I would like to grasp is the system of limits and exclusion which we practice without realizing it; I would like to make the cultural unconscious apparent. Therefore, the more I travel, the more I remove myself from my natural and habitual centers of gravity, the greater my chance of grasping the foundations I am obviously standing on. To that extent any trip—not, of course, in the sense of a sightseeing trip nor even a survey— any movement away from my original frame of reference, is fruitful. It is always good for me to change language and country. A simple example: in New York I was struck, as any foreigner would be, by the immediate contrast between the "good sections" and the poverty, even the misery, that surround them on the right and the left, North and South. I well know that one finds that same contrast in Europe, and that you too, when in Europe, are certainly shocked by the great misery in the poor sections of Paris, Hamburg or London, it doesn't matter where. Having lived in Europe for years, I had lost a sense of this contrast and had ended up believing that there had been a general rise in the standard of living of the whole population; I wasn't far from imagining that the proletariat was becoming middle class, that there were really no more poor people, that the social struggle, the struggle between classes, consequently, was coming to an end. Well, seeing New York, perceiving again suddenly this vivid contrast that exists everywhere but which was blotted out of my eyes by familiar forms of it, that was for me a kind of second revelation; the class struggle still exists, it exists more intensely.

Translated by J. K. Simon

---

1 Peter Weiss, *The Persecution and Assassination of Jean-Paul Marat, as performed by the Inmates of the Asylum of Charenton, under the Direction of the Marquis de Sade.* (New York: Atheneum, 1966). [Ed.]

2 The C.G.T. (General Confederation of Workers) then was a powerful trade-union closely linked to the French Communist Party. Cf. A. Belden Fields, *Trotskyism and Maoism: Theory and Practice in France and the United States* (New York: Autonomedia, 1988). [Ed.]

10

Intellectuals and Power

MICHEL FOUCAULT: A Maoist once said to me: "I can easily understand Sartre's purpose in siding with us; I can understand his goals and his involvement in politics; I can partially understand your position, since you've always been concerned with the problem of confinement. But Deleuze is an enigma." I was shocked by this statement because your position has always seemed particularly clear to me.

GILLES DELEUZE: Possibly we're in the process of experiencing a new relationship between theory and practice. At one time, practice was considered an application of theory, a consequence; at other times, it had an opposite sense and it was thought to inspire theory, to be indispensable for the creation of future theoretical forms. In any event, their relationship was understood in terms of a process of totalization. For us, however, the question is seen in a different light. The relationships beween theory and practice are far more partial and fragmentary. On one side, a theory is always local and related to a limited field and it is applied in another sphere, more or less distant from it. The relationship which holds in the application of a theory is never one of resemblance. Moreover, from the moment a theory moves into its proper domain, it begins to encounter obstacles, walls, and blockages which require its relay by another type of discourse (it is through this other discourse that it eventually passes to a different domain). Practice is a set of relays from one theoretical point to another, and theory is a relay from one practice to another. No theory can develop without eventually encountering a wall, and practice is necessary for piercing this wall. For example, your work began in the theoretical analysis of the context of confinement, specifically with respect to the psychiatric asylum within a capitalist society in the 19th century. Then you became aware of the necessity for confined individuals to speak for themselves, to create a relay (it's possible, on the contrary, that your function was already that of a relay in relation to them); and this group is found in prisons—these individuals are imprisoned. It was on this basis that you organized the Group of Information on Prisons (G.I.P.),[1] the object being to create conditions that permit the prisoners themselves to speak. It would be

74

absolutely false to say, as the Maoist implied, that in moving to this practice you were applying your theories. This was not an application; nor was it a project for initiating reforms or an enquiry in the traditional sense. The emphasis was altogether different: a system of relays within a larger sphere, within a multiplicity of parts that are both theoretical and practical. A theorising intellectual, for us, is no longer a subject, a representing or representative consciousness. Those who act and struggle are no longer represented, either by a group or a union that appropriates the right to stand as their conscience. Who speaks and acts? It is always a multiplicity, even within the person who speaks and acts. All of us are "groupuscules." Representation no longer exists; there's only action—theoretical action and practical action which serve as relays and form networks.

FOUCAULT: It seems to me that the political involvement of the intellectual was traditionally the product of two different aspects of his activity: his position as an intellectual in bourgeois society, in the system of capitalist production and within the ideology it produces or imposes (his exploitation, poverty, rejection, persecution, the accusations of subversive activity, immorality, etc); and his proper discourse to the extent that it revealed a particular truth, that it disclosed political relationships where they were unsuspected. These two forms of politicization did not exclude each other, but, being of a different order, neither did they coincide. Some were classed as "outcasts" and others as "socialists." During moments of violent reaction on the part of the authorities, these two positions were readily fused: after 1848, after the Commune, after 1940. The intellectual was rejected and persecuted at the precise moment when the facts became incontrovertible, when it was forbidden to say that the emperor had no clothes. The intellectual spoke the truth to those who had yet to see it, in the name of those who were forbidden to speak the truth: he was conscience, consciousness, and eloquence.

In the most recent upheaval,[2] the intellectual discovered that the masses no longer need him to gain knowledge: they know perfectly well, without illusion; they know far better than he and they are certainly capable of expressing themselves. But there exists a system of power which blocks, prohibits, and invalidates this discourse and this knowledge, a power not only found in the manifest authority of censorship, but one that profoundly and subtly penetrates an entire societal network. Intellectuals are themselves agents of this system of power—the idea of their responsibility for "consciousness" and discourse forms part of the system. The intellectual's role is no longer to place himself "somewhat ahead and to the side" in order to express the stifled truth of the collectivity; rather, it is to struggle against the forms of power that transform him into its object and instrument in the sphere of "knowledge," "truth," "consciousness," and "discourse."[3]

In this sense theory does not express, translate, or serve to apply practice: it is practice. But it is local and regional, as you said, and not totalizing. This is a struggle against power, a struggle aimed at revealing and undermining power where it is most invisible and insidious. It is not to "awaken consciousness" that we struggle (the masses have been aware for some time that consciousness is a form of knowledge; and consciousness as the basis of subjectivity is a prerogative of the bourgeoisie), but to sap power, to take power; it is an activity conducted alongside those who struggle for power, and not their illumination from a safe distance. A "theory" is the regional system of this struggle.

DELEUZE: Precisely. A theory is exactly like a box of tools. It has nothing to do with the signifier. It must be useful. It must function. And not for itself. If no one uses it, beginning with the theoretician himself (who then ceases to be a theoretician), then the theory is worthless or the moment is inappropriate. We don't revise a theory, but construct new ones; we have no choice but to make others. It is strange that it was Proust, an author thought to be a pure intellectual, who said it so clearly: treat my book as a pair of glasses directed to the outside; if they don't suit you, find another pair; I leave it to you to find your own instrument, which is necessarily an instrument for combat. A theory does not totalize; it is an instrument for multiplication and it also multiplies itself. It is in the nature of power to totalize and it is your position, and one I fully agree with, that theory is by nature opposed to power. As soon as a theory is enmeshed in a particular point, we realize that it will never possess the slightest practical importance unless it can erupt in a totally different area. This is why the notion of reform is so stupid and hypocritical. Either reforms are designed by people who claim to be representative, who make a profession of speaking for others, and they lead to a division of power, to a distribution of this new power which is consequently increased by a double repression; or they arise from the complaints and demands of those concerned. This latter instance is no longer a reform but revolutionary action that questions (expressing the full force of its partiality) the totality of power and the hierarchy that maintains it. This is surely evident in prisons: the smallest and most insignificant of the prisoners' demands can puncture Pleven's pseudoreform.[4] If the protests of children were heard in kindergarten, if their questions were attended to, it would be enough to explode the entire educational system. There is no denying that our social system is totally without tolerance; this accounts for its extreme fragility in all its aspects and also its need for a global form of repression. In my opinion, you were the first—in your books and in the practical sphere—to teach us something absolutely fundamental: the indignity of speaking for others. We ridiculed representation and said it was finished, but we failed to draw the consequences of this "theoretical" conversion—to appreciate the theoretical fact that only those directly concerned can speak in a practical way on their own behalf.

FOUCAULT: And when the prisoners began to speak, they possessed an individual theory of prisons, the penal system, and justice. It is this form of discourse which ultimately matters, a discourse against power, the counter-discourse of prisoners and those we call delinquents—and not a theory about delinquency. The problem of prisons is local and marginal: not more than 100,000 people pass through prisons in a year. In France at present, between 300,000 and 400,000 have been to prison. Yet this marginal problem seems to disturb everyone. I was surprised that so many who had not been to prison could become interested in its problems, surprised that all those who had never heard the discourse of inmates could so easily understand them. How do we explain this? Isn't it because, in a general way, the penal system is the form in which power is most obviously seen as power? To place someone in prison, to confine him there, to deprive him of food and heat, to prevent him from leaving, from making love, etc.—this is certainly the most frenzied manifestation of power imaginable. The other day I was speaking to a woman who had been in prison and she was saying: "Imagine, that at the age of forty, I was punished one day with a meal of dry bread." What is striking about this story is not the childishness of the exercise of power but the cynicism with which power is exercised as power, in the most archaic, puerile, infantile manner. As children we learn what it means to be reduced to bread and water. Prison is the only place where power is manifested in its naked state, in its most excessive form, and where it is justified as moral force. "I am within my rights to punish you because you know that it is criminal to rob and kill...." What is fascinating about prisons is that, for once, power doesn't hide or mask itself; it reveals itself as tyranny pursued into the tiniest details; it is cynical and at the same time pure and entirely "justified," because its practice can be totally formulated within the framework of morality. Its brutal tyranny consequently appears as the serene domination of Good over Evil, of order over disorder.

DELEUZE: Yes, and the reverse is equally true. Not only are prisoners treated like children, but children are treated like prisoners. Children are submitted to an infantilization which is alien to them. On this basis, it is undeniable that schools resemble prisons and that factories are its closest approximation. Look at the entrance to a Renault plant, or anywhere else for that matter: three tickets to get into the washroom during the day. You found an 18th-century text by Jeremy Bentham proposing prison reforms; in the name of this exalted reform, he established a circular system where the renovated prison serves as a model and where the individual passes imperceptibly from school to the factory, from the factory to prison and vice versa. This is the essence of the reforming impulse, of reformed representation. On the contrary, when people begin to speak and act on their own behalf, they do not oppose their representation (even as its reversal) to another; they do not oppose a new representativity to the false representativity of power. For example, I remember your saying that there is no popular justice against justice; the reckoning takes place at another level.

FOUCAULT: I think that it is not simply the idea of better and more equitable forms of justice that underlies the people's hatred of the judicial system, of judges, courts, and prisons, but—aside from this and before anything else—the singular perception that power is always exercised at the expense of the people. The antijudicial struggle is a struggle against power and I don't think that it is a struggle against injustice, against the injustice of the judicial system, or a struggle for improving the efficiency of its institutions. It is particularly striking that in outbreaks of rioting and revolt or in seditious movements the judicial system has been as compelling a target as the financial structure, the army and other forms of power. My hypothesis—but it is merely an hypothesis—is that popular courts, such as those found in the Revolution, were a means for the lower middle class, who were allied with the masses, to salvage and recapture the initiative in the struggle against the judicial system. To achieve this, they proposed a court system based on the possibility of equitable justice, where a judge might render a just verdict. The identifiable form of the court of law belongs to the bourgeois ideology of justice.

DELEUZE: On the basis of our actual situation, power emphatically develops a total or global vision. That is, all the current forms of repression (the racist repression of immigrant workers, repression in the factories, in the educational system, and the general repression of youth) are easily totalized from the point of view of power. We should not only seek the unity of these forms in the reaction to May '68, but more appropriately in the concerted preparation and organization of the near future. French capitalism now relies on a "margin" of unemployment and has abandoned the liberal and paternal mask that promised full employment. In this perspective, we begin to see the unity of the forms of repression: restrictions on immigration, once it is acknowledged that the most difficult and thankless jobs go to immigrant workers—repression in the factories, because the French must reacquire the "taste" for increasingly harder work; the struggle against youth and the repression of the educational system, because police repression is more active when there is less need for young people in the work force. A wide range of professionals (teachers, psychiatrists, educators of all kinds, etc.) will be called upon to exercise functions that have traditionally belonged to the police. This is something you predicted long ago, and it was thought impossible at the time: the reinforcement of all the structures of confinement. Against this global policy of power, we initiate localized counter-responses, skirmishes, active and occasionally preventive defenses. We have no need to totalize that which is invariably totalized on the side of power; if we were to move in this direction, it would mean restoring the representative forms of centralism and a hierarchical structure. We must set up lateral affiliations and an entire system of networks and popular bases; and this is especially difficult. In any case, we no longer define reality as a continuation of politics in the traditional sense of competition and the distribution of power, through the so-called representative agencies of the Communist Party or the General Workers Union.[5] Reality is what actually happens in factories, in schools, in barracks, in prisons, in police stations. And this action carries a type of information which is altogether different from that found in newspapers (this explains the kind of information carried by the Agence de Presse Libération).

FOUCAULT: Isn't this difficulty of finding adequate forms of struggle a result of the fact that we continue to ignore the problem of power? After all, we had to wait until the 19th century before we began to understand the nature of exploitation, and to this day, we have yet to fully comprehend the nature of power. It may be that Marx and Freud cannot satisfy our desire for understanding this enigmatic thing which we call power, which is at once visible and invisible, present and hidden, ubiquitous. Theories of government and the traditional analyses of their mechanisms certainly don't exhaust the field where power is exercised and where it functions. The question of power remains a total enigma. Who exercises power? And in what sphere? We now know with reasonable certainty who exploits others, who receives the profits, which people are involved, and we know how these funds are reinvested. But as for power... We know that it is not in the hands of those who govern. But, of course, the idea of the "ruling class" has never received an adequate formulation, and neither have other terms, such as "to dominate," "to rule," "to govern," etc. These notions are far too fluid and require analysis. We should also investigate the limits imposed on the exercise of power—the relays through which it operates and the extent of its influence on the often insignificant aspects of the hierarchy and the forms of control, surveillance, prohibition, and constraint. Everywhere that power exists, it is being exercised. No one, strictly speaking, has an official right to power; and yet it is always exerted in a particular direction, with some people on one side and some on the other. It is often difficult to say who holds power in a precise sense, but it is easy to see who lacks power. If the reading of your books (from *Nietzsche* to what I anticipate in *Capitalism and Schizophrenia*)[6] has been essential for me, it is because they seem to go very far in exploring this problem: under the ancient theme of meaning, of the signifier and the signified, etc., you have developed the question of power, of the inequality of powers and their struggles. Each struggle develops around a particular source of power (any of the countless, tiny sources—a small-time boss, the manager of a "H.L.M.,"[7] a prison warden, a judge, a union representative, the editor-in-chief of a newspaper). And if pointing out these sources—denouncing and speaking out—is to be a part of the struggle, it is not because they were previously unknown. Rather, it is because to speak on this subject, to force the institutionalized networks of information to listen, to produce names, to point the finger of accusation, to find targets, is the first step in the reversal of power and the initiation of new struggles against existing forms of power. If the discourse of inmates or prison doctors constitutes a form of struggle, it is because they confiscate, at least temporarily, the power to speak on prison conditions—at present, the exclusive property of prison administrators and their cronies in reform groups. The discourse of struggle is not opposed to the unconscious, but to the secretive. It may not seem like much; but what if it turned out to be more than we expected? A whole series of misunderstandings relates to things that are "hidden," "repressed," and "unsaid"; and they permit the cheap "psychoanalysis" of the proper objects of struggle. It is perhaps more difficult to unearth a secret than the unconscious. The two themes frequently encountered in the recent past, that "writing gives rise to repressed elements" and that "writing is necessarily a subversive activity," seem to betray a number of operations that deserve to be severely denounced.

DELEUZE: With respect to the problem you posed: it is clear who exploits, who profits, and who governs, but power nevertheless remains something more diffuse. I would venture the following hypothesis: the thrust of Marxism was to define the problem essentially in terms of interests (power is held by a ruling class defined by its interests). The question immediately arises: how is it that people whose interests are not being served can strictly support the existing power structure by demanding a piece of the action? Perhaps, this is because in terms of investments, whether economic or unconscious, interest is not the final answer; there are investments of desire that function in a more profound and diffuse manner than our interests dictate. But of course, we never desire against our interests, because interest always follows and finds itself where desire has placed it. We cannot shut out the scream of Wilhelm Reich: the masses were not deceived; at a particular time, they actually wanted a fascist regime! There are investments of desire that mold and distribute power, that make it the property of the policeman as much as of the prime minister; in this context, there is no qualitative difference between the power wielded by the policeman and the prime minister. The nature of these investments of desire in a social group explains why political parties or unions, which might have or should have revolutionary investments in the name of class interests, are so often reform oriented or absolutely reactionary on the level of desire.

FOUCAULT: As you say, the relationship between desire, power, and interest are more complex than we ordinarily think, and it is not necessarily those who exercise power who have all interest in its execution; nor is it always possible for those with vested interests to exercise power. Moreover, the desire for power establishes a singular relationship between power and interest. It may happen that the masses, during fascist periods, desire that certain people assume power, people with whom they are unable to identify since these individuals exert power against the masses and at their expense, to the extreme of their death, their sacrifice, their massacre. Nevertheless, they desire this particular power; they want it to be exercised. This play of desire, power, and interest has received very little attention. It was a long time before we began to understand exploitation; and desire has had and continues to have a long history. It is possible that the struggles now taking place and the local, regional, and discontinuous theories that derive from these struggles and that are indissociable from them stand at the threshold of our discovery of the manner in which power is exercised.

DELEUZE: In this context, I must return to the question: the present revolutionary movement has created multiple centers, and not as the result of weakness or insufficiency, since a certain kind of totalization pertains to power and the forces of reaction. (Vietnam, for instance, is an impressive example of localized counter-tactics). But how are we to define the networks, the transversal links between these active and discontinuous points, from one country to another or within a single country?

FOUCAULT: The question of geographical discontinuity which you raise might mean the following: as soon as we struggle against exploitation, the proletariat not only leads the struggle but also defines its targets, its methods, and the places and instruments for confrontation; and to ally oneself with the proletariat is to accept its positions, its ideology, and its motives for combat. This means total identification. But if the fight is directed against power, then all those on whom power is exercised to their detriment, all who find it intolerable, can begin the struggle on their own terrain and on the basis of their proper activity (or passivity). In engaging in a struggle that concerns their own interests, whose objectives they clearly understand and whose methods only they can determine, they enter into a revolutionary process. They naturally enter as allies of the proletariat, because power is exercised the way it is in order to maintain capitalist exploitation. They genuinely serve the cause of the proletariat by fighting in those places where they find themselves oppressed. Women, prisoners, conscripted soldiers, hospital patients, and homosexuals have now begun a specific struggle against the particularized power, the constraints and controls, that are exerted over them. Such struggles are actually involved in the revolutionary movement to the degree that they are radical, uncompromising and nonreformist, and refuse any attempt at arriving at a new disposition of the same power with, at best, a change of masters. And these movements are linked to the revolutionary movement of the proletariat to the extent that they fight against the controls and constraints which serve the same system of power.

In this sense, the overall picture presented by the struggle is certainly not that of the totalization you mentioned earlier, this theoretical totalization under the guise of "truth." The generality of the struggle specifically derives from the system of power itself, from all the forms in which power is exercised and applied.

DELEUZE: And which we are unable to approach in any of its applications without revealing its diffuse character, so that we are necessarily led—on the basis of the most insignificant demand—to the desire to blow it up completely. Every revolutionary attack or defense, however partial, is linked in this way to the workers' struggle.

Translated by Donald Bouchard and Sherry Simon

----

[1] "Groupe d'Information des Prisons": Foucault's books *I, Pierre Rivière* and *Discipline and Punish* result from this association.

[2] May '68, popularly known as the "events of May."

[3] See *The Order of Things*.

[4] René Pleven was the prime minister of France in the early 1950s.

[5] "Confédération Générale des Travailleurs."

6 *Nietzsche and Philosophy* [French, 1962] (New York: Columbia University Press, 1983).*Capitalism and Schizophrenia,* Vol. I, *Anti-Oedipus* (Minneapolis: The University of Minnesota Press, 1983) in collaboration with F. Guattari, was published in French at the time of this interview, in 1972.

7 "Low Income Housing."

11

Confining Societies

JEAN-MARIE DOMENACH: Here is our first question. Until recently, a-social or anti-social behavior has been thought of and dealt with in legal terms (prisoners, the confined, the criminally insane, etc.). More and more, they are thought of and dealt with in clinical terms (the emotionally disturbed, mentally ill, psychopath, etc.). To what is this evolution due?

JACQUES DONZELOT: The formulation of this question bothers me. I would say the opposite. Isn't it putting the cart before the horse to speak of a-social or anti-social behavior when the behavior is first determined by a certain institutional distribution? People who are placed in institutions are there in compliance with a power relation which the legal and the clinical only confirm, since they go hand in hand.

PHILIPPE MEYER: Yes, but is it of no consequence whether emphasis is placed on the clinical, as it is now, or on the legal, as it was before?

MICHEL FOUCAULT: I would like to make a small historical point. I don't know if it will change the position of the problem. I think, as Donzelot does, that legal categories of exclusion usually do have their medical or clinical correlatives. What is deceptive is that legal terms, for a number of reasons, are rather stable and constant, whereas clinical categories are relatively unstable and have changed rapidly.

It is true that the notion of emotional disturbance is recent, but that does not mean that legal-clinical doubling, or the re-use of a legal category in a clinical category, is a recent phenomenon, because before emotionally disturbed people, there were degenerates, and before degenerates, there were monomaniacs, and these notions are as much legal as medical. On the other hand, there was a great police sorting out process which, I believe, began in the West in the 15th century—namely, the hunting down of vagrants, beggars, and the idle; this practice of police selection, exclusion and imprisonment remained outside the field of the judicial, legal practice. The Paris Parliament was in charge of policing vagrants and beggars in the capital for a number of years, but this was soon relinquished, and institutions and apparatus completely different from the normal legal apparatus assumed these duties. And then, at the beginning of the 19th century, the police enforcement of social selection was reintegrated into the judicial practice because, in the Napoleonic State, police, justice and penitential institutions were linked to each other, and just as these practices were being integrated into the judicial, thus police, practice, new psychological, psychiatric, and sociological categories appeared at the same time in order to justify them, to double them, to give them another reading (not to give them another readability).

MEYER: Then, two remarks: the difference, it seems, between the emotionally disturbed person of today and the degenerate of the past is that the degenerate did not call for a whole host of experts on relations, rehabilitation, readjustment, etc. Moreover, you say that there was first a penal apparatus and that this was then doubled by the psychiatric apparatus; isn't it currently the reverse?

FOUCAULT: I agree with you. It is certain that the interplay between the penal and the psychiatric, the legal and the psychological has certainly changed a lot in the past 150 years, but I think nevertheless that both are born of social practices, those of selection, of exclusion, that they were both born of police practices that were integrated into the legal world rather late. When you say: now there are experts in charge of treating the emotionally disturbed whereas the degenerates were not treatable, you are absolutely right. But around 1820-1830, just as large prisons and large psychiatric hospitals came into being, when juries had to deal with parricide or the murder of a child, the jurors were in an awkward position: they had to choose between the prison and the hospital, two solutions that were ultimately fairly equivalent. The problem was: the guy had to be locked up in any case; what sort of confinement would be the most secure—that of the prison or the hospital? Doctor-police communication is long standing.

PAUL VIRILIO: There's something very interesting to me in what Foucault just said: that sociatry[1] preceded psychiatry. That interests me because where are the asylums of today? Are they closed, are they open? If you look at what has recently happened in Great Britain with the House of Commons' decision to abolish all asylums within twenty years, this is very important. We're back to the situation you describe in *Madness and Civilization,* in the Middle Ages, before confinement; but not under exactly the same conditions. That is, the mad, the deviants, are "freed" to roam the territory, but this time the territory is completely controlled, contrary to the medieval period. What do you think of this notion of sociatry, in the largest sense of the word, preceding psychiatry?

FOUCAULT: The House of Commons' decision is indeed remarkable, it is even stupefying, and I wonder if they know where it will lead, unless they realize very well where it won't lead. Because capitalist societies, and until now societies that call themselves non-capitalist as well, are nevertheless confining societies. If one classified societies according to how they got rid not of their dead but of their living, one would have a classification of massacre societies or murder ritual societies, exile societies, reparation societies, and confinement societies. These seem to me to be the four main types. That capitalist society is a confinement society is a fact that I think has been very difficult to explain. Why indeed is it necessary for this society, where the work force is sold, to be a confining society? Idleness, vagrancy, the migrations of those seeking better salaries elsewhere—all of this leads to the control of this mass, the possibility of putting it back on the employment market; all of this is inscribed in the very practice of confinement, so that when a society, even a capitalist one like the English society, declares that there is no longer confinement, at least for the mad, I ask myself this: does this mean that the other great half of confinement, the prison, will disappear, or is it that, on the contrary, it will occupy the space left vacant by the asylum? Is England not doing the opposite of what the Soviet Union is in the process of doing? The USSR is generalizing the psychiatric hospital; it is making it assume the role of prisons. Won't England be led to expand the function of prisons, even if they are tremendously improved?

DONZELOT: It doesn't seem to me to be a matter of eliminating confinement; I simply think that it has been devalued and that we are witnessing an outward diffusion of confinement procedures that preserves places of confinement as a resting point. Reducing the prison, but on the basis of a system of control and surveillance meant to keep people in their place, which would have the same function.

FOUCAULT: That's why your question interested me very much, with some qualifications. If one reduces the problem to these two terms, the legal and the psychological, one ends up saying this: either psychological discourse reveals the truth of what legal practice did blindly—a positivist conception that you find very frequently among medical historians and psychologists when they say to you, What do you think witches were? They were neurotics—or else, if one does a purely relativist analysis, one admits that the legal and the psychological are two readings of one and the same phenomenon, a reading that in the 19th century was above all legal, that in the 20th is psychological, without the psychological being better founded than the legal. As for me, I would introduce a third term that I would superficially call police: a practice that is selective, exclusive, confining, etc. upon which legal, psychological, etc., practices and discourses are built.

DONZELOT: Before, one proceeded with the means at hand, and that was exclusion. But now there is a very good system which is relegation through the school; school, as we well know, allows people to remain in the place that has been assigned them according to the demands of the system, and this according to their social origin. There is a book that discusses this very well: *L'Ecole capital-*

iste en France. It talks about two school networks: the high school-college network, and the pre-professional network; there is perhaps a third, which would be the legal-clinical network, a sort of new layer, a new educative strata that is being set up in order to absorb the old products of exclusion somewhat. There would therefore be a sort of dialectic—though I don't like this word very much—between exclusion and relegation; when things are fine, when one has the means, relegation is done through schooling; when that is not enough, one resorts to exclusion. To me, that is the whole problem, it's no more complicated than that.

JACQUES JULLIARD: In short, confinement, as we understand it, is a substitute for previous closed societies; as these societies open up, they no longer have the sorts of internal regulations that pre-capitalist societies had and at that moment we have types of confinement such as the asylum and the prison.

FOUCAULT: That was an important technique in the growth of capitalism, much more so, in fact, than at its budding stage.

MEYER: I do not agree with Donzelot when he says it doesn't matter whether emphasis is placed on penalty or psychiatry. As long as law finds its expression in a legal form, in the largest sense of the word, transgression is possible, definable, perhaps even called for, in a way, if one accepts Mauss's reasoning on taboo. It's different when law is expressed and transmitted in a way that above all concerns what is unspoken. I'll give an example: the incest taboo. It is actually written in the penal code, it happened rather late, I think, and in any case, no one ever taught us that it was forbidden to sleep with one's mother, father, brother or little sister; on the other hand, hitting them on the head or treating them badly is something we were constantly told not to do. The greatest difficulty of transgression within a social group concerns the implicit norm. The fact that we have passed from social control that took on legal and penal aspects to social control that takes on clinical or "therapeutic" aspects leads us to a diffusion of the norm and to a control of the norm that escapes the representation and apprehension of both individuals and the community. I think this is how the treatment of deviance has been socialized, and this seems to me to be a negative socialization, a socialization in the same sense of control, but this time much more grave.

SOCIAL WORK AND POLICE CONTROL

DOMENACH: This is the direction of our second question: Social work is constantly increasing its scope. It started as volunteer work to help eradicate tuberculosis and sexually transmitted diseases, and became professional social assistance in underprivileged or para-proletarian environments. Today it is widely established in companies and administrations. Its most recent evolution has led it to take charge of community activities in "ordinary" populations, particularly in cities. Do you think this growth and evolution of social work has a relation to the nature and evolution of our economic system? Is there really a continuity between the social work that stemmed from the police, psychiatric, or rehabilitative treatment of deviants, and social action among the mass population? What do we call social work today?

PAUL THIBAUD: For about ten years, we have been emerging more and more from a "welfare state," that is, from a certain economy mostly controlled by the state whose professed social goal is full employment. When there is work for everyone and blind belief in growth is accepted, the economic sphere can be the general mode of control of society. With the opening of borders, the formation of multinational companies, the emphasis on competitive capabilities, etc., full employment is no longer the basis of the economic credo at all: not only does unemployment increase, but phenomena like overeducation in relation to what the production or the innumerable social "nuisances" require manifest a sort of detachment of the economic from the social. Thus the social has to be controlled or made to exist independently, by its own means and not through the economy which goes its own way. Between production and the population a gulf is created. A new terrain of debates and conflicts appear. The outcome could just as well be more control as more autonomy.

DONZELOT: The welfare system that had relative autonomy is now systematically tied to the legal; there is a continuity from custody aid, court assistance, etc. So, roughly speaking, we have the following two facts: a considerable number of agents increasingly dependent on the legal apparatus, and the diffusion of a systematic model of interpretation of human problems, which is psychologism, but which functions above all ideologically.

JEAN-RENÉ TREANTON: What makes you say that social workers are linked to the legal system?

DONZELOT: Laws.

TREANTON: Absolutely not.

MEYER: If you want a number taken from a recent survey, 50% of social workers are directly paid by the State and 19% paid by Social Security; that makes 69% paid by the State or Social Security. The least we can say is that we are moving toward a grouping of forces...

VIRILIO: I thought we should reflect on social assistance that is developing and starting to enter new sectors. Couldn't we question the legitimacy of this? You talk as though this were self-evident, these 90,000 social workers, these health identity cards, this psychiatric overseeing of the territory, community policing, this generalized surveillance by every means, electronic and otherwise. For me, this is a problem.

THIBAUD: I did not say that this was self-evident at all. I simply said that before asserting that social workers are in the service of the police, the question still had to be asked: what do social workers do? And I wanted to protest against the answer that was immediately given: social workers are working for the cops. I said: this has to be looked at more closely. Take the case of Madame d'Escrivan, the social worker in the Fresnes prison: she was dismissed by the Penal Administration because she had denounced the mistreatment of a prisoner; she was therefore not in the service of the police. This is not a matter of shoving people into drawers.

FOUCAULT: Nevertheless, when you give us, as an example of social workers not being employed by the police, the fact that Madame d'Escrivan was sent packing on police orders with the support of the Red Cross, I think this is a topical example of the way power prescribes social work in our society. I think some individuals in that situation say no and take the offensive, as Madame Rose and Madame d'Escrivan did. This does not prevent their expulsion, and the fact that their expulsion was accepted by everyone—not only, of course, by the administration, but by their colleagues—proves how programmed and determined social work currently is.

JULLIARD: I think the word police has created a false debate. Indeed, in the case of prison, the connection to the police, which is a particularly operational instrument of coercion, is very clear. If you take teachers—at the point we're at now, they could be considered social workers—you see that a growing number of them find that aside from their explicit function, which is communication, they have an implicit function, which is the maintenance of order. And it seems to me the problem today comes from the fact that this implicit function becomes explicit for a number of people, insofar as they realize that some of the actions they would like to carry out in order to fulfill their explicit, necessary and legitimate function, brings them to question what remains implicit in it. And then they come up against the external authority which indeed determines them and which—I don't want to say manipulates them, that would be too strong, but which is their guarantor in the last analysis.

RENÉ PUCHEU: But then, is a counselor inevitably a police officer in current society?

MEYER: No, but the mandate he receives is that of a controller.

VIRILIO: And he reinforces the harmful assumption that we can no longer counsel ourselves and recreate ourselves. That's terrible; it's trading favors, that's the whole problem. This accusation on the basis of supposed intentions which the social worker implicitly makes against us, through his function, through the mass of social workers, this accusation we cannot accept; this is the problem of social work. We act as if society didn't create itself, as if it were treated, acted upon only from the outside. It seems as though we go through three states: the self-regulation of primitive societies, the regulation of our societies, and that we are headed toward a sort of "deregulation," through the urbanization you spoke of just now, which in itself is a new phenomenon since now we talk about world cities.

FOUCAULT: I would like to add a word to what Julliard was saying: it is obvious that we never said that such and such social worker, the social worker as an individual, was salaried by the police; it is absolutely not the case. I think, on the other hand, what is important is that social work is inscribed within a larger function which for centuries has not ceased to take on new dimensions, which is the function of surveillance-correction. Surveilling individuals, and correcting them, in both senses of the term, that is, punishing them or teaching them.

This function of surveillance-correction was insured, even in the 19th century, by various institutions, by the Church among others, then by schoolteachers. We say that the social worker started out as a volunteer to help eradicate tuberculosis and venereal disease; I wonder if his origin is not rather in the function of the educator, the "instituteur" properly speaking.[2] He indeed had that role, next to the priest, opposite the priest, against the priest; the republic developed through their opposition. In the 19th century, this function of surveillance-correction was relatively autonomous in relation to political power. Political power played on their opposition, their conflicts, their autonomy, and now it is overseeing this again very closely, and all the more rigorously now that the Church on the one hand and intellectuals on the other are beginning to elude its grasp. The great betrayal of intellectuals in terms of the bourgeois State is sanctioned by the fact that social workers are being made to play the role that, for some time now, the schoolteacher, the high school teacher, the intellectual no longer play, the paradox being that these social workers are trained by these intellectuals. Hence the fact that the social worker can't help betraying the function that he has been assigned.

DOMENACH: The political meaning of social work is to be determined in terms of another problem, which our third question raises. How do we situate in social theory those who are currently considered maladjusted? Problems or subjects? Capitalism's army reserve or the revolution's?

TREANTON: Most social workers are experiencing a sort of malaise now, because they are beginning to realize that they are contributing, most of the time implicitly and without wanting to, to the maintenance of order. So there is an internal tension. Hence, a consciousness of the fact that to act on the individual level is absolutely illusory as long as certain political problems are not addressed.

MEYER: Let's take the example of delinquents. (I did preventive work for three years in an underprivileged environment.) What one finds in Marx and Engels is not particularly soft on the underclass. Do we have to accept this

Marxist logic, namely that the best thing that can happen to young sub-proletarians is to become proletarians?

JULLIARD: You've stated the question very well: a reading of Marxism, which is, alas, probably the correct one, would consider these problems as very marginal, insofar as social, political, and trade-union action, as deduced from Marxism, rests on the same type of logic as capitalism itself, that is the defense or the will to take over a part of the surplus value. If one situates oneself within this universe, one understands very well why Marx and Engels were not interested in the sub-proletariat: because it's not a producer of surplus, thus it's not a social agent, and not to be defended as such. The sub-proletariat is, in their eyes, a by-product of the overall society, its dominant part as well as its dominated part. This logic, this productivist logic, is what we're presently questioning.

Nevertheless the problem still remains of knowing if the marginals, the delinquents, the prisoners, the mentally ill, etc., can become one of the essential agents of political action or not. If the goal of political action remains the taking or the exercise of power, it can only be the act of groups that are significant in society, that is, producers, those who have a precise social or economic function. Only we are discovering that there are no longer the marginals and the producers, but that a growing number of producers are becoming marginal one after another, that is, they are experiencing different forms of exclusion. And this is perhaps where there is a possibility of bringing the real marginal into social and political action which would be that of all workers.

DONZELOT: I agree with this process of dividing up and categorizing people in general, but ultimately I think we would have to look at the fundamental dividing lines. There is one that is decisive, the one that separates the honorable, working, trade-union proletariat from the ignoble, imprisoned, non-trade-union proletariat; and indeed this dividing line is what makes the functioning of the economic and political system possible; it is fundamental.

FOUCAULT: I agree with your analysis of Marx, but where I don't follow you is when you say: here's the proletariat on one side, and on the other, the marginals, and you have gathered under this rubric (it was not an exhaustive list) prisoners, the mentally ill, delinquents, etc. So can one define the non-proletarian, non-proletarianized plebeian by the list of the mentally ill, the delinquent, the imprisoned, etc.? Shouldn't we say instead that there is a split between the proletariat on the one hand and the extra-proletarian, non-proletarianized plebeian on the other? We should not say: there is the proletariat and then there are these marginals. We should say: there is in the overall mass of the plebeians a split between the proletariat and the non-proletarianized plebeian, and I think that institutions like the police, the courts, the penal system are some of the ways that are constantly used to deepen this rift which capitalism needs.

Because basically what capitalism is afraid of, rightly or wrongly, since 1789, since 1848, since 1870, is insurrection and riot: the guys who take to the streets with their knives and their guns, who are ready for direct and violent action. The bourgeoisie was haunted by this vision and it wants to let the proletariat know this is no longer possible: "It is not in your own interests to ally yourselves with people ready to spearhead your insurrections." And all this mobile population, prepared to take to the streets, to cause riots, these people were held up, in a way, as negative examples by the penal system. And all the legal and moral devalorization of violence, of theft, etc., all this moral education that the teacher gave in positive terms to the proletariat, the courts provide in negative terms. This is how the rift was constantly reproduced and reintroduced between the proletariat and the non-proletarianized world, because it was assumed that contact between the two was a dangerous ferment of riots.

JULLIARD: I agree enough to say that, from this point of view, the Marxist perspective must be broken with, which is centered solely on the producer.

TREANTON: Marxist and Darwinist, because 19th-century bourgeois thought was profoundly marked by Darwinism, and in that respect, Marx and Darwin concur. The lumpenproletariat, in Marxist theory, is a sort of residue. I totally agree with your analysis there. The courts, the police do their best to "stigmatize" the lumpenproletariat. But social workers, in this case, do the opposite. Generally, perhaps, the social worker maintains a certain social order, but social work breaks totally, in its technique and in its spirit, with the process and procedure of stigmatization. We have to look at how social work developed. It was not born in France, but in Anglo-Saxon countries, in reaction against Darwinist thought which was: "Let them all croak, otherwise you're going against the natural order." Historically that was it, and I think the techniques of social work have precisely consisted of trying to reintegrate the lumpenproletariat through individual action, but simultaneously of attenuating or erasing the border based on stigmatization.

DONZELOT: The function of all apparatus, of all authority, is to mark out a territory and establish limits, to divide things up. The function of social assistants is this: to divide things up. A family which a social assistant has visited is a family designated as belonging to a certain rejected or disposable population, whose participation is no longer wanted because it is already outside the law.

FOUCAULT: There are two ways of erasing the dividing line between the non-proletarianized plebeian and the proletariat. One is to address this proletarianized plebeian and to inculcate in it a certain number of values, principles, norms so that it accepts unquestioningly values that are ultimately bourgeois values, which are also, in many cases, values that the bourgeoisie has inculcated in the proletariat. Thanks to which the plebeian finds itself disarmed since it will have lost its specificity in face of the proletariat and it will cease to be dangerous as a ferment, a center of riots, of possible insurrection, for the bourgeoisie. There is another way to bypass the division, which is to say to the proletariat and to the plebeian at the same time: what is this system of values being inculcated in you if not precisely a system of power, an instrument of power in the hands of the bourgeoisie? When you are told that stealing is bad, you are given a certain definition of private property, which is accorded a certain value in the bourgeoisie. When you are taught not to like violence, to be for peace, not to want vengeance, to prefer justice to struggle, what are you being taught? You are being taught to prefer bourgeois justice to social struggle. You are being taught that it is better to have a judge than vengeance. This is the work that intellectuals and schoolteachers have done, to great effect, and this is the work that social workers, on their level, are continuing.

TREANTON: This type of alliance between proletarians and sub-proletarians is absolutely traditional in periods of violent revolution. Only it's an ephemeral alliance; once past the period of vacillation which accompanies the substitution of one power for another, traditional exclusion returns. The heroes of the riot find themselves in prison. The question seems therefore to conclude an alliance between the proletariat and sub-proletariat based on something besides values of revolt, on a common social project. Without which, after the day of rage, the alliance will prove ephemeral, a deception as usual.

FOUCAULT: When I said that the problem was precisely to show the proletariat that the justice system being proposed to it, being imposed on it, is in fact an instrument of power, it was precisely so that this alliance with the plebeian not be simply a tactical alliance for one day or night, but that between the proletariat which absolutely does not have the same ideology as the plebeian and a plebeian which absolutely does not have the social practices of the proletariat, there could actually be something else besides a meeting of circumstance.

DONZELOT: I think the place where this meeting between the insurgent plebeian and the proletariat subjected to bourgeois values can happen is on the extra-professional level, on the level of housing problems, unemployment, life in certain neighborhoods, isolation, on the level of health problems, on the level of confronting police control, the link can be made on all of this.

VIRILIO: Julliard just said that the margin is becoming massive and we're not talking about it, while the state seems to have envisaged it through the development of social work. As soon as the margin becomes massive, classic police treatment will be impossible, or else it will be civil war. The only possible treatment, especially since the intelligentsia fled, let's say after 1968, is to repatriate the popular ideologists who are social workers. With the crisis not only of capitalist society but also industrial society, the real question is this: what happens if marginalization becomes a mass phenomenon? Just now, we gave the characteristics of this abandoned, anomic segment of the population. In the 19th century, it was a tiny segment of society; let's admit that now these characteristics apply to millions of people in the suburbs of the continental metropolises we just spoke of.

FOUCAULT: I would like to ask a question: what if it is the mass that marginalizes itself? That is, if it is precisely the proletariat and the young proletarians that refuse the ideology of the proletariat? At the same time that the margins become massive, the masses might well marginalize themselves; contrary to what we expected, the people who go before the courts are not really all unemployed. They are young workers who say: why should I sweat my whole life for $2000 a month, when I could... At that point, it's the mass that is becoming marginal.

MEYER: When a young proletarian marginalizes himself, he ends up in court sooner or later, or at a psychiatrist's. The court will consider the penal dimension of his marginalization; the psychiatrist, the individual dimension. Who will make him aware of the political dimension of this marginalization? Surely not the so-called "social" worker who only intervenes as the psychiatrist's or the judge's underling. Certain militant groups, like the G.I.P [Group for Information on Prisons], allowed the underclass and their families to situate themselves socially and politically, to know who their allies and who their adversaries were. Wasn't this sort of G.I.P. action at once a critique of social work and a critique of political militantism?

DONZELOT: Indeed, on two levels there is a refusal of the classic militant practice: first, classic militantism was systematically pedagogical; the G.I.P. only gives people the means to express themselves, restores a certain amount of expressive possibilities. Second, emphasis is placed on divisions within the proletariat and not on unification whose rhetoric has occupied the political arena for the past 150 years.

JULLIARD: Do you find that very positive politically? On the first count, OK: it's a matter of letting people express themselves, rather than instructing them. But when you say: "let's stress the differences rather than the pseudo-unanimity that might exist between them" I wonder if this is not politically very demobilizing. Your action would end up being a safety valve for society as a whole.

I tend to think that only insofar as working classes and dangerous classes can come together will something be possible. This is not easy at all: this implies that the working classes, who I think remain determinant, come to see themselves as something other than productive classes. That is, that they arrive at a universal awareness that their position as a productive class is prohibitive, for as productive classes, they are only a segment of society, which necessarily complements some and excludes others, as you pointed out.

So insofar as the productive class—that is, ultimately, the majority of the population—considers the problems of the marginals as its own, in different forms (not all marginalism is represented by delinquency or mental illness) can this junction come to be. Yet market society imposes increasingly specific and increasingly demanding social models of behavior and consumption. If you don't look like a young, dynamic, 30-year-old executive, married with two children, in good social standing, you are potentially a marginal. Insofar as the social model becomes increasingly rigorous and increasingly exclusive, producers as a whole could refuse it and come to a new type of universality by considering the problems of the marginal as their own—that we are all German Jews, if you prefer.[3]

DONZELOT: We are not all German Jews, we are not all homosexuals, we do not all want to be, we are not all this or that; these are forms that, as such, have to be expressed, and I think types of political action and political movements were always conceived on a religious mode, that is, people unified on the basis of transcendental values and not on the basis of real life, of this or that real problem of theirs. We do not stress opposition in order to engender differences but precisely so that, once differences are recognized, the alliances that are concluded are real alliances and not mythical alliances, that end in the usual way.

Translated by Jeanine Herman

---

[1] *Sociatry* is the psychotherapy of social behavior. [Trans.]

[2] An "instituteur" is a primary school teacher. Primary school teachers were the backbone of the French Republic, against Royalists and the Clergy. [Ed.]

[3] A well-known May '68 motto in defense of Daniel Cohn-Bendit—"Danny the Red"—who had been expelled to Germany by the French Government. [Ed.]

12

AN HISTORIAN OF CULTURE

Q: Professor Foucault, you have said that philosophy, as a discourse, is above all a diagnostic enterprise. I would like to ask you a question about this. Doesn't performing a diagnosis perhaps involve placing oneself outside, elevating oneself to a different level of reflection, a level superior to the level of the objective field to which the diagnosis is applied?

MF: I would like to add that there exist various means of knowing diagnostically. By diagnostic knowledge I mean, in general, a form of knowledge that defines and determines differences. For example, when a doctor makes a diagnosis of tuberculosis, he does it by determining the differences that distinguish someone sick with tuberculosis from someone sick with pneumonia or any other disease. In this sense diagnostic knowledge operates within a certain objective field defined by the sickness, the symptoms, etc.

Q: Yet it is outside the sickness: the doctor speaks of the sickness but doesn't live it; and his discourse is not in fact a symptom of this or that sickness.

MF: Yes, within an objective field yet outside of the sickness. However, there are forms of diagnostic knowledge that are not located within an objective field but which, on the contrary, permit a new objective field to appear. For example, when Saussure defined what *langue* was with respect to *parole* or what synchronic was with respect to diachronic, he opened up a new sector of potential studies, a new objective field which did not exist before.[1] And this too is knowledge through diagnosis, though much different from the first type.

Q: At any rate, it is necessary to resort to a metalanguage, a language to describe a language.

MF: Not always. It depends on the science with which one is dealing. I do not believe that one can call a medical diagnosis a metalanguage.

Q: If we consider the symptoms of a sickness as signs, the doctor's discourse is metalinguistic with respect to these signs.

MF: If you give to metalanguage the very general meaning of a discourse about a system of signs, it is true that one is dealing with a metalanguage. But only if one accepts this very general definition.

Q: Metalanguage is a discourse about a discourse.

MF: Yes, but now I am a little worried because today the term metalanguage is employed in a very wide and general sense which lacks rigor. One speaks of metalanguage in dealing with literary criticism, the history of science, the history of philosophy, etc. Naturally, one can talk about it in dealing with medicine as well. I wonder whether it might not be preferable to return to the more rigorous definition of metalanguage, one which says that it is the discourse through which the elements and the rules of construction of a language are defined.

Q: In fact, in mathematics, metalanguage is the language through which mathematics is formalized. But beyond the definition, the most important aspect of the question is something else: that is, that the structure of the metalanguage can be different from that of the language.

MF: Possibly.

Q: But I am constructing my discourse within the *epistemè* of my civilization, or outside it?

MF: What meaning are you giving to the term *epistemè?*

Q: The same one you gave to it.

MF: Yes, and I'd like to know what that meaning is.

Q: For my part, as a good neo-Kantian, I intend to refer to the categories.

MF: Now we're at the crux. What I called *epistemè* in *The Order of Things* has nothing to do with historical categories, that is with those categories created in a particular historical moment. When I speak of *epistemè,* I mean all those relationships which existed between the various sectors of science during a given epoch. For example, I am thinking of the fact that at a certain point mathematics was used for research in physics, while linguistics or, if you will, semiology, the science of signs, was used by biology (to deal with genetic messages). Likewise the theory of evolution was used by, or served as a model for historians, psychologists, and sociologists of the 19th century. All these phenomena of relationship between the sciences or between the various scientific sectors constitute what I call the *epistemè* of an epoch. Thus for me *episteme* has nothing to do with the Kantian categories.

Q: Yet when you speak of the concept of "order" in the 17th century, aren't you dealing with a category?

MF: I simply noted that the problem of order (the problem, not the category), or rather the need to introduce an order among series of numbers, human beings, or values, appears simultaneously in many different disciplines in the 17th century. This involves a communication between the diverse disciplines, and so it was that someone who proposed, for example, the creation of a universal language in the 17th century was quite close in terms of procedure to somoeone who dealt with the problem of how one could catalog human beings. It's a question of relationships and communication among the various sciences. This is what I call *epistemè,* and it has nothing to do with the Kantian categories.

Q: I call these categories, because they are formal, universal, and empty.

MF: Do you consider historicity, for example, to be a category?

Q: Yes, it's a category of 19th century culture.

MF: But this isn't Kant's meaning of "category."

Q: It depends on how one reads Kant.

MF: Then I recognize that even my own are categories in this sense.

Q: Let's go on now to another topic. I would like to ask you a question concerning your interest in Nietzsche. What is the Nietzsche that you like?

MF: Clearly, it is not that of *Zarathustra.* It is that of *The Birth of Tragedy,* of *The Genealogy of Morals.*

Q: The Nietzsche of origins, then?

MF: I would say that in Nietzsche I find a questioning of the historical type which does not refer in any way to the "original" as do many of the analyses of Western thought. Husserl and Heidegger bring up for discussion again all of our knowledge and its foundations, but they do this by beginning from that which is original. This analysis takes place, however, at the expense of any articulated historical content. Instead, what I liked in Nietzsche is the attempt to bring up again for discussion the fundamental concepts of knowledge, of morals, and of metaphysics by appealing to a historical analysis of the positivistic type, without going back to origins. But clearly this is not the only thing that interests me in Nietzsche.

In your writings, I find another more important aspect: the return to the discussion of the primacy, or, if you prefer, of the privilege of the subject in the Cartesian or Kantian sense, of the subject as consciousness.

Q: It's precisely on that point that I wanted to ask you another question. I have the impression that for you, as for the majority of French philosophers, the subject coincides with consciousness.

MF: For me this isn't true; but it is true that the overwhelming majority of philosphers from the 17th to the 19th century has equated subject and consciousness. I would say, rather, that this holds true also for the French philosophers of the 20th century, including Sartre and Merleau-Ponty. I think that this equation of subject-consciousness at the transcendental level is a characteristic of Western philosophy from Descartes to our own time. Nietzsche launched one of the first, or at least one of the most vigorous, attacks against this equation.

Q: It's a question of consciousness as the subject of "I think." But what I don't understand is the position of consciousnenss as object of an *episteme*. The consciousness, if anything, is "epistemizing," not "epistemizable."

MF: Are you speaking of the transcendental consciousness?

Q: Yes.

MF: Well, I am not Kantian or Cartesian, precisely because I refuse an equation on the transcendental level between subject and thinking "I." I am convinced that there exist, if not exactly structures, then at least rules for the functioning of knowledge which have arisen in the course of history and within which can be located the various subjects.

Q: I am afraid that all this may be a trap in which we are prisoners. What you are saying is undoubtedly true, but on the other hand, it is exactly this transcendental consciousness which conditions the formation of our knowledge. It is true that transcendental consciousness arises in a particular phase of our history and civilization, in a particular situation; but it is also true that, once arisen, it manifests itself as a constituting and not a constituted thing.

MF: I understand your position, but it is exacty on this point that our views diverge. You seem to me Kantian or Husserlian. In all of my work I strive instead to avoid any reference to this transcendental as a condition of possibility for any knowledge. When I say that I strive to avoid it, I don't mean that I am sure of succeeding. My procedure at this moment is of a regressive sort, I would say; I try to assume a greater and greater detachment in order to define the historical conditions and transformations of our knowledge. I try to historicize to the utmost in order to leave as little space as possible to the transcendental. I cannot exclude the possibility that one day I will have to confront an irreducible *residuum* which will be, in fact, the transcendental.

Q: Let's try to look at the question from another point of view. Since it is said that you are a structuralist (forgive me for saying this), I would like to know whether you think that some kind of relationship exists between the concept of "structure" and the Freudian notion of the "unconscious."

MF: I'll answer you in an offhand way, though I will begin by making a statement of principles: I am absolutely not a structuralist.

Q: I know that, but public opinion has linked you to the structuralists.

MF: I am obliged to repeat it continually. I have never used any of the concepts which can be considered characteristic of structuralism. I have mentioned the concept of structure several times, but I have never used it. Unfortunately critics and journalists are not like philosophers; they do not recognize the difference between "mention" and "use." Thus if I now speak of structure and the unconscious I do so from a completely external standpoint; nor do I consider myself bound by the answer that I give. Anyway I am quite incompetent in this field. I will say that it seems to me that in recent years (I am speaking as a historian of culture) an unexpected discovery has occurred: I mean the discovery of the existence of formal relationships, which can indeed be called structures, exactly in areas that appear in all respects under the control of consciousness, for example in language and formal thought. It has also been observed that these relationships existed and operated even when the subject was not truly conscious of them—conscious first in the psychological sense of the word, but also in the Kantian or Cartesian sense. Thus through linguistics, logic and ethnology one arrives at the discovery of a sector which stands outside consciousness in the usually accepted meaning of that word. Is it necessary to fit this sector into the realm of the unconscious, understood in the Freudian sense? Students of psychoanalysis have found themselves with two choices. The first involves asserting that this "structural" unconscious, if we want to term it that, is subordinate to the Freudian unconscious. Fortunately many investigators have avoided this error, or should I say ingenuousness, and have put the problem in different terms. The problem is to find out whether the Freudian unconscious is not itself a locus in which this system of formal relationships operates. These relationships are operative in language, in formal thought, and even in certain social structures. Perhaps the Freudian unconscious as well is, shall we say, "touched" by this structural unconscious. This is the point at which many psychoanalytic investigations have arrived.

Q: But doesn't this "structural" unconscious perhaps coincide with the unconscious as defined by Jung?

MF: Certainly not. One can say with confidence that we are not speaking of an individual unconscious, in the sense that psychoanalysis generally understands that notion. Yet neither is it a collective unconscious, which would be a kind of collection or reservoir of archetypes at the disposal of everyone. The "structural" unconscious is neither of these things.

Q: Please explain to me your interest in a writer like Sade. Does it have to do with the dissolution of the "ego" in his work, or perhaps with his eroticism, with that kind of algebraic combination which eroticism undergoes in his work?

MF: Sade's great experiment, even with all that might be considered pathetic in it, lies in the fact that he seeks to introduce the disorder of desire into a world dominated by order and classification. This is precisely the meaning of what he calls "libertinism." The libertine is a man gifted with a desire strong enough and a mind cold enough to allow him to succeed in fitting all the potentialities of his desire into an absolutely exhaustive combination of events.

Q: But according to you, doesn't one perhaps arrive at the death of desire in Sade? These combinations which know neither time nor the dynamics of desire, but only some abstract sexual acts—don't these combinations of all possible modes of behavior lead us perhaps to a situation in which Eros no longer exists, in which Eros becomes only a pretext?

MF: I'll say only a few things in reference to this. It is evident that if I want to make love (or rather, when I want to make love) I do not resort to Sade's prescribed methods, to his combinations; not so much because I wouldn't like to try, but because I've never had the opportunity. Thus I agree with you that in these perfect successive combinations it is not possible that desire should be multiplied or divided as it is in Sade's works. But in Sade I don't seek a formula for making love or a stimulus leading to it. For me Sade is a symptom of a curious movement which becomes evident within our culture at that moment when a thought, which was basically dominated by representation, calculation, order and classification, gives way, simultaneously with the French Revolution, to an element which up to then had never been conceived in this way, that is desire or voluptuousness...

Q: Thus, according to you, Sade is the last defender of the *esprit de géometrie*?

MF: Exactly. I see in Sade the last representative of the 18th century (the milieu from which he came also testifies to this), rather than a prophet of the future. Perhaps the real question is why we today should be so passionately interested in him. At any rate, I don't make Sade out to be a god, and I don't make him the prophet of our age; my interest in him has been constant principally because of the historical position he occupies, which is at a point of transition between two forms of thought.

Q: Why is our era so interested in Sade?

MF: The reason probably is that Sade sought to insert into the combinations of representations the infinite power of desire, and when he did so he was obliged, almost as an afterthought, to take away the ego's privileged position. The ego became just one element within a combination. In the philosophy of the 17th and 18th centuries, the ego was king. Later, in the 19th century, with the philosophy of will, the ego remains king, though in a different way. Yet at the moment at which these two currents are joined, the ego is dissociated and dispersed among the various combinations. I believe that one of the most noteworthy characteristics of our era is that the sovereignty of the ego has been put in doubt. The dissociation which characterizes our own time was already present in Sade.

Q: But don't you think that the popularity of Sade is due rather to the pansexuality which reigns in our day, the opposition to all order and all morality? I feel that for many people Sade represents above all the liberation of Eros, a spirit that mocks virtuousness, or the victory of the anarchistic Juliette ("Vice") over the timid and conformist Justine ("Virtue").

MF: That's true. However, I maintain that the desire to liberate oneself from sexual taboos has always existed, in all epochs. People have always been famished, from the sexual point of view; there are no societies which do not regulate sex, and thus all societies create the hope of escaping from such regulations. The point is to decipher what form that hope takes today. It's true, today we set Juliette against Justine. But when we do that, aren't we perhaps admitting, or agreeing to, a kind of sexuality which goes beyond the subject, which stands behind the ego, so to speak, or which supersedes it? Thus the kind of sexuality that we recognize today in practice contributes to the dissociation of the ego, at least in the form in which that term is understood from Descartes onward. So we see that in fact the basic theme of Sade's *Juliette* is this: "I will do with you anything that my desire wants, though it is agreed that you will do the same with me. No part of you will escape my desire, but the same goes for me." Thus neither of the two controls his or her own body anymore, and the loss of one communicates with the loss of the other even if the subject itself does not exercise any real control. It is exactly this orgiastic quality of contemporary sexuality that has raised the question of the subject's position.

Q: But many, for example Marcuse, speak of the liberation of Eros as an affirmation of the ego.

MF: I think that Marcuse is trying to use the ancient themes inherited from the 19th century to salvage the ego, understood in the traditional sense.

Q: Again, for me things appear differently. Pansexuality is a phenomenon analogous to protest; it is a refusal of authority, of morality. The struggle is not so much against the subject as against constituted society, the "establishment."

MF: When I speak of the particular forms which erotocism assumes today, I don't mean to say that it is the only factor leading to a dissolution of the individual. I believe that we are passing through a profound crisis of our civilization, in the course of which the ego, the individual person as understood in traditional terms, has come to be questioned.

Q: You have written that moral problems today are entirely reducible to political and sexual problems. Why?

MF: It often happens that I say something just so that I won't have to think about it anymore; then, for this reason, I have some trouble in justifying it. Nevertheless, I made this statement because I was thinking about it and also in order to continue thinking about it.

Q: But you went further; you said that sexuality could ultimately be connected to politics.

MF: This I stated simply as hypothesis. But here is what I meant. Today, in our time (and I speak to you as a historian, even if my goal is to be a historian of the present), moral problems concern sex and politics exclusively. I'll give you an example. For a very long time, in the 17th and 18th centuries, the problem of work, or the lack of work, was or seemed to be a moral problem by nature. Those who did not work were not considered unfortunates who could not find work, but lazy evil creatures who did not want to work. In short, there existed a work ethic but it's hardly necessary for me to say this, because Max Weber said it all, and much better than I could. Today we know quite well that whoever is not working cannot find work, is unemployed. Work has left the domain of morality and entered into that of politics.

Q: It's clear that you are not Italian.

MF: Be that as it may, to me it seems difficult to deny that today work is no longer a moral problem. In short, I would like you to give me an example of a moral problem recognized as such by everyone or by many people, and one which is not connnected to sex or politics. Do you think that my reduction is a bit too radical?

Q: I'm from another school. For me, morality is a hierarchy of values, of all values; every time we are forced to choose between values we find ourselves in the midst of a moral problem.

MF: But don't you believe that in the present world sex and politics define these values?

Q: They define the most visible and most discussed part of moral problems. I would say that they define rather the ethicality (Hegel's *Sittlichkeit*). You're right as far as *Sittlichkeit* is concerned, but not for the case of morality (Hegel's *Moralität*). The two things are not identical. Ethicality is custom: habitual behavior, or at least the behavior expected from a person within a social group, in his relations with the members and the institutions of that group, in his dealings with them. Custom has its duties and its prohibitions, its idols and its taboos, which vary through our history, from epoch to epoch, from place to place (a customs barrier suffices to mark a change in ethics). Morality is much wider, and includes ethics as one of its particular, determined aspects. But it actually signifies a general respect for values as such (for "all" values) inasmuch as they are objects of the will ("ends"); moreover, it is a respect for the hierarchy of values, and whenever the realization of some of these values appears impossible, there will be a conflict (the necessity of choosing). Robinson Crusoe, on his desert island, doesn't have ethical problems; but he continues to have a morality, and eventually moral problems as well. Morality is a category of the objective spirit, while ethicality is only a particular value (and perhaps it is merely an instrumental thing, if it is true, as I happen to think, that the individual represents a higher value than the group).

MF: Here we find ourselves dealing with the same problem as before; you believe in the transcendental and I don't.

Q: But how, in your view, can sexuality be reduced to politics?

MF: This is a question that I have asked myself, but I am not really sure. Perhaps one could say that, if certain aspects of our sexual lives (marriage, the family, the corruption of minors, etc.) raise moral problems, that happens as a function of the particular political situation.

Q: But everything we do has a relationship to the political situation. We are no longer in the midst of Rousseau's forest; in all aspects of our lives we are confronted with laws and institutions.

MF: I wasn't speaking of that. I was wondering how sexuality could raise moral problems; I'm not talking about problems of repression, but exclusively of moral problems. In what sense can leaving a woman or not leaving her constitute a moral problem? I'm not thinking of laws, which vary from one country to another. I think that such things can be because certain acts have connections with the political relationships that define our societies.

Q: According to you, what is the difference between political and social relationships?

MF: I label political everything that has to do with class struggle, and social everything that derives from and is a consequence of the class struggle, expressed in human relationships and in institutions.

Q: For me politics is everything connected to the struggle for power and therefore constitutes perhaps only one aspect of class struggle. The social refers to everything connected to relationships between people in general.

MF: If we give to the term "political" the meaning that you attribute to it—and yours is the more precise definition, I must admit—then my definition cannot stand. I also want to give politics the meaning of a struggle for power; but it's not power understood only as government or state, but economic power as well.

Translated by Jared Becker and James Cascaito.

---

[1] Ferdinand de Saussure, *Course in General Linguistics,* trans. Wade Baskin (New York: McGraw Hill, 1966). *Langue* (language) is the system of language; *parole* (speech) is the individual utterance. [Ed.]

13

Equipments of Power:

Towns, Territories and Collective Equipments

1. Establishing "Logical Categories"

GILLES DELEUZE: There is not a single category that comes out of the text you propose. For example, one could have considered three types of structures in collective equipments—structures of investment, structures of public service and structures of assistance or pseudo-assistance—and posit that there can be oppositional relationships between these different structures. Thus, the highway constitutes an investment structure, with police assistance, and the disappearance of any notion of public service.

The method used in the text, on the contrary, has historical sequences but not logical categories: that is why there is no plan that comes out of it.

One could have taken the example of country dances. In the country, a dance is a collective equipment: young people are also subjected to a kind of racket from swindlers; that's the repressive assistance. And there, it's the right to use which should define the collective equipment, and not, as is the case, the right to consume. These two dimensions oppose each other in the collective equipment: the consumer, actually the one who does not have the right to use, is clearly opposed to the user.

FÉLIX GUATTARI: In order to be able to place decoded fluxes of work in production, fluxes of women or fluxes of children, a number of equipments have to be installed to allow for the preformation of these fluxes.

This conception allows one to take a course which opposes the present approach to collective equipments, which proceeds by fundamental categories, such as the function in the Athens Charter (to live, to circulate, to recreate oneself, to work, as natural categories). Collective equipments must respond to these categories.

Here, it is the exact opposite since: to educate, to put in daycare, in the hospital, circulate, etc... these are not functions at all, faculties of a separated, general instrument, but rather these are axioms which are not comprehensible unless they are determined in terms of each other. Therefore, far from understanding the nature of an equipment according to the spatialized form it takes, it is necessary to first understand what kind of axiomatic is implied. In this way, we are going to see correlative modifications of the conception of an office, a thoroughfare, rooms facing a director's office, the conception of an entrance way, a courtyard...

Perhaps we have to find some synchronism: where there is a kind of mutation that implies that the city, as a body without organs, and the collective equipments, as axioms of capital, imply a mutation (a massive incursion of decoded fluxes: factory work, etc.), everything is going to be correlatively modified. One may be able to see how, in specific examples, this "personologization" of fluxes is obtained. For example, a certain type of relationship of women in production is going to modify the conception of daycare and consequently, twenty years later, that of the school, even professional training, maybe the prison. It is therefore necessary to have a tree of implication, from a given mutation. Another example: the incidence on collective equipments of the entrance of women into the work force during the war of 1914.

In and of itself, there is no such thing as an equipment: there is a constellation of equipments: just as, in and of itself, there is no such thing as a city, but a constellation of cities.

MICHEL FOUCAULT: What appeals to me in your text is the manner in which you establish the non-operative character of the notion of the city. It seems to me that one can show three functions of collective equipments that can intersect perfectly in the same equipment. I would like to try to designate them for one single example, the roadway.

First function of the roadway: to produce production. It is a matter of making sure that there can be production with a surplus and thus, allowing for a deduction. A roadway that attracts labor, that permits instruments to be brought in, to transport raw materials, to take away payments. A road from the fields or from the mines, from the harvest and the tithes. This road has been one of the elements of crystallization of state power. Around this primary function of the roadway, two characters: the agent of power, the tax collector, the payment agent or "fiscal agent": in short, the one who levies fees. Facing him, like an antithetical character, is the bandit, someone who also subtracts fees, but against the agent of power—the looter.

Second function of the roadway: to produce demand. It is a question of constituting a maximal demand or at least a demand which responds to the surpluses of production. The roadway leads to the market, it engenders market places, it transports merchandise, buyers and sellers. A whole set of rules is linked to this function, what one can put on the market, the prices practiced, the places where one can do business. Two characters face off: the inspector, the controller, the customs and tollbooth agent; and on the other side, the smuggler of contraband goods, the peddler. The mandrel does not lift merchandise, on contrary, he offers it up, abundantly, tax free and lawlessly. This function of the collective equipment call for the establishment of a mercantilist State.

Third function: to normalize, to adjust the production of production and the production of demand. The roadway is part of "land planning" (l'amenage-ment du territoire): or, in an even more restricted way, the highway "consumes" the cars whose production it ensures. At one end of the roadway, there is the engineer from Public Works, a regulator—agent and subject of normality (engineering schools authenticate knowledge, attribute power and provide social models; to be a polytechnician)—and at the other end, the one who is cut off or "off-circuit," either because he is ever on-the-move, the vagabond who goes nowhere, or because he is the "laggard," immobile in his spot, an archaic and wild relic predating the roadway: in both cases, abnormal. Hence the necessity of a disciplinary State, the correlative of the industrial State. This is not the same chronology. This is a way of identifying the functional elements in a given collective equipment selected as an example. We could have taken another one. Education produces producers, it produces those who demand and at the same time, it normalizes, classes, divides, imposes rules and indicates the limit of the pathological.

DELEUZE: What Michel has just said is a typical case of categories of collective equipments which are not confused with species. Is not the objective actually to assign categories which, in each historical context and in each case, are like to vary with each other? Thus there are cases where the production aspect overshadows the demand, according to a given economic, political situation, etc...

One must make a set of variable categories, in which the relationships are variable. Let us pinpoint three aspects of collective equipments, close to the distinction proposed by Michel.

First aspect: investment. It is close to the production of production. The daycare center is the production of production and at the same time investment, in that it allows women to work. That always consists of treating someone as a producer, at least a potential one.

Second aspect: control, assistance, partitioning, with, as necessary, collective equipments which privilege this aspects. This consists of always treating someone as a consumer.

Third aspect: it's the public service aspect. It is completely evacuated in a capitalist regime. It consists of considering the citizen as a user, it defines itself by the right to use, that is, the democratic right par excellence outside of all partitioning operations. The right to use is the community. Investment is the State, the police. The highway today is channeled nomadism, a partitioning into a grid, while public service implies a general nomadism. So, one should ask each collective equipment what its role is, production of production, production of demand, regulation. The more public service there is, the less consumption, the less call for consumption and assistance.

FOUCAULT: There is a period when the formation of instruments of production of production, such as the windmill, could only be entrusted to a political power which was also a fiscal power pertaining to them. It did not come under private property. Then, we see a sudden change: the instruments of production of production shift under the regime of private property: the State then becomes responsible for the production of demand. It is only then that public services (markets, roads, post offices...) are created for use; there is no private investment in these public services, only users. At present, it has become clear that this production of demand is profitable, and that one can invest in it. It was run by the State and started up by functionaries; it has since entered into the circuit of private profit; thus advertising, privatization of highways, maybe even the telephone company.

The new state function that appears is that of the balancing of production of production with the production of demand. The role of the State is going to be enlarged more and more; the police, the hospital, the separation of insane/not-insane. And then, normalization, maybe the psychiatric hospitals and even the prisons will be directly run by the pharmaceutical industry, when the patients are all treated with neuroleptic drugs. We see the de-statization of collective equipments that had been the anchoring pins of the power of the State.

The difference between socialist utopias and capitalist utopias is that the capitalist utopias worked. In 1840, 40,000 workers used to live in factory-convents run by nuns. In the North, the city, the dwellings, the road, everything belonged to the factory (and still does today, for example, in the mining village at Bruay-en-Artois). This hooked into the state in two ways: through the banking system and through the army (the industrialists asked the State to establish barracks around the large industrial centers: the case of Lyon after 1834). Now this form of repression has been privatized; it has been given the form of a type of control of the normal: the psychologist, the private police of guard, unions, company committees: the army is no longer called in. Instead, the State is entrusted with a number of collective equipments which, in the past, were reserved for the private sector: there are no more workers' cities, there are "housing projects" which depend on the State apparatus. The deck has been reshuffled.

2. IS THE CITY A PRODUCTIVE OR ANTI-PRODUCTIVE FORCE?

GUATTARI: If the city is a point in time where there is a density of equipments, then one can say that it is the body without organs of these equipments. Equipments hang on to the incomprehensible pseudo-totalization of this body without organs which is only that of desire in dreams, dreams of cities from German expressionist cinema or heavenly Jerusalem. The body without organs-city is more generally like capital, city-military town, city of commercial capital, etc. But given what it is, in fact, a body without organs of desire, all reterritorializations of political power are made on the city.

The city is the totalizing structure of equipments, themselves machines of the socius. The city is the threshold of density for machines of the socius. It doesn't matter then that the definitions of collective equipment link it to the city or to the State, it doesn't even matter that the equipment appears outside of the city (the flotilla of Athens, for example). One can imagine nomad cities, like those of the Toureg. They bear a powerful city because they carry political power that can re-center the machines of the socius.

The city would be everywhere if the threshold of its emergence were not defined: the Urstaat and the writing machine mark this threshold, the threshold of the city and the totalization of collective equipments. It is the despotic signifier. Below this, there are structures of political power, village territorialities, but not collective equipments. It is from the point where a signifier takes off that the territoriality of the city becomes deterritorialization of fluxes. The city is the place where primitive communities are deterritorialized, it is the detached object of primitive communities, and the flux allowing possible definitions of the city, according to the conjunction of deterritorialized fluxes, from writing, money, capital or others. The city and the body without organs of capital are increasingly identified with one another: from the capitol to capital. Equipments as machines are reterritorialized at the same time. Deterritorialized fluxes constitute the city, material fluxes support deterritorialized fluxes, and the city reterritorializes the most deterritorialized fluxes of any given period; legislation in Venice during the Middle Ages prevented the birth of capital.

Collective equipments, as such, are the social unconscious. There is no other kind. They work on all structures of representation. The collective equipment is only apprehended in the universe of representation. The concept of collective equipment refers precisely to representation because it is totalizing. But the first collective equipment is language which allows for the encoding of disjointed elements. A city without writing, does that exist? The flux of writing allows a surface of inscription to be deployed, a body without organs, a detached object of a flux which is more deterritorialized than the others, which is able to connect to them all, these fluxes of rocks, of duties, etc., a re-distributor which will only function like a landowner's independent machine by ensuring the encoding of deterritorialized fluxes. The city is the body without organs of the writing machine.

FRANÇOIS FOURQUET: The first form of writing is accounting, the quantification of something that has no reason for being what it is: fluxes. But not all fluxes: only those that the despot retains and detaches to stock them. In the same way, capital is nothing but crystallized overproduction. The city joins all these fluxes, gathers them, cuts them and re-cuts them every which way and regardless of their nature: fluxes of material objects, informational fluxes, etc. This is the function of collective equipments: to record, fix, stock the fluxes. There is no other social machine. This differs from the current use of the term "collective equipments" which in the language of planners is opposed to "activities" (factories, offices, businesses, etc.) which are nevertheless the prime examples of actual collective equipments!

GUATTARI: Equipments of production and collective equipments are only opposed in the framework of a whole which encompasses them. Next, one can distinguish between equipments of anti-production and equipments of production. However, in capitalism, it is almost impossible to tell the difference. On the contrary, in eastern despotism, all equipments are anti-production, production being for the most part on primitive territorialities. They only become collective equipments in terms of their functioning for the despot. The essence of the despotic city is its anti-productive activity, encoding, despotic overcoding that regulates the productive fluxes. It is the surface of inscription of all systems of coding deterritorialized fluxes in relation to the previously territorialized productive systems. There is therefore no specific work of production in the city, but a political specification of the city, that soon explodes in productive segments which are the collective equipments. It functions as a body without organs, unengendered stasis of the totalization of all the decoded fluxes. It soon explodes into a thousand pieces which are productive entities, collective equipments, which are distinct from other types of production in that they depend on despotic encoding.

FOURQUET: The excess of the despot who measures the fluxes... After the emergence of the city, we only see the monstrous body of the state (Egypt, Sumeria) and its military bulimia. The excessive extension of the State as such, born from the city and soon to destroy it.

GUATTARI: The body without organs is made to flatten, grasp, retain: but it's impossible—everything leaks out from all sides. Like all machine systems, it breaks down. The scribe, for example, who is there to count, like a jerk, the perverse bastard starts to play with signs and write poems. That which is used to contain things is even more dangerous than the previous situation: writing is used to seal a segmentarity, and this becomes scientific equipment, mathematics... The city is the body without organs of writing, but not just any kind. Once that was chucked into the system, there was no getting rid of writing.

The city shouldn't exist; the despot is enough. The ideal of despotism is Genghis Khan; destroy everything (except the craftsmen). But, without a city, he could not manage to overcode primitive territorialities. Capital is also anti-productive—it too would build itself pyramids if it could: but the pyramid of capital runs ahead of it, the signs pop up and disperse in all directions. The body without organs of capital is the ideal of mastering decoded fluxes: it is always running behind the machine, always late in innovating. To use Hjelmslev's distinction, all forms of expression of capital are there to contain its ideal meaning: the capitalists are there to prevent capital from being spread around, but they can't do it. The capitalist expropriates himself in the very movement of capital: the capitalist class has the same function as the Urstaat.

The city is a spatial projection, a form of reterritorialization, of blockage. The original despotic city is a military camp where soldiers are enclosed to prevent the flux of soldiers from spreading out... closure of the city. The idea of the reterritorialization of decoded fluxes is incarnated in the ideal of the Urstaat. But this is not possible: the activated fluxes begin to function, to turn around.

These are collective equipments. They start working all by themselves. They disperse and swarm about. The collective equipment is there to hold something that, by its very nature, cannot be held.

FOURQUET: The city is not a simple projection in inert space of fluxes that have their logic elsewhere. The city, as such, is a productive force: in and of itself, in its spatiality, it has a productive function, it is something more than the sum of juxtaposed collective elements. We cannot limit its definition to criteria of dispersion, proximity and distance, density and concentration... It is a means of production, a use value for production.

GUATTARI: The function of the collective equipment is to produce the socius, the city. The Roman military camp produced towns on borders. The town is made of a connection of confluent machine systems. It defines a material logic, an internal ordering. In the medieval city, the driving force could be religious, royal, noble, military, commercial, etc. We can think about the initial accumulation of the socius of the city, a "surplus value of the code" pre-existing the constitution of a decoded "surplus value of the flux." Generally speaking, new cities today are no longer only accumulated capital.

FOUCAULT: I would like to indicate some questions that must be raised about any collective equipment.

1. What type of property defines the collective equipment? The master's windmill in the Middle Ages is private, but in one way only. One also has to distinguish collective appropriation from collective use. The property status of these equipments is to be studied. Medieval collective equipments were comprised of the windmill, the road, but also the monastic library, the body of agricultural knowledge located in the monastery, for example. The mode of appropriation of collective equipments varies a great deal.

2. The function of the collective equipment is to be a service, but how does this service function? To whom is it open or reserved? What are the criteria limiting it? Further: what profit can be gained by those who use it? But also what profit (and not necessarily economic profit) if gained by the one who ensures the establishment of the collective equipment? Briefly, the double direction, or rather, multiple directions of the collective equipment.

3. The collective equipment has a productive effect. The ford of a river, the roadway and the bridge enable the increase of wealth. But what type of production is involved? Or what place in the system of production?

4. A relationship of power underlies the existence of the collective equipment and its functioning (for example, the toll highway or the communal windmill actualize a certain relationship of power; the school, another).

5. The genealogical implication: how do a number of effects get diversified from there? It will be a question of showing, for example, how urbanization stems from the collective equipment. The city and the collective equipment are not equivalent. What indications and crystallizations grow out of the private

estate or the national forest, a town meadow and places or production like a cement factory? How does the process of urbanization connect with the collective equipment? Either it pre-exists it (bridge-windmill), or it is constituted as an urban collective equipment.

Translated by Lysa Hochroth

14

ON ATTICA

Q: We have just recently visited the prison at Attica and I know that in addition to your studies about exclusion—exclusion of the sick, exclusion of all sorts—you have been interested for a year or a year and a half in prison reform in France. I would like to know your reactions toward this visit. It's the first visit of a prison that you have made, I believe.

MF: Well yes, since in France one does not have the right to visit prisons. You can enter a prison only if you are yourself a prisoner, a guard, or a lawyer, and I have not, practically speaking, belonged to any of these three categories. I have never been detained by the police for more than twelve hours, and consequently I have not really been able to get to know prisons in France. It is thanks to you that I was able, for the first time in my life, to enter a prison, and obviously, for a Frenchman, the sight of Attica is completely overwhelming. Even though I have never entered French prisons, I have heard a lot about them from people who have spent time there, and I know that they are decrepit and dilapidated places, with the prisoners often crammed on top of one another in cells that are repellent with filth.

Attica is obviously not that at all. At Attica what struck me perhaps first of all was the entrance, that kind of phony fortress à la Disneyland, those observation posts disguised as medieval towers with their *machicoulis*. And behind this rather ridiculous scenery which dwarfs everything else, you discover it's an immense machine. And it's this notion of machinery that struck me most strongly—those very long, clean heated corridors which prescribe, for those who pass through them, specific trajectories that are evidently calculated to be the most efficient possible and at the same time the easiest to oversee, and the most direct. Yes, and all of this ends in those huge workshops, like the metallurgical one, which are clean and appear to be close to perfection. A former Attica prisoner whom I saw the day before yesterday told me that in reality those famous workshops that they display so willingly are very dangerous, that a lot of people are hurt in them. But actually, at first sight you have the impression you are visiting more than just a factory, that you are visiting a machine, the inside of a machine.

So the question one obviously asks is what does the machine produce, what is that gigantic installation used for and what comes out of it. At the time of the creation of Auburn and of the Philadelphia prison which served as models (with rather little change until now) for the great machines of incarceration, it was believed that something indeed was produced: "virtuous" men. Now we know, and the administration is perfectly aware, that no such thing is produced. That nothing at all is produced. That it's a question simply of a great trick of sleight of hand, a curious mechanism of circular elimination: society eliminates by sending to prison people whom prison breaks up, crushes, physically eliminates; and then once they have been broken up, the prison eliminates them by "freeing" them and sending them back to society; and there, their life in prison, the way in which they were treated, the state in which they come out insures that society will eliminate them once again, sending them to prison which in turn... Attica is a machine for elimination, a kind of prodigious stomach, a kidney which consumes, destroys, breaks up and then rejects, and which consumes in order to eliminate what it has already eliminated. You remember that when we visited Attica they spoke to us about the four wings of the building, the four corridors, the four large corridors A, B, C, and D. Well, I learned, again through the same former prisoner, that there is a fifth corridor which they didn't talk to us about, it's the corridor E. And you know which that one is?

Q: No.

MF: Ah, well, it is quite simply the machine of the machine, or rather the elimination of the elimination, elimination in the second degree: it's the psychiatric wing. That's where they send the ones who cannot even be integrated into the machine and whom the machinery cannot succeed in assimilating according to its norms, that it cannot crush in accordance with its own mechanical process. Thus they need an additional mechanism.

Q: You have studied the process of exclusion as a sort of abstract concept, and I know that you are acquainted with the inside of hospitals and other institutions. To have visited a place like this—I mean physically visited—did that effect any emotional change in your attitude toward the process of exclusion? Or has the visit simply reinforced your ideas about exclusion?

MF: No, they have rather been undermined; in any case a problem has arisen for me which is rather different from ones that I had been puzzling over formerly; the change was perhaps not absolutely determined by the visit to Attica, but the visit surely precipitated it. Until then I envisioned exclusion from society as a sort of general function, a bit abstract, and I tried to plot that function as in some way constitutive of society, each society being able to function only on condition that a certain number of people are excluded from it. Traditional sociology, sociology of the Durkheim type presented the problem rather in this way: How can society hold individuals together? What is the form of relationship, of symbolic or affective communication that is established among individuals? What is the organizational system which permits society to constitute a totality? I was interested by the somewhat opposite problem, or, if you will, by the opposite response to this problem, which is: through what system of exclusion, by eliminating whom, by creating what division, through what game of negation and rejection can society begin to function?

Well, the question that I ask myself now is the reverse: prison is an organization that is too complex to be reduced to purely negative functions of exclusion; its cost, its importance, the care that one takes in administering it, the justifications that one tries to give for it seem to indicate that it possesses positive functions. The problem is then to find out what role capitalist society has its penal system play, what is the aim that is sought and what effects are produced by all these procedures for punishment and exclusion? What is their place in the economic process, what is their importance in the exercise and the maintenance of power? What is their role in the class struggle?

Q: I wondered precisely to what degree you remained conscious of the political context while walking through the corridors of Attica. I myself was so terrified by the purely human side, by the sense of latent suffering and repression that there were moments, paradoxically perhaps, when I completely forgot the political context.

MF: It is very difficult for me to reply on the matter of the human and virtually physical horror of what goes on at Attica. I believe that I had the same impression as you; but possibly I am less sensitive than you and perhaps a bit thick-skinned. When you go through those long corridors which are—let me repeat—clean, a Frenchman has the impression of being in a somewhat austere private or parochial school; after all, 19th century *lycées* and *collèges* were not that much more pleasant. But finally, after thinking it over, what appeared most terrifying to me at Attica was the strange relationship between the periphery and the inner part. I mean the double game of bars: those which separate the prison from the outside and those which, inside the prison, set apart each of the individual cells. The former, the bars on the gates, I am well aware how prison theoreticians justify them: society must be protected. (Of course, one might say that the greatest dangers for society are not produced by car thieves, but by wars, famines, exploitation and all those who permit and provoke them, but let that pass...). Once the first bars have been passed through, you might expect to find a place where the prisoners are "readapted" to community life, to a respect for law, to a practice of justice, etc. Well, you perceive instead that the place where prisoners spend ten to twelve hours a day, the place where they consider themselves "at home," is a terrifying animal cage: about two yards by one and a half yards, entirely grated on one side. The place where they are alone, where they sleep and where they read, where they dress and take care of their needs, is a cage for wild animals. And there lies the entire hypocrisy of the prison. One suspects that the representative of the administration who conducts the visit must really be giggling inside. You have the impression that he must be saying to himself and also to us something like: "You have handed over to us robbers and murderers because you thought of them as wild beasts—you asked us to make domesticated sheep of them on the other side of the bars which protect you; but there is no reason why we, the guards, the representatives of 'law and order,' we, the instruments of your morality and your prejudices, would not think of them as wild animals, just the same as you. We are identical with you; *we* are *you*; and consequently in this cage where you have put us with them, we build cages which re-establish between them and us the relationship of exclusion and power that the large prison establishes between them and you. You signaled to us that they are wild beasts; *we* signal in turn to *them*. And when they will have learned it well behind their bars, we will send them back to you."

The only way for prisoners to escape from this system of training is by collective action, political organization, rebellion. It appears that American prisons, much more easily than European prisons, can be a place for political action. American prisons in fact play two roles: a role as a place of punishment, as there has existed now for centuries, and a role of "concentration camp" as there existed in Europe during the war and in Africa during the European colonization (in Algeria, for example, during the period when the French were there). One must not forget that there are more than a million prisoners in the United States out of two hundred twenty million inhabitants, to be compared with thirty thousand in France for fifty million inhabitants. The proportion is not at all the same. Then, in the United States, there must be one out of thirty or forty black men in prison: it is here that one can see the function of massive elimination in the American prison. The penal system, the entire pattern of even minor prohibitions (too much drinking, speeding, smoking hashish) serves as an instrument and as a pretext for this practice of radical concentration. It is hardly surprising that the political struggle for penal justice has progressed further in the United States than in France.

Q: One of the things that occurred to me was the question whether such a prison, in the context of American society, might be considered as a symbol simply as a microcosm of society in general or—you said a moment ago that the prison resembled schools as they were formerly...

MF: In Europe, in Europe...

Q: Yes, in Europe, but in America, now you have become acquainted with many no man's lands, areas on the outskirts of cities, suburbs; you have spoken to me in rather precise terms of drug stores in airports, places which seem to be nowhere. And, of course, there are bars everywhere in our society like those in prison. Is it such a big jump from the center of a city, from a ghetto, for example, to the situation of a prison that the latter cannot be naturally encompassed as a normal part of American society or, on the contrary, isn't the prison simply an extension of this society, an extremity of it, as it were?

MF: I think that your question is very much to the point because indeed Attica does resemble America in a profound way, in any event America such as it is viewed by a European who is a little bit lost and not very resourceful like me; that is to say, gigantic, technological, a little terrifying, that Piranesi aspect which permeates the view that many Europeans have of New York. It is true that what we have seen resembles American society but you cannot, I think, simply be satisfied to say, "Oh yes, American prisons are the image of American society, just as European prisons are the image of Europe"; for, if you say that too much, you finally are saying this, that ultimately we are all in prison, that, after all, in the street, in a factory, in a dormitory, one is similarly in prison. It is true that we are caught in a system of continuous surveillance and punishment. But prison is not only punitive; it is also part of an eliminative process. Prison is the physical elimination of people who come out of it, who die of it sometimes directly, and almost always indirectly in so far as they can no longer find a trade, don't have anything to live on, cannot reconstitute a family anymore, etc., and finally passing from one prison to another or from one crime to another end up by actually being physically eliminated.

Q: Well then, where does one begin to reform prisoners, because just as with the Vietnam war, those who seek to reform prisons may be deluding themselves in feeling that they are cleaning up the source of evil simply by making the most visible symptom of it disappear. Is it not then an illusion to hope for reform inside prisons? Are not the prisons so much a part of the fabric of society that nothing can be achieved by beginning there?

MF: The group that we have formed in France is not primarily concerned with the reform of prisons. Our project is, I think, even quite radically different. In France (I know that in America the situation is a little bit different because of the army) the penal system and imprisonment weighs in a privileged and most insistent manner upon a certain fringe of the population which is really not integrated into the working class, controlled to a certain extent by the large unions. We have often been told, on behalf of certain political organizations, that the problem of prisons is not part of the proletarian conflict. There are several reasons for that. The first one is that the fringe of the lower class which is constantly in contact with the police and law is to a large extent made up of people who are outside the factory. Whether their unemployment is voluntary or involuntary, their form of opposition to bourgeois society does not express itself in demonstrations, politically organized struggles, and professional or economic pressures such as strikes. The second reason is that the bourgeoisie often uses this fringe of the population against the working people: it may be made into a temporary work force or even recruited for the police. The third reason is that the proletariat has been fully imbued with the bourgeois ideology concerning morality and legality, concerning theft and crime.

So we are currently at a stage where different strata of the people seek to overcome conflicts and oppositions which had been established and maintained between them by the capitalist system; where struggles in the factories are linked more than they used to be with struggles outside the factories (concerning housing, the question of the "quality of life," etc.); where it is recognized that the general ideological struggle is an integral part of the political struggle. For all these reasons, the isolation of that fringe of the lower class, at the outset under the domination of police pressure, is in the process of slowly disappearing. Its reintegration into political struggles is the prime objective of our group.

Q: In this regard the story that you told us about Genet and the distinction which was made between certain types of prisoners—has that sort of thing become better recognized by the proletariat in France as well as in America?

MF: You are evidently referring to what Genet told me one day about prisons. During the war he was in prison at the Santé and he had to be transferred to the Palais de Justice in order to be sentenced; at that time the custom was to handcuff the prisoners two by two to lead them to the Palais de Justice; just as Genet was about to be handcuffed to another prisoner, the latter asked the guard "Who is this guy you're handcuffing me to?" and the guard replied: "It's a thief." The other prisoner stiffened at that point and said, "No, I'm a political prisoner, I'm a Communist, I won't be handcuffed with a thief." And Genet said to me that from that day on, with regard to all forms of political movements and actions that we have known in France, he has had not merely a distrust but a certain contempt....

Q: I wonder to what extent since that time those who are involved in politics have become aware of the lack of distinction among different forms of prisoners, of the possibility that these other prisoners, victims of social problems which are at the source of their own political struggle, are not political prisoners in the proper sense of the word but are still more profoundly prisoners, politically, than they themselves.

MF: I believe that there has been a historical mutation, if you will, in the course of the 19th century. It is almost certain that labor movements and their leaders, in Europe and particularly in France, in order to escape from police repression in its more violent and savage form, were obliged to distinguish themselves from the entire criminal population. Efforts were made to present these labor movements as organizations of murderers, as hired killers, thieves, alcoholics, etc. There was thus the necessity to avoid falling victim to these accusations and to the consequent punishments; thus also the obligation they felt to take up, as if it were their own, the responsibility for a whole system of morality which came from the ruling class, and finally to accept the bourgeois division between virtue and vice, respect for the property of others, and so on. They were obliged to recreate for themselves a sort of moral puritanism which was for them a necessary condition for survival and a useful instrument in the struggle as well. That kind of moral rigorism finally remained with them as a part of the proletariat's daily ideology, and still now, until recent times, the proletariat and its union or political leaders had certainly continued to grant that separation between the offenders of common law and political prisoners. And after all, you must keep in mind all the struggles, all the efforts that were necessary in the 19th century so that the leaders of the workers were not treated and punished like crooks.

The change occurred a short while ago in France at the time of the imprisonment of certain Maoists. When Maoists were put in prison, they began, it must be said, by reacting a little like the traditional political groups, that is to say: "We do not want to be assimilated with the criminals of common law, we do not want our image to be mixed with theirs in the opinion of people, and we ask to be treated like political prisoners with the rights of political prisoners." This was, I think, a sort of political mistake which was rather quickly felt, there were discussions on this subject, and it was at this time that we founded our group; the Maoists quickly understood that ultimately the prison's elimination of common law prisoners was part of the system of political elimination of which they were themselves the victims. If one makes the distinction, if one accepts the difference between political law and common law, that means that fundamentally one recognizes morality and law as far as respect for the property of others, respect for traditional moral values, etc., are concerned. The cultural revolution in its widest sense implies that, at least in a society like ours, you no longer make the division between criminals of common law and political criminals. Common law is politics, it's after all the bourgeois class which, for political reasons and on a basis of its political power, defined what is called common law.

Q: Then, what the Maoists understood was not simply a political mistake that they had committed—I mean, in the eyes of the public, the idea that they were excluding themselves, that they intended to remain an elite in prison—but this was something they learned as usual in connection with politics in a much deeper sense.

MF: That's right, I believe that it was for them an important deepening of their understanding, the discovery that ultimately the penal system in its entirety and ultimately the entire moral system both were the result of a power relationship established by the bourgeoisie and constituted an instrument for exercising and maintaining that power.

Q: In listening to you I am reminded of a scene in the film *The Battle of Algiers*.[1] This is simply one example among others, but there is a certain asceticism on the part of revolutionaries which results in their refusing to indulge in drugs and looking with disgust upon prostitution. I am reminded of that film where the heroes were sketched as being very pure, and one of them refused to go off with a prostitute. This attitude seems still to prevail in Algeria, as a matter of fact. To what extent does that asceticism on the part of certain revolutionaries who want to remain pure (and which is very likely the product of a bourgeois education) become a quality which prevents the true revolutionary from eventually succeeding in being accepted within a popular movement?

MF: One can say in reply to your first question that the rigorism of the revolutionary certainly reveals his bourgeois origins or in any case a cultural and ideological affinity with the bourgeoisie. Nevertheless, I think that we must link that to an historical process; it seems to me that until the beginning of the 19th century, and even during the French Revolution, popular uprisings were led at one and the same time by peasants, small craftsmen, by the first laborers and then by that category of restless elements poorly integrated into society that might be highway robbers, smugglers, and so on—at any rate all who had been rejected by the reigning system of legality, the law of the state. And in the 19th century, in the course of political struggles which permitted the proletariat to have itself recognized as a power with compelling demands, which permitted the proletariat to escape, all the same, from violent elimination and constraint, in the course of these political struggles the proletariat was obliged in some way to establish a separation between it and that other "agitated" population. When labor unionization was founded, in order to have itself recognized, it needed to dissociate itself from all the seditious groups and from all those who refused the legal system: We are not the murderers, we are not attacking either people or goods; if we stop production, it is not in an outburst of absolute destruction, but in conjunction with very precise demands. Family morality which had absolutely no currency in popular circles at the end of the 18th century had become by the beginning of the 19th century one of the means by which the proletariat was able in some way to establish its respectability. Popular virtue, the "good" worker, good father, good husband respectful of the legal system, that is the image which since the 18th century the bourgeoisie proposed and imposed on the proletariat in order to turn it away from any form of violent agitation, insurrection, any attempt to usurp power and its rules. That image the proletariat took up and used as a matter of fact in an often very efficient way to support its struggles. That "morality" was up to a certain point the marriage contract between the proletariat and the petty bourgeoisie during the entire second half of the 19th century, from 1848 to Zola and Jaurès.

Now your second question: Isn't this puritanism an obstacle for the revolutionary leader? I would say, currently, yes. There exists indeed—at least that's the opinion of our group in any event—there exists today in our societies truly revolutionary forces made up of just those strata which are poorly integrated into society, those strata which are perpetually rejected and which in their turn reject the bourgeois moral system. How can you work with them in the political battle if you do not get rid of those moral prejudices which are ours? After all, if one takes into account the habitually unemployed who say, "Me, I prefer not working to working"; if one takes into account women, prostitutes, homosexuals, drug addicts, etc., there is a force for questioning society that one has no right, I think, to neglect in the political struggle.

Q: If one followed your line of thought logically, one would say almost that those who are involved with the rehabilitation of prisoners are perhaps the most virulent enemies of the revolution. And then, that fellow who guided us through Attica, if I may come back to my first question, and who gave us the impression of being a very well intentioned guy, "decent" as you would say, but totally devoid of imagination, he would be the most dangerous enemy.

MF: Yes, I think what you say is profoundly true. Look, I do not want to go further, because you have presented the problem very well, but this man who is responsible for the cultural programs at Attica and who took care of our visit, I think that one can say also that he is dangerous in an immediate sense. One of the former prisoners of Attica whom I saw after our visit said to me: "He is one of the most vicious among the guards."

But afterwards we met some psychologists who were clearly very nice people, very liberal, who saw things with a good deal of accuracy. For them, stealing the property of someone else, pulling off a holdup in a bank, committing prostitution, sleeping with a man if one is male, etc.—if those acts are psychological problems that they must help the individual to resolve, are they not also fundamentally accomplices of the system? Aren't they masking the fact that ultimately committing a misdemeanor, committing a crime questions the way society functions in a most fundamental way? So fundamental that we forget that it's social, that we have the impression that it's moral, that it involves peoples' rights....

And you see in what way one can present the problem. So that I subscribe completely to what you say, doesn't everything that concerns reintegration, everything that is a psychological or individual solution for the problem, mask the profoundly political character both of society's elimination of these people and of those people's attack on society. All of that profound struggle is, I believe, political. Crime is "a *coup d'état* from below." That phrase is from *Les Misérables.*

Translated by John Simon

------

1 *The Battle of Algiers* (1984) is a film by Gillo Pontecorvo (France) [Ed.]

15

FILM AND POPULAR MEMORY

Q: Let's start from the journalistic phenomenon of the "retro" style, the current fad for the recent past. Basically, we can put the question like this: how is it that films like Louis Malle's *Lacombe Lucien* or *The Night Porter*[1] can be made today? Why do they meet with such a fantastic response? We think the answer has to be sought on three levels:

(1) Giscard d'Estaing has been elected. A new kind of approach to politics, to history, to the political apparatus is coming into existence, indicating very clearly—in such a way that everyone can see it—that Gaullism is dead. So it's necessary, insofar as Gaullism remains very closely linked to the period of the Resistance, to look at how this is translated in the films which are being made.

(2) How is it possible for bourgeois ideology to attack the weak points of orthodox Marxism (rigid, economistic, mechanical—the terms don't matter much) which has for so long provided the only framework for interpreting social phenomena?

(3) Lastly, what does all this mean for political militants? Given that militants are consumers and sometimes also makers of films. The thing is, that after Marcel Ophuls' film *The Sorrow and the Pity,* the floodgates have been open. Something hitherto completely repressed or forbidden has flooded out. Why?

MF: I think this comes from the fact that the history of the war, and what took place around it, has never really been written except in completely official accounts. To all intents and purposes, these official histories are centered on Gaullism, which, on the one hand, was the only way of writing history in terms of an honorable nationalism; and, on the other, the only way of introducing the Great Man, the man of the right, the man of the old 19th-century nationalisms, as an historical figure. It boils down to the fact that France was exonerated by de Gaulle, while the right (and we know how it behaved at the time of the war) was purified and sanctified by him. What has never been described is what was going on in the very heart of the country from 1936, and even from the end of the 1914 war, up until the Liberation.

Q: So what has come about since *The Sorrow and the Pity* is some kind of return to truth in history. The point is really whether it is the truth.

MF: This has to be linked to the fact that the end of Gaullism means an end to this exoneration of the right by de Gaulle and by this brief period. The old right of Pétain and Maurras, the old reactionary and collaborating right, which disguised itself behind de Gaulle as best it could, now feels entitled to write its own history. This old right which, since Tardieu, had been upstaged both historically and politically, is now coming back into the limelight.

It openly supported Giscard. There's no longer any need for it to rely on disguises, it can write its own history. And among the factors which account for the present acceptance of Giscard by half of France (a majority of 200,000), we must not forget to include films like those we're discussing—whatever their makers' intentions. The fact that it's been possible to show everything has enabled the right to carry out a certain regrouping. In the same way that, conversely, it's really the healing of the breach between the national right and the collaborating right which has made these films possible. The two are inextricably linked.

Q: This history, then, is being rewritten both in the cinema and on television. It seems this rewriting of history is being carried out by film-makers who are thought of as more or less left-wing. This is a problem we should look at more closely.

MF: I don't think it's that simple. What I've just said is very schematic. Let's go over it again.

There's a real fight going on. Over what? Over what we can roughly describe as popular memory. It's an actual fact that people—I'm talking about those who are barred from writing, from producing their books themselves, from drawing up their own historical accounts—that these people nevertheless do have a way of recording history, or remembering it, of keeping it fresh and using it. This popular history was, to a certain extent, even more alive, more clearly formulated in the 19th century, where, for instance, there was a whole tradition of struggles which were transmitted orally, or in writing or songs, etc.

Now, a whole number of apparatuses have been set up ("popular literature," cheap books and the stuff that's taught in school as well) to obstruct the flow of this popular memory. And it could be said that this attempt has been pretty successful. The historical knowledge the working class has of itself is continually shrinking. If you think, for instance, of what workers at the end of the 19th century knew about their own history, what the trade union tradition (in the strict sense of the word) was like up until the 1914 war, it's really quite remarkable. This has been progressively diminished, but although it gets less, it doesn't vanish.

Today, cheap books aren't enough. There are much more effective means like television and the cinema. And I believe this was one way of reprogramming popular memory, which existed but had no way of expressing itself. So people are shown not what they were, but what they must remember having been.

Since memory is actually a very important factor in struggle (really, in fact, struggles develop in a kind of conscious moving forward of history), if one controls people's memory, one controls their dynamism. And one also controls their experience, their knowledge of previous struggles. Just what the Resistance was, must no longer be known...

I think we have to understand these films in some such way. Their theme is, roughly, that there's been no popular struggle in the 20th century. This assertion has been successively formulated in two ways. The first, immediately after the war, simply said: "What a century of heroes the 20th century is! There's been Churchill, de Gaulle, those chaps who did the parachuting, the fighter squadrons, etc.!" It amounted to saying: "There's been no popular struggle, because this is where the real struggle was." But still no one said directly, "There's been no popular struggle." The other, more recent formulation —skeptical or cynical, as you prefer—consists in proceeding to the blunt assertion itself: "Just look at what happened. Where have you seen any struggles? Where do you see people rising up, taking up rifles?"

Q: There's been a sort of half-rumor going around since, perhaps, *The Sorrow and the Pity,* to the effect that the French people, as a whole, didn't resist the Germans, that they even accepted collaboration, that they took it all lying down. The question is what all this finally means. And it does indeed seem that what is at stake is popular struggle, or rather the memory of that struggle.

MF: Exactly. It's vital to have possession of this memory, to control it, to administer it, tell it what it must contain. And when you see these films, you find out what you have to remember: "Don't believe all that you've been told. There aren't any heroes. And if there aren't any, it's because there's no struggle." So a sort of ambiguity arises: to start with, "there aren't any heroes" is a positive debunking of the whole war-hero mythology à la Burt Lancaster. It's a way of saying, "No, that's not what war is about." So your first impression is that history is beginning to reappear; that eventually they're going to tell us why we're not all obliged to identify with de Gaulle or the members of the Normandy-Niemen squadron, etc. But beneath the sentence "There are no heroes" is hidden a different meaning, its true message: "There was no struggle." This is what the exercise is all about.

Q: There's another phenomenon which explains why these films are so successful. The resentment of those who really did struggle is used against those who didn't. The people who formed the Resistance, watching *The Sorrow and the Pity* for example, see the passive citizens of a town in central France, and they recognize their passivity. And then the resentment takes over: they forget that they themselves did struggle.

MF: In my view, the politically important phenomenon is, rather than any one particular film, that of the series, the network established by all these

films and the place—excuse the pun—they "occupy." In other words, the important thing is to ask: "Is it possible at the moment to make a positive film about
the struggles of the Resistance?" Well, clearly the answer's no. One gets the
impression that people would laugh at a film like this, or else quite simply
wouldn't go to see it.

Q: Yes. It's the first thing to be brought up against us when we attack a
film like Malle's. The response is always, "What would you have done, then?"
And you're right; it's impossible to answer. We should be beginning to
develop—how shall I put it—a left-wing perspective on all this, but it's true that
one doesn't exist ready-made. Alternately, this restates the problem of how one
is to produce a positive hero, a new type of hero.

MF: The problem's not the hero, but the struggle. Can you make a film
about a struggle without going through the traditional process of creating
heroes? It's a new form of an old problem.

Q: Let's go back to the "retro" style. From its own standpoint, the bourgeoisie has largely concentrated its attention on one historical period (the 40s)
which throws into focus both its strong and weak points. For on the one hand, this
is where it's most easily exposed (it's the bourgeoisie which created the breeding
ground of Nazism or of collaboration with it); while on the other hand, it's here
that it's currently trying to justify its historical behavior—in the most cynical
ways. The difficulty is how to reveal what, for us, is the positive content of this
same historical period—for us, that is, the generation of the struggles of 1968 or
LIP.2 Is the period of the Resistance really a weak point to be attacked, the point
where some different kinds of ideological hegemony could emerge? For it's a fact
that the bourgeoisie is simultaneously defensive and offensive about its recent
history: strategically defensive, but tactically offensive because it's found this
strong point from which it can best sow confusion. But do we have to be
restricted (which is to be on the defensive) to simply re-establishing the truth
about history? Isn't it possible to find some weak point where we might attack the
ideology? Is this point necessarily the Resistance? Why not 1789 or 1968?

MF: Thinking about these films and their common subject, I wonder
whether something different couldn't be done. And when I say "subject," I don't
mean showing the struggles or showing they didn't exist. I mean that it's historically true that while the war was going on there was a kind of rejection of it
among the French masses. Now where did this come from? From a whole series
of episodes that no one talks about—the right doesn't, because it wants to hide
them, and the left doesn't, because it's afraid of being associated with anything
contrary to "national honor."

A good seven or eight million men went through the 1914-18 war. For
four years they lived a horrifying existence, seeing millions upon millions of
men die all around them. And what do they find themselves facing again in

1920? The right-wing in power, full-scale economic exploitation and finally an economic crisis and the unemployment of 1932. How could these people, who'd been packed into the trenches, still feel attracted by war in the two decades of 1920-30 and 1930-40? If the Germans still did, it's because defeat had reawakened such a national feeling in them that the desire for revenge could overcome this sort of repulsion. But even so, people don't enjoy fighting these bourgeois wars, with middle-class officers and these kind of benefits resulting from them. I think this was a crucial experience for the working class. And when in 1940, these guys tossed their bikes into the ditch and said, "I'm going home"—you can't simply say "They're scabs!" and you can't hide from it either. You have to find a place for it in this sequence of events. This non-compliance with national instructions has to be fitted in. And what happened during the Resistance is the opposite of what we're shown. What happened was that the process of repoliticization, remobilization and a taste for fighting reappeared little by little in the working class. It gradually reappeared after the rise of Nazism and the Spanish Civil War. Now what these films show is just the opposite process: namely, that after the great dream of 1939, which was shattered in 1940, people just gave up. This process did really take place, but as part of another, much more extended process which was going in the opposite direction: starting from a disgust with war, it ended up, in the middle of the occupation, as a conscious awareness of the need to struggle.

I think there was a positive political meaning to this noncompliance with the demands of the national armed struggles. The historical theme of *Lacombe Lucien* and his family takes on a new light if you look back to Ypres and Douaumont....

Q: This raises the problem of popular memory: of a memory working at its own pace, a pace quite detached from any seizure of central power or from the outbreak of any war....

MF: This has always been the aim of the history taught in schools: to teach ordinary people that they got killed and that this was very heroic. Look at what's been made of Napoleon and the Napoleonic wars....

Q: A number of films, including those of Malle and Cavani, leave off talking about history or the struggle over Nazism and fascism; usually, they talk instead, or at the same time, about sex. What's the nature of this discourse?

MF: But don't you make a sharp distinction between *Lacombe Lucien* and *Night Porter* on this? It seems that the erotic, passionate aspect of *Lacombe Lucien* has a quite easily identifiable function. It's basically a way of making the antihero acceptable, of saying he's not as anti as all that.

In fact, if all the power relations in his life are distorted, and if it's through him that they keep on running, on the other hand, just when you think he's distorting all the erotic relations, a true relationship suddenly appears and he loves the girl. On the one hand, there's the machinery of power which, starting with a flat tire, carries Lacombe closer and closer to something crazy. On the other hand, there's the machinery of love, which seems hooked up to it, which seems distorted, but which, on the contrary, has just the opposite effect and in the end restores Lucien as the handsome naked youth living in the fields with a girl.

So there's a fairly elementary antithesis between power and love. While in *Night Porter* the question is—both generally and in the present situation—a very important one: love for power.

Power has an erotic charge. There's an historical problem involved here. How is it that Nazism—which was represented by shabby, pathetic puritanical characters, laughably Victorian old maids, or at best, smutty individuals—how has it now managed to become, in France, in Germany, in the United States, in all pornographic literature throughout the world, the ultimate symbol of eroticism? Every shoddy erotic fantasy is now attributed to Nazism. Which raises a fundamentally serious problem: how do you love power? Nobody loves power any more. This kind of affective, erotic attachment, this desire one has for power, for the power that's exercised over you, doesn't exist any more. The monarchy and its rituals were created to stimulate this sort of erotic relationship towards power. The massive Stalinist apparatus, and even that of Hitler, were constructed for the same purpose. But it's all collapsed in ruins and obviously you can't be in love with Brezhnev, Pompidou or Nixon. In a pinch you might love de Gaulle, Kennedy or Churchill. But what's going on at the moment? Aren't we witnessing the beginnings of a re-eroticization of power, taken to a pathetic, ridiculous extreme by the porn-shops with Nazi insignia that you can find in the United States, and (a much more acceptable but just as ridiculous version) in the behavior of Giscard d'Estaing when he says, "I'm going to march down the streets in a lounge suit, shaking hands with ordinary people and kids on half-day holidays"? It's a fact that Giscard has built part of his campaign not only on his fine physical bearing but also on a certain eroticizing of his character, his stylishness.

Q: That's how he's portrayed himself on an electoral poster—one where you see his daughter turned towards him.

MF: That's right. He's looking at France, but she's looking at him. It's the restoration to power of seduction.

Q: Something that struck us during the electoral campaign, particularly at the time of the big televised debates between François Mitterand and Giscard, was that they weren't at all on the same level. Mitterand appeared as the old type of politico, belonging to the old left, let's say. He was trying to sell ideas, which were themselves dated and a bit old-fashioned, and he did it with a lot of style. But Giscard was selling the idea of power, exactly like an advertiser sells cheese.

MF: Even quite recently, it was necessary to apologize for being in power. It was necessary for power to be self-effacing, for it not to show itself as power. To a certain extent, this is how the democratic republics have functioned, where the aim was to render power sufficiently invisible and insidious for it to be impossible to grasp, to grasp what it was doing or where it was.

Q: Perhaps we have to talk about a certain powerlessness of traditional Marxist discourse to account for fascism. Let's say that Marxism has given an historical account of the phenomenon of Nazism in a deterministic fashion, while completely leaving aside what the specific ideology of Nazism was. So it's scarcely surprising that someone like Louis Malle, who's pretty familiar with what's going on on the left, can benefit from this weakness, and rush into the breach.

MF: Marxism has given a definition of Nazism and fascism: "an overt terrorist dictatorship of the most reactionary fraction of the bourgeoisie." It's a definition that leaves out an entire part of the content and a whole series of relationships. In particular, it leaves out the fact that Nazism and fascism were only possible insofar as there could exist within the masses a relatively large section which took on the responsibility for a number of state functions of repression, control, policing, etc. This, I believe, is a crucial characteristic of Nazism; that is, its deep penetration inside the masses and the fact that a part of the power was actually delegated to a specific fringe of the masses. This is where the word "dictatorship" becomes true in general, and relatively false. When you think of the power an individual could possess under a Nazi regime as soon as he was simply S.S. or signed up in the Party! You could actually kill your neighbor, steal his wife, his house! This is where *Lacombe Lucien* is interesting, because it's one side it shows up well. The fact is that contrary to what is usually understood by dictatorship—the power of a single person—you could say that in this kind of regime the most repulsive (but in a sense the most intoxicating) part of power was given to a considerable number of people. The S.S. was that which was given the power to kill, to rape...

Q: This is where orthodox Marxism falls down. Because it's obliged to talk about desire.

MF: About desire and power...

Q: It's also where films like *Lacombe Lucien* and *Night Porter* are relatively "strong." They can talk about desire and power in a way which seems coherent...

MF: It's interesting to see in *Night Porter* how under Nazism the power of a single person is taken over and operated by ordinary people. The kind of mock trial which is set up is quite fascinating. Because on the one hand, it has all the trappings of a psychotherapy group, while in fact having the power structure of a secret society. What they re-establish is basically an S.S. cell, endowed with a judicial power that's different from, and opposed to, the central power.

You have to bear in mind the way power was delegated, distributed within the very heart of the population; you have to bear in mind this vast transfer of power that Nazism carried out in a society like Germany. It's wrong to say that Nazism was the power of the great industrialists carried on under a different form. It wasn't simply the intensified central power of the military—it was that, but only on one particular level.

Q: This is an interesting side of the film, in fact. But what in our view seems very open to criticism is that it appears to say: "If you're a typical S.S. man, you'll act like this. But if, in addition, you have a certain inclination for the job, it will offer you incredible erotic experiences." So the film keeps up the seductiveness.

MF: Yes, this is where it meets up with *Lacombe Lucien.* Because Nazism never gave people any material advantages, it never handed out anything but power. You still have to ask why it was, if this regime was nothing but a bloody dictatorship, that on May 3rd, 1945, there were still Germans who fought to the last drop of blood; whether these people didn't have some form of emotional attachment to power. Bearing in mind, of course, all the pressuring, the denunciations... In *Lacombe Lucien,* as in *Night Porter,* this excess of power they're given is converted back into love. It's very clear at the end of *Night Porter,* where a miniature concentration camp is built up around Max in his room, where he starves to death. So here love has converted power, surplus power, back into a total absence of power. In one sense, it's almost the same reconciliation as in *Lacombe Lucien* where love turns the excess of power in which he's been trapped into a rustic poverty far removed from the Gestapo's shady hotel, and far removed, too, from the farm where the pigs were being butchered.

Q: So we now have the beginnings of an explanation for the problem you were posing at the start of our discussion: why is Nazism, which was a repressive, puritanical system, nowadays associated with eroticism? There's a sort of shift of emphasis: the central problem of power, which one doesn't want to confront head on, is dodged, or rather shoved completely into the question of sexuality. So that this eroticising is ultimately a process of evasion, or repression...

MF: The problem's really very difficult and it hasn't been studied perhaps enough, even by Reich. What leads to power being desirable, and to actually being desired? It's easy to see the process by which this eroticising is transmitted, reinforced, etc. But for the eroticising to work, it's necessary that the attachment to power, the acceptance of power by those over whom it is exerted, is already erotic.

Q: It's that much more difficult since the representation of power is rarely erotic. De Gaulle or Hitler are not particularly seductive.

MF: True—and I wonder if the Marxist analyses aren't victims to some extent to the abstractedness of the notion of liberty. In a regime like the Nazi regime, it's a fact that there's no liberty. But not having liberty doesn't mean not having power...

There's a battle for and around history going on at this very moment which is extremely interesting. The intention is to reprogram, to stifle what I've called the "popular memory," and also to propose and impose on people a framework in which to interpret the present. Up to 1968, popular struggles were part of folklore. For some people, they weren't even part of their immediate concept of reality. After 1968, every popular struggle, whether in South America or in Africa, has found some echo, some sympathetic response. So it's no longer possible to keep up their separation, this geographical "quarantine." Popular struggles have become for our society, not part of the actual, but part of the possible. So they have to be set at a distance. How? Not by providing a direct interpretation of them, which would be liable to be exposed. But by offering an historical interpretation of those popular struggles which have occurred in France in the past, in order to show that they never really happened! Before 1968, it was: "It won't happen here because it's going on somewhere else." Now it's: "It won't happen here because it never has! Take something like the Resistance even, this glorious past you've talked about so much, just look at it for a moment...Nothing. It's empty, a hollow facade!" It's another way of saying, "Don't worry about Chile, it's no different; the Chilean peasants couldn't care less. And France too: the bulk of the population isn't interested in anything a few malcontents might do."

Q: When we react to all this—against it all—it's important that we don't limit ourselves to re-establishing the truth, to saying, about the Resistance, for example, "No, I was there and it wasn't like that!" If you're going to wage any effective ideological struggle on the kind of ground dictated by these films, we believe you have to have a much broader, more extensive and positive frame of reference. For many people this consists in reappropriating the "history of France" for instance. It was with this in mind that we undertook a close reading of *I, Pierre Rivière*; because we realized that, paradoxically enough, it was useful to us in understanding *Lacombe Lucien,* that their comparison was not unproductive. A significant difference between them, for example, is that Pierre Riviere is someone who writes, who commits a murder and who has a quite extraordinary memory. While Malle, on the other hand, treats his hero as a half-wit, as someone who goes through everything—history, the war, collaboration—without accumulating any experience. This is where the theme of memory, of popular memory, can help to separate off someone like Pierre Rivière from the character created by Malle (and Patrick Modiano, in *La Place de l'Etoile*).[3] Pierre Rivière, having no way of making his voice heard, takes the floor and is obliged to kill before he wins the right to speak. While Malle's character proves, precisely by making nothing of what has happened to him, that there's nothing worth the trouble of remembering. It's a pity you haven't seen *The Courage of the People*. It's a

Bolivian film made with the explicit aim of becoming evidence on a criminal record. The characters in this film—which has been shown throughout the world (but not in Bolivia, thanks to the regime)—are played by the very people who were part of the real drama it re-enacts (a miner's strike and its bloody repression). They themselves take charge of their picture, so that nobody shall forget...

There are two things going on in the cinema at the moment. On the one hand there are historical documents, which have an important role. In *A Whole Life*, for instance, they play a very big part. Or again, in the films of Marcel Ophuls, or of Harris and Sedouy, it's very moving to watch the reality of Duclos in action in 1936 or 1939. And on the other hand, there are fictional characters who, at a given moment of history, condense within themselves the greatest possible number of social relations, of links with history. This is why *Lacombe Lucien* is so successful. Lacombe is a Frenchman during the occupation, an ordinary Joe with concrete connections to Nazism, to the countryside, to local power, etc. And we shouldn't ignore this way of personifying history, of incarnating it in a character or a collection of characters who embody, at a given moment, a privileged relation to power.

There are lots of figures in the history of the workers' movement that aren't known; there are plenty of heroes in the history of the working class who've been completely driven out of memory. And I think there's a real issue to be fought here. There's no need for Marxism to keep on making films about Lenin. We've got plenty already.

MF: What you say is important. It's a trait of many Marxists nowadays—ignorance of history. All these people, who spend their time talking about the misrepresentation of history, are only capable of producing commentaries on texts. What did Marx say? Did Marx really say that? Look, what is Marxism but a different way of analyzing history itself? In my opinion, the left in France has no real grasp of history. It used to have one. At one time in the 19th century, Michelet might have been said to represent the left. There was Jaures, too, and after them there grew up a kind of tradition of left-wing, social democratic historians (Mathiez, etc.). Nowadays it's dwindled to a trickle; whereas it could be a formidable wave, carrying along writers, film-makers. True, there has been Aragon and Les Cloches de Bâle—a very great historical novel. But there are relatively few things, compared to what it could be like in a society where, after all, one can say that the intellectuals are more or less impregnated with Marxism.

Q: In this respect, the cinema offers something new: history captured "Live." How do people in America relate to history, seeing the Vietnam war on television every evening while they're eating?

MF: As soon as you start seeing pictures of war every evening, war becomes totally acceptable. That's to say, thoroughly tedious, you'd really love to see something else. But when it becomes boring, you put up with it. You don't even watch it. So how is this particular reality on film to be reactivated as an existing, historically important reality?

Q: Have you seen *Les Camisards?*

MF: Yes, I liked it very much. Historically, it's impeccable. It's well made, intelligent and it makes a lot of things clear.

Q: I think that's the direction we have to take in making films. To come back to the films we were talking about at the beginning—we must raise the question of the extreme left's confusion in the face of certain aspects of *Lacombe Lucien* and *Night Porter,* particularly the sexual one; and how this confusion can be of benefit to the right...

MF: As for what you call the extreme left, I find myself in considerable difficulty. I'm not at all sure that it still exists. Nonetheless, there really needs to be a thorough summing-up of what the extreme left has done since 1968, both negatively and positively. It's true that this extreme left has been the means of spreading a whole number of important ideas: on sexuality, women, homosexuality, psychiatry, housing, medicine. It's also been the means of spreading methods of action, where it continues to be of importance. The extreme left has played as important a role in the forms of activity as in its themes. But there's also a negative summing-up to be made, concerning certain Stalinist and terrorist organizational practices. And a misunderstanding, too, of certain broad and deeply-rooted processes which recently resulted in 13 million people backing Mitterrand, and which have always been disregarded, on the pretext that this was the politics of the politicians, that this was the business of the parties. A whole heap of things have been ignored; notably, that the desire to defeat the right has been a very important political factor within the masses for a number of months and even years. The extreme left hasn't sensed this desire, thanks to a false definition of the masses, a wrong appreciation of what this will to win really is. Faced with the risks a co-opted victory would involve, it prefers not to take the risk of winning. Defeat, at least, can't be co-opted. Personally, I'm not so sure.

Translated by Martin Jordin

---

1 *Lacombe Lucien*, a film by Louis Malle, is the story of a French collaborator during the German occupation. *Night Porter*, a film by Liliana Cavani, is a sado-masochistic love story involving a former Nazi camp worker and prisoner. [Ed.]

2 LIP, a *cause célèbre* in France, involved the take-over by workers of a factory. Cf. A. Belden Field, *Trotskyism and Maoism: Theory and Practice in France and the United States.* (New York: Autonomedia, 1988) [Ed.]

3 Pierre Modiano, *La Place de l'Etoile* (Paris: Gallimard, 1968). [Ed.]

16

TALK SHOW

Q: Michel Foucault, you are a professor at the Collège de France, a philosopher and thinker. Many people consider you one of the greatest thinkers of our time. You are forty-eight years old. You are steeped in knowledge. To students and humanists, you are someone who has written and spoken. What a responsibility! What I would like to know is how, precisely, does one come to knowledge? Is there a particular way of going about it?

MF: How does one come to knowledge? Well, you're born to it. For someone like me, brought up as a provincial petty bourgeois, you drink learning in with your baby formula before even getting to primary school. It was an environment where the rule of life, the road to advancement, lay in knowledge, in knowing a little more than the next person, being a bit better in class. I grew up with competition, with doing more than the next person, even taking your bottle better, walking before other children, etc. So I didn't come to knowledge, I've always been splashing around in it.

Q: You were lucky.

MF: What is luck? When I say that I've been splashing around in knowledge, I mean it in the sense that I would really rather try to dispense with it. But since I can't do that, I look for other angles, I try to get around the problem, to find something that is not a part of knowledge but deserves to be. The other day Philippe Gavy, who is one of the editors of *Libération* and a friend of mine, told me that, oddly enough, May '68 was ultimately an uprising against learning, an insurrection in support of not knowing. I told him that this was not the case, that I believed the very opposite to be true. It was, rather, a revolt against a certain type of learning that was itself a prohibition against knowing certain things. It's incredible how little was taught through the educational system, how slight the required, institutional knowledge was before May 1968. You should have seen what they were being taught in the universities; it was less than nothing! So May '68 was actually a huge break with all of that; it was the crumbling of walls, the destruction of prohibitions, the setting aside of barriers and the incursion of a new type of knowledge and new content to be learned. I feel rather at home in all this. I have always been interested in the underside, the "lower depths" as Nietzsche would say—in madness, but not in the noble sense, not madness in its great struggle with reason but ordinary, everyday madness as it is subdued, disqualified, enclosed, despised and vilified.

Q: Misunderstood, especially.

MF: Also misunderstood. Having been concerned with these issues, I find myself at home in what is happening today. I am certainly not going to call myself a great contemporary thinker. It's just that the people I have concerned myself with for the past fifteen to twenty years are now starting to resurface. I was in my diving bell on the ocean floor...

Q: You were ahead of others.

MF: Ahead of others? Not at all. I was below them, on the ocean floor in my diving bell. And now that the underside's come up, I find myself almost at the surface. It's as simple as that.

Q: Your education led you to learn a little more than others less privileged than yourself. Have you learned *too much*? Or have you learned *poorly*?

MF: Yes in both cases. Too much, hence poorly; poorly, hence too much. For a number of years I had the privilege of teaching in Tunisia. My audience, my students, were people who had grown up in a truly illiterate environment. Their parents were unable to read or write. There were no books in the house, nor any electricity. So there was no question of working at home. We who have been fed on the kind of petty competitive knowledge that, in my view, surrounds most or all of us, we cannot imagine what access to learning means to people like that.

Q: You have quite a few degrees?

MF: I suppose.

Q: A degree, or a satchelful of them, is pretty burdensome?

MF: No. There are certain ones that are very burdensome. Those are the ones I had to work really hard for, in other words, the ones I deserve. The ones you haven't deserved are gratifying, they're the only ones you remember with pleasure. But the ones you truly deserve—after three years of cramming, your style gets cramped, you get caught up in conventional ways of thinking, and this is really hard to get rid of.

Q: What do you think, for example, of those children who could have gone far in life but who had to stay and look after the farm or go to work in a factory? They may have been among the most gifted, but their intelligence came to a halt the moment they quit school.

MF: But precisely, they still display a keen intelligence, a sharp mind not subdued by the institution or mired in ordinary ways of thinking. I am not saying that they are the ones who become union leaders [laughter], we all know how they are recruited. They're the ones who stand up whenever there's a problem—a strike or some other confrontation—who correctly analyze the situation, who know what to do, who see things as they are.

Q: You teach?

A: I lecture in a rather special place, the Collège de France, whose function is precisely not to teach. What I find very pleasing about the situation is that I don't feel like I'm teaching, that is, I don't feel that I am in a relationship of power with my students. A teacher is someone who says: "There are a certain number of things you don't know, but you should know." He starts off by making the students feel guilty. And then he places them under an obligation, saying: "I'm the one who knows these things that you should know and I'm going to teach them to you. And once I've taught them to you, you're going to have to know them. And I'm going to verify whether you really do know them." So there's verification, a whole series of relationships of power. But at the Collège de France, students take only the courses they want to take. And anybody can sit in on classes, anybody from retired army officers to fourteen-year-old *lycéens*. They come if they are interested, otherwise they stay home. So who is tested, who is under the other's power? At the Collège de France, it's the teacher.

Q: The teacher is tested?

MF: He is tested. He is paid to work year round, so twelve times a year he has to give an account of his work to his students. At any rate, each time I go to give a lecture I get terrible stage fright, the same as when I used to write exams, because I feel deep down that the public is coming to check up on my work. And if they don't find it interesting I feel quite dejected.

Q: As a rule, school is a place where you're obliged to learn. Whereas school, we all agree, should be like a celebration. You should be happy to go there, because it's a place that satisfies your curiosity. So there must be things that it's essential to learn. What are these things?

MF: The first thing one should learn—that is, if it makes any sense to learn such a thing—is that learning is profoundly bound up with pleasure.

Certainly, learning can be made an erotic, highly pleasurable activity. Now, that a teacher should be incapable of revealing this, that his job should virtually consist of showing how unpleasant, sad, dull and unerotic learning is—to me, this is an incredible achievement. But it is an achievement that certainly has its *raison d'être*. We need to know why our society considers it so important to show that learning is something sad; maybe it's because of the number of people who are excluded from it. Imagine what it would be like if people were crazy about learning the way they are about sex. They would knock each other over in a rush to get into school. It would be a complete social disaster! However, if you want to keep the number of people with access to learning at a minimum, then you have to present it as this perfectly disagreeable thing and induce people to learn solely by means of such social perks as the ability to compete and high-paying jobs at the finish line. I believe, however, that there is an intrinsic pleasure in learning, a *libido sciendi* as it is called by scholars—[in an undertone] I don't include myself.

Q: In your opinion what is the role of parents in the proper education of children?

MF: I think parents make children really anxious about learning just by the interest they show in their children's education. Because they put their own glory, their own sacrifices, their own plans for the future, and their own vindication as well, into their children's education. Children are generally very quick to perceive the anxiety of adults, that's definitely what they pick up best. And it weighs very heavily on them.

Q: There still has to be a sanction, and that sanction is the degree.

MF: Bah!

Q: How else could it be done?

MF: The degree simply serves to create a kind of market value for knowledge, to make those who don't have degrees feel they have no right to knowledge, are not capable of knowledge. Everyone who gets a degree knows perfectly well it's useless, it has no content, it's empty. But those who don't have degrees are the ones who set great store by them. Degrees are precisely for those that don't have them.

Q: If you, Michel Foucault, didn't have any degrees, would you be where you are today?

MF: If I didn't have any degrees, my first publisher would not have accepted my first book. And then, you can go back indefinitely. I wouldn't even have been able to gain access to the material I used to write my books.

Q: You've always said that one should refrain from thinking in terms of good and evil. How do you feel now about this maxim?

MF: All those who say you should stop thinking in terms of good and evil are themselves thinking entirely in terms of good and evil!

Q: Nietzsche.

MF: Of course. Fortunately he provides his own example [laughter]. Who better than Nietzsche could say what was good and what was evil? To want not to think in terms of good and evil is to want not to think in terms of this good and that evil, in their *current* meaning. I think it is important to shift the boundaries, to make them indefinite, shake them up, make them fragile, to allow for crossovers and osmosis. It isn't possible not to think in terms of good and evil, true and false. But you have to say every time: and if it were the opposite, what if the lines were elsewhere...

Q: You're always working at the boundary of the serious and the unserious. And sometimes it's hard to follow you.

MF: It makes me a little sad when I'm told that. All I want is that when someone does me the honour, the favour, gives me the pleasure of reading me, that they first of all understand exactly what I am saying. Ultimately, I'd rather say less than not be accessible. And I would like people to enjoy reading me. I'm often told, "Your writing is too refined, too complicated and baroque." I don't deny that this is intentional. I would like to write in such a way that people feel a kind of physical pleasure in reading me. I would almost say that this is the writer's sense of courtesy.

Q: Do you consider yourself a philosopher? Before, you shied away from the word "scholar."

MF: "Scholar" has a very specific meaning: a man of knowledge, a man who manipulates various forms of knowledge, who reveals some parts of knowledge and disqualifies others, who moves within this kind of knowledge game. You're born into the game. The problem is making it work, knowing what to attach it to, and knowing whether the purely ludic game to which you are ultimately dedicated can still actually communicate with certain processes outside the game, serious processes, historical processes. That where the problem comes in, and the pleasure.

Q: The book that launched your career was *Madness and Civilization.* Why madness? You remake everything and you accept the absence ...

MF: Alas, they are absent, those people who by the thousands and, if you follow the course of history, hundreds of thousands were actually shut away, who fell into the hole and suffered, spoke and cried out! It happens that for biographical reasons I have known what asylum are all about. I have heard those voices and, like anyone, I was overwhelmed by those voices. I say, anyone; I was about to say, with the exception of doctors and psychiatrists. And that's not at all out of hostility toward them. I mean that their legalistic functioning filters out so much of the cry in the madman's words that they no longer hear anything other than the intelligible or unintelligible part of the discourse. The cry has become inaccessible to them precisely because their established knowledge and information acts as a filter.

Q: You've just spoken of the asylum. Is the asylum still your world?

MF: No, not really. I would say that it's through the asylum that I first became aware of a problem that still haunts me, I mean the problem of power. It's not true that knowledge can function or that we can discover the truth, the reality, the objective reality of things without calling into play a certain form of power, of domination and subjection. To know and to subject, to know and command, are intimately linked, and I found this in its purest form in the asylum, where medical knowledge, the ostensibly serene and speculative knowledge of the psychiatrist, is absolutely inseparable from an extraordinarily meticulous, shrewdly hierarchical power which is deployed in the asylum, which *is* the asylum.

Q: Was this painful?

MF: Yes, of course. But it's a form of suffering that emanates from all asylums and, now, you know, absolutely everybody knows about it, there's only a rear guard of psychiatrists who don't know the sum of suffering, or of revolt, that the knowledge-power they wield in the asylum carries with it.

Q: Sometimes we use "mad" as an ordinary word. We should accord it a different importance.

MF: The word "mad" is not the most treacherous. It's so overused now that it no longer has much power. The term I'm afraid of is "mentally ill." From the moment this indefinite character that was excluded and laughed at but ultimately accepted as part of the social fabric, from the moment this individual received a specific status, became "ill," then as an ill person he had to be respected, but he also fell under the canonical and institutional power of the doctor. What interests me is the transition of the madman to the ill person, which appears to be a change in terminology but which at another level is a seizure of power.

Q: Michel Foucault, you have so much inside your head, so much knowledge, and you continue to learn every day, and you perhaps have a greater ability to learn than other people, that at a certain point—one can be afraid of oneself, isn't that true? Isn't it hard to put it all together?

MF: Yes, but do I put it together? I don't try to do so, and I precisely would not want to do so. What interests me much more is those fragments of knowledge that you can bring back and give a current political meaning to. That can be used as weapons; knowledge that would at the same time be a strategy, an armour or an offensive weapon, that's what interests me. Making a synthesis, reconstituting the history of the West or describing its curve or determining its destiny, those are not things that interest me. But what, finally, in the depth of our history, in the night of forgotten historical memories, can now be fished out, salvaged, brought into the light and used, now that's what interests me.

Q: You've thought a lot about the birth of mental illness. Was there a birth?

MF: Yes, the birth of this complex entity that consists of a form of illness considered mental illness, a category of doctors called psychiatrists, and a series of institutions including asylums, of course, but also medical-psychological institutes and psychoanalysts' and psychiatrists' offices. The birth of mental illness is this whole phenomenon; it is madness as an institution in our society.

Q: But do we need all these organizations?

MF: [Laughter] You have to believe they were considered necessary by our whole society because look how widespread they are. At the outset, I was interested in asylums, these very frightening spaces with high walls that are usually next to prisons in the centre or on the outskirts of cities, impenetrable spaces, holes you go into but much more rarely get out of, in which this power reigns that is undoubtedly attentive, undoubtedly punctilious, undoubtedly endorsed by "Science," but that in the end still represents extraordinary exceptions to the general rules and norms of social functioning. And then, isn't this psychiatric power ultimately all the more powerful for being insidious? When you encounter it elsewhere than in its birthplace, when it functions outside its normal realm, which is that of mental illness: the psychiatrist at school who probes the emotional drama, the family problem, the delay in psycho-physiological or psycho-neurological development that has led to the little boy's lack of success in his exams. You have an adolescent, his sexual problems: what does the family do, it sends him to the psychiatrist or psychoanalyst. A child commits a delinquent act, and it's prison and a psychological examination. He appears in court, it's a mandatory psychological examination.

Q: Then the problem is, maybe we're all mad?

MF: No! The problem is: aren't all powers currently connected to one specific power, that of normalization? Aren't the powers of normalization, the techniques of normalization, a kind of instrument found just about everywhere today, in the educational institution, the penal institution, in shops, factories and administrations, as a kind of general instrument, generally accepted because scientific, which makes possible the domination and subjection of individuals? In other words, psychiatry as a general instrument of subjection and normalization—that, in my view, is the problem.

Q: In *Discipline and Punish,* you analyzed the relation between crime and the methods used by society to punish it. This raises the question: when did we start punishing?

MF: There is probably no human society without punishment. On the other hand, what seems especially characteristic of our society is surveillance. To tell the truth, I should have called my book *Punishment and Surveillance*[1] surveillance being, curiously, one of the ways, not exactly of punishing but of exercizing punitive power. It seems to me that, even in eighteenth-century society, the number of people who actually escaped the laws under which they normally would have fallen was enormous. The penal power, the power to punish, was discontinuous, full of holes. This explains why, when they actually got hold of a criminal, the punishment was all the more formidable—because others were escaping and they had to "set an example." The fear of the ordeal must have made up for the discontinuity of the punishment. It seems to me that the quest for a punitive power began at the end of the 18th century or the beginning of the 19th.

Q: There's always power in what you do.

MF: Yes, always… They sought a punitive power, which could be more lenient precisely because it was more continuous and in principle nobody escaped it.

Q: Today, we seem to consider the criminal over the victim.

MF: We actually have great difficulty in punishing now. Formerly it was neither a moral nor a political problem. Today, on the other hand—of course the magistrates punish, and punish heavily—but if you should ask them why they punish, how they justify the fact of punishing, it's rarely in terms of chastisement, it's never in terms of expiation. They'll say that when they punish, it's to set an example, but primarily to correct, to improve. They see themselves as technicians of behaviour, the behaviour of the person punished, who in principle must be improved by the punishment; it's also the correction of the behaviour of others, who, through this example, must understand that it is not in their interest to commit such an act. Thus the magistrate is not the agent of sovereignty or of the sovereign who requires the expiation of a crime, he is the technician of behaviour who must measure the punishment for the corrective effect it will have—on the guilty party or others. So he doesn't punish, he says, "I correct. Therefore I am a kind of doctor."

Q: *Discipline and Punish* begins in horror, with a description of the slow torture and death of Damian the regicide. It's incredible what was done to him! He had killed, maybe he deserved to be killed, but to be killed in that way! And the spectacle of his ordeal involved an audience, who was pleased. Could people today enjoy watching something like that?

MF: That's a serious question. It's absolutely certain that, things being what they are, society being what it is, if punishments were left to free choice, to the free will of what we call public opinion, it would be terrible. Terrible. I have a specific memory. There was a meeting on the death penalty at the Porte de Versailles four years ago. And I went to it with some friends, most of whom had just gotten out of prison. We went for a drink in a café, we were talking about the meeting and we asked the patrons and the waiters about it. They said, "A meeting against the death penalty? But what about people who steal purses from little old ladies, they should be guillotined! Death to everybody!" And this was the general cry surrounding this meeting that brought together thousands of people demanding the abolition of the death penalty.

Q: A death for a death.

MF: I feel that, very deeply, the penal system as it functions is absolutely not accepted. It is not accepted by any of us, neither those who bear the brunt of it nor the others. It's an administrative apparatus that has absolutely not been integrated or assimilated by our social conscience since it came into existence a hundred and fifty years ago.

Q: Still, surely we've progressed since the torture of Damian.

MF: Certainly. You want me to say we no longer use torture. That's true, but only in the penal system. Torture has moved elsewhere now: the police, which is also a new institution, originated precisely when torture disappeared. From the time the watchword stopped being "A few major spectacular ordeals, let the other criminals go," and became "Everyone must be punished systematically, every crime must effectively be punished"—from that time, the justice system had to be backed up by the new institution of the police. And the police increasingly use violent means to find out the truth, as you know very well. The police torture, and when it carries out police duties, as it did in Algeria under generals Massu or Bigeard, the army tortures. Thus there has been a functional displacement of torture but not a disappearance of torture in our society.

Q: It must be acknowledged that torture is not the privilege of the West: it's found in Siberia, China, and many other countries. So we can ask, is punishment exemplary?

MF: It's interesting to see that this mechanism consisting of surveillance, detailed social plotting, imprisonment in detention centres, camps, work camps, etc., this model has been, and is, used in all political and social contexts. It has been such a marvelous, formidable invention that it has spread almost like the steam engine. And you could easily trace the history, the historico-geographic development of this institution of punitive imprisonment which originated in Europe in the second half of the eighteenth century and which has now become a form of general supervision in most modern societies, whether they are capitalist or socialist. There I am in complete agreement with you.

Q: But you won't eliminate from people's minds the idea that a crime must be sanctioned by suffering. Unfortunately that is still the case today.

MF: Indeed, when people are attacked, when their money is taken or a member of their family killed, it's absolutely clear that people demand what Nietzsche would call revenge. But what is not acknowledged, what remains as an abstraction that's hard for people to tolerate, is that this need for revenge has in a sense been confiscated by a form of political power and that the penal system is now fused with a general form of political control over the whole of society. This need for a response, revenge, a confrontation with the person who has attacked you, has been transferred to a social institution and a general political form in which people do not recognize themselves.

Q: Michel Foucault, do you have children?

MF: No, no, no. I'm not married.

Q: Well, if you did have children, and if your daughter or son were harmed or killed, how would you react? Did you think about that while writing this book?

MF: Yes, yes, yes. I can't say I thought about it. Maybe my book isn't clear enough.

Q: No, it's quite clear.

MF: This book is absolutely not an apology for crime. On the contrary. Since the beginning of the nineteenth century, there has been a whole literature that I would call bourgeois, in praise of crime, a sort of esthetic of crime, assassination seen as a fine art. I think that this literature was part of the system of control and general oppression. It also seems to me, and this is important, that modern society, nineteenth-century society, really began to organize and to plan a free space for delinquency, because delinquents are useful in a society. They're good for a whole lot of things. There is a genuine de facto tolerance for delinquency, or at least for certain forms of illegal activity. Therefore my book should definitely not be read as saying: it's very bad to punish, if a person knocks somebody off, let's give him a prize.

Q: You merely want to humanize punishment.

MF: No! I want to show that the way we currently punish is very closely connected to a certain form of power and political control in both capitalist societies and socialist societies. And that's why people do not tolerate, do not understand, do not identify profoundly with this system of punishment although they indeed demand that people be punished when they do certain things.

Q: But in the past punishment met a taste for atrocity, for rubbing salt in the wound. Was that out of ignorance?

MF: Oh, no, it wasn't ignorance. On the contrary, it was a very specific ritual linked to another form of political power exercised in the name of the sovereign and around his physical person. In the monarchies of the late Middle Ages and the seventeenth and eighteenth centuries, any person who contravened a law attacked the will of the sovereign, because the law was the will of the sovereign. So there was a grain of regicide in the heart of the most petty of criminals. The great ceremony of torture should be seen as a sort of political ritual. The coronation of the king was a political ritual, his entry into a city was also a political ritual. Extreme corporal punishments were a much more common sort of political ritual which demonstrated the physical, material power of the king in all its splendor and violence. And the body of the person punished had to show by its wounds, its cries, its howls, the overwhelming power of the sovereign.

Q: The punishment is the affirmation of a power. There will always be punishment since there will always be power everywhere, regardless of the regime. You are in favour of a hierarchy...

MF: [Laughter] The problem is knowing if power is necessarily related to the forms of hierarchy we know. Or to hierarchy at all.

Q: But will there ever come a day when every citizen will be free to do what he wants?

MF: No! Individual relationships are still relations of power. If there is anything polemical in what I have said or written, it is simply that on both sides we have too often tended not to take into account the existence of these relations of power. In traditional academic spiritualist philosophy, relations among individuals are viewed essentially as dialogues, relations of understanding, verbal, discursive: either you understand each other or you don't. And then you have the Marxist type of analysis, which tries to define relations among people essentially in terms of relations of production. It seems to me that there are relations of power as fundamental as economic or discursive relations, that absolutely structure our lives. When people make love, they put in play these relations of power.

What I think we must try to avoid is failing to take these relations of power into account, ignoring them, allowing them to play uncontrollably or on the other hand to be confiscated by a state or class power. At any rate, we should argue against that. To reveal relations of power is, in my opinion at any rate, to put them back in the hands of those who exercise them.

Q: In a society, who re-establishes the balance, the dominator or the dominated?

MF: Relations of power are strategic relations. Every time one side does something, the other one responds by deploying a conduct, a behaviour that counter-invests it, tries to escape it, diverts it, turns the attack against itself, etc. Thus nothing is ever stable in these relations of power.

Q: But you have a terrible faith in man. You consider that man can become better, and in all cases, even when he has done the worst.

MF: Become better...

Q: First of all, is it becoming better?

MF: I'm going to say something extremely naive, but everything I've been saying has been naive, so it will just make one more thing. [Laughter] I would say, perhaps not becoming better. He must be able to be happier. He must be able to increase the amount of pleasure he is capable of in his life. After all, we don't have that much pleasure in our lives. You have to look hard for it, it's pretty rare.

Q: That's a pretty pessimistic assessment for you.

MF: No, it's not pessimistic!

Q: Because you're telling something about yourself in saying that.

MF: If you mean my description of what can be done in the present situation, I would say yes, I am pessimistic. But you have to be pessimistic, to make the situation look darker to make the task appear more urgent and the possibilities for the future livelier and brighter. On the other hand, I'll be vain enough to say I believe the events in which I've tried to get mixed up in one way or another are quite important. I remember when we started to get involved with madness, in the 60s, we were pretty alone. Who really thought that psychiatric power was something that threatened us, even us, normal people, in our daily lives? Very few. You know who accepted my book in France—Maurice Blanchot, Roland Barthes. No psychiatrist was interested in it. There was one who got up during a radio broadcast and said to me: "You have no right to speak, you are not a doctor!" And the

Marxists, none of them talked about what I was trying to do on psychiatry or medicine. Do you think that people concerned with plus value were going to bother with anything as trivial as mental illness, madness. They were concerned with finding out if Pavlov and conditioned reflexes could be used in psychiatry, that was the problem for them. Finally it was the English anti-psychiatrists Laing and Cooper who put the problem of psychiatry in the news. And then it was the political groups before May '68, and especially after. I feel that the struggle against the "psychiatrization" of our lives is important today, and here I am perhaps being vain; but what I am doing and saying on this process doesn't strike me as very important. If I and my books were suppressed, it wouldn't make much difference. I rather like this feeling, which to me is not at all negative—I feel almost a physical pleasure in thinking that the things I'm involved in go beyond me, that there are a thousand people and a thousand books being written, a thousand people talking and a thousand things being done, that go in exactly the same direction I am and that ultimately surpass me.

Q: Michel Foucault, I have the impression that now you would like to free yourself of your great burden of knowledge, to go elsewhere. That you are almost tempted to start over again from scratch.

MF: Insofar as I have this feeling of pleasure in being surpassed, in seeing things go faster and farther than I, yes, a very great feeling of relief, of freedom and, finally, a desire to take a small bag and go somewhere else.

Q: But have you ever defined this "elsewhere"?

MF: No, not at all! Maybe I won't do it, maybe I'll keep treading the same ground, with my stories and fighting against these normalizations that hem us in. Maybe I'm just more normalized than I think, more than I'd like to be.

Q: We've talked about power, but do you accept direction? Do you like to take orders?

MF: To take orders or to give orders?

Q: You asked the question, so you like to give orders.

MF: I said before that when you're making love, relations of power become charged with eroticism. Now that's an area that has been studied very little, and that should be studied some day. There's so much pleasure in giving orders, and there's also much pleasure in taking orders. So this pleasure in power should be examined.

Translated by Phillis Aronov and Dan McGrawth

---

1 The French title literally means *Surveillance and Punishment*.

17

FROM TORTURE TO CELLBLOCK

Q: In its function and contemporary form, the prison might pass for an unexpected and isolated invention, having appeared at the end of the 18th century. You demonstrate, on the contrary, that its birth is to be situated within a more profound shift. Which one?

MF: By reading the great historians of the classic period, one can see how much the monarchy's administration, however centralized and bureaucratized one imagines it to have been, was despite everything an irregular and discontinuous power, leaving to individuals and groups a certain leeway in their dealings with the law, their adaptations to custom, and their sliding between obligations. The Ancient Regime dragged with it hundreds and thousands of ordonnances never applied, rights that no one exercized, and rules bypassed by masses of people. For example, the most traditional fiscal fraud, as well as the most flagrant smuggling, were a basic part of the economic life of the kingdom. In short, during this period a constant transaction between legality and illegality was one of the conditions of the functioning of power.

In the second half of the 18th century this system of tolerance changed. New economic demands, the political fear of popular movements, which were going to become insistent in France after the Revolution, made a different kind of social control necessary. The exercise of power had to become denser and more discriminating; from the central decision-making to the targeted individual, a network as continuous as possible had to be formed. Hence the appearance of the police, an administrative hierarchy, and the bureaucratic pyramid of the Napoleonic State.

Well before 1789 jurists and "reformers" were already dreaming of a society with uniform penalties, where punishments would be inevitable, necessary, and equal, with no possible exception or escape. As a result, the great rituals of punishment, these tortures meant to provoke terror and to serve as examples and from which many of the guilty escaped, disappeared before the demand for a system of universal punishment concretized in the penitentiary system.

Q: But why the prison and not some other system? What social role does the confinement of the "guilty" assume?

MF: Where does the prison come from? I would say, a little from everywhere. There was an "invention," no doubt, but an invention of a whole technique—of surveillance, control, the identification of individuals, and a mapping of their gestures, activities, and their effectiveness. And that took place from the 16th or 17th century, in the army, the colleges, the schools, the hospitals, the workshops. It was a refined and everyday technology of power, a technology that operated on the body. The prison is the last figure of this age of disciplines.

As for the social role of confinement, it has to do with the delinquent, this social type who begins to be defined in the 19th century. The constitution of a space of delinquency is absolutely correlative with the existence of the prison. There was an effort to create at the heart of the masses a small kernel of people who would be, so to speak, the privileged and exclusive title-bearers of illegal behavior. People rejected, despised and feared by everyone.

In the classical period, on the contrary, violence, petty theft, small acts of fraud were widely current and finally tolerated by everyone. The lawbreaker succeeded very well, it seems, in merging with society. And if he happened to get caught, the penal procedures were expeditious: death, life in the galleys, banishment. The criminal milieu thus did not have this self-enclosed quality essentially organized by the prison, by this kind of "marinade" within the carceral system, whereby a micro-society was formed, where people established a real solidarity that would permit them, once outside, to find help for one another.

Thus the prison is an instrument for the recruitment of an army of delinquents. That's the purpose it serves. For two centuries it has been said that the prison fails because it produces delinquents. I would say, rather, it succeeds because that is what is demanded of it.

Q: However, it is repeatedly said that the prison, at least ideally, "takes care of" and "rehabilitates" delinquents. It is—or ought to be, so it is said—more therapeutic than punitive.

MF: Criminal psychology and psychiatry risk being the great alibi behind which the same system will be maintained. They couldn't constitute a serious alternative to the prison regime, for the simple reason that they were born with it. The prison that one sees being set up immediately after the penal code is established, claims from the outset the status of psychological correction. It's already a medico-judiciary space. One can therefore put the incarcerated in the therapists's hands, but that will change nothing in the system of power and generalized surveillance set up at the beginning of the 19th century.

Q: We still don't know what "benefit" the class in power extracts from the constitution of this army of delinquents you were talking about.

MF: Well, it allows this class to break the continuity of popular illegalities. In effect, it isolates a small group of people that can be controlled, kept under surveillance, known inside and out, and who are exposed to the hostility and distrust of the popular milieu out of which they came. For the victims of minor, everyday delinquencies are still the people at the bottom, the poor.

And the result of this operation, in the final analysis, is a huge economic and political profit. An economic profit from the fabulous sums brought in by prostitution, the sale of drugs, etc. A political profit from the fact that the more deliquents there are, the more easily the population accepts political control; not to mention a steady employment for those who do the dirty political work: billstickers, electoral agents, strike-breakers, etc. In the Second Empire the workers knew very well that "the scabs" imposed on them, exactly like Louis-Napoleon's anti-riot squads, were ex-cons.

Q: All the scheming and turmoil around "reforming" and "more humane" prisons would thus be a lure?

MF: It seems to me that the real political issue is not whether the prisoners get a piece of chocolate for Christmas or are allowed Easter leave. What has to be denounced is less the "human" character of the prison than its real social function, as a constituent element of a delinquent milieu that the ruling classes strive to control. The true problem is to know if the self-enclosure of this milieu can be brought to an end, and whether or not this milieu will remain cut off from the popular masses. In other words, the way the penal system and the judicial apparatus function in society should be the target of the struggle. For they are the ones that manage the illegalities, and play them off against one another.

Q: How is this "management of illegalities" to be defined? The phrase assumes an unusual conception of the law, of society, and of their relationship.

MF: Only a fiction can make us believe that the laws are made to be respected, the police and judges meant to insure that they are respected. Only a theoretical fiction can make us believe that we have subscribed once and for all to the laws of the society to which we belong. Everyone also knows that the laws are made by some and imposed on others.

But it seems to me that one can take a step further. Illegality is not an accident, a more or less unavoidable imperfection. It's an absolutely positive element of social functioning, whose role is allocated in the general strategy of society. Every legislative arrangement has brought about protected and profitable spaces where the law can be violated, others where it can be ignored, and others finally where infractions are sanctionned. If pushed, I would say that the law is not made to prevent any particular type of behavior, but to differentiate among ways of finding a loophole in the law itself.

Q: For example?

MF: The laws against drugs. From the U.S. agreement with Turkey (linked in part with an authorization to cultivate opium) to the police stake-outs in the Latin District, the drug traffic expands like on a chess-board, with controlled and free squares, prohibited and tolerated squares, squares permitted to some but forbidden to others. Only the pawns are positioned on and occupy dangerous squares. For huge profits, the way is clear.

Q: *Discipline and Punish*, like your previous books, is based on a considerable quantity of archival work. Does Michel Foucault have a "method"?

MF: I believe that today there is such a prestige attached to projects of the Freudian type that very often the analysis of historical texts takes as its objective the "non-spoken" of a discourse, the "repressed" or "unconscious" of a system. It is good to abandon this attitude and to be at once more modest and more of a rummager. For when one looks at the documents, it is striking to see with what cynicism the bourgeoisie of the 19th century said exactly what it was doing, what it was going to do, and why. For it, as the holder of power, cynicism was a form of pride. And the bourgeoisie, except in the eyes of the naive, is neither stupid nor cowardly. It is intelligent and bold. It stated perfectly what it wanted.

To rediscover this explicit discourse obviously implies leaving behind the university and scholarly material of the "great texts." It is neither in Hegel nor Auguste Comte that the bourgeoisie speaks directly. Adjacent to these consecrated texts, a strategy that is absolutely conscious, organized, and deliberate is clearly inscribed in a mass of unknown documents which constitute the effective discourse of a political action. For the logic of the unconscious, therefore, we must substitute a logic of strategy. For the logic accorded today to the signifier and its chains, we must substitute tactics and their unfolding.

Q: What struggles can your works serve?

MF: My discourse is obviously that of an intellectual, and as such it functions in the networks of power presently in place. But a book is made to serve ends not defined by the one who wrote it. The more there are new, possible, unforeseen uses for it, the happier I'll be.

All my books, whether *Madness and Civilization* or this one we're talking about, are, if you like, little tool boxes. If people want to open them, use a particular sentence, idea, or analysis like a screwdriver or wrench in order to short-circuit, disqualify or break up the systems of power, including eventually the very ones from which my books have issued...well, all the better!

Translated by John Johnston

18

ON LITERATURE

Q: What is the place or status of literary texts in your research?

MF: In *Madness and Civilization* and in *The Order of Things,* I only mention literary texts, or point to them in passing, as a kind of dawdler who says, "Now, there you see, one cannot fail to speak of *Rameau's Nephew.*"[1] But these allusions play no role in the economy of the process. For me, literature was each time the object of a report, not part of an analysis nor a reduction nor an integration into the domain of analysis. It was a point of rest, a halt, a blazon, a flag.

Q: You didn't want these texts to play the role of expressing or reflecting historical processes?

MF: No...The question would have to be broached on another level. There has never really been an analysis of how, given the mass of things that are spoken, given the set of discourses actually held, a certain number of these discourses (literary discourse, philosophical discourse) are sacralized and given a particular function. It seems that traditionally literary or philosophical discourse has been made to function as a substitute or as a general envelope for all other discourses. Literature had to assume the value for all the rest. People have written histories of what was said in the 18th century by passing through Fontenelle, Voltaire, Diderot or *The New Heloise,*[2] etc. Or else they have thought of these texts as the expression of something that in the end failed to be formulated on a more quotidian level.

In regard to this attitude, I passed from a state of uncertainty—citing literature where it was, without indicating its relationship with the rest—to a frankly negative position, by trying to make all the non-literary or para-literary discourses that were actually constituted in a given period reappear positively, and by excluding literature. In *Discipline and Punish* I only deal with bad literature.

Q: How does one distinguish good from bad?

MF: Exactly. That's just what will have to be considered one day. We will have to ask ourselves just what is this activity that consists of circulating fictions, poems, and narratives in a society. We also ought to analyze a second operation: among all these narratives, what is it that sacralizes some and makes them begin to function as "literature"? They are quickly taken up within an institution that was very different at its origin: the institution of the university. Now it begins to be identified with the literary institution

This is a very visible line of decline in our culture. In the 19th century the university was the medium at the center of which a literature said to be classical was constituted. This literature, by definition, was not a contemporary literature, and was valorized simultaneously as both the only base for contemporary literature and as its critique. Hence a very curious play in the 19th century between literature and the university, between the writer and the academic.

And then, little by little, the two institutions, which underneath their petty squabbles were in fact profoundly akin, tended to become completely indistinguishable. We know perfectly well today that the literature said to be avant-garde is only ever read by academics; that a writer over thirty has students around him who are doing their theses on his work; and that writers live for the most part by giving courses and by being academics. Thus the truth about something is already evident there, in the fact that literature functions thanks to a play of selection, sacralization, and institutional valorization of which the university is at once both the operator and the receiver.

Q: Are there intrinsic criteria for evaluating texts, or is it only a matter of sacralization by the university as institution?

MF: I know nothing about it. I would simply say this: in order to break with a number of myths, like the one of literature's expressive character, it has been very important to establish the great principle that literature is concerned only with itself. If it has anything to do with its author, it's according to a mode of death, silence, and the very disappearance of the one who writes.

The reference here to Blanchot or Barthes matters little. The essential thing is the importance of the principle: the intransitivity of literature. It was indeed the first stage thanks to which one could get rid of the idea that literature was the place of all transits, or the point where all transits ended up the expression of totalities.

But it seems to me that this was still only a stage. Yet, to maintain the analysis at this level is to risk not dismantling the set of sacralizations which affected literature. On the contrary, one risks sacralizing it even worse. And that's actually what has happened, even up to 1970. We have seen a number of the themes of Blanchot and Barthes used for a kind of exaltation, at once ultra-lyrical and ultra-rationalizing, of literature as a structure of language susceptible to analysis only in itself and in its own terms.

The political implications were not absent from this exaltation. Thanks to it, one succeeded in saying that literature in itself at this point was freed from all determinations, that the fact of writing in itself was subversive, that the writer possesses, in the very gesture of writing, an imprescribable right to subversion! Consequently, the writer was a revolutionary, and the more the writing claimed to be Writing, the more it dipped into intransitivity, the more revolutionary it was! You know that these things were unfortunately said...

In fact, Blanchot's and Barthes' trajectory tended to desacralize literature by breaking the connections that put it in a position of absolute expression. This rupture implied that the next movement would desacralize it absolutely, and try to understand how, in the general mass of what was said, at a given moment and in a certain mode, this particular area of language could be constituted, an area that shouldn't be asked to bear the decisions of a culture, but rather how was it that a culture has decided to give it this position so singular and so strange.

Q: Why strange?

MF: Our culture assigns literature a part which is in one sense extraordinarily limited: how many people read literature? What place does it actually have in the general expansion of discourse? But this same culture imposes on all its children, as a ticket to culture, this passage through a whole ideology, a whole theology of literature, during their studies. There is a kind of paradox there.

And it's not unrelated to the affirmation that writing is subversive. That someone states it, in such and such a periodical, has no importance and no effect. But if at the same moment all instructors, from high school teachers to university professors tell you, explicitly or not, that the great decisions of a culture, the points where it changes drastically... these must be found in Diderot, Sade, Hegel or Rabelais, this makes you realize that it finally amounts to the same thing. Both make literature function in the same way. At this level, the effects of reinforcement are reciprocal. The so-called avant-garde groups and the large mass at the university are in agreement. That leads to a very heavy political blockage.

Q: How have you escaped this blockage?

MF: I tackled the problem on the one hand with the book on Raymond Roussel and then above all the with book on Pierre Rivière. Both pursue the same investigation: what is this threshold starting from which a discourse (whether that of a sick person, a criminal, etc.) begins to function in a field described as literature?

In order to know what is literature, I would not want to study internal structures. I would rather grasp the movement, the small process through which a non-literary type of discourse, neglected, forgotten as soon as it is spoken, enters the literary domain. What happens there? What is released? How is this discourse modified by the fact that it is recognized as literary?

Q: You have, however, devoted texts to literary works about which this question is not raised. I am thinking notably of your essays in "Critique" on Blanchot, Klossowski and Bataille. If they were collected in a single volume, perhaps they would give your transversal an unexpected image...

MF: Yes, but.... It would be rather difficult to speak of them. At bottom, Blanchot, Klossowski and Bataille, who were finally the three who interested me in the 1960s, for me were much more than literary works or discourses interior to literature. They were discourses exterior to philosophy.

Q: That is to say...

MF: Let's take Nietzsche, if you like. In relation to academic philosophical discourse, which ceaselessly refers to him, Nietzsche represents the outside edge. Of course a whole strain of Western philosophy can be found in Nietzsche's works. Plato, Spinoza, the philosophers of the 18th century, Hegel...all that goes through Nietzsche. And yet, in relation to philosophy, there is in Nietzsche's work a roughness, a rustic simplicity, an outsideness, a kind of mountain peasantness that allows him, with a shrug of the shoulder and without appearing in any way ridiculous, to say with unavoidable force: "What nonsense all that is!"

To rid oneself of philosophy necessarily implies such an offhandedness. It's not by remaining in philosophy, it's not by refining it to the maximum, it's not by turning it against itself that one exits from it. No. It's by opposing it with a kind of astonished and joyful stupidity, a sort of incomprehensible burst of laughter that in the end understands, or in any case, breaks. Yes...it breaks more than it understands.

To the extent that, in spite of everything, I was an academic, a professor of philosophy, what remained of traditional philosophical discourse hampered me in the work I had done on madness. There was an Hegelianism there that was still lingering on. To bring out objects as derisory as the relations with the police, the measures of internment and the cries of the mad, that wasn't enough to exit from philosophy. For me Nietzsche, Bataille, Blanchot and Klossowski were ways of exiting from philosophy.

In the violence of Bataille, in the sort of insidious and disturbing softness of Blanchot, in Klossowski's spirals, there was something that began with philosophy, put it into play and into question, then left it and returned... Something like the theory of breathing in Klossowski is connected by God knows how many lines to the entirety of Western philosophy. And then, through the staging, the formulation, the way in which all that functions in *Le Baphomet,* philosophy leaves it altogether.

These comings and goings around the position of philosophy finally rendered permeable—and thus finally derisory—the frontier between philosophy and non-philosophy.

Translated by John Johnston

---

1 *Rameau's Nephew* is by Diderot. [Ed.]

2 *The New Héloïse* is a novel by Jean-Jacques Rousseau. [Ed.]

3 *Critique* is a French magazine originally founded by Georges Bataille. [Ed.]

19

Schizo–Culture: Infantile Sexuality

I have taken on a piece of work that is a sort of sequel to my book on the history of madness

I once had the idea of writing something like a history of sexual repression, a history of the sexual anomaly, the mechanisms that both designate and repress it.

I failed to go through with this piece of work for a number of reasons: I have been trying for a long time to figure out what these reasons are.

The first reason I gave myself was this: that I couldn't find the necessary documents. But in fact if I couldn't find the documents, it was probably simply because such documents didn't exist—that is, that what I was looking for was not there to be deciphered in terms of the body of mechanisms that we call repression.

It seems to me that a number of people before me, and I too, followed a definite schema of analysis which was elaborated from 1920 to 1930 around the person and the work of Wilhelm Reich.

Now I have the feeling that this schema, whose validity I admit, and though it has given rise to a certain number of works, researches, analyses, and, to a certain point, to very interesting discoveries, still will not lead our historical research toward success.

Van Hussel has written a recent book in a rather Reichian style on the history of sexual repression. It is an interesting book, but it strikes me as rather limited in its results, and above all it fails to take account of the whole of a historical reality. I am going to try only to indicate a few of the principal characteristics of this reality.

I now see the Reichian schema as an obstacle rather than an instrument. What does this schema consist of?

Caricaturing it a bit, I would say that according to this schema we are now living, in fact we have been living since the 18th century at least, under a sexual regime that could be called Victorian. The Queen's scowl, the pout of the imperial prude, could serve as the emblem of our unhappy, hypocritical, and silent sexuality.

In general, for this Reichian schema, for the style of analysis that I will call anti-repressive, up until the beginning of the 17th century sexuality was the beneficiary of a sort of franchise, a franchise in both senses of the word, since it involved both a non-repressed sexual practice, an open and above–board sexual practice, and a free and joyful prattle, a kind of discourse free of reticences and disguises, about this sexuality. Reference is usually made (especially by Van Hussel) to Erasmus' famous dialogue in which he instructs a young man on how to get on in life, how one should make love to a prostitute, etc.

This golden age of loquacious and sunny sexuality gave way to a twilight that took us into the heart of the 19th century, the Victorian night (the Victorian night in which all cats are gray), when love could be made only in the shadows, out of the hay, behind life's cellar stairs; when love could only be spoken through veiled words, in words carefully coded according to a well-established rhetoric.

In brief, from the beginning of the 17th century a sexuality of shadows would have begun to spread itself over the western world, a sexuality trapped in the spatial metonymy of the brothel and in the obligatory metaphors of discourse, from which Freud would have finally rescued us.

This schema, which I am caricaturing, is based on a methodological principle and an explanatory hypothesis.

The methodological principle is this: it is the possibility that is established in these "anti-repressive" analyses, at any rate in this style of writing the history of sexual repression, the possibility of making use of a whole set of notions like those of interdiction, of censorship, of suppression (*refoulement*), of repression, to decode this great repressive process.

Consequently this anti-repressive holds that in studying processes *without a subject*—in a society, the exercise and discourse of sexuality—it is valid to use categories worked out by Freud or his followers for the analysis of the speaking subject or the subject of desire.

I believe that this vast myth of Victorianism, this vast fresco of Victorianism, little by little taking over our sexuality and plunging it into darkness, carries with it the burdensome methodological hypothesis that the processes of history and the mechanisms of the subject are continuous with each other.

And, moreover, it was Reich himself who said that the main Freudian categories, or at least those categories by which Freud analyzed the mechanisms of the superego, were social categories.

There, I think, lies the methodological hypothesis that can be found throughout this analysis of repression, or of the history of repression. To this methodological hypothesis is linked an explanatory hypothesis:

That the great censorship we can see developing in the course of the 16th, 17th, and 18th centuries, to triumph at last in the 19th, can best be seen as an effect caused by the development of capitalism.

Capitalism, at least in its early period, could not afford the luxury of a sexuality that was both visible and verbal. Several reasons have been given for this.

The most simple–minded ones, advanced, for example, by Van Hussel, are that capitalism requires a certain number of well-defined mechanisms to assure the reproduction of the labor power it needs to feed perpetually into the labor market. This called for the organization and rigorous coding of a conjugal family oriented entirely around the production of children, i.e. the reproduction of labor power. Get married and have a lot of children to help boost production.

This explanation runs up against a number of blatant historical difficulties—the fact, for instance, that birth control got started in Europe at exactly the same time as the great development of capitalism at the end of the 18th century.

To this rather simplistic explanation one could oppose the one given by Reich a long time ago, when he explained that sexual repression was necessary for capitalism because the latter had to mobilize individuals' psychic forces for the job of the suppression of sexuality. Once occupied with internal tasks, the individual's psychological forces would no longer be available for external political and social tasks like rebellions, political struggle, etc.

The disciplining of individuals during the capitalist period would have taken place, according to Reich, because of this need to mobilize psychological energy for the suppression of sexuality.

It makes little difference whether you accept Reich's explanation or Van Hussel's; in general we can say that according to this schema there was a period from the end of the 18th century to the beginning of the 20th during which we lived under Capitalism the Repressor.

Thus there would have been a sort of propensity toward Victorianism essential to capitalist society, at least during its first phase. The only love that capitalism can stand is love for Queen Victoria or a love within the boundaries of her modesty.

These are considerable themes, they have had a very great political importance for the last fifty years, and I do not plan to discuss them here. There can be no question of dismissing them with a few pirouettes. For fifty years *Sex-Politik* has been sustained by this analysis; for fifty years the struggle for sexual liberation has been animated by these themes.

All of this should be taken into consideration, even if it is easy to denounce a sort of facile, barely disguised Hegelianism behind it: capitalism, the negative moment, bound for a proximate *Aufhebung*.

All right, at the risk of passing for a pessimist, I will say that capitalism is a great deal more than this, that it is not just a negative moment.

It is this notion of repression that I would like to try to analyze, because it seems to run through all the historical analyses that have been attempted according to the Reichian schema. It is the demolition or at any rate the putting into question of this notion that I would like to sketch out now.

* * * * *

Under the notion of repression I think we can group a number of important postulates, namely:

First Postulate, which is, I believe, necessarily at work in the entire repressive discourse I've been talking about: There is a necessary parallelism, a simultaneity, an interlocking between, on the one hand, the rejection of desire or the drive (*la pulsion*) from reality, and, on the other hand, their exclusion outside discourse and discursive practices.

When the Reichians (which I mean in a very general sense) speak of repression, they always assume that to silence and to forbid, to exclude from discourse and to exclude from reality, are, on the whole, in the end, the same thing. They suppose that what is involved is all kinds of ways of barring sexuality access to manifestation, whether this is manifestation in reality or manifestation in discourse.

It seems to me that the analysis of repression within this schema always more or less assumes the use of this somewhat confused notion of manifestation. Repression would be whatever keeps sexuality from manifesting itself either in discourse or in reality.

And it seems to me that in the same way they fit the analysis of historical processes, they fit the analysis of what happened to sexuality and its repression at the end of the 18th century, into a sort of "hysterical" model; that is, they suppose that in this period a sort of mechanism of hysterical suppression got started, for which we can to some extent find the law and the scale model among real people who are hysterics.

We can also understand why in this analysis it is absolutely necessary to find a sort of point of articulation between, on the one hand, that which allows exclusion from the order of reality, and, on the other, that which allows exclusion from the order of discourse. Whence the need to find a support either in the symbolic field or in the signifying chain, a symbolic field and a signifying chain that are at once linguistic structures and supports for reality.

The notion of the signifying chain makes it possible to think in a single thought both the rejection of the drive outside reality and its exclusion from the field of discourse.

What I would like to show is that mechanisms of rejection are without a doubt all the more powerful for the very fact that they operate through more widely deployed discursive practices; in other words, we can suppose that discourse—the discourse that names, that describes, that designates, that analyzes, that recounts, that metaphorizes, etc.—constitutes the field of the object and at the same time creates power effects that make it possible for subjugation to take place.

In a word, it would be a question of disconnecting barriers in the order of reality from exclusions in the order of discourse; and we would have to look in the direction of the deployment of discourse, in the direction of its very abundance, for the barrier–mechanisms that are at work in reality. And at the same time we would have to abandon the hysterical model and we would also have to replace exclusion outside the signifying chain (as an analytical category) by the deployment of discourses and of their power effects.

Consequently it would be necessary to envisage a history of sexuality that would take for its basic model not a simultaneous blocking both in the order of discourse and in the order of reality, but, on the contrary, that would take as its point of attack the newer effects that come into being through the very deployment and overabundance of discourse.

In other words: the more talking goes on, the more power there is; and it is not power that reduces speech to silence.

A *Second Postulate* which I think is linked to the notion of repression, and is equally present throughout the analyses made in the name of anti-repressive discourse:

In all the analyses that I have been talking about and from which I want to differentiate myself, *power* is always analyzed in a reduced, schematic, I was going to say pejorative, at any rate a *negative* form. Which is to say that these analyses assume that power exerts itself basically in the form of an interdiction and an exclusion: thou shalt not say, thou shalt not do. In this we are supposed to have the essential aspect of the mechanism of power; in a word, penal law would be the very essence of power in its exercise and it is precisely the importance given to the law that allows all the mechanisms of power to be absorbed into the thin, schematic, empty form of the interdiction, the ban. Repression would then be power acting as the law of interdiction, pursuing and prosecuting all those who violate the ban.

In the first postulate we immediately noticed the use of a hysterical model to make an analysis of historical processes. And indeed it seems to me that here, by reducing power to the law and the law to a taboo, the Reichian approach has fit the analysis of historical processes into the model that psychoanalysis developed to analyze obsessional neurosis and the legalistic niceties of its mechanism.

Now it seems to me that power does something very different from just *forbidding*.

And this is precisely what makes it so formidable, what makes it so difficult to defend oneself from it and triumph over it. Things would be very nice and political work would be very easy if the essential role and function of power was just to say no, if the only role and function of power was to prevent and exclude.

But what gives power its force, what makes it so hard to get around and master, is that power is positive in its effects.

Power invents, power creates, power produces. It produces more than a law that forbids desire—it produces desire itself, power induces and produces desire, power gives desire its objects, power, indeed, is desirable. Power not only produces desire; to an equal degree, and this goes much farther, beyond the law that is imposed on the subject, power produces the very form of the subject, it produces what makes up the subject. The form the subject takes is, precisely, determined by power.

Power produces desire and the subject.

Power must not be seen simply as law and interdiction. Power relations point out the lines of desire, positions for the subject, places of enunciation, fields of objectification, etc.

Rather than reducing the exercise of power to the single juridical and legalistic form of the interdiction, I think we must try to analyze it in military rather than juridical terms, in terms of strategy and tactics. Whence, if you will, a second imperative, a second methodological prescription that I would propose: to study the strategies of power rather than the interdictions of the law.

A *Third Postulate* linked to the notion of repression and assumed when one does an anti-repressive analysis:

This postulate is that power, especially repressive power, would always and essentially produce effects of misrecognition (*méconnaissance*). In acting as a ban, in barring access to manifestation, the major effect of repressive power would be to prevent the formation of knowledge: to prevent it in the strongest sense, by producing the unconscious; or to prevent it in a weaker and more superficial sense, by bringing about a whole series of effects on the order of denial of reality, ignorance, blindness, or false consciousness.

In brief, the major effect of power would be *not knowing*, or at any rate the impossibility of access to the truth. Power would be that which bars access to the truth. And it strikes me that here, just as we noted in the use of the hysterical model and the model of obsessional neurosis, the Reichians apply a model to historical material which was constructed to deal with the mechanisms of denial and misrecognition among paranoiacs.

So, I think that the hysterical model, the obsessional model, the paranoiac model are what we find behind the three great postulates that are linked to the use of the notion of repression:

The first postulate: the symbolic chain which allows both exclusion outside of reality and exclusion outside of discourse.

The second postulate: which confounds or merges the exercise of power and the application of taboos.

Finally, the third postulate: which supposes that wherever there is power the green grass of knowledge cannot grow.

Now, I wonder if it wouldn't be possible, just as we reversed the first two postulates, to also reverse the last one and say that power, with the discursive practices that bear it and pronounce its effects, is the producer of knowledge. Power not only creates true discourses, but what is much more important, it creates the constraints that allow us to separate true discourse from false discourse.

And, consequently, instead of denouncing the misrecognitions that we would like to blame on the interdiction, we should try to reconstitute and study the ties that might exist among strategies of power, discursive practices, and the production of knowledge. This is the third methodological prescription that I would propose.

Thus the history of sexuality would not be the analysis of the mechanisms that have repressed it and buried it in darkness since the 17th century, that have sworn it to silence, to interdiction and misrecognition. The historical study of sexuality would be the analysis of the discursive practices and the knowledge that allowed the strategies of power to invade (*investir*) this sexuality.

It would therefore mean the abandonment of the whole set of notions that are necessarily at work in an analysis in the negative terms of repression, the symbolic and manifestation, the law and the interdiction, the unconscious and misrecognition, to get rid of all this and try to begin an analysis of discourses, strategies, and knowledge.

One more word before turning to how this sort of analysis can be done.

A word on how it is that analysis in terms of repression could have received such privileges for such a long time—why these privileges were granted to the law, interdiction, misrecognition, in the deciphering of the historical process.

There are good reasons for this. I could mention several, but there is one that I want to insist on: this is what I will call the payoff (*le bénéfice*) of the enunciator. A payoff that must be taken into consideration is the critique of a discourse, but which must not be understood as the personal interest of the individual who is speaking.

To situate the enunciator's payoff within anti-repressive discourse I will say this: the first postulate linked to the notion of repression (the postulate of parallelism between exclusion from discourse and exclusion from reality) allows whoever is making the analysis of repression, whoever is discoursing on anti-repressive themes, to think and make others think is real whatever he can observe as an event in discourse; or, again, it lets him think and makes others think that what appears, what reappears, what returns in his own discourse at the moment he speaks also returns in reality, precisely because it is working inside a symbolic chain in which the effects of discourse are at the same time effects of reality.

At one blow the enunciator, he who is speaking the anti-repressive discourse, gives his discourse a sort of fundamental justification and a kind of immediate access to reality; what I say in my discourse is at the same time inscribed in reality. Quite a payoff.

The second postulate (the postulate that reduces the effects of power to the form of an interdiction) allows the analyst who is speaking an anti-repressive discourse to think and make others think that the lifting of the interdiction is an attack on the fundamental mechanisms of power. This postulate lets him valorize all transgressions of the law, those he formulates in his discourse and eventually those that he practices, as an immediate subversion of power.

Finally, the third and last postulate (the postulate of a link between power effects and misrecognitions) lets him valorize his own discourse about truth as being liberating and disalienating, that is, that analyses of repression in the style I have been talking about permit whoever performs them to define for himself, immediately, and therefore in a Utopian way, a subversive position. I am speaking, so they'd better watch out.

This is the position of him who only speaks, and whose discourse alone is supposed to produce truth beyond all power, to leap the ban at a single bound, attain a new law, and bring about real effects.

This position, as you have no doubt recognized, is held every day in well-known institutions, by both the professor and the psychoanalyst.

Basically, in using the notion of repression, one puts oneself in relation to history, in relation to society, in relation to reality, in the position of what I might call the professorial analyst, at the same time in the professor's armchair and behind the analyst's couch. One becomes the professorial analyst of culture, condemned to do nothing else, and enraptured by having nothing to do but to speak in place of, or to make speak, the silence of hysterics, of undergraduates, and all of history's speechless oppressed, speak.

It lets one do nothing else, and be enraptured by having nothing else to do than to alleviate the legalistic scruples of obsessional neurotics (if you're a psychoanalyst), the zeal of graduate students (if you're a professor), or the obsequiousness of loquacious moralists (if you're a historian), by presenting the example of one's own verbal dance.

Finally, this allows the denunciation by a critique in terms of truth of denials of the paranoiac (if you're a psychiatrist), the misrecognitions of faculty colleagues who are always fooling themselves (if you're a professor), ideology (if you're a historian)—all of these provide ways to bring power effects back into one's own discourse.

So this is what I would call, in general, the "enunciator's payoffs", payoffs assured to whoever speaks by means of "anti-repressive" theory, which he himself is helping to develop. These conditions explain the fact that "anti-repressive" discourse would be a genre that circulates so obstinately between university auditorium and analytic couch.

* * * * *

Let us try now to look at how to begin the analysis of these enigmatic historical processes that involve the status, the functioning, the "repression" of sexuality.

If I have been led to try (without, of course any guarantee of the outcome) to get rid of this notion of repression, it is because I actually found myself faced with a very simple empirical difficulty: repression, silencing, the whole mechanism by which sexuality is supposed to have been banished both from discourse and from reality since the 17th century—I looked for it, and I didn't find it.

Certainly when rummaging through juridical works one can find plenty of strict, severe, cruel, barbaric laws on adultery, rape, the corruption of minors, homosexuality, etc. But when one tries to see what their juridical effects have been, it is very surprising to find that although these famous laws on adultery, dating from the end of the Middle Ages, have produced a certain number of condemnations per year, a certain number of confessions, a considerable number of commitments to convents—still all of this is not very serious, and you could hardly say that we have pinned down the mechanism of repression. Everyone knows that homosexuals were burned at the stake until Cambacérès (for his own personal reasons) had the law against homosexuality removed from the French penal code in 1810—it looks like you, too, are going to benefit from this in the next few days. Now, up until 1789, homosexuals were supposed to end up at the stake; in fact, how many homosexuals were actually condemned to the stake in a country like France in the 15th century? A few individuals—not a few individuals a year, but a few individuals a century. Which doesn't say much for the honor of the sect, even if "a few individuals" are quite enough for it to stand.

Thus at this level it is very difficult to grasp the mechanism of repression itself; and, on the other hand, while the mechanism of repression and the way it really works escape us (above all from the 17th century on, the beginning of the period of Victorianism), we can observe a number of other, remarkable, things.

This one first of all: birth control, destined for such great import both in history and in the very biology of the human species, was empirically a popular practice, which developed among the peasants of England and the south of France during the second half of the 18th century. Consequently the knowledge of birth control, the exchange of instruction, information, techniques, all were developing at a time that is supposed to be the period of absolute interdiction.

This same epoch saw the development of illegitimate birth as an institution, and the development of infanticide, and above all this was a period that witnessed the growth of a mass of discourse about sexuality.

From the 18th century on, we are dealing with a veritable explosion of sexual discourse. Of course, this didn't appear out of a situation of total silence; and one can say, or at least one can suppose, that literature became a bit more prudish at this time, but after all, literature is only one infinitely limited part of the immense field of discursive practices.

While literature may have been more modest, sexuality was bursting into a whole series of other kinds of discourses, including scientific discourse. It was at this moment that demography appeared. Sexuality made an equally important entry into medicine in the 18th century, it entered into biology in the 17th and 18th centuries. And not only do we see it taking its place in a whole series of new discourses, but we also see it appearing on the horizon of a whole series of preoccupations: the texts of urban planners and architects, for example, at the end of the 18th century, are haunted by the problem of sexuality; and philanthropists, who were the first social workers, were haunted by sexuality. They thought about nothing else; they talked about nothing else.

The 18th century is also the period when we see the sexuality of the child and the adolescent become a problem.

I certainly don't intend to make this explosion of discourse, of knowledge, of information, of controls, of preoccupations about sexuality, into a proof for some kind of liberation. We are dealing with something else—but what we are dealing with is not a simple repression, and the notion of a simple repression that is also a silencing and the beginning of an age of prudery is out of the question.

I believe, if you will, that it is time to put an end to this kind of dualism, of Manicheanism, which puts discourse, freedom, truth, broad daylight on one side, and on the other silence, repression, ignorance, night.

Instead of making this division we must try to reunite all these elements and describe what I would call a technological constellation (*ensemble*), which would be a three-dimensional constellation including discourse, knowledge, and power, within which modern sexuality would have been caught (I was going to say "produced"), that is, both invaded and controlled, constituted as an object, formulated in "truth" and defined as an object, as the target of a possible knowledge. Sexuality was not "repressed"—I would say rather that it was "expressed," not in the sense that it finally got translated into words, but in the sense that at that moment a discourse on sexuality came into being. A discourse on sexuality that was at once a power relationship and an object relation. The theme, the general form of this piece of work would consequently be, not the repression of sexuality as a fundamental mechanism that we must start from to understand all the others; the theme of this research should be the ensemble of the technology of sexuality, or the ensemble of explicit sexual systems.

Two remarks preliminary to this study:

First remark: Interdiction, barriers, silences, definitely had their place in this technological ensemble, but instead of being its kernel, instead of constituting the very center of the mechanism, it seems to me that this ensemble (barring, exclusion, etc.) is only one part of the mechanism. For example, the mere fact of sexual repression in literary discourse does not mean that the contemporary growth of discourse on sexuality in the sciences, medicine, etc., was a derivation from, or a compensation for literature.

What we have to try to consider is the ensemble constituted both by the discourses in which sexuality does not appear and by the other simultaneous discourses in which, on the contrary, sexuality does appear under a certain form. It is this relationship among discourses, this inter-discursive framework or web, that we should try to analyze, without determining the point where or the moment when sexuality is not given the privilege of being the root cause of everything else. In the same way it is not a question of explaining brothels by Queen Victoria and saying that, of course, sexuality had to pop up in brothels since it had been marked by repression and prudery; instead, we should begin to see brothels and Queen Victoria as twin brothers.

Second Remark: Certainly this technology of sexuality was not first invented in the 18th century in European society.

Every society has its own sexual technology, its forms of discourse, knowledge and power concerning sexuality.

*   *   *   *   *

In this third and final section of my talk, I am going to try and show you how I see the general form of this sexual technology, whose reality I would like to put in place of the rather dull and dismal notion of repression.

What is the sexual technology within which we are living?

I will mention only four of its essential traits.

The First Trait did not begin in the 18th century; it is far older than that...

The first trait is already found in the Middle Ages; it is the fact that in the Western world sexuality is not something that isn't talked about. On the contrary it is something that is talked about a great deal, even something that *has to be talked about*. That is, one must talk about one's sexuality and talk about it in a specific way: within a very precise discursive operation, that of *confession* (*l'aveu*). In the West sexuality has not been something that you hide but something that you confess. And it is to the degree that sexuality has been caught within the techniques of confession that it must consequently become silent at a particular moment or in a particular situation.

Thus we would have to do a whole history of confession since the Middle Ages:

—the judicial confession, of fairly recent importance (the Inquisition);

—the penitential confession, also recent;

—the confession of sins against the Sixth and Ninth Commandments. These led to a whole series of very intricate and precise elaborations of technique to find out how, in what conditions, why this confession should be made...

In any case, confession was certainly one of the parts of the apparatus into which sexuality penetrated. Even in theology and in the priesthood, this sexual confession worked its way in, in more and more subtle forms and it is the obligation to make this confession that we will find prolonged and displaced, from the 18th century on, in a completely different context—that of medical power and familial power.

A very clear example of this is provided by masturbation. Between 1720 and 1760, masturbation became one of the great European problems, one could say the major problem of medical psychology. One of the themes that immediately appeared was that in order to cure someone of this new disease, it was absolutely necessary that he confess it. You could find out whether he masturbated, you could find out the remedies to cure him, you could learn the techniques to keep him from doing it; but in the end he could never be cured if he didn't confess. And throughout the huge mass of literature put out by the anti-masturbation crusade for a century, you can find advice to parents on how to drag a confession out of their children, how to creep into Junior's bedroom at night or in the morning on tiptoe, there were even handbooks to describe the color of the stain according to types of sheet... A technique for the confession of sexuality by child to parents, doubled, controlled by the confession to the doctor—for the doctor too had to get a confession. In fact one very interesting book written at the beginning of the 19th century says that it's not enough to make a confession to the family, nor even enough to make one to the family doctor—in order to cure, confession must be made to a doctor specializing in sexuality.

This same confessional technique appears in general medicine at the end of the 18th century.

This same technique of confession, transposed into the Christian technique, will be taken up again and put in control of psychiatry, with a far wider scope and greater rigor. In 19th century psychiatry, the sexual confession became one of the cornerstones of the "curative" operation. It is this same confessional practice that Freud brought back in the technique of psychoanalysis.

So you see that, for the last six or seven centuries, sexuality has been less something that you do than something that you confess, by which and through which are established a whole set of obligatory procedures of elocution, enunciation and confession; the obligations of silence are doubtless the counterpart of these.

So that is what the first trait of this technology of sexuality is: sexuality is something that must be talked about inside a ritual discourse organized around a power relationship.

The Second Trait, more recent in the technology of sexuality, is what I will call the tendency toward somatization.

What I mean is this: if you take the legislation, the constraints and obligations of discourse about sexuality that appear in confessional manuals up to about the middle of the 16th century, you will see that the only thing that was considered, the only thing that had to be confessed, the only thing that had to be controlled, the only thing that was pertinent in any way for discourse on sexuality and its power over sexuality, was what had to do with the relationship between individuals. People were supposed to confess to adultery, to rape, to incest, sodomy, bestiality; the question was who you had sexual relations with and what kind of relations they were, how you got an orgasm, etc...

Now, starting in the 16th century, we can see the appearance and the growing importance of a sin which was certainly part of the traditional list, but in the midst of others. This was the sin of *la mollitiesse,* i.e. of masturbation, of caressing oneself. And if this was a sin in the priesthood and the moral theology of the Middle Ages and the Renaissance, it was because it too was a relational sin. You were supposed to have a sexual relationship with someone, yet you reached the "effusio seminis" outside such a relationship. It is a sin against the relationship by default.

Starting in the 16th century, this sin takes on a completely different position, related to a completely different function. *Mollitiesse,* no longer masturbation itself as much as the caress of oneself, relations with one's own body, bodily complicity in one's own desire, is on its way to becoming the definitive sin of lust. The violation of the Sixth and Ninth Commandments was no longer having a wicked relationship with a married woman or a forbidden woman, the first sin was to have directed hand or gaze to oneself. In moral theology, the relationship with one's own body became the heart and root of all the sins of lust; this is what becomes the pertinent element of any confession, and in 16th and 17th century confessional manuals, the confessor is told to always ask the penitent first of all about sins against the Sixth Commandment: Did you happen to stroke yourself? Did your hand end up somewhere it shouldn't?

So the body becomes present, the relationship with one's own body, and at the same time the entire body becomes the object of sexual observation and sexual control. Sexuality is not what links you with someone else by a carnal relationship, but something that implicates the entire body; and, parallel to this, a whole new kind of analysis is coming into being, in which desire, concupiscence, complicity, consent, imagination, will all be put through an extraordinarily fine analysis, an extremely precise grid that will constitute, if you will, the global organization of the desiring body. It is this desiring body and no longer the forbidden relationship that will be the object of the new sexual technology that is getting established in the 17th century.

Desire and the body, desire in the body, the body as the place of desire, as the surface and volume of the deployment of desire, it is this, and no longer the relation to another and the law that prescribes or forbids that relation, which I think is the target of this technology.

This transformation takes place at the same time as the increase in control over individuals by the mechanisms of sermons, confessions, direction of the conscience. It corresponds to the establishment of a widespread, subtle, analytical power that defines individuals as individuals and constitutes them as individuals on the level of their bodies. From the 17th century on, it is the body as a whole that is to be accounted for in sexuality, in the knowledge of sexuality, in the power exercised over sexuality.

The Third Trait: the "pedocentrism" that dates from the 18th century.

From this time on, the privileged point of control, of discourse, and of knowledge of sexuality will be the child. The 18th century literally invented childhood sexuality. It was the 18th century that constituted it both as an object of knowledge and as the target for power relations, for control.

The first form of this technology of infantile sexuality was a campaign against masturbation beginning around 1710-1720 in England, 1740 in Germany, and 1760 in France. Its interest lies in the fact that there we see joined, on the one hand, the old practice of the examination of conscience and, on the other hand, the obligation of confession, and, thirdly, the disciplinary technique of surveillance, particularly in schools and high schools. The consequences of this episode were capital for three reasons: 1) the colonization of sexuality by medicine: for the first time sexuality becomes a medical object and the doctor obtains the privileged right of observation vis-à-vis sexuality. The second major consequence is that the sexuality of the child receives a causal power that is, in a sense, limitless since infantile masturbation is thought to lead to and entail innumerable pathologies up until one's last days. The third consequence, finally, the family in the restricted sense, i.e. the mother and the father, are made responsible for the life and for the health of their child through their sexuality. Watching over this childhood sexuality, observing it, diagnosing it, discovering it when it is hidden has now become a fundamental obligation of the parents. Parents, in their children, don't merely have an heir, they have before them and within their group a sexual object. Through the intermediary of the controls that weigh on the child's body, the familial space has become, from the 18th century on, a sexually saturated space. The prohibition against masturbation, which is a fundamental ethnological fact in our society—doubtless more important than the prohibition against incest—has as a correlative the obligation of incestuous intention on the part of the parents towards their child. In our society, the prohibition against masturbation as a relation of pleasure is doubled by an obligation of incest as a relation of power.

The Fourth Trait that joins all the others is the fact that the sexual technology is constituted at the beginning of the 19th century as a *scientia sexualis*. Doubtless every society has constituted for itself a knowledge of sexuality, but one can distinguish two major types of sexual knowledge: the first type which would be an *ars erotica*, and whose example is to be found in ancient China. Here I am referring to Von Gulick's book. In this case, the knowledge of sexuality has as its basic function the intensification of pleasure. This knowledge is in a relation with medicine, but this medicine is understood as a technique of medicines and drugs, as an art of intensifying sensations by prolonging life. This knowledge is also linked to pedagogy, but the latter is understood as an initiation and a transmission of the secret. In the West, on the contrary, the *scientia sexualis* does not have the function of intensifying pleasure, but rather that of causing relations of power to function in the finest and most intricate elements of the body and its conduct. Sexuality is linked to truth, not because it would be an access to truth, but because truth permits access to sexuality and permits its subjugation as an object.

* * * * *

We can now trace some consequences of all this:

First, in relation to Freud, we can point out the sexual etiology of behavior problems, infantile sexuality, a libido and a desire that are not fixed to a procreative, heterosexual relationship, and a practice of sexual discursivity in the form of a confession.

These things existed before Freud, not as a theory but as constituent elements of this particular technology of this specific arrangement of discourse, knowledge, and power, which took over sexuality in our society in the 18th century.

Secondly, this sketch of the history of sexual technology shows that what has happened since the 18th century is an immense explosion, a continuing explosion, on the question of sexuality; and that it is impossible to reduce this event to a simple silencing, to the mechanisms of the law, to interdictions and censorship.

We are dealing with a complex strategy that connects the exercise of power and the constitution of knowledge, that connects relations of subjugation and object relations.

Consequently, anti-repressive discourse seems inadequate to account for the history of sexuality.

20

SCHIZO-CULTURE: ON PRISONS AND PSYCHIATRY

RONALD D. LAING: We are talking about what we do to people who lose whatever protection they can get in our society. When that protection is lost, we see how unbridled the attack on people is.

Supposing someone is mentally ill, then all the more reason not to be treated in that way. All the more reason not to attack people with terror and add more of the same. The most prevailing anxiety, terror, fear that I find going around the world is another thing that has got no name for it. What most people are frightened of is other people. We are frightened of each other. And we have got good reason to be frightened of each other because we can see what happens to any of us when other people have got the chance to do us in. They do us in. If one is in a position of not being able to defend oneself (I suppose you could call that being mentally ill, in our society) then there is all the more chance that one will be done in.

People come to London from all over the world in the hope of finding some place where they can just get into, where the heat will be off, where they are not going to be walked over. No one is going to do anything to them and there is no hassle. It is a place where it is not against the law to be terrified, or to feel. A lack of feeling of and for each other is what is cultured in our society. When I was last over in this country, I met a lot of students and was asked a lot of questions on everything from Transcendental Meditation to Behavior Modification. The single most frequent question I was asked though was: How do we get in touch with our feelings? People feel their feelings have become numb.

What we call tranquilizers were originally employed on rats and laboratory animals. You first try these things out on some remote population, say Kashmir East, then you try them out on prisoners, especially Black prisoners; then you try them out on mental patients, then you try them out on ourselves, on our own children. These drugs were employed, and are still employed as a chemical variable to enhance conditionability. In other words, they are drugs that were introduced into the human population because they were found to make rats more amenable to be conditioned. And of course you have to have a nice term, which has got nothing to do with their reality: you call them "tranquilizers." They are not tranquilizers, they are *drugs of conditionability.*

In England, there was only one chair of psychiatry before World War I. A psychiatrist then wrote a paper called the "Economic Use of Manpower in the British Army." We ought, he said, to treat soldiers in the same way we treat tanks and the rest of our equipment. A doctor once told me, when my wife wasn't very well: you should take better care of your wife, she is your most important single piece of equipment.... We instrumentize ourselves, we mechanize ourselves. We are not, however, just analogues of machines, we *are* machines, but rather poorly constructed machines, all that gristle and flesh and so on, we are not nearly as functionally effective as a real, proper machine, we are a rather inadequate machine. But we've got to be aware of the ideological warfare, we've got to be aware of the whole nexus. It's not just a matter of winning one victory; although this is very important. As soon as they have got to stop hacking up people in one domain, then it goes on in another way. Every time it gets a bit more subtle every time it gets a bit more technicalized and, from their point of view, effective.

To keep one's feelings going and still act upon them and challenge the system in whatever skillful means it presents itself through a comprehensive awareness of the nature of our society as a whole, is very largely a function of the intellectual. This isn't a trivial function, it does cut ice, it does make a difference. It is an endless task but this doesn't mean that we are going to let the bastards get away with it.

HOWIE HARP: I would like to add that if there is such a thing as "mental illness." I believe that it is a reaction to present social and economic conditions. A normal reaction to abnormal conditions.

In this society, showing emotions is considered a weakness or a sign of instability. In order to be considered "normal," you have to go to work, to school, you have to become some sort of a machine or a robot. Many people in society, as a result, never get a chance to express themselves, to express their creativity.

There is such a thing as problems in living and sometimes it manifests itself in people being "incoherent" and "psychotic", and all these kinds of things. As R. D. Laing said, it all depends how you treat this, and my opinion is that when someone goes through a psychotic break or a schizophrenic reaction, I think it's *a learning experience.* I don't think it should be called mental illness, it should be called just that: a learning experience, a change in a person's head. There is no such thing as an emotional disturbance that has no relationship at all to the outside environment. I personally believe that everything we think, everything we feel is directly caused by our environment. We live in a very repressive society, and in this society it's very easy to freak out, or rather it is very hard to freak out because you end up in a hospital... But a lot of people want to freak out. Very often I ask people, as I would ask people in this audience, how many of you have at one time or another wanted to get up and start yelling and screaming? I'm sure that everyone here has wanted to do that. But how many people have actually done it?

LAING: It's an extraordinary society where yelling and screaming are regarded as freaking out! It's a perfectly natural thing to do. It's one of the things that anyone normally adjusted to the world should do: to raise one's voice to full volume at least once or twice a day. But that's called freaking out...

HARP: That's called freaking out in our society and when you do it, you're locked up, you're given thorazine, shock treatment, seclusion, restrain, psychosurgery, alienation, etc. People have problems, people have emotional crises and inasmuch as psychology has any value, it brings about some understanding of the workings of the human mind. It is one thing, though, to understand what's going on in the mind and it is another to place value judgements on it, such as: this is abnormal-sick, this is normal-healthy. In doing this, the practice of psychology becomes oppressive and a knowledge that psychology holds becomes abused. Institutional psychiatry is the total abuse of that knowledge, since it coercively enforces those value judgements on the individuals. I believe, from my own experiences as well as those of hundreds of people I have known, that no one freaks out without any relationship at all to what has been going on in their lives. We should not put the blame on the individual and say: there is something wrong with you. We at *Project Release* start out by saying: O.K., if you're upset, what's going on in your life that's causing you to be upset. In this society, institutional psychiatry lays the blame and lays the emphasis on the individual and not on the environment, on society as a whole. If somebody's upset, we ask: where are you not being treated the way you should be, or where are you being prevented from doing something you want to do? I've worked in crisis centers and I have found that it is a better way to deal with people's problems.

As far as the genetic root of illness, I've heard a lot about that. As a matter of fact, I was put in an institution for a few months to try to prove that my mental illness was genetic because a lot of my relatives had been in mental hospitals: I was sort of following a family tradition... I don't know of anybody in this room who doesn't have some kind of chemical imbalance because of the processed food we eat, with all its chemicals, and the pollution in the air. If vitamins can help solve this chemical imbalance, if they work, fine. When someone is upset, it has been shown that there is a *change* in his chemical make-up. But whether this is an imbalance is quite another thing...

I just resent anybody telling me that I'm mentally ill because my mother's mentally ill. I think it's a lot of bullshit. I think my mother was reacting to very oppressive conditions, and so was I.

JUDY CLARK: I want to follow up on some of the things Howie Harp was saying. People look for some abstract situation when the basic realities of society are taken away. They wonder if there is a chemical imbalance, if there is something that is genetic because they don't look at the basic realities.

The lives of the people I work with in the prison movement were determined from the time they were born. It was determined that they would end up in a series of institutions. It usually started out at youth homes, often times with a stop-over in a mental institution, and ended up in the prison. The basic conditions that will determine you ending up there have to do with poverty.

People who are trained to work in those institutions are part of them. They are taught to hate the patients, to hate the inmates, to hate the kids who are in those institutions. Professionals are made to be antisocial beings. We are all social animals but, what you are taught to do in colleges like this (Columbia University) is to separate yourself out and hate those you are treating or those you are housing, or those you are guarding. The main thing professionals do is to not separate themselves out. There are basic social movements going on from the bottom up in every one of those institutions. They can begin to identify with those base-up movements of resistance instead of going through a lot of intellectual trauma about "Is there a use for me in this society?" Well, the use is to resocialize ourselves, resocialize people who have become professionals by embedding ourselves more in the realities, and in that reality of existence that people from the base up are involved in. In this city, in every institution, in every hospital, there is a mounting pressure and a mounting resistance and professionals are needed to be apart of it, not separated from it.

One way you are trained in this university is to hate the environment around you. When I used to live in New York City, Columbia University was a very political institution. When I came back from jail, I was shocked to find there was a student rally on this campus asking for more police to protect them from the community around them. This is what students in these institutions are being taught to do, to feel that they need to be protected from communities around them that are pretty angry because of what is been done in their lives by these institutions.

LAING: I would like to make two brief responses to the question of heredity and mental illness. My last book is a detailed analysis of some of the work done on so-called genetics. I don't think a single piece of scientific work ever established anywhere that the so-called schizophrenia is a genetic condition. All these studies beg the very questions we are challenging, and I don't think it stands up to a detailed critique.

My second response is that we certainly are social beings and our chemistry is social. The idea that our chemistry somehow happens in some arcane, in some environmental isolated place, that it has nothing to do with other people and with our social environment is absolutely ridiculous.

Just as much as our thinking is always in relationship to the world, so are our chemistry, our minds, our emotions. There is nothing that changes the chemistry of my body so much as going into a safe room, an easy welcoming situation. If it is a tight, anxious, hostile environment, then I am sure that a needle in my veins would record the fluctuations of my chemistry, it would also be changing. Studies of chemistry should be studies of *social* chemistry. Chemists haven't gotten around to that and sociologists haven't got around to that. This is a purely artificial development: we section ourselves up, we institutionalize these sections, we study bit and pieces and then we try to put it all together! When so-called tranquilizers first came into a mental hospital in the 50s, I remember a staff meeting in which one of the patients, a so-called manic woman, was discussed. She had been put on a lot of tranquilizers. A woman in the staff asked: Do these new drugs have any effect on height? She was asked what she exactly meant. Well, she said, I am sure this woman shrunk at least three inches since she is on tranquilizers. This is a very interesting observation in a social system. You put a chemical in the body of one person and through a mediating link this actually affects the perception of someone else on a quantitative as well as a qualitative way. When you put chemistry into the skin of a person, not only is that person's chemistry social but this is a social act because it's affecting the whole social system. Until we get such an awareness, until it leads to some decent research on this subject, we haven't got anywhere to go.

MICHEL FOUCAULT: I completely agree with what Ronald Laing said about the power of the medical profession, and the extension of it at the present time. On the basis of these two authorities, therefore, Howie Harp and Ronald Laing, I would like to introduce a problem which is perhaps still alien, too alien, to many occupations.

A few days ago I was in Latin America, in Brazil, where, as you know, there are a large number of political prisoners. Several hundred journalists, students, professors, intellectuals and lawyers have been arrested there during these last few weeks. And in Brazil, of course, arrested also mean tortured. But one thing is quite remarkable. It seemed that recently, techniques of torture have been developed and perfected to a considerable extent with the help of American technicians. One of the characteristics of the new techniques of torture is this: the person who does the torturing is not the same as the one who poses the questions. Someone sits in one room with just a computer in front of him, and, on the basis of the computer, determines what questions he should put to the victim. He then writes the question down and transmits it to another person, his subordinate, who applies the torture in another room until the answer is obtained. Once he gets an answer, it is fed back into the computer to verify whether it is consistent with information already obtained.

Forgive this digression which appears to be speaking only incidentally about mental hospitals and not about medicine at all. Except that a new character has been introduced in this new technique, which is now constantly present in the ritual of torture: the doctor. A doctor is now present at practically all the important tortures. His role is first of all to say what torture will be most effective, and, secondly, to give medical examinations to make sure that the patient is not a heart case, for example, and in risk of dying. Thirdly, the doctor administers various kinds of injections to revive the patient so that he can physically withstand the tortures and, at the same time, suffer them psychologically in the harshest manner.

This is certainly just one example of what happens in many other countries of the world besides Latin America. So, on this basis, I would like to make a few remarks. I am completely astonished—well, not astonished in fact, but apparently, rhetorically, astonished—to see how fiercely the different medical associations of the world, be they in the United States, France, Europe, South America—how carefully they claim the right to determine themselves, for the doctor, the rights of life and death. Look what happened in France with abortion. The doctors said: our profession consists in preserving life and must never decide in favor of death. Look what happened in the United States in the case that was judged four or five days ago, the Quinlin case, where the doctors said: we are committed to preserving life and to not causing death in any event. Do you ever see these medical associations which get so aroused about abortion denounce the political role of medicine in the prisons, the police stations, the torture chambers? Is there a group or association of doctors that demands the exclusion of doctors who serve this kind of function, from the medical profession?

I should add that in these torture sessions not just general doctors serve as technical advisers, but also sometimes psychiatrists, and even psychoanalysts. In Rio there is a psychoanalyst who belongs to, shall we say, the most sophisticated school of psychoanalysis and who is an official adviser to the police on torture. I do not think that this Freudian school has ever denounced this person.

Since we have before us the example of a group which defends former mental patients, do you not think one could create an association of people, tied to medicine in one way or another, either as doctors, nurses, students, etc. whose function and role it would be to denounce, wherever it might occur, this explicit effective, nominal, individual collaboration of doctors with police practices?

The other thing I would like to add is this. It seems to me that the participation of doctors in politics and judicial affairs poses a whole series of serious questions in a more general way than in the examples I have just said. I think that the role of psychiatrist-experts in law courts is not a medical activity at all. It is impossible to give a medical meaning to the diagnosis, judgement, description or clinical picture given by an expert in a criminal law court. The medical-legal discourse is not medical at all, but completely legal. Since, at the moment, we are talking about a critique of medical power, don't you think that right now would be the time to begin a specific action against the presence and functioning of the medical person in legal and police practices?

I will end simply with a question: what, in your opinion, is the best method to use, the best kind of organization to choose to begin this action at a local level as well as a national or international one?

CLARK: I want to talk about the prison movement in the United States. I work on a paper called "Midnight Special". It is written by prisoners and sent back into the prisons all over the country. The movement is very developed. It involves widely different activities, from study groups to breaking down the class divisions and racist usages inside prisons, up to the events that hit the headlines when rebellions occur. I could talk about the whole spectrum of reality within the prisons. I will choose, within the context of this conference, to talk about oppression inside the prison system: behavior modification.

Behavior modification is the use of physical and psychological terror against people who are organizing inside and rebelling against the conditions inside. It began as a reform under the basic assumption that prisoners are in prison not because they can't survive on the streets, but because of some maladjustments. So they should be readjusted. This is a very new trend that has taken over a lot of the prisons inside. It happens in many women's prisons, in the State prisons and it's most highly developed in the Federal prison system—first in Springfield, Missouri, and then in Marion, Illinois under the Start Program and the Care Program. A new prison in Butler, North Carolina was set up as an institute where prisoners will be sent from all over the country. They will experiment on them, try various methods against them.

When we first got letters in "Midnight Special" about behavior modification, they came from places like Vaccaville in California. They were using shock treatment and drugs as well as certain kinds of "therapeutic means" against prisoners. Nerve-deadening drugs administered would create a death-like state. They have permanent effects on people. I have worked with people who have been administered these drugs over the years, and it affects their central nervous system, it affects their capability of operating, it creates paranoia, and that was at the first onslaught what they began to use. A lot of that was exposed in California a few years ago. A number of psychiatrists who were involved in these programs finally freaked out, they were using torture methods against prisoners. They attended a big psychological conference in California and exposed it, and a movement started to be built against the use of these kinds of drugs.

Then we started to get letters that informed us that this program had a lot more to it than just the use of drugs, that it was a more subtle kind of development. The best example was the Start Program in Marion, Illinois, and what they do is exactly what they say they are trying to do: they are trying to modify the behavior of prisoners. First of all, who was sent to those programs? The people who have been actively organizing inside. Many prisoners who were involved in the Attica rebellion or in political work inside, or detained on political charges, were sent to a behavior modification program they tried to start in New York State. This is a step by step program. You're first thrown into a strip cell where you have nothing. You have no clothes, no recreation, no reading materials. You are not allowed to receive letters from the outside. You're not allowed to talk to anyone else. You have no privileges. Then they give you certain ways to show that you will be cooperative. If you're not cooperative, you're kept in step one. You never leave it. If you are cooperative, you get to step two.

What cooperation usually means is that you will involve yourself in therapy groups. What they do in these therapy groups, the main tactic they use is *attack therapy*. People in a group will be informed of your own history, on your childhood, on various realities in your life. The group will focus on one person, and you are supposed to scream at him about these things in his past, about these practices that are terrible, that are "anti-social," or against the prison administration. If you don't accept this role you are thrown back into the strip cell. If you do accept it, you are allowed into step two of a program.

In step two, you get a few more privileges. You get your clothes back, or a better diet. You will be able to see a doctor if there is anything wrong with your medical care. Maybe you will be able to get letters from your family. You have more privileges, but also more responsibilities. Behavior modification is just that: if you modify your behavior, if you do exactly what they tell you to do and attack new people coming into the programs, you can get to the next step. You can't go before a parole board and get out of prison until you get to the last step of this program.

The program is designed to break down the will of people inside; it forces them to see each other, and to maintain unity with each other, as their only means of survival. This is exactly what it means to modify your behavior. It means to cooperate with the administration against other prisoners. The end result is to produce someone who will follow the rules of a prison and therefore, when let out, follow the rules of society no matter what the rules are in the prison and when you get out. Someone who will turn against those who are in your same situation. What it teaches you, in other words, is pure capitalist ethic: the way you get ahead is to stamp on someone below you.

That system is being used in many places now. Most people who go into those program , though, will not accept the system. So they are put in "control units." Control units are what they always had inside prisons, that is, segregation. You are kept in there; you are in isolation and you never get out of that isolation. There are rules in prisons according to which people should not be put into permanent isolation. Isolation is a punishment; they have to give you a hearing to prove that there is a reason to punish you before they can put you in these kinds of units. But since these are behavior modification programs, they say that it is not for punishment, it is for your own treatment that they are putting you into them! Whatever due process exists inside the prisons is eliminated in the name of therapy. They actually keep people in isolation for years and years.

There is a law suit in Marion Penitentiary against the use of long term segregation and the control unit. Two years ago the struggle against the Start Program culminated. It began when they sent six prisoners into the Start Program, including a prisoner named Eddy Sanchez, who is a guy who had been in jail most of his life, who started out when he was a kid. When Eddy got inside he knew that this was a hook-up and he was not going to accept it. He organized six other people, three Black men, two Puerto Ricans and one white man, who refused to have anything to do with the program. Three years ago they went on a 42 day hunger strike. They got the word to the outside and people started writing letters to Norman Carlson, who was at that time the head of the Federal Bureau of Prisons. They began to develop momentum against the program by taking the kind of stand they did, which is a pretty extreme stand, of refusing to eat for 42 days. They felt it was the only way they could dramatize the situation. And they were successful. It began to develop into a movement. As a result, they were chained to their beds and beaten, then thrown back into their cells. They set fire to their cells. Each time they did something, the administration would respond, and they would counterrespond while word would be going to the outside so that the pressure would mount both from the inside and from outside. Their example disrupted the entire situation because the whole program is based on setting up the kind of coercive situation that will force everyone to go along with the game. These people wouldn't go along with the game, no matter what they did to them, and it mounted into a movement inside the Start Program as well as outside. Eddy is a fantastic writer, and a great strategist. He just sent out word all over the country and Carlson found himself with letters mounting up by the hundreds to his office, and with psychiatrists calling him up and with law students calling him up and lawyers filing suits. People inside were able to successfully mount that kind of campaign but with great risk to their own lives.

Eventually a suit was put into court that broke open and allowed liberal psychologists and also church groups to come inside the prisons to check out what were the conditions of these therapeutic programs. What they found was that they were horror shows! There is no way that you could define them as "treatment." Evidence started to come out in court and the prison system had to close down the Start Program. That was a major victory, and it was won by a lot of blood and struggle.

When they closed down Start, they tried to say, "Well, we found out that a few things were wrong with this kind of program, so we closed this one down." So now everyone can go home and forget about it. But in fact what they did was to decentralize these programs and put them all over the different prisons instead of keeping them in one. They also kept all the people who were in the control unit in Marion in the control unit. Some people have been in isolation cells in Marion, Illinois for over three years.... There's a suit fighting the use of the control unit as a mere continuation of the behavior modification technique meant to isolate the most political elements inside from the rest of the population. Hearings on that suit took place all summer long. Some of it hit the press, but most of it didn't. And we're still waiting for a decision.

Behavior modification is called a reform because instead of "hacks," guards (we call them "hacks" inside, that is, going up through the ranks and becoming wardens of prisons) now psychologists are becoming wardens of prisons. That is true in Marion and it is true in Butler, North Carolina. It amounts to show that, "We're bringing in real professionals who really know, they're not just going to use brute force, they are professionals!" It throws some strange light on the use of professionals or what professionals will allow themselves to be used to do inside the prisons.

The other reason for developing the Butler center in North Carolina is that the personnel used in these experimental programs come from the three universities in the area, including Duke University. Students who learn psychological means and methods are actually being used to develop terror campaigns inside Butler, North Carolina. Butler really is the crystallization of all these various techniques. They will use drugs, they will use the most outright kind of psychological means, and they will also use the whole step-by-step program. In Butler you start out in cold isolation and if you graduate all the way through you end up on the part of the prison grounds that looks like a college campus. If you go along with the game, you end up being rehabilitated, you end up in the true American dream of being on a college campus. What you have to do is simply to go along with the technique of putting down people who are with you. This is why they make it like a college campus. They say they want to help people learn how to survive on the outside, get them used to the kind of lives they could live if they became normal citizens in the United States of America. So they take people who were first inside prisons because they are Black, Third World and poor, and they say they are helping them get used to life on the outside by ending up being on this college campus. Now you know, and I know, that it is not the type of life on the outside that people who are in prison, or most people who aren't in prison, have to learn to survive with when they get outside. They may graduate to this college campus inside, but when they get outside they are going to graduate to welfare, the unemployment lines, to methadone centers, and to the streets. They have learned very little about survival on the outside. What they have learned is that what the Man says is: You play my game or you get your ass kicked! This is a big movement inside right now and one of the reasons we are trying to develop it as a movement is the fact that the ultimate tool of these kinds of reforms is to set people up against each other. We see this as just one dimension of what they use on the outside all the time. Prisoners think that it is important for them to resist inside these behavior modification programs if these *can* be instituted inside, they will be instituted on the outside.

It is actually just one step from utilizing them in schools. A prisoner once wrote to us that he was in a behavior modification program being given drugs inside. His son was defined as a hyperactive child on the outside and was being given Ridilin. He said, "What's the difference? The reason I have got to resist inside is that they just practice inside what they are going to use on the population on the outside…"

Another area where behavior modification comes down very sharply is in women's prisons. There is definitely something wrong with everyone who goes as far as the administration is concerned, but particularly so for a woman. It means that she is anti-social, she is not playing her role. As a result, they often don't use the same kind of physical terror against women inside. Rather psychological terror. The use of drugs inside of Women's prisons is enormous. When I was at Cook County Jail, the doctor came in to see us once a week. If there was anything wrong with you on a Monday, that was your problem. He wasn't going to come until Thursday anyway. When you did finally get to see him, there were two drugs he gave out. One was aspirin. They did give you aspirin. And the other was thorazine.

Many people are inside because they are drug addicts. They kick heroin when they are inside, but they get addicted to drugs like thorazine. Thorazine is used on a massive scale because it slows people down, it slows their reactions down so it keeps them quiet, keeps them muted. When people are rebellious, especially when they get into fights they will give them intravenous thorazine. They call it "drug assaults". These are used massively in Women's prisons. In many Women's jails, you can't ever come before the Parole board unless you are first willing to see a psychiatrist for a certain amount of time.

In Bedford Hills, which is the State Women's penitentiary in New York, there was a mounting resistance around a whole lot of conditions inside. They said: What is wrong with these women who are complaining about bad medical care is that they have psychological problems. They took six of the ringleaders and they sent them to Mattawan State Hospital, which is a mental hospital. One of them was a woman named Carol Crux. She is a small woman but very powerful, and she beat up a couple of guards. They then assaulted her. They sent eleven male guards into her cell one night and they beat the shit out of her. The other women on her wing heard that she was being beaten up so the next day, when they were in the yard, they refused to go back into the cells. They said, "We won't go until we can go to the warden and see what happened to Carol Crux. Why did they do what they did to Carol Crux?" That was what precipitated them sending six of those sisters to Mattawan. Most of those women had no one on the outside to fight for them, so they did it without any kind of legal redress. They were sent to Mattawan and immediately put on high doses of drugs. The only thing that stopped it is that these women just were not going to take them.

Bronx Legal Services, which is a community organization in the Bronx, took up the case of these women and managed to get it into Federal Court. The courts are not going to institute a great ruling for these women, but they have become a way of exposing what is happening inside. Women were able to come on the stand to testify about what had been going on against them, the drugs that were being used against them and the long term segregation that was inflicted on them without due process. This is something prisons don't like, when word about it gets outside because pressure from the outside starts to mount up. Eventually they won that suit and the women were sent back to Bedford. What you find inside, therefore, is the development of a very terrifying institution of behavior modification.

It has many different manifestations besides the step by step programs I described and use of drugs. We learned a lot from prisoners. People who developed these programs studied the use of brainwashing techniques during warfare on prisoners of war in different countries. They wrote up all the various techniques they found successful in breaking people's will to survive, to resist, to act as individuals. They listed, I think, 22 techniques. For instance, prisoners would never receive their mail. Then the guards would tell the prisoners, "Oh, your people on the outside are abandoning you." Or simply the use of deprivation, perceptual deprivation—being kept inside a strip cell. Not only are you isolated from other people but you hear no voices. Sometimes a light will be kept on 24 hours a day. Sometimes the light will be off for a week, so that you lose your sense of time and space. These techniques have only one goal: to break down people's own individual capacities and spirits.

On the one hand, it is very terrifying. On the other hand, what you learn from the prison system is that they can set up the most monolithic and terrifying kinds of systems of oppression, people will continue to resist them. The human spirit does not get broken. It maintains itself by building a unity among each other. People define the problem and understand it. They analyse the conditions used against them and realize that their major weapon is their own unity. They realize that their unity is in fact greater than the technology used against them and that, in the protracted struggle, the prisoners will win. This is a lesson that we could put to use on the outside. The more you learn about this lesson, the more you can respond to it both by looking at our own lives and the way our behavior is modified in this society. Whether people's resistance inside will survive technology developed to break out spirits as human beings is thus a key question to us.

When I get letters from Eddy Sanchez, I feel I have a large stake in his capability of resisting. It is a mirror image, it reflects my own sense of my capability of resisting. The fact that Eddy has almost singlehandedly been able to mount the kind of campaign he has, gather the kind of support he has, been able to disrupt even his being kept in isolation in a State prison in Washington state is a victory to people's ability to resist.

The reason I wanted to focus on behavior modificiation is that it is liberals who are instituting that technique, and it's professionals who are utilizing it in the name of developing a more humane kind of system. It teaches us what professionalism and the science mean in this society, how they get distorted, the way they are utilized and what we can do to resist. They know now whatever they use will be found out by people and that pressure on the outside will mount against it.

FOUCAULT: The problem for the generation which turned twenty in the 1930s was how to fight fascism, how to fight the fascists, how to fight the different forms, the different milieux in which fascism appeared. Depending on the balance of powers, depending on the global political and economic situation, forms of struggle, the struggle against fascism between the years 1930 and 1945 was a specific kind of struggle. I think that what has happened since 1960 is characterized by the appearance of new forms of fascism, new forms of fascist consciousness, new forms of description of fascism, and new forms of the fight against fascism. And the role of the intellectual, since the sixties, has been precisely to situate, in terms of his or her own experiences, competence, personal choices, desire—situate him or herself in such a way as to both make apparent forms of fascism which are unfortunately not recognized, or too easily tolerated, to describe them, to try to render them intolerable, and to define the specific form of struggle that can be undertaken against fascism.

Look, for example, at what has been happening concerning psychiatry and mental hospitals. You have a whole series of works which were essentially concerned, ostensibly, with either the actual functioning of hospitals, their origin, or their psychiatric effects, yet at the same time these works have all been tied to forms of contestation, of struggle, of transformation of medical practice. The same thing can be said about the work that has been done on prisons. If you compare, for example, the reform projects that emerged during the last hundred years with what has been happening during the last ten years, you see considerable differences. For the last ten years the problem of prisons has been posed in term which are theoretical and practical at the same time, descriptive and organizational terms, if you will, and to that extent I think the question "Are you a writer or a militant?" is *passé* today. And in any case, the specificity of what has been undertaken recently precludes theoretical or historical analysis being separate from concrete struggle.

The problem I posed a little while ago concerning Brazil is not a question about what I, as an individual, can do about the current situation in Brazil. Medicine functions in some kind of police or judicial capacity in all countries. What would be interesting, I think, would be to determine just what kinds of struggle could be undertaken in each country against the medical participation in repressive legal institutions.

21

PAUL'S STORY

MF: When I saw your film, I rubbed my eyes. I rubbed my eyes because I recognized professional actors; but what I was seeing in the film, I can't say that it was like an asylum, it was the asylum. I wondered if you hadn't spent many weeks or months in an asylum with your actors studying what was going on there, observing gestures, listening to dialogues. You explained to me that nothing of the sort had taken place, that you left your actors to somehow follow a kind of line, a thread, their own inclinations, which you had spotted in them; and that it was in working with them on this line that was theirs, that you were able to get out of them these characters who typically belong to the asylum. Is that really how it happened?

RENÉ FERÉT: We didn't need the actors to go do training internships in psychiatric hospitals, but from the beginning of the conception, even before shooting the film, while writing the scenario, the team had already met together and could rely on real experiences of people who had been interned in asylums. From the beginning, we wanted to construct a film from the point of view of the insane. In studying these real experiences, we reflected upon the institution of the asylum and the actors immediately got involved. I wrote for them based upon my intimate knowledge of them. During the fifteen days of rehearsals, they were situated in the settings, costumes and with the accessories which belong to the asylum environment. With the help of a videotape recorder, we were able to control, enrich, and develop the themes that we had elaborated. The actors lived the conditions of an asylum.

MF: You took actors, you put them in a space, in the middle of a system of coexistence, with clothing from the asylum, and you let them follow their thread; we take the insane, dress them and distribute them as you have done, let them follow their lines and we have the same thing. There is an effect which belongs to the space of the asylum, to the walls, to coexistence, to the asylum's hierarchy, and you release them, you make them gush forth the same way in someone who is ill, in someone who is in a state of horrible anguish, or in someone who, after all, is earning his living as a professional actor. There is then a surprising experiment about the force and plastic effects of the mental institution's power. The behaviour of these characters, so typical and stereotypical, are not exactly symptoms or illnesses, they are the vegetation and fauna of the asylum: the laugher, with his sardonic laugh, his agitation which is sometimes good-natured and sometimes anxious; the anguished questioner; the one who says his prayers. Each of those people is on his own path; the paths do not truly intersect; it's a little like those highways where, when you look at them from above, it looks like they cross one another, but in fact, the highways are passing under or over one another, in such a way that they never meet. Each is therefore on his own path that intersects the others but does not meet up with them; but, taken together in their pseudo-crossing, these solitary lines form "scenes" that do not truly belong to communication but rather indicate juxtaposition and solitude: ping-pong games, a game of cards, meals. You are going to encounter some criticism with the problem of the doctors, because they are caricatures; they are in fact the only characters which are caricatures (the attendants aren't). Grotesque are the cavalcading across the rooms of the asylum, the interrogating and not asking for answers; this is not the reality of medical practice in asylums.

RF: During the preparation of the film, we talked a lot about the role of the doctors and it is true that some doctors are not always happy when they see the film. The difference between the portrayal of the attendants and that of the doctors comes from the fact that the attendants and the mentally ill are two groups which flirt with each other a bit, because promiscuity between them is no doubt greater and in the film, in any case, they belong to the same social class. For the doctors, it's different, more so because we showed them from the point of view of the patients, assuming the role they have in relation to the mentally ill with their power, their knowledge, their intermittent visits. Faced with the objective reality of practicing physicians, we developed the subjective perception that the mentally ill have of them.

MF: In short, what you wanted to show was that it is enough for medical power to be administered in a homeopathic dose, it is enough for the doctor to come by, ask a question, give an order, for the system to crystallize; it's the little keystone that holds everything together. The doctors are seen from below, in a certain way, from the frog's perspective, described by Nietzsche. The world is seen from bottom to top, and it is therefore this character who is at once inaccessible, fleeting, or enigmatic, with enormous feet and hands, a microscopic head, a loud-speaker voice, both all-powerful and always elided, present by virtue of all the effects in the asylum, and yet, always absent.

RF: Some people criticize me by saying: you are content to describe; however, in describing, you don't seem to take a position, you show neither the causes nor the solutions, you only describe the effects. You do not have a constructive attitude with which to confront this problem.

MF: You know, I think that describing is already something important. And you have done more. You remember the experiments done in California, during which a number of students who were considered mentally sound were sent with false medical diagnoses into several hospitals, and the problem was to find out how much time it would take for them to be recognized as not mentally ill. They were immediately recognized by the patients, but it took the medical staff several weeks. Personally, I think that you have done the inverse experiment, since you took healthy people, you reconstituted the asylum environment around them and you showed what happens there. Because of this, insofar as it is an experiment, I would say that it is highly constructive; because one can understand from there a whole series of mechanisms and effects that are specific to institutional asylums. An experiment like that on the real effects of the institutional fiction that had never been done before.

RF: At the center of this "objective" experiment, I wanted to situate Paul's subjective experience; this was to allow the viewer to enter into the asylum himself

MF: The character is not a blank page. He has various circles that spin over his head. Immediately around him, around his bed, there is the circle of the mentally ill, a little above and standing up, is the circle of the attendants, and then, going like that, like spiraling on clouds, the doctors. So, we know strictly nothing about what brought him to the asylum, except the shot of the water which comes back many times and which, I think, designates the suicide that he committed or wanted to commit. I think it may also signify the insular character of the asylum, the water was crossed, it is now in the middle of this water and each time that he leaves the asylum, while sleeping and dreaming, he finds this water which separates him, and it's the mark of his subjectivity and the perspective character of the film.

RF: The shots of the water have the meanings you give them, they are also Paul's problems which will never be tackled within the asylum. They appear in moments of crisis and the film ends with a long shot of the water which does not want to say anything more, that cannot say anything more about it in a place where in no way, Paul's problems will be able to be dealt with, understood, unraveled.

MF: The asylum itself has the nature of water: water that makes you sleep and water that sleeps. Since the advent of neuroleptic medications, there is institutional sweetness, I cannot say that there is no longer violence, moreover, you showed some of it, in the middle of this felt-covered environment, in this sort of softness of the storm, at certain moments, lightening, thunder, and fighting are released. But there is a great sweetness in the asylum and the height of this sweetness is the food. In traditional mythology, the asylum was a place of violent repression and it was at the same time an environment of physical misery, of lacking, penury, hunger, emaciation, etc., starving people in a cage. Paul's mother comes to bring food, and moreover, everyone comes with bags filled with oranges, cakes, chocolates and they come to feed the sick, as if to compensate for the internment and its lacking. But it's redundant to reproduce the requirements inside the asylum in the name of the outside for everything in the asylum, and that, it seems to me you showed very well, everything in the asylum pivots around absorption. One has to absorb food and medicine, the good patient is the one who eats.

RF: From beginning to end, Paul's integration in the asylum is being read in terms of the food. Paul starts off by refusing all food, he is then punished and rejected by the mentally ill themselves, in the room where the "problem patients" are kept. In this room, the patients literally force Paul to ingest food; Paul, obliged to accept, returns to the first room. He is finally accepted, because he accepts eating. He then begins to integrate himself into the institution.

MF: The very beautiful scene with the crêpes seems to be the turning point. It's the moment where Paul accepts both the food that comes from his mother and the food given to him at the hospital. He consequently accepts the fact of being put away by his family and he accepts being a good patient in the hospital. The hospital functions like an immense digestion apparatus, inside which people digest; it's a big food channel, it's Jonah's whale. The medicine that must be absorbed is simultaneously the prize, the guarantee, this mixture of pleasure and duty. The patients congregate around a table when the medicine arrives. There is even a patient who says: "And what about me, how is it that I only have one today? I had two yesterday, why do I only have one!"
The great beauty of your film, where each gesture is carried by stripping it down to its maximum intensity, is also sustained by everyone's terrible irony—the patients, attendants, except the doctors perhaps with respect to this madness in which they work.

RF: Why wouldn't humor have its place in a subject like that, and why wouldn't we make it into a show, since the actors' work is one of its essential elements? Sometimes people laugh, people also shudder—I hope they do—and then they talk about it and perhaps think about it. The humor of the insane, their irony, these things exist and the actors approached them with their own sense of humor, their own irony.

MF: One might think that it's a little bit the opposite of these fools' festivals that went on in some Swiss psychiatric hospitals and I think in certain areas in Germany: the day of the carnival, the mentally ill wore costumes and went out into town, of course not the ones who were gravely ill; they organized a carnival where the population attended at a distance and with some trepidation, and it was finally rather terrible after all, that the only day they were permitted to go out together en masse was the day they had to disguise themselves and literally act crazy, like how non-crazy people act crazy. You have made the opposite experiment with the actors: "You are not crazy, so, go ahead and play the insane and be crazy!..."

RF: "...But careful, play the insane according to the rules of the asylum in order to better show its effects..."

MF: That's it, and "make madness according to the rules just as it is played and as you would play it if you were inside an asylum." So that gave it this funny side that doesn't at all contradict the reality of the asylum, and one feels that the actors, I couldn't say that they have fun acting, but they convey an intensity, a gravity of pleasure which is very palpable throughout the film.

Translated by Lysa Hochroth.

22

SADE: SARGEANT OF SEX

Q: When you go to the movies, are you struck by the sadism of some recent films, whether they take place in a hospital, or, as in the last Pasolini, in a false prison?

MF: I have been struck—at least until recently—by the absence of sadism, and the absence of Sade, the two not being equivalent. There can be Sade without sadism and sadism without Sade. But let's leave aside the problem of sadism, which is more delicate, and focus on Sade. I believe that there is nothing more allergic to the cinema than the work of Sade. Among the numerous reasons, this one first: the meticulousness, the ritual, the rigorous ceremonial form that all the scenes of Sade assume exclude the supplementary play of the camera. The least addition or suppression, the smallest ornament, are intolerable. No open fantasy, but a carefully programed regulation. As soon as something is missing or superimposed, all is lost. There is no place for an image. The blanks must not be filled except by desires and bodies.

Q: In the first part of Jodorowsky's *El Topo*, there is a bloody orgy, a rather revealing cutting up of bodies. Isn't the cinema's sadism first a way of treating actors and their bodies? And particularly women in the cinema—are they not (mis)treated as appendices of a male body?

MF: The way in which the body is treated in contemporary cinema is something very new. Look at the kisses, the faces, the cheeks, the eyebrows, the teeth in a film like Werner Schroeter's *The Death of Maria Malibran*. To call that sadism seems to me completely false, except through the detour of a vague psychoanalysis involving a partial object, a body in pieces, the *vagina dentata*. It's a rather vulgar Freudianism that reduces to sadism this way of celebrating the body and its wonders. What Schroeter does with a face, a cheekbone, the lips, an expression of the eyes has nothing to do with sadism. It's a question of multiplying and burgeoning of the body, an exaltation, in some way autonomous, of its least parts, of the least possibilities of a body fragment. There is an anarchizing of the body, in which hierarchies, localizations and designations, organicity if you like, is being undone. Whereas in sadism it's very much the organ as such that is relentlessly targeted. You have an eye that looks, I tear it from you. You have a tongue that I have taken between my lips and bitten, I'm going to cut it off. With these eyes you will no longer be able to see, with this tongue you will no longer be able to eat or speak. The body in Sade is still strongly organic, anchored in this hierarchy, the difference being of course that the hierarchy is not organized, as in the old fable from the head, but from sex.

Whereas in some contemporary films, the way of making the body escape itself is of a completely different type. The goal is to dismantle this organicity: this is no longer a tongue but something completely different that comes out of the mouth. It's not the organ of a mouth that has been soiled and meant for someone else's pleasure. It's an "unnameable" thing that can't be used outside of all programs of desire. It's the body made entirely malleable by pleasure: something that opens itself, tightens, palpitates, beats, gapes. In *The Death of Maria Malibran*, the way in which the two women kiss each other, what is it? Sand dunes, a desert caravan, a voracious flower that advances, insect mandibles, a grassy crevice. All that is anti-sadism. The cruel science of desire has nothing to do with these unformed pseudopods, which are the slow movements of pleasure-pain.

Q: Have you seen the "snuff films" in New York? There's one in which a woman is cut into pieces.

MF: No, but apparently the woman is really cut up alive.

Q: It's purely visual, without any words. A cold medium in relation to cinema, which is a hot medium. No more literature on the subject of the body: it's only a body in the act of dying.

MF: It's no longer cinema. It's part of a private erotic circuit, made only to kindle desire. It's just a matter of being "turned on," as Americans say, by a kind of stimulation that comes only from images but is no less potent than reality—although of another kind.

Q: Would you say that the camera is the master who treats the actor's body as the victim? I am thinking of Marilyn Monroe falling over and over again at Tony Curtis's feet in *Some Like it Hot*. Surely the actress experienced that as a sadistic sequence.

MF: The relationship between the camera and the actress in the film you're talking about seems to me still very traditional. One finds it in the theater: the actress taking upon herself the sacrifice of the hero and accomplishing it even in her own body. What seems new in the cinema I was speaking about is this discovery-exploration of the body that happens with the camera. I imagine that the cinematography in these films is very intense. It's an encounter at once calculated and aleatory between the bodies and the camera, discovering something, breaking up an angle, a volume, a curve, following a trace, a line, possibly a ripple. And then suddenly the body derails itself, becomes a landscape, a caravan, a storm, a mountain of sand, etc. It's the contrary of sadism, which cut up the unity. What the camera does in Schroter's films is not to detail the body for desire, but to knead the body like a dough out of which images are born, images of pleasure and images for pleasure. At the point of an always unforseen encounter between the camera (and its pleasure) and the body (throbbing with its own pleasure) these images and pleasures with multiple entries are born.

Sadism was anatomically wise, and, if it gave way to mania, it was within a very reasonable manual of anatomy. There is no organic madness in Sade. To try to adapt Sade, this meticulous anatomist, in precise images does not work. Either Sade disappears or one makes old-fashioned family entertainment.

Q: An old-fashioned cinema, in the proper sense, since recently one tends to associate fascism and sadism, in the name of "retro" or a nostalgic return. Thus Liliana Cavani in *The Night Porter* and Pasolini in *Salo*. Yet this representation is not History. The bodies are dressed up in period costumes. They would have us believe that Himmler's henchmen correspond to the Duke, the Bishop, and his Excellency in Sade's text.

MF: It's a complete historical error. Nazism was not invented by the great erotic madmen of the 20th century but by the most sinister, boring and disgusting petit-bourgeois imaginable. Himmler was a vaguely agricultural type, and married a nurse. We must understand that the concentration camps were born from the conjoined imagination of a hospital nurse and a chicken farmer. A hospital plus a chicken coop: that's the phantasm behind the concentration camps. Millions of people were murdered there, so I don't say it to diminish the blame of those responsible for it, but precisely to disabuse those who want to superimpose erotic values upon it.

The Nazis were chairwomen in the bad sense of the term. They worked with brooms and dusters, wanting to purge society of everything they considered unsanitary, dusty, filthy: syphilitics, homosexuals, Jews, those of impure blood, Blacks, the insane. It's the foul petit bourgeois dream of racial hygiene that underlies the Nazi dream. Eros is absent.

That said, it's not impossible that locally, within this structure, there were erotic relationships that formed in the bodily confrontation between victim and executioner. But it was accidental.

The problem raised is why we imagine today to have access to certain erotic phantasms through Nazism. Why these boots, caps, and eagles that are found to be so infatuating, particularly in the United States? Is it our incapacity to live out this great enchantment of the disorganized body that we project onto a meticulous, disciplinary, anatomical sadism? Is the only vocabulary that we possess to rewrite this great pleasure of the body in explosion this sad tale of a recent political apocalypse? Are we unable to think the intensity of the present except as the end of the world in a concentration camp? You see how poor our treasure of images really is! And how urgent it is to fabricate another instead of whining about "alienation" and vilifying the "spectacle."

Q: Directors see Sade like the maidservant, the night porter, the floorscrubber. At the end of Pasolini's film the victims are seen through a glass. The floorscrubber sees through a glass what happens far off in a medieval courtyard.

MF: You know that I am not for Sade's absolute deification. After all, I would be willing to admit that Sade formulated an erotism proper to a disciplinary society: a regulated, anatomical, hierarchical society whose time is carefully distributed, its spaces partitioned, characterized by obedience and surveillance.

It's time to leave all that behind, and Sade's eroticism with it. We must invent with the body, with its elements, surfaces, volumes, and thicknesses, a non-disciplinary eroticism: that of a body in a volatile and diffused state, with its chance encounters and unplanned pleasures. It bothers me that in recent films certain elements are being used to resuscitate through the theme of Nazism an eroticism of the disciplinary type. Perhaps it was Sade's. Too bad then for the literary deification of Sade, too bad for Sade: he bores us. He's a disciplinarian, a sargeant of sex, an accountant of the ass and its equivalents.

Translated by John Johnston

23

THE POLITICS OF SOVIET CRIME

Q: Guard towers, barbed-wire fences, police dogs, prisoners transported in trucks like so many animals... When the first filmed reports of life in a Soviet detention camp to reach the West were shown on French television, these were some of the scenes witnessed by viewers—scenes all too characteristic of our century. Soviet spokesmen at first denied the film's authenticity. Later admitting the existence of the camp in question, they added, by way of justification, that only nonpolitical prisoners were interned there. The response of the French public was on the whole one of relief: "Oh well, since they're only common criminals...." What were your reactions to the film and to the responses it elicited?

MF: One early statement on the part of the Soviet authorities impressed me enormously. They claimed that the very existence of the camp in plain view in the middle of a city proved that there was nothing shocking about it. As though the fact that a concentration camp could exist undisguised in the middle of Riga constituted an excuse. (The Germans, after all, sometimes felt the need to hide their camps.) As though the shamelessness of not hiding from the people of Riga what they do in that city entitled the Soviet authorities to demand silence everywhere else and to enforce their demand. It's the logic of Cyrano de Bergerac, cynicism as censorship: "You're not allowed to mention my nose because it's right in the middle of my face." As though it were possible not to see the Riga camp for what it is, a symbol of shamelessly exercized power, just as we see our own city halls, courts, and prisons as emblems on the escutcheon of power.

Setting aside for a moment the question of whether its inmates are political or non-political prisoners, the camp's high visibility and the fear inherent in that visibility are in themselves political. Barbed wire, searchlight beams, and the echoing footsteps of prison guards—that is political. And that is policy.

I was also struck by the Soviet rationalization you quoted: "These are not political prisoners; they are common criminals." Now, as a matter of fact, the Soviet vice-minister of Justice has said that the notion of political imprisonment does not even exist in his country. The only ones who may be prosecuted are those who seek to weaken the social order and the state by means of high treason, espionage, terrorism, vilifying propaganda, or the dissemination of misinformation. In short, he defines as non-political precisely those acts which the rest of the world considers political.

The Soviet definition is at once logical and bizarre. The obliteration of the distinction between political and nonpolitical offenses in the Soviet Union would be a logical development. But at that point, it seems to me, all offenses become political. In a socialist state, any breach of law—robbery, the most petty of thefts—is not a crime against private property, but against the property of the people, against society itself, socialist production, and the body politic. I would understand if the Soviet authorities had said that there were no longer any non-political prisoners because all crime is by definition political. As it is, we must not only accuse the vice minister of lying (because he knows there are political prisoners in the Soviet Union), but also ask him how after sixty years of socialism they still have a criminal code for non-political crimes.

However, if we define criminality in purely political terms, we necessarily forego the traditional contempt for "common" criminals that is an essential element of the penal system itself. And if we consider all crime to be political, then our response to it must be equally political. But in fact, the guard towers, the police dogs, and the endless gray barracks are only "political" in so far as they are sinister evocations of Hitler and Stalin, who used them to dispose of their enemies. The penal methods themselves—incarceration, deprivation, forced labor, brutality, humiliation—are not far removed from those invented by 18th-century Europe. Those who break the laws of the Soviet Union are subject to bourgeois penal techniques some two hundred years old. And far from changing these techniques, the Soviets have made them more atrocious and carried them to their logical extreme. What so moved those who saw the Riga documentary was not only the specter of Dachau, but beyond it, the endless procession of human beings condemned to penal servitude—a two-hundred year spectacle used by those in power for the purpose of instilling fear.

Q: I think the explanation of these paradoxes lies in the fact that the Soviet Union claims to be a socialist state but is in reality not at all socialist. The hypocrisy of Soviet leaders and the incoherence of their official statements follows logically from this fact. It has been evident for some time now that if the Soviet Union has been unable to evolve along lines that the Twentieth Congress seemed to suggest, it is because the weaknesses of the Soviet society are structural and lie in the mode of production, and not simply in a more-or-less bureaucratized leadership.

MF: It is undoubtedly true that although the Soviets indeed changed the distribution of property and the role of the state in the control of production, they merely adopted certain power and management techniques perfected by 19th-century European capitalism. The particular morality, esthetic forms, and disciplinary methods that already functioned effectively by 1850 in European bourgeois society—its forms of social control—were adopted wholesale by the

Soviets. I think the system of imprisonment was invented as a generalized penal system during the 18th century and consolidated in the 19th century in connection with the development of capitalist societies and states. Moreover, the prison system was only one of the techniques of power necessary to the development and control of the forces of production. The disciplined life—discipline in school, at work, in the army—is also a technical innovation of that period. And techniques are easily transplanted. Just as the Soviets adopted the principles of scientific management and other related management techniques developed in the West, they also adopted our disciplinary techniques, adding one new weapon—party discipline—to the arsenal we had perfected.

Q: It seems to me that Soviet citizens have even more difficulty than Europeans in understanding the political significance of these mechanisms. I see proof of this in the unfortunate prejudice of Soviet dissidents against non-political prisoners. Solzhenitsyn's descriptions of the latter are absolutely chilling. His "ordinary" criminals are subhuman creatures incapable of expressing themselves in any known language. The least we can say about his attitude is that he shows them no compassion.

MF: The hostility shown toward "ordinary" criminals by those who consider themselves political prisoners can seem shocking to those of us who think that poverty, rebellion, and the rejection of exploitation and humiliation are at the root of delinquency. But we must try to look at things in terms of their tactical relevance. We must take into account the fact that in the Soviet Union, just as in France or elsewhere, the criminal element is controlled, infiltrated, and manipulated by those in power. Among criminals as among non-criminals, rebels are a minority and conformists a majority. Do you think that a system of punishment that provides recidivism could have been maintained if criminal behavior did not serve some function? Early in the 19th century it became obvious that in most cases imprisonment turned the condemned into lifetime offenders. Other methods of punishment would certainly have been invented, were it not for the fact that the professionalization of crime created a kind of reserve army useful to those in power for providing services such as prostitution, for example, and for providing informers, strike-breakers, lackeys, agents-provocateurs, and even bodyguards for electoral, and even presidential candidates. In short, there is a historical conflict between political and non-political offenders—insofar as those in power have always sought to implicate both groups in the same base, selfish, and savage criminality.

I do not mean to imply that non-political criminals are the faithful handmaidens of the Soviet regime. But given the extreme difficulty of the dissidents' struggle, I wonder whether it is not necessary for them to distinguish themselves from the others, to show that their cause is not that of the "thieves and murderers" with which the regime tries to identify them. This may be only a tactical maneuver on the part of the dissidents. In any case, I find it difficult to condemn the attitude of the Soviet dissenters who are careful not to be confused with the "ordinary" criminals. I believe there were many members of the French resistance who when arrested refused—for political reasons—to be taken for black-marketeers, even though the latter could expect a far less cruel fate.

However, if you were to ask me about a country like France, my answer would be different. Here I must point out the existence of a broad spectrum of illegalities that extends from the sometimes honored, always tolerated wheelings and dealings of politicians and the merchant princes of drugs and munitions (who all use the law), to the prosecuted and punished offenses of the small-time thief who rebels against the law, is ignorant of it, or even baited by it. And we must also point out the unequal treatment handed out by our penal system. The important distinction here is not between political and nonpolitical offenders, but between the profitable illegalities perpetrated with impunity by those who use the law, and the simple illegalities that the penal system uses to create a standing army of criminals.

Q: But it is also true that in the Soviet Union, just as in France, there is a profound rupture between the ordinary people and those found guilty of petty crimes. I recently saw a program on Italian television that ended with scenes of a prison cemetery where those who died while serving their sentences are buried in tombs hardly worthy of the name. The prisoners' families almost never claim their dead—undoubtedly because transportation is too expensive, but also because they are ashamed. For me, the scene had profound social implications.

MF: The break between public opinion and criminals has the same origin as the prison system itself. Or, rather, it is one of the great benefits that the power structure has reaped from that system. In fact, the hostile relationship that we see today between criminals and the lower strata of society did not exist until the 18th century—and in some parts of Europe not until the 19th or even early 20th century.

The gap between rich and poor was so wide that the thief—the redistributor of wealth—was welcome among the poor. Until the 17th century, thieves and bandits were popular heroes, some of whom remain as shadowy but positive figures in our mythology. The same is true of the bandits of Corsica and Sicily and the thieves of Naples. But in an urban industrial setting, pilfering and petty theft became too costly, and these infractions tolerated by the masses began to be seen as a serious threat. At that point, a new form of economic discipline calling for honesty, accuracy, punctuality, thrift, and an absolute respect for property was imposed at all levels of society. It became necessary on the one hand to insure more efficient protection of wealth, and on the other to create in the popular mind an openly hostile attitude toward illegality. Thus, with the aid of prisons, those in power created a hard core of criminals who had no real communication with the masses and were no longer tolerated by them. This isolation facilitated both the infiltration of the criminal element by the police and the development, in the course of the 19th century, of an underworld ideology. The contempt, suspicion, and hatred aroused by criminals should not come as any surprise: it is the result of 150 years of effort on the part of politicians, ideologues, and the police. One should not be surprised either by the fact that the same phenomenon is found in the USSR.

Q: One month after the Riga documentary was shown on French television, the release of the mathematician Leonid Plyushch focused attention on another all too familiar aspect of Soviet repression: the imprisonment of dissidents in psychiatric hospitals.

MF: The internment of dissidents in mental hospitals constitutes an extraordinary paradox in a country that calls itself socialist. In the case of a murderer or child molester, a search for the psychological roots of the crime and an attempt to cure the perpetrator can be justified; the procedure in any case is not illogical. But the dissenter—I mean the one who does not accept the regime, repudiates it, or does not understand it—is of all Soviet citizens the one who should not be considered mentally ill. Instead, he should be the object of political instruction designed to make him open his eyes, to raise his level of consciousness, to make him understand in what way Soviet reality is intelligible and necessary, desirable and pleasant. However, dissidents are subjected to psychiatric treatment more frequently than anybody else. Does this not mean that it is not possible to convince someone in rational terms, that his opposition is unfounded? Does it not mean that the only way that Soviet reality can be made acceptable to those who don't like it is by authoritarian methods—through the use of drugs that affect hormones and neurons? The paradox is a revealing one: Soviet reality is only pleasant under the effects of Thorazine. And if only tranquilizers can make it acceptable, then perhaps there is a real cause for anxiety. Haven't the Soviet leaders renounced the rationality of their revolution, worrying only about maintaining docility? The punitive techniques employed in the Soviet Union reveal this renunciation of all that is basic to a socialist project.

Q: But there has been a certain amount of change in the Soviet Union. There is less repression now. In Stalin's time, everyone was terrified; one day you were the head of a factory, the next day you found yourself in a prison camp. Now, a certain element can act with impunity. If you are an academician, you no longer go to prison. Not only is Sakharov still free, but out of a total of 600 Soviet academicians, only seventy signed the denunciation of him. This means that the others felt free to refuse to sign. Twenty years ago this would have been unthinkable.

MF: I agree that the reign of terror has abated somewhat. However, terror is not the apogee of discipline, but rather its failure. Under Stalin, the head of the NKVD himself could be executed as he left a cabinet meeting. (In fact, no head of the NKVD ever died of natural causes.) Change and upheaval were inherent in the system itself. Fear is circular: those who unleash terror inevitably become its victims. But once the ministers, police officials, academicians, and other party leaders become entrenched and no longer fear for themselves, discipline in the ranks below them will function effectively without even the slightest risk of upheaval.

I would like to return to the issue of punishment in a more general sense. The questions of what to punish and how to punish have been debated for a long time. Now, however, we are beginning to ask ourselves some strange new questions. "Is punishment necessary?" "What do we mean by punishment?" "Why is there a connection—until now taken for granted—between crime and punishment?" The idea that crime must be punished is so familiar, so necessary to us, and yet, there is something somewhere that makes us doubt. Consider the cowardly relief of judge, jury, journalists, spectators, etc., when a psychiatrist or psychologist tells them not to be afraid to find a defendant guilty, that they will not be punishing the offender, but merely providing for his/her rehabilitation and cure. The defendant is found guilty, sentenced, imprisoned. The court is acquitted.

To suggest an alternative to punishment is to avoid the issue, which is not the judicial context of punishment, nor its techniques, but the power structure that punishes. This is why I find the problem of criminal justice in the Soviet Union so interesting. It is easy to mock the theoretical contradictions that characterize the Soviet penal system, but these are theories that kill, and blood-stained contradictions. One can also be surprised that they weren't able to come up with new ways of dealing with crime and political opposition; one must be indignant that they adopted the method of the bourgeoisie in its most rigid period, at the beginning of the 19th century. and that they pushed it to a degree of meticulousness that is overwhelming.

Their dimensions unknown, the mechanisms of power in the Soviet Union—systems of control, of surveillance, punishment—are versions of those used on a smaller scale and with less consistency by the bourgeoisie as it struggled to consolidate its power. One can say to many socialisms, real or dreamt: between the analysis of power in the bourgeois state and the idea of its future withering away, there is a missing term—the analysis, criticism, destruction, and overthrow of the power mechanism itself. Socialism and socialist societies have no need for new declarations of human rights and freedoms: simple, thus unnecessary. But if they want to be worthy of love and no longer rejected, they must address themselves to the question of power and its exercise. Their task is to invent a way in which power can be exercised without instilling fear. That would be a true innovation.

Translated by Mollie Horwitz

24

THE SOCIAL EXTENSION OF THE NORM

Q: Does this study by Szasz, *The Manufacture of Madness,*[1] challenge *Madness and Civilization* which you wrote fifteen years ago? You were following another filiation, another equivalence: not the one between the sorcerer and the madman, but the one between the leper and the mentally ill. How do these two branches connect to a common trunk?

MF: In fact, in *Madness and Civilization,* I didn't speak about witchcraft at all. I was wary of a theme usually found in the work of hasty historians: this idea that the insane used to be taken for witches, since one was incapable of recognizing them as sick people. Doctors, both from their own knowledge and out of a good heart, would have reacted: sorcery is illness denied. Let's no longer going to burn the witches, let's treat them. I had wanted to demolish this myth after *Madness and Civilization,* then...

Szasz's book (and that's why it is interesting) does not say: the madman was the sorcerer of the past, or the sorcerer of yesteryear is today's madman. He says something else, which is more important historically and politically: the practice through which one used to pick out a certain number of people, by which one suspected them, isolated them, interrogated them, by which one "identified" them as witches—this technique of power, used by the Inquisition, has been found again (after transformation) in psychiatric practice. It is not the madman who is the sorcerer's son, but the psychiatrist who is the descendant of the inquisitor. Szasz situates his history at the level of power techniques, not at the level of pathological identity. For him, it is not the sick person who unmasks the truth of the sorcerer, after the fact. It is anti-witchcraft which tells the truth of psychiatry, ahead of time. Szasz deals with the techniques of detection, diagnostics, interrogations. I deal with techniques of dividing things up (sharing) between society and the police. These two histories are not incompatible, to the contrary.

Q: All the more so that you both indicate the central role of medical practice in the mechanisms of social repression. What does this teach us about power set-ups (*dispositifs*)?

MF: We have entered a type of society where the power of law is not regressing but rather merging into a much more general power: roughly, that of the norm. Look at the trouble the penal institution is having today in actually carrying out a sentence, the purpose for which it is made. As if punishing a crime no longer had any meaning. The criminal is increasingly assimilated to a sick individual, and the condemnation tries to pass itself off as a therapeutic prescription. This is characteristic of a society which is no longer a juridical society essentially ruled by the law. We are becoming a society which is essentially defined by the norm.

This implies another system of surveillance, another kind of control. An incessant visibility, a permanent classification of individuals, the creation of a hierarchy qualifying, establishing limits, providing diagnostics. The norm becomes the criterion for evaluating individuals. As it truly becomes a society of the norm, medicine, *par excellence* the science of the normal and the pathological, assumes the status of a royal science. Szasz says: medicine is the religion of the modern age. I would modify the proposition a bit. It seems to me that the power of religion, from the Middle Ages to the Late Renaissance, was juridical, with its orders, its courts of law and its forms of penitence. Rather than a succession religion-medicine, I see a succession law-norm.

Q: In what way does the critique of psychiatry as a form of social control affect medicine as such?

MF: Psychiatry was one of the forms of social medicine that appeared in the 19th century. The history of psychiatry written by Szasz—another one of his merits—discloses the social function of medicine in a society of normalization. Medical power is at the heart of a society of normalization. Its effects can be seen everywhere: in the family, in schools, in factories, in courts of law, on the subject of sexuality, education, work, crime. Medicine has taken on a general social function: it infiltrates law, it plugs into it; it makes it work. A sort of juridico-medical complex is presently being constituted, which is the major form of power.

But what permits medicine to function with such force is that, as opposed to religion, it is part of the scientific institution. It is not enough to indicate the disciplinary effects of medicine. Medicine may very well function as a mechanism of social control, but it also assumes technical and scientific functions. This is why we cannot speak of medicine and psychiatry in one breath because psychiatry only has an imaginary relationship with scientific knowledge. The critique is not situated at the same level.

Q: How far does historical analysis of madness go? Szasz dismantles the social mechanisms of production of mental illness. He does not deal with the specific issue of madness.

MF: If madness is not a mental illness charted on a nosographic[2] table, if madness has a specific reality that shouldn't be pathologized or medicalized, then, what is it? Anti-psychiatry is now confronting this thing that must be coded, neither in terms of mental illness nor in terms of social normativity, but, nevertheless, remains a problem. Anti-psychiatry demolishes the medicalization of madness within the institution and the conscience of doctors. But from this very fact, the question of madness comes back to us after this long colonization by medicine and psychiatry. What can we make of it?

Hasty leftist discourses which are lyrically anti-psychiatric, or meticulously historical are only imperfect ways of approaching this incandescent core. With the illusion, sometimes, that from there, the "truth," our poor truths, may be able to light up with a devouring flame. It is illusory to believe that madness—or deliquency or crime—speak to us from a position of absolute exteriority. Nothing is more interior to our society, nothing is more within the effects of its power, than the affliction of a crazy person or the violence of a criminal. In other words, we are always on the inside. The margin is a myth. The word from beyond is a dream that we keep renewing. The "crazies" are placed in an outside space of creativity or monstrosity. And nonetheless, they are caught in the network, they are shaped and function within the mechanisms of power.

Q: From this point of view, isn't historical analysis in a retreating position? Are not the blind spots in the theory and practice of Szasz noticeable in this retreat? In terms of psychoanalysis, for example.

MF: It should be said that, without psychoanalysis, our criticism of psychiatry, even from a historical perspective, would not have been possible. That being said, psychoanalysis, not only in the United States, but also in France, functions massively as a medical practice: even if it is not always practiced by doctors, it certainly functions as therapy, as a medical type of intervention. From this point of view, it is very much a part of this network of medical "control" which is being established all over. If it has played a critical role, at another level, psychoanalysis plays harmoniously with psychiatry. You absolutely have to read Robert Castel's book, *Le psychanalysme,*[3] which dismantled the psychiatric-psychoanalytic network. Psychoanalysis superbly requires a specific historical dismantling, but of the same type as psychiatry. It doesn't have to play the role of a blind spot in relation to history.

Another question, then: in a period during which the burning flame of revolutionary struggles has been extinguished, is there not a temptation to retreat into historical speculation? Historical analysis is not in a retreating position, but rather in an instrumental position, from the moment it is used as an instrument within a political field. Historical analysis is a way of avoiding the sacralization of theory: it allows one to erase the threshold of scientific untouchability. It is necessary to play it against former and recent epistemology, which asked itself: in a science, what is the irreducible core of the scientific? Historical analysis has to determine what the nonscientificity of science is, or rather, since the problem scientificity/non-scientificity is not the important thing, it has to ask itself what is the force of a science, how, in our society, the truth-effects of truth of a science are at the same time effects of power.

Q: What does the contradiction between the theoretical positions and the practical and political positions of Thomas Szasz mean to you?

MF: There was a period of "ideological" criticism which was one of "denunciation," of diagnostics and disqualification invoking more or less secret faults. When someone was speaking, one would spot in his vocabulary, in what he was saying, even worse, in what he was not saying and which was precisely the unspoken in his discourse, how to characterize him and shut him up: criticism by theoretical pox. At one point in time, for example, if one wanted to refer to Nietzsche, one felt obliged to say that Nietzsche was not an anti-Semite.

I prefer using the technique of intentional pirating. Thoughts and discourses are very much organized by systems. But these systems must be considered as the internal effects of power. It is not the systematic nature of discourse which holds its truth, but rather its possibility of dissociation, of reutilization, of reimplantation elsewhere. Szasz's historical analyses can be reused in anti-psychiatric discourse. Szasz felt perfectly the deep resonance between the control functions of medicine, psychiatry and state structures of control established since the 19th century. It seems, however, that he is deluding himself if he thinks that liberal medicine is free from all that, when it is merely the extension of these state structures, their support and their antenna.

PW: You're not embarrassed by Szasz's positions on the "potential of private psychiatry"?

MF: The problem of private practice in Szasz is both simple and topical. For him, the mystification of psychiatry is in believing that madness, the suffering of the insane, is the illness. And therefore, making the "crazy person" believe that he needs a doctor. In short, he means: "Since I do not want to believe that it is as a doctor that I am intervening, since I do not pretend that a free exchange with a voluntary client is a medical act, I do not participate in this charade. I listen to the client, I free him from the pathological framework; I do not receive him as a sick person, I do not present myself as a doctor: I only sell him my time. He pays me at the end of a free contract."

We can say a lot of things against this deduction and the profits it authorizes. It is an exclusively dual and resolutely mercenary social interaction. Psychiatrists were selling the status of illness they gave to their clients at a rather high price. Szasz sells non-illness to people who think they are sick. The problem: must one sell what is precious?

Translated by Lysa Hochroth

---

[1] Thomas Szasz, *The Manufacture of Madness*, a comparative study of the Inquisition and the mental health movement. (New York: Harper and Row, 1970)

[2] Nosography, from the Greek, *nosos,* illness and *graphe,* description: description of illness.

[3] Robert Castel, *Le Psychanalysme* (Paris: Maspero, 1973).

25

SORCERY AND MADNESS

Q: For twenty years Thomas S. Szasz has developed the theme that there are fundamental analogies between the persecution of heretics and witches in former times and the persecution of the mad and mentally ill today. It's the principal subject of his book *The Manufacture of Madness*,[1] which shows that the therapeutic state has been substituted for the theological state. Psychiatrists and more generally workers in the field of mental health have succeeded in bringing back the Inquisition and in setting it up as a new scientific panacea. Does the parallel between the Inquisition and psychiatry appear to you to be historically justified?

MF: When will we be delivered from these witches and misunderstood madnesses that a society without psychiatrists unfortunately condemned to the stake? When will we be rid of this commonplace that so many books are still recounting today? What's strong and important in Szasz's work is to have shown that the historical continuity doesn't go from witches to madness, but from the institution of witches to the one of psychiatrists. It's not the witch, with her tawdry chimeras and power over the shades, who has finally been recognized as the alienated one by a tardy but beneficent science.

Szasz shows that a certain kind of power is exercised through the surveillances, interrogations and decrees of the Inquisition; and that through successive transformations it interrogates us still, questions our desires and our dreams, disturbs our nights, hunts down secrets and traces boundaries, designates what's abnormal, undertakes purifications and insures the functioning of order. Szasz, I hope, has definitively displaced the old question—were witches the mad ones?— and reformulated it in these terms: What, in the psychiatric set-up, is still recognizable as the effect of a power linked to the prying work of the Inquisitors, with their long muzzles and sharp teeth? *The Manufacture of Madness*, I think, is an important book in the history of the related techniques of power and knowledge.

Q: In *The Manufacture of Madness* Szasz describes the insatiable curiosity of the Inquisitors concerning the sexual fantasies and activities of their victims, the witches, and compares it to that of psychiatrists. Do you think this comparison is justified?

MF: We're really going to have to rid ourselves of the "Marcuseries" and "Reichianisms" which encumber us and which would have us believe that of all things sexuality is the most obstinately "repressed" and "overrepressed" by our "bourgeois," "capitalist," "hypocritical" and "Victorian" society. Since the Renaissance there is nothing that has been more studied, questioned, extorted, brought to light and into discourse, forced into confession, required to express itself and praised, finally, when it found the words. No civilization has chattered so much about sexuality as ours. And many people still believe that they are subverting it when they are only obeying this injunction to confess, this secular requisition that subjects us—we other men of the West—to say all about our desire. Since the Inquisition, through penitence, the examination of conscience, spiritual guidance, education, medicine, hygiene, psychoanalysis and psychiatry, sexuality has always been suspected of holding over us a decisive and profound truth. Tell us what your pleasure is, don't hide anything of what happens between your heart and your sex, and we will know what you are and what you are worth.

Szasz has seen very clearly, I think, how the "questioning" of sexuality was not simply the morbid interest of Inquisitors crazed by their own desire, but that what was taking shape there was a modern kind of power and control over individuals. Szasz is not an historian and perhaps one can quarrel with him, but at a time when the discourse on sexuality fascinates so many historians, it was good that a psychoanalyst retraced in historical terms the interrogation of sexuality. And many of Szasz's intuitions confirm what Le Roy Ladurie reveals in his remarkable book *Montaillou*.[2]

Q: What do you think of Szasz's idea that in order to understand the psychiatric institution—and all mental health movements—it's advisable to study the psychiatrists themselves and not the so-called sick?

MF: If it's a question of studying the psychiatric institution, he's obviously right. But I think Szasz goes much further. Everyone dreams of writing a history of the mad, of going over to the other side and tracing the great evasions or the subtle retreats into delirium from the beginning. Yet, under the pretext of tuning in and letting the mad themselves speak, one already accepts the division between the two as a fact. It's necessarily better to put oneself at the point where the machinery that makes these qualifications and disqualifications is actually operative, and putting the mad and the non-mad on two sides facing each other. Madness is no less an effect of power than non-madness; it doesn't dart through the world like a furtive beast until its course is halted and it's put in the cage of an asylum. It's a tactical response, in the form of an infinite spiral, to the tactics that invest it. In another of Szasz's books, *The Myth of Mental Illness*,[3] there's a chapter that, I think, is exemplary on this subject, where hysteria is shown to be a product of psychiatric power, but also as the response that opposes it and the trap into which it falls.

Q: If the therapeutic state has replaced the theological state, and if medicine and psychiatry have today become equally the most restrictive and underhanded means of social control, isn't it necessary from the point of view of an individualist and libertarian like Szasz to fight for the separation of medicine and state?

MF: On this point I have some difficulty. I wonder if Szasz is not identifying, in a way that's too forced, power with the State. Perhaps this identification is explained by Szasz's double experience: the European experience, in a totalitarian Hungary where all forms and mechanisms of power were jealously controlled by the State, and an experience of an America penetrated with this conviction that liberty begins where the centralized intervention of the State ceases.

In fact, I don't believe that power is only the State or that the non-State is therefore liberty. It's true (here Szasz is right) that the circuits of psychiatricalizing and psychologizing, even if they pass through the parents, the peer group and the immediate surroundings, are finally supported by a vast medico-administrative complex. But the "free" medicine of the "liberal" doctor, the private psychiatrist or home psychologist are not an alternative to institutional medicine. They are part of the network, even in the case where they are poles apart from the institution. Between the therapeutic State Szasz talks about and "liberated" medicine there is a whole play of support and complex cross-reference.

The analyst listening silently in his chair is not so foreign to the insistent questioning and the close surveillance in the asylum. I don't think one can apply the world "libertarian"—Does Szasz himself do it? I don't remember—to a doctor who is "liberal," that is, linked to an individual profit that the State protects all the more since it profits from it too. Szasz cites very effectively the anti-State interventions of these liberal doctors, and they have had salutory effects. But it seems to me that there you have the combative utilization—against "general abuses"—of a medicine whose destination rather is to assure, conjointly with the State and with its support, the smooth functioning of a normalizing society. Rather than the therapeutic State, it's the normalizing society, with its institutional and private wheels, that it is necessary to study and criticize. Robert Castel's book *Le Psychanalysme*4 seems to me to have cast a very accurate light on this great continuous web which reaches from the sad dormitory to the profit-making couch.

Translated by John Johnston

---

1 Thomas Szasz, *The Manufacture of Madness* (New York: Harper & Row, 1974).

2 Foucault's *History of Sexuality*, which takes this anti-Reichian stand, came out at the time of this interview.

3 Thomas Szasz, *The Myth of Mental Illness* (New York: Harper & Row, 1977).

4 Robert Castel, *Le Psychanalysme* (Paris: Maspero, 1973).

26

I, Pierre Rivière

Q: If you like, we can begin by discussing your interest in the publication of the dossier on Pierre Rivière, and in particular your interest in the fact that, at least in part, it has been made into a film.

MF: For me the book was a trap. You know how much people are talking now about delinquents, their psychology, their drives and desires, etc. The discourse of psychiatrists, psychologists and criminologists is inexhaustible on the phenomenon of delinquency. Yet it's a discourse that dates back about 150 years, to the 1830s. Well, there you had a magnificent case: in 1836 a triple murder, and then not only all the aspects of the trial but also an absolutely unique witness, the criminal himself, who left a memoir of more than a hundred pages. So, to publish this book was for me a way of saying to the shrinks in general (psychiatrists, psychoanalysts, psychologists): well, you've been around for 150 years, and here is a case contemporary with your birth. What do you have to say about it? Are you better prepared to discuss it than your 19th century colleagues?

In a sense I can say I won; I won or I lost, I don't know, for my secret desire of course was to hear criminologists, psychologists, and psychiatrists discuss the case of Rivière in their usual insipid language. Yet they were literally reduced to silence: not a single one spoke up and said: "Here is what Rivière was in reality. And I can tell you now what couldn't be said in the 19th century." Except for one fool, a psychoanalyst, who claimed that Rivière was an illustration of paranoia as defined by Lacan. With this exception no one had anything to say. But I must congratulate them for the prudence and lucidity with which they have renounced discussion of Rivière. So it was a bet won or lost, as you like. . .

Q: But more generally, it's difficult to discuss the event itself, both its central point which is the murder and also the character who instigates it.

MF: Yes, because I believe that Rivière's own discourse on his act so dominates, or in any case so escapes from every possible handle, that there is nothing to be said about this central point, this crime or act, that is not a step back in relation to it. We see there nevertheless a phenomenon without equivalent in either the history of crime or discourse: that is to say, a crime accompanied by a discourse so strong and so strange that the crime ends up not existing anymore; it escapes through the very fact of this discourse held about it by the one who committed it.

Q: Well how do you situate yourself in relation to the impossibility of this discourse?

MF: I have said nothing about Rivière's crime itself and once more, I don't believe anyone can say anything about it. No, I think that one must compare Rivière with Lacenaire, who was his exact contemporary and who committed a whole heap of minor and shoddy crimes, mostly failures, hardly glorious at all, but who succeeded through his very intelligent discourse in making these crimes exist as real works of art, and in making the criminal, that is, Lacenaire himself, the very artist of criminality. It's another tour de force if you like: he managed to give an intense reality, for dozens of years, for more than a century, to acts that were finally very shoddy and ignoble. As a criminal he was a rather petty type, but the splendor and intelligence of his writing gave a consistency to it all. Rivière is something altogether different: a really extraordinary crime which was revived by such an even more extraordinary discourse that the crime ended up ceasing to exist, and I think moreover that this is what happened in the minds of the judges.

Q: Well then, do you agree with the project of René Allio's film, which was centered on the idea of a peasant seizing the opportunity for speech? Or had you already thought about that?

MF: No, it's to Allio's credit to have thought of that, but I subscribe to the idea completely. For by reconstituting the crime from the outside, with actors, as if it were an event and nothing but a criminal event, the essential would be lost. It was necessary that one be situated, on the one hand, inside Rivière's discourse, that the film be a film of memory and not the film of a crime, and on the other hand that this discourse of a little Normand peasant of 1835 be taken up in what could be the peasant discourse of that period. Yet, what is the closest to that form of discourse, if not the same one that is spoken today, in the same voice, by the peasants living in the same place. And finally, across 150 years, it's the same voices, the same accents, the same maladroit and raucous speech that recounts the same thing with almost nothing transposed. In fact Allio chose to commemorate this act at the same place and almost with the same characters who were there 150 years ago; these are the same peasants who in the same place repeat the same act. It was difficult to reduce the whole cinematic apparatus, the whole filmic apparatus, to such a thinness, and that is really extraordinary, rather unique I think in the history of the cinema.

What's also important in Allio's film is that he gives the peasants their tragedy. Basically, the tragedy of the peasant until the end of the 18th century was still hunger. But, beginning in the 19th century and perhaps still today, it was, like every great tragedy, the tragedy of the law, of the law and the land. Greek tragedy is a tragedy that recounts the birth of the law and the mortal effects of the law on men. The Rivière affair occurred in 1836, that is, twenty years after the Code Civil was set into place: a new law is imposed on the daily life of the peasant and he struggles in this new juridical universe. The whole drama of Rivière is a drama about the law, the code, legality, marriage, possessions, and so forth. Yet, it's always within this tragedy that the peasant world moves. And what is important therefore is to show peasants today this old drama which is at the same time the one of their lives: just as Greek citizens saw the representation of their own city on the stage.

Q: What role can this fact play, the fact that the Normand peasants of today can keep the spirit, thanks to the film, of this event, of this period?

MF: You know that there is a great deal of literature about the peasants, but very little peasant literature, or peasant expression. Yet, here we have a text written in 1835 by a peasant, in his own language, that is, in one that is barely literate. And here is the possibility for these peasants today to play themselves, with their own means, in a drama which is of their generation, basically. And by looking at the way Allio made his actors work you could easily see that in a sense he was very close to them, that he gave them a lot of explanations in setting them up, but that on the other side, he allowed them great latitude, in the manner of their language, their pronunciation, their gestures. And, if you like, I think it's politically important to give the peasants the possibility of acting this peasant text. Hence the importance also of actors from outside to represent the world of the law, the jurors, the lawyers, etc., all those people from the city who are basically outside of this very direct communication between the peasant of the 19th century and the one of the 20th that Allio has managed to visualize, and, to a certain point, let these peasant actors visualize.

Q: But isn't there a danger in the fact that they begin to speak only through such a monstrous story?

MF: It's something one could fear. And Allio, when he began to speak to them about the possibility of making the film, didn't dare tell them what was really involved. And when he told them, he was very surprised to see that they accepted it very easily; the crime was no problem for them. On the contrary, instead of becoming an obstacle, it was a kind of space where they could meet, talk and do a whole lot of things which were actually those of their daily lives. In fact, instead of blocking them, the crime liberated them. And if one had asked them to play something closer to their daily lives and their activity, they would have perhaps felt more theatrical and stagey than in playing this kind of crime, a little far away and mythical, under the shelter of which they could go all out with their own reality.

Q: I was thinking rather of a somewhat unfortunate symmetry: right now it's very fashionable to make films about the turpitudes and monstrosities of the bourgeoisie. So in this film was there the risk of falling into the trap of the indiscreet violence of the peasantry?

MF: And link up again finally with this tradition of an atrocious representation of the peasant world, as in Balzac and Zola...I don't think so. Perhaps just because this violence is never present there in a plastic or theatrical way. What exists are intensities, rumblings, muffled things, thicknesses, repetitions, things hardly spoken, but not violence...There is none of that lyricism of violence and peasant abjection that you seem to fear. Moreover, it's like that in Allio's film, but it's also like that in the documents, in history. Of course there are some frenetic scenes, fights among children that their parents argue about, but after all, these scenes are not very frequent, and above all, running through them there is always a great finesse and acuity of feeling, a subtlety even in the wickedness, often a delicacy. Because of this, none of the characters have that touch of unrestrained savagery of brute beasts that one finds at a certain level in the literature on the peasantry. Everyone is terribly intelligent in this film, terribly delicate, and, to a certain point, terribly reserved.

Translated by John Johnston

27

POWER AFFECTS THE BODY

Q: Michel Foucault, *The Will for Knowledge,* the first volume of your *History of Sexuality* strikes me as astounding in all respects. The thesis you defend in it, unexpected and straightforward at first glance, is progressively revealed to be very complex. Let's say to sum it up that, from power to sex, the relation is not one of repression, on the contrary. But before going any further, let's look at your first course at the Collège de France in December 1970. You analyze the processes that control the production of discourse. Among these are the forbidden, then the old division of reason/madness, finally the will for truth. Would you point out the links between *The Will for Knowledge* and *The Order of Things* and tell us if, throughout your demonstration, the will for knowledge and the will for truth overlap?

MF: I think I mixed two conceptions in this "Order of Things" or rather, I proposed an inadequate response to a question I think is legitimate (the meshing of facts of discourse with the mechanisms of power). This text I wrote at a moment of transition. Until then, it seems to me that I accepted the traditional conception of power, power as an essentially legal mechanism, what the law says, that which forbids, that which says no, with a whole string of negative effects: exclusion, rejection, barriers, denial, dissimulation, etc. Now I find that conception inadequate. It was enough for me, however, in *Madness and Civilization* (not that this book was satisfactory or sufficient in itself), for madness is a privileged case: during the classical period, power was exercised over madness primarily in the form of exclusion; one saw then a great reaction of rejection which involved madness. So that analyzing this fact, I was able to use, without too many problems, a purely negative conception of power. It seemed to me, after a while, that this was insufficient, and this occurred to me in the course of a concrete experience I had around 1971-72, regarding prisons. Prisons convinced me that power should not be considered in terms of law but in terms of technology, in terms of tactics and strategy, and it was this substitution of a technical and strategical grid for a legal and negative grid that I tried to set up in *Discipline and Punish,* and then use in *History of Sexuality.* So that I would rather willingly abandon everything in the order of discourse that might present the relations of power to discourse as negative mechanisms of rarefaction.

Q: The reader who remembers your *Madness and Civilization* retains an image of great baroque madness locked up and reduced to silence. In all of Europe, in the middle of the 17th century, asylums were hurriedly being built. Is that to say that modern history, if it has imposed silence on madness, has untied the tongue on sex? Or else has a similar obsessive fear—about madness, about sex—resulted in opposite outcomes, on both the level of discourse and action, for one and the other, and why?

MF: I do think there is a series of historical relations between madness and sexuality that are important and that I certainly did not see when I wrote *Madness and Civilization.* At that time, I had in mind to do two parallel histories: on the one hand, the history of the exclusion of madness and the divisions that resulted from it; on the other hand, a history of demarcations in the arena of sexuality (permitted and forbidden sexuality, normal and abnormal, women's and men's, adults' and children's); I thought of a whole series of binary divisions that would in their way cash in on the great "reason–madness" split I tried to reconstruct in terms of madness. But I don't think this is enough; if madness, at least for a century, was essentially the object of negative processes, sexuality, from that century on, was a product of much more precise and positive investments. But starting in the 19th century, an absolutely fundamental phenomenon occurred: the enmeshing, the interweaving of the two great technologies of power—the one that wove sexuality, and the one that divided madness. The technology concerning madness went from negative to positive, from binary to complex and multifaceted. A great technology of the psyche was then born, which is one of the fundamental traits of our 19th century and our 20th century: it makes sex at once a hidden truth of the reasonable conscience, and the decipherable meaning of madness—their common meaning, and therefore that which allows a hold on both, according to the same modalities.

Q: Perhaps we should do away with three possible misunderstandings. Your refutation of the repressive hypothesis seems to involve neither a simple shift in emphasis nor an acknowledgement of denial or ignorance on the part of power. Take the Inquisition, for example. Instead of emphasizing the repression to which it subjected the heretic, one could stress the "will for knowledge" that presides over the torture. Aren't you going in that direction? Aren't you saying that power denies its own interest in sex or that sex speaks unbeknownst to power?

MF: I don't think my book corresponds with any of these themes and objectives you speak of as so many misunderstandings. And the word misunderstanding might be somewhat severe to designate these interpretations or rather these demarcations of my book. Take the first: I did in fact want to shift the emphasis and to make positive mechanisms appear where ordinarily the negative are emphasized.

So in terms of penitence, people always underscore that Christianity sanctions sexuality, that it only authorizes certain forms and punishes all the others. But we also have to notice, I think, that at the heart of Christian penitence, there is confession, thus, avowal, the examination of conscience, and through this, a whole extrusion of knowledge and discourse on sex that induced a series of theoretical effects (for example, the great analysis of concupiscence in the 17th century) and practical effects (sexual education was subsequently secularized and medicalized). Just as I talked about how different instances or different resting points of power were caught, in a way, in the pleasure of their exercise. There is, in surveillance, or more precisely in the gaze of those surveilling, something not extraneous to the pleasure of surveillance and to the pleasure of surveilling pleasure, etc. I wanted to say this, but this is not the whole of my purpose. I also stressed the backlashes that you spoke of. It is certain, for example, that the explosions of hysteria manifested in psychiatric hospitals in the second half of the 19th century were indeed a backlash, a repercussion of the very exercise of psychiatric power: the psychiatrists got their patients' hysterical body full in the face (I mean in full knowledge and in full ignorance) without wanting it, without even knowing how it happened. These elements are certainly in my book, but they do not constitute the essential part; one must, it seems to me, understand them based on the deployment of power exercised on the body itself. What I am trying to do is to show how power relations can get through to the very depths of bodies, materially, without having been relayed by the representation of subjects. If power affects the body, it is not because it was first internalized in people's consciousness. There is a network of bio-power, of somatic-power that is itself a network from which sexuality is born as a historical and cultural phenomenon within which we both recognize and lose ourselves.

Q: In *History of Sexuality*, responding, it seems, to the reader's expectations, you distinguish Power—as a set of institutions and apparatuses—from power as a multiplicity of relations of force immanent to the domain in which they are inscribed. You portray this power, this power game, as happening constantly, everywhere, in every relationship. And this power, if I understand you correctly, is not external to sex, just the contrary?

MF: For me, the essential part of the work is a reworking of the theory of power, and I am not sure that the pleasure of writing on sexuality alone would have been enough to motivate me to start this series of six volumes (at least), had I not felt the need to reconsider this question of power. It seems to me that too often, and according to a model prescribed by the legal-philosophical thought of the 16th and 17th centuries, we reduce the problem of power to sovereignty: What is a sovereign? How is the sovereign constituted? What links individuals to the sovereign? This problem, considered by monarchist or antimonarchist jurists from the 13th century to the 19th century, continues to haunt us and seems to me to discredit a whole series of fields of analysis; I know that they can seem very empirical, and secondary, but after all they concern our bodies, our existences, our daily life. Against this privilege of sovereign power I wanted to try to emphasize an analysis that would go in the other direction. Between each point of a social body, between a man and a woman, in a family, between a teacher and his student, between the one who knows and the one who does not know, power relations come into play which are not the projection pure and simple of the great sovereign power on individuals; rather, they are the shifting and solid ground in which it has taken root, the conditions under which it can function. The family, even today, is not the simple reflection, the extension of state power; it is not the representative of the state for the children, just as the male is not the representative of the state for the woman. For the state to function as it does, the relationship of domination between the man and woman or the adult and child has to be a very specific, with its own configuration and relative autonomy.

I think one has to be wary of a whole thematics of representation that encumbers analyses of power. For a long time it was the question of knowing how individual will could be represented in or through general will. The assertion that the father, the husband, the boss, the adult, the professor "represents" State power which itself "represents" the interests of a class has been repeated so often. This does not take into consideration the complexity of the mechanisms, or their specificity, or the support, complementarities, and sometimes blockages that this diversity encompasses. More broadly, I don't think power is built on "wills" (individual or collective) or that it derives from interests. Power is constructed and functions out of powers, multitudes of questions and effects of power. It is this complex domain that has to be studied. This does not mean that it is independent, and that it can be deciphered outside the economic process and relations of production.

Q: In reading what could be considered in your text as an attempt to elaborate a new conception of power, one is divided between the image of the computer and that of the isolated, or supposedly isolated, individual, also the holder of a specific power.

MF: The idea that an explanation for all the arrangements of power must be gotten from the source, or the point of accumulation of power—the State—seems to me to be without great historical fecundity, or let's say its historical fecundity has been exhausted. The opposite approach currently appears richer. I'm thinking of studies such as Jacques Donzelot's on the family. He shows how absolutely specific forms of power exercised within families have been penetrated by more general, state-like mechanisms thanks to schooling, but how state-like powers and familial powers have maintained their specificity and have only truly become enmeshed insofar as each of their mechanisms were kept intact. Similarly François Ewald is doing a study on mines, the setting up of systems of owner control and the way in which this owner control was relayed but without losing its efficiency in large state administrations.

Q: Is it possible, given this reevaluation of what we call "power," to look at it from a political point of view? You present sexuality as a political arrangement. Would you define the meaning that you give to "political"?

MF: If it is true that all power relations in a given society constitute the domain of the political, and that a policy is more or less a global strategy that tries to coordinate and finalize these power relations, I think your questions can be answered in the following way:

The political is not what ultimately determines (or overdetermines) elementary relations, which are "neutral" by nature. All relations of force imply a power relation (which, in a way, instantly provides an analysis of it) and each power relation can be referred to the political sphere of which it is a part, both as its effect and as its condition of possibility. To say that "everything is political" is to acknowledge this omnipresence of relations of force and their immanence to the political field; but it requires untangling this indefinite skein, a task still barely sketched out. Such an analysis should not be crushed in individual guilt (the kind that was practiced a few dozen years ago especially, in the existentialism of self-flagellation—you know, each person is responsible for everything, there is no injustice in the world in which we are not ultimately accomplices). Nor should we dodge it through those displacements we so gladly practice today—all of this derives from a market economy, or capitalist exploitation, or simply this rotten society (thus, problems of sex, or delinquency, or madness reflect an "other" society). Political analysis and critique, for the most part, have to be invented—but so do strategies that will allow both modifying these relations of force and coordinating them in such a way that this modification will be possible and register in reality. That is to say that the problem is not really defining a political "position" (which brings us back to a choice on a chessboard that is already set up), but to imagine and to bring out new schemas of politicization. If "to politicize" means going back to standard choices, to pre-existing organizations, all these relations of force and these mechanisms of power that analysis mobilizes, then it's not worth it. The great new techniques of power (which correspond to multinational economies or bureaucratic states) must be opposed by new forms of politicization.

Q: One of the phases and consequences of your research involves distinguishing between sex and sexuality in a very perplexing manner. Could you explain this distinction and tell us how, from now on, we should read the title of your *History of Sexuality*?

MF: This question was the central difficulty of my book; I had begun to write it as a history of the way we have covered and costumed sex with this sort of fauna, this strange vegetation that would be sexuality. I think this opposition of sex and sexuality reflected a position of power as law and interdiction: power would have set up a system of sexuality in order to say no to sex. My analysis remained caught in the legal conception of power. I had to reverse my position: I hypothesized that the idea of sex was internal to the system of sexuality and that, as a result, what one necessarily finds at its root is not the refusal of sex, but a positive economy of bodies and pleasure.

There is a fundamental feature in the economy of pleasures as it functions in the West, which is that sex serves as its principle of intelligibility and measurement. For thousands of years, we have been made to believe that the law of all pleasure is, secretly at least, sex. And this is what justifies the need for its moderation, and creates the possibility of its control. These two themes that at the bottom of all pleasure there is sex, and that the nature of sex would have it be devoted and limited to procreation, are not initially Christian themes, but Stoic ones; and Christianity was forced to take up these themes when it endeavored to integrate itself into the state structures of the Roman empire, of which Stoicism was the quasi-universal philosophy. Sex then became the "code" of pleasure. In the West (in societies endowed with an erotic art, the intensification of pleasure instead tends to desexualize the body), it was this codification of pleasure by the "laws" of sex that ultimately gave rise to the whole arrangement of sexuality. And this makes us think that we are "liberating" ourselves when we "decode" all pleasure in terms of sex finally brought into the open. Whereas we should be striving, rather, toward a desexualization, to a general economy of pleasure that would not be sexually normed.

Q: Your analysis casts the genesis of psychoanalysis in a somewhat suspect and shameful light. Psychoanalysis reveals its dual, primordial adherence to inquisitorial confession, on the one hand, and psychiatric medicalization, on the other. Is that indeed your point of view?

MF: One could say, of course, that psychoanalysis is a part of the tremendous growth and institutionalization of confessional procedures so characteristic of our civilization. In the short term, it is part of this medicalization of sexuality, which is also a strange phenomenon: while in erotic art, the means (pharmaceutical or somatic) that serve to intensify pleasure are medicalized, we have in the West a medicalization of sexuality itself as if it were a zone of pathological fragility particular to the human existence. Every sexuality risks both being sick and inducing countless sicknesses. One cannot deny that psychoanalysis finds itself at the crossing point of these two processes. I will try to look at how psychoanalysis managed to take shape when it did in subsequent volumes. I just fear that what happened in terms of psychiatry when I tried to do the "History of madness" [the French title of *Madness and Civilization*] will happen in terms of psychoanalysis; I had attempted to account for what had happened until the beginning of the 19th century; then psychiatrists took my analysis to be an attack against psychiatry. I don't know what will happen with psychoanalysts but I am afraid they will take as "anti-psychoanalysis" something that is only meant to be a genealogy.

Why would an archeology of psychiatry function as "anti-psychiatry" while an archeology of biology does not function as anti-biology? Is it because of the partial character of the analysis? Or isn't it rather because of a certain "bad relationship" between psychiatry and its own history, a certain inability on psychiatry's part, given what it is, to accomodate its own history? We will certainly see how psychoanalysis receives the question of its own history.

Q: Do you feel your *History of Sexuality* will advance women's issues? I'm thinking of what you say in terms of the hystericalization and psychiatricalization of the woman's body.

MF: I have a few ideas, but they're tentative, not final. The discussion and criticisms following each volume will perhaps bring them out. But it's not up to me to establish users' rules.

Q: In *History of Sexuality*, it is a matter of facts and discourse; facts and discourse themselves are caught in your own discourse, in this order of your discourse which presents itself rather as a dis-order, provided one detaches the prefix. You fly from one point to another in your demonstration, you yourself incite those who might contradict you, as if the locus of your analysis preexisted and preempted what you would say. Your writing, moreover, tries to present the reader with distant and abstract relations. Do you agree with the dramatization of your analysis and its fictional quality?

MF: This book has no demonstrative function. It is there as a prelude, in order to explore the keyboard and sort of sketch out the themes and see how people are going to react, where it will be criticized, where it will be misunderstood, where it will make people angry. I wrote this first volume to make the other volumes permeable, in a way, to all these reactions. As for the matter of fiction, it is very important to me. I am quite aware that I have never written anything but fictions. I'm not saying for all that that this is outside truth. It seems to me the possibility exists to make fiction work in truth, to induce effects of truth with a discourse of fiction, and to make it so that the discourse of truth creates, "fabricates" something that does not yet exist, therefore "fictionalizes." One "fictionalizes" history starting from a political reality that makes it true, one "fictionalizes" a political outlook that does not yet exist starting from an historical truth.

Translated by Jeanine Herman

28

THE END OF THE MONARCHY OF SEX

Q: You inaugurate with *The History of Sexuality* a study of monumental proportions. How do you justify today, Michel Foucault, an enterprise of such magnitude?

MF: Of such magnitude? No, no, rather of such exiguity. I don't wish to write the chronicle of sexual behaviors throughout so many ages and civilizations. I want to follow a much finer thread: the one which has linked in our societies for so many centuries sex and the search for truth.

Q: In precisely what sense?

MF: The problem in fact is the following: how is it that in a society such as ours, sexuality is not simply that which permits us to reproduce the species, the family, and the individual? Not simply something which procures pleasure and enjoyment? How is it that sexuality has been considered the privileged place where our deepest "truth" is read and expressed? For this is the essential fact: that since Christianity, Western civilization has not stopped saying, "To know who you are, know what your sexuality is about." Sex has always been the center where our "truth" of the human subject has been tied up along with the development of our species.

Confession, the examination of conscience, all of the insistence on the secrets and the importance of the flesh, was not simply a means of forbidding sex or of pushing it as far as possible from consciousness, it was a way of placing sexuality at the heart of existence and of connecting salvation to the mastery of sexuality's obscure movements. Sex was, in Christian societies, that which had to be examined, watched over, confessed and transformed into discourse.

Q: Hence the paradoxical thesis which supports the first volume: far from making sexuality their taboo, their major interdiction, our societies have not ceased to speak about sexuality, to make it speak...

MF: They could speak well and often about it, but only to forbid it. But I wished to underline two important things. First, that the bringing to light, the "clarification" of sexuality, did not happen only in discussions, but in the reality of institutions and practices. Secondly, that numerous strict prohibitions exist. But they are part of an economic complex where they might mingle with incitements, manifestations and valorizations. These are the prohibitions that we always insist upon. I would like to refocus the perspective somewhat: seizing in any case the entire complex of operative mechanisms.

And then, you know all too well, that they've made me into the melancholy historian of prohibitions and repressive power, someone who recounts history according to two categories: insanity and its incarceration, anomaly and its exclusion, delinquence and its imprisonment. But my problem has always been on the side of another category: truth. How did the power unfolding in insanity produce psychiatry's "true" discourse? The same thing applies to sexuality: how to recapture the will to know how power exerted itself on sex? I don't want to write the sociological history of a prohibition but rather the political history of a production of "truth."

Q: A new revolution in the concept of history? The dawn of another "new history"?

MF: A few years ago, historians were very proud to have discovered that they could write not only the history of battles, of kings and institutions, but also of the economy. Now they're all dumbfounded because the shrewdest among them learned that it was also possible to write the history of feelings, of behaviors and of bodies. Soon they'll understand that the history of the West cannot be disassociated from the way in which "truth" is produced and inscribes its effects.

We live in a society which is marching to a great extent "towards truth"—I mean a society which produces and circulates discourse which has truth as its function, passing itself off as such and thus obtaining specific powers. The establishment of "true" discourses (which however are incessantly changing) is one of the fundamental problems of the West. The history of "truth"—of the power proper to discourses accepted as true—has yet to be written. What are the positive mechanisms which, producing sexuality in this or that fashion, bring with them misery? In any case, what I would like to study for my part, are all of these mechanisms in our society which invite, incite and force us to speak about sex.

Q: Some would answer that, despite such discourse, repression and sexual misery still exist...

MF: Yes, that objection has been made. You're right: we live more or less in this state of sexual misery. With this said, it's true that this objection is never treated in my book.

Q: Why? Is that a deliberate choice?

MF: When I undertake concrete studies in subsequent volumes on women, children and perverts, I will try to analyze the forms and conditions of misery. But for the moment, it is a question of establishing a method. The problem is to know whether this mystery should be explained negatively by fundamental interdiction or by a prohibition relative to an economic situation ("Work, don't make love") or whether this misery is the effect of procedures which are much more complex and positive.

Q: What could a "positive" explanation be in this case?

MF: I'm going to make a presumptuous comparison. What did Marx do when in his analysis of capital he encountered the problem of working-class misery? He refused the usual explanation which regarded this misery as the effect of a rare natural cause or of a concerted theft. And he said in effect: given what capitalist production is in its fundamental laws, it can't help but to produce misery. Capitalism's raison d'être is not to starve the workers but it cannot develop without starving them. Marx substituted the analysis of production for the denunciation of theft.

Other things being equal, that's approximately what I wanted to say. It's not a question of denying sexual misery, but it's also not a question of explaining it negatively by repression. The whole problem is to understand which are the positive mechanisms that, producing sexuality in such or such a fashion, result in misery.

Here is one example that I will treat in a future volume: at the beginning of the eighteenth century enormous importance was suddenly accorded to childhood masturbation, which was persecuted everywhere as a sudden terrible epidemic threatening to compromise the whole human race. Must we admit that childhood masturbation had suddenly become unacceptable for a capitalist society in the process of development? This is the position of certain recent "Reichians." It does not appear to me to be a satisfying one. On the contrary, what was important at the time was the reorganization of the relations between children and adults, parents and educators: it was an intensification of intra-familial relationships, it was childhood which was at stake for the parents, the educational institutions, for the public health authorities; it was childhood as the breeding ground for the generations to come. At the crossroads of body and soul, of health and morality, of education and training, children's sexuality became at the same time a target and an instrument of power. A specific "children's sexuality" was established: it was precarious, dangerous, to be watched over constantly.

From this resulted a sexual misery of childhood and adolescence from which our generations still have not recovered. The objective was not to forbid. It was to constitute, through childhood sexuality suddenly become important and mysterious, a network of power over children.

Q: This idea that sexual misery arises from repression, and that in order to be happy we must liberate our sexualities, is a fundamental one for sexologists, doctors, and vice squads...

MF: Yes, and that is why they set a fearsome trap for us. They basically tell us: "You have a sexuality, this sexuality is both frustrated and mute, hypocritical prohibitions repress it. So, come to us, show us, confide in us your unhappy secrets..." This type of discourse is in fact a formidable tool of control and power. As always, it uses what people say, feel and hope for. It exploits their temptation to believe that to be happy, it suffices to cross the threshhold of discourse and remove a few prohibitions. It ends up in fact repressing and controlling movements of revolt and liberation.

Q: From this I suppose comes the misunderstanding of certain commentators: "According to Foucault, the repression and liberation of sexuality amounts to the same thing..." Or elsewhere: "Pro-abortion and pro-life movements employ basically the same discourse...."

MF: Yes! These matters have yet to be cleared up. They've had me saying in effect that there is no real difference between the language of condemnation and that of contra-condemnation, between the discourse of prudish movements and that of sexual liberation. They claimed that I was putting them all in the same bag to drown them like a litter of kittens. Completely false: that's not what I wanted to say. The important thing is, however, I didn't say it at all.

Q: But you agree all the same that there are some common standards and components...

MF: But a statement is one thing, discourse another. There are common tactics and opposing strategies.

Q: For example?

MF: I believe the so-called "sexual liberation" movements must be understood as movements of affirmation "beginning with" sexuality. Which means two things: these are movements which take off from sexuality, from the apparatus of sexuality within which we're trapped, which make it function to the limit; but at the same time, these movements are displaced in relation to sexuality, disengaging themselves from it and going beyond it.

Q: What do these outbursts resemble?

MF: Take the case of homosexuality. In the 1870s psychiatrists began to make it into a medical analysis: certainly a point of departure for a whole series of new interventions and controls. They began either to incarcerate homosexuals in asylums or attempted to cure them. They were formerly perceived as libertines and sometimes as delinquents (from this resulted condemnations which could be very severe—with burning at the stake still occurring in the 18th century, although very rarely). In the future we'll all see them in a global kinship with the insane, suffering from sickness of the sexual instinct. But taking such discourses literally, and thereby even turning them around, we see responses appearing in the form of defiance: "All right, we are what you say we are, whether by nature or sickness or perversion, as you wish. And so if we are, let it be, and if you want to know what we are, we can tell you better than you can." An entire literature of homosexuality, very different from libertine narratives, appeared at the end of the 19th century: think of Oscar Wilde and Gide. It is the strategic return of a "same" will to truth.

Q: That's what is happening in fact for all minorities, women, youths, black Americans...

MF: Yes, of course. For a long time they tried to pin women to their sexuality. They were told for centuries: "You are nothing other than your sex." And this sex, doctors added, is fragile, almost always sick and always inducing sickness. "You are the sickness of man." And towards the 18th century this very ancient movement quickened and ended up as the pathologization of woman: the female body became the medical object par excellence. I will try later to write the history of this "gynecology" in the largest sense of the term.

But the feminist movements have accepted the challenge. Are we sex by nature? Well then, let it be but in its singularity, in its irreducible specificity. Let us draw the consequences from it and reinvent our own type of political, cultural and economic existence... Always the same movement: take off from this sexuality in which movements can be colonized, go beyond them in order to reach other affirmations.

Q: This strategy of double detente which you are describing, is it still a strategy of liberation in the classic sense? Or shouldn't it rather be said that to liberate sex is henceforth to hate it and go beyond it?

MF: A movement is taking shape today which seems to me to be reversing the trend of "always more sex," of "always more truth in sex," a trend which has doomed us for centuries: it's a matter, I don't say of rediscovering, but rather of fabricating other forms of pleasure, of relationships, coexistences, attachments, loves, intensities. I have the impression of hearing today an "anti-sex" grumbling (I'm not a prophet, at most a diagnostician), as if a thorough effort were being made to shake this great "sexography" which makes us decipher sex as the universal secret.

Q: Some symptoms for this diagnosis?

MF: Only one anecdote. A young writer, Hervé Guibert, had written some children's stories. No editor wanted them. He wrote another text, moreover very remarkable and apparently very "sexy." This was the condition for being heard and published (the book is *La Mort propagande*[1]). Read it: it seems to me to be the opposite of the sexographic writing that has been the rule in pornography and sometimes in good literature: to move progressively toward mentioning what is most unmentionable in sex. Hervé Guibert opens with the worst extreme—"You want us to speak about it, well then, let's go, and you will hear more about it than you ever have before"—and with this infamous material he constructs bodies, mirages, castles, fusions, acts of tenderness, races, intoxications... The entire heavy coefficient of sex has been volatilized. But this here is only one example of the "anti-sex" challenge, of which many other symptoms can be found. It is perhaps the end of this dreary dessert of sexuality, the end of the monarchy of sex.

Q: Provided that we aren't devoted or chained to sex as if to a fatal destiny. And since early childhood, as they say...

MF: Exactly. Look at what is happening as far as children are concerned. Some say: children's life is their sex life. From the bottle to puberty, that's all it is. Behind the desire to learn to read or the taste for comic strips, there is still and will always be sexuality. Well, are you sure that this type of discourse is actually liberating? Are you sure that it doesn't lock children into a sort of sexual insularity? And what after all if they just couldn't care less? If the liberty of not being an adult consisted exactly in not being enslaved to the law of sexuality, to its principles, to its commonplace, would it be so boring after all? If it were possible to have polymorphic relationships with things, people and bodies, wouldn't that be childhood? To reassure themselves, adults call this polymorphism perversity, coloring it thus with the monotonous monochrome of their own sexuality.

Q: Children are oppressed by the very ones who claim to liberate them?

MF: Read the book by René Scherer and Guy Hocquenghem[2]: it shows very well that the child has a flow of pleasure for which the "sex" grid is a veritable prison.

Q: Is this a paradox?

MF: This ensues from the idea that sexuality is fundamentally feared by power; it is without a doubt more a means through which power is exerted.

Q: Look at authoritarian states however. Can we say that there power is exerted not against but through sexuality?

MF: Two recent facts, apparently contradictory. About ten months ago, China began a campaign against children's masturbation, along exactly the same lines as that carried out in 18th century Europe (masturbation prevents work, causes blindness, leads to the degeneration of the species...). On the other hand, before the year is out, the Soviet Union is going to host a congress of psychoanalysts for the first time (the Soviet Union has to host them, since they have none of their own). Liberalization? A thaw on the side of the subconscious? Springtime of the Soviet libido against the moral bourgeoizification of the Chinese?

In Peking's antiquated stupidities and the Soviet Union's new curiosities, I see mainly a double recognition of the fact that, formulated and prohibited, spoken and forbidden, sexuality is a relay station which no modern system of power can do without. We should greatly fear socialism with a sexual face.

Q: In other words, power is no longer necessarily that which condemns and encloses?

MF: In general terms, I would say that the interdiction, the refusal, the prohibition, far from being essential forms of power, are only its limits: the frustrated or extreme forms of power. The relations of power are, above all, productive.

Q: This is a new idea compared with your previous books.

MF: If I wanted to pose and drape myself in a slightly fictive coherence, I would tell you that this has always been my problem: effects of power and the production of "truth." I have always felt ill at ease with this ideological notion which has been used so much in recent years. It has been used to explain errors or illusions, shaded representations—in short, everything that impedes the formation of true discourses. It has also been used to show the relationship between what goes on in peoples' heads and their place in the relations of production. In all, the economy of untruth. My problem is the politics of truth. I have taken a lot of time in realizing it.

Q: Why?

MF: For several reasons. First, because power in the West is what diplays itself the most, and thus what hides itself best. What we have called "political life" since the nineteenth century is (a bit like the court in the age of monarchy) the manner in which power gives itself over to representation. Power is neither there, nor is that how it functions. The relations of power are perhaps among the most hidden things in the social body.

On the other hand, since the 19th century, the critique of society has been essentially carried out, starting with the actual determining nature of the economy. Certainly a healthy reduction of "politics," but also with the tendency to neglect the relations of elementary power that could be constitutive of economic relations.

The third reason is the tendency, common to institutions, political parties, and an entire current of revolutionary thought and action, which consists in not seeing power in any other form than that of the state apparatus.

All of which leads, when one turns to individuals, to finding power only in their heads (under the form of representation, acceptation, or interiorization).

Q: And what did you want to do in the face of this?

MF: Four things: investigate what might be most hidden in power relations; anchor them in their economic infrastructures; trace them not only in their governmental forms but also in their infra-governmental or para-governmental ones; and recuperate them in their material play.

Q: At what point did you begin this type of study?

MF: If you want a bibliographical reference, it was in *Discipline and Punish*. But I would rather say that it began with a series of events and experiences since 1968 concerning psychiatry, delinquency, the schools, etc. I believe that these elements themselves would never have been able to take their direction and intensity if there had not been those two gigantic shadows of fascism and Stalinism behind them. If proletarian misery—this sub-existence—caused political thought of the nineteenth century to revolve around the economy, then these super-powers, fascism and Stalinism, induce political anxiety about our present-day societies.

Hence two problems. Power—how does it work? Is it enough that it imposes strong prohibitions in order to function effectively? And does it always move from above to below and from the center to the periphery?

Q: I saw this in *The History of Sexuality,* this shifting, this essential sliding. This time you made a clean break with the diffuse naturalism that haunts your previous books...

MF: What you call "naturalism" designates two things, I believe. A certain theory, the idea that underneath power with its acts of violence and its artifice we should be able to recuperate things themselves in their primitive vivacity: behind the asylum walls, the spontaneity of madness; through the penal system, the generous fever of delinquence; under the sexual interdiction, the freshness of desire. And also a certain aesthetic and moral choice: power is evil, it's ugly, poor, sterile, monotonous, dead; and what power is exercised upon is right, good, rich.

Q: Yes. And finally the theme common to the orthodox Marxist and to the New Left: "Under the cobblestones lies the beach."[3]

MF: If you like. There are moments when such simplifications are necessary. Such a dualism is provisionally useful to change the scenery from time to time and move from pro to contra.

Q: And then comes the time to stop, the moment of reflection and of regaining equilibrium?

MF: On the contrary. The moment of new mobility and displacement must follow. Because these reversals of pro to contra are quickly blocked, unable to do anything except repeat themselves and form what Jacques Rancière calls the "Leftist doxa." As soon as we repeat indefinitely the same refrain of the anti-repressive ditty, things remain in place—anyone can sing the tune, without anyone paying attention. This reversal of values and of truths, which I was speaking about a while ago, has been important to the extent that it does not stop with simple cheers (long live insanity, delinquency, sex), but it permits new strategies. You see, what often bothers me today, in fact, what really troubles me, is that all the work done in the past fifteen years or so, often under hardship and solitude, functions only for some as a sign of belonging on the "good side" of insanity, children, delinquency, sex.

Q: There is no good side?

MF: One must pass to the other side—the "good side"—but in order to extract oneself from these mechanisms which make two sides appear, in order to dissolve the false unity, the illusory "nature" of this other side with which we have taken sides. This is where the real work begins, that of the historian of the present.

Q: You already have defined yourself several times as an historian. What does it mean? Why "historian" and not "philosopher"?

MF: Under a form as naive as a child's tale, I will say that the question of philosophy has been for a long time: "In this world where all perishes, what doesn't pass away? Where are we, we who must die, in relation to that which doesn't?" It seems to me that, since the 19th century, philosophy has not ceased asking itself the same question: "What is happening right now, and what are we, we who are perhaps nothing more than what is happening at this moment?" Philosophy's question is the question of this present age which is ourselves. This is why philosophy is today entirely political and entirely historical. It is the politics immanent in history and the history indispensable for politics.

Q: But isn't there also a return today to the most classical, metaphysical kind of philosophy?

MF: I don't believe in any form of return. I would say only this, and only half-seriously. The thinking of the first Christian centuries would have had to answer the question: "What is actually going on today? What is this age in which we live? When and how will this promised return of God take place? What can we do with this intervening time which is superfluous? And what are we, we who are in this transition?

One could say that on this slope of history, where the revolution is supposed to hold back and has not yet come, we ask the same question: "Who are we, we who are superfluous in this age where what should happen is not happening?" All modern thought, like all politics, has been dominated by this question of revolution.

Q: Do you continue, as far as you are concerned, to raise this question of revolution and reflect upon it? Does it remain in your eyes the question par excellence?

MF: If politics has existed since the 19th century, it's because there was revolution. The current one is not a variant or a sector of that one. It's politics that always situates itself in relation to revolution. When Napoleon said, "The modern form of destiny is politics," he was only drawing the consequences from this truth, for he came after the revolution and before the eventual return of another one.

The return of revolution—that is surely our problem. It is certain that without its return, the question of Stalinism would be only an academic one— a mere problem of the organization of societies or of the validity of the Marxist scheme of things. But it's really quite another question concerning Stalinism. You know very well what it is: the very desirability of the revolution is the problem today.

Q: Do you want the revolution? Do you want something more than the simple ethical duty to struggle here and now, at the side of one or another group of mental patients and prisoners, oppressed and miserable?

MF: I have no answer. But I believe that to engage in politics—aside from party politics—is to try to know with the greatest possible honesty whether or not the revolution is desirable. It is in exploring this terrible molehill that politics runs the danger of caving in.

Q: If the revolution were no longer desirable, would politics remain what you say it is?

MF: No, I don't believe so. It would be necessary to invent another one or something which could be a substitute for it. We are perhaps living the end of politics. For it's true that politics is a field which was opened by the existence of the revolution, and if the question of revolution can no longer be raised in these terms, then politics risks disappearing.

Q: Let's return to your politics in *The History of Sexuality*. You say: "Where there is power, there is resistance." Are you not thus bringing back this nature which a while back you wanted to dismiss?

MF: I don't think so, because this resistance I am speaking of is not a substance. It is not anterior to the power which it opposes. It is coextensive with it and absolutely its contemporary.

Q: The reverse of power? That would come to the same thing. Always the cobblestones under the beach...

MF: It isn't that either. For if it were only that, it wouldn't resist. To resist, it would have to operate like power. As inventive, mobile and productive power. Like power, it would have to organize, coagulate, and solidify itself. Like power, it would have to come from "underneath" and distribute itself strategically.

Q: "Where there is power, there is resistance." It's almost a tautology, consequently...

MF: Absolutely. I am not positing a substance of resistance in the face of power. I am simply saying: as soon as there is a power relation, there is the possibility of resistance. We are never trapped by power: we can always modify its grip in determinate conditions and according to a precise strategy.

Q: Power and resistance...tactics and strategy...Why this stock of military metaphors? Do you think that power from now on must be thought of in the form of war?

MF: For the moment, I really don't know. One thing seems certain to me; it is that in order to analyze the relationships of power, at present we have only two models at our disposal: the one proposed by law (power as law, interdiction, the institution) and the military or strategic model in terms of power relations. The first has been much used and has proven its inadequate character, I believe. We know very well that law does not describe power.
I know that the other model is also much discussed. But we stop with words: we use ready-made ideas or metaphors ("war of all against all," "struggle for life"), or again formal schemata (strategies are very much in fashion among certain sociologists or economists, especially Americans). I believe that this analysis of power relations should be tightened up.

Q: This military conception of power relations, was it already used by the Marxists?

MF: What strikes me about Marxist analyses is that it's always a question of "class struggle," but less attention is paid to one word in this expression, namely "struggle." Here again qualifications must be made. The greatest of the Marxists (starting with Marx himself) insisted a great deal on "military" problems (the army as an instrument of the state, armed insurrection, revolutionary war). But when they speak of "class struggle" as the mainspring of history, they worry especially about defining this class, where it is situated, who it encompasses, but never concretely about the nature of the struggle. With one exception, however: Marx's own non-theoretical, historical texts, which are better in this regard.

Q: Do you think that your book can fill such a gap?

MF: I don't make any such claim. In a general way, I think that intellectuals—if this category exists, if it should exist at all, which is not certain nor perhaps even desirable—are renouncing their old prophetic function.

And by that I'm not thinking only of their claim to say what is going to happen, but also of the legislative function which they've aspired to for so long: "See what must be done, see what is good, follow me. In the turmoil you're all in, here is the pivotal point, it's where I am." The Greek sage, the Jewish prophet, and the Roman legislator are still models that haunt those who practice today the profession of speaking and writing. I dream of the intellectual destroyer of evidence and universalities, the one who, in the inertias and constraints of the present, locates and marks the weak points, the openings, the lines of power, who incessantly displaces himself, doesn't know exactly where he is heading nor what he'll think tomorrow because he is too attentive to the present; who, in passing, contributes the raising of the question of knowing whether the revolution is worth it, and what kind (I mean what kind of revolution and what effort), it being understood that they alone who are willing to risk their lives to bring it about can answer the question.

As for all the questions of classification and programming that we are asked: "Are you a Marxist?" "What would you do if you had power?" "Who are your allies and where are your sympathies?"—these are truly secondary questions compared with the one that I have just indicated. That is the question of today.

Translated by Dudley M. Marchi

---

1 Hervé Guilbert, *La Mort propagande* (Paris: R. Deforges, 1977).

2 René Schérer and Guy Hocquenghem, *Co-ire* (Paris: Recherches, 1976).

3 A well-known motto of May '68.

29

THE EYE OF POWER

JEAN-PIERRE BAROU: Jeremy Bentham's *Panopticon* is a work published at the end of the 18th century that has remained largely unknown yet you've called it "an event in the history of the human mind," "a revolutionary discovery in the order of politics." And you described Bentham, an English jurist, as "the Fourrier of a police society." This is all very intriguing for us, but as for you, how did you fall upon the *Panopticon?*

MICHEL FOUCAULT: It was while I was studying the origins of clinical medicine. I was considering a study on hospital architecture in the second half of the 18th century, when a major reform of medical institutions was under way. I wanted to know how medical observation, the observing gaze of the clinician became institutionalized; how it was effectively inscribed in social space; how the new hospital structure was at one and the same time the effect of a new type of gaze and its support. And I came to realize, while examining the different architectural projects that resulted from the second fire at the Hotel-Dieu in 1772, to what extent the problem of the total visibility of bodies, of individuals and things, under a system of centralized surveillance, had been one of the most constant guiding principles. In the case of hospitals, this problem raised yet another difficulty: one had to avoid contacts, contagions, physical proximity and overcrowding, while at the same time insuring proper ventilation and circulation of air: the problem was to divide space and leave it open, in order to insure a form of surveillance at once global and individualizing, while carefully separating the individuals under observation. For quite some time I believed these problems to be specific to 18th century medicine and its beliefs.

Later, while studying the problems of the penal system, I became aware that all the major projects for the reorganization of prisons (projects that date, incidentally, from slightly later, from the first half of the 19th century) took up the same theme, but almost always in reference to Jeremy Bentham. There were few texts or projects concerning prisons where Bentham's "device," the "panopticon," did not come up.

The principle is simple: on the periphery runs a building in the shape of a ring; in the center of the ring stands a tower pierced by large windows that face the inside wall of the ring; the outer building is divided into cells, each of which crosses the whole thickness of the building. These cells have two windows: one corresponding to the tower's windows, facing into the cell; the other, facing outside, thereby enabling light to traverse the entire cell. One then needs only to place a guard in the central tower, and to lock into each cell a mad, sick or condemned person, a worker or a pupil. Owing to the back-lighting effect, one can make out the little captive silhouettes in the ring of the cells. In short, the principle of the dungeon is reversed: bright light and the guard's observing gaze are found to impound better than the shadows which in fact provided a sort of protection.

One is already struck by the fact that the same concern existed well before Bentham. It seems that one of the first models of this system of isolating visibility was instituted in the dormitories of the Military Academy of Paris in 1751. Each of the pupils was assigned a glassed-in cell where he could be observed all night long without any possible contact with his fellow students or even the domestic help. In addition there was a very complicated mechanism whose sole purpose was to enable the barber to comb each of the cadets without touching him physically: the pupil's head extended from a kind of hatch while his body remained on the other side of the glass partition, allowing a clear observation of the entire process. Bentham told how it was his brother who first had the idea of the panopticon while visiting the Military Academy. In any case, the theme clearly was in the air at this time. Claude-Nicolas Ledoux's constructions, most notably the salt-plant he constructed at Arc-et-Senans, tended to provide the same effect of visibility, but with one important addition, namely, that there be a central observation-point that would serve as the seat of the exercise of power as well as the place for recording observations and acquiring knowledge. At all events, while the idea of the panopticon antidates Bentham, it was he who actually formulated it, and baptised it. The very word *panopticon* can be considered crucial, for it designates a comprehensive principle. Bentham's conception was therefore more than a mere architectural figure meant to resolve a specific problem, such as that raised by prisons or schools or hospitals. Bentham himself proclaims the panopticon to be a "revolutionary discovery," that it was "Columbus' egg." And indeed it was Bentham who proposed a solution to the problem faced by doctors, penologists, industrialists and educators: he invented a technology of power capable of resolving the problems of surveillance. It is important to note that Bentham considered his optical procedure to be *the* major innovation needed for the easy and effective exercise of power. As a matter of fact, this discovery has been widely employed since the end of the 18th century. But the procedures of power resorted to in modern societies are far more numerous and diverse and rich. It would be false to say that the principle of visibility has dominated the whole technology of power since the 19th century.

MICHELLE PERROT: So the key was architecture. What about architecture as a mode of political organization then? For everything is spatial, not only mentally but also materially, in this 18th century current of thought.

FOUCAULT: In my opinion, it is at the end of the 18th century that architecture begins to concern itself closely with problems of population, health and urbanism. Before that time, the art of building responded firstly to the need to make power, divinity and might manifest. The palace and the church were the two major architectural forms, to which we must add fortresses. Architecture manifested might, the Sovereign, God. It developed for a long while according to these requirements. Now, at the end of the 18th century, new problems emerge: the arrangement of space is to be used for political and economic ends.

A specific type of architecture arises during this period. Philippe Ariès has written some very important things on the subject of the house which, according to him, remains an undifferentiated space until the 18th century. There are rooms that can be used interchangeably for sleeping, eating or receiving guests. Then, little by little, space becomes specified and functional. A perfect illustration can be found in the development of working-class housing projects between the 1830s and 1870s. The working-class family is to be fixed; by assigning it a living space (a room that serves as kitchen and dining room), the parents' bedroom (the place of procreation), and the children's bedroom, one prescribes a form of morality for the family. Sometimes, in the most favorable of situations, there will be a boy's room and a girl's room. A whole "history of *spaces*" could be written, that would be at the same time a "history of the powers" (both these terms in the plural), from the great strategies of geopolitics to the little tactics of housing, institutional architecture, from the classroom to the hospital organization, by way of all the political and economic implantations. It is surprising how long it took for the problem of spaces to be viewed as an historical and political problem. For a long time space was either referred to "nature"—to what was given, the first determining factor—or to "physical geography"; it was referred to a kind of "prehistoric" stratum. Or it was conceived as the residential site or the field of expansion of a people, a culture, a language or a State. In short, space was analyzed either as the *ground* on which people lived or the area in which they existed; all that mattered were *foundations* and *frontiers*. It took the work of historians like Marc Bloch and Fernand Braudel to develop a history of rural and maritime spaces. This work must be expanded, and we must cease to think that space merely predetermines a particular history which in return reorganizes it through its own sedimentation. Spatial arrangements are also political and economic forms to be studied in detail.

I will mention only one of the reasons why a certain neglect regarding spaces has prevailed for so long, and this concerns the discourse of philosophers. At the precise moment when a serious-minded politics of spaces was developing (at the end of the 18th century), the new achievements of theoretical and experimental physics removed philosophy's privileged right to speak about the world, the *cosmos,* space, be it finite or infinite. This double investment of space by political technology and a scientific practice forced philosophy into a problematic of time. From Kant on it is time that occupies the philosopher's reflection, in Hegel, Bergson and Heidegger for example. Along with this occurs a correlative disqualification of space in human understanding. I recall some ten years ago discussing these problems of a politics of spaces and someone remarked that it was very reactionary to insist so much on space, that life and progress must be measured in terms of time. I must add that this reproach came from a psychologist: here we see the truth and the shame of 19th century philosophy.

PERROT: We might perhaps mention in passing the importance of the notion of sexuality in this context. You pointed this out in the case of surveillance of cadets and, there again, the same problem surfaces with respect to the working-class family. No doubt the notion of sexuality is fundamental.

FOUCAULT: Absolutely. In these themes of surveillance, and especially school surveillance, it seems that control of sexuality becomes directly inscribed in the architectural design. In the case of the Military Academy, the struggle against homosexuality and masturbation is written on the walls.

PERROT: Talking about architecture, doesn't it strike you that people like doctors, whose social involvement is considerable at the end of the 18th century, played in a sense the role of spatial "arrangers"? This is when social hygiene is born; in the name of cleanliness and health, the location of people is controlled. And with the rebirth of Hippocratic medicine, doctors are among those most sensitized to problems of environment, milieu, temperature, etc., which were already givens in John Howard's investigation into the state of prisons.[1]

FOUCAULT: Doctors were indeed, in part, specialists of space. They raised four fundamental problems: the problem of locations (regional climates, the nature of the soil, humidity and aridity: they applied the term "constitution" to this combination of local determinants and seasonal variations that at a given moment favor a particular type of illness); the problem of coexistence (the coexistence of people among themselves, questions the density or proximity; of people and things, water, sewage and ventilation; or the coexistence of humans and animals, slaughter-houses and cattle-sheds; and finally, the coexistence of the living and the dead, involving cemeteries); the problem of housing (habitat, urbanism); and the problem of displacements (the migration of people, the spreading of illnesses). Doctors and military men were the prime administrators of collective space. But the military thought essentially in terms of the space of "military campaigns" (and thus of "passages") and of fortifications. Doctors, for their part, thought above all in terms of the space of housing and cities. I cannot recall who it was that sought the major stages of sociological thought in Montesquieu and Auguste Comte, which is a very uninformed approach. For sociological knowledge is formed, rather, within practices such as that of doctors. In this context Guépin, at the very beginning of the 19th century, wrote a marvelous study of the city of Nantes.

The intervention of doctors was indeed of such crucial importance at this particular time because they had to deal with a whole range of new political and economic problems, which accounts for the importance of demographic facts.

PERROT: A prominent feature of Bentham's thinking is the question of numbers. He keeps making the claim that he had solved the problem of how to control a great number of people with just a few.

FOUCAULT: Like his contemporaries, Bentham encountered the problem of the accumulation of people. But whereas economists posed the problem in terms of wealth (population-as-wealth, since it is manpower, the source of economic activity and consumption; and population-as-poverty, when it is in excess or idle), Bentham considered it in terms of power: population as the target of the relations of domination. I think it could be said that the power mechanisms at work even in an administrative monarchy as developed as it was in France, were full of holes: it was a global system, but erratic and uneven woth little hold on details, that either exercised its controls over established groups or resorted to the method of examplary intervention (as is clear in the fiscal system or criminal justice), and therefore had a low "resolution," as they say in photography. Power was incapable of practicing an exhaustive and individuating analysis of the social body. Now, the economic mutations of the 18th century made it necessary for the effects of power to circulate through finer and finer channels, taking hold of individuals, their bodies, their gestures, every one of their daily activities. Power was to be as effectively exercised over a multiplicity of people as if it were over one individual.

PERROT: The demographic upswings of the 18th century undoubtedly contributed to the development of such a form of power.

BAROU: Is it surprising then to learn that the French Revolution, through people like La Fayette, favorably welcomed the project of the panopticon? He actually helped Bentham become a "Citizen of France" in 1791.

FOUCAULT: To my mind Bentham is the complement to Rousseau. For what is in fact the Rousseauian dream that captivated the revolutionary era, if not that of a transparent society, at once visible and legible in every one of its parts, a society where there were no longer any zones of obscurity established by the privileges of royal power or the prerogatives of a given body, spaces of disorder: the dream was that each man, from his own position, could see the whole of society, that hearts should communicate directly and observations carried out unobstructed, and that opinion reigned supreme over each. Jean Starobinski made some very interesting comments on this subject in *Transparency and Obstruction* and in *The Emblem of Reason*.[2] Bentham is at once close to this Rousseauian notion, and the complete opposite. He poses the problem of visibility, but in his conception visibility is organized completely around a dominating and observing gaze. He initiates the project of a universal visibility that would function on behalf of a rigorous and meticulous form of power. In this sense the technical idea of the exercise of an "all-seeing" power, which is Bentham's obsession, is connected to the great Rousseauian theme, which is in a sense the Revolution's lyricism: the two themes interlock perfectly—Bentham's obsession and Rousseau's lyricism.

PERROT: What about this quote from the *Panopticon:* "Each comrade becomes an overseer"?

FOUCAULT: Rousseau would probably have said the opposite: each overseer must be a comrade. In *L'Emile,* for example, Emile's tutor is an overseer, but he must also be a friend.

BAROU: The French Revolution did not interpret Bentham's project as we do today; it even perceived humanitarian aims in this project.

FOUCAULT: Precisely. When the Revolution examines the possibilities of a new form of justice, it asks what is to be its mainspring. The answer is public opinion. The Revolution's problem once again was not just that wrongdoers be punished, but that they could not even act improperly, being submerged in a field of total visibility where the opinion of one's fellow men, their observing gaze, and their discourse would prevent one from doing evil or detrimental deeds. This idea is ever present in the texts written during the Revolution.

PERROT: The immediate context also played a part of the Revolution's adoption of the Panopticon; the problem of prisons was then a high priority. Since 1770, in England as in France, there was a strong sense of uneasiness surrounding this issue, which is clear in Howard's investigation of prisons. Hospitals and prisons are two major topics of discussion in the Parisian salons and the enlightened circles. It was viewed as scandalous that prisons had become what they were: schools of crime and vice so lacking in decent hygiene as to seriously threaten one's chances of survival. Doctors began to talk about the degeneration of bodies in such places. With the Revolution, the bourgeoisie in turn undertook an investigation on a European scale. One Duquesnoy was entrusted with the task of reporting on the "establishments of humanity," a term designating hospitals as well as prisons.

FOUCAULT: A definite fear prevailed during the second half of the 18th century: the fear of a dark space, of a screen of obscurity obstructing the clear visibility of things, of people and of truths. It became imperative to dissolve the elements of darkness that blocked the light, demolish all of society's somber spaces, those dark rooms where arbitrary political rule foments, as well as the whims of a monarch, religious superstitions, tyrants' and priests' plots, illusions of ignorance and epidemics. From even before the Revolution, castles, hospitals, charnel houses, prisons and convents gave rise to a sometimes over-valued distrust or hatred; it was felt that the new political and moral order could not be instituted until such places were abolished. During the period of the Revolution,

Gothic novels developed a whole fanciful account of the high protective walls, darkness, the hide-outs and dungeons that shield, in a significant complicity, robbers and aristocrats, monks and traitors. Ann Radcliffe's landscapes are always mountains, forests, caverns, mined castles, frighteningly dark silent convents. Now, these imaginary spaces are like the negative of the transparency and visibility that the new order hoped to establish. The reign of "opinion" so frequently invoked during this period is a way of exercising power on the sole basis of things being known and people seen by a kind of immediate observing gaze that is at once collective and anonymous. A form of power whose *primum mobile* is public opinion could hardly tolerate zones of darkness. Bentham's project aroused such a great interest because it provided the formula, applicable in a wide variety of domains, for a form of "power through transparency," a subjugation through a process of "illumination." The Panopticon to a certain extent was the form of the "castle" (a dungeon surrounded by high protective walls) to paradoxically create a space of exact legibility.

BAROU: The Age of Enlightenment would also have liked to abolish the somber areas of darkness within man.

FOUCAULT: Absolutely.

PERROT: One is also struck by the techniques of power used within the Panopticon itself. Essentially there is the observing gaze, but also speech, for there are those well known "tin tubes" that connect the chief inspector to each of the cells in which, according to Bentham, not one prisoner but small groups of prisoners are confined. What is very striking in Bentham's text is the importance attributed to dissuasion: "It is necessary for the inmate," he writes, "to be constantly be under the eyes of an inspector; this prevents the capacity of any wrong doing, even the wish to commit wrong." This is one of the major preoccupations of the Revolution: to keep people from doing evil, and even wanting to: not being able and not wanting to do evil.

FOUCAULT: Two different things are involved here: the observing gaze, the act of observation on the one hand, and internalization on the other. And isn't this the problem of the cost of power? Power is only exercised at a cost. There is obviously the economic cost, which Bentham discusses: "How many guardians will the Panopticon need? How much will the machine cost?" But there is also the specifically political cost. If power is exercised too violently, there is the risk of provoking revolts; or if the intervention is too discontinuous, there could be resistance and disobedience, phenomena of great political cost. This is how monarchic power operated. The judicial apparatus, for example, arrested only a ridiculously small proportion of criminals; from which it was deduced that punishment had to be spectacular so as to instill fear in those present. Therefore monarchic power was violent and resorted to glaring examples to insure a continuous mode of operation. To this conception of power the new theoreticians of the 18th century retorted: this power was too costly in proportion to its results. These great expenditures of violence only had exemplary value; multiplying the violence, one had to multiply the revolts.

PERROT: This is what happened during the gallows riots

FOUCAULT: On the other hand there is a form of surveillance which requires very little in the way of expenditures. No need for arms, physical violence, or material restraints. Just an observing gaze that each individual feels weighing on him, and ends up internalizing to the point that he is his own overseer: everyone in this way exercises surveillance over and against himself. An ingenious formula: a continuous form of power at practically no cost! When Bentham realizes what he has discovered, he calls it as a "Copernican revolution in the order of politics," a formula that is exactly the reverse of monarchic power. And it is true that among the techniques of power developed in modern times, observation has had a major importance but, as I said earlier, it is far from being the only or even the principal system.

PERROT: It seems that Bentham envisaged the problem of power essentially in terms of small groups of individuals. Why? Did he consider that the part already is the whole, that if one succeeds at the level of small groups this can be extended to society as a whole? Or is it that society as a whole and power on that scale had not yet been grasped in their specificity then?

FOUCAULT: The whole problem for this form of power is to avoid stumbling blocks and obstructions presented in the Ancien Regime by the established bodies, and the privileges of certain categories, the clergy, the trade guilds, magistrature. The bourgeoisie was perfectly aware that a new legislation or constitution won't be enough to guarantee its hegemony. A new technology had to be invented that would insure the free-flow of the effects of power within the entire social body down to its most minute of levels. And it is by such means that the bourgeoisie not only achieved a political revolution, but also managed to establish a form of social hegemony which it has never relinquished since. This is why all of these inventions were so important, and why Bentham was surely among the most exemplary inventors of power technologies.

BAROU: Yet it is not immediately clear who could profit from the organized space that Bentham advocated, even for those who occupied or visited the central tower. Bentham's proposals confronts us with an infernal world from which there is no escape, neither for those who are being watched, nor for those who are observing.

FOUCAULT: This is perhaps the most diabolical aspect of the idea and of all the applications it brought about. Power here isn't totally entrusted to someone who would exercise it alone, over others, in an absolute fashion;

rather this is a machine in which everyone is caught, those who exercise the power as well as those who are subjected to it. It seems to me this is the major characteristic of the new societies established in the 19th century. Power is no longer substantially identified with a particular individual who possesses it or exercises it by right of birth. It becomes a machinery that no one controls. Obviously everyone in this machine occupies a different position; some are more important than others and enable those who occupy them to produce effects of supremacy, insuring a class domination to the extent that they dissociate political power from individual power.

PERROT: The way the Panopticon operates is somewhat contradictory from this point of view. There is the principal inspector who keeps watch over the prisoners from a central tower. But he also watches his subordinates as well, the guards, in whom he has no confidence. He often speaks rather disparagingly of them, even though they are supposed to be his auxiliaries. Doesn't this constitute an aristocratic form of thought? Actually supervision was a crucial problem for industrial society. Finding foremen and technicians capable of regimenting and supervising the factories was no easy task for the bosses.

FOUCAULT: This was an enormous problem, as is clear in the case of the 18th century army when it was necessary to create a corps of NCO's competent enough to marshal the troops effectively during often very difficult tactical maneuvers involving the rifle, which had just been perfected. Movements, displacements and formations of troops, as well as marches required a disciplinary personnel of that kind. Workplaces posed the same problem in their own right, as did school, with its head masters, teachers, and disciplinarians. The Church was then one of the rare social bodies where such competent small corps of disciplinarians existed. The not too literate, but not too ignorant monk and the vicar joined forces against children to school hundreds of thousands of children. The State only devised comparable cadres much later, as for hospitals. Until recently, the majority of their staff were nuns.

PERROT: Nuns played a considerable part in women's work. In the 19th century the well-known residential establishments housed a female work-force supervised by nuns specially trained to maintain factory discipline.
The *Panopticon* is also preoccupied with these issues as is apparent when it deals with the chief inspector's surveillance of his staff and his surveillance of everyone through the control tower's windows, an uninterrupted succession of observations that call to mind the dictum: "Each comrade becomes a guardian." One has the vertiginous sense of being in the presence of an invention no longer mastered by its creator. Yet it is Bentham who begins by relying on a unique, central form of power. Who did he mean to put in the tower? The eye of God? Yet God is barely present in his texts, for religion only plays a utilitarian part. So who is in the tower? In the last analysis it must be admitted that Bentham himself is not too clear about who should be entrusted with this power.

FOUCAULT: He cannot entrust it to anyone in that no person can, or may, be a source of power and justice as the king was in the former system. In the theory of the monarchy it was implicit that one owed allegiance to the king. By his very existence, willed by God, the king was the source of justice, law and authority. Power in the person of the king could only be good; a bad king was equivalent to an historical accident or to a punishment inflicted by the absolutely good sovereign, God. On the other hand, no single individual could be trusted if power and is as a complex machine where it's an individual's place, and not his nature, that is the determining factor. If the machine were such that someone could stand outside it or had the sole responsibility for its management, power would be identified with that person and one would be back to the monarchic system of power. In the *Panopticon,* everyone is watched, according to his position within the system, by all or by certain of the others. Here we have an apparatus of total and mobile distrust, since there is no absolute point. A certain sum of malevolence was required for the perfection of surveillance.

BAROU: A diabolical machine, as you said, that spares no one. Could it be the image of power today? But, according to you, how did we get to this point? What sort of "will" was involved, and whose?

FOUCAULT: The question of power is greatly impoverished if posed solely in terms of legislation, or the constitution, or the state, the state apparatus. Power is much more complicated, much more dense and diffuse than a set of laws or a state apparatus. One cannot understand the development of the productive forces of capitalism, nor even conceive of their technological development, if the apparatuses of power are not taken into consideration. For example, take the case of the division of labor in the major work-places of the 18th century; how would this distribution of tasks have been achieved had there not been a new distribution of power on the very level of the productive forces? Likewise for the modern army: it was not enough to possess new types of armaments or another style of recruitment: this new form of power called discipline was also required, with its hierarchies, its commands, its inspections, its exercises, its conditionings, its drills. Without this the army such as it functioned since the 18th century would never have existed.

BAROU: And yet is there nevertheless an individual or a group of individuals who provide the impetus for this disciplinary system?

FOUCAULT: A distinction must be made. It is clear in the organization of an army or a work-place, or some other institution that the network of power adopts a pyramidal form. Therefore there is a summit. But even in a simple case, this "summit" is not the "source" or the "principle" from which the totality of power derives as from a focal point (such as the monarch's throne). The summit and the lower elements of the hierarchy stand in a relationship of reciprocal support and conditioning: they "hold together" (power as a mutual and indefinite "extortion"). But if you ask me whether the new technology of power has its historical roots in a specific individual or in a group who would decide to apply this technology in their own interests and in order to shape the social body according to their designs, then I would have to say no. These tactics were invented and organized according to local conditions and particular urgencies. They were designed piece by piece before a class strategy solidified them into vast and coherent ensembles. It should also be noted that these ensembles do not consist in a homogenization but rather in a complex interplay of support among the different mechanisms of power which nonetheless remain quite specific. Thus where children are concerned at the present time the interplay between the family, medicine, psychiatry, psychoanalysis, the school, and the judicial system does not homogenize these different agencies, but establishes connections, cross-references, complementarities and determinations that presuppose that each one of them maintains, to a certain extent, its own modalities.

PERROT: You have opposed the idea of power as a superstructure, but not the idea that this power is in a sense consubstantial to the development of the productive forces, of which it is a part.

FOUCAULT: Correct. And power is constantly being transformed along with the productive forces. The Panopticon was a utopian program. But already in Bentham's time the theme of a spatializing, observing, immobilizing—i.e. disciplinary, power, was in fact outflanked by much more subtle mechanisms allowing for the regulation of population phenomena, the control of their oscillations, and compensation for their irregularities. Bentham's thought is "archaic" insofar as he attaches so much importance to observation; he is completely modern when he stresses the importance of the techniques of power in our societies.

PERROT: There is no global State in Bentham; rather the emergence of micro-societies, microcosms.

BAROU: Is the distribution of forces in the Panopticon attributable to industrial society, or should we consider capitalist society to be responsible for this form of power?

FOUCAULT: Industrial or capitalist society? I don't know what to answer, except perhaps that these forms of power are also present in socialist societies: the transference was immediate. But on this point, I would rather have the historian among us speak.

PERROT: It is true that the accumulation of capital was accomplished by an industrial technology and by the erection of an entire apparatus of power. But it is also true that a similar process can be found in the Soviet socialist society. In certain respects, Stalinism also corresponds to a period of accumulation of capital and to the establishment of a strong form of power.

BAROU: The notion of profit comes to mind here—how valuable some can find Bentham's inhuman machine.

FOUCAULT: Obviously! We would have to share the rather naive optimism of 19th century "dandies" to think that the bourgeoisie is stupid. On the contrary, we must acknowledge its master strokes, among which, precisely, there is the fact that it succeeded in constructing machines of power allowing circuits of profit, which in turn reinforced and modified the mechanisms mostly operated through capital levies and expenditures, drained itself. Bourgeois power perpetuates itself not by conservation, but by successive transformations, which accounts for the fact that its arrangement is not inscribed within history as the feudal arrangement is. This both accounts for its precariousness and its inventive resiliency. And it explains, finally, how the possibility of its downfall as well as the possibility of Revolution have been an intimate part of its history from the beginning.

PERROT: Bentham assigns an important place to the question of work, and keeps coming back to it.

FOUCAULT: This is due to the fact that the techniques of power were invented to meet the demands of production, in the largest sense of the term (including the "production" of a destruction, as in the army).

BAROU: When you speak of "work" in your books, this rarely refers to productive work...

FOUCAULT: This is because I have been mainly dealing with people situated outside the circuits of productive labor: the mad, the sick, prisoners, and now children. For them, work, such as they are supposed to accomplish it, is mostly valued for its disciplinary effects.

BAROU: Isn't work always a form of drill (*dressage*)?

FOUCAULT: Of course, the triple function of work is always present: the productive function, the symbolic function and the training, or disciplinary function. The productive function is near zero for the categories with which I am concerned, whereas the symbolic and disciplinary functions are quite important. But in most instances the three components coexist.

PERROT: In any case, Bentham strikes me as very self-confident in the penetrating power of the gaze. One feels in fact that he doesn't fully appreciate the degree of opacity and resistance of the material to be corrected and reintegrated into society, namely the prisoners. Doesn't Bentham's *Panopticon* share, to a certain extent, in the illusion of power?

FOUCAULT: It is the illusion shared by practically all of the 18th-century reformers who invested public opinion with considerable power. Public opinion had to be good since it was the immediate conscience of the entire social body; they really believed people would become virtuous owing to their being observed. For them, public opinion represented a spontaneous re-actualization of the social contract. They failed to recognize the real conditions of public opinion, the "media," i.e. a materiality caught in the mechanisms of economy and power in the forms of the press, publishing, and then films and television.

PERROT: When you say that they disregarded the media, you mean they failed to appreciate their importance.

FOUCAULT: They also failed to understand that the media would necessarily be controlled by economic and political interests. They did not perceive the material and economic components of public opinion. They thought that public opinion would be just by its very nature, that it would spread on its own accord, and provide a kind of democratic surveillance. It was essentially journalism—a crucial innovation of the 19th century—that manifested the utopian characteristics of this entire politics of the gaze.

PERROT: Thinkers generally miscalculate the difficulties they will encounter in trying to make their system take effect; they are not aware that there will always be loopholes and that resistances will always play a part. In the domain of prisons, inmates have not been passive; and yet Bentham leads us to believe quite the opposite. Penal discourse itself unfolds as if it concerned no one in particular, except perhaps a tabula rasa in the form of subjects to be rehabilitated and then returned to the circuits of production. In reality there is a material, the inmates, who resist in a formidable manner. The same could also be said of Taylorism, the extraordinary invention of an engineer who wanted to fight loafing, everything that slows downs production. But we might finally ask whether Taylorism ever really worked?

FOUCAULT: Another element does indeed make Bentham's project unreal: people's effective capacity to resist, studied so carefully by you, Michelle Perrot. How did people in workshops and housing projects resist the system of continual surveillance and recording of their activities? Were they aware of the compulsive, subjugating, unbearable nature of this surveillance, or did they accept it as natural? In short, were there revolts against the observing gaze of power?

PERROT: Yes, there were. The repugnance workers had to living in housing projects is well-documented. These projects were failures for quite a long while, as was the compulsory distribution of time, also present throughout the *Panopticon.* The factory and its time schedules aroused a passive resistance; the workers' simply stayed home. Witness the extraordinary story of the 19th century

"Holy Monday," a weekly break invented by the workers. There were multiple forms of resistance to the industrial system, so many, in fact, that in the beginning management had to back off. Another example is found in the systems of micro-powers which were not instituted immediately either. This type of surveillance and supervision was first of all developed in the mechanized sectors composed mainly of women and children, hence of people accustomed to obeying; women obeying husbands and children their parents. But in the "male" sectors such as the iron-works, the situation was quite different. Management did not succeed in installing its surveillance system right away: during the first half of the 19th century it had to delegate its powers; it worked out contracts with the teams of workers through the foremen, who were often the most qualified workers or those with most seniority. A veritable counter-power developed among the professional workers, which sometimes had two facets: one directed against the management, in defense of the workers' community, and the other against the workers themselves insofar as the foreman oppressed his apprentices and comrades. The workers' forms of counterpower continued to exist until management were able to mechanize the functions that escaped their control; it was then able to abolish the skilled workers' power. There are numerous examples of this: in the rolling-mills the shop steward had the means at his disposal to resist the boss until the time when semi-automated machines were installed. Thermal control, for instance, replaced the worker's mill-hand. It became possible to determine whether the material was at the right temperature simply by glancing at a thermometer.

FOUCAULT: This being the case, one must analyze the constellation of resistances to the Panopticon in terms of tactics and strategies and bear in mind that each offensive on one level serves to support a counter-offensive on another level. The analysis of power-mechanisms does not seek to demonstrate that power is both anonymous and always victorious. Rather it was a matter of locating the positions and the modes of action of everyone involved as well as the various possibilities for resisting and counter-attacks on either side.

BAROU: Of battles, actions and reactions, offensives and counter-offensives, you talk like a strategist. Are resistances to power essentially physical in nature according to you? What then becomes of the content of the struggles and the aspirations they manifest?

FOUCAULT: This indeed is a very important theoretical and methodological question. One thing strikes me in particular: certain political discourses make constant use of a vocabulary of the relations of forces. "Struggle" is a word that comes up most frequently. Now, it seems to me that people sometimes refuse to see the consequences of such a vocabulary or even to consider the problem it raises: namely, whether or not one should analyze these "struggles" in terms of the vicissitudes of a war, decipher them according to a strategical, tactical grid? Is the relationship of forces in the order of politics a relationship of war? I personally am not prepared to respond categorically with a yes or a no. It only seems to me at this point that the pure and simple affirmation of a "struggle" cannot be viewed as a final explanation in an analysis of power relations. This theme of the struggle is only operational if one concretely establishes in each case who is struggling, for what reasons, how the struggle is developing, in what locations, with what instruments and according to what kind of rationality. In other words, if one wishes to take seriously the assertion that struggle is at the core of the relations of power, one should realize that the good, old "logic" of contradictions is no longer sufficient to account for the real processes involved.

PERROT: Put another way, and getting back to the *Panopticon,* Bentham not only projects a utopian society but also describes an existing society.

FOUCAULT: He describes, in the utopian form of a general system, particular mechanisms that really exist.

PERROT: Then does it make sense for the inmates to take over the observation tower?

FOUCAULT: Yes, provided that this is not the end of the operation. Do you believe that things would be much better if the inmates seized control of the Panopticon and occupied the tower, rather than the guards?

Translated by Mark Seem

---

[1] John Howard made the results of this investigation public in his study: *The State of the Prisons in England and Wales, with Preliminary Observations and an Account of some Foreign Prisons and Hospitals,* 1777.

[2] Jean Starobinski, *Transparency and Obstruction.* (Chicago: University of Chicago Press, 1988); *The Emblem of Reason.* (MIT Press, 1988).

30

THE ANXIETY OF JUDGING

JEAN LAPLANCHE: The death penalty is absolute, in the sense that it abolishes the criminal at the same time as the crime.[1] Yet we no longer have the theological certainty, the blind faith, that would authorize us to pronounce such a penalty. For me it would be enough to know that, out of a thousand people condemned to death there was a single innocent, to make the abolition of the death penalty essential. When the court makes a mistake, there's no way to make reparations, since its "object"—the condemned man—no longer exists. I am therefore personally and unambiguously in favor of the suppression of the death penalty.

That said, my article was born of a disturbing astonishment. I perceived that in this great debate there was a tacit agreement to refer only to utilitarian arguments. To me that was particularly shocking on the part of people who, claiming to be mostly on the left, consider themselves partisans of the abolition of the death penalty. Before the deluge of statistics "showing" that the death penalty doesn't discourage crime and that it has no dissuasive power, I asked myself: how can something so serious be discussed only from the point of view of the fear it provokes, even if it is meant to show that the latter is ineffective? And if other statistics were to "demonstrate" that the penalty is dissuasive? Your conviction wouldn't change a bit.

ROBERT BADINTER: In your article you alluded to the role of the defense in the jury trial and you reproach me for using "utilitarian" arguments. There's much to say about that. But, before everything, I must make clear that for me a plea for the defense is dead the very moment it's uttered. It's an action, not a reflection. It can't be dissociated from the trial of which it is part. I had a stenographer record all the debates in Patrick Henry's trial. I thought, like everyone, that it was going to end with his death sentence. I wanted—and this will not surprise Michel Foucault—the debates to remain, as an historic document. Had Henry been condemned to death, I would have published this text immediately.

MICHEL FOUCAULT: You just said something very important: no one really knows what happens in the course of a trial. Which is surprising if nothing else, insofar as it's a public procedure, in principle. Because of the distrust of the secret and the written word—which were the two principles of penal justice under the monarchy—our trials since 1794 have supposedly been oral and public. The indictments of the prosecution are only preparatory documents. All must be played out in a theater with the public supposedly present. Yet, concretely, only fifty people, some journalists, a hurried judge, and an overwhelmed jury participate. There is no doubt that in France justice is a secret. And, after the verdict, it remains as such. It is nevertheless extraordinary that every day dozens of indictments are pronounced in the name of the "French people," who are essentially ignorant of them.

A debate like the one at Troyes was extremely important. For months Patrick Henry's crime was made the object of an unprecedented dramatization in all the press. And then, and I don't know if we should be congratulating ourselves, during the trial the history of the death penalty became involved in the issue. Yet, in spite of all that, no one really knows what was said about it, what argument hit home. In my opinion the uncensored publication of the debates is indispensable, whatever your reserves.

BADINTER: What you just said encourages me to ask Jean Laplanche a preliminary question, a minor but very important question: Have you ever witnessed a great criminal trial?

LAPLANCHE: No, never.

BADINTER: You neither, Michel Foucault?

FOUCAULT: Never a big criminal trial. And "Le Nouvel Observateur" never asked me to cover the Troyes trial, which I regret...

BADINTER: Jean Laplanche has only seen artifice and cleverness where all those who were present at the trial felt exactly the contrary. In fact, for me it was only a matter of leading the jury to a state of lucidity about what the death penalty represented for them as human beings.

I said to myself: the true problem for the jury member is his personal, secret relationship to death. I wanted to make them feel that they represented, finally, only themselves, facing a man seated very close to them. And that they had the aberrant and exorbitant power to prohibit this man from continuing to live. Of course, I spoke of the man "cut in two." But, contrary to what Jean Laplanche imagines, this was not done out of a taste for oratorical effect. I am horrified by every rhetorical exploitation of the guillotine and torture. It was precisely to avoid any description that I sought the barest image to represent the decapitation of a man. And however you interpret it, at the end of the execution this man is in two pieces in the courtyard of the Santé prison. That's all. So, instead of going into a wealth of disturbing details—they're going to cut off his head and put it into a basket—I chose extreme bareness.

That this image evokes fundamental notions like castration for a psychoanalyst is possible. But in what concerns me, it's the opposite of rhetorical artifice. That's why this article shocked and wounded me.

LAPLANCHE: Badinter seems to think that I reproached him for techniques and "effects." But it's not the sincerity of the law yer that's in question. At bottom, it hardly matters whether or not I was present at the trial. The trials like the one at Troyes are spectator trials: all citizens, not just the audience, are summoned to them.

And this leads to my second remark: you are necessarily in a compromised position between your function as a defender of a man and your mission as reformer of a law. I very much admired your book, *L'Exécution*,[2] where you show that the defense of a man can be only an absolute witnessing, body to body, that no longer has to be concerned with justice. It's a redoubtable and admirable position. Assuming you have used certain "effects" to this end, I see nothing more to add. But your position is untenable when, at the same moment, you intend to take action against the death penalty. One of two things: either you still situate yourself in reference to the law and to justice—but that impedes your absolute defense; or it's the very notion of penalty that you contest; yet the critic of the death penalty who emphasizes its "efficiency" presupposes that justice has only the administration of the best possible relationships between men as its object.

BADINTER: But finally the problem of the death penalty is not posed only in itself, abstractly. It is first posed very concretely at the moment when a man is there next to you, at risk of being condemned to death. It takes on all its meaning, believe me, only at the last bloody minute in the court of Sante. There's nothing theoretical about it, alas!

LAPLANCHE: You tell us that each jury member finally represents only himself. But one can claim the same thing for every pronouncement of a penalty, whatever it is. Let's suppose that the death penalty is abolished. Isn't it the same situation? Isn't the jury member then the person who slides the bolt on the prison cell? Don't we return, as in the case of the death penalty, to a "man-to-man" situation where no decision can be conceived but the one of vengeance? That's very much the reason why justice is only possible when rendered "in the name of..." If you suppress this reference that transcends the individual, you suppress justice. But what is substituted for it is not liberty, but the obligatory administration of men, with its multiple faces: technical, psychiatric, the police, etc.

BADINTER: At no moment in his life does a man dispose of a power comparable to the one when he says: "What am I going to do with him? Am I going to send him to prison for five years? Ten years?" And from that moment on, of course, a lawyer's first duty is to remind the jury the immensity of those five years. But, in the case of a prison term, which can easily be changed, nothing is really final. The trial will proceed in the shadow or within the framework of detention, sometimes a pardon or conditional freedom, etc. When it's a matter of death the choice is radical: it changes nature. After the decision—except for the possibility of pardon—it's all over. When the jurors have to pronounce a sentence, it's death that looks them straight in the face. And it is conjured away, erased, masked by the whole judicial ceremony.

LAPLANCHE: The ceremony is ridiculous and absolute only when deprived of its symbolic significance, of its reference "in the name of..." You insist on individualizing the judifical decision. But, by doing that, you render every decision impossible—or criminal. Every day, aren't there numerous circumstances in which the decision of a single person leads to the death of thousands? Imagine that you are President of the Republic and that you have to decide whether to lower the speed limit on highways to 55 miles/hour. There's reason to spend a few bad nights. There again, the filing of a charge is not a vain trifle but what allows guilt to be tied to every decision. Presidents, judges, jurors are obsessionally made to feel guilty: is that what we want? But then, in turn, police superintendents, technocrats, and the specialists "of the human soul" will disburden themselves of all scruples...

BADINTER: I don't see the connection. How can the fact that certain political or strategic decisions invoking the life and death of others justify the judicial decision to put someone to death? It's true that the decision to keep a man in prison for five more years is a serious one. But how are we to admit the death penalty into today's system? At Troyes Patrick Henry saved his life. But Ranucci had just been guillotined, and, a week after Troyes, Carrein was sentenced, perhaps because some jurors felt frustrated by Henry's release. This relativism alone suffices to condemn capital punishment.

So, why not use all the arguments one has at one's disposal? There is the prosecutor, standing before you, saying: "If you don't condemn this man to death, other innocent children will be savagely murdered." At that point of the trial, if you don't respond in kind, if you don't destroy his argument—which in reality is only a disguise for the death drive that works within us all—you are lost. Of course, criminals aren't executed in order to protect other potential victims. They are killed for other reasons, reasons that I would like to hear you, as a psychoanalyst, explain to us. But before getting to the heart of the issue, these pseudo-rational arguments have to be destroyed. If we don't take that approach, it's not worth the trouble trying to save a man.

LAPLANCHE: To be sure, you're in touch with the reality of the court. But I wonder if this milieu of the court, with its arguments that move in a closed circle, is really connected to this other reality, that of the social body, and its need for justice that you have wrongly reduced to a need for vengeance. The exemplarity or inefficiency of the penalty—that's not what resonates at the level of the population. Or rather, to make a finer distinction, we ought to distinguish between two aspects of what is called "exemplarity." One is purely utilitarian:

man is compared to a rat that one trains in a maze. If he gets a shock, he'll go in another direction. We know that this kind of conditioning—fortunately—is for man greatly inefficient. And there is a different exemplarity that one can call symbolic, which attests to the durability of a certain network of values: the value of human life for example. So I think that, if you go to the heart of things, the "real" dissuasion doesn't particularly interest the people who clamor, sometimes in a frightful or vehement way, for criminals to be punished. What they want, simply, is that the crime be punished; the "example" of the punishment is there to attest to the durability of certain "taboos." Yet, on that level, you're not responding to them; you never say to them, at any point: "Do you really understand what the punishment is? Do you really know why you desire it so much?"

FOUCAULT: Badinter's defense plea at Troyes seemed strong to me on precisely those points that Jean Laplanche is contesting. But I don't think that you, Monsieur Badinter, are giving but a minimal interpretation of what you have done. You said to the jurors: "In the end your conscience doesn't allow you to condemn someone to death." And you said equally: "You don't know this individual; the psychiatrists haven't been able to tell you anything about him, and you're going to condemn him to death." You also have criticized the exemplarity of the punishment. Yet these arguments are possible only because penal justice doesn't function so much as the application of a law or a code than as a sort of corrective mechanism in which the psychology of the defendant and the conscience of the jurors interfere with one another.

If your strategy appears shrewd to me, it's because it puts the way penal justice has worked since the beginning of the 19th century into a trap. You have taken it literally. You have said to yourself: "According to our justice the jurors, these people chosen randomly, are reputed to be the universal conscience of the people. But there is no reason that twelve people can suddenly, by a kind of judicial grace, begin to function as the universal conscience." Having raised this challenge, you have said to them: "Monsieur John Doe, you have your moods, your mother-in-law, your little life. Can you take it upon yourself, such as you are, to kill someone?" And you were right to speak to them like that. For justice functions on the equivocation between the juror as universal conscience, as abstract citizen, and the individual juror drawn randomly according to a certain number of criteria.

Similarly, you have said: "At bottom, we judge people not so much according to their acts as according to their personality." The best proof: we bring in a psychiatrist, character witnesses, we ask the little sister if the accused was nice, we question his parents about his childhood. We judge the criminal more than the crime. And it's the knowledge we gain of the criminal that justifies whether we inflict such and such a punishment. But, continuing to raise the challenge, you have drawn the consequences: "The psychiatrists have not been capable of telling us about Patrick Henry. We don't really know him. Therefore we cannot kill him."

Your arguments were tactically skillful, to be sure. But above all they had the merit of openly making use of the logic of the current penal system, and of turning it back against itself. You have demonstrated that the death penalty couldn't function within such a system. But then Jean Laplanche intervenes by saying that this system is dangerous.

LAPLANCHE: If I say that it's dangerous, it's because it leads us to a conformism much worse than that of the law: that of conformity. Foucault emphasizes an evolution but he pushes also in the direction of the latter. The law whose death he announces is replaced, in an insidious way, by the manipulation of man in the name of a "norm" claimed to be rational. And the "norm" will not be so easily put off: it's the crabgrass that ceaselessly pushes back the ground "liberated" from the law.

FOUCAULT: Let's imagine a justice that functions only according to a code: if you steal, your hand is cut off; if you commit adultery, your sex organs are slit; if you murder, your head is cut off. It's a system of arbitrary and obligatory relationships between the acts and the punishment that sanctions the crime in the person of the criminal. Thus it is possible to condemn someone to death.

But, if justice is concerned with correcting an individual, of gripping the depths of his soul in order to transform him, then everything is different: it's a man who is judging another and the death penalty is absurd. Monsieur Badinter has proved it; his defense, in this sense, is unarguable.

LAPLANCHE: Not only does the death penalty become impossible but no punishment is truly possible.

FOUCAULT: That's right. Today two systems are superimposed on one another. On the one hand, we are still living under the old traditional system which says: we punish because there is a law. And then, on top of that, a new system has penetrated the first: we punish according to the law but in order to correct, to modify, to redress; for we are dealing with deviants and the abnormal. The judge thinks of himself as a therapist of the social body, a worker in the field of "public health" in the larger sense.

LAPLANCHE: I think it's a little exaggerated to proclaim that we have finished with the law in order to enter the universe of the norm—even if we intend to contest it in turn. In spite of everything, for the people, the notion of justice remains intact. There's justice, there's no justice. This man has acted badly, he must be punished: we hear this everywhere, all around us—the need for law manifesting itself in this great collective murmur. It's striking to see our jurists and modern criminologists treat with contempt the notion of punishment as "retribution."

In order to trace this current course or degradation back a little I alluded to Hegel, who anticipated the major objection: if one keeps to the level of materiality, of suffering, nothing justifies the addition of another crime and the further suffering that is imposed on the criminal. It doesn't change anything, it doesn't bring back the dead. The evil, far from being balanced, is only added to. Yet this objection, so powerful, can be transcended only through reference to another level, that of the law. The punishment, Hegel forcefully says, only makes sense if it symbolically abolishes the crime. But that, in turn, is only comprehended because the crime itself does not lie in the material violence where it is manifested. It only exists in and through the law. We are animals dedicated to symbols and the crime adheres to our skin, like the law...

BADINTER: A little while ago I evoked the relationship established between the one whose task is to judge and the decision. You say to me: the law survives. It's true. Only we must not forget the extenuating circumstances. For the same crime you can be condemned to death or to three years in prison with a suspended sentence. Of course, the range of possible sentences is not infinite, but all the same it's very large. The diversity of possible decisions confers on judges a great power.

In fact, if one has thus been oriented toward an expansion of the possible, it's because the judicial institution has been demanding it. Recall the thesis of Montesquieu and the Constituent Assembly: the judge must be "the mouth of the law." It was infinitely easy for him. It sufficed that he ask himself the question: guilty or not guilty? If he were convinced that the accused was guilty, he pronounced the penalty provided by the texts. And he had the comforting feeling of having applied the general will. That must have been agreeable. But too easy. Today the judge, groping and uncertain, assumes responsibility for the decision. But it's infinitely preferable to this automatic cleaver of abstract retribution.

The drama is that we haven't gone to the end of personalization. Of course, we talk about treatment, reeducation, rehabilitation. But we are given a caricature of treatment. We talk of the social rehabilitation of the convicted. And, in fact, we witness a political exploitation of the fight against crime. No government has ever wanted to provide itself with the means to carry out these beautiful statements.

LAPLANCHE: We march in giant steps toward a total psychiatricalization of justice.

BADINTER: No, psychiatry is only one means among others available to judges.

LAPLANCHE: I would mention psychoanalysis, which seems to me just as serious. Psychoanalysis is not there to cure delinquency on order.

FOUCAULT: I will go further: what is this strange postulate according to which, from the moment someone has committed a crime, it signifies that he is sick? This symptomatization of the crime is the problem...

BADINTER: Don't make me say what I didn't say: it would be a gross caricature of my thinking. Crime is a social sickness. But it's not by killing the patients or by confining them separately from the so-called healthy that one fights the sickness.

FOUCAULT: Perhaps, but it's not a caricature of what all of criminology has been saying since 1880. We still have, in appearance, a legal system which punishes the criminal. In fact, we have a justice that proves itself innocent of punishing by pretending to treat the criminal.

It is around this substitution of criminal for the crime that things have pivoted and that we have begun to think: "if we are dealing with a criminal, to punish him doesn't make a lot of sense unless the punishment is inscribed in a technology of human behavior." And it is there that the criminologists of the 1880s and 90s began to advance strangely modern statements: "The crime cannot be, for the criminal, but an abnormal, disturbed behavior. If he upsets society, it's because he himself is upset." They have drawn two kinds of conclusions: in the first place, "the judicial apparatus is no longer useful." The judges, as men of law, are no longer competent to treat so difficult a matter, one so little juridical and so properly psychological as the criminal. Therefore, for the juridical apparatus we must substitute technical commissions of psychiatrists and doctors. Very specific projects were elaborated in this direction.

Second consequence: "We must certainly treat this individual who is dangerous only because he is sick. But, at the same time, we must protect society against him." Hence the idea of an internment with a mixed function: therapeutic and social preservation.

These projects aroused very lively reactions from judicial and political authorities in the 1900s. However, in our day they have found a very large field of application, and the USSR—once more "exemplary"—is not the exception.

BADINTER: But all the same, one cannot advocate a return to the abstract retribution of the penalty. You speak of crime, Michel Foucault, but it's the criminal one judges. One can try to make reparations for a crime but it's the criminal that one punishes. The judges couldn't refuse to go in the direction of judicial treatment. How could they refuse the idea that one was going to change the criminal by bringing him back to the norm? What was there to do? Throw him into a hole for twenty years? It's not possible any longer. Cut him in half? It's not possible. What then? Reintegrate him by normalizing him. From the point of view of judicial technology—judge or lawyer—there is no other possible approach. And it's not necessarily practiced according to the Soviet system.

The other aspect of the thing that really upsets me is this rising clamor: "Death! Death! Let's hang them, let's torture them, let's castrate them!" Why? If I was so disappointed by reading Laplanche's article, it was because he didn't respond to the question. At bottom, the only interesting approach to the problem of the death penalty is not that of the technicians of justice, nor that of the moralists, nor of the philosophers. It is another that I would like to see born and that will respond to all those investigating the secret function of the death penalty.

The death penalty, in France, concerns only a very small number of criminals. In the last nine years, there have been only five executions. Considering these figures, look at the enormity of the passions vented. Why does one receive, as soon as one publishes an article on the death penalty, two hundred letters of insult and delirium. For the Patrick Henry case, I'm still receiving an unbelievable amount of mail: "You filth, if you think you're gonna save your own skin after letting him go—that monster!" Threats of torture against my wife and children then follow. Can you explain this anguish? Why do non-criminals have such a need for expiatory sacrifice?

FOUCAULT: I think you are integrating two things into the same question. It's certain that spectacular crimes set off a general panic; it's the irruption of danger in daily life, a resurgence exploited shamelessly by the press.

On the other hand, you can't imagine the efforts needed to interest people even a little in what you will agree is the real problem of criminal punishment, that is, the flagrant offences, the diet in correctional institutions, the trial-a-minute where some kid, because he has stolen a piece of scrap iron off some vaguely defined lot, finds himself spending eighteen months in prison, which means that he will have to start over again, etc. The intensity of feelings that surround the death penalty is intentionally maintained by the system, since it allows it to mask the real scandals.

We have then three superimposed phenomena out of keeping with one another: a penal discourse that claims to treat rather than punish, a penal apparatus that never ceases to punish, and a collective consciousness that demands several singular punishments and is ignorant of the daily punishment that is silently exercised in its name.

LAPLANCHE: It seems arbitrary to me to separate so distinctly the population of delinquents from that of the non-delinquents. There exists, on both sides, depths of common anguish and guilt. The great waves of anguish you were speaking of are not linked to fear but to something much deeper and harder to pinpoint. If people investigate the death penalty so much, it's because they are fascinated by their own aggressivity. Because they know in a vague way that they bear the crimes in themselves and that they resemble the monster that confronts them.

As for the criminals—whom I don't know so well as Monsieur Badinter—they themselves remain faithful to the law. Don't you hear, from one cell to another: "It's not fair, he got too heavy a rap," or "He got what was coming to him!"

No, there isn't on one side a population white as snow who's afraid of lawbreakers and wants them punished, and on the other a group of criminals who live only in and through lawbreaking. Well, what's there to say, if not that there exists a gap between the unnameable anguish that comes from our own death drive and a system that introduces the law? And that it's just this gap that permits a certain psychic equilibrium. I don't think at all that the application of the law is an element that exists implicitly, even in the one who violates it. Inversely, the crime exists in each one of us, but what is psychically devastating is to treat someone as an "irresponsible child" when he manifests this implicit crime in his acts. One could refer here to psychoanalysis and to its evolution in relation to the problems of education: it has been observed that the absence of law—or at least its partial deficiency, or its ambiguity—is very anguishing, indeed "psychotizing" for the child brought up in a "permissive" environment.

BADINTER: There's no question of suppressing the law. It has not only a technical and repressive function but also an expressive function, in the sense that it expresses what the collective conscience judges to be proper.

LAPLANCHE: I would say, in the strongest sense, that it has a subjective function that operates in each of us; that of prohibitions that we respect—in our unconscious—like parricide and incest.

FOUCAULT: For Laplanche, the subject is constituted because there is law. Suppress the law and there will be no subject.

BADINTER: I'm very sorry that psychoanalysts haven't investigated any further the origin of the need for punishment that they seem to assume is a given. To say that, at the same time, there is identification with the criminal and anguish in this identification are just words...

FOUCAULT: It appears to me to be dangerous to demand the reason and foundation of the social act of punishment from psychoanalysts.

BADINTER: Not reason and foundation but explication and clarity.

LAPLANCHE: Psychoanalysts, and Freud first of all, have studied this question at length. If one had to try and summarize their point of view in two sentences, I would say that there exists two levels of guilt: the one where it is co-extensive with the anguish of our own self-aggression; and the other where it comes to be symbolized in the constitutive systems of our social being: linguistic, juridical, religious. The need for punishment is already a way of making a primordial anguish pass into something expressible, and, consequently, "negotiable." That which can be expiated can be abolished, compensated for symbolically...

BADINTER: We are content then to accept the need for punishment as a given without looking for the causes. But, once the public has been informed about a punishment, the second aspect of things begins: the treatment, the personalized approach to the criminal. The judiciary must then satisfy the collective need for punishment, without forgetting about rehabilitation. Obviously that sometimes grates on nerves, and the public becomes indignant: "He was con-

demned to twenty years and he's being let go after eight!" But why should he be
kept longer if he's been reformed?

LAPLANCHE: One might even wonder if it's absolutely necessary to punish some criminals if we are sure they are reformed before being punished.

BADINTER: We ought not. But the public demands punishment. And if
the judicial institution did not satisfy the need for punishment, that would produce a formidable frustration, which would be taken out in other forms of violence. That said, once the judicial dramaturgy is performed, the substitution of
treatment for punishment allows the accused to be reinserted without affecting
the ritual. And so the game is played.

FOUCAULT: Of course, that grates, but see also how well oiled everything is. Of course, there's someone there to punish the crime, but the president,
with his ermine and his cap, what does he say? He leans over toward the delinquent: "What was your childhood like? Your relationship with your mother?
Your little sisters? Your first sexual experience?" What do these questions have
to do with the crime he has committed? Naturally, that has to do with psychology. Psychiatrists are brought in to make everyone feel stupid, with discussions
as much from the psychiatric point of view as from the judicial, and that everyone pretends to consider as highly competent exposés. At the end of this great
juridico-psychological liturgy, the jurors finally accept this enormous thing: to
punish with the feeling that they have accomplished an act of social security and
public health, that one deals with "evil" by sending a fellow to prison for five
years. The incredible difficulty of punishing someone is dissolved into theatricality. It doesn't function badly at all.

BADINTER: I'm not as sure as you are that the juror allows himself to be
seduced by this medical approach. He thinks more simply: "He was abandoned by
his mother? Let's take two years off the sentence." Or again: "His father beat him?
Then reduce the solitary confinement by four years. He had a praiseworthy childhood? Then take off three years. He deserted his wife and children? Then add on
three years." And so it goes. I'm caricaturing the situation a little, but not so much.

LAPLANCHE: Psychiatric expertise, such as I've known it, has been preoccupied above all with the protection of society. What would be most effective
from that point of view? Therapeutics didn't have much to do with it? I saw
cases involving minor offenses: knowing that the prison term would be very
short, the expert advises to intern the delinquent, even recommending that the
authorities not follow the advice of the top doctor who may be too intelligent
and let him go free.

FOUCAULT: There is a circular on this subject that dates from after the
war, according to which the psychiatrist must respond in court to three questions

in addition to the traditional "Was he of sound mind?" These questions are extraordinary if one considers them: (1) Is the individual dangerous? (2) Can he be given criminal punishment? (3) Is he curable or can he be rehabilitated? Three questions which make no sense judicially. The law has never pretended to punish someone because he is "dangerous," but because he was a criminal. But in the realm of psychiatry the question isn't any more meaningful: as far as I know "danger" is not a psychiatric category, nor is the concept of "rehabilitation." Here we have before us a strange mixed discourse where the only thing that matters is the danger to society. This is the game that psychiatrists have agreed to play. How is it possible?

LAPLANCHE: Indeed, when psychiatry submits to this game, it assumes a double role: of repression and adaptation. For what concerns psychoanalysis, things are a little different. It is dedicated neither to an expertise nor to rehabilitation. Criminality in itself is certainly not a motive for analytic cure; with all the more reason if the delinquent was sent to the analyst by the authorities. However, one could easily imagine a delinquent undertaking an analytic cure in prison. If he expresses such a wish, there is no reason not to try to accommodate him. But in no case could the treatment be an alternative to the punishment: "If you get better, you will be freed sooner..."

FOUCAULT: Certain legislation has foreseen judicial decisions for mandatory treatment, as in the case of drug addicts and trials for minors.

LAPLANCHE: That's aberrant. One knows how very difficult it is to approach addicts, even when they agree to be treated...

BADINTER: It's not an aberration from the judge's point of view. Even so, it's more valuable than keeping the addict locked up for several months.

LAPLANCHE: But, precisely in this respect, to want to remove the addict from a possible confrontation with a prison term is to put oneself in the worst conditions, from the point of view of psychotherapy. Psychotherapy could not be an alternative to prison without undermining itself.

BADINTER: That said, our justice never really intended to go all the way with treatment.

LAPLANCHE: It's not because the penitential framework is detestable that it must be replaced by a no less detestable psychiatric one.

BADINTER: I'm not talking about a psychiatric framework. It's not a matter of giving psychiatry full power. What I'm saying is that one can't be ignorant of it. Up to the present it has been used as an alibi. Never for curative purposes.

FOUCAULT: You seem to think of psychiatry as a system that might really exist, like a marvelous instrument prepared in advance. "Ah, if finally the psychiatrists would come to work with us, how good that would be!" Yet I believe that psychiatry is not capable of responding to such a demand, and that it never will be. It is incapable of knowing if a crime is a sickness or of transforming a delinquent into a non-delinquent.

It would be serious if justice washed its hands of its responsibilities by delegating them to psychiatrists. Or if the sentence became a kind of transactional decision between an archaic code and an unjustified knowledge.

BADINTER: It's certainly not a question of delegating responsibilities. Psychiatry is one instrument among many, badly or hardly utilized up till now in judicial matters.

FOUCAULT: Its value is exactly what has to be put into question.

BADINTER: But then must all psychiatric research be excluded from judicial concerns? Do we return to the beginning of the 19th century? To prefer the penal colony, to get rid of them by sending them as far away as possible where they can starve in indifference would be a frightful regression.

LAPLANCHE: Psychiatry is more and more infiltrated with psychoanalytic concepts. Yet psychoanalysis can in no case make pronouncements about the irresponsibility of a delinquent. On the contrary: one of the postulates of psychoanalysis is that those analyzed must become responsible again, as subjects of their acts. Using psychoanalysis to make them "irresponsible" would be an absurd reversal.

FOUCAULT: It suffices to listen to these "experts" who come to analyze a fellow. They say just what anyone in the street would say: "You know he had an unhappy childhood. He's a difficult person..." Of course all that is dressed up in technical terms, which doesn't fool anybody. Yet it works. Why? Because everyone—the prosecuting attorney, the lawyer, the presiding judge—needs a modulator for the punishment. It allows one to make the code function as one wants, and to retain a good conscience. In fact, the psychiatrist doesn't discuss the delinquent's psychology: it's to the judge's liberty that he addresses himself. It's a question not of the criminal's unconscious but of the judge's consciousness. When we publish some of the psychiatric testimony we have gathered over the past few years, one will be able to determine to what extent psychiatric relationships constitute tautologies: "He killed a little old lady? Well then, he's an aggressive subject!" Do we need psychiatry to perceive that? No. But the judge needs psychiatry in order to reassure himself.

This "modulator" effect works moreover in both directions; it can also increase the sentence. I saw expert testimony on homosexual subjects formulated in such terms as: "These are abject individuals." But "abject" is not an accepted technical term. It's a way of reintroducing, under the honorable cloak of psychiatry, certain connotations of homosexuality in a trial where they don't belong. Take Tartuffe at Elmira's knees proposing "a love without scandal and a pleasure without fear." Substitute prison term and punishment for pleasure and love and you have psychiatric tartufferie at the feet of the court of justice. Nothing works better against the anxiety of judging.

BADINTER: But it *is* anguishing to judge. The judicial institution can function only to the extent that the judge is liberated from his anxiety. To succeed in it he must know in the name of what values he condemns or absolves. Until a recent period everything was simple. Political regimes changed, but not the values of society. The judges were comfortable. But today, in this uncertain society, in the name of what does one judge, by means of what values?

FOUCAULT: I fear that is is dangerous to allow judges to continue to judge alone, by liberating them from their anxiety and allowing them to avoid asking themselves in the name of what they judge, by what right, by what acts, and who are they, those who judge. Let them become anxious like we become anxious when we meet so few who are disturbed. The crisis of the function of justice has just been opened. Let's not close it too quickly.

Translated by John Johnston

---

1 On February 28, 1977, Jean Laplanche published an article on the then-current trial of Patrick Henry, provoking numerous reactions. The renowned psychoanalyst, in essence, dismissed both adversaries and advocates of capital punishment. Robert Badinter, the lawyer (later Socialist Minister of Justice) who contributed to saving Patrick Henry from the guillotine, here debates the issue of the death penalty and capital punishment with Laplanche and Michel Foucault. [Ed.]

2 Robert Badinter, *L'Exécution* (Paris: Grasset, 1973).

31

CLARIFICATIONS ON THE QUESTION
OF POWER

Q: Your research since, let us say, *Discipline and Punish,* has begun to extend into and bring to light the realm of power relationships and the technology of power; this fact has created problems and difficulties now that these analyses have started to have echoes in the political and intellectual fields. In the United States they are wondering into which university discipline your work ought to be placed; in Italy they want rather to know what is the political effect of your ideas.

1. How would you define the field of your work today, and what might its political implications be?

2. In your analyses there would be no difference between ideology and the process of power, between ideology and reality. This type of analysis, this *mise à plat* [flattening out of the issues]—for which you are criticized—would be nothing more than an echo of what already exists, a confirmation of the real.

3. The metaphor of Bentham's Panopticon—to which one attempts to reduce all your analyses—would take us back to an absolute transparency of power which is all-seeing.

4. The concept of resistance can easily function as *repoussoir,* as the external limit of an analysis which would bring to light in the presence of this concept the notion of Power with a capital P. In reality, you are probably thinking the opposite, in particular in *The History of Sexuality.* But this is a problem to which we shall undoubtedly have to return.

MF: By way of introduction, it is perhaps worth it to say something on this problem of the "amalgam," because I think it might be an important factor. I have the impression that the whole operation can be summarized in this way: there is no difference between what Deleuze says, what Foucault says and what the "new philosophers" say.[1] I suppose, though it would have to be verified, that yet a fourth adversary has been assimilated here, the theory of radical needs, which is, I believe, rather important in Italy today and of which the PCI would also like to rid itself. Here we find something worth emphasizing: these are the old tactics, both political and ideological, of Stalinism, which consist of having at all times only one adversary. Also, or rather above all, when you strike on several fronts, you must do it in such a way that the battle seems like a battle against one and the same adversary. There are a thousand devils, the Church used to say, but there is only one Prince of Darkness... And they do the same thing. This produced, for example, social-fascism, in the very moment when it was necessary to fight against fascism; but they wanted at the same time to attack social democracy. There has been the category of Hitlerian–Trotskyism; or Titoism as the unchanging element of all the adversaries. So they maintain absolutely the same procedure.

Secondly, it has to do with a judiciary procedure, and one which has acted out a very precise role in all the trials, those of Moscow, those of the post-war popular democracies; that is, the role of saying: since you are nothing more than one and the same enemy, we shall ask you above all to account not only for what you have said, but also for everything you have not said, if it is one of your so-called allies or accomplices who has said it. Hence a totalization of sins on each of the accused heads. And then: as you can well see, you contradict yourselves, since, even though you are all one and the same adversary you say one thing but you also say the opposite. So you must account for what has been said and for the opposite of what has been said.

There is also a third element which seems important to me and which consists of the act of assimilating the enemy and the danger. Every time something appears which represents a danger (with respect to given situations, affirmed tactics and dominant ideological themes)—that is, a given problem or the need for a change of analysis, you never have to take it as a danger or as an event; you need only denounce it immediately as an adversary. To give a precise example, I believe that these analyses of power held nothing more than a relatively restricted place in the institutionalized discourse of Marxism. It is a new event, the fact that the problem has been opened up, and not by me, but by many other events, other people and other trials. The various communist parties, the Italian party in particular, did not respond to this by saying: perhaps we ought to take it into consideration; rather, the response was: if it is something new, it is a danger and therefore an adversary.

In my opinion, these elements deserve to be stressed as supports of the current polemics.

In the same vein with what I have just said, the operation of "reduction to system" must be added. In the presence of analyses of this kind, in the presence of the problems, with respect to which, however, these analyses are nothing more than imperfect and awkward attempts to come up with an answer—and here I do not delude myself—one tries to extract immediately a certain number of theses, no matter how caricaturish they may be, no matter how arbitrary the link between the "extracted" theses and what has actually been said. The goal is to arrive at a formulation of theses which might permit something like a condemnation; a condemnation which is produced solely upon the basis of the comparison between these theses and those of Marxism, or, in any case, the "just" theses.

I believe that all of these procedures can be found in the enormous network of fiction which some communists have constructed around what I was doing. There is hardly any relationship between what I have actually said and the things they attribute to me. This, I believe, can be asserted with complete objectivity. For example, a naturalistic conception of desire was attributed to me: enough to make you split your sides with laughter. Perhaps one could accuse them of stupidity, and certainly this is being done; but I think that the problem, in spite of everything, should be examined instead at the very level of their cynicism. I mean that they are well-skilled in telling lies, and that this can easily be demonstrated. They know very well that every honest reader, reading what has been written about me and what I myself have written, will see that these theses are lies. But their problem, as well as their strength, lies in the fact that what interests them is not what they themselves say, but what they do when they say something. And what they do is precisely this: to constitute a singular enemy, to utilize a judiciary proceeding, to begin a procedure of condemnation, in the politico-judiciary sense; and this is the only thing that interests them. Just so the individual is condemnable and condemned. The nature of the evidence upon which he is condemned is of little importance, since, as we well know, the essential thing in a condemnation is not the quality of the evidence but the force of the one who presents the evidence.

In reference to the reduction of my analyses to that simplistic figure which is the metaphor of the Panopticon, I think that here too a response can be made on two levels. We can say: let us compare what they attribute to me with what I have said; and here it is easy to show that the analyses of power which I have made cannot at all be reduced to this figure, not even in the book where they went searching for it, that is, *Discipline and Punish*. In fact, if I show that the Panopticon was a utopia, a kind of pure form elaborated at the end of the 18th century, intended to supply the most convenient formula for the constant, immediate and total exercising of power; and if, then, I have revealed the genesis, the formulation of this utopia, its *raison d'être;* it is also true that I immediately showed that what we are talking about is precisely a utopia which had never functioned in the form in which it existed, and that the whole history of the prison—its reality—consists precisely of its having come near this model. Certainly there was a functionalism in Bentham's dream, but there has never been a real functionality of the prison. The reality of the prison has always been grasped in diverse strategic and tactical connections which took into account a dense, weighty, blind, obscure reality. It is thus necessary to be in absolute bad faith in order to say that I presented a functionalist conception of the transparency of power. As far as the other books are concerned, the same thing is true. In *The Will to Knowledge* I tried to indicate how analyses of power ought to be made, just how they can be oriented—and all of these indications revolved around the theme of power as a series of complex, difficult and never-functionalized relationships, a series of relationships which in a certain sense never functions at all. Power is not omnipotent or omniscient—quite the contrary! If power relationships have produced forms of investigation, of analysis, of models of knowledge, etc., it is precisely not because power was omniscient, but because it was blind, because it was in a state of impasse. If it is true that so many power relationships have been developed, so many systems of control, so many forms of surveillance, it is precisely because power was always impotent. On the level of the nature itself of my analyses, it is easy to show that what is being attributed to me is a pure and simple lie. What must be done, then, is precisely to take things at another level and to try to understand what they are doing when they tell a lie which can be so easily unmasked—and here I believe they are utilizing the technique of the inversion of reproach.

Ultimately, it is true that the question I posed was raised in reference to Marxism, as well as to other conceptions of history and politics; and the question was this: isn't it possible, with reference to production, for example, that power relationships do not represent a level of reality which is simultaneously complex and relatively, but only relatively, independent? In other words, I was putting forth the hypothesis that there was a specificity to power relationships, a density, an inertia, a viscosity, a course of development and an inventiveness which belonged to these relationships and which it was necessary to analyze.

I was simply saying this: maybe everything is not as easy as one believes; and in order to say this I was basing my message on analyses and experience at the same time. The experience is that of the Soviet Union, but also that of the Communist parties, because sixty to seventy years of contemporary experience have taught us that the idea of taking over the apparatus of the State, of the deterioration of the State, of democratic centralism, that all of this was nothing more than a marvelously simple set of formulas, but ones which absolutely did not take into account what was happening at the level of power. And this is true for the Soviet Union just as it is for any Communist party. Furthermore, this affirmation was not as simple as some people thought, because I was basing it upon historical analyses. It is evident, for example, that since the 16th century the problem of the art of governing, of how to govern, with what techniques, with what instruments, has been a decisive problem for the entire West. How are we to govern, how are we to accept being governed, etc.

So then, my problem was one of saying: look, the problem of power is complicated; and it was the problem of showing in what sense this was true, with all the consequences resulting therefrom all the way up to current politics. This has been the answer of the Communists: you speak of simplicity and yet you hold that things are more complicated than one thinks? But it is you who hold the most simplistic conception. And they have reduced everything I said to the simple form of the Panopticon, which was only one element of my analysis. Inversion of reproach: the technique of lawyers.

Another point which could be talked about here is the reduction of the analyses of the technology of power to a kind of metaphysics of Power with a capital P, by which technology is led back to a dualism in which the things confronted are this Power and the silent, deaf resistance to it, of which no one would ever say anything. What would be reconstructed in this is a kind of dual clash.

First of all, I never use the word power with a capital P; they are the ones who do that. In the second place, some French "Marxists" maintain that power for me is "endogenous," and that I would like to construct a real and true ontological circle, deducing power from power. This is a stupid and ridiculous affirmation, since I have always tried to do just the opposite. Let's take, for example, *Madness and Civilization*, my very first book, in which I tried somewhat to deal with this problem. I was then involved with some psychiatric institutions, where the power of the administration, of the director, of the doctors, of the family, etc., functioned absolutely, with reference to the mentally ill. If I had wanted to make, as they say, an ontology of Power with a capital P, I would have tried to establish the origin of these great institutions of power; I would have placed my analysis exclusively on the level of the institution and of the law, and on the power relationship, more or less regulated, with which the violence against madness or madmen would have been exercised.

Instead, I tried to show how these *découpages,* these relationships of force, these institutions and this entire network of power were able to establish themselves at a given moment. And beginning from what? Beginning from those economic and demographic processes which appear clearly at the end of the 16th century, when the problem of the poor, of the homeless, of fluctuating populations, is raised as an economic and political problem; and an attempt is made to resolve it with an entire arsenal of implements and arms (the laws concerning the poor, the more-or-less forced isolation and, finally, imprisonment of these people—in particular, what took place in France and in Paris in 1660-1661).

I tried to see, then, how this set of power relationships which encircled madness and defined it as a mental illness was something completely different from a pure and simple power relationship, from a pure and simple tautological affirmation of the following type: I, reason, exercise power over you, madness. Just as, in the opposite sense, a power relationship was born from within a very different transformation, which was at the same time the condition allowing for the regulation and control of these relationships and these economic processes, etc. It is precisely the heterogeneity of power which I wanted to demonstrate, how it is always born of something other than itself.

The same can be said, for example, of the prison. To make an analysis of power in terms of an ontological affirmation would have meant to question oneself as to what penal law is and to deduce the prison from the essence itself of the law which condemns the crime. Instead, I was attempting to reinsert the prison within a technology which is the technology of power, but which has its birth in the 17th and 18th centuries, that is, when an entire series of economic and demographic problems poses once again the problem of what I have called the economy of power relationships.

Could the feudal type systems or the systems of the great administrative monarchies still be considered valid when it is a question of irrigating the power relationships in a social body whose demographic dimensions, whose population shifts, whose economic processes are those which they have become? All of this is born from out of something else; and there is no Power, but power relationships which are being born incessantly, as both effect and condition of other processes.

But this is only one aspect of the problem which I wanted to confront; the other is the one of resistance. If mine were an ontological conception of power, there would be, on one side, Power with a capital P, a kind of lunar occurrence, extra-terrestrial; and on the other side, the resistance of the unhappy ones who are obligated to bow before power. I believe an analysis of this kind to be completely false, because power is born out of a plurality of relationships which are grafted onto something else, born from something else, and permit the development of something else.

Hence the fact that these power relationships, on one hand, enter into the heart of struggles which are, for example, economic or religious—and so it is not against power that struggles are fundamentally born.

On the other hand, power relationships open up a space in the middle of which the struggles develop. For example, in reference to criminality, to the penal system, and to the judicial bureaucracy, there was in the 18th century an entire series of interesting struggles: the struggles of the people against the upper echelons, struggles of the intellectuals against the old bureaucracies, struggles of the judiciary bureaucracy against the new political and technocratic classes which exerted power, at least in some states, and which sought to sweep away the old structures.

If there are class struggles, and certainly there have been, these struggles cover this field, they divide it, plough it, organize it. But we must reposition the power relationships within the struggles and not suppose that power might exist on one side, and that on the other side lies that upon which power would exert itself; nor can we suppose that the struggle develops between power and non-power.

Instead of this ontological opposition between power and resistance, I would say that power is nothing other than a certain modification, or the form, differing from time to time, of a series of clashes which constitute the social body, clashes of the political, economic type, etc. Power, then, is something like the stratification, the institutionalization, the definition of tactics, of implements and arms which are useful in all these clashes. It is this which can be considered in a given moment as a certain power relationship, a certain exercising of power. As long as it is clear that this exercising (to the degree to which it is, in the end, nothing other than the instant photograph of multiple struggles continuously in transformation)—this power, transforms itself without ceasing. We need not confuse a power situation, a certain distribution or economy of power in a given moment, with the simple power institutions, such as the army, the police, the government, etc.

Finally, there is another thing for which I am criticized. By freeing myself of the old concept of ideology, which permitted playing reality against false interpretations of reality, which permitted functioning on the basis of the device of demystification—things are not as they are presented, but exist in a different way—they say I would perform a *mise à plat* of the discussions concerning reality, reducing my analyses to a simple reproduction of reality, in such a way that my discussion would be nothing more than a kind of reactionary echo which would do nothing but confirm things as they are.

Here once again we must understand what they are doing when they say something like this. Because, we have to ask what it means when they say: you do nothing but repeat reality. Above all, it can mean: you do nothing but repeat what has been said. I would answer: show me that it has been said. Did you say it? If they say to me: you do nothing but repeat reality—in the sense that what I say is true, then I agree with them and thank them for this recognition. It is true, I decided to say exactly what has happened. But I would only thank them half-way, because after all, that is not exactly what I decided to do.

This is what others would say of the analyses I perform and of that opinion which claims that these analyses simply reproduce reality: this is not at all true; it is all pure and simple imagination. The French psychiatrists, of more or less Marxist inspiration, tried to say this about *Madness and Civilization,* with dubious success, however. They tried to say that it was a fable.

In reality, what I want to do, and here is the difficulty of trying to do it, is to solve this problem: to work out an interpretation, a reading of a certain reality, which might be such that, on one hand, this interpretation could produce some of the effects of truth; and on the other hand, these effects of truth could become implements within possible struggles. Telling the truth so that it might be acceptable. Deciphering a layer of reality in such a way that the lines of force and the lines of fragility come forth; the points of resistance and the possible points of attack; the paths marked out and the shortcuts. It is the reality of possible struggles that I wish to bring to light.

This is what I wanted to do in *Madness and Civilization.* It is, however, rather curious that all the psychiatrists have read this as a book of anti-psychiatry—a book which says explicitly: I shall speak of what has happened with regard to madness and mental illness between the middle of the 17th century and the beginning of the 18th, roughly speaking—and I have not gone beyond Pinel. As if the book were speaking about the mental situation!

Those psychiatrists were right and wrong at the same time. Wrong because it simply was not true; I was not speaking about the mental situation. Nonetheless, there was something of the truth in this superficial and angry reaction of theirs since, in reality, reading history in that way meant, in essence, tracing within contemporary reality some possible paths which later became, with the indispensable transformations, paths actually followed.

This polemics of reality is the effect of truth which I want to produce. The same holds true for the prison, for the problem of criminality. This too is a book which deals with seventy years of the history of penal institutions: 1760–1830/40. In nearly all the reviews it was said that this book speaks about the current situation, but that it does not speak sufficiently about it because things have changed since then. But I am not speaking about the current situation. I am making an interpretation of history, and the problem is that of knowing—but I don't resolve the problem—how these analyses can possibly be utilized in the current situation.

At this point I think we need to bring into the discussion the problem of the function of the intellectual. It is absolutely true that when I write a book I refuse to take a prophetic stance, that is, the one of saying to people: here is what you must do—and also: this is good and this is not. I say to them: roughly speaking, it seems to me that things have gone this way; but I describe those things in such a way that the possible paths of attack are delineated. Yet even with this approach I do not force or compel anyone to attack. So then, it becomes a completely personal question when I choose, if I want, to take certain courses of action with reference to prisons, psychiatric asylums, this or that issue. But I say that political action belongs to a category of participation completely different from these written or bookish acts of participation. It is a problem of groups, of personal and physical commitment. One is not radical because one pronounces a few words; no, the essence of being radical is physical; the essence of being radical is the radicalness of existence itself.

Now then, returning to the Communists, I would say that this radicalness is what they don't have. They don't have it because for them the problem of the intellectual is not one of telling the truth, because the intellectuals of the PC were never asked to tell the truth. They were asked to take a prophetic stance, to say: this is what must be done—which implies simply that what must be done must adhere to the PC, must do as the PC does, must be with the PC or vote for the PC. In other words, what the PC demands is that the intellectual be the intermediary that transmits the intellectual, moral and political imperatives of which the party can make direct use.

But it is a different story for the intellectual who takes a completely opposite position, which consists of saying to the people: I would like to produce some effects of truth which might be used for a possible battle, to be waged by those who wish to wage it, in forms yet to be found and in organizations yet to be defined. The people of the PC clearly do not talk about this freedom which I leave here at the end of my discussion for anyone who wants or does not want to get something done.

This is exactly the opposite of what they would have me do; because for the PC the real intellectual is the one who calms down reality, explaining how it ought to be and saying immediately how it will have to be on that day when everyone will do as the Communist party does. A position exactly contrary to my own; and it is in this sense that they do not pardon me.

They really do understand what I am doing, but they don't understand what I am saying. Or, at least, they take the risk—and this, once again, is truly surprising—of letting everyone see that they don't understand what I am saying. But this does not worry them, because their problem is one of covering up what I do, of condemning it and thereby preventing the people from doing or accepting what I do; theirs is the task of making what I do unacceptable. And in the moment when they cannot say: what he is doing is unacceptable, they say: what he is saying is false. But in order to say this they are obligated to lie and to make me say what I am not saying.

For this reason, I don't think there's much to discuss concerning these words poured on top of my own. Rather, what we need to do is to grasp clearly the reason for this attack of theirs. And if they do understand what I am doing, then I would like to make clear what they are doing when they tell these lies.

Translated by James Cascaito

———

[1] The "New Philosophers" were the first French intellectuals of the younger generation to openly link Marxism as a philosophy to totalitarian politics. Its main proponents were Bernard-Henri Lévy and André Glucksman, with whom Foucault seemed to be close at the time. Gilles Deleuze, a friend and ally of Foucault, on the other hand, came out strongly against the simplifications of the "New Philosophers" the year before. (Cf. Deleuze, "Entrietien sur les Nouveaux Philosophes," June 5, 1977. Distributed as hand–out.) [Ed.]

32

The Danger of Child Sexuality

MICHEL FOUCAULT: All three of us agreed to take part in this broadcast (it was agreed in principle several months ago) for the following reason. Things had evolved on such a wide front, in such an overwhelming and at first sight apparently irreversible way, that many of us began to hope that the legal regime imposed on the sexual practices of our contemporaries would at last be relaxed and broken up. This regime is not as old as all that, since the penal code of 1810[1] said very little about sexuality, as if sexuality was not the business of the law; and it was only during the 19th century and above all in the 20th, at the time of Pétain or of the Mirguet amendment (1960),[2] that legislation on sexuality increasingly became oppressive. But, over the last ten years or so, a movement in public opinion and sexual morals has been discernible in favor of reconsidering this legal regime. A Commission for the Reform of Penal Law was even set up, whose task it was to revise a number of fundamental articles in the penal code. And this commission has actually admitted, I must say with great seriousness, not only the possibility, but the need to change most of the articles in our present legislation concerning sexual behavior. This commission, which has now been sitting for several months, considered this reform of the sexual legislation last May and June. I believe that the proposals it expected to make were what may be called liberal. However, it would seem that for several months now, a movement in the opposite direction has begun to emerge. It is a disturbing movement—firstly, because it is not only occurring in France. Take, for example, what is happening in the United States, with Anita Bryant's campaign against homosexuals, which has almost gone so far as to call for murder. It's a phenomenon observable in France. But in France we see it through a number of particular, specific facts, which we shall talk about later (Jean Danet and Guy Hocquenghem will certainly provide examples), but ones that seem to show that in both police and legal practice we are returning to tougher and stricter positions. And this movement, observable in police and legal practice, is unfortunately very often supported by press campaigns, or by a system of information carried out in the press. It is therefore in this situation, that of an overall movement tending to liberalism, followed by a phenomenon of reaction, of slowing down, perhaps even the beginnings of a reverse process, that we are holding our discussion this evening.

GUY HOCQUENGHEM: Six months ago we launched a petition demanding the abrogation of a number of articles in the law, in particular those concerning relations between decriminalization of relations between minors and adults below the age of fifteen. A lot of people signed it, people belonging to a wide range of political positions, from the Communist Party to Mme. Dolto.[3] So it's a petition that has been signed by a lot of people who are suspect neither of being particularly pedophiles themselves nor even of entertaining extravagant political views. We felt that a certain movement was beginning to emerge, and this movement was confirmed by the evidence submitted to the commission reforming the penal code. What we can now see, then, is not only that this kind of movement is something of a liberal illusion, but that in fact it does not amount to a profound transformation in the legal system, either in the way a case is investigated or in the way it is judged in court. Furthermore, at the level of public opinion, at the level of the mass media, the newspapers, radio, television, etc., it is rather the opposite that is beginning to take place, with new arguments being used. These new arguments are essentially about childhood, that is to say, about the exploitation of popular sentiment and its spontaneous horror of anything that links sex with the child. Thus an article in the *Nouvel Observateur* begins with a few remarks to the effect that "pornography involving children is the ultimate American nightmare and no doubt the most terrible in a country fertile in scandals." When someone says that child pornography is the most terrible of present-day scandals, one cannot but be struck by the disproportion between this—child pornography, which is not even prostitution—and everything that is happening in the world today—what the Black population has to put up with in the United States, for instance. This whole campaign about pornography, about prostitution, about all those social phenomena, which are in any case controversial—nobody here is advocating child pornography or prostitution—only leads to one fundamental question: it's worse when children are consenting and worse still if it is neither pornographic nor paid for, etc. In other words, the entire criminalizing context serves only to bring out the kernel of the accusation: you want to make love with consenting children. It serves only to stress the traditional prohibition and to stress in a new way, with new arguments, the traditional prohibition on sexual relations without violence, without money, without any form of prostitution, that may take place between adults and minors.

JEAN DANET: We already know that some psychiatrists consider that sexual relations between children and adults are always traumatizing. And that if a child doesn't remember them, it is because they remain in his unconscious, but in any case the child is marked forever, the child will become emotionally disturbed. So what takes place with the intervention of psychiatrists in court is a manipulation of the children's consent, a manipulation of their words. Then there is another use, a fairly recent one, I think, of repressive legislation, which should be noted because it may be used by the legal system as a temporary tactic to fill in the gaps. Indeed in the traditional disciplinary institutions—prisons, schools, and asylums—the nurses, teachers, and so on, followed a very strict regimen. Their superiors kept as close a watch on them as on the inmates. On the other hand, in the new agencies of social control, control through hierarchy is much more difficult. Indeed we may well wonder whether we are not witnessing a use of common-law legislation; incitement of a minor to commit an immoral act, for example, can be used against social workers and teachers. And I would point out in passing that Villerot is a teacher, that Gallien was a doctor even if the acts did not take place at a time when he was practicing his profession; that in 1976, in Nantes, a teacher was tried for inciting minors to immoral acts, when in fact what he had done was to supply contraceptives to the boys and girls in his charge. So the common law appears to have been used this time to repress teachers and social workers who were not carrying out their task of social control as their respective hierarchies wished. Between 1830 and 1860, there already were laws directed specifically at teachers: certain judgments stated this explicitly. Article 334 of the Penal Code—which applied to certain persons, teachers, for example, and concerned the incitement of minors to commit immoral acts—was invoked in a case that did not involve a teacher. So we can see the extent to which such legislation is ultimately looking for places where perverts likely to corrupt young people might slip in. The judges were obsessed with this. They were unable to come up with a definition of the perversions. Medicine and psychiatry were to do it for them. In the mid-19th century they had one obsession: if the pervert was everywhere, then they must start tracking him down in the most dangerous institutions, the institutions at risk, among the populations at risk, though the term had not yet been invented. If it has been possible to believe for a time that there was to be a withdrawal of legislation, it was not because we thought we were living in a liberal period but because we knew that more subtle forms of sexual supervision would be set up—and perhaps the apparent freedom that camouflaged these more subtle, more diffuse social controls was going to extend beyond the field of the juridical and the penal. This is not always necessarily the case, and it is quite possible to believe that traditional repressive laws will function side-by-side with much more subtle forms of control, a hitherto unknown form of sexology that would invade all institutions, including educational ones.

FOUCAULT: Indeed it seems to me that we have reached an important point. It is true that we are witnessing a real change: it is probably not true that this change will be favorable to any real alleviation of the legislation on sexuality. As Jean Danet has shown, a very large body of legislation was gradually promulgated, though not without difficulty, throughout the 19th century. But this legislation was characterized by the odd fact that it was never capable of saying exactly what it was punishing. Harrassments were punished, but were never defined. Outrageous acts were punished; nobody ever said what an outrage was. The law was intended to defend decency (*pudeur*); nobody ever knew what pudeur was. In practice, whenever a legislative intervention into the sphere of sexuality had to be justified, the law on pudeur was always invoked. And it may be said that all the legislation on sexuality introduced since the 19th century in France is a set of laws on pudeur. It is certainly a fact that this legislative apparatus, aimed at an undefined object, was never used except in cases when it was considered to be tactically useful. Indeed there has been a whole campaign against teachers. There was a time when it was used against the clergy. This legislation was used to regulate the phenomenon of child prostitution, so important throughout the 19th century between 1830 and 1880. We are now aware that this instrument, which possessed the advantage of flexibility, since its object was undefined, could no longer survive when these notions of *pudeur, outrage,* and harrassment were seen as belonging to a particular system of value, culture, and discourse; in the pornographic explosion and the profits that it involves, in this new atmosphere, it is no longer possible to use these words and to make the law function on this basis. But what is emerging—and indeed why I believe it was important to speak about the problem of children—what is emerging is a new penal system, a new legislative system, whose function is not so much to punish offenses against these general laws concerning decency, as to protect populations and parts of populations regarded as particularly vulnerable. In other words, the legislator will not justify the measures that he is proposing by saying: the universal decency of mankind must be defended. What he will say is: there are people for whom others' sexuality may become a permanent danger. In this category, of course, are children, who may find themselves at the mercy of an adult sexuality that is alien to them and may well be harmful to them. Hence there is a legislation that appeals to this notion of a vulnerable population, a "high-risk population," as they say, and to a whole body of psychiatric and psychological knowledge imbided from psychoanalysis—it doesn't really matter whether the psychoanalysis is good or bad—and this will give the psychiatrists the right to intervene twice. Firstly, in general terms, to say: yes, of course, children do have a sexuality, we can't go back to those old notions about children being pure and not knowing what sexuality is. But we psychologists or psychoanalysts or psychiatrists, or teachers, we know perfectly well that children's sexuality is a specific sexuality, with its own forms, its own periods of maturation, its own highpoints, its specific drives, and its own latency periods, too. This sexuality of the child is a territory with its own geography that the adult must not enter. It is virgin territory, sexual territory, of course, but territory that must preserve its virginity. The adult will therefore intervene as guarantor of that specificity of child sexuality in order to protect it. And, on the other hand, in each particular case, he will say: this is an instance of an adult bringing his own sexuality into the child's sexuality. It could be that the child, with his own sexuality, may have desired that adult, he may even have consented, he may even have made the first moves. We may even agree that it was he who seduced the adult; but we specialists with our psychological knowledge know perfectly well that even the seducing child runs a risk, in every case, of being damaged and traumatized by the fact that he or she has had sexual dealings with an adult.

Consequently, the child must be protected from his own desires, even when his desires turn him towards an adult. The psychiatrist is the one who will be able to say: I can predict that a trauma of this importance will occur as a result of this or that type of sexual relation. It is therefore within the new legislative framework—basically intended to protect certain vulnerable sections of the population with the establishment of a new medical power—that a conception of sexuality and above all of the relations between child and adult sexuality will be based; and it is one that is extremely questionable.

HOCQUENGHEM: There is a whole mixture of notions that makes it possible to fabricate this notion of crime or offence against decency, a highly complex mixture, which we do not have time here to discuss at length, but which comprises both the religious prohibitions concerning sodomy and the completely new notions, to which Michel Foucault has just referred, about what people think they know of the total difference between the world of the child and the world of the adult. But today's overall tendency is indisputably not only to fabricate a type of crime that is quite simply the erotic or sensual relationship between a child and an adult, but also, since this may be isolated in the form of a crime, to create a certain category of the population defined by the fact that it tends to indulge in those pleasures. There exists then a particular category of the pervert, in the strict sense, of monsters whose aim in life is to practice sex with children. Indeed they become perverts and intolerable monsters since the crime as such is recognized and constituted, and now strengthened by the whole psychoanalytical and sociological arsenal. What we are doing is constructing an entirely new type of criminal, a criminal so inconceivably horrible that his crime goes beyond any explanation, any victim. It is rather like that kind of legal monster, the term *attentat sans violence:* an attack without violence that is unprovable in any case and leaves no trace, since even the anuscope is unable to find the slightest lesion that might legitimate in some way or other the notion of violence. Thus, in a way, public outrage to decency also realizes this, insofar as the offense in question does not require a public in order to be committed. In the case of *attentat sans violence,* the offense in which the police have been unable to find anything, nothing at all, in that case, the criminal is simply a criminal because he is a criminal, because he has those tastes. It is what used to be called a crime of opinion. Take the case of Parajanov. When a delegation arrived in Paris to see the representative of the Soviet embassy to hand in a protest, the Soviet representative replied: in fact you don't really know why he was condemned; he was condemned for raping a child. This representative read the press: he knew very well that this term inspired more fear than any other. The constitution of this type of criminal, the constitution of this individual perverse enough to do a thing that hitherto had always been done without anybody thinking it right to stick his nose into it, is an extremely grave step from a political point of view. Even if it has not reached the same dimensions as the campaigns against the terrorists, there are nevertheless several hundred cases going before the courts each year. And this campaign suggests that a certain section of the population must henceforth be regarded a priori as criminals, may be pursued in operations of the "help the police" type, and this is what happened in the case of Villerot. The police report noted with interest that the population took part in the search, that people used their cars to look for the pervert. In a way the movement feeds upon itself. The crime vanishes, nobody is concerned any longer to know whether in fact a crime was committed or not, whether someone has been hurt or not. No one is even concerned any more whether there actually was a victim. The crime feeds totally upon itself in a man-hunt, by the identification, the isolation of the category of individuals regarded as pedophiles. It culminates in that sort of call for a lynching sent out nowadays by the gutter press.

DANET: It is true that lawyers defending these cases have a lot of problems. But I should like to say something specifically about such problems. In cases like the Croissant affair, the terrorists' lawyers were regarded immediately as dangerous accomplices of the terrorists.[4] Anyone who came into contact with the affair became implicated. Similarly, the defense of someone found guilty of an indecent act with a minor, especially in the provinces, has extremely serious problems, because many lawyers simply cannot take on such a defense, avoid doing so, and prefer to be appointed by the court. For, in a way, anyone who defends a pedophile may be suspected of having some sympathy for that cause. Even judges think to themselves: if he defends them, it's because he isn't really as much against it himself. It's a serious matter, though it's almost laughable really, it's a fact known to anyone who has had to deal with such cases whether in the provinces or in Paris: it is extremely difficult both for the lawyer to defend such a case and even sometimes to find a lawyer willing to do so. A lawyer will be quite happy to defend someone accused of murdering ten old ladies. That doesn't bother him in the least. But to defend someone who has touched some kid's cock for a second, that's a real problem. That is part of the whole set up around this new sort of criminal, the adult who has erotic relations with children.

I apologize for referring to history once again, but I think in this matter one can usefully refer to what happened in the 19th and early 20th centuries. When an open letter to the commission for the reform of the penal code was published and signatures placed at the bottom of this letter, it was remarked that a number of psychologists, sexologists, and psychiatrists had signed. What they were demanding, then, was the decriminalization of immoral act with minors over the age of fifteen, a different regime for immoral acts with minors between fifteen and eighteen, abolition of the offense of public outrage etc., etc. The fact that psychiatrists and psychologists demanded that the law be brought up to date on this point did not mean that they were on the side of those who were subjected to such repression.What I mean is, just because one is involved in a struggle against some authority, in this instance, the legal authorities, this does not mean one is on the side of those who are subjected to it. This is proved by the example of Germany, where from the 19th century onwards, from 1870, a whole movement protested against a law that was aimed at homosexuals, paragraph 175 of the German penal code. It was not even a habitual crime. There was no need to be an acknowledged homosexual; a single homosexual act was enough, whatever it may be. So a whole movement developed, made up of homosexuals, but also of doctors and psychiatrists, to demand the abolition of this law. But if one reads the literature published by these doctors and psychiatrists it becomes absolutely clear that they expected only one thing from the abolition of this law, namely, to be able to take over the perverts for themselves and to treat them with all the knowledge that they claimed to have acquired since around 1860. With Morel's *Treatise On Degeneracy* what we have is the setting up of a whole nosography of the perversions; and these psychiatrists were demanding in fact that the perverts be handed over to them, that the law should give up any dealings it may have with sexuality, which it speaks of so badly, in so unscientific a way, and that they should be able to treat cases in a perhaps less aggressive, less systematic, less blind way than the law; they alone could say in each case who was guilty, who was sick, and calmly decide what measures were to be taken.[5] I'm not saying that things were reproduced in the same way, but it is interesting to see how the two authorities could be in competition to get hold of that population of perverts.

FOUCAULT: I'm certainly not going to sum up everything that has been said. I think Hocquenghem has shown very clearly what was developing in relation to the strata of the population that had to be "protected." On the other hand, there is childhood, which by its very nature is in danger and must be protected against every possible danger, and therefore any possible act or attack. Then, on the other hand, there are dangerous individuals, who are generally adults of course, so that sexuality, in the new system that is being set up, will take on quite a different appearance from the one it used to have. In the past, laws prohibited a number of acts, indeed acts so numerous one was never quite sure what they were, but, nevertheless, it was acts that the law concerned itself with. Certain forms of behavior were condemned. Now what we are defining and, therefore, what will be found by the intervention of the law, the judge, and the doctor, are dangerous individuals. We're going to have a society of dangers, with, on the one side, those who are in danger, and on the other, those who are dangerous. And sexuality will no longer be a kind of behavior hedged in by precise prohibitions, but a kind of roaming danger, a sort of omnipresent phantom, a phantom that will be played out between men and women, children and adults, and possibly between adults themselves, etc. Sexuality will become a threat in all social relations, in all relations between members of different age groups, in all relations between individuals. It is on this shadow, this phantom, this fear that the authorities would try to get a grip through an apparently generous and, at least general, legislation and through a series of particular interventions that would probably be made by the legal institutions, with the support of the medical institutions. And what we will have there is a new regime for the supervision of sexuality; in the second half of the 20th century it may well be decriminalized, but only to appear in the form of a danger, a universal danger, and this represents a considerable change. I would say that the danger lay there.

DISCUSSION

PIERRE HAHN: I simply would like to mention a work that appeared about ten years ago, but which seems to me to be rather important in the present context. It is a work on the personality of exhibitionists. On the one hand, then, there is this classification that leads to excluding a certain type of exhibitionist from what I would call the system of psychoanalytic reeducation and, on the other hand, it actually consists in returning, but in rather different ways, apparently to the notion of the born criminal. I just would like to quote this sentence from the book, because it seems to me significant and then I shall say why: "The exhibitionist perversion is a category of exhibitionistic perverts—exhibitionistic perversion corresponds here to a phenomenon of radical amputation from part of the instincts, and this amputation takes place at a stage that is neither genital nor non-genital in sexual development, but in that still mysterious area where personality and instinct seem to me to be potential."

Yes, we are back to Lombroso's notion of the born criminal, which the author himself had just quoted.[6] It really is something present before birth, something that appears to be in the embryo; and if I mention the embryo it is because at the present time we are seeing a strong return of old methods, though perhaps wrapped up in new forms: methods such as psycho-surgery, in which, for example, homosexuals, pedophiles, and rapists might be operated on in the brain. On the other hand, certain genetic manipulations are being carried out: we had proof of this quite recently, especially in East Germany. All this seems to me very disturbing. Of course, it is pure repression. But, on the other hand, it is also evidence of a certain use of the critique of psychoanalysis that is in a sense quite reactionary, I would say, in inverted commas.

The expert referred to in the text I have quoted is called Jacques Stephani, a psychiatrist in Bordeaux who has contributed to the study of the exhibitionist personality. The expert actually says that the judge must act as one element in a process of therapeutic reeducation, except in the extreme case where the subject is regarded as beyond rehabilitation. This is the moral madman, Lombroso's born criminal. Indeed this idea that legislation, the legal system, the penal system, even medicine must concern themselves essentially with dangers, with dangerous individuals rather than acts, dates more or less from Lombroso and so it is not at all surprising if one finds Lombroso's ideas coming back into fashion. Society has to defend itself against dangerous individuals. There are dangerous individuals by nature, by heredity, by genetic code, etc.

Q: I would just like to ask Guy Hocquenghem, who gave us an outline of some examples of the repression associated today with this type of act, how can we create strategic alliances to fight in that area? The natural allies of this type of movement—which are, let's say, the progressive groups—are somewhat reticent about getting mixed up in this sort of business. Movements such as the women's movement are focusing their activities on such problems as rape and are succeeding in increasing the penalization of such acts.

HOCQUENGHEM: We were very careful in the text of the Open Letter to the Penal Code. We took great care to speak exclusively of an indecent act not involving violence and incitement of a minor to commit an indecent act. We were extremely careful not to touch, in any way, on the problem of rape, which is totally different. Now I agree with you on one thing, and that is that we have all seen the television program on rape and were all shocked by the reactions it aroused in France, some of which even went so far as telephone calls requesting the chemical castration of the rapists. There are two problems here. There is the problem of rape in the strict sense, on which the women's movement and women in general have expressed themselves perfectly clearly, but there is the other problem of the reactions at the level of public opinion. One triggers off secondary effects of man-hunting, lynching, or moral mobilization.

DANET: I should like to add something in reply to the same question. When we say that the problem of consent is quite central in matters concerned with pedophilia, we are not, of course, saying that consent is always there. But—and this is where one may separate the attitude of the law with regard to rape and with regard to pedophilia—in the case of rape, judges consider that there is a presumption of consent on the part of the women and that the opposite has to be demonstrated. Whereas where pedophilia is concerned, it's the opposite. It's considered that there is a presumption of non-consent, a presumption of violence, even in a case where no charge of an indecent act with violence has been made, that is, in a case in which the charge used is that of indecent act without violence, that is, with consenting pleasure—because it has to be said that this act without violence is the repressive, legal translation of consenting pleasure. It's pretty clear how the system of proof is manipulated in opposite ways in the case of rape of women and in the case of indecent assault on a minor.

Q: Public opinion, including enlightened opinion such as that of the doctors of the Institute of Sexology, asked at what age there can said to be definite consent. It's a big problem.

FOUCAULT: Yes, it is difficult to lay down barriers. Consent is one thing; it is a quite different thing when we are dealing with the likelihood of a child being believed when, speaking of his sexual relations, his affections, his tender feelings, or his contacts (the sexual adjective is often an embarrassment here, because it does not correspond to reality), a child's ability to explain what his feelings are, what actually happened, how far he is believed, these are quite different things. Now, where children are concerned, they are supposed to have a sexuality that can never be directed towards an adult, and that's that. Secondly, it is supposed that they are not capable of talking about themselves, of being sufficiently lucid about themselves. They are unable to express their feelings about the whole thing. Therefore they are not believed. They are thought to be incapable of sexuality and they are not thought to be capable of speaking about it. But, after all, listening to a child, hearing him speak, hearing him explain what his relations actually were with someone, adult or not, provided one listens with enough sympathy, must allow one to establish more or less what degree of violence if any was used or what degree of consent was given. And to assume that a child is incapable of explaining what happened and incapable of giving his consent are two abuses that are intolerable, quite unacceptable.

Q: If you were a legislator, you would fix no limit and you would leave it to the judges to decide whether or not an indecent act was committed with or without consent? Is that your position?

FOUCAULT: In any case, an age barrier laid down by law does not have much sense. Again, the child may be trusted to say whether or not he was subjected to violence. An examining magistrate, a liberal, told me once when we were discussing this question: after all, there are eighteen-year-old girls who are practically forced to make love with their fathers or their stepfathers; they may be eighteen, but it's an intolerable system of constraint. And one, moreover, that they feel as intolerable, if only people are willing to listen to them and put them in conditions in which they can say what they feel.

HOCQUENGHEM: On the one hand, we didn't put any age limit in our text. In any case, we don't regard ourselves as legislators, but simply as a movement of opinion that demands the abolition of certain pieces of legislation. Our role isn't to make up new ones. As far as this question of consent is concerned, I prefer the terms used by Michel Foucault: listen to what the child says and give it a certain credence. This notion of consent is a trap, in any case. What is sure is that the legal form of an intersexual consent is nonsense. No one signs a contract before making love.

FOUCAULT: Consent is a contractual notion.

HOCQUENGHEM: It's a purely contractual notion. When we say that children are "consenting" in these cases, all we intend to say is this: in any case, there was no violence, or organized manipulation in order to wrench out of them affective or erotic relations. It's an important point, all the more important for the children because it's an ambiguous victory in that to get a judge to organize a ceremony in which the children come and say that they were actually consenting is an ambiguous victory. The public affirmation of consent to such acts is extremely difficult, as we know. Everybody—judges, doctors, the defendant— knows that the child was consenting—but nobody says anything, because, apart from anything else, there's no way it can be introduced. It's not simply the effect of a prohibition by law: it's really impossible to express a very complete relationship between a child and an adult—a relation that is progressive, long, goes through all kinds of stages, which are not all exclusively sexual, through all kinds of affective contacts. To express this in terms of legal consent is an absurdity. In any case, if one listens to what a child says and if he says "I didn't mind," that doesn't have the legal value of "I consent." But I'm also very mistrustful of that formal recognition of consent on the part of a minor, because I know it will never be obtained and is meaningless in any case.

Translated by Alan Sheridan

---

1 Penal Code of 1810: Part of the Napoleonic Code. This group of 485 articles defines crimes, offenses, and misdemeanors as well as the resulting punishments. Promulgated February 12, 1810.

2 Mirguet amendment: Promulgated July 18, 1960 as amendment to article 38 of the 1958 French constitution (October 4, 1958). It declared the necessity to fight against all threats to public hygiene and specifically names tuberculosis, cancer, alcoholism, prostitution and homosexuality as objects of attack.

3 Françoise Dolto. French clinical psychoanalyst whose research on children focuses particularly on the theoretical aspects of early maladjustment [Lawrence D. Kritzman]

4 Klaus Croissant. The lawyer of the Red Army Fraction. He sought asylum in France but was the victim of extradition to Germany in 1978. Foucault took on the cause of Croissant and wrote many articles on his behalf in the *Nouvel Observateur.*

5 Bénédict-Auguste Morel (1809-1873). He studied the institution of the insane asylum in Europe and reformulated the coercive procedures used against the mentally ill.

6 Cesar Lombroso (1836-1909). Italian founder of the science of criminology. Postulated a theory that distinguishes "normal" individuals from criminal types.

33

The Impossible Prison

WHY THE PRISON?

Q: Why do you see the birth of the prison, and in particular this process you call "hurried substitution" which in the early years of the 19th century establishes the prison at the centre of the new penal system, as being so important?

Aren't you inclined to overstate the importance of the prison in penal history, given that other quite distinct modes of punishment (the death penalty, the penal colonies, deportation) remained in effect too? At the level of historical method, you seem to scorn explanation in terms of casuality or structure, and sometimes to prioritise a description of a process which is purely one of events. No doubt it's true that the preoccupation with "social history" has invaded historians' work in an uncontrolled manner, but, even if one does not accept the "social" as the only valid level of historical explanation, is it right for you to throw out social history altogether from your "interpretative diagram"?

MF: I wouldn't want what I may have said or written to be seen as laying any claims to totality. I don't try to universalize what I say; conversely, what I don't say isn't meant to be thereby disqualified as being of no importance. My work takes place between unfinished abutments and lines of dots. I like to open up a space of research, try it out, and then if it doesn't work, try again somewhere else. On many points—I am thinking especially of the relations between dialectics, genealogy and strategy—I am still working and don't yet know whether I am going to get anywhere. What I say ought to be taken as "propositions", "game openings" where those who may be interested are invited to join in; they are not meant as dogmatic assertions that have to be taken or left *en bloc*. My books aren't treatises in philosophy or studies of history: at most, they are philosophical fragments put to work in a historical field of problems.

I will attempt to answer the questions that have been posed. First, about the prison. You wonder whether it was as important as I have claimed, or whether it acted as the real focus of the penal system. I don't mean to suggest that the prison was the essential core of the entire penal system; nor am I saying that it would be impossible to approach the problems of penal history—not to speak of the history of crime in general—by other routes than the history of the prison. But it seemed to me legitimate to take the prison as my object, for two reasons. First, because it had been rather neglected in previous analyses; when people had set out to study the problems of "the penal order" *(pénalité)*—a confused enough term in any case—they usually opted to prioritize one of two directions: either the sociological problem of the criminal population, or the juridical problem of the penal system and its basis. The actual practice of punishment was scarcely studied except, in the line of the Frankfurt School, by Rusche and Kirchheimer. There have indeed been studies of prisons as institutions, but very few of imprisonment as a general punitive practice in our societies.

My second reason for wanting to study the prison was the idea of reactivating the project of a "genealogy of morals," one which worked by tracing the lines of transformation of what one might call "moral technologies." In order to get a better understanding of what is punished and why, I wanted to ask the question: how does one punish? This was the same procedure as I had used when dealing with madness: rather than asking what, in a given period, is regarded as sanity or insanity, as mental illness or normal behaviour, I wanted to ask how these divisions are enforced. This method seems to me to yield, I wouldn't say the maximum of possible illumination, but at least a fairly fruitful kind of intelligibility.

There was also, while I was writing this book, a contemporary issue relating to the prison and, more generally, to the numerous aspects of penal practice which were being brought into question. This development was noticeable not only in France but also in the United States, Britain and Italy. It would be interesting incidentally to consider why all these problems about confinement, internment, the penal dressage of individuals and their distribution, classification and objectification through forms of knowledge, came to be posed so urgently at this time, well in advance of May '68: the themes of antipsychiatry were formulated around 1958 to 1960. The connection with the matter of the concentration camps is evident—look at Bettelheim. But one would need to analyze more closely what took place around 1960.

In this piece of research on the prisons, as in my other earlier work, the target of analysis wasn't "institutions," "theories" or "ideology," but practices—with the aim of grasping the conditions which make these acceptable at a given moment; the hypothesis being that these types of practice are not just governed by institutions, prescribed by ideologies, guided by pragmatic circumstances—whatever role these elements may actually play—but possess up to a point their own specific regularities, logic, strategy, self-evidence and "rationale." It is a question of analysing a "regime of practices"—practices being understood here as places where what is said and what is done, rules imposed and reasons given, the planned and the taken for granted meet and interconnect.

To analyse "regimes of practices" means to analyse programmes of conduct which have both prescriptive effects regarding what is to be done (effects of "jurisdiction"), and codifying effects regarding what is to be known (effects of "veridiction").

So I was aiming to write a history, not of the prison as an institution, but of the practice of imprisonment. To show its origin, or, more exactly, to show how this way of doing things—ancient enough in itself—was capable of being accepted at a certain moment as a principal component of the penal system, thus coming to seem an altogether natural, self-evident and indispensable part of it.

It's a matter of shaking this false self-evidence, of demonstrating its precariousness, of making visible, not its arbitrariness but its complex interconnection with a multiplicity of historical processes, many of them of recent date. From this point of view I can say that the history of penal imprisonment exceeded my wildest hopes. All the early 19th century texts and discussions testify to the astonishment at finding the prison being used as a general means of punishment—something which had not at all been what the 18th century reformers had had in mind. I did not at all take this sudden change—which was what its contemporaries recognised it as being—as marking a result at which one's analysis could stop. I took this discontinuity, this in a sense "phenomenal" set of mutations, as my starting-point and tried, without eradicating it, to account for it. It was a matter not of digging down to a buried stratum of continuity but of identifying the transformation which made this hasty passage possible.

As you know, no one is more of a continuist than I am: to recognise a discontinuity is never anything more than to register a problem that needs to be solved.

Q: What you have just said clears up a number of things. All the same, historians have been troubled by a sort of equivocation in your analyses, a sort of oscillation between "hyper-rationalism" and "infra-rationality."

MF: I am trying to work in the direction of what one might call "eventualization." Even though the "event" has been for some while now a category little esteemed by historians, I wonder whether, understood in a certain sense, "eventalisation" may not be a useful procedure of analysis. What do I mean by this term? First of all, a breach of self-evidence. It means making visible a singularity at places where there is a temptation to invoke a historical constant, an immediate anthropological trait, or an obviousness which imposes itself uniformly on all. To show that things "weren't as necessary as all that," it wasn't as a matter of course that mad people came to be regarded as mentally ill; it wasn't self-evident that the only thing to be done with a criminal was to lock him up; it wasn't self-evident that the causes of illness were to be sought through the individual examination of bodies; and so on. A breach of self-evidence, of those self-evidences on which our knowledges, acquiescences and practices rest. This is the first theoretico-political function of "eventualization."

Secondly, eventualization means rediscovering the connections, encounters, supports, blockages, plays of forces, strategies and so on which at a given moment establish what subsequently counts as being self-evident, universal and necessary. In this sense one is indeed effecting a sort of multiplication or pluralisation of causes.

Does this mean that one regards the singularity one is analysing simply as a fact to be registered, a reasonless break in an inert continuum? Clearly not, since that would amount to treating continuity as a self-sufficient reality which carries its own raison d'etre within itself.

Causal multiplication consists in analysing an event according to the multiple processes which constitute it. So to analyse the practice of penal incarceration as an "event" (not as an institutional fact or ideological effect) means to determine the processes of "penalisation" (that is, progressive insertion into the forms of legal punishment) of already existing practices of internment; the processes of "carceralisation" of practices of penal justice (that is, the movement by which imprisonment as a form of punishment and technique of correction becomes a central component of the penal order); and these vast processes themselves need to be further broken down: the penalisation of internment comprises a multiplicity of processes such as the formation of closed pedagogical spaces functioning through rewards and punishments, etc.

As a procedure for lightening the weight of causality, "eventualization" thus works by constructing around the singular event analysed as process a "polygon" or rather a "polyhedron" of intelligibility, the number of whose faces is not given in advance and can never properly be taken as finite. One has to proceed by progressive, necessarily incomplete saturation. And one has to bear in mind that the further one decomposes the processes under analysis, the more one is enabled and indeed obliged to construct their external relations of intelligibility. (In concrete terms: the more one analyses the process of "carceralisation" of penal practice down to its smallest details, the more one is led to relate them to such practices as schooling, military discipline, etc.). The internal analysis of processes goes hand in hand with a multiplication of analytical "salients."

This operation thus leads to an increasing polymorphism as the analysis progresses:

—A polymorphism of the elements which are brought into relation: starting from the prison, one introduces the history of pedagogical practices, the formation of professional armies, British empirical philosophy, techniques of use of firearms, new methods of division of labour.

—A polymorphism of relations described: these may concern the transposition of technical models (such as architectures of surveillance), tactics calculated in response to a particular situation (such as the growth of banditry, the disorder provoked by public tortures and executions, the defects of the practice of penal banishment), or the application of theoretical schemas (such as those representing the genesis of ideas and the formation of signs, the Utilitarian conception of behaviour, etc.).

—A polymorphism of domains of reference (varying in their nature, generality, etc.), ranging from technical mutations in matters of detail to the attempted emplacement in a capitalist economy of new techniques of power designed in response to the exigencies of that economy.

Forgive this long detour, but it enables me better to reply to your question about hyper- and hypo-rationalisms, one which is often put to me.

It is some time since historians lost their love of events, and made "de-eventualization" their principle of historical intelligibility. The way they work is by ascribing the object they analyse to the most unitary, necessary, inevitable and (ultimately) extrahistorical mechanism or structure available. An economic mechanism, an anthropological structure or a demographic process which figures as the climactic stage in the investigation—these are the goals of de-eventualized history. (Of course, these remarks are only intended as a crude specification of a certain broad tendency.)

Clearly, viewed from the standpoint of this style of analysis, what I am proposing is at once too much and too little. There are too many diverse kinds of relations, too many lines of analysis, yet at the same time there is too little necessary unity. A plethora of intelligibilities, a deficit of necessities.

But for me this is precisely the point at issue, both in historical analysis and in political critique. We aren't, nor do we have to put ourselves under the sign of a unitary necessity.

THE PROBLEM OF RATIONALITIES

Q: I would like to pause for a moment on this question of eventualization, because it lies at the centre of a certain number of misunderstandings about your work. (I am not talking about the misguided portrayal of you as a "thinker of discontinunity.") Behind the identifying of breaks and the careful, detailed charting of these networks of relations that engender a reality and a history, there persists from one book to the next something amounting to one of those historical constants or anthropologico-cultural traits you were objecting to just now: this version of a general history of rationalisation spanning three or four centuries, or at any rate of a history of one particular kind of rationalisation as it progressively takes effect in our society. It's not by chance that your first book was a history of reason as well as of madness, and I believe that the themes of all your other books, the analysis of different techniques of isolation, the social taxonomies, etc., all this boils down to one and the same meta-anthropological or meta-historical process of rationalisation. In this sense, the "eventualization" which you define here as central to your work seems to me to constitute only one of its extremes.

MF: If one calls "Weberians" those who set out to take on board the Marxist analyses of the contradictions of capital, treating these contradictions as part and parcel of the irrational rationality of capitalist society, then I don't think I am a Weberian, since my basic preoccupation isn't rationality considered as an anthropological invariant. I don't believe one can speak of an intrinsic notion of "rationalisation" without, on the one hand, positing an absolute value inherent in reason, and on the other taking the risk of applying the term empirically in a completely arbitrary way. I think one must restrict one's use of this word to an instrumental and relative meaning. The ceremony of public torture isn't in itself more irrational than imprisonment in a cell; but it's irrational in terms of a type of penal practice which involves new ways of envisaging the effects to be produced by the penalty imposed, new ways of calculating its utility, justifying it, graduating it, etc. One isn't assessing things in terms of an absolute against which they could be evaluated as constituting more or less perfect forms of rationality, but rather examining how forms of rationality inscribe themselves in practices or systems of practices, and what role they play within them. Because it's true that "practices" don't exist without a certain regime of rationality. But, rather than measuring this regime against a value-of-reason, I would prefer to analyse it according to two axes: on the one hand, that of codification/prescription (how it forms an ensemble of rules, procedures, means to an end, etc.), and on the other, that of true or false formulation (how it determines a domain of objects about which it is possible to articulate true or false propositions).

If I have studied "practices" like those of the sequestration of the insane, or clinical medicine, or the organisation of the empirical sciences, or legal punishment, it was in order to study this interplay between a "code" which rules ways of doing things (how people are to be graded and examined, things and signs classified, individuals trained, etc.) and a production of true discourses which serve to found, justify, and provide reasons and principles for these ways of doing things. To put the matter clearly: my problem is to see how men govern (themselves and others) by the production of truth (I repeat once again that by production of truth I mean not the production of true utterances but the establishment of domains in which the practice of true and false can be made at once ordered and pertinent).

Eventualizing singular ensembles of practices, so as to make them graspable as different regimes of "jurisdiction" and "veridiction." That, to put it in exceedingly barbarous terms, is what I would like to do. You see that this is neither a history of knowledge-contents *(connaissances)* nor an analysis of the advancing rationalities which rule our society, nor an anthropology of the codifications which, without our knowledge, rule our behavior. I would like, in short, to resituate the production of true and false at the heart of historical analysis and political critique.

Q: It's not an accident that you speak of Max Weber. There is in your work, no doubt in a sense you wouldn't want to accept, a sort of "ideal type" which paralyses and mutes analysis when one tries to account for reality. Isn't this what led you to abstain from all commentary when you published the memoir of Pierre Rivière?

MF: I don't think your comparison with Max Weber is exact. Schematically one can say that the "ideal type" is a category of historical interpretation; it's a structure of understanding for the historian who seeks to integrate, after the fact, a certain set of data: it allows him to recapture an "essence"

(Calvinism, the State, the capitalist enterprise), working from general principles which are not at all present in the thought of the individuals whose concrete behaviour is nevertheless to be understood on their basis.

When I try to analyse the rationalities proper to penal imprisonment, the psychiatrisation of madness, or the organisation of the domain of sexuality, and when I lay stress on the fact that the real functioning of institutions isn't confined to the unfolding of this rational schema in its pure form, is this an analysis in terms of "ideal types"? I don't think so, for a number of reasons.

The rational schemas of the prison, the hospital or the asylum are not general principles which can be rediscovered only through the historian's retrospective interpretation. They are explicit programmes; we are dealing with sets of calculated, reasoned prescriptions in terms of which institutions are meant to be reorganised, spaces arranged, behaviours regulated. If they have an ideality, it is that of a programming left in abeyance, not that of a general but hidden meaning.

Of course this programming depends on forms of rationality much more general than those which they directly implement. I tried to show that the rationality envisaged in penal imprisonment wasn't the outcome of a straightforward calculation of immediate interest (internment turning out to be, in the last analysis, the simplest and cheapest solution) but that it arose out of a whole technology of human training, surveillance of behaviour, individualisation of the elements of a social body. "Discipline" isn't the expression of an "ideal type" (that of "disciplined man"); it's the generalization and interconnection of different techniques themselves designed in response to localised requirements (schooling; training troops to handle rifles).

These programmes don't take effect in the institutions in an integral manner; they are simplified, or some are chosen and not others; and things never work out as planned. But what I wanted to show is that this difference is not one between the purity of the ideal and the disorderly impurity of the real, but that in fact there are different strategies which are mutually opposed, composed and superposed so as to produce permanent and solid effects which can perfectly well be understood in terms of their rationality, even though they don't conform to the initial programming: this is what gives the resulting apparatus *(dispositif)* its solidity and suppleness.

Programmes, technologies, apparatuses—none of these is an "ideal type." I try to study the play and development of a set of diverse realities articulated onto each other; a programme, the connection which explains it, the law which gives it its coercive power, etc., are all just as much realities—albeit in a different mode—as the institutions that embody them or the behaviors that more or less faithfully conform to them.

You say to me: nothing happens as laid down in these "programmes"; they are no more than dreams, utopias, a sort of imaginary production that you aren't entitled to substitute for reality. Bentham's *Panopticon* isn't a very good description of "real life" in 19th century prisons.

To this I would reply: if I had wanted to describe "real life" in the prisons, I wouldn't indeed have gone to Bentham. But the fact that this real life isn't the same thing as the theoreticians' schemas doesn't entail that these schemas are therefore Utopian, imaginary, etc. That would be to have a very impoverished notion of the real. For one thing, the elaboration of these schemas corresponds to a whole series of diverse practices and strategies: the search for effective, measured, unified penal mechanisms is unquestionably a response to the inadequation of the institutions of judicial power to the new economic forms, urbanisation, etc; again, there is the attempt, very noticeable in a country like France, to reduce the autonomy and insularity of judicial practice and personnel within the overall workings of the State; there is the wish to respond to emerging new forms of criminality; and so on. For another thing, these programmes induce a whole series of effects in the real (which isn't, of course, the same as saying that they take the place of the real): they crystallize into institutions, they inform individual behaviour, they act as grids for the perception and evaluation of things. It is absolutely true that criminals stubbornly resisted the new disciplinary mechanism in the prison; it is absolutely correct that the actual functioning of the prisons, in the inherited buildings where they were established and with the governors and guards who administered them, was a witches' brew compared to the beautiful Benthamite machine. But if the prisons were seen to have failed, if criminals were perceived as incorrigible, and a whole new criminal "race" emerged into the field of vision of public opinion and "Justice," if the resistance of the prisoners and the pattern of recidivism took the forms we know they did, it's precisely because this type of programming didn't just remain a utopia in the heads of a few projectors.

These programmings of behaviour, these regimes of jurisdiction and veridiction aren't abortive schemas for the creation of a reality. They are fragments of reality which induce such particular effects in the real as the distinction between true and false implicit in the ways men "direct," "govern" and "conduct" themselves and others. To grasp these effects as historical events—with what this implies for the question of truth (which is the question of philosophy itself)—this is more or less my theme. You see that this has nothing to do with the project—an admirable one in itself—of grasping a "whole society" in its "living reality."

The question which I won't succeed in answering here but have been asking myself from the beginning is roughly the following: "What is history, given there is continually being produced within it a separation of true and false?" By that I mean four things. Firstly, in what sense is the production and transformation of the true/false division characteristic and decisive for our historicity? Secondly, in what specific ways has this relation operated in "Western" societies which produce scientific knowledge whose forms are perpetually changing and whose values are posited as universal? Thirdly, what historical knowledge is possible of a history which itself produces the true/false distinction on which such knowledge depends? Fourthly, isn't the most general of political problems the problem of truth? How can one analyse the connection between ways of distinguishing true and false and ways of governing oneself and others? The search for a new foundation for each of these practices, in itself and relative to the other, the will to discover a different way of governing oneself through a different way of dividing up true and false—this is what I would call "political spirituality."

The Anaesthetic Effect

Q: There is a question here about the way your analyses have been transmitted and received. For instance, if one talks to social workers in the prisons, one finds that the arrival of *Discipline and Punish* had an absolutely sterilizing, or rather anaesthetizing effect on them, because they felt your critique had an implacable logic which left them no possible room for initiative. You said just now, talking about eventualization, that you want to work towards breaking up existing self-evidentnesses, to show both how they are produced and how they are nevertheless always unstable. It seems to me that the second half of the picture—the aspect of instability—isn't clear.

MF: You're quite right to pose this problem of anaesthesis, one which is of capital importance. It's quite true that I don't feel myself capable of effecting the "subversion of all codes," "dislocation of all orders of knowledge," "revolutionary affirmation of violence," "overturning of all contemporary culture," these hopes and prospectuses which currently underpin all those brilliant intellectual ventures which I admire all the more because the worth and previous achievements of those who undertake them guarantees an appropriate outcome. My project is far from being of comparable scope. To give some assistance in wearing away certain self-evidentnesses and commonplaces about madness, normality, illness, crime and punishment; to bring it about, together with many others, that certain phrases can no longer be spoken so lightly, certain acts no longer, or at least no longer so unhesitatingly performed, to contribute to changing certain things in people's ways of perceiving and doing things, to participate in this difficult displacement of forms of sensibility and thresholds of tolerance—I hardly feel capable of attempting much more than that. If only what I have tried to say might somehow, to some degree, not remain altogether foreign to some such real effects... And yet I realise how much all this can remain precarious, how easily it can all lapse back into somnolence.

But you are right, one has to be more suspicious. Perhaps what I have written has had an anaesthetic effect. But one still needs to distinguish on whom.

To judge by what the psychiatric authorities have had to say, the cohorts on the Right who charge me with being against any form of power, those on the Left who call me the "last bulwark of the bourgeoisie" (this isn't a "Kanapa phrase";[1] on the contrary), the worthy psychoanalyst who likened me to the Hitler of *Mein Kampf,* the number of times I've been "autopsied" and "buried" during the past fifteen years—well, I have the impression of having had an irritant rather than anaesthetic effect on a good many people. The epidermi bristle with a constancy I find encouraging. A journal recently warned its readers in deliciously Petainist style against accepting as a credo what I had had to say about sexuality ("the importance of the subject," "the personality of the author" rendered my enterprise "dangerous"). No risk of anaesthetic in that direction. But I agree with you, these are trifles, amusing to note but tedious to collect. The only important problem is what happens on the ground.

We have known at least since the 19th century the difference between anaesthesis and paralysis. Let's talk about paralysis first. Who has been paralysed? Do you think what I wrote on the history of psychiatry paralysed those people who had already been concerned for some time about what was happening in psychiatric institutions? And, seeing what has been happening in and around the prisons, I don't think the effect of paralysis is very evident there either. As far as the people in prison are concerned, things aren't doing too badly. On the other hand, it's true that certain people, such as those who work in the institutional setting of the prison—which is not quite the same as being in prison—are not likely to find advice or instructions in my books that tell them "what is to be done." But my project is precisely to bring it about that they "no longer know what to do," so that the acts, gestures, discourses which up until then had seemed to go without saying become problematic, difficult, dangerous. This effect is intentional. And then I have some news for you: for me the problem of the prisons isn't one for the "social workers" but one for the prisoners. And on that side, I'm not so sure that what's been said over the last fifteen years has been quite so—how shall I put it?—demobilising.

But paralysis isn't the same thing as anaesthesis—on the contrary. It's in so far as there's been an awakening to a whole series of problems that the difficulty of doing anything comes to be felt. Not that this effect is an end in itself. But it seems to me that "what is to be done" ought not to be determined from above by reformers, be they prophetic or legislative, but by a long work of comings and goings, of exchanges, reflections, trials, different analyses. If the social workers you are talking about don't know which way to turn, this just goes to show that they're looking, and hence not anaesthetised or sterilised at all—on the contrary. And it's because of the need not to tie them down or immobilize them that there can be no question for me of trying to tell them "what is to be done." If the questions posed by the social workers you spoke of are going to assume their full amplitude, the most important thing is not to bury them under the weight of prescriptive, prophetic discourse. The necessity of reform mustn't be allowed to become a form of blackmail serving to limit, reduce or halt the exercise of criticism. Under no circumstances should one pay attention to those who tell you: "Don't criticise, since you're not capable of carrying out a reform." That's ministerial cabinet talk. Critique doesn't have to be the premise of a deduction which concludes: this then is what needs to be done. It should be an instrument for those who fight, those who resist and refuse what is. Its use should be in processes of conflict and confrontation, essays in refusal. It doesn't have to lay down the law for the law. It isn't a stage in a programming. It is a challenge directed to what is.

The problem, you see, is one for the subject who acts—the subject of action through which the real is transformed. If prisons and punitive mechanisms are transformed, it won't be because a plan of reform has found its way into the heads of the social workers; it will be when those who have to do with that penal reality, all those people, have come into collision with each other and with themselves, run into dead ends, problems and impossibilities, been through conflicts and confrontations; when critique has been played out in the real, not when reformers have realised their ideas.

Q: This anaesthetic effect has operated on the historians. If they haven't responded to your work it's because for them the "Foucauldian schema" was becoming as much of an encumbrance as the Marxist one. I don't know if the "effect" you produce interests you. But the explanations you have given here weren't so clear in *Discipline and Punish.*

MF: I really wonder whether we are using this word "anaesthetise" in the same sense. These historians seemed to me more to be "aesthetised," "irritated" (in Broussais' sense of the term, of course). Irritated by what? By a schema? I don't believe so, because there is no schema. If there is an "irritation" (and I seem to recall that in a certain journal a few signs of this irritation may have been discreetly manifested), it's more because of the absence of a schema. No infra- or superstructure, no Malthusian cycle, no opposition between State and civil society: none of these schemas which have bolstered historians' operations, explicitly or implicitly, for the past hundred or hundred and fifty years.

Hence no doubt the sense of malaise and the questions enjoining me to situate myself within some such schema: "What do you do with the State? What theory do you offer of the State?" Some say I neglect its role, others that I see it everywhere, imagining it capable of minutely controlling individuals' everyday lives. Or that my descriptions leave out all reference to an infrastructure—while others say that I make an infrastructure out of sexuality. The totally contradictory nature of these objections proves that what I am doing doesn't correspond to any of these schemas.

Perhaps the reason why my work irritates people is precisely the fact that I'm not interested in constructing a new schema, nor in validating one that already exists. Perhaps it's because my objective isn't to propose a global principle for analysing society. And it's here that my project has differed since the outset from that of the historians. They—rightly or wrongly, that's another question—take "society" as the general horizon of their analysis, the instance relative to which they set out to situate this or that particular object ("society, economy, civilisation," as the *Annales* have it). My general theme isn't society but the discourse of true and false, by which I mean the correlative formation of domains and objects and the verifiable, falsifiable discourses that bear on them; and it's not just their formation that interests me, but the effects in the real to which they are linked.

I realise I'm not being clear. I'll take an example. It's perfectly legitimate for the historian to ask whether sexual behaviours in a given period were supervised and controlled, and to ask which among them were heavily disapproved of. (It would, of course, be frivolous to suppose that one has explained a certain intensity of "repression" by delaying the age of marriage; here one has scarcely even begun to outline a problem: why is it that the delay in the age of marriage takes effect thus and not otherwise?) But the problem I pose myself is a quite different one; it's a matter of how the rendering of sexual behaviour into discourse comes to be transformed, what types of jurisidiction and "veridiction" it's subject to, and how the constitutive elements are formed of this domain which comes—and only at a very late stage—to be termed "sexuality." Among the numerous effects the organisation of this domain has undoubtedly had, one is that of having provided historians with a category so "self-evident" that they believe they can write a history of sexuality and its repression.

The history of the "objectification" of those elements which historians consider as objectively given (if I dare put it thus: of the objectification of objectivities), this is the sort of circle I want to try and investigate. It's a difficult tangle to sort out: this, not the presence of some easily reproducible schema, is what doubtless troubles and irritates people. Of course, this is a problem of philosophy to which the historian is entitled to remain indifferent. But if I am posing it as a problem within historical analysis, I'm not demanding that history answer it. I would just like to find out what effects the question produces within historical knowledge. Paul Veyne saw this very clearly[2]: it's a matter of the effect on historical knowledge of a nominalist critique formulated elsewhere, but by way of a historical analysis.

Translated by Colin Gordon

[1] Jean Kanapa was a leader of the French PC. [Ed.]

[2] Cf. "Foucault révolutionne l'histoire", in Paul Veyne, *Comment on écrit l'histoire.*(Paris: Seuil, 1978). [Ed.]

34

White Magic and Black Gown*

MICHEL FOUCAULT: Experts are attacked. I do not want to defend experts, but I wonder if there is not a question to ask psychiatry in general. What is striking in the history of psychiatric expertise in criminal matters, is the fact that psychiatrists were the ones who absolutely imposed themselves on the penal system which wanted nothing to do with it and which tried everything to get rid of them. Psychiatrists forced themselves on it and now have it under their thumb. *But what is this desire for the criminal on the part of the psychiatrist?* In psychiatry, there has been a desire to annex criminality for two centuries now. And we cannot understand how psychiatric expertise functions today if we do not account, on one hand, for the criminal justice system, but, also, on the other hand, for psychiatry and the need psychiatric practice in general has for medical-legal expertise. Psychiatric practice as a whole needs there to be experts, psychiatric interventions as such in the area of criminal justice.

And I think that the reason, mentioned before (the law of 1838), is that at the time when psychiatrists gave themselves the right to confine an individual as dangerous, they had to show that madness was dangerous... They established that at the heart of every crime there was a bit of madness and, from the moment one shows that behind the crime, there is the danger of madness, reciprocally, behind madness, there is the danger of crime.

But, between the law of 1838 and medical-legal expertise, there is mutual reinforcement. One must account for that, and consider the experts necessary for the law to function.

There are two institutions which are in charge of the dangers represented by individuals: medicine and law. The psychiatrist is the person in charge of individual dangers.

---

*The participants in this panel are described as follows: André Bompart—psychiatrist, psychoanalyst; Michel Foucault—professor at the Collège de France and author of books on madness; Pierre Gay—psychiatrist who always refused to be officially listed as an expert-specialist in psychiatry; Jacques Hassoun—director of the publication *Garde-Fous;* J. Lafon—Head psychiatrist at Sainte-Anne Hospital, specialist in psychiatry and professor at the Institute of Criminology in Paris; Philippe Sphyras—lawyer, Court of Appeals, Paris.

LAFON: Now, lawyers run after psychiatrists and judges systematically ask for expert testimony.

FOUCAULT: Crime has become a privileged object for psychiatric analysis, it is a clear, constant fact. Psychiatry needs to annex criminality for itself in order to function as it does.

PIERRE GAY: Except if one introduces a kind of psychiatry that no longer needs to prove that madness is dangerous.

JACQUES HASSOUN: It is something that may seem unpleasant, this accusation against the expert. But I think that psychiatric expertise is the symptom of psychiatry. If one formulates the problem in political terms, psychiatry tries to stick to events, medical psychiatry is repressive.

LAFON: Expert = the *de facto* judge—therefore in what way can the lawyer organize his defense in terms of this omnipresence of the *de facto* judge who is the expert and dominates the legal judge?

Q: Question: to what degree, disguised as psychiatric expertise, does one end up having the expert play a traditionally repressive role, without any of the guarantees provided for in the Penal Code?

PHILIPPE SPHYRAS: The accused has the same feelings for the expert as for a judge, and so, shouldn't there be another kind of expertise practiced differently?

COSSARD: Down deep, what appalls lawyers, trial lawyers in particular, is to see themselves dispossessed of some of their power because they can assist their clients the day of the interrogation, but the day of the psychiatric evaluation, they are not there. We attack the expert evaluations because we are completely dispossessed by them.

LAFON: What lawyers accuse us the most, is of not automatically coming on the side of the defense.

COSSARD: Not necessarily. But a number of guarantees for the defense *no longer exist.*

LAFON: One has to know the facts. The way in which the facts are presented has a great deal of importance for psychological and psychiatric determinations as well as the way in which they were lived.

COSSARD: I do not see the connection between this and the answers you have to give in your expert psychiatric evaluations and which are the three questions the judge asks you for in his binding order, that is: 1. to specify if the accused presents any mental, psychic or character anomalies. And if so, to describe them and specify the afflictions linked to them; 2. to say if the accused was in a *state of dementia (insane)* as per article 64 of the Penal Code, at the moment of the crime; and if not, to say if the anomalies observed are of the sort which can attenuate his responsibility; 3. to say if (the accused) has access to a criminal punishment, if he is *curable and can be rehabilitated,* if his placement in a psychiatric hospital is advisable, either in his interest or in that of the general public.

LAFON: *What is access to criminal punishment?* Definition: it is the fact of knowing whether an individual is capable of understanding that he has committed an anti-social act and that this act is theoretically punished under the penal code. Hence people who are not insane are "accessible" to criminal punishment.

FOUCAULT: In the beginning in the practice of psychiatric expertise (article 64) the question asked was: was the individual insane at the moment when the act was committed? In this case, there is no longer a crime; in the beginning, the psychiatrist never intervened at the level of sentencing, but simply at the procedural level. Bit by bit, he started to intervene at the level of attenuating circumstances to eventually modulate the sentence, and starting in 1832, the psychiatrist's report modulates the sentence, then it intervenes, since he has to say whether the responsibility of the individual is attenuated, which juridically speaking makes no sense, and begins not to make sense medically, when previously insanity made sense. Therefore, attenuated responsibility has no juridical meaning and no medical meaning, and we arrive at the three questions of 1958 which are dangerousness, accessibility to the sentence, the possibility of rehabilitation or adaptability. These three notions are neither psychiatric notions nor are they juridical notions, but their effect within the criminal justice system is enormous.

Q: What can indicate whether someone can be rehabilitated or not? Or rather, what does it mean to be "unadaptable"?

LAFON: There are many, many people about which one cannot say that they cannot be rehabilitated. They are, on the contrary, very well adapted to their careers (mobsters for example), but of course not according to society's norms. There are also people who have never been "unadaptable," The psychiatrist is there to sort out the "crazies" and to protect them for the influence of justice. That is the initial idea which was later modified, and in the end, psychiatrists were asked to do something else. And, as long as they are in the free will system, they have to proceed in this fashion. If one accepts being an expert in court, one cannot sabotage expert evaluations. One must admit that *a priori* people are responsible for their actions, with the exception of those who are mad.

FOUCAULT: We have to get back to an important question raised by lawyers: does the accused belong to justice or not? If the expert answers yes, he goes to court; if the expert answers no, the accused is taken out of the hands of justice. But, once again since 1832, the psychiatrist intervenes in order to say what kind of sentence there will be. Therefore, he has a judiciary role within the very unfolding of justice, and the discomfort of lawyers is linked to just this fact. For the lawyer is now dealing with two judges, including this pseudojudge who is going to modify the sentence, and, the greater the role of modulator of the sentencing in penal psychiatry, the less the concepts utilized by these psychiatrists are medical ones.

LAFON: That is precisely what makes psychiatric expertise so difficult. A good expert evaluation is one which does not attempt to take sides, one which remains as objective as possible.

DUPONT MONOD: I think that expert testimony as such has retarded and perhaps even prevented justice from becoming aware of its own repressive character. It allows the judge to say in an extremely easy way: you are the defender, I am not the one responsible for my appreciation of the facts, it's the expert. The expert is a screen for the judge.

COSSARD: Down deep, the judge's dream would be to leave it entirely up to the experts.

HASSOUN: Psychiatry as a whole handles concepts such as readaptability, dangerousness, responsibility. Psychiatry is now entirely molded by these concepts.

FOUCAULT: Where do these notions of dangerousness, accessibility to sentencing and rehabilitation come from after all? They aren't from medicine or law. These notions are neither juridical, nor psychiatric or medical, but rather disciplinary. There are all those little disciplines in school, in the barracks, in reform schools, the factory, which have taken on greater and greater importance. All these institutions, by proliferating, expanding, ramifying their networks throughout society, have made these notions emerge which were originally unbelievably empirical and which are now found to be doubly sacred. On one hand, through the psychiatric and medical discourse, therefore apparently scientific, which uses them and on the other hand, by the judiciary effect they have, since it is in their name that someone is condemned. I think that criminology drags along these notions.

LAFON: These notions which you call disciplinary, I will simply call them ideological. These are notions which refer to a dominant ideology, and therefore, the expert, the judge, the lawyer, all play exactly the same role, which is that of society defending itself. There is clearly no mentally ill person, no delinquant, there is, each time, the product of a society.

FOUCAULT: It's the word "ideology" and how you use it that I don't agree with at all. If it were simply a question of rehashing an ideology, that wouldn't be too serious. The word "disciplinary" is more important because it is a type of power. In inscribing these notions in law and in psychiatry, one authenticates them, makes them sacred.

ANDRÉ BOMPART: Can what Mr. Foucault is saying be connected to Legendre's work on canonical law?

FOUCAULT: That interesting book does not touch on this human materiality of mechanisms of power.

Translated by Lysa Hochroth

35

"Paris – Berlin"

Q: Hundreds of visitors waited in line, often for hours, to attend the "Paris-Berlin" exhibition at the Centre Pompidou. The reviewers were enthusiastic. Even "Le Monde," a paper which has not been particularly friendly to Germany in the past few years, wrote: "This exhibition has a significance which could be termed historic." What's the meaning of this euphoria?

MF: I wouldn't term it euphoria but instead enormous astonishment. Suddenly we French no longer find what we regarded as our "identity." We see that we were very similar to the Germans when we were killing each other, and very far apart from each other when we drew closer. We feel very close to their past and—as they do—quite distant from the recent past.

Q: So that the connections which existed between Paris and Berlin only now become clear to the exhibit visitor?

MF: A question comes to mind when entering the exhibition: Who were they, these people on the other side? And a different question arises while looking at the exhibition: Who are we, they and we, who have paired like the genes of two cells to form a third according to some set of bizarre laws? Since the Franco-Prussian War of 1870, we have had such a distrustful relationship with Germany that entire epochs of German culture were systematically hidden, while others appeared to us as sporadically surfacing fragments.

Q: With the result that, say, Brecht, Freud, Marcuse, Klee do not represent German culture or the German language for some French people. Haven't they instead become something like stateless figures of the world stature?

MF: Yes. For a long time, and especially since the First World War, the French accepted Germans or representatives of German culture only on the condition that they demonstrate sufficient distance from Germany, its institutions, and its history. Once "de-Germanized," they could be acknowledged. Brecht was acceptable because he was a Marxist, Marcuse because he had become an

American, Freud from the moment he was driven out of Vienna by the Germans, Thomas Mann because he lived in Switzerland and the USA.

Q: Is this exhibition the turning point? Is it really—as "Le Monde" wrote—"an opportunity to get acquainted and perhaps understand each other"?

MF: After the war, Europeans were constantly pulled back and forth between one side, the Atlantic, and the other, the Vistula. You were a European, but of the Eastern Community. Reduced to nothing or next to nothing at the end of the war, Europe sought its Metropolis in the East and the West, to the right and to the left. In the process, the center and the cause of all of the agonies of our entire history could be ignored. Today the world is regionalizing, and Europe has to think about itself.

Q: And do the French have to recognize in this exhibition that there was not a direct line from Bismarck to Hitler?

MF: In France, one way of diffusing the political and cultural problems posed by Germany has always been to simply ignore it. We opposed the good German to the bad German, the cultivated to the militaristic, the Germanic to the European Germany. The division has been even more simplified in the past few years: the pure, hardworking, ordered Germany, face-to-face with a handful of terroristic nihilists; immovable fullness and the exploding void.

Q: Wasn't it primarily filmmakers such as Fassbinder and Herzog who finally corrected the image of the supposed German police state strangling the art and at the most permitting Heinrich Böll to breathe?

MF: The German film very definitely gave us a new concept of what was going on in German society, not by showing a "different" Germany, but by showing a tense and disturbing one.

Q: Haven't the French up to now seen cultural Germany in classical terms, between Goethe and Hesse, Beethoven and Heine, Brahms and Wagner? Such Expressionists as Macke and Beckman were probably first discovered in this exhibition.

MF: Since the end of Impressionism, French painting has been tending ever more strongly in a descending line in the direction of formalism, abstraction. Painting as a powerful form of expression, as a lyrical protest, was unknown in France. We only just discovered it through such painters as Bacon. The exhibition "Paris-Berlin" shows us the roots of this type of painting—so new to us—in German Expressionism.

Q: Were these painters new to you as well?

MF: As they were for every good, average Frenchman. I experience this art as very contemporary. Perhaps prompted by the general trend in France, I have recently begun reading very systematically those German philosophers and writers of the 20th century whom I scarcely knew. It's often said in France that we're still living in the 19th century. When I looked at "Paris-Berlin" and read the German authors of the years 1910 to 1930, I became conscious that the 20th century actually does exist with its own ideas, problems, specific cultural forms. To my mind, this exhibition is proof of the 20th century.

Translated by J. D. Steakley

36

THE SIMPLEST OF PLEASURES

"Homosexuals often commit suicide," reports a psychiatric study. This word "often" fascinates me. We might imagine tall, slender, pallid creatures unable to cross over the threshhold to the opposite sex, in a faceoff with death all through life, only to end it finally by slamming the door with a loud bang (which never fails to annoy the neighbors). Instead of marrying the opposite sex they marry death. The other sex is replaced by the other side. But, the story goes, they're just as incapable of dying as they are of really living. In this ludicrous account suicide and homosexuals are portrayed so as to make each other look bad.

So let's see what there is to say in favor of suicide. Not so much in support of legalizing it or making it "moral." Too many people have already belabored these lofty things. Instead, let's say something against the shady affairs, humiliations, and hypocrisies that its detractors usually surround it with: hastily getting boxes of pills together, finding a solid, old-fashioned razor, or licking gun store windows and entering some place pretending to be on the verge of death.

In my opinion a person should have the right not to be rushed, which is very bothersome. Indeed, a great deal of attention and competence are required. You should have the chance to discuss at length the various qualities of each weapon and its potential. It would be nice if the salesperson were experienced in these things, with a big smile, encouraging but a little bit reserved (not too chatty), and sophisticated enough to understand that they were dealing with a person who's basically good-hearted, but somewhat clumsy, never having had the idea before of employing a machine that shoots people. It would also be convenient if the salesperson's enthusiasm didn't stop them from advising you about the existence of alternative ways, ways that were more chic, more your style. This kind of business-like discussion is worth a thousand times more than the chatter that goes on around the corpse among the employees of the funeral parlor.

Some people that we didn't even know, and who didn't know us either, arranged it so that one day we started existing. They pretended to believe, no doubt sincerely, that they were waiting for us. In any case they prepared for our entry into the world with great care (and often with a sort of second-hand seriousness). It's quite inconceivable that we not be given the chance to prepare ourselves with all the passion, intensity and detail that we wish, including the little extras that we've been dreaming about for such a long time, since childhood perhaps or just some warm summer evening. Life it seems is quite fragile in the human species and death quite certain. Why must we make of this certainty a mere happenstance (which might suggest, by virtue of its suddenness or inevitability, an air of punishment)?

The philosophies that promise to teach us what to think about death and how to die bore me to tears. I'm not at all moved by those things that are supposed to "prepare us for it". One has to prepare it bit by bit, decorate it, arrange the details, find the ingredients, imagine it, chose it, get advice on it, shave it into a work without spectators, one which exists only for oneself, just for that shortest little moment of life. Those who survive, of course, see suicide as nothing but superficial traces, solitude, awkwardness, and unanswered cries. These people can't help but ask "why?": the only question about death that shouldn't be asked.

"Why? Because I wanted to." It's true that suicide often leaves discouraging traces. But who's to blame? Do you think it's pleasant to have to hang yourself in the kitchen with your tongue hanging out all bluish? Or to close yourself in the garage and turn on the gas? Or to leave a tiny bit of your brain lying on the sidewalk for the dogs to come and sniff at? I believe that we're witnessing in these times a "suicide spiral" because many people are so depressed at the thought of all these nasty things that are forced on someone who's aspiring to suicide (things including the police, the ambulance, the elevator man, the autopsy and what not), that many prefer to commit suicide rather than continue to think about it all.

Some advice to the lovers of humanity. If you really want to see a decrease in the number of suicides, support only those potential suicides which are committed with forethought, quietly and without wavering. Suicide must not be left to unhappy people who might bungle it or make a mess of it. In any case there are lots fewer happy than unhappy people. It's always struck me as strange that people say that death is nothing to worry about, because between life and nothingness death is nothing but a border. But is it true that this all there is to the game? Make something of it, something fine.

No doubt we've missed out on a lot of pleasures and we've had some that were pretty mediocre: others we've let slip by out of laziness or lack of attention, imagination or persistence. We should consider ourselves lucky to have at hand (with suicide) an extremely unique experience: it's the one which above all the rest deserves the greatest attention—not that it shouldn't worry you (or comfort you)—but rather so that you can make of it a fathomless pleasure whose patient and relentless preparation will enlighten all of your life.

Suicide festivals or orgies are just two of the possible methods. There are others more intricate and learned. When I see the funeral "homes" in American cities I'm not just appalled by how dreadfully banal they are, as if death had to smother any attempt at imagination, but also I think it's a pity that they serve only cadavers and their glad-to-still-be-alive families. Let there be some alternatives for those of little means and those who have grown weary of too much reflection so that they don't have to rely on these prepackaged, boring and expensive expedients. For example, alternatives like those the Japanese have devised (they're called "love hotels") for having sex. They know a lot more about suicide than we do.

If you have the chance to go to the Chantily in Tokyo you'll see what I mean. You'll sense there the existence of places without maps or calendars where you can enter into the most absurd decors with anonymous partners to look for an opportunity to die free of all stereotypes. There you'd have an indeterminate amount of time—seconds, weeks, months perhaps—until the moment presents itself with a compelling clearness. You'd recognize it immediately. You couldn't miss it. It would have the shapeless shape of utterly simple pleasure.

37

TRUTH IS IN THE FUTURE

Q: In France your work is well known, part of the popular culture. Here you are known only in academic circles—the fate, it seems, of almost all intellectual critics in the United States. How do you account for this difference?

MF: Since 1964 in France the university has been in a deep crisis, both political and cultural. There have been two movements: a movement among the students to try to get rid of the purely academic life, a movement also identified with other movements such as feminism and gay rights. The second movement has been among the teachers, away from the university. There has been an attempt among them to try to express their ideas in other places—to write books, to speak on radio or television. And then, French newspapers have always been much more interested in discussing ideas of this kind than American newspapers.

Q: In your lectures you spoke of the necessity for individual self-realization. In the U.S. there has been for some time, of course, a large movement for self-realization, an apolitical one, connected with encounter groups or groups like EST or groups of other kinds. Do you make a distinction between that "self-realization" and your use of the word?

MF: In France too there is a movement of the same type and of the same intensity. I think of subjectivity in another way. I think that subjectivity and identity and individuality have been a great political problem since the 1960s. I think there is a danger in thinking of identity and subjectivity as quite deep and quite natural and not determined by political and social factors. The psychological subjectivity that the psychoanalysts deal with—we have to be liberated from this kind of subjectivity. We are prisoners of certain conceptions about ourselves and our behavior. We have to liberate our own subjectivity, our own relation to ourselves.

Q: You said something in your talk about the tyranny of the modern state as it relates to war and welfare.

MF: Yes, if we think about the way in which the modern state began to worry about individuals—about the lives of individuals—there is a paradox in this history. At the same moment the state began to practice its greatest slaughters, it began to worry about the physical and mental health of each individual. The first great book on public health in France was written in 1784, five years before the Revolution, and ten years before the Napoleonic wars. This game between death and life is one of the main paradoxes of the modern state.

Q: Is the situation different in other societies, in socialist or Communist countries?

MF: It is not very different in the Soviet Union and China from this point of view. The control over individual life in the Soviet Union is very strong. Apparently nothing in the life of the individual is a matter of indifference to the government. The Soviets killed 16 million people to build socialism. Mass slaughter and individual control are two deep characteristics of all modern societies.

Q: There are critics in this country who are also concerned with the questions of the manipulation of individuals by the state and by other institutions. I think of Thomas Szasz, for example. How do you think of your work in relation to theirs?

MF: This kind of problem I write about is not a new problem. It is not my own invention. One thing struck me in the American review of my books, particularly the review of my book on prisons. They say I am trying to do the same thing as Erving Goffman in his work on asylums, that I try to do the same thing but not as well. I am not a social scientist. I don't want to do the same thing. His problem is the way a certain type of institution works, the total institution—the asylum, the school, the prison. My problem is to show and analyze the way in which a set of power techniques is related to forms, political forms like states, or social forms. Goffman's problem is the institution itself. My problem is the rationalization of the management of the individual. My own work is not a history of institutions or a history of ideas, but the history of rationality as it works in institutions and in the behavior of people.

All human behavior is scheduled and programmed through rationality. There is a logic in institutions and in behavior and in political relations. In even the most violent ones there is a rationality. What is most dangerous in violence is its rationality. Of course violence itself is terrible. But the deepest root of violence and its permanence come out of the form of the rationality we use. The idea has been that if we live in the world of reason, we can get rid of violence. This is quite wrong. Between violence and rationality there is no incompatibility. My problem is not to put reason on trial, but to know what is this rationality so compatible with violence.

It is not reason in general that I am fighting. I could not fight reason.

Q: You say you are not a scientist. Some people say you are an artist. But then I was present when a student came up to you with a copy of *Discipline and Punish* and asked you to sign it, and you said, "No, only artists should sign their work. And I am not an artist."

MF: An artist? When I was a boy I never thought of becoming a writer. Now when a book is a piece of art, that is something important. Somebody like me, it is always to do something, to change even a small part of the reality—to write a book about madness, to change even the smallest part of our reality—people's ideas.

I am not an artist, I am not a scientist. I am somebody who tries to deal with reality through those things which are always—often—far from reality.

Q: I understand that you have worked and taught in Sweden, Poland, Germany, and Tunis. Did working in those countries have an important influence on you?

MF: Because of my theoretical interests the time I spent in Sweden, Poland, and Germany, those societies near my own—but a little different—were very important. They looked sometimes like an exaggeration or an exacerbation of my own society. In 1955 to 1960, Sweden was, from a welfare, social-political point of view, much in advance of France. And a lot of the trends in France which were not perceptible were visible to me there—though the Swedes were blind to them themselves. I had a foot ten years back and a foot ten years ahead.

I was in Poland for a year. From a psychological and cultural point of view, Poland is deeply related to France, but they live in a socialist system. The contradiction was very clear to me.

If I had been in the Soviet Union, on the other hand, that would have been a different case. There, under a political system that has lasted more than fifty years, the behavior of the people is much more modeled by the government.

Q: When you speak of modeling, are you implying that it is inescapable, or do you believe that there is something in human beings that resists such modeling?

MF: In human societies one can't find political power without domination. But no one wants to be commanded—though very often in a lot of situations, people accept it. If you take a historical view in most societies we know, the political structure is unstable. I am not speaking of non-historical societies—primitive societies. Their history is nothing like our own. But in all the societies that belong to our tradition there has been instability and revolution.

Q: Your thesis about the pastoral shape of power is based upon the idea of an Old Testament God who guards and watches a people who obey. But what of the times the Israelites did not obey?

MF: The fact that the flock doesn't follow the shepherd is quite normal. The problem is to know how people experience their relation to God. In the Old Testament, God as a shepherd is the way in which the Jews experienced that relationship. In the Greek city, the relationship to God was much more similar to that between a pilot and the passengers of a boat.

Q: It is very odd—this may sound very strange—but it seems to me that even though many of your assumptions appear contradictory, there is something persuasive about your approach and your convictions.

MF: I am not merely a historian. I am not a novelist. What I do is a kind of historical fiction. In a sense I know very well that what I say is not true. A historian could say of what I've said, "That's not true." I should put it this way: I've written a lot about madness in the early 1960s—a history of the birth of psychiatry. I know very well that what I have done from a historical point of view is single-minded, exaggerated. Perhaps I have dropped out some contradictory factors. But the book had an effect on the perception of madness. So the book and my thesis have a truth in the nowadays reality.

What I am trying to do is provoke an interference between our reality and the knowledge of our past history. If I succeed, this will have real effects in our present history. My hope is my books become true after they have been written—not before.

My English is not very good, so with this kind of sentence I've said, people will say, "You see, he's a liar." But let me try to say it another way. I have written a book about prisons. I have tried to underline trends in the history of prisons. "Only one trend," people could say. "So that's not exactly true."

But two years ago there was turmoil in several prisons in France, prisoners revolting. In two prisons, the prisoners in their cells read my book. They shouted the text to other prisoners. I know it's pretentious to say, but that's a proof of a truth—a political and actual truth—which started after the book was written.

I hope that the truth of my books is in the future.

38

THE MASKED PHILOSOPHER

Q: Allow me first to ask why you have chosen to remain anonymous?[1]

MF: You know the story of the psychologist who went to a little village in the depths of Africa to show a film to its inhabitants. He then asked them to recount the story exactly as they had understood it. Well, in this anecdote with three characters they had only been interested in one thing: the passage of light and shadows through the trees. For us, the characters establish the laws of perception. Our eyes naturally focus on the figures who come and go, arise and disappear.

Why have I suggested that I remain anonymous? Out of nostalgia for the time when, being completely unknown, what I said had some chance of being heard. The surface contact with some possible reader was without a wrinkle. The effects of the book rebounded in unforeseen places and outlined forms I hadn't thought about. The name is a facility.

I will propose a game: the year without names. For one year books will be published without the author's name. The critics will have to manage with an entirely anonymous production. But I suspect that perhaps they will have nothing to say: all the authors will wait until the next year to publish their books.

Q: Do you think intellectuals today speak too much? That they encumber us with their discourse at every opportunity and most often inopportunely?

MF: The word "intellectual" is foreign to me. I have never encountered any intellectuals. I have known people who write novels, and others who take care of illnesses; some who do economic studies and others who compose electronic music. I have encountered people who teach, people who paint, and people who do I don't know what. But intellectuals, never.

On the other hand, I have met many people who talk about intellectuals. And, as a result of hearing them, I have formed an idea of what this animal might be. It's not difficult: an intellectual is one who is guilty. Guilty of a little of everything: of speaking, of remaining silent, of doing nothing, of mixing in everywhere. In short, the raw material for a verdict, a sentencing, a condemnation, an exclusion...

I don't find that intellectuals talk too much, since they don't exist for me. But I do find the discourse of intellectuals very intrusive and not very reassuring.

I have a regrettable mania. When people speak, like that, idly, I try to imagine what would result if their words were transcribed into reality. When they "criticize" someone, when they "denounce" his ideas, when they "condemn" what he writes, I imagine them in an ideal situation where they would have complete power over him. I let the first meaning of the words they use return: to demolish, beat down, reduce to silence, bury. And I catch sight of the radiant city where the intellectual would be in prison, and hanged of course, if in addition he were a theoretician. To be sure, we don't live in a regime where intellectuals are sent to the rice-fields. But in fact, tell me, have you heard of a certain Toni Negri? Isn't he in prison for being an intellectual?[2]

Q: Well then, what has led you to entrench yourself behind anonymity? The fact that philosophers use their names, or allow their names to be used, for some advertising?

MF: That doesn't shock me at all. I saw great men in plaster in the halls of my *lycée*. And now I see at the bottom of the first page of a newspaper the photograph of a thinker. I don't know if the aesthetics have improved. The economic rationality, surely...

At bottom I am very touched by a letter that Kant wrote when he was already very old. He was hurrying, he writes, against age and his worsening eyesight and muddled ideas, in order to finish one of his books for the Leipzig fair. I recount the story to show that all that has no importance. Advertising or not, Leipzig fair or not, the book is something else. I will never be persuaded that a book is bad because its author was seen on television. Or that it is good for the same reason.[3]

If I have chosen anonymity, it is not in order to criticize such and such, which I have never done. It's a way of addressing more directly the possible reader, the only character here who interests me: "Since you don't know who I am, you will not be tempted to look for the reasons for which I state what you are reading: let yourself go to the point of simply saying to yourself: this is true, this false. That I like, that I don't. One point, that's all."

Q: But doesn't the public wait for the critic to supply it with a precise appreciation of a work's value?

MF: I don't know if the public waits or not for the critic to judge the works and authors. The judges were there, I think, before it could say what it wanted.

It seems that Courbet had a friend who woke up during the night screaming: "To judge, I want to judge." It's crazy, that people like to judge. It's everywhere, all the time. No doubt it's one of the simplest things that humanity has been given to do. And you know that the last man, when finally the last radiation has reduced his last adversary to cinders, will take a wobbly table, sit down behind it and begin the trial of those responsible.

I can't help thinking of the critic who would not try to judge, but bring into existence a work, a book, a phrase, an idea. He would light the fires, watch the grass grow, listen to the wind, snatch the passing dregs in order to scatter them. He would multiply, not the number of judgments, but the signs of existence; he would call out to them, he would draw them from their sleep. Would he sometimes invent them? So much the better. The sententious critic puts me to sleep. I would prefer a critic of imaginative scintillations. He would not be sovereign, nor dressed in red. He would bear the lightning flashes of possible storms.

Q: Well, there are so many things to make known, so many interesting works, that the media ought to discuss philosophy all the time.

MF: No doubt there is a traditional uneasiness between the "critic" and those who write books. The ones feel themselves badly understood and the others believe we want to keep them under control. But that's the game. It seems to me that the situation today is rather peculiar. We have institutions for the poor, whereas we are in a situation of over abundance.

Everyone has noticed the exaltation which often accompanies the publication (or the re-edition) of works that moreover are sometimes interesting. They are never less than the "subversion of all the codes," the "exact contrary of contemporary culture," the "radical questioning of all our ways of thinking." The author must be an unknown marginal.

And in return, we must be assured that the others are sent back to the night from which they ought never have left; they were only the dregs of "pathetic fashion," a simple product of the institution, etc.

A Parisian phenomenon, it is said, and superficial. I perceive there rather the effects of a profound anxiety. The feeling of "no place left," "him or me," "each his turn." One is in single file because of the extreme meagerness of places where one can listen and make oneself heard.

This leads to a kind of anguish that bursts out in a thousand symptoms, amusing or less droll. It leads, in those who write, to the feeling of their impotence before the media which they reproach for controlling the world of books and for bringing into existence those who please them or making those who don't disappear. It leads, also, to the feeling in the critics that they will not make themselves understood unless they raise the tone and draw a rabbit out of their hats every week. It leads to a pseudo-politicization that masks, under the necessity of leading the "ideological combat" or of disabusing us of "dangerous ideas," the profound fear of neither being read nor understood. It leads to the fantastic phobia of power: every person who writes exercises a disturbing power on which limits, if not an end, must be imposed. It leads equally to the somewhat incantatory affirmation that everything today is void and desolate, without interest or importance: an affirmation that evidently comes from those who, doing nothing themselves, find that others are "too much."

Q: Don't you believe, however, that our period really lacks minds who are equal to its problems, that we lack great writers?

MF: No, I don't believe in the refrain of decadence, the absence of great writers, the sterility of thought, the restricted and bleak horizon. I think on the contrary that there is a plethora. And that we don't suffer from the void, but from too few means to think about all that is happening. Whereas there is an abundance of things to know: essential or terrible, marvelous or droll, minuscule and outstanding at the same time. And then there is an immense curiosity, a need or desire to know. One always complains that the media cram peoples' heads, but there is a misanthropy in this idea. I think on the contrary that people are reacting; the more one wants to convince them, the more they want to investigate. The mind is not soft wax; it's a reactive substance. And the desire to know more, and better, and something else, grows with this attempt to stuff our skulls.

If you admit this, and add to it the fact that at the university and elsewhere a crowd of people is being formed who can serve as an interchange between this mass of things and this avidity to know, you will quickly deduce that the unemployment of students is the most absurd thing there is. The problem is to multiply the canals, the bridges, the means of information, the television and radio networks, the newspapers.

Curiosity is a vice that has been stigmatized in turn by Christianity, by philosophy, and even by a certain conception of science. Curiosity, futility. The word, however, pleases me. To me it suggests something altogether different: it evokes "concern"; it evokes the care one takes for what exists and could exist; a readiness to find strange and singular what surrounds us; a certain relentlessness to break up our familiarities and to regard otherwise the same things; a fervor to grasp what is happening and what passes; a casualness in regard to the traditional hierarchies of the important and the essential.

I dream of a new age of curiosity. We have the technical means for it; the desire is there; the things to be known are infinite; the people who can employ themselves at this task exist. Why do we suffer? From too little: from channels that are too narrow, skimpy, quasi-monopolistic, insufficient. There is no point in adopting a protectionist attitude, to prevent "bad" information from invading and suffocating the "good." Rather, we must multiply the paths and the possibility of comings and goings. No Colbertism in this area![4] Which doesn't mean, as it is often feared, the homogenization and leveling from below. But on the contrary, the differentiation and simultaneity of different networks.

Q: At that level the media and the university, instead of opposing each other, could begin to play complementary roles.

MF: You remember Sylvain Levi's admirable phrase: teaching is when one has a listener; as soon as there are two, it's vulgarization. Books, the university, professional journals—they are also media. One ought to guard against calling every channel of information to which one cannot have or doesn't want access the media. The problem is to know how to play out the differences; and to know if it is necessary to establish a reserved zone, a "cultural park" for the fragile species of scholar threatened by great ravages of information, while all the remaining space would be a vast market for the shoddy products. Such a division doesn't appear to me to correspond to the reality. And worse: it's not at all desirable. To implement useful differentiations, there must be no division.

Q: Let's risk making some concrete proposals. If everything is going badly, where do we start?

MF: But no, it's not all going badly. In any case, I think it's necessary not to confuse the useful critic who is against things with the repetitive jeremiahs who are against people. As for concrete proposals, they can only appear as gadgets, if several general principles are not admitted first. And above all this one: that the right to knowledge must not be restricted to certain stages in life or to certain categories of individuals. One must be able to exercise it continuously and in multiple forms.

Q: Isn't this desire to know a little ambiguous? In fact, what are people going to do with the knowledge they acquire? How would they be able to use it?

MF: One of the principle functions of teaching was that the formation of the individual be accompanied by the determination of his place in society. Today we ought to conceive it in such a way that it would permit the individual to modify himself according to his own will, which is possible only on the condition that teaching be a "permanently open" possibility.

Q: In short, you are for a learned society?

MF: I am saying that the connection people make with culture must be continuous and as polymorphic as people are. There ought not to be this formation that one submits to on the one hand and this information one is exposed to on the other.

Q: In this learned society what becomes of "eternal" philosophy? Does one still need it, with its imponderable questions and silences before the unknowable?

MF: What is philosophy if not a way of reflecting not so much on what is true and false but on our relationship to the truth? One sometimes complains that there is no dominant philosophy in France. So much the better. No sovereign philosophy, but a philosophy, or rather a from-philosophy-to-activity. From this philosophy comes the movement through which, not without effort and fumblings, dreams and illusions, one detaches oneself from what are the received truths and seeks other rules of the game. From philosophy comes the displacement and transformation of the limits of thought, the modification of received values and all the work done to think otherwise, to do something else, to become other than what one is. From this point of view, it's a period of more intense philosophical activity than the last thirty years. The interference between analysis, research, scholarly or theoretical "critique" and the changes in behavior, the actual conduct of people, their relationships with themselves and with others has been instant and considerable.

I would say at this point that philosophy is a way of reflecting on our relation to the truth. But it must not end there. It's a way of asking oneself, if such is the relation that we have with truth, then how should we conduct ourselves? I think that it has done and continues today to do a very considerable and multiple labor, which modifies at the same time both our connection to the truth and our way of conducting ourselves. And this in a complex conjunction between a whole series of researches and a whole set of social movements. It's the very life of philosophy.

One understands that certain people are crying about the vacuum today and that in the realm of ideas they wish for a little monarchy. But those who, once having found a new tone in their lives, a new way of looking, another way of doing, will never experience, I don't think, the need to lament that the world is full of error, history encumbered with inauthenticities, and that it's time that everybody else shut up so that the tinkling of their censure can be heard.

Translated by John Johnston

---

1 In this interview given to *Le Monde*, Foucault's identity was not divulged. [Ed.]

2 Toni Negri, the well-known Italian philosopher of the "Autonomia" movement, was accused of being the mastermind of the Red Brigades. Arrested in 1979, he was imprisoned until the summer of 1983, after being elected to the Italian legislature. He is currently in political exile in Paris. See Semiotext(e)'s *Italy: Autonomia (Post-Political Politics)* (New York: Semiotext(e), 1980); Félix Guattari and Toni Negri, *Communists Like Us* (New York: Semiotext(e) Foreign Agents Series, 1989); and Toni Negri, *Marx Beyond Marx* (New York: Autonomedia, 1989). [Ed.]

3 An apparent allusion to the popular French literary program on TV "Apostrophes," conducted by Bernard Pivot. [Ed.]

4 Jean–Baptiste Colbert, 1619-83, adviser to Louis XIV after 1661, is credited with inaugurating the politics of centralism and tight bureaucratic regulation that has become the hallmark of French society. [Ed.]

39

FRIENDSHIP AS A WAY OF LIFE

Q: You're in your fifties. You're a reader of "Le Gai Pied," which has been in existence now for two years. Is the kind of discourse you find there something positive for you?

MF: That the magazine exists is the positive and important thing. In answer to your question I could say that I don't have to read it to voice the question of my age. Yet reading it does force me to ponder the question; and I haven't been very satisfied with the way I have been led to do it. Very simply I have no place there.

Q: Perhaps the problem is the age group of those who contribute to it and read it; the majority are between 25 and 35.

MF: Of course. The more it is written by young people the more it concerns young people. But the problem is not to make room for one age group along side another, but to find out what can be done in relation to the quasi-identification between homosexuality and the love among young people.

Another thing to distrust is the tendency to relate the question of homosexuality to the problem of "Who am I?" and "What is the secret of my desire?" Perhaps it would be better to ask oneself, "What relations, through homosexuality, can be established, invented, multiplied and modulated?" The problem is not to discover in oneself the truth of sex but rather to use sexuality henceforth to arrive at a multiplicity of relationships. And no doubt that's the real reason why homosexuality is not a form of desire but something desirable. Therefore we have to work at becoming homosexuals and not be obstinate in recognizing that we are. The development towards which the problem of homosexuality tends is the one of friendship.

Q: Did you think so at twenty, or have you discovered it over the years?

MF: As far back as I remember, to want boys was to want relations with boys. That has always been important for me. Not necessarily in the form of a couple, but as a matter of existence: how is it possible for men to be together? To live together, to share their time, their meals, their room, their leisure, their grief, their knowledge, their confidences? What is it, to be "naked" among men, outside of institutional relations, family, profession and obligatory camaraderie? It's a desire, an uneasiness, a desire-in-uneasiness that exists among a lot of people.

Q: Can one say that desire and pleasure, and the relationships one can have, are dependent on one's age?

MF: Yes, very profoundly. Between a man and a younger woman the marriage institution makes it easier: she accepts it and makes it work. But two men of noticeably different ages—what code would allow them to communicate? They face each other without terms or convenient words, with nothing to assure them about the meaning of the movement that carries them towards each other. They have to invent, from A to Z, a relationship that is still formless, which is friendship: that is to say, the sum of everything through which they can give each other pleasure.

One of the concessions one makes to others is not to present homosexuality as a kind of immediate pleasure, of two young men meeting in the street, seducing each other with a look, grabbing each other's asses and getting each other off in a quarter of an hour. There you have a kind of neat image of homosexuality without any possibility of generating unease, and for two reasons: it responds to the reassuring canon of beauty and it cancels everything that can be uncomfortable in affection, tenderness, friendship, fidelity, camaraderie and companionship, things which our rather sanitized society can't allow a place for without fearing the formation of new alliances and the tying together of unforeseen lines of force. I think that's what makes homosexuality "disturbing": the homosexual mode of life much more than the sexual act itself. To imagine a sexual act that doesn't conform to law or nature is not what disturbs people. But that individuals are beginning to love one another—there's the problem. The institution is caught in a contradiction; affective intensities traverse it which at one and the same time keep it going and shake it up. Look at the army, where love between men is ceaselessly provoked and shamed. Institutional codes can't validate these relations with multiple intensities, variable colors, imperceptible movements and changing forms. These relations short-circuit it and introduce love where there's supposed to be only law, rule or habit.

Q: You were saying a little while ago: "Rather than crying about faded pleasures, I'm interested in what we ourselves can do." Could you explain that more precisely?

MF: Asceticism as the renunciation of pleasure has bad connotations. But the askesis is something else: it's the work that one performs on oneself in order to transform oneself or make the self appear that happily one never attains.

Can that be our problem today? We've rid ourselves of asceticism. Yet it's up to us to advance into a homosexual askesis that would make us work on ourselves and invent, I do not say discover, a manner of being that is still improbable.

Q: That means that a young homosexual must be very cautious in regard to homosexual imagery; he must work at something else?

MF: What we must work on, it seems to me, is not so much to liberate our desires but to make ourselves infinitely more susceptible to pleasure. We must escape and help others escape the two ready-made formulas of the pure sexual encounter and the lovers' fusion of identities.

Q: Can one see the first fruits of strong constructive relationships in the United States, in any case in the cities where the problem of sexual misery seems under control?

MF: To me it appears certain that in the United States, even if the basis for sexual misery still exists, the interest in friendship has become very important: one doesn't enter a relationship simply in order to be able to consummate it sexually, which happens very easily. But towards friendship people are very polarized. How can a relational system be reached through sexual practices? Is it possible to create a homosexual mode of life?

This notion of mode of life seems important to me. Will it require the introduction of a diversification different from the ones due to social class, differences in profession and culture, a diversification which would also be a form of relationship and which would be a "way of life"? A way of life can be shared among individuals of different age, status and social activity. It can yield intense relations not resembling those that are institutionalized. It seems to me that a way of life can yield a culture and an ethics. To be "gay," I think, is not to identify with the psychological traits and the visible masks of the homosexual, but to try to define and develop a way of life.

Q: Isn't it a myth to say: here we are enjoying the first fruits of a socialization between different classes, ages and countries?

MF: Yes, like the great myth of saying: there will no longer be any difference between homo- and heterosexuality. Moreover, I think that it's one of the reasons that homosexuality presents a problem today. Many sexual liberation movements project this idea of "liberating yourself from the hideous constraints that weigh upon you." Yet the affirmation that to be a homosexual is for a man to love another man—this search for a way of life runs counter to the ideology of the sexual liberation movements of the '60s. It's in this sense that the mustached "clones" are significant. It's a way of responding: "Have nothing to fear; the more one is liberated, the less one will love women, the less one will founder in this poly-sexuality where there are no longer any differences between the two." It's not at all the idea of a great community fusion.

Homosexuality is an historic occasion to re-open affective and relational virtualities, not so much through the intrinsic qualities of the homosexual, but due to the biases against the position he occupies; in a certain sense diagonal lines that he can trace in the social fabric permit him to make these virtualities visible.

Q: Women might object: what do men together have to win compared to the relations between a man and a woman or between two women?

MF: There is a book that just appeared in the U.S. on the friendships between women.[1] The affection and passion between women is well documented. In the Preface the author states that she began with the idea of unearthing homosexual relationships but that she perceived that not only were these relationships not always present but that it was uninteresting whether relationships could be called homosexual or not. And by letting the relationship manifest itself as it appeared in words and gestures other very essential things also appeared: dense, bright, marvelous loves and affections or very dark and sad loves. The book shows the extent to which woman's body has played a great role, and the importance of physical contact between women: women do each other's hair, help each other with make up, dress each other. Women have had access to the bodies of other women: they put their arms around each other, kiss each other. Man's body has been forbidden to other men in a much more drastic way. If it's true that life between women was tolerated, it's only in certain periods and since the 19th century that life between men not only was tolerated but rigorously necessary: very simply during war.

And equally in prison camps. You had soldiers and young officers who spent months and even years together. During WWI men lived together completely, one on top of another, and for them it was nothing at all, insofar as death was present and finally the devotion to one another and the services rendered were sanctioned by the play of life and death. And apart from several remarks on camaraderie, the brotherhood of spirit, and some very partial observations, what do we know about these emotional uproars and storms of feeling that took place in those times? One can wonder how, in these absurd and grotesque wars and infernal massacres, the men managed to hold on in spite of everything. Through some emotional fabric no doubt. I don't mean that it was because they were each other's lovers that they continued to fight. But honor, courage, not losing face, sacrifice, leaving the trench with the captain—all that implied a very intense emotional tie. It's not to say: "Ah, there you have homosexuality!" I detest that kind of reasoning. But no doubt you have there one of the conditions, not the only one, that has permitted this infernal life where for weeks guys floundered in the mud and shit, among corpses, starving for food, and were drunk the morning of the assault.

I would like to say finally that something like a publication that is reflected upon voluntarily ought to make possible a homosexual culture, that is to say the instruments for polymorphic, varied, and individually modulated relationships. But the idea of a program of proposals is dangerous. As soon as a program is presented, it becomes a law and there's a prohibition against inventing. There ought to be an inventiveness special to a situation like ours and to these feelings that Americans call "coming out," that is, showing oneself. The program must be open. We have to dig deeply to show how things have been historically contingent, for such and such reason intelligible but not necessary. We must make the intelligible appear against a background of emptiness, and deny its necessity. We must think that what exists is far from filling all possible spaces. To make a truly unavoidable challenge of the question: what can we make work, what new game can we invent?

Translated by John Johnston

---

[1] Lilian Faderman, *Surpassing the Love of Men* (New York: William Morrow, 1980).

40

PASSION ACCORDING
TO WERNER SCHROETER

MICHEL FOUCAULT: Watching *The Death of Maria Malibran* and *Willow Springs*, it struck me that these films are not about Love but about Passion.

WERNER SCHROETER: *Willow Springs* is based on the idea of an obsession of dependence linking four characters, with none of them knowing the exact reasons for the dependence. For example, Ila von Hasperg, who plays the role of the servant and the maid, doesn't know why she's the victim of a relationship of dependence with Magdalena. I see it as an obsession.

FOUCAULT: Except for a single word, I think we're talking about the same thing. First, one can't say that these two women love each other. Nor is it love in *Maria Malibran*. What is passion? It's a state, something that falls on you out of the blue, that takes hold of you, that grips you for no reason, that has no origin. One doesn't know where it comes from. Passion arrives like that, a state that is always mobile but never moves toward a given point. There are strong and weak moments, moments when it becomes incandescent. It floats, it evens out. It's a kind of unstable time that is pursued for obscure reasons, perhaps through inertia. In the extreme, it tries to maintain itself and to disappear. Passion gives itself all the conditions necessary to continue, and, at the same time, it destroys itself. In a state of passion one is not blind, one is simply not oneself. To be oneself no longer makes sense. One sees things differently.

In a state of passion there is also a quality of pleasure-pain that is very different from what one can find in desire or in what is called sadism and masochism. I see no sadistic or masochistic relationship between the women, whereas there exists a completely indissociable state of pleasure-pain. These are not two qualities that are mixed together, but a single and same quality. In each one of the characters, there is a great suffering. One cannot say that one of them makes the other suffer. It's three types of permanent suffering, which, at the same time, are entirely willed, for there is no necessity there that they be present.

These women have been entwined in a state of suffering that links them, and from which they don't succeed in detaching themselves even though they do everything to liberate themselves from it. All that is different from love. In love, there is, in some way or another, a beloved, whereas passion circulates between the partners..

SCHROETER: Love is less active than passion.

FOUCAULT: The state of passion is a mixed state among different partners.

SCHROETER: Love is a state of grace, of distance. In a discussion several hours ago with Ingrid Caven, she was saying that love is an egotistical feeling because it doesn't consider the partner.

FOUCAULT: One can perfectly well love without being loved in return. It's an affair of solitude. For that reason, love is always full of solicitations toward the other. That's its weakness, for it always demands something of the other, whereas in a state of passion among two or three people it's something that allows intense communication.

SCHROETER: Which means that passion contains in itself a great communicative force, whereas love is an isolated state. I find it very depressing to know that love is a creation and interior invention.

FOUCAULT: Love can become passion, that is to say, the kind of state we have talked about.

SCHROETER: And therefore this suffering.

FOUCAULT: This state of mutual and reciprocal suffering—it truly is communication. It seems to me what happens between these women. Their faces and bodies are not traversed by desire, but by passion.

SCHROETER: In a discussion several years ago someone said to me that *Willow Springs* was like Albert Camus's *Malentendu*.

FOUCAULT: I was thinking that your film came from Camus's book. It's the old story that one finds in many narratives of European literature about the red auberge run by women who kill travelers wandering into their domain. Camus used it in his novel.

SCHROETER: I didn't know the story when I was shooting *Willow Springs*. Later, when I read Camus's book, I realized that what mattered in the narrative was the mother/son relationship. The auberge was run by a mother and sister who were waiting for the son. When the son returns, the mother and sister kill him because they don't recognize him.

Willow Springs was instigated by Christine Kaufmann, who had just been working with me on the mise en scene for Gotthold Ephraim Lessing's *Emilia Galotti*. One day, Tony Curtis, her ex-husband, came to take their two children, whom she had cared for for five years. We didn't have the money to fight this irresponsible husband. At that moment I had proposed a small budget film for German television intitled *The Death of Marilyn Monroe*. I left for America with Christine Kaufmann, Magdalena Montezuma and Ila von Hasperg, for I had the idea, with Christine, of getting the kids back. It was my first time in Los Angeles and California. The idea for *Willow Springs* came during my sessions with the lawyers, and while discovering the area. In Germany, certain people saw in it a critique of the fear of homosexuals. In the end we found ourselves in the same situation as the protagonists of the film. We were in a little hotel six miles from Willow Springs and completely cut off.

FOUCAULT: Why are the three women living together?

SCHROETER: What I want to say first is that we were together. *Willow Springs* is the reflection of the situation we were living and that I had felt, while working for several years with the three women, Magdalena, Ila and Christine. In a poetic way, Ila put her ugliness up front, Christine was coldly beautiful and very friendly, and the third, Magdalena, very depressive and dominant. The situation had been created in a very unfavorable political space, with fascists living all around. The town was run by an American Nazi. A really scary place...

Do you have a tendency for passion or love?

FOUCAULT: Passion.

SCHROETER: The conflict between love and passion is the subject of all my plays. Love is a lost force, a force that must lose itself immediately because it is never reciprocal. It is always suffering, total nihilism, like life and death. The authors I love are all suicides: Kleist, Holderlin—who is someone I think I understand, but outside the literary context...

Ever since childhood I've known I had to work, not because I was told it was necessary—I was too anarchistic and turbulent to believe that—but because I knew that there were so few possibilities to communicate in life that it was necessary to profit from work to express oneself. In fact, to work is to create. I knew a very creative prostitute whose behavior, with her clientele, was very artistic and socially creative. It's my dream. When I don't attain this state of passion, I work...

What about your life?

FOUCAULT: Very wise.

SCHROETER: Can you speak to me about your passion?

FOUCAULT: I lived for eighteen years in a state of passion in relation to someone, for someone. Perhaps at a certain moment this passion took a turn toward love. In truth, it's a matter of a passion between the two of us, a permanent state with no other reason to end than itself, which passes through me, and in which I am fully invested. I believe there isn't a single thing in the world, nothing whatever, that would stop me when it's a question of finding him again, of speaking to him.

SCHROETER: What differences have you noticed between a passion lived by a man and a passion lived by a woman?

FOUCAULT: I would tend to say that it's not possible to know if it's stronger among homosexuals, in this state of communication without transparency that is passion, when one doesn't know what the other's pleasure is, what the other is, what is happening with the other.

SCHROETER: I have my passion in Italy. It's a passion not definable in exclusively sexual terms. It's a boy who has his friends, who has his lovers. It's someone who also, I believe, has a passion for me. That would be too beautiful if true! I have been saying it since my childhood: for me it's an advantage to be a homosexual because it's beautiful.

FOUCAULT: We have objective proof that homosexuality is more interesting than heterosexuality: there are a considerable number of heterosexuals who would like to become homosexuals but very few homosexuals who really feel like becoming heterosexuals. It's like passing from East Germany to West Germany. We could love a woman, have an intense relationship with a woman, perhaps more intense than with a boy, but never feel like becoming heterosexuals.

SCHROETER: My great friend Rosa von Praunheim, who has made many films on the subject of homosexuality, said to me one day: "You're an unbearable coward" because I refused to sign a petition against the repression of homosexuals. In response to a press campaign launched by the magazine "Der Stern," homosexuals had to declare their coming out. To Rosa I replied: "I will gladly sign your petition but I cannot write something against the repression of homosexuals, for if there is one thing for which I have never suffered in my life, it is my homosexuality." As I was already much loved by women, they were even more attentive to me personally since they knew that I was homosexual.
Perhaps I filmed *Willow Springs* out of guilt, for I have made a lot of films and plays with women. I see very clearly the difference between my passion for a woman like Magdalena Montezuma, with whom I will maintain a deep friendship until the end of my days and my passion for my Italian friend. Perhaps psychologically—and I know nothing about psychology—it's anxiety with men and guilt with women. My motivation is quite strange. I can't define it. In Prague, for my film *Der Tag der Idioten*, I worked with thirty women from among all those with whom I have collaborated since I was thirteen years old.

FOUCAULT: Could you say why?

SCHROETER: No.

FOUCAULT: One of the most striking things about your film is that one knows nothing about what goes on among the women, about the nature of these little worlds, and yet, at the same time, there is a kind of clarity about the facts.

SCHROETER: I can't define the cause of my feelings. For example, when I saw this Italian friend again, it put me in a state of passion.

FOUCAULT: Consider this example. When I see a film by Bergman, who is equally a film-maker obsessed by women and the love between women, I'm bored. Bergman bores me because I think he wants to try to see what goes on between women. Whereas in your work there is a kind of immediate evidence which doesn't try to say what is happening and allows one not to even raise the question. And your way of exiting altogether from psychological film seems fruitful to me. At that exact moment one sees bodies, faces, lips, eyes. You make them the evidence of passion.

SCHROETER: Psychology doesn't interest me. I don't believe in it.

FOUCAULT: We have to go back to what you were saying a little while ago about creativity. One is lost in life, in what one writes, in the film one makes, precisely when one wants to investigate the nature of the identity of something. At that exact point one "fails," for one enters into classifications. The problem is to create precisely something that happens between ideas, and to which one can't give a name. At every instant, therefore, it's trying to give a coloration, a form and intensity to something that never says what it is. That's the art of living. The art of living is to eliminate psychology, to create, with oneself and others, individualities, beings, relations, unnameable qualities. If one fails to do that in one's life it isn't worth living. I don't distinguish between people who make of their existence a work and those who make a work during their existence. An existence can be a perfect and sublime work. That's something the Greeks understood, whereas we have completely forgotten it, above all since the Renaissance.

SCHROETER: It's the system of psychological terror. The cinema is made up solely of psychological drama, of films of psychological terror. I have no fear of death. It's perhaps arrogant to say it but it's the truth. Ten years ago I was afraid of death. To look death in the face is an anarchist feeling dangerous to established society, which depends on terror and fear.

FOUCAULT: One of the things that has preoccupied me for some time is the realization how difficult it is to kill oneself. Let's consider the small number of means of suicide we have available, each one more disgusting than the others:

gas is dangerous for the neighbors, hanging is disagreeable for the maid who discovers the body the next morning, throwing oneself out the window dirties the sidewalk. Moreover, suicide is considered in the most negative way possible by society. Not only are we told that it's not good to kill ourselves but also that if someone commits suicide it's because things were going badly.

SCHROETER: It's strange, what you are saying, because I had a discussion with my friend Alberte Barsacq, the clothes-designer for my films and plays, about two friends who committed suicide not long ago. I don't understand how somebody very depressed would have the strength to commit suicide. I could kill myself only in a state of grace or extreme pleasure, but above all not in a state of depression.

GERARD COURANT: The thing that surprised some people about the suicide of Jean Eustache[1] is that in the days before his suicide he was feeling better.

FOUCAULT: I'm sure that Jean Eustache killed himself when he was in good shape. People don't understand it because he was feeling well. Actually, it's something one can't admit. I am a partisan of a true cultural combat for re-instructing people that there is no conduct more beautiful, that merits more reflection with as much attention, than suicide. One should work on one's suicide all one's life.

SCHROETER: Do you know Amery, the German writer who wrote a book several years ago about suicide and who proposed something like the same ideas? Afterwards, he killed himself.

We live in a system that functions on guilt. Consider sickness. I lived in Africa and in India where people feel no compunction about exhibiting their sickness to society. Even the lepers exhibit themselves. In our western society the moment one is sick, one must be afraid, hide oneself, and no longer live. It would be ridiculous if sickness were not a part of life. I have a completely schizoid relationship with psychology. If I pick up my lighter and a cigarette, it's a banal act. The important thing is the gesture. It's what gives me my dignity. Knowing that my mother smoked too much when I was five years old has no bearing on knowledge about my own personality.

FOUCAULT: It's one of the fundamental choices that one has now in relation to western societies. We have been taught throughout the 20th century that one can do nothing if one knows nothing about oneself. The truth about oneself is a condition of existence, whereas you have societies where one could perfectly imagine that there is no attempt at all to regulate the question of what one is and where it makes no sense, while the important thing is: what is the art of putting into a work what one does, for being what one is. An art of the self which would be the complete contrary of oneself. To make of one's being an object of art, that's what is worth the effort.

SCHROETER: I recall the phrase from your book *The Order of Things* that I love very much: "If these arrangements [of the episteme] were to disappear..., then it would be a good bet that man would be effaced, like a face drawn in sand at the edge of the sea." I have never been angry with anyone. I do not understand how one can accept the bourgeois system of psychology which ceaselessly plays one individual against another. I can easily argue with someone and the next day return to normal relations. (I'm not talking about a relationship of love or passion.) Each day I am another. Psychology, for me, is a mystery. Freud constructed a very dangerous system above our heads, one that all western society can use.

I'd like to cite a revealing example of a harmless act that would be negatively interpreted in a Freudian sense. When I returned from America after the shooting of *Willow Springs*, I was very tired and my mother wanted to wash me, because it gave her pleasure. At a certain moment I began to pee in the bathtub. Imagine the situation: a mother of sixty years and her son of twenty-seven. I laughed a lot. (In any case, I always pee in the bathtub.) Why not pee? It's the only thing to say. Ours is not an incestuous relationship; we're like buddies; I've never imagined an erotic relationship with my mother. I see no problem there unless I reduce the action to a bourgeois psychological context....

Novalis wrote a poem that I love: *Night Elegies*. He explains why he prefers the night to the day. That's German Romanticism....

When I shot *Lohengrin* three years ago in Kassel, they asked me about my idea of mise en scene. My only response was to say that the music of *Lohengrin* is extremely beautiful, that it's a romantic music that can be forced because Wagner already had the consciousness of the industrial century. I explained that I would not give them the pleasure of playing with them the little devil who denounces Wagner's work and music, for I found it so overcharged with interpretations, above all ideological, that I decided to give it a rather childish representation in a very primitive mise en scene like the Marionnette theater. The sky was studded with a thousand bright stars above a golden pyramid and sparkling costumes. I worked almost alone with the orchestra director to make the music as beautiful as possible. My left-wing friends from Berlin asked me how I could do Wagner in this way. I responded that I refuse to do Wagner like Patrice Chéreau, who uses evening gowns and industrial machines in the *Ring of the Nibelungen* in order to denounce Wagner, to make of him a precursor of the Third Reich.

FOUCAULT: I don't think Chéreau would have wanted to do as you say.[2] What seemed to me strong in Chéreau's work is not that because he makes industrial visions appear that he is denouncing something. To say that there are elements of that reality present in Wagner is not a simple critique and denunciation of the type: "Look at Wagner's reality, it's bourgeois society."

SCHROETER: I always work with the ambience. The Kassel theater where I did the mise en scene has a good musical ambience. I made the mise en scene a function of the actors and singers. If there is an enormous singer in the cast, like the one Elsa played, I don't try to camouflage her with a black shadow and white clothing. I conceived the mis en scene in such a way that when Elsa, in the first act, is accused of having assassinated Godefroi and she recounts her visions, I show them as collective visions, as if Elsa with vision made up part of a loving, passionate collective. At the end, when Lohengrin is discovered as a masculine being, one realizes that he is someone real and it's no longer a question of a collective vision. At that moment Elsa commits suicide and Ortrude, who represents the old culture, triumphs. For me, Ortrude is the positive passionate woman of the piece.

It's a music that one has to "attack" naively. I very much like the way Boulez directs Wagner, but it's not at all the way I see Wagner's music. His interpreters have shamefully missed his genius...and finally they miss everything. Wagner was like everyone else, with a lot of talent and a great idea, to be sure. One should not begin by respecting him, although one should respect the quality of the work, but the genius that is behind it. The music of *Lohegrin* is very musical, like Viennese music. That's what I tried to show in the mise en scene, for I don't like either the luxuriousness or Bayreuth.

FOUCAULT: When you shot *Maria Malibran*, did you think first about the music?

SCHROETER: Before anything else, I was thinking about suicide, about the people I loved and with whom I experienced passion, like Maria Callas, whom I've always loved. *The Death of Maria Malibran* also came into existence as a result of reading a Spanish book on Maria Malibran, a text on Janis Joplin's death, and another on Jimi Hendrix's death—people I admired enormously.

Maria Callas was the erotic vision of my childhood. At fourteen, in my erotic dreams, I imagined her pissing while I watched her. This was always outside the image of Maria Callas, for whom I felt friendliness and respect. She was *the* erotic woman. Maria Callas was a total passion. Oddly, she never frightened me. I remember a discussion I had with her in Paris in 1976, when she told me that the only people she knew were afraid of her. I asked her: "How is it possible to be afraid of you?" She had an exceptional gentleness, like a little American Greek girl. At fifty she was the same thing. I asked her if she wanted an article published in "France-Soir," "Maria Callas looking for a man"? You will see a hundred men turn up. She laughed. People were so afraid of her that they didn't come to see her. She lived a very solitary life. Which was too bad, since, her genius apart, she possessed a sympathy and fabulous gentleness.

One thing fascinates me, which I find unimaginable. For the twelve years I have worked with the same dozen people, within this group there has been practically no interest on the part of one member for another. There is no deep interest between Magdalena Montezuma and Christine Kaufman, between Christine and Ingrid Caven, etc. Between Magdalena and Ingrid, who love and admire one another, there is a vital interest, but it's the exception. If there were no director among them there would be no vital communication.

Translated by John Johnston

---

1 Jean Eustache, a French filmmaker, author of *The Mother and the Whore*,
committed suicide on November 4, 1981. [Ed.]

2 See Michel Foucault, "19th Century Imaginations" in *The German Issue*.
Semiotext(e), No. 11, 1982. [Ed.]

41

SEXUAL CHOICE, SEXUAL ACT

Q: Let me begin by asking you to respond to John Boswell's recent book on the history of homosexuality from the beginning of the Christian era through the Middle Ages.[1] As an historian yourself, do you find his methodology valid? To what extent do you think the conclusions he draws contribute to a better understanding of the contemporary homosexual experience?

MF: This is certainly a very important study whose originality is already evident in the way in which it raises the question. Methodologically speaking, the rejection by Boswell of the categorical opposition between homosexual and heterosexual, which plays such a significant role in the way our culture conceives of homosexuality, represents an advance not only in scholarship but in cultural criticism as well. His introduction of the concept of "gay" (in the way he defines it) provides us both with a useful instrument of research and at the same time a better comprehension of how people actually conceive of themselves and their sexual behavior. On the level of investigative results, this methodology has led to the discovery that what has been called the repression of homosexuality does not go back to Christianity properly speaking, but developed within the Christian era at a much later date. In this type of analysis it is important to be aware of the way in which people conceived of their own sexuality. Sexual behavior is not, as is too often assumed, a superimposition of, on the one hand, desires which derive from natural instincts, and, on the other, of permissive or restrictive laws which tell us what we should or shouldn't do. Sexual behavior is more than that. It is also the consciousness one has of what one is doing, what one makes of the experience, and the value one attaches to it. It is in this sense that I think the concept "gay" contributes to a positive (rather than a purely negative) appreciation of the type of consciousness in which affection, love, desire, sexual rapport with people have a positive significance.

Q: I understand that your own recent work has led you to a study of sexuality as it was experienced in ancient Greece.

MF: Yes, and precisely Boswell's book has provided me with a guide for what to look for in the meaning people attached to their sexual behavior.

Q: Does this focus on cultural context and people's discourse about their sexual behavior reflect a methodological decision to bypass the distinction between innate predisposition to homosexual behavior and social conditioning; or do you have any conviction one way or the other on this issue?

MF: On this question I have absolutely nothing to say. "No comment."

Q: Does this mean you think the question is unanswerable, or bogus, or does it simply not interest you?

MF: No, none of these. I just don't believe in talking about things that go beyond my expertise. It's not my problem and I don't like talking about things that are not really the object of my work. On this question I have only an opinion; since it is only an opinion it is without interest.

Q: But opinions can be interesting, don't you agree?

MF: Sure, I could offer my opinion, but this would only make sense if everybody and anybody's opinions were also being consulted. I don't want to make use of a position of authority while I'm being interviewed to traffic in opinions.

Q: Fair enough. We'll shift directions then. Do you think it is legitimate to speak of a class consciousness in connection with homosexuals? Ought homosexuals to be encouraged to think of themselves as a class in the way that unskilled laborers or black people are encouraged to in some countries? How do you envision the political goals of homosexuals as a group?

MF: In answer to the first question, I would say that the homosexual consciousness certainly goes beyond one's individual experience and includes an awareness of being a member of a particular social group. This is an undeniable fact that dates back to ancient times. Of course, this aspect of their collective consciousness changes over time and varies from place to place. It has, for instance, on different occasions taken the form of membership in a kind of secret society, membership in a cursed race, membership in a segment of humanity at once privileged and persecuted, all kinds of different modes of collective consciousness, just as, incidentally, the consciousness of unskilled laborers has undergone numerous transformations. It is true that more recently certain homosexuals have, following the political model, developed or tried to create a certain class consciousness. My impression is that this hasn't really been a success, whatever the political consequences it may have had, because homosexuals do not constitute a social class. This is not to say that one can't imagine a society in which homosexuals would constitute a social class. But in our present economic and social mode of organization I don't see this happening.

As for the political goals of the homosexual movement, two points can be made. First, there is the question of freedom of sexual choice that must be addressed. I say freedom of sexual choice and not freedom of sexual acts because there are sexual acts like rape which should not be permitted whether they involve a man and a woman or two men. I don't think we should have as our objective some sort of absolute freedom or total liberty of sexual action. However, where freedom of sexual choice is concerned one has to be absolutely intransigent. This includes the liberty to manifest that choice or not to manifest it. Now, there has been considerable progress in this area on the level of legislation, certainly progress in the direction of tolerance, but there is still a lot of work to be done.

Second, a homosexual movement could adopt the objective of raising the question of the place in a given society which sexual choice, sexual behavior and the effects of sexual relations between people could have with regard to the individual. These questions are fundamentally obscure. Look, for example, at the confusion and equivocation that surround pornography, or the lack of eluci- dation which characterizes the question of the legal status which might be attached to the liaison between two people of the same sex. I don't mean that the legalization of marriage among homosexuals should be an objective; rather, that we are dealing here with a whole series of questions concerning the insertion and recognition—within a legal and social framework—of diverse relations among individuals which must be addressed.

Q: I take it, then, that your point is that the homosexual movement should not only give itself the goal of enlarging legal permissiveness but should also be asking broader and deeper questions about the strategic roles played by sexual preferences and how they are perceived. It is your point that the homosex- ual movement should not stop at liberalizing laws relating to personal sexual choice but should also be provoking society at large to rethink its own presuppo- sitions regarding sexuality? In other words, it isn't that homosexuals are deviants who should be allowed to practice in peace, but rather that the whole conceptual scheme which categorizes homosexuals as deviants must be dismantled. This throws an interesting light on the question of homosexual educators. In the debate which arose in California, regarding the rights of homosexuals to teach primary and secondary school, for example, those who argued against permitting homo- sexuals to teach were concerned not only with the likelihood of homosexuals constituting a threat to innocence in that they may be prone to seducing their stu- dents, but also that they might preach the gospel of homosexuality.

MF: The whole question, you see, has been wrongly formulated. Under no circumstances should the sexual choice of an individual determine the profes- sion he is allowed, or forbidden, to practice. Sexual practices simply fall outside the pertinent factors related to the suitability for a given profession. "Yes," you might say, "but what if the profession is used by homosexuals to encourage others to become homosexuals?"

Well, let me ask you this, do you believe that teachers who for years, for decades, for centuries, explained to children that homosexuality is intolerable; do you believe that textbooks that purged literature and falsified history in order to exclude various types of sexual behavior, have not caused ravages at least as serious as a homosexual teacher who speaks about homosexuality and who can do no more harm than explain a given reality, a lived experience?

The fact that a teacher is a homosexual can only have electrifying and intense effects on the students to the extent that the rest of society refuses to admit the existence of homosexuality. A homosexual teacher should not present any more of a problem than a bald teacher, a male teacher in an all-female school, a female teacher in an all-male school, or an Arab teacher in a school in a fashionable district in Paris.

As for the problem of a homosexual teacher who actively tries to seduce his students, all I can say is that in all pedagogical situations the possibility of this problem is present; one finds instances of this kind of behavior much more rampant among heterosexual teachers—for no other reason than there are a lot more heterosexual teachers.

Q: There is a growing tendency in American intellectual circles, particularly among radical feminists, to distinguish between male and female homosexuality. The basis of this distinction is two-fold. If the term homosexuality is taken to denote not merely a tendency toward affectional relations with members of the same sex but an inclination to find members of the same sex erotically attractive and gratifying, then it is worth insisting on the very different physical things that happen in the one encounter and the other. The second basis for the distinction is that lesbians seem in the main to want from other women what one finds in stable heterosexual relationships: support, affection, long-term commitment, and so on. If this is not the case with male homosexuals, then the difference may be said to be striking, if not fundamental. Do you think the distinction here a useful and viable one? Are there discernible reasons for the difference noted so insistently by many prominent radical feminists?

MF: (Laughs.) All I can do is explode with laughter.

Q: Is the question funny in a way I don't see, or stupid, or both?

MF: Well, it is certainly not stupid, but I find it very amusing, perhaps for reasons I couldn't give even if I wanted to. What I will say is that the distinction offered doesn't seem to me convincing, in terms of what I observe in the behavior of lesbian women. Beyond this, one would have to speak about the different pressures experienced by men and women who are coming out or are trying to make a life for themselves as homosexuals. I don't think that radical feminists in other countries are likely to see these questions quite in the way you ascribe to such women in American intellectual circles.

Q: Freud argued in "Psychogenesis of a Case of Hysteria in Woman" that all homosexuals are liars. We don't have to take this assertion seriously to ask whether there is not in homosexuality a tendency to dissimulation that might have led Freud to make this statement. If we substitute for the word "lie" such words as metaphor or indirection, may we not be coming closer to the heart of the homosexual style? Or is there any point in speaking of a homosexual style or sensibility? Richard Sennett, for one, has argued that there is no more a homosexual style than there is a heterosexual style. Is this your view as well?

MF: Yes, I don't think it makes much sense to talk about a homosexual style. Even on the level of nature, the term homosexuality doesn't have much meaning. I'm reading right now, as a matter of fact, an interesting book which came out recently in the U.S. called *Proust and the Art of Love*.[2] The author shows how difficult it is to give meaning to the proposition "Proust was a homosexual." It seems to me that it is finally an inadequate category. Inadequate, that is, in that we can't really classify behavior on the one hand, and the term can't restore a type of experience on the other. One could perhaps say that there is a "gay style" or at least that there is an ongoing attempt to recreate a certain style of existence, a form of existence or art of living, which might be called "gay."

In answer to the question about dissimulation, it is true that, for instance, during the nineteenth century it was, to a certain degree, necessary to hide one's homosexuality. But to call homosexuals liars is equivalent to calling the resistors under a military occupation liars. It's like calling Jews "money lenders," when it was the only profession they were allowed to practice.

Q: Nevertheless, it does seem evident, at least on a sociological level, that there are certain characteristics one can discern in the gay style, certain generalizations which (your laughter a moment ago notwithstanding) recall such stereotypifications as promiscuity, anonymity between sexual partners, purely physical relationships, and so on.

MF: Yes, but it's not quite so simple. In a society like ours where homosexuality is repressed, and severely so, men enjoy a far greater degree of liberty than women. Men are permitted to make love much more often and under less restrictive conditions. Houses of prostitution exist to satisfy their sexual needs. Ironically, this has resulted in a certain permissiveness with regard to sexual practices between men. Sexual desire is considered more intense for men and therefore in greater need of release; so, along with brothels, one saw the emergence of baths where men could meet and have sex with each other. The Roman baths were exactly this, a place for heterosexuals to engage in sexual acts. It wasn't until the 16th century, I believe, that these baths were closed as places of unacceptable debauchery. Thus even homosexuality benefited from a certain tolerance toward sexual practices, as long as it was limited to a simple physical encounter. And not only did homosexuality benefit from this situation but, by a curious twist often typical of such strategies—it actually reversed the standards in such a way that homosexuals came to enjoy even more freedom in their physical relations than heterosexuals. The effect has been that homosexuals now have the luxury of knowing that in a certain number of countries—Holland, Denmark, the United States, and even as provincial a country as France—the opportunities for sexual encounters are enormous. There has been, you might say, a great increase in consumption on this level. But this is not necessarily a natural condition of homosexuality, a biological given.

Q: The American sociologist Philip Rieff, in an essay on Oscar Wilde entitled "The Impossible Culture," sees Wilde as a forerunner of modern culture. The essay begins with an extensive quotation from the transcript of the trial of Oscar Wilde, and goes on to raise questions about the viability of a culture in which there are no prohibitions, and therefore no sense of vital transgression. Consider, if you will, the following:

"A culture survives the assault of sheer possibility against it only so far as the members of a culture learn, through their membership, how to narrow the range of choices otherwise open."
"As culture sinks into the psyche and become character, what Wilde prized above all else is constrained: individuality. A culture in crisis favors the growth of individuality; deep down things no longer weigh so heavily to slow the surface play of experience. Hypothetically, if a culture could grow to full crisis, then everything would be expressed and nothing would be true."
"Sociologically, a truth is whatever militates against the human capacity to express everything. Repression is truth."

Is Rieff's response to Wilde and to the idea of culture Wilde embodied at all plausible?

MF: I'm not sure I understand Professor Rieff's remarks. What does he mean, for instance, by "repression is truth?"

Q: Actually, I think this idea is similar to claims you make in your own books about truth being the product of a system of exclusions, a network, or episteme, that defines what can and cannot be said.

MF: Well, the important question here, it seems to me, is not whether a culture without restraints is possible or even desirable but whether the system of constraints in which a society functions leaves individuals the liberty to transform the system. Obviously constraints of any kind are going to be intolerable to certain segments of society. The necrophiliac finds it intolerable that graves are not accessible to him. But a system of constraint becomes truly intolerable when the individuals who are affected by it don't have the means of modifying it. This can happen when such a system becomes intangible as a result of its being considered a moral or religious imperative, or a necessary consequence of medical science. If Rieff means that the restrictions should be clear and well-defined, I agree.

Q: Actually, Rieff would argue that a true culture is one in which the essential truths have been sunk so deep in everyone that there would be no need to articulate them. Clearly, in a society of law, one would need to make explicit a great variety of things that were not to be done, but the main credal assumptions would for the most part remain inaccessible to simple articulation. Part of the thrust of Rieff's work is directed against the idea that it is desirable to do away with credal assumptions in the name of a perfect liberty, and also the idea that restrictions are by definition what all must aim to clear away.

MF: There is no question that a society without restrictions is inconceivable, but I can only repeat myself in saying that these restrictions have to be within the reach of those affected by them so that they at least have the possibility of altering them. As to credal assumptions, I don't think that Rieff and I would agree on their value or on their meaning or on the devices by which they are taught.

Q: You're no doubt right about that. In any case, we can move now from the legal and sociological spheres to the realm of letters. I would like to ask you to comment on the difference between the erotic as it appears in heterosexual literature and the manner in which sex emerges in homosexual literature. Sexual discourse, as it appears in the great heterosexual novels of our culture—I realize that the designation "heterosexual novels" is itself dubious—is characterized by a certain modesty and discretion that seems to add charm to the works. When heterosexual writers treat sex too explicitly it seems to lose some of the mysteriously evocative quality, some of the potency we find in novels like *Anna Karenina*. The point is made with great cogency in a number of essays by George Steiner, as a matter of fact. In contrast to the practice of the major heterosexual novelists, we have the example of various homosexual writers. I'm thinking for example of Cocteau's *The White Paper*, where he succeeds in retaining the poetic enchantment, which heterosexual writers achieve through veiled allusion, while depicting sexual acts in the most graphic terms. Do you think such a difference does exist between these two types of literature, and if so, how would you account for it?

MF: That's a very interesting question. As I mentioned earlier, over the past few years I have been reading a lot of Latin and Greek texts that describe sexual practices both between men and between men and women; and I've been struck by the extreme prudishness of these texts (with certain exceptions, of course). Take an author like Lucien. Here we have an ancient writer who talks about homosexuality but in an almost bashful way. At the end of one of his dialogues, for instance, he evokes a scene where a man approaches a boy, puts his hand on the boy's knee, slides his hand under his tunic and caresses the boy's chest; then the hand moves down to the boy's stomach and suddenly the text stops there. Now I would attribute this prudishness, which generally characterizes homosexual literature in ancient times, to the greater freedom then enjoyed by men in their homosexual practices.

Q: I see. So the more free and open sexual practice is, the more one can afford to be reticent or oblique in talking about it. This would explain why homosexual literature is more explicit in our culture than heterosexual literature. But I'm still wondering how one could use this explanation to account for the fact that the former manages to achieve the same effect in the imagination of the reader as the latter achieves with the exact opposite tools.

MF: Let me try to answer your question another way. The experience of heterosexuality, at least since the Middle Ages, has always consisted of two panels: on the one hand, the panel of courtship in which the man seduces the woman; and, on the other, the panel of the sexual act itself. Now the great heterosexual literature of the West has had to do essentially with the panel of amorous courtship, that is, above all, with that which precedes the sexual act. All the work of intellectual and cultural refinement, all the aesthetic elaboration of the West, were aimed at courtship. This is the reason for the relative poverty of literary, cultural, and aesthetic appreciation of the sexual act as such.

In contrast, the modern homosexual experience has no relation at all to courtship. This was not the case in ancient Greece, however. For the Greeks, courtship between men was more important than between men and women. (Think of Socrates and Alcibiades.) But in Western Christian culture homosexuality was banished and therefore had to concentrate all its energy on the act of sex itself. Homosexuals were not allowed to elaborate a system of courtship because the cultural expression necessary for such an elaboration was denied them. The wink on the street, the split-second decision to get it on, the speed with which homosexual relations are consummated: all these are products of an interdiction. So when a homosexual culture and literature began to develop it was natural for it to focus on the most ardent and heated aspect of homosexual relations.

Q: I'm reminded of Casanova's famous expression that "the best moment of love is when one is climbing the stairs." One can hardly imagine a homosexual today making such a remark.

MF: Exactly. Rather, he would say something like: "The best moment of love is when the lover leaves in the taxi."

Q: I can't help thinking that this describes more or less precisely Swann's relations with Odette in the first volume of Proust's great novel.

MF: Well, yes. That is true. But though we are speaking there of a relationship between a man and a woman, we should have to take into account in describing it the nature of the imagination that conceived it.

Q: And we would also then have to take into account the pathological nature of the relationship as Proust himself conceives it.

MF: The question of pathology I would as well omit in this context. I prefer simply to return to the observation with which I began this part of our exchange, namely, that for a homosexual, the best moment of love is likely to be when the lover leaves in the taxi. It is when the act is over and the boy is gone that one begins to dream about the warmth of his body, the duality of his smile, the tone of his voice. This is why the great homosexual writers of our culture (Cocteau, Genet, Burroughs) can write so elegantly about the sexual act itself, because the homosexual imagination is for the most part concerned with reminiscing about the act rather than anticipating it. And, as I said earlier, this is all due to very concrete and practical considerations and says nothing about the intrinsic nature of homosexuality.

Q: Do you think this has any bearing on the so-called proliferation of perversions one sees today? I am speaking of phenomena like the S & M scene, golden showers, scatological amusements and the like. We know these practices have existed for some time but they seem much more openly practiced these days.

MF: I would say they are much more widely practiced also.

Q: Do you think this general phenomenon and the fact that homosexuality is "coming out of the closet," making public its form of expression, have anything to do with each other?

MF: I would advance the following hypothesis: In a civilization that for centuries considered the essence of the relation between two people to reside in the knowledge of whether one of the two parties was going to surrender to the other, all the interest and curiosity, the cunning and manipulation of people was aimed at getting the other to give in, to go to bed with them. Now, when sexual encounters become extremely easy and numerous, as is the case with homosexuality nowadays, complications are only introduced after the fact. In this type of casual encounter it is only after making love that one becomes curious about the other person. Once the sexual act has been consummated you find yourself asking your partner, "By the way, what was your name?"

What you have, then, is a situation where all the energy and imagination, which in the heterosexual relationship were channeled into courtship, now become devoted to intensifying the act of sex itself. A whole new art of sexual practice develops which tries to explore all the internal possibilities of sexual conduct. You find emerging in places like San Francisco and New York what might be called laboratories of sexual experimentation. You might look upon this as the counterpart of the medieval courts where strict rules of proprietary courtship were defined.

It is because the sexual act has become so easy and available to homosexuals that it runs the risk of quickly becoming boring, so that every effort has to be made to innovate and create variations that will enhance the pleasure of the act.

Q: Yes, but why have these innovations taken the specific form they have? Why the fascination with excretory functions, for instance?

MF: I find the S & M phenomenon in general to be more surprising than that. That is to say, sexual relations are elaborated and developed by and through mythical relations. S & M is not a relationship between he (or she) who suffers and he (or she) who inflicts suffering, but between the master and the one on whom he exercises his mastery. What interests the practitioners of S & M is that the relationship is at the same time regulated and open. It resembles a chess game in the sense that one can win and the other lose. The master can lose in the S & M game if he finds he is unable to respond to the needs and trials of his victim. Conversely, the servant can lose if he fails to meet or can't stand meeting the challenge thrown at him by the master. This mixture of rules and openness has the effect of intensifying sexual relations by introducing a perpetual novelty, a perpetual tension and a perpetual uncertainty which the simple consummation of the act lacks. The idea is also to make use of every part of the body as a sexual instrument.
Actually, this is related to the famous phrase "animal triste post coitum." Since in homosexuality coitus is given immediately the problem becomes "what can be done to guard against the onset of sadness?"

Q: Would you venture an explanation for the fact that bisexuality among women today seems to be much more readily accepted by men than bisexuality among men?

MF: This probably has to do with the role women play in the imagination of heterosexual men. Women have always been seen by them as their exclusive property. To preserve this image a man had to prevent his woman from having too much contact with other men, so women were restricted to social contact with other women and more tolerance was exercised with regard to the physical rapport between women. By the same token, heterosexual men felt that if they practiced homosexuality with other men this would destroy what they think is their image in the eyes of their women. They think of themselves as existing in the minds of women as master. They think that the idea of their submitting to another man, of being under another man in the act of love, would destroy their image in the eyes of women. Men think that women can only experience pleasure in recognizing men as masters. Even the Greeks had a problem with being the passive partner in a love relationship, for a Greek nobleman to make love to a passive male slave was natural, since the slave was by nature an inferior. But when two Greek men of the same social class made love it was a real problem because neither felt he should humble himself before the other.

Today homosexuals still have the same problem. Most gays feel the passive role is in some way demeaning. S & M has actually helped alleviate this problem somewhat.

Q: Is it your impression that the cultural forms growing up in the gay community are directed very largely to young people in that community?

MF: I think that is largely the case, though I'm not sure there is much to make of it. Certainly, as a fifty-year-old man, when I read certain publications produced by and for gays I find that I am not being taken into account at all, that I don't belong somehow. This is not something on the basis of which I would criticize such publications, which after all do what their writers and readers are interested in. But I can't help observing that there is a tendency among articulate gays to think of the major issues and questions of life-style as involving typically people in their twenties.

Q: Might not this constitute the basis of a criticism, not only of particular publications but of gay life generally?

MF: I didn't say that one might not find grounds for criticism, only that I don't choose to or think it useful.

Q: Why not consider the worship of the youthful male body as the center of the standard homosexual fantasy, and go on to speak of the denial or ordinary life processes entailed in this, particularly aging and the decline of desire?

MF: Look, these are not new ideas you're raising, and you know that. As to the worship of youthful bodies, I'm not convinced that it is peculiar at all to gays or in any way to be regarded as a pathology. And if that is the intention of your question, then I reject it. But I would also remind you that gays are not only involved in life processes, necessarily, but are very much aware of them in most cases. Gay publications may not devote as much space as I would like to questions of gay friendship and to the meaning of relationships when there are no established codes or guidelines. But more and more gay people are having to face these questions for themselves. And you know, I think that what most bothers those who are not gay about gayness is the gay lifestyle, not sex acts themselves.

Q: Are you referring to such things as gays fondling or caressing one another in public, or their wearing flashy clothing, or adopting clone outfits?

MF: These things are bound to disturb some people. But I was talking about the common fear that gays will develop relationships that are intense and satisfying even though they do not at all conform to the ideas of relationship held by others. It is the prospect that gays will create as yet unforeseen kinds of relationships that many people can not tolerate.

Q: You are referring, then, to relationships that don't involve possessiveness or fidelity—to name only two of the common factors that might be denied?

MF: If the relationships to be created are as yet unforeseeable, then we can't really say that this feature or that feature will be denied. But you can see how, in the military for example, love between men can develop and assert itself in circumstances where only dead habit and rules were supposed to prevail. And it is possible that changes in established routines will occur on a much broader scale as gays learn to express their feelings for one another in more various ways and develop new life-styles not resembling those that have been institutionalized.

Q: Do you see it as your role to address the gay community especially on matters of general importance such as you have been raising?

MF: I am of course regularly involved in exchanges with other members of the gay community. We talk, we try to find ways of opening ourselves to one another. But I am wary of imposing my own views, of setting down plans or programs. I don't want to discourage invention, don't want gay people to stop feeling it is up to them to adjust their own relationships by discovering what is appropriate in their situations.

Q: You don't think there is some special advice, or a special perspective, that a historian or archeologist of culture like yourself can offer?

MF: It's always useful to understand the historical contingency of things, to see how and why things got to be as they are. But I'm not the only person equipped to show these things, and I want to avoid suggesting that certain developments were necessary or unavoidable. Gays have to work out some of these matters themselves. There are useful things I can contribute, but again, I want to avoid imposing my own scheme or plan.

Q: Do you think that in general intellectuals are more tolerant towards, or receptive to, different modes of sexual behavior than other people? If so, is this due to a better understanding of human sexuality? If not, how do you think that you and other intellectuals can improve this situation? In what way can the rational discourse on sex best be reoriented?

MF: I think that where tolerance is concerned we allow ourselves a lot of illusions. Take incest, for example. Incest was a popular practice, and I mean by this, widely practiced among the populace, for a very long time. It was towards the end of the 19th century that various social pressures were directed against it. And it is clear that the great interdiction of incest is an invention of the intellectuals.

Q: Are you referring to figures like Freud and Lévi-Strauss or to the class of intellectuals as a whole?

MF: No, I'm not aiming at anyone in particular. I'm simply pointing out that if you look for studies by sociologists or anthropologists of the 19th century on incest you won't find any. Sure, there were scattered medical reports, but the practice of incest didn't really seem to pose a problem at the time.

It is perhaps true that in intellectual circles these things are talked about more openly but that is not necessarily a sign of greater tolerance. Sometimes it means the reverse. I remember ten or fifteen years ago, when I used to socialize within the bourgeois milieu, that it was rare indeed for an evening to go by without some discussion of homosexuality and pederasty—usually even before dessert. But these same people who spoke so openly about these matters were not likely to tolerate their sons being pederasts.

As for prescribing the direction rational discourse on sex should take, I prefer not to legislate such matters. For one thing, the expression "intellectual discourse on sex" is too vague. There are very stupid things said by sociologists, sexologists, psychiatrists, doctors and moralists and there are very intelligent things said by members of those same professions. I don't think it's a question of intellectual discourse on sex but a question of asinine discourse and intelligent discourse.

Q: And I take it that you have lately found a number of works that are moving in the right direction?

MF: More, certainly, than I had any reason to expect I would some years ago. But the situation on the whole is still less than encouraging.

Translated by James O'Higgins

1 John Boswell, *Christianity, Social Tolerance, and Homosexuality.* (Chicago: University of Chicago Press, 1980). [Ed.]

2 Julius Edwin Rivers, *Proust and the Art of Love* (New York: Columbia University Press, 1980). [Ed.]

42

SPACE, KNOWLEDGE AND POWER

Q: In your interview with geographers at *Herodote,*[1] you said that architecture beocomes political at the end of the 18th century. Obviously, it was political in earlier periods, too, such as during the Roman Empire. What is particular about the 18th century?

MF: My statement was awkward in that form. Of course I did not mean to say that architecture was not political before, becoming so only at that time. I only meant to say that in the 18th century one sees the development of reflection upon architecture as a function of the aims and techniques of the government of societies. One begins to see a form of political lietarature that addresses what the order of a society should be, what a city should be, given the requirements of the maintenance of order; given that one should avoid epidemics, avoid revolts, permit a decent and moral family life, and so on. In terms of these objectives, how is one to conceive of both the organization of a city and the construction of a collective infrastructure? And how should houses be built? I am not saying that this sort of reflection appears only in the 18th century, but only that in the 18th century a very broad and general reflection on these questions takes place. If one opens a police report of the times—the treatises that are devoted to the techniques of government—one finds that architecture and urbanism occupy a place of considerable importance. That is what I meant to say.

Q: Among the Ancients, in Rome or Greece, what was the difference?

MF: In discussing Rome one sees that the problem revolves around Vitruvius. Vitruvius was reinterpreted from the 16th century on, but one can find in the 16th century—and no doubt in the Middle Ages as well—many considerations of the same order as Vitruvius; if you consider them as *reflections upon.* The treatises on politics, on the art of government, on the manner of good government, did not generally include chapters or analyses devoted to the organization of cities or to architecture. The *Republic* of Jean Bodin (Paris, 1577) does not contain extended discussions of the role of architecture, whereas the police treatises of the 18th century are full of them.

Q: Do you mean that there were techniques and practices, but the discourse did not exist?

MF: I did not say that discourse upon architecture did not exist before the 18th century. Nor do I mean to say that discussions of architecture before the eighteenth century lacked any political dimension or significance. What I wished to point out is that from the 18th century on, every discussion of politics as the art of government of men necessarily includes a chapter or a series of chapters on urbanism, on collective facilities, on hygiene, and on private architecture. Such chapters are not found in the discussions of the art of government of the 16th century. This change is perhaps not in the reflections of architects upon architecture, but it is quite clearly seen in the reflections of political men.

Q: It was not necessarily a change within the theory of architecture itself?

MF: That's right. It was not necessarily a change in the minds of architects, or in their techniques—although that remains to be seen—but in the minds of political men in the choice and the form of attention that they bring to bear upon the objects that are of concern to them. Architecture became one of these during the 17th and 18th centuries.

Q: Could you tell us why?

MF: Well, I think it was linked to a number of phenomena, such as the question of the city and the idea that was clearly formulated at the beginning of the 17th century that the government of a large state like France should ultimately think of its territory on the model of the city. The city was no longer perceived as a place of privilege, as an exception in a territory of fields, forests, and roads. The cities were no longer islands beyond the common law. Instead, the cities, with the problems that they raised, and the particular forms that they took, served as the models for the governmental rationality that was to apply to the whole of the territory.

There is an entire series of utopias or projects for governing territory that developed on the premise that a state is like a large city; the capital is like its main square; the roads are like its streets. A state will be well-organized when a system of policing as tight and efficient as that of the cities extends over the entire territory. At the outset, the notion of police applied only to the set of regulations that were to assure the tranquility of a city, but at that moment the police become the very *type* of rationality for the government of the whole territory. The model of the city became the matrix for the regulations that apply to a whole state.

The notion of police, even in France today, is frequently misunderstood. When one speaks to a Frenchman about police, he can only think of people in uniform or in the secret service. In the 17th and 18th centuries, "police" signified a program of government rationality. This can be characterized as a project to create a system of regulation of the general conduct of individuals whereby everything would be controlled to the point of self-sustenance, without the need of intervention. This is a rather typically French effort of policing. The English did not develop a comparable system, mainly because of parliamentary traditions on the one hand, and traditions of local, communal autonomy on the other, not to mention the religious system.

One can place Napoleon almost exactly at the break between the old organization of the 18th-century police state (understood, of course, in the sense we have been discussing, not in the sense of the "police state" as we have come to know it) and the forms of the modern state, which he invented. At any rate, it seems that, during the 18th and 19th centuries, there appeared—rather quickly in the case of commerce and more slowly in all the other domains—this idea of a police that would manage to penetrate, to stimulate, to regulate, and to render almost automatic all the mechanisms of society.

This idea has been abandoned. The question has been turned around. No longer do we ask, What is the form of governmental rationality that will be able to penetrate the body politic to its most fundamental elements? But rather, How is government possible? That is, what is the principle of limitation that applies to governmental actions such that things will occur for the best, in conformity with the rationality of government, and without intervention?

It is here that the question of liberalism comes up. It seems to me that at that very moment it became apparent that if one governed too much, one did not govern at all—that one provoked results contrary to those one desired. What was discovered at that time—and this was one of the great discoveries of political thought at the end of the 18th century—was the idea of *society*. That is to say, that government not only has to deal with a territory, with a domain, and with its subjects, but that it also has to deal with a complex and independent reality that has its own laws and mechanisms of disturbance. This new reality is society. From the moment that one is to manipulate a society, one cannot consider it completely penetrable by police. One must take into account what it is. It becomes necessary to reflect upon it, upon its specific characteristics, its constants and its variables…

Q: So there is a change in the importance of space. In the 18th century there was a territory and the problem of governing people in this territory: one can choose as an example *La Métropolite* (1682) of Alexandre LeMaitre—a utopian treatise on how to build a capital city—or one can understand a city as a metaphor or symbol for the territory and how to govern it. All of this is quite spatial, whereas after Napoleon, society is not necessarily so *spatialized*…

MF: That's right. On one hand, it is not so spatialized, yet at the same time a certain number of problems that are properly seen as spatial emerged.

Urban space has its own dangers: disease, such as the epidemics of cholera in Europe from 1830 to about 1880; and revolution, such as the series of urban revolts that shook all of Europe during the same period. These spatial problems, which were perhaps not new, took on a new importance.

Secondly, a new aspect of the relations of space and power were the railroads. These were to establish a network of communication no longer corresponding necessarily to the traditional network of roads, but they nonetheless had to take into account the nature of society and its history. In addition, there are all the social phenomena that railroads give rise to, be they the resistances they provoked, the transformations of population, or changes in the behavior of people. Europe was immediately sensitive to the changes in behavior that the railroads entailed. What was going to happen, for example, if it was possible to get married between Bordeaux and Nantes? Something that was not possible before. What was going to happen when people in Germany and France might get to know one another? Would war still be possible once there were railroads? In France a theory developed that the railroads would increase familiarity among people and that the new forms of human universality made possible would render war impossible. But what the people did not foresee—although the German military command was fully aware of it, since they were much cleverer than their French counterpart—was that, on the contrary, the railroads rendered war far easier to wage. The third development, which came later, was electricity.

So, there were problems in the links between the exercise of political power and the space of a territory, or the space of cities—links that were completely new.

Q: So, it was less a matter of architecture than before. These are sorts of technics of space...

MF: The major problems of space, from the 19th century on, were indeed of a different type. Which is not to say that problems of an architectural nature were forgotten. In terms of the first ones I referred to—disease and the political problems—architecture has a very important role to play. The reflections on urbanism and on the design of workers' housing—all of these questions—are an area of reflection upon architecture.

Q: But architecture itself, the Ecole des Beaux-Arts, belongs to a completely different set of spatial issues.

MF: That's right. With the birth of these new technologies and these new economic processes one sees the birth of a sort of thinking about space that's no longer modeled upon the police state of the urbanization of the territory, but that extends far beyond limits of urbanism and architecture.

Q: Consequently, the Ecole des Ponts et Chaussées...

MF: That's right. The Ecole des Ponts et Chaussées and its capital importance in political rationality in France are part of this. It was not architects, but engineers and builders of bridges, roads, viaducts, railways, as well as the Polytechnicians (who practically controlled the French railroads)—those are the people who thought out space.

Q: Has this situation continued up to the present, or are we witnessing a change in relations between the technicians of space?

MF: We may well witness some changes, but I think that we have until now remained with the developers of the territory, the people of the Ponts et Chaussées, etc.

Q: So architects are not necessarily the masters of space that they once were, or believed themselves to be.

MF: That's right. They are not the technicians or engineers of the three great variables—territory, communication, and speed. These escape the domain of architects.

Q: Do you see any particular architectural projects, either in the past or the present, as forces of liberation or resistance?

MF: I do not think that it is possible to say that one thing is of the order of "liberation" and another of the order of "oppression." There are a number of things that one can say with some certainty about a concentration camp to the effect that it is not an instrument of liberation, but one should still take into account—and this is not generally acknowledged—that aside from torture and execution, which preclude any resistance, no matter how terrifying a given system may be, there always remain the possibilities of resistance, disobedience, and oppositional groupings.

On the other hand, I do not think that there is anything that is functionally—by its very nature—absolutely liberating. Liberty is a practice. So there may, in fact, always be, a number of projects whose aim is to modify some constraints, to loosen, or even to break them, but none of these projects can, simply by its nature, assure that people will have liberty automatically: that it will be established by the project itself. The liberty of men is never assured by the institutions and laws that are intended to guarantee them. This is why almost all of these laws and institutions are quite capable of being turned around. Not because they are ambiguous, but simply because "liberty" is what must be exercised.

Q: Are there urban examples of this? Or examples where architects succeeded?

MF: Well, up to a point there is Le Corbusier, who is described today—with a sort of cruelty that I find perfectly useless—as a sort of crypto-Stalinist. He was, I am sure, someone full of good intentions, and what he did was in fact dedicated to liberating effects. Perhaps the means that he proposed were in the end less liberating than he thought, but, once again, I think that it can never be inherent in the structure of things to guarantee the exercise of freedom. The guarantee of freedom is freedom.

Q: So you do not think of Le Corbusier as an example of success. You are simply saying that his intention was liberating. Can you give us a successful example?

MF: No. It *cannot* succeed. If one were to find a place, and perhaps there are some, where liberty is effectively exercised, one would find that this is not owing to the order of objects, but, once again, owing to the practice of liberty. Which is not to say, after all, one may as well leave people in slums thinking that they can simply exercise their rights there.

Q: Meaning that architecture in itself cannot resolve social problems?

MF: I think it can and does produce positive effects when the liberating intentions of the architect coincide with the real practice of people in the exercise of their freedom.

Q: But the same architecture can serve other ends.

MF: Absolutely. Let me bring up another example: The *Familistère* of Jean-Baptiste Godin at Guise (1859). The architecture of Godin was clearly intended for the freedom of people. Here was something that manifested the power of ordinary workers to participate in the exercise of their trade. It was a rather important sign and instrument of autonomy for a group of workers. Yet no one could enter or leave the place without being seen by everyone—an aspect of the architecture that could be totally oppressive. But it could only be oppressive if people were prepared to use their own presence in order to watch over others. Let's imagine a community of unlimited sexual practices that might be established there. It would once again become a place of freedom. I think it is somewhat arbitrary to try to dissociate the effective practice of freedom by people, the practice of social relations, and the spatial distributions in which they find themselves. If they are separated, they become impossible to understand. Each can only be understood through the other.

Q: Yet people have often attempted to find utopian schemes to liberate people, or to oppress them.

MF: Men have dreamed of liberating machines. But there are no machines of freedom, by definition. This is not to say that the exercise of freedom is completely indifferent to spatial distribution, but it can only function when there is a certain convergence; in the case of divergence or distortion it immediately becomes the opposite of that which had been intended. The panoptic qualities of Guise could perfectly well have allowed it to be used as a prison. Nothing could be simpler. It is clear that, in fact, the *Familistère* may well have served as an instrument for discipline and a rather unbearable group pressure.

Q: So once again the intention of the architect is not the fundamental determining factor.

MF: Nothing is fundamental. That is what is interesting in the analysis of society. That is why nothing irritates me as much as these inquiries—which are by definition metaphysical—on the foundations of power in a society or the self-institution of a society, etc. These are not fundamental phenomena. There are only reciprocal relations, and the perpetual gaps between intentions in relation to one another.

Q: You have singled out doctors, prison wardens, priests, judges, and psychiatrists as key figures in the political configurations that involve domination. Would you put architects on this list?

MF: You know, I was not really attempting to describe figures of domination when I referred to doctors and people like that, but rather to describe people through whom power passed or who are important in the fields of power relations. A patient in a mental institution is placed within a field of fairly complicated power relations, which Erving Goffman analyzed very well. The pastor in a Christian or Catholic church (in Protestant churches it is somewhat different) is an important link in a set of power relations. The architect is not an individual of that sort.
After all, the architect has no power over me. If I want to tear down or change a house he built for me, put up new partitions, add a chimney, the architect has no control. So the architect should be placed in another category—which is not to say that he is totally foreign to the organization, the implementation, and all the techniques of power that are exercised in a society. I would say that one must take him—his mentality, his attitude—into account as well as his projects, in order to understand a certain number of the techniques of power that are invested in architecture, but he is not comparable to a doctor, a priest, a psychiatrist, or a prison warden.

Q: "Post-modernism" has received a great deal of attention recently in architectural circles. It is also being talked about in philosophy, notably by Jean-François Lyotard and Jurgen Habermas. Clearly, historical reference and language play an important role in the modern *epistemè*. How do you see post-modernism, both as architecture and in terms of the historical and philosophical questions that are raised by it?

MF: I think there is a widespread and facile tendency, which one should combat, to designate that which has just occurred as the primary enemy as if this were always the principal form of oppression from which one had to liberate oneself. Now, this simple attitude entails a number of dangerous consequences: first, an inclination to seek out some cheap form of archaism or some imaginary past forms of happiness that people did not, in fact, have at all. For instance, in the area that interests me, it is very amusing to see how contemporary sexuality is described as something absolutely terrible. To think that it is only possible now to make love after turning off the television! And in mass-produced beds! "Not like the wonderful time when..." Well, what about those wonderful times when people worked eighteen hours a day and there were six people in a bed, if one was lucky enough to have a bed! There is in this hatred of the present or the immediate past a dangerous tendency to invoke a completely mythical past. Secondly, there is the problem raised by Habermas: if one abandons the work of Kant or Weber, for example, one runs the risk of lapsing into irrationality.

I am completely in agreement with this, but at the same time, our question is quite different. I think that the central issue of philosophy and critical thought since the 18th century has been, still is, and will, I hope, remain the question, *What* is this Reason that we use? What are its historical effects? What are its limits, and what are its dangers? How can we exist as rational beings, fortunately committed to practicing a rationality that is unfortunately crisscrossed by intrinsic dangers? One should not forget—and I'm not saying this in order to criticize rationality, but in order to show how ambiguous things are—it was on the basis of the flamboyant rationality of Social Darwinism that racism was formulated, becoming one of the most enduring and powerful ingredients of Nazism. This was, of course, an irrationality, but an irrationality that was at the same time, after all, a certain form of rationality...

This is the situation that we are in and that we must combat. If intellectuals in general are to have a function, if critical thought itself has a function, and, even more specifically, if philosophy has a function within critical thought, it is precisely to accept this sort of spiral, this sort of revolving door of rationality that refers us to its necessity, to its indispensability, and at the same time, to its intrinsic dangers.

Q: All that being said, it would be fair to say that you are much less afraid of historicism and the play of historical references than someone like Habermas is; also that this issue has been raised in architecture as almost a crisis of civilization by the defenders of modernism, who contend that if we abandon modern architecture for a frivolous return to decoration and motifs, we are somehow abandoning civilization. On the other hand, some post-modernists have claimed that historical references per se are somehow meaningful and are going to protect us from the dangers of an overly rationalized world.

MF: Although it may not answer your question, I would say this: one should totally and absolutely suspect anything that claims to be a return. One reason is a logical one; there is in fact no such thing as a return. History, and the meticulous interest applied to history, is certainly one of the best defenses against this theme of the return. For me, the history of madness or the studies of the prison...were done in that precise manner because I knew full well—this is in fact what aggravated many people—that I was carrying out an historical analysis in such a manner that people *could* criticize the present, but it was impossible for them to say, "Let's go back to the good old days when madmen in the eighteenth century..." or, "Let's go back to the days when the prison was not one of the principal instruments..." No; I think that history preserves us from that sort of ideology of the return.

Q: Hence, the simple opposition between reason and history is rather silly...choosing sides between the two...

MF: Yes. Well, the problem for Habermas is, after all, to make a transcendental mode of thought spring forth against any historicism. I am, indeed, far more historicist and Nietzschean. I do not think that there is a proper usage of history or a proper usage of intrahistorical analysis—which is fairly lucid, by the way—that works precisely against this ideology of the return. A good study of peasant architecture in Europe, for example, would show the utter vanity of wanting to return to the little individual house with its thatched roof. History protects us from historicism—from a historicism that calls on the past to resolve the questions of the present.

Q: It also reminds us that there is always a history; that those modernists who wanted to suppress any reference to the past were making a mistake.

MF: Of course.

Q: Your next two books deal with sexuality among the Greeks and the early Christians. Are there any particular architectural dimensions to the issues you discuss?

MF: I didn't find any; absolutely none. But what is interesting is that in Imperial Rome there were, in fact, brothels, pleasure quarters, criminal areas, etc., and there was also one sort of quasi-public place of pleasure: the baths, the *thermes*. The baths were a very important place of pleasure and encounter, which slowly disappeared in Europe. In the Middle Ages, the baths were still a place of encounter between men and women as well as of men and men and women with women, although that is rarely talked about. What was referred to and condemned, as well as practiced, were the encounters between men and women, which disappeared over the course of the 16th and 17th centuries.

Q: In the Arab world it continues.

MF: Yes; but in France it has largely ceased. It still existed in the 19th century. One sees it in *Les Enfants du Paradis,* and it is historically exact. One of the characters, Lacenaire, was—no one mentions it—a swine and a pimp who used young boys to attract older men and then blackmailed them; there is a scene that refers to this. It required all the naivete and antihomosexuality of the Surrealists to overlook that fact. So the baths continued to exist, as a place of sexual encounters. The bath was a sort of cathedral of pleasure at the heart of the city, where people could go as often as they wanted, where they walked about, picked each other up, met each other, took their pleasure, ate, drank, discussed...

Q: So sex was not separated from the other pleasures. It was inscribed in the center of the cities. It was public; it served a purpose...

MF: That's right. Sexuality was obviously considered a social pleasure for the Greeks and the Romans. What is interesting about male homosexuality today—this has apparently been the case of female homsexuals for some time— is that their sexual relations are immediately transferred into social relations and the social relations are understood as sexual relations. For the Greeks and the Romans, in a different fashion, sexual relations were located within social relations in the widest sense of the term. The baths were a place of sociality that included sexual relations.

One can directly compare the bath and the brothel. The brothel is in fact a place, and an architecture, of pleasure. There is, in fact, a very interesting form of sociality that was studied by Alain Corbin in *Les Filles de Noces* (Aubier, 1978). The men of the city met at the brothel; they were tied to one another by the fact that the same women passed through their hands, that the same diseases and infections were communicated to them. There was a sociality of the brothel; but the sociality of the baths as it existed among the ancients—a new version of which could perhaps exist again—was completely different from the sociality of the brothel.

Q: We now know a great deal about disciplinary architecture. What about confessional architecture—the kind of architecture that would be associated with a confessional technology?

MF: You mean religious architecture? I think that it has been studied. There is the whole problem of a monastery as xenophobic. there one finds precise regulations concerning life in common; affecting sleeping, eating, prayer, the place of each individual in all of that, the cells. All of this was programmed from very early on.

Q: In a technology of power, of confession as opposed to discipline, space seems to play a central role as well.

MF: Yes, space is fundamental in any form of communal life; space is fundamental in any exercise of power. To make a parenthetical remark, I recall having been invited, in 1966, by a group of architects to do a study of space, of something that I called at that time "heterotopias," those singular spaces to be found in some given social spaces whose functions are different or even the opposite of others. The architects worked on this, and at the end of the study someone spoke up—a Sartrean psychologist—who firebombed me, saying that *space* is reactionary and capitalist, but *history* and *becoming* are revolutionary. This absurd discourse was not at all unusual at the time. Today everyone would be convulsed with laughter at such a pronouncement, but not then.

Q: Architects in particular, if they choose to analyze an institutional building such as a hospital or a school in terms of its disciplinary function, would tend to focus primarily on the walls. After all, that is what they design. Your approach is perhaps more concerned with space, rather than architecture, in that the physical walls are only one aspect of the institution. How would you characterize the difference between these two approaches, between the building itself and space?

MF: I think there is a difference in method and approach. It is true that for me, architecture, in the very vague analyses of it that I have been able to conduct, is only taken as an element of support, to insure a certain allocation of people in space, a *canalization* of their circulation, as well as the coding of their reciprocal relations. So it is not only considered as an element in space, but is especially thought of as a plunge into a field of social relations in which it brings about some specific effects.

For example, I know that there is an historian who is carrying out some interesting studies of the archeology of the Middle Ages, in which he takes up the problem of architecture, in terms of the problem of the chimney. I think that he is in the process of showing that from a certain time on it was possible to build a chimney inside the house—a chimney with a hearth, not simply an open room or a chimney outside the house; that at that moment all sorts of things changed and relations between individuals became possible. All of this seems very interesting to me, but the conclusion that he presented in an article was that the history of ideas and thoughts is useless.

What is, in fact, interesting is that the two are rigorously indivisible. Why did people struggle to find the way to put a chimney inside the house? Or why did they put their techniques to this use? So often in the history of techniques it takes years or even centuries to implement them. It is certain, and of capital importance, that this technique was a formative influence upon new human relations, but it is impossible to think that it would have been developed and adapted had there not been in the play and strategy of human relations something which tended in that direction. What is interesting is always interconnection, not the primacy of this over that, which never has any meaning.

Q: In your book *The Order of Things* you constructed certain vivid spatial metaphors to describe structures of thought. Why do you think spatial images are so evocative for these references? What is the relationship between these spatial metaphors describing disciplines and more concrete descriptions of institutional spaces?

MF: It is quite possible that since I was interested in the problems of space I used quite a number of spatial metaphors in *The Order of Things,* but usually these metaphors were not ones that I advanced, but ones that I was studying as objects. What is striking in the epistemological mutations and transformations of the 17th century is to see how the spatialization of knowledge was one of the factors in the constitution of this knowledge as a science. If the natural history and the classifications of Linneas were possible, it is for a certain number of reasons: on the one hand, there was literally a spatialization of the very object of their analyses, since they gave themselves the rule of studying and classifying a plant only on the basis of that which was visible. They didn't even want to use the microscope. All the traditional elements of knowledge, such as the medical functions of the plant, fell away. The object was spatialized. Subsequently, it was spatialized insofar as the principles of classification had to be found in the very structure of the plant: the number of elements, how they were arranged, their size, etc., and other elements, like the height of the plant. Then there was the spatialization into illustrations within books, which was only possible with some printing techniques. Then the spatialization of the reproduction of the plants themselves, which was represented in books. All of these are spatial techniques, not metaphors.

Q: Is the actual plan for a building—the precise drawing that becomes walls and windows—the same form of discourse as, say, a hierarchical pyramid that describes rather precisely relations between people not only in space but in social life?

MF: Well, I think there are a few simple and exceptional examples in which the architectural means reproduce, with more or less emphasis, the social hierarchies. There is the model of the military camp, where the military hierarchy is to be read in the ground itself, by the place occupied by the tents and the buildings reserved for each rank. It reproduces precisely through architecture a pyramid of power; but this is an exceptional example, as is everything military—privileged in society and of an extreme simplicity.

Q: But the plan itself is not always an account of relations or power.

MF: No. Fortunately for human imagination, things are a little more complicated than that.

Q: Architecture is not, of course, a constant: it has a long tradition of changing preoccupations, changing systems, different rules. The *savoir* of architecture is partly the history of the profession, partly the evolution of a science of construction, and partly a rewriting of aesthetic theories. What do you think is particular about this form of *savoir*? Is it more like a natural science, or what you have called a "dubious science"?

MF: I can't exactly say that this distinction between sciences that are certain and those that are uncertain is of no interest—that would be dodging the question—but I must say that what interests me more is to focus on what the Greeks called the *technè,* that is to say, a practical rationality governed by a conscious goal. I am not even sure if it is worth constantly asking the question of whether government can be the object of an exact science. On the other hand, if architecture, like the practice of government and the practice of other forms of social organization, is considered as a *technè,* possibly using elements of sciences like physics, for example, or statistics, etc…that is what is interesting. But if one wanted to do a history of architecture, I think that it should be much more along the lines of that general history of the *technè,* rather than the histories of either the exact sciences or the inexact ones. The disadvantage of this word *technè,* I realize, is its relation to the word "technology," which has a very specific meaning. A very narrow meaning is given to "technology": one thinks of hard technology, the technology of wood, of fire, of electricity. Whereas government is also a function of technology: the government of individuals, the government of souls, the government of the self by the self, the government of families, the government of children, and so on. I believe that if one placed the history of architecture back in this general history of *technè,* in this wide sense of the word, one would have a more interesting guiding concept than by considering opposition between the exact sciences and the inexact ones.

Translated by Christian Hubert

1 "Questions on Geography," from *Hérodote* 1 (1976), reprinted in *Power/ Knowledge: Selected Interviews and Other Writings by Michel Foucault, 1972-1977,* ed. Colin Gordon (New York: Pantheon Books, 1980), p. 69.

43

HOW MUCH DOES IT COST FOR REASON TO TELL THE TRUTH

Q: What is the origin of what we loosely call Post-Structuralism?

MF: Indeed, why not this term? In regard to Structuralism, neither the exponents of this movement nor those who were designated "Structuralists" knew what it was about. Those who used the structural method in very limited areas like linguistics or comparative mythology knew that it was structuralism. But as soon as one went beyond these very limited areas, nobody knew what that was. I am not certain it would be very interesting to attempt to redefine what was called Structuralism then. Instead it seems interesting to me to study Formal Thinking, the different types of Formalism, which have traversed Western culture during all of the 20th century.

I'm thinking of the unusual skill of Formalism in painting, the formal research in music, the significance of Formalism in the analysis of folklore, the sagas, architecture, the application of some of its forms to theoretical thinking. Formalism was probably in general one of the most powerful and complex forces in 20th century Europe. Moreover, Formalism was associated very often with conditions and even political movements, which were certainly equally stimulating each time. The relationship between Russian Formalism and the Russian Revolution should definitely be investigated precisely anew. The role of formal thinking and formal art at the beginning of the 20th century, its ideological value, its ties to various political movements should be analyzed. What strikes me about the so-called structuralist movement in France and in Western Europe during the 1960s: it was really like an echo of the efforts of certain countries in the East and particularly Czechoslovakia to free themselves from dogmatic Marxism. While in a country like Czechoslovakia, the old tradition of prewar European Formalism was revived—around 1955 or in the 1960s—so-called Structuralism arose at about the same time in Western Europe—that is, I believe, a new form, a new modality of this thinking, of this formalistic investigation. That's the way I would classify this structural phenomenon—through its revitalization in the great stream of formal thought.

Q: There is no longer a direct connection between Critical Theory and the student movement in the Federal Republic of Germany. Perhaps the student movement rather made instrumental use of Critical Theory. It sought refuge there. In the same way, perhaps there is no direct causality anymore between Structuralism and '68.

MF: That's right.

Q: But would you say that Structuralism was like a necessary forerunner?

MF: No, nothing is necessary in this order of ideas. But one could say very roughly that formalistic culture, thought, and art in the first third of the 20th century were generally associated with critical political movements of the Left—and even with revolutionary movements—and Marxism obscured all that. Marxism devoted itself to an angry criticism of Formalism in art and in theory which has become manifest since 1930. Thirty years later you can see in a few Eastern countries and in France, how people have attacked dogmatic Marxism, in that they use forms and types of analysis which are obviously inspired by Formalism. The events in France and other countries in 1968 are to the same degree as highly exciting as they are ambiguous; and ambiguous because they are exciting. It's a matter of movements, which often clearly showed a definite respect toward Marxism while at the same time strongly criticizing the dogmatic Marxism of parties and institutions. And the play between a certain pro-Marxist form of thought and Marxist references created room in which the student movements developed. Eventually they brought the revolutionary Marxist discourse to the height of exaggeration. At the same time they were possessed by an antidogmatic impetuosity which prohibits any type of discourse.

Q: In Freud's camp or in Structuralism's camp.

MF: That's right. I would like to return to the history of Formalism and the small Structuralist episode in France, which was relatively, with widely dispersed forms, embedded in the heart of Formalism in the 20th century which is in my opinion as significant as Romanticism or Positivism in the 19th century. Marxism constituted in France a kind of horizon, which Jean-Paul Sartre once considered impassable. At that time Marxism was in fact a rather closed and in any case a controlling mental horizon. From 1945 to 1955 the entire French university life—the group university life in order to differentiate it from the university tradition—was busy with or even fully engrossed in achieving something; not Freud/Marx, rather Husserl/Marx, the relationship to Phenomenological Marxism. That was the beginning of the discussion and the efforts of a whole group of people: Maurice Merleau-Ponty, Sartre, who came to Marxism by way of Phenomenology, and also Jean-Toussaint Dessanti.[1]

Q: Mikel Dufresne, even Jean-François Lyotard.[2]

MF: Paul Ricoeur, who is certainly no Marxist, but who was a phenomenologist and not inclined to ignore Marxism.[3] Then one attempted to combine Marxism with Phenomenology and, as a certain form of structural thought and structural method began to develop, Structuralism took the place of Phenomenology, in order to couple itself with Marxism. The transition from Phenomenology to Structuralism occurred and focused basically on the problem of language. It was a significant moment, as Merleau-Ponty discovered the problem of language. You know that Merleau-Ponty's last efforts were directed to this end: I remember exactly a lecture in which he began to speak about Saussure, who even though he had been dead for only about 50 years, had been completely ignored by the cultivated public—not to mention the French philologists and linguists. The problem of language arose and it became obvious that phenomenology could not do it as much justice as the structural analysis of signification which could be produced by a structure of a linguistic nature, a structure in which the subject in the phenomenological sense could not be engaged as a creator of meaning and naturally, since the phenomenological bride did not understand how to speak about language, she was let go. Structuralism became the new bride. That's the way it happened. Psychoanalysis also brought—mostly due to the influence of Jacques Lacan—a problem to the fore, which was indeed very different, but not without analogy to the above. The problem was the unconscious, which cannot fit into an analysis of a phenomenological nature. The best proof, that it could not be included in phenomenology, not at least into the one constructed by the French, is the following. Sartre or Merleau-Ponty—I don't want to speak about others—have sought indefatigably to dethrone what they called "Positivism." And when the question of language arose, Lacan said: Your efforts are in vain, the activity of the unconscious cannot be reduced to the effects of giving meaning, for which phenomenology is suited. Then Lacan formulated an absolutely symmetrical problem for the linguists. The phenomenological subject was disqualified a second time by psychoanalysis, as it had already been disqualified by linguistic theory. One understands why Lacan could say at this moment that the unconscious was structural like a language. It's the same type of problem. So one had a structural Freudo-Marxism. While phenomenology is excluded on the basis of the above reasons, there are now many more suitors who give Marx their hands and that's a merry group. What I described here was done and embraced by a number of people, but there was a whole group of individuals who did not follow this movement. I'm thinking of those who participated in the history of science, those who showed by aligning themselves with Comte a noteworthy tradition, particularly those around Canguilhem,[4] who had a decidedly influential effect on the young French university life. Many of his students were neither Marxist nor Freudians or Structuralists. If you wish, I'm speaking about myself here. At that time I was a Freudian. I was never a Marxist and never a Structuralist.

Q: How about giving us some dates.

MF: I wrote my first book at the end of my student days, around 1956–1957. That was *Madness and Civilization,* which I wrote between 1955 and 1960. This book is neither Freudian nor Structuralist or Marxist. In 1953, I read Nietzsche and indeed—equally unusual as Nietzsche himself—in his perspective of an examination of the history of knowledge, the history of reason: How can one write the history of rationality, that as the problem of the 19th century.

Q: Knowledge, reason, rationality.

MF: Knowledge, reason, rationality: the possibility of writing a history of rationality. With a man like Alexandre Koyré[5] one still encounters phenomenology: a historian of science with a German education, who settled in France around 1930–1935 and developed a historical analysis of the forms of rationality and knowledge in a phenomenological perspective. For me the problem presents itself in analogous terms as those I've just recalled: can a transhistorical subject of a phenomenological kind be accounted for by the history of reason? Here the writings of Nietzsche cause a break, a rupture (*coupure*) for me. There is a history of the subject as there is a history of reason. One cannot expect this history of reason to evolve from the initial founding act of a rationalistic subject. I read Nietzsche a bit by chance. Remarkably it was through Canguilhem—at that time the most influential French historian of science.

Q: But he shows no detectable traces of Nietzsche.

MF: On the contrary. Without a doubt, there are even expressed references, clearer in his later texts than his earlier ones. In France the relationship to Nietzsche—even the relationship of all 20th century thought—was difficult, for understandable reasons. But I keep talking about myself. One must also speak about Gilles Deleuze. Deleuze wrote his book on Nietzsche around 1960. It was published in 1965.[6] I am quite certain that he is in debt to Hume since he is interested in empiricism and also in the same question: is the theory of the subject presented by phenomenology satisfying? He escapes this question through Hume's subterfuge of empiricism. I am convinced that he met Nietzsche under the same conditions. Everything which happened in the 1960s came from this dissatisfaction with phenomenology's theory of the subject with various digressions, escapes and breakthroughs, according to whether one understood an expression to be positive or negative—to linguistics, to psychology, to Nietzsche.

Q: In any case, Nietzsche represented a certain experience in order to offer the founding act of a subject a check.

MF: Exactly. And here French authors like Maurice Blanchot and Georges Bataille are very important for us. As I just said, I asked myself why I read Nietzsche. I do know why I read Nietzsche. I read Nietzsche because of Bataille and I read Bataille because of Blanchot. It's not true at all that Nietzsche first appeared in French philosophy in the 1970s. At first his influence appeared in the discourse of people who were Marxists in the 1960s and left Marxism as a result of Nietzsche. But those who first reached back to Nietzsche didn't want to leave Marxism. They were not Marxists. They wanted to leave phenomenology.

Q: They spoke one after the other of historians of science and then about writing a history of knowledge, a history of rationality, a history of reason. Before we return to Nietzsche one can certainly summarize these four terms: one can assume that is a matter of quasi-synonyms.

MF: No, not at all. I have described a movement which encompassed many parts and many different problems. I didn't identify the problems. I'm speaking about relationships of research and the proximity of the people who practice them.

Q: Can one attempt to ascertain their relationships?

MF: That's not easy to do in an interview. The history of science played a significant role in the philosophy of France. If modern philosophy of the 19th and 20th centuries derives primarily from the Kantian question, namely "What is Enlightenment?" and if one admits that modern philosophy took up the test of every historical moment, since reason in the form of "maturity" and "without guardian" could appear, under its principle functions, so the function of philosophy of the 19th century consists of the question after the moment in which reason finds access to autonomy, what history means to reason and which value the sway of reason in the modern world straight through the three great forms of objective thought, of technical apparatus and political organization, must be accorded. That was a great task for philosophy since the test of these three domains signifies a reckoning or introducing an unsettling question into the realm of reason. It meant, continuing the Kantian question of "What is Enlightenment?" This taking up against this reiteration of Kant's question in France has found a certain and by the way inadequate form: "What is the history of science? What has happened since Greek mathematics to modern physics, since this universe of science has been erected?" From Auguste Comte until the 1960s it was the philosophical task of history of science to take up this question again. In Germany the question of the history of reason or the history of forms of rationality in Europe manifested itself not so much in the history of science as much more in that stream of thought, which, talking in generalities, stretches from Max Weber to Critical Theory.

Q: Yes, reflection on norms and values.

MF: From Max Weber to Habermas. It seems to me that there the same questions arise about the history of reason, about the various forms of exercising this sway of reason. Surprisingly, France knew little, indirectly or not at all the stream of Weber's thought, Critical Theory or the Frankfurt School. By the way, that presents a small historical problem, which vexes me and I cannot escape from it. It's known that many representatives of the Frankfurt School came to Paris in 1935 to find refuge. But they left again fairy rapidly, most likely repelled—some have said this—in any case sad and disheartened that they had not found acclaim again. The 1940s came, but they had already left for England or North America, where they were really received much better. A small agreement was struck between the Frankfurt School and a French philosophical thought, which would have been able to come to an understanding over the history of science, as well as the question of the history of rationality. I can assure you, that during my student days none of my professors mentioned the Frankfurt School.

Q: That's amazing.

MF: If I had known the Frankfurt School at the right time, I would have been spared a lot of work. Some nonsense, I wouldn't have expressed and taken many detours as I sought not to let myself be led astray when the Frankfurt School had already opened the ways. There is a remarkable problem of non-penetration of two forms of thought, which are akin to each other. Perhaps it is this proximity which explains the non-penetration. Nothing obscures a common problem more than two related ways of approaching it.

Q: It is interesting that you say you would have avoided certain things if you had been familiar with the Frankfurt School and Critical Theory, especially since Habermas and Negt have applauded your efforts. In a conversation with Habermas, he praised to me your idea of the bifurcation of reason—that in every moment reason is supposed to be divided in two. Despite that I asked myself if you would agree with the bifurcation of reason as Critical Theory conceives of it. That is, with the dialectic of reason according to which reason is perverted by the effect of its own power, is transformed and reduced to a type of thought which is technical thought. The ruling thought in Critical Theory is that of a dialectical continuity of reason, with a perversion, which changes it completely suddenly and which serves to correct it, which should be the beginning of the battle for emancipation. The will to knowledge has made in its own way a lot of trust in history ambiguous (*bifurquer*). The word *bifurquer* is perhaps not the right word. Reason has divided knowledge many times.

MF: Yes, one has often tried to blackmail all criticism of reason and every critical test of the history of rationality so that one either recognizes reason or casts it into irrationalism—as if it were not possible to write a rational criticism of rationality, a rational history of all ambiguity and bifurcations, a contingent history of rationality. Since Max Weber in the Frankfurt School and in every case with many historians of science like Canguilhem it was a matter of determining the form of rationalism, which is presented as the ruling one and to which one gives the status of reason, in order to let it appear as one of the possible forms of rational work. In this history of French science, which is considerably significant, Gaston Bachelard also plays a central role.

Q: Despite that the hymns of praise are a bit poisoned. According to Habermas you described the moment of the bifurcation of reason splendidly. This bifurcation is supposed to be a one-time occurrence, you had determined, as reason took a turn, which led to technical rationalism, to a self-diminution, to a self-limiting. If this bifurcation is also a split, then it could only have happened a single time in history, in order to divide two realms as one has called them since Kant. This analysis of bifurcation is Kantian. There is knowledge of understanding, the knowledge of reason, technical reason and moral reason. In order to judge this bifurcation one accepts the position of moral-practical reason. Therefore, a one-time bifurcation, a division between technical and practical which governs all of the history of thought in Germany. You just said that this tradition stems from the question "What is Enlightenment?" This praise seems to diminish your assessment of the history of ideas.

MF: In fact, I do not speak of a bifurcation of reason. Rather I speak of multiple bifurcations. I speak of an endless prolific division. I am not speaking of the moment when reason became technical. At the present, in order to give an example I am researching the problem of technology of self in Greco-Roman antiquity. How men, life, self were objects of a number of *technai,* which can be compared completely, in their compelling rationality, to a production technology.

Q: But without including the entire society.

MF: Without including the entire society. What a *technai* or technology of self brings to development is a historical phenomenon, which is completely analyzable and determinable and is not the bifurcation of reason. In the prolific division, breaks, caesuras, this was an occurrence, a significant epoch, which had noteworthy consequences, but is not a one-time phenomenon.

Q: If one assumes then that the phenomenon of the self-perversion of reason is not a one-time occurrence, didn't it occur just once in history that reason lost something essential, something substantial—as Weber would say—and does your work aim to rehabilitate fruitful reason? Is there another kind of conception of reason in your work, another concept of rationality as that which is accepted by us today.

MF: Yes. But here I would like to free myself from phenomenology which was my starting point. I don't believe that there is here a kind of founding act through which reason in its essence discovers or would be engaged and afterwards could be broken off from any occurrence. I believe that there is a self-creation of reason and therefore I am trying to analyze the forms of rationality: various proofs, various formulations, various modifications by which rationalities educe each other, contradict one another, chase each other away, without one therefore being able to designate a moment in which reason would have lost its basic design or changed from rationalism to irrationalism. Very schematically, in the 1960s I wanted to give up the phenomenological thesis as well as the Marxist thesis (Lukàcs). There was a rationality which was the exemplary form of reason itself and had been led into a crisis by a number of social necessities (capitalism or even more the transition of one form of capitalism to another). That is, into a forgetting of reason and a descent into irrationalism. That is the second great model, schematically correct and unjust, from which I tried to free myself.

Q: According to this model there was a one-time bifurcation, be it after a forgetting, be it after an expropriation by a class. Therefore the emancipation movement in history did not just consist of a retaking of what had been expropriated in order to re-expropriate it, but rather on the contrary in that reason was given back its entire truth, given back its status of absolute universal science. It is clear that you have no proposal of a new science or an expanded science.

MF: Absolutely not.

Q: But you show that every time a form of rationality asserts itself, it occurs through division, that is, through closure or alienation, through the demarcation of a boundary between itself and another. Does your proposal include a wish to rehabilitate this other one? For example, when you embrace the silence of a madman, do you consider it a language which expresses itself comprehensively on the necessities of the creation of works?

MF: Yes. What interested me in this general framework were the forms of rationality, which the human subject applied to himself. While the historian of science in France busied himself primarily with the problem of the constitution of scientific objects, I asked myself another question. How does it happen that the human subject makes himself into an object of possible knowledge, through which forms of rationality, through which historical necessities, and at what price? My question is this: How much does it cost the subject to be able to tell the truth about itself? How much does it cost the subject as madman to be able to tell the truth about itself? About the cost of constituting the madman as the absolute other and in that it not only pays this theoretical price, but also an institutional and even economic price as the organization of psychiatry allows it to be determined. A complex and multilayered totality with an institutionalized game, class relationships, class conflicts, modalities of knowledge and finally a whole history, subjects and reason are involved in it. That is what I tried to reconstitute. That is perhaps a completely crazy, very complex project, of which I could only observe a few moments, a few special points, like the problem of the insane subject. How can one tell the truth about an insane subject? Those were my first two books. *The Order of Things* asked, what is the cost of problematizing and analyzing the speaking, working, living subject. That's why I transferred the same kinds of questions to criminals and penal institutions. How can one tell the truth about oneself as a criminal. And I want to continue that in respect to sexuality. How can the subject tell the truth about itself as a subject of sexual gratification, and at what cost?

Q: It is in no way a matter of exhuming, using archaeology, something archaic which existed before history.

MF: No. Absolutely not. When I use the word archaeology, which I don't do anymore, then I use it to say that the type of analysis which I conduct was displaced, not in time but by the level at which it is determined. My problem is not to study the evolution of the history of ideas, but rather much more to observe the ideas, how this or that object could appear as a possible object of perception. Why for example insanity became at one time an object of perception, which corresponded to a type of recognition. This displacement between the ideas about insanity and the constitution of insanity as object I wanted to delineate through the use of the word archaeology as opposed to history.

Q: I asked this question because there are now tendencies, under the guise that the New German Right is influenced by Nietzsche, to assume that French Nietzscheanism comes from the same vein. One mixes everything together in order to renew basically the fronts of a new theoretical class war, which is very difficult to find these days.

MF: There is not just *one* Nietzscheanism. One cannot say there is a true Nietzscheanism and that this one is truer than the other. But those who found Nietzsche a tool more than 25 years ago, to change their position in regard to the body of philosophical thought ruled by one of phenomenology or Marxism, have nothing to do with those who use Nietzsche today. Gilles Deleuze wrote a powerful book about Nietzsche and Nietzsche is present in his work in general, but without noisy reference and without the desire to flaunt Nietzsche's banner for a rhetorical or political effect. It is impressive that someone like Deleuze simply turned to Nietzsche and took him seriously. I also wanted to do that: what serious use can one make of Nietzsche? I gave a lecture about Nietzsche and have written a little about him.[7] The only honor I accorded him, weakly, was naming the first part of *The History of Sexuality* "The Will to Knowledge."

Q: Motivated by this will to knowledge there was always a rapport or relationship. I suspect you avoid both these words because they are colored by Hegelianism. Perhaps we should speak about evaluation, as Nietzsche did; a way to evaluate truth and the power to give it structure to create it; a power which does not exist as archaically as reason or source, but rather a relationship of powers—perhaps already a relationship of power in the act of constituting all knowledge.

MF: No, I wouldn't say that. That is too complicated. My problem is the relationship of self to self and that of saying the truth. What I thank Nietzsche for, I owe more to his texts of around 1880 in which the question of truth, of the truth of history and the will to truth were central for him. The first text which Sartre wrote as a young student was a Nietzschean text. "The History of Truth," a tiny text which appeared for the first time around 1925 in a *gymnasium* journal. His departure point was from the same problem. And it is very noteworthy that his way led from the history of truth to phenomenology while the way of the subsequent generation to which we belong, arose particularly to severe itself from phenomenology in order to return to the question of the history of truth.

Q: You admit to an affinity to Deleuze, to a certain extent. Does this include Deleuze's concept of desire?

MF: No.

Q: It seems to me that desire by Deleuze is a productive desire and gives the species its form-giving reason for genesis.

MF: I don't want to take a position or say what Deleuze meant.[8] People say what they want to or what they can. When a system of thought is created it always becomes fixed and identified in the heart of a cultural tradition. It is perfectly normal that this cultural tradition takes it up and restricts it, does what it wants with it, has it express what it didn't say, but with the allusion that it is only another form of what one intended to say. That's what culture does. But that cannot be my relationship to Deleuze. I will not say what he wanted to say. His problem was the problem of desire. Probably we will find in the theory of desire the effect of a relationship to Nietzsche. While my problem always was truth. *Wahr-Sagen* and the relationship between it and the forms of reflexivity, the reflexivity of self on self.

Q: Yes, I think Nietzsche did not differentiate thoroughly enough the will to knowledge from the will to power.

MF: There's a noticeable shifting in Nietzsche's text between those who are governed by the question about the will to knowledge and the will to power. But I didn't want to debate this for a simple reason. I haven't read Nietzsche for a good many years.

Q: The elaboration seemed to be important for me because of the truly confused reception of Nietzsche abroad, as characterized by the way also in France.

MF: My relationship to Nietzsche is not a historical relationship. I am not so interested in Nietzsche's history of thought as in this quality of the challenge, which I felt—rather long ago—as I read Nietzsche for the first time. If one reads *"Frohliche Wissenschaft"* or *"Morgenrote"* while one is being formed by the great and old university tradition of Descartes, Kant, Hegel, Husserl, then one stumbles on these witty, strange, and impudent texts and says to oneself, good, I won't do it the way my friends, colleagues, and professors do it, peering in arrogance from on high. What is the epitome of philosophical intensity and what are the actual philosophical effects, which we can find in these texts. That for me is the challenge of Nietzsche.

Q: In the actual reception there is a second confusion, that is post-modernism, to which not insignificant people refer and which played a certain role in Germany, since Habermas took up this expression and criticized it. Do you see a tendency in it? Can you ascertain a place for yourself in it?

MF: I must say, I find that difficult to answer. First, because I never really understood how modernism is defined in France. It's clear by Baudelaire, but after that it seems to lose meaning for me. I don't know in what sense Germans speak of modernism. I know that Americans are planning a kind of seminar with Habermas and me and Habermas proposed modernism as the topic. I'm at a loss; I don't know what that means nor what the problematic is. As much as I recognize behind the expression Structuralism, the problem of the subject and its transformation, as little do I see the common problematic between post-modernism or post-structuralism.

Q: Accepting modernism or rejecting it is not only ambiguous, it truncates modernism. Also it has at least three definitions: the definition of the historian, Weber's definition, and Adorno's which alludes to Benjamin's *Baudelaire*. Habermas seems to prefer here against Adorno the tradition of reason, that is, Weber's definition of modernism. Therefore he perceives in post-modernism the decline of reason, so that reason basically becomes a form of the will to knowledge, among other things.

MF: That isn't my problem. I don't at all identify reason with the totality of the forms of rationality. The latter could until recently dominate in the types of knowledge, the forms of technology and the modalities of governance. The application of rationality occurs primarily in these areas. I don't deal with the problem of art, it is too complicated. For me no given form of rationality is reason. Therefore I don't see how one can say that the forms of rationality, which have governed these three realms, break apart and disperse. I simply see multiple transformations—but why should one call that the demise of reason? Endlessly other forms of rationality are born. Therefore I claim that reason is a long narrative, which ends today and makes room for another, and makes no sense.

Q: The field is open for many forms of narratives.

MF: We hit here upon one of the most destructive habits of contemporary thought. Perhaps even one of the most destructive of modern thought—in any case, of post-Hegelian thought. That is that the moment of the present is considered in history as the break, the climax, the fulfillment, the return of youth, etc. The solemnity with which everyone who has a philosophical discourse reflects his own time seems a stigma to me. I say this particularly because it happens to me and one finds it constantly in Nietzsche. One must probably find the humility to admit that the time of one's own life is not the one-time, basic, revolutionary moment of history, from which everything begins and is completed. At the same time humility is needed to say without solemnity that the present time is rather exciting and demands an analysis. We must ask ourselves the question, What is today? In relation to the Kantian question, "What is Enlightenment?" one can say that it is the task of philosophy to explain what today is and what we are today, but without breast-beating drama and theatricality and maintaining that this moment is the greatest damnation or daybreak of the rising sun. No, it is a day like every other, or much more, a day which is never like another.

Q: That brings up a lot of questions which you have raised yourself. What is today? Can one characterize this epoch despite everything as a great fragmentation in regard to others, through deterritorialization and schizophrenia?

MF: I want to say about the task of a diagnosis of today that it does not consist only of a description of who we are, rather a line of fragility of today to follow and understand, if and how what is, can no longer be what it is. In this sense, the description must be formulated in a kind of virtual break, which opens room, understood as a room of concrete freedom, that is possible transformation.

Q: Does the practical work of intellectuals focus on this place of the crack?

MF: I believe so. The work of the intellect is to show that what is, does not have to be what it is. Therefore this designation and description of reality never has the value of a prescription according to the form "because this is, that is." Therefore the return to history makes sense in the respect that history shows that that which is not always was so. It unites casual movements into threads of a fragile and uncertain history. Thus things were formed which give the impression of the greatest self-evidence. What reason considers its necessity or much more what various forms of rationality claim to be their necessary existence, has a history which we can determine completely and recover from the tapestry of contingency. But this doesn't mean that these forms of rationality are irrational. They rest upon a foundation of human practices and human faces, because they are made they can be unmade—of course, assuming we know how they were made.

Q: This work on the breaks is both descriptive and practical, a work on a particular place.

MF: Perhaps a place and perhaps work which must return as a result of the questions asked there so far back into historical analysis.

Q: Is the work on the place of the break what you call microphysics of power or analysis of power?

MF: Somewhat. These forms of rationality in the process of dominance must be analyzed for themselves. They are alien to other forms of power like recognition or technology. On the contrary, there is an exchange, transfer, interference. But it is impossible, however, to designate these three realms as the only and constant form of rationality. We find the same types again displaced, dense manifold circuits, but still no isomorphism.

Q: Sometimes or always?

MF: There are no universal rules which establish the types of relationship between rationality and the processes of governance.

Q: I asked this question because a number of critics express the same criticism—like Jean Baudrillard[9]—which claims the beginning of microphysics reflects a situation in which power has been rendered irreparable through dissemination. That you speak up at a point in time when capitalism has decomposed the subject to such extent that it is possible to realize that all that remains of it, it appears, is a multiplicity of positions.

MF: I'll talk about that soon but I started with something else. First, when I examine the rationality of governance, I seek to establish circuits which are not isomorphisms. Second, when I speak about the relationships of power and the forms of rationality, which regulate and govern these, then I'm not speaking about the power, which governs all of society and superimposes its rationality on it. Relationships of power are manifold. They have various forms which can be executed within the family, inside an institution, an administration, between a ruling and subservient class in specific and common forms of rationality. It is a matter of a field of analysis and not a reference to a unique instance. Third, when I examine relationships of power, I create no theory of power. I examine how relationships of power interact, are determining elements in every relationship. The question I raise between the reflexivity of the subject and the discourse of truth is: How can the subject tell the truth about itself? That is obvious for my examination of insanity. The subject was able to tell the truth about his insanity, because the structures of the Other allowed him to. That was possible as a result of a specific kind of dominance, which some persons exerted over others.

I am no theoretician of power. The question of power in itself doesn't interest me. I did speak often about this question of power because the given political analysis of the phenomenon of power could not be properly addressed from the fine and small appearances which I wanted to recall, when I asked the question of the *"dire-vrai"* (telling the truth) about oneself. If I "tell the truth" about myself, I constitute myself as subject by a certain number of relationships of power, which weigh upon me and which I lay upon others. I am not creating a theory of power or an analysis of contemporary power, I am working on the way the reflexivity of self to self has been established and which discourse of truth is tied to it. When I speak about the institutions of confinement in the 18th century, then I am speaking about the point in time of existing relationships of power. I take contemporary psychiatry for examination. A number of problems arise in the interdependences of function of the institution. They point to a relatively ancient history, which encompasses several centuries. I write the history or archaeology of the kind of way one tried in the 17th or 18th century to tell the truth about insanity. I want to show it as it existed at that time. For example, when I wanted to describe the criminal and system of punishment in the 18th century I researched the forms and practices of power in a handful of 18th century institutions, which can serve as a model. Therefore, I do not find it correct at all to say that power is no longer the same.

Translated by Mia Foret and Marion Martius.

---

1 Jean–Toussaint Dessanti had been one of Foucault's teachers. A remarkable Spinozist and phenomenologist of science (together with Cavaillès, Koyré and Canguilhem), but also a hard–core Stalinist, he published *La Philosophie silencieuse* (Paris: Editions du Seuil, 1975) and *Le Philosophe et les pouvoirs* (Paris: Calmann–Lévy, 1976). [Ed.]

2 Mikel Dufresne, *The Sciences of Art* (Westport, Conn.: Greenwood, 1963); Jean-François Lyotard, *Driftworks* (New York: Semiotext(e) Foreign Agents Series, 1984).[Ed.]

3 Paul Ricoeur wrote extensively on hermeneutics. See, for example, *The Conflict of Interpretations* (Chicago: Northwestern University Press, 1974), and *Interpretation Theory: Discourse and the Surplus of Meaning* (Texas Christian University Press, 1976).[Ed.]

4 Georges Canguilhem, a well-known French epistomologist and seminal teacher, author of *Essais sur quelques problèmes concernant le normal et le pathologique* (Clermont-Ferrand: La Montagne, 1943) and *La Connaissance de la vie* (Paris: J. Vrin, 1985).[Ed.]

5 Alexandre Koyré, historian of the ideas of science, author of *From the Closed World to the Infinite Universes* (Baltimore: The Johns Hopkins Press, 1957) and *The Astronomical Revolution: Copernicus, Kepler, Borelli* (Ithaca, NY: Cornell University Press, 1983).[Ed.]

6 Gilles Deleuze, *Nietzsche and Philosophy*, trans. Hugh Tomlinson, (New York: Columbia University Press, 1983). See also *On the Line,* trans. John

Johnston (New York: Semiotext(e) Foreign Agents Series, 1983).[Ed.]

7 Michel Foucault, "Nietzsche, Geneaology, History," *Semiotext(e)* (Vol III, No. 1, 1978).[Ed.]

8 For a later clarification [1994], see Gilles Deleuze, "Desire and Pleasure," *More & Less*, No., 2, 1996 (Pasadena: Art Center) [Ed.]

9 Jean Baudrillard, *Forget Foucault* (New York: Semiotext(e) Foreign Agents Series, 1987).[Ed.]

44

HISTORY AND HOMOSEXUALITY

Q: K.J. Dover's book *Greek Homosexuality*[1] presents a new elucidation of homosexuality in ancient Greece.

MF: It seems to me that the most important thing about this book is that Dover shows that our division of sexual behavior between homo- and heterosexuality is absolutely not relevant for the Greeks and the Romans. That means two things: on the one hand that they lacked the notion or *concept* of this division, and on the other that they didn't have the experience. A person who went to bed with another of the same sex did not experience himself as a homosexual. This seems to me fundamental.

When a man made love with a boy, the moral issue revolved around the question: was this man active or passive, and did he make love with a beardless boy—the appearance of a beard defined a cut-off point? The combination of these two types of dichotomy institutes a very complex profile defining morality and immorality. Thus it makes no sense to say that homosexuality was tolerated by the Greeks. Dover brings out the complexity of this very coded relationship between men and boys. It had to do with flight and protection for the boys, and pursuit and courtship for the men. Thus there existed a whole civilization of pederasty, of man-boy love, which necessitated, as always happens with this type of coding, the valorization or devalorization of certain kinds of behavior.

That is what I would take from Dover's book. It dispenses with a lot of things in historical analysis regarding the famous sexual taboos, the very notion of the taboo. You have to take things differently, that is to say, write the history of a family of experiences, of different ways of life, a history of the diverse kinds of relationships between people of the same sex, according to age, etc. In other words, the condemnation of Sodom shouldn't serve as the historical model.

I would add something that is not found in Dover's book, an idea that came to me last year. There is a whole theoretical discourse on the love of boys in Greece, from Plato to Plutarch, Lucian, etc. And what me struck in this series of theoretical texts is this: it is very difficult for a Greek or a Roman to accept the idea that a boy brought up, by virtue of his condition, as a free man born of a noble family to exercise familial and social responsibilities and assume power over others—as Roman senator, man of politics, Greek orator—to accept the idea that this boy has been *passive* in his relationship with a man. It's something unthinkable within their moral values, one that can't be assimilated to the status of a taboo either. That a man pursues a boy goes without saying, and that this boy be a slave, in Rome particularly, is only natural. As the saying goes: "to be fucked is a necessity for a slave, a shame for a free man, and a favor returned for an emancipated slave." In contrast, then, it's immoral for a free young man to be fucked. It's in this context that one can understand the law forbidding ex-prostitutes to exercise any political function. One calls a prostitute not a streetwalker but someone who has been supported successively and publicly by different people. That he has been passive, an object of pleasure, makes it inadmissable that he exercize any authority. That's what the theoretical texts always butt up against. For them it's a matter of edifying a discourse, which consists in proving that the only true love must exclude sexual relations with a boy and stick to affective pedagogical relations, of a quasi-paternal nature. This is, in fact, a way of making acceptable the practice of love between free men and free boys, while denying and transposing what actually happens in reality. Therefore one should not interpret the existence of this discourse as the sign of a tolerance toward homosexuality, in practice as in thought, but rather as the sign of an *obstruction*. One speaks of it because there's a problem, for one must retain the following principle: it's not because one speaks about something in society that it is admissible. If one accounts for a discourse, one should not investigate the reality of which this discourse would be the reflection, but the reality of the problem that forces people to speak about it. What makes it mandatory to speak of these man-boy relations— whereas one speaks much less about marriage relations with women—is very much the fact that these relations were difficult to accept morally.

Q: It was difficult to accept morally and yet the whole of Greek society was founded on these pederastic relations, let's say pedagogical in the widest sense. Isn't there an ambiguity there?

MF: Actually, I have simplified things a bit. What is necessary to take into account in the analysis of these phenomena is the existence of a monosexual society, since there was a very clear separation between men and women. Certainly there were relations between women that were very close, but which are not well known because there is practically no theoretical, reflective text written by women about love and ancient sexuality. I set apart the texts of several pythagorians and neo-pythagorians written between the first and eighth centuries B.C. and poetry. In contrast, we have all sorts of evidence that refers to a monosexual masculine society.

Q: How would you explain the fact that these monosexual relations finally disappeared with Rome, well before Christianity?

MF: In fact, it seems to me that one can only observe the disappearance on a massive scale of monosexual societies in 18th century Europe. In Rome, one finds a society where the woman in a distinguished family had a very important role at the familial, social and political level. But it's not so much the increased importance of the wife's role that provoked the dislocation of monosexual societies; it was rather the establishment of new political structures that prevented friendship from continuing to have the political and social functions that it had had up to that point; if you like, the development of institutions of political life made relations of friendship no longer possible, as they had been in an aristocratic society. But this is only an hypothesis...

Q: What you are saying leads me to raise a question about the origin of homosexuality, and here I must separate male from female homosexuality. The problem is this: in Greece, masculine homosexuality can only exist in a highly hierarchical society, with women occupying the lowest level. It seems to me that in taking up again the Greek ideal, masculine gay society of the 20th century thus legitimates a misogyny that rejects women.

MF: Actually I do think that this Greek myth plays a role, but it only plays the role that one wants it to play: it's not because one refers to it that one assumes a certain behavior, but because one assumes a certain behavior that one will refer to it while remodelling it. I find very striking the fact that, in America, homosexual society is a monosexual society with ways of life, organizations at the professional level, a certain number of pleasures that are not of the sexual order. Thus that you have homosexuals who live in a group or community, in a relation of constant exchange, reveals completely the return of monosexuality. Women also have lived in monosexual groups, but clearly in many cases they were forced to; it was a response, often novel and creative, to a status that was imposed upon them. I am thinking specifically of a very interesting book by an American, *Surpassing the Love of Men*. The author, Lillian Faderman,2 studies women's friendships from the 18th century to the first half of the 19th on the following basis: "I will never raise the question whether or not these women had sexual relations. I will simply consider on the one hand the network of these friendships or the very history of a friendship, see how it unfolds, how the couple lives it, what kinds of behavior it entails, and how the women were linked to one another; and on the other hand, what is the lived experience, the type of affect, of attachment linked to that."
Thus a whole culture of feminine monosexuality appears, of a life among women that is fascinating.

Q: However, what you were saying in *Gay-Pied* and what you are saying now seem problematic to me in this respect: to study the feminine monosexual groupings without posing the question of their sexuality would seem to continue the attitude that confines women to the domain of feeling, with its eternal stereotypes: their freedom of contact, their free emotions, their friendships, etc.

MF: Perhaps I will appear too lax to you, but I think that the phenomena that one would like to study are so complex and pre-coded by grids of analysis already in place that one must accept certain methods, incomplete to be sure, but generative of new reflections and which allow new phenomena to appear. Such methods allow one to go beyond the completely hackneyed terms current in the 1970s: taboos, the law, repression. These terms were very effective politically and useful in terms of knowledge, but one can attempt to renew the instruments of analysis. From this point of view, the freedom of trajectory appears to me to be much greater in America than in France. Which does not mean that one must regard it as sacred.

Q: Perhaps you could speak about John Boswell's book, *Christianity, Social Tolerance and Homosexuality.*[3]

MF: It's an interesting book because it reconsiders things already known and brings new things to light. Things already known that it develops: that what is called Christian or indeed Judeo-Christian sexual morality is a myth. It suffices to consult the documents: this famous morality that localizes sexual relations in marriage, that condemns adultery and all non-procreative and non-matrimonial behavior, was well established before Christianity. You find all these formulations in the texts of the Stoics and Pythagorians and these formulations are already so "Christian" that the Christians take them up as they are. What is rather surprising is that this philosophical morality comes in a certain sense retrospectively, after a real movement in society to valorize matrimony and marriage and affective relations between spouses... Marriage contracts dating from the Hellenistic period have been found in Egypt in which women demanded the husband's sexual fidelity, which he promised. These contracts did not emanate from the noble families but from an urban and somewhat popular milieu.

Since the documents are rare, one can hypothesize that the Stoic texts on this new matrimonial morality distilled in cultivated circles what was already taking place in the popular milieu. That shakes up completely the whole familiar landscape of a Greco-Roman world of marvelous sexual license destroyed by Christianity in a single blow.

Beginning from this perspective, Boswell was very struck to see to what point Christianity remained in conformity with what existed before it, particularly on the question of homosexuality. Until the 4th century Christianity takes up the same type of morality; it simply tightens up the bolts. There, however, beginning precisely in the 4th century, new problems will be raised with the development of monasticism. The demand for virginity then emerges. First, in the ascetic Christian texts there is an insistence on the problem of abstinence, of not eating too much, of not thinking too much about eating; slowly a haunting by libidinal images, images of concupiscence, develops. One then finds a certain type of experience, of a relationship to desires and to sex which is rather new. As for homosexuality, even if you find for example in the work of Basile de Cesaree a condemnation of friendship between boys as such, that doesn't carry against the whole of society. It seems to me certain that the great condemnation of homosexuality properly speaking dates from the Middle Ages, between the 8th and 12th centuries. Boswell states clearly that it is the 12th century, but already it appears in a certain number of penitential texts in the 8th and 9th centuries. In any case, it is necessary to break up the image of a Judeo-Christian morality and account for the fact that these elements were put into place at different epochs around certain practices and institutions passing from certain milieus to others.

Q: To return to Boswell, what seems surprising to me is that he speaks about a gay subculture in the 12th century which had for one of its members the monk A. de Rievaulx.

MF: Actually, there was already in antiquity a pederastic culture that appears to diminish with the shrinking of the man-boy relation in the Roman Empire. One of Plutarch's dialogues accounts for this transformation; all the modern values are put on the side of the woman who is older than the boy; it's their relation that is valorized. When two boy lovers show up, they are slightly ridiculed. They are clearly the story's rejects, and moreover they disappear from the end of the dialogue. Thus the pederastic culture was shrinking. But incidentally, one must not forget that Christian monasticism presented itself as the continuation of philosophy; one was dealing therefore with a monosexual society. As the highly elevated ascetic demands of the first monasticism rapidly relaxed and if one admits that beginning in the Middle Ages the monasteries alone were the titularies of culture, one has all the elements that would explain why one can speak of a gay subculture. Add the elements of spiritual guidance, thus of friendship and an intense affective relation between old and young monks, considered as a possibility for salvation, and they had there a form of the Platonic type predetermined in antiquity. If one admits that until the 12th century it was very much Platonism that constituted the cultural base for this monastic and ecclesiastic elite, I think the phenomenon is explained.

Q: I understood that Boswell was postulating the existence of a conscious homosexuality.

MF: Boswell begins with a long chapter in which he justifies his trajectory, why he takes the gays and gay culture as the guiding thread of his history. At the same time he is absolutely convinced that homosexuality is not a transhistoric constant. His idea is the following: if men have sexual relations among themselves, whether between an adult and a young man in the city or in the monastery, it is not only because of the tolerance of others vis-a-vis a certain form of sexual act; it implies necessarily a culture, that is to say, modes of expression, valorizations, etc., and thus the recognition by the subjects themselves of the specific nature of these relations. One can admit this idea as long as it doesn't imply a constant sexual or anthropomorphic category, but a cultural phenomenon that changes in time while maintaining itself in its general formulation: a relation between individuals of the same sex that entails a mode of life in which the consciousness of being singular among others is present. Beyond a certain point it's also an aspect of monosexuality. One could imagine an equivalent hypothesis, a feminine subculture in which the fact of being a woman would assume that one has the possibility of a relationship with other women which is given neither to men nor even to other women. It seems to me that around Sapho and the myth of Sapho there was this form of a subculture.

Q: Actually some recent feminist research goes in this direction, concerning in particular the women troubadors, whose texts are addressed to other women. But interpretation is difficult since one doesn't know if they were only the mouthpieces for certain noblemen like the male Troubadors. But certain texts exist in any case that speak like Christine de Pisan of the "feminine sex" and that prove that there was a certain awareness of an autonomous feminine culture, imperiled moreover by the society of men. Should one speak here of a feminine gay culture? Applied to women the term "gay" as doesn't seem to me to be very operative.

MF: Actually the term has a much stricter meaning in France than in America. In any case, it seems to me that in postulating at least a masculine gay culture, Boswell does not contradict himself in relation to the thesis that would have it that homosexuality is not an anthropomorphic constant which is sometimes repressed and sometimes accepted.

Q: In *The History of Sexuality* you analyze the discursification of sex, as it proliferates in the modern epoch, yet in this discourse on sex it appears that homosexuality is absent, at least until around 1850.

MF: I would like to understand how certain sexual behaviors become problems at a given moment, give rise to analyses, constitute objects of knowledge. One tries to decipher these behaviors, understand them and classify them. The interesting thing is not so much a social history of sexual behaviors, a historical psychology of attitudes in regard to sexuality, but a history of the problematisation of these behaviors. There are two golden ages in the problematisation of "homosexuality" or "monosexuality," that is to say, relations between men and men, and men and boys. The first is the one of the Greek, Hellenistic period that ends roughly during the Roman Empire. Its last great witnesses are Plutarch's dialogue, Maxime de Tyr's dissertations, and Lucian's dialogue. My hypothesis is that—although it is a current practice—they spoke a great deal about it because it created a problem.

In European societies the problematisation has been much more institutional than verbal: a set of measures, prosecutions, condemnations have been taken in regard to those whom one didn't yet call homosexuals but, from the 17th century on, sodomites. It's a very complicated history and I would say that it has three stages.

Since the Middle Ages a law against sodomy carrying the death penalty has been in existence, but it was seldom applied. One ought to study the economy of this problem, the existence of the law, the framework in which it was applied, and the reasons for which it was only applied in some cases. The second aspect is the practice of the police in regard to homosexuality, very clear in France in the mid 17th century, an epoch when cities actually exist, where a certain type of police surveillance is in place and where, for example, one observes the arrest, relatively massive, of homosexuals—in the Jardin du Luxembourg, Saint-Germain-des-Pres, or the Palais Royal. One observes dozens of arrests; names are taken down, people are arrested for several days or are simply released. Some remain "in the hole" without a trial. A whole system of traps and threats is set up, with cops and police spies, a little world is put into place very early, in the 17th and 18th centuries. The files at the Arsenal library speak clearly: workers, priests, soldiers as well members of the lower nobility are arrested. This is all inscribed within the framework of a surveillance and organisation of a world of prostitutes—kept women, dancers, actresses—fully developing in the 18th century. But it seems to me that the surveillance of homosexuality began a little earlier.

Finally, the third stage: it's obviously the noisy entry of homosexuality into the field of medical reflection in the mid-19th century. It had happened more distinctly during the 17th and in the beginning of the 19th centuries. This is a social phenomenon of great scale, more complicated than a simple invention of doctors.

Q: Do you think, for example, that the classifications and medical work of Hirschfeld, at the beginning of the 20th century, isolated homosexuals?

MF: These categories were used, it is true, to pathologize homosexuality, but they were equally categories of defense, in the name of which one could claim rights. The problem is still very current: between the affirmation "I am homosexual" and the refusal to say it, lies a very ambiguous dialectic. It's a necessary affirmation since it is the affirmation of a right, but at the same time it's a cage and a trap. One day the question "Are you homosexual?" will be as natural as the question "Are you a bachelor?" But after all, why would one subscribe to this obligation to choose? One can never stabilize oneself in a position; one must define the use that one makes of it according to the moment.

Q: In an interview in the journal *Gay-Pied* you say that one must "be set on becoming homosexual," and at the conclusion you speak of varied and polymorphic relations. Isn't that a contradiction?

MF: Saying "one must be set on being gay" puts oneself in a dimension where the sexual choices that one makes are present and have their effects over the whole of our life. I also meant that these sexual choices must at the same time be creative of ways of life. To be gay means that these choices spread across a whole life; it's also a certain way of refusing existing life styles; making sexual choice the operator of a change of existence. Not to be gay is to say: "How am I going to be able to limit the effects of my sexual choice in such a way that my life doesn't change in any way?" I would say that one must use sexuality to discover or invent new relations. To be gay is to be in a state of becoming. To respond to your question, I would add that it is not necessary to be homosexual but it is necessary to be set on being gay.

Q: Is that why you affirm that homosexuality is not a form of desire but something desirable?

MF: Yes, and I believe that it's the central point. To question ourselves on our relation to homosexuality is more than simply having the desire for a sexual relation with someone of the same sex, even if it is important; it's desiring a world where these relations are possible.

Translated by John Johnston

------

[1] Kenneth James Dover, *Greek Homosexuality* (Cambridge, MA: Harvard University Press, 1978).

[2] Lillian Faderman, *Surpassing the Love of Men.* (New York: William Morrow, 1980)

[3] John Boswell, *Christianity, Social Tolerance, and Homosexuality.* (Chicago: University of Chicago Press, 1980)

45

AN ETHICS OF PLEASURE

Q: One of the many things that a reader can unexpectedly learn from your work is to appreciate silence. You write about the freedom it makes possible, its multiple causes and meanings. For instance, you say in your last book that there is not one but many silences. Would it be correct to infer that there is a strongly autobiographical element in this?

MF: I think that any child who has been educated in a Catholic milieu just before or during the Second World War had the experience that there were many different ways of speaking as well as many forms of silence. There were some kinds of silence which implied very sharp hostility and others which meant deep friendship, emotional admiration, even love. I remember very well that when I met the filmmaker Daniel Schmidt who visited me, I don't know for what purpose, we discovered after a few minutes that we really had nothing to say to each other. So we stayed together from about three o'clock in the afternoon to midnight. We drank, we smoked hash, we had dinner. And I don't think we spoke more than twenty minutes during those ten hours. From that moment a rather long friendship started. It was for me the first time that a friendship originated in strictly silent behaviour.

Maybe another feature of this appreciation of silence is related to the obligation of speaking. I lived as a child in a petit bourgeois, provincial milieu in France and the obligation of speaking, of making conversation with visitors, was for me something both very strange and very boring. I often wondered why people had to speak. Silence may be a much more interesting way of having a relationship with people.

Q: There is in North American Indian culture a much greater appreciation of silence than in English-speaking societies and I suppose in French-speaking societies as well.

MF: Yes, you see, I think silence is one of those things that has unfortunately been dropped from our culture. We don't have a culture of silence; we don't have a culture of suicide either. The Japanese do, I think. Young Romans or young Greeks were taught to keep silent in very different ways according to the people with whom they were interacting. Silence was then a specific form of experiencing a relationship with others. This is something that I believe is really worthwhile cultivating. I'm in favour of developing silence as a cultural ethos.

Q: You seem to have a fascination with other cultures and not only from the past: for the first ten years of your career you lived in Sweden, West Germany and Poland. This would seem a very atypical career for a French academic. Can you explain why you left France and why, when you returned in about 1961, from what I have heard, you would have preferred to live in Japan?

MF: There is a snobbism about antichauvinism in France now. I hope what I say is not associated with those kinds of people. Maybe if I were an American or a Canadian I would suffer from some features of North American culture. Anyway, I have suffered and I still suffer from a lot of things in French social and cultural life. That was the reason why I left France in 1955. Incidentally, in 1966 and 1968 I also spent two years in Tunisia for purely personal reasons.

Q: Could you give some examples of the aspects of French society that you suffered from?

MF: Well, I think that, at the moment when I left France, freedom for personal life was very sharply restricted there. At this time Sweden was supposed to be a much freer country. And there I had the experience that a certain kind of freedom may have, not exactly the same effects, but as many restrictive effects as a directly restrictive society. That was an important experience for me. Then I had the opportunity of spending one year in Poland where, of course, the restrictions and oppressive power of the Communist party are really something quite different. In a rather short period of time I had the experience of an old traditional society, as France was in the late 1940s and early 1950s, and the new free society which was Sweden. I won't say I had the total experience of all the political possibilities but I had a sample of what the possibilities of Western societies were at that moment. That was a good experience.

Q: Hundreds of Americans went to Paris in the 1920s and 1930s for exactly the same reasons you left in the 1950s.

MF: Yes. But now I don't think they come to Paris any longer for freedom. They come to have a taste of an old traditional culture. They come to France as painters went to Italy in the 17th century to see a dying civilization. Anyway, you see, we very often have the experience of much more freedom in foreign countries than in our own. As foreigners we can ignore all those implicit obligations which are not in the law but in the general way of behaving. Secondly, merely changing your obligations is felt or experienced as a kind of freedom.

Q: If you don't mind, let us return for a while to your early years in Paris. I understand that you worked as a psychologist at the Hôpital Sainte-Anne in Paris.

MF: Yes, I worked there a little more than two years, I believe.

Q: And you have remarked that you identified more with the patients than the staff. Surely that's a very atypical experience for anyone who is a psychologist or psychiatrist. Why did you feel, partly from that experience, the necessity of radically questioning psychiatry when so many other people were content to try to refine the concepts which were already prevalent?

MF: Actually, I was not officially appointed. I was studying psychology in the Hôpital Sainte-Anne. It was the early 1950s. There was no clear professional status for psychologists in a mental hospital. So as a student in psychology (I studied first philosophy and then psychology) I had a very strange status there. The head psychiatrist was very kind to me and let me do anything I wanted. But nobody worried about what I should be doing: I was free to do anything. I was actually in a position between the staff and the patients, and it wasn't owed to my merit, it wasn't because I had a special attitude, it was the consequence of this ambiguity in my status which forced me to maintain a distance from the staff. I am sure it was not my personal merit because I felt all that at the time as a kind of malaise. It was only a few years later when I started writing a book on the history of psychiatry that this malaise, this personal experience, took the form of historical criticism or a structural analysis.

Q: Was there anything unusual about the Hôpital Sainte-Anne? Would it have given an employee a particularly negative impression of psychiatry?

MF: Oh no. It was as typical a large hospital as you could imagine and I must say it was better than most of the large hospitals in provincial towns that I visited afterwards. It was one of the best in Paris. No, it was not terrible. That was precisely the thing that was important. Maybe if I had been doing this kind of work in a small provincial hospital I would have believed its failures were the result of its location or its particular inadequacies

Q: As you have just mentioned the French provinces, where you were born, in a sort of derogatory way, do you, nevertheless, have fond memories of growing up in Poitiers in the 1930s and 40s?

MF: Oh yes. My memories are rather, one could not exactly say strange, but what strikes me now when I try to recall those impressions is that nearly all the great emotional memories I have are related to the political situation. I remember very well that I experienced one of my first great frights when Chancellor Dollfuss was assassinated by the Nazis in, I think, 1934. It is something very far from us now. Very few people remember the murder of Dollfuss. I remember very well that I was really scared by that. I think it was my first strong fright about death. I also remember refugees from Spain arriving in Poitiers. I remember fighting in school with my classmates about the Ethiopian War. I think that boys and girls of this generation had their childhood formed by these great historical events. The menace of war was our background, our framework of existence. Then the war arrived. Much more than the activities of family life, it was these events concerning the world which are the substance of our memory. I say 'our' because I am nearly sure that most boys and girls in France at that time had the same experience. Our private life was really threatened. Maybe that is the reason why I am fascinated by history and the relationship between personal experience and those events of which we are a part. I think that is the nucleus of my theoretical desires. (Laughs.)

Q: You remain fascinated by the period, though you don't write about it.

MF: Yes, sure.

Q: What was the origin of your decision to become a philosopher?

MF: You see, I don't think I ever had the project of becoming a philosopher. I did not know what to do with my life. And I think that is also something rather typical for people of my generation. We did not know when I was ten or eleven years old, whether we would become German or remain French. We did not know whether we would die or not in the bombing and so on. When I was sixteen or seventeen I knew only one thing: school life was an environment protected from exterior menaces, from politics. And I have always been fascinated by living protected in a scholarly environment, in an intellectual milieu. Knowledge is for me that which must function as a protection of individual existence and as a comprehension of the exterior world. I think that's it. Knowledge as a means of surviving by understanding.

Q: Could you tell me a bit about your studies in Paris? Is there anyone who had a special influence upon the work that you do today or any professors you are grateful to for personal reasons?

MF: No, I was a pupil of Althusser, and at that time the main philosophical currents in France were Marxism, Hegelianism and phenomenology. I must say I have studied these but what gave me for the first time the desire of doing personal work was reading Nietzsche.

Q: An audience that is non-French is likely to have a very poor understanding of the aftermath of the May Rebellion of '68 and you have sometimes said that it resulted in people being more responsive to your work. Can you explain why?

MF: I think that before '68, at least in France, you had to be as a philosopher a Marxist, or a phenomenologist or a structuralist and I adhered to none of these dogmas. The second point is that at this time in France studying psychiatry or the history of medicine had no real status in the political field. Nobody was interested in that. The first thing that happened after '68 was that Marxism as a dogmatic framework declined and new political, new cultural interests concerning personal life appeared. That's why I think my work had nearly no echo, with the exception of a very small circle, before '68.

Q: Some of the works you refer to in the first volume of *The History of Sexuality,* such as the Victorian book *My Secret Life,* [1] are filled with sexual fantasies. It is often impossible to distinguish between fact and fantasy. Would there be a value in your focusing explicitly upon sexual fantasies and creating an archeology of them rather than one of sexuality?

MF: (Laughs.) No, I don't try to write an archeology of sexual fantasies. I try to make an archeology of discourse about sexuality which is really the relationship between what we do, what we are obliged to do, what we are allowed to do, what we are forbidden to do in the field of sexuality and what we are allowed, forbidden, or obliged to say about our sexual behaviour. That's the point. It's not a problem or fantasy: it's a problem of verbalization.

Q: Could you explain how you arrived at the idea that the sexual repression that characterized 18th and 19th century Europe and North America, and which seemed so well-documented historically, was in fact ambiguous and that there were beneath it forces working in the opposite direction?

MF: Indeed, it is not a question of denying the existence of repression. It's one of showing that repression is always a part of a much more complex political strategy regarding sexuality. Things are not merely repressed. There is about sexuality a lot of defective regulations in which the negative effects of inhibition are counterbalanced by the positive effects of stimulation. The way in which sexuality in the 19th century was both repressed but also illuminated, underlined, analyzed through techniques like psychology and psychiatry shows very well that it was not simply a question of repression. It was much more a change in the economics of sexual behaviour in our society.

Q: In your opinion what are some of the most striking examples which support your hypothesis?

MF: One of them is children's masturbation. Another is hysteria and all the fuss about hysterical women. These two examples show, of course, repression, prohibition, interdiction and so on. But the fact that the sexuality of children became a real problem for the parents, an issue, a source of anxiety, had a lot of effects upon the children and upon the parents. To take care of the sexuality of their children was not only a question of morality for the parents but also a question of pleasure.

Q: A pleasure in what sense?

MF: Sexual excitement and sexual satisfaction.

Q: For the parents themselves?

MF: Yes. Call it rape, if you like. There are texts which are very close to a systemization of rape. Rape by the parents of the sexual activity of their children. To intervene in this personal, secret activity, which masturbation was, does not represent something neutral for the parents. It is not only a matter of power, or authority, or ethics; it's also a pleasure. Don't you agree with that? Yes, there is enjoyment in intervening. The fact that masturbation was so strictly forbidden for children was naturally the cause of anxiety. It was also a reason for the intensification of this activity, for mutual masturbation and for the pleasure of secret communication between children about this theme. All this has given a certain shape to family life, to the relationship between children and parents, and to the relations between children. All that has, as a result, not only repression but an intensification both of anxieties and of pleasures. I don't want to say that the pleasure of the parents was the same as that of the children or that there was no repression. I tried to find the roots of this absurd prohibition.

One of the reasons why this stupid interdiction of masturbation was maintained for such a long time was because of this pleasure and anxiety and all the emotional network around it. Everyone knows very well that it's impossible to prevent a child from masturbating. There is no scientific evidence that it harms anybody. One can be sure that it is at least (Laughs.) the only pleasure that really harms nobody. Why has it been forbidden for such a long time then? To the best of my knowledge, you cannot find more than two or three references in all the Greco-Latin literature about masturbation. It was not relevant. It was supposed to be, in Greek and Latin civilization, an activity either for slaves or for satyrs. (Laughs.) It was not relevant to speak about it for free citizens.

Q: We live at a point in time when there is great uncertainty about the future. One sees apocalyptic visions of the future reflected widely in popular culture. Louis Malle's *My Dinner with André,* for example. Isn't it typical that in such a climate sex and reproduction come to be a preoccupation and thus writing a history of sexuality would be symptomatic of the time?

MF: No. I don't think I would agree with that. First, the preoccupation with the relationship between sexuality and reproduction seems to have been stronger, for instance, in the Greek and Roman societies and in the bourgeois society of the 18th and 19th centuries. No. What strikes me is the fact that now sexuality seems to be a question without direct relation with reproduction. It is your sexuality as your personal behaviour which is the problem.

Take homosexuality, for instance. I think that one of the reasons why homosexual behaviour was not an important issue in the 18th century was due to the view that if a man had children, what he did besides that had little importance. During the 19th century you begin to see that sexual behaviour was important for a definition of the individual self. And that is something new. It is very interesting to see that before the 19th century forbidden behaviour, even if it was very severely judged, was always considered to be an excess, a "libertinage," as something that came on top of everything else. Homosexual behaviour was only considered to be a kind of excess of natural behaviour, an instinct that is difficult to keep within limits. From the 19th century on you see that behaviour like homosexuality came to be considered an abnormality. When I say that it was libertinage I don't say that it was tolerated. I think that the idea of characterizing individuals by their sexual behaviour or desire is not to be found, or very rarely, before the 19th century. "Tell me your desires, I'll tell you who you are." This question is typical of the 19th century.

Q: It would not seem any longer that sex could be called the secret of life. Has anything replaced it in this respect?

MF: Of course it is not *the* secret of life now, since people can show at least certain general forms of their sexual preferences without being plagued or condemned. But I think that people still consider, and are invited to consider, that sexual desire is able to reveal what is their deep identity. Sexuality is not *the* secret but it is still a symptom, a manifestation of what is the most secret in our individuality.

Q: The next question I would like to ask may at first seem odd and if it does I'll explain why I thought it was worth asking. Does beauty have special meaning for you?

MF: I think it does for everyone. (Laughs.) I am near-sighted but not blind to the point that it has no meaning for me. Why do you ask? I'm afraid I have given you proof that I am not insensitive to beauty.

Q: One of the things about you which is very impressive is the sort of monachal austerity in which you live. Your apartment in Paris is almost completely white; you also avoid all the "objets d'art" that decorate so many French homes. While in Toronto during the past month you have on several occasions worn clothes as simple as white pants, a white T-shirt and a black leather jacket. You suggested that perhaps the reason you like the colour white so much is that in Poitiers during the '30s and '40s it was impossible for the exterior of houses to be genuinely white. You are staying here in a house whose white walls are decorated with black cut-out sculptures and you remarked that you especially appreciated the straightforwardness and strength of pure black and white. There is also a noteworthy phrase in *The History of Sexuality*: "that austere monarchy of sex." You do not fit the image of the sophisticated Frenchman who makes an art out of living well. Also, you are the only French person I know who has told me he prefers American food.

MF: Yes. Sure. (Laughs.) A good club sandwich with a coke. That's my pleasure. It's true. With ice cream. That's true. Actually, I think I have real difficulty in experiencing pleasure. I think that pleasure is a very difficult behaviour. It's not as simple as that (Laughs.) to enjoy one's self. And—I must say that's my dream—I would like and I hope I'll die of an overdose (Laughs.) of pleasure of any kind. Because I think it's really difficult and I always have the feeling that I do not feel the pleasure, the complete total pleasure and, for me, it's related to death.

Q: Why would you say that?

MF: Because I think that the kind of pleasure I would consider as *the* real pleasure would be so deep, so intense, so overwhelming that I couldn't survive it. I would die. I'll give you a clearer and simpler example. Once I was struck by a car in the street. I was walking. And for maybe two seconds I had the impression that I was dying and it was really a very, very intense pleasure. The weather was wonderful. It was 7 o'clock on a summer day. The sun was coming down. The sky was very wonderful and blue and so on. It was, it still is now, one of my best memories. (Laughs.)

There is also the fact that some drugs are really important for me because they are the mediation to those incredibly intense joys that I am looking for and that I am not able to experience, to afford by myself. It's true that a glass of wine, of good wine, old and so on, may be enjoyable but it's not for me. A pleasure must be something incredibly intense. But I think I am not the only one like that.

I'm not able to give myself and others those middle range pleasures that make up everyday life. Such pleasures are nothing for me and I am not able to organize my life in order to make room for them. That's the reason why I'm not a social being, why I'm not really a cultural being, why I'm so boring in my everyday life. (Laughs.) It's a bore to live with me. (Laughs.)

Q: A frequently quoted remark of Romain Rolland is that the French Romantic writers were "visual." For them music was only a noise.This remark is an obvious exaggeration, but most recent scholarship tends to support it. Many references to paintings occur in some of your books but few to music. Are you also representative of this characteristic of French culture that Rolland called attention to?

MF: Yes, sure. Of course French culture gives no room to music, or nearly no room. But it's a fact that in my personal life music played a great role. The first friend I had when I was twenty was a musician. Then afterwards I had another friend who was a composer and who is dead now. Through him I know all the generation of Boulez. It has been a very important experience for me. First, because I had contact with a kind of art which was, for me, really enigmatic. I was not competent at all in this domain; I'm still not. But I felt beauty in something which was quite enigmatic for me. There are some pieces by Bach and Webern which I enjoy but for me, what is real beauty is a musical phrase, a piece of music that I cannot understand, something I cannot say anything about. I have the opinion, maybe it's quite arrogant or presumptuous, that I could say something about any of the most wonderful paintings in the world. For this reason they are not absolutely beautiful. Anyway, I have written something about Boulez. What has been for me the influence of living with a musician for several months. Why it was important even in my intellectual life.

Q: If I understand correctly, artists and writers responded to your work more positively at first than philosophers, sociologists or other academics.

MF: Yes, that's right.

Q: Is there a special kinship between your kind of philosophy and the arts in general?

MF: Well, I think I am not in a position to answer. You see, I hate to say it, but it's true that I am not a really good academic. For me intellectual work is related to what you could call aestheticism, meaning transforming yourself. I believe my problem is this strange relationship between knowledge, scholarship, theory and real history. I know very well, and I think I knew it from the moment when I was a child, that knowledge can do nothing for transforming the world. Maybe I am wrong. And I am sure I am wrong from a theoretical point of view for I know very well that knowledge has transformed the world.

But if I refer to my own personal experience I have the feeling that knowledge can't do anything for us and that political power may destroy us. All the knowledge in the world can't do anything against that. All this is related not to what I think theoretically (I know that's wrong) but I speak from my personal experience. I know that knowledge can transform us, that truth is not only a way of deciphering the world (and maybe what we call truth doesn't decipher anything) but that if I know the truth I will be changed. And maybe I will be saved. Or maybe I'll die but I think that is the same anyway for me. (Laughs.)

You see, that's why I really work like a dog and I worked like a dog all my life. I am not interested in the academic status of what I am doing because my problem is my own transformation. That's the reason also why, when people say, "Well, you thought this a few years ago and now you say something else," my answer is, (Laughs,) "Well, do you think I have worked like that all those years to say the same thing and not to be changed?" This transformation of one's self by one's own knowledge is, I think, something rather close to the aesthetic experience. Why should a painter work if he is not transformed by his own painting?

Q: Beyond the historical dimension is there an ethical concern implied in *The History of Sexuality*? Are you not in some ways telling us how to act?

MF: No. If you mean by ethics a code which would tell us how to act, then of course *The History of Sexuality* is not an ethics. But if by ethics you mean the relationship you have to yourself when you act, then I would say that it intends to be an ethics, or at least to show what could be an ethics of sexual behaviour. It would be one which would not be dominated by the problem of the deep truth of the reality of our sex life. The relationship that I think we need to have with ourselves when we have sex is an ethics of pleasure, of intensification of pleasure.

Q: Many people look at you as someone who is able to tell them the deep truth about the world and about themselves. How do you experience this responsibility? As an intellectual, do you feel responsible toward this function of seer, of shaper of mentalities?

MF: I am sure I am not able to provide these people with what they expect. (Laughs.) I never behave like a prophet. My books don't tell people what to do. And they often reproach me for not doing so (and maybe they are right) and at the same time they reproach me for behaving like a prophet. I have written a book about the history of psychiatry from the 17th century to the very beginning of the 19th. In this book I said nearly nothing about the contemporary situation but people still have read it as an anti-psychiatry position. Once, I was invited to Montreal to attend a symposium about psychiatry. At first I refused to go there since I am not a psychiatrist, even if I have some experience, a very short experience as I told you earlier. But they assured me that they were inviting me only as a historian of psychiatry to give an introductory speech. Since I like Quebec I went. And I was really trapped, I was introduced by the president as the representative of French anti-psychiatry. Of course there were nice people there who had never read a line of what I had written and they were convinced that I was an anti-psychiatrist.

I have done nothing else than write the history of psychiatry until the beginning of the 19th century. Why should so many people, including psychiatrists, believe that I am an anti-psychiatrist? It's because they are not able to accept the real history of their institutions which is, of course, a sign of psychiatry being a pseudo-science. A real science is able to accept even the shameful, dirty stories of its beginning. (Laughs.)

So you see, there really is a call for prophetism. I think we have to get rid of that. People have to build their own ethics, taking as a point of departure the historical analysis, sociological analysis and so on, one can provide for them. I don't think that people who try to decipher the truth should have to provide ethical principles or practical advice at the same moment, in the same book and the same analysis. All this prescriptive network has to be elaborated and transformed by people themselves.

Q: For a philosopher to have made the pages of *Time* magazine, as you did in November 1981, indicates a certain kind of popular status. How do you feel about that?

MF: When newsmen ask me for information about my work I consider that I have to respond. You see, we are paid by society, by the taxpayers (Laughs.) to work. And really I think that most of us try to do our work as best we can. I think it is quite normal that this work, as far as it is possible, is presented and made accessible to everybody. Naturally, a part of our work cannot be accessible to anybody because it is too difficult. The institution which I belong to in France (I don't belong to the university but to the College de France) obliges its members to make public lectures, open to anyone who wants to attend, in which we have to explain our work. We are both researchers and people who have to explain publicly our research. I think there is in this very old institution—it dates from the 16th century—something very interesting. The deep meaning is, I believe, very important. When a newsman comes and asks for information about my work, I try to provide it in the clearest way I can. Anyway, my personal life is not at all interesting. If somebody thinks that my work cannot be understood without reference to such and such a part of my life, I accept to consider the question. (Laughs.) I am ready to answer if I agree. As far as my personal life is uninteresting, it is not worthwhile making a secret of it. (Laughs.) By the same token, it may not be worthwhile publicizing it.

---

[1] *My Secret Life*. (New York: Grove Press, 1966). [Ed.]

46

SEX, POWER AND THE POLITICS OF IDENTITY

Q: You suggest in your work that sexual liberation is not so much the uncovering of secret truths about one's self or one's desire as it is a part of the process of defining and constructing desire. What are the practical implications of this distinction?

MF: What I meant was that I think what the gay movement needs now is much more the art of life than a science or scientific knowledge (or pseudo-scientific knowledge) of what sexuality is. Sexuality is a part of our behavior. It's a part of our world freedom. Sexuality is something that we ourselves create—it is our own creation, and much more than the discovery of a secret side of our desire. We have to understand that with our desires, through our desires, go new forms of relationships, new forms of love, new forms of creation. Sex is not a fatality: it's a possibility for creative life.

Q: That's basically what you're getting at when you suggest that we should try to become gay—not just to reassert ourselves as gay.

MF: Yes, that's it. We don't have to discover that we are homosexuals.

Q: Or what the meaning of that is?

MF: Exactly. Rather, we have to create a gay life. To *become*.

Q: And this is something without limits?

MF: Yes, sure, I think when you look at the different ways people have experienced their own sexual freedoms—the way they have created their works of art—you would have to say that sexuality, as we now know it, has become one of the most creative sources of our society and our being. My view is that we should understand it in the reverse way: the world [regards] sexuality as the secret of the creative cultural life; it is rather a process of our having to create a new cultural life underneath the ground of our sexual choices.

Q: Practically speaking, one of the effects of trying to uncover that secret has meant that the gay movement has remained at the level of demanding civil or human rights around sexuality. That is, sexual liberation has remained at the level of demanding sexual tolerance.

MF: Yes, but this aspect must be supported. It is important, first, to have the possibility—and the right—to choose your own sexuality. Human rights regarding sexuality are important and are still not respected in many places. We shouldn't consider that such problems are solved now. It's quite true that there was a real liberation process in the early '70s. This process was very good, both in terms of the situation and in terms of opinions, but the situation has not definitely stabilized. Still, I think we have to go a step further. I think that one of the factors of this stabilization will be the creation of new forms of life, relationships, friendships in society, art, culture and so on, through our sexual, ethical and political choices. Not only do we have to defend ourselves, not only affirm ourselves as an identity but as a creative force.

Q: A lot of that sounds like what, for instance, the women's movement has done, trying to establish their own language and their own culture.

MF: Well, I'm not sure that we have to create our *own* culture. We have to *create* culture. We have to realize cultural creations. But in doing so, we come up against the problem of identity. I don't know what we would do to form these creations, and I don't know what forms these creations would take. For instance, I am not at all sure that the best form of literary creations by gay people is gay novels.

Q: In fact, we would not even want to say that. That would be based on an essentialism that we need to avoid.

MF: True. What do we mean for instance, by "gay painting"? Yet, I am sure that from the point of departure of our ethical choices, we can create something that will have a certain relationship to gayness. But it must not be a translation of gayness in the field of music or painting or what have you, for I do not think this can happen.

Q: How do you view the enormous proliferation in the last 10 or 15 years of male homosexual practices: the sensualization, if you like, of neglected parts of the body and the articulation of new pleasures? I am thinking, obviously, of the salient aspects of what we call the ghetto—porn movies, clubs for S/M or fistfucking, and so forth. Is this merely an extension into another sphere of the general proliferation of sexual discourses since the 19th century, or do you see other kinds of developments that are peculiar to this present historical context?

MF: Well, I think what we want to speak about is precisely the *innovations* that those practices imply. For instance, look at the S/M subculture, as our good friend Gayle Rubin would insist. I don't think that this movement of sexual practices has anything to do with the disclosure or the uncovering of S/M tendencies deep within our unconscious, and so on. I think that S/M is much more than that; it's the real creation of new possibilities of pleasure, which people had no idea about previously. The idea that S/M is related to a deep violence, that S/M practice is a way of liberating this violence, this aggression, is stupid. We know very well what all those people are doing is not aggressive; they are inventing new possibilities of pleasure with strange parts of their body—through the eroticization of the body. I think it's a kind of creation, a creative enterprise, which has as one of its main features what I call the desexualization of pleasure. The idea that bodily pleasure should always come from sexual pleasure is the root of *all* our possible pleasure. I think *that's* something quite wrong. These practices are insisting that we can produce pleasure with very odd things, very strange parts of our bodies, in very unusual situations, and so on.

Q: So the conflation of pleasure and sex is being broken down.

MF: That's it precisely. The possibility of using our bodies as a possible source of very numerous pleasures is something that is very important. For instance, if you look at the traditional construction of pleasure, you see that bodily pleasure, or pleasures of the flesh, are always drinking, eating and fucking. And that seems to be the limit of the understanding of our body, our pleasures. What frustrates me, for instance, is the fact that the problem of drugs is always envisaged only as a problem of freedom and prohibition. I think that drugs must become a part of our culture.

Q: As a pleasure?

MF: As a pleasure. We have to study drugs. We have to experience drugs. We have to do *good* drugs, which can produce very intense pleasure. I think this puritanism about drugs, which implies that you can either be for drugs or against drugs, is mistaken. Drugs have now become a part of our culture. Just as there is bad music and good music, there are bad drugs and good drugs. So we can't say we are "against" drugs any more than we can say we're "against" music.

Q: The point is to experiment with pleasure and its possibilities.

MF: Yes. Pleasure also must be a part of our culture. It is very interesting to note, for instance, that for centuries people generally, as well as doctors, psychiatrists and even liberation movements, have always spoken about desire, and never about pleasure. "We have to liberate our desire," they say. No! We have to create new pleasure. And then maybe desire will follow.

Q: Is it significant that there are, to a large degree, identities forming around new sexual practices, like S/M? These identities help in exploring such practices and defending the right to engage in them. But are they also limiting in regards to the possibilities of individuals?

MF: Well, if identity is only a game, if it is only a procedure to have relations, social and sexual–pleasure relationships that create new friendships, it is useful. But if identity becomes the problem of sexual existence, and if people think that they have to "uncover" their "own identity," and that their own identity has to become the law, the principle, the code of their existence; if the perennial question they ask is "Does this thing conform to my identity?" then, I think, they will turn back to a kind of ethics very close to the old heterosexual virility. If we are asked to relate to the question of identity, it has to be an identity to our unique selves. But the relationships we have to have with ourselves are not ones of identity, rather they must be relationships of differentiation, of creation, of innovation. To be the same is really boring. We must not exclude identity if people find their pleasure through this identity, but we must not think of this identity as an ethical universal rule.

Q: But up to this point, sexual identity has been politically very useful.

MF: Yes, it has been very useful, but it limits us and I think we have (and can have) a right to be free.

Q: We want some of our sexual practices to be ones of resistance in a political and social sense. Yet, how is this possible, given that control can be exercised by the stimulation of pleasure? Can we be sure that these new pleasures won't be exploited in the way advertising uses the stimulation of pleasure as a means of social control?

MF: We can never be sure. In fact, we can always be sure *it will happen,* and that everything that has been created or acquired, any ground that has been gained will, at a certain moment be used in such a way. That's the way we live, that's the way we struggle, that's the way of human history. And I don't think that is an objection to all those movements or all those situations. But you are quite right in underlining that we always have to be quite careful and to be aware of the fact that we have to move on to something else, that we have other needs as well. The S/M ghetto in San Francisco is a good example of a community that has experimented with, and formed an identity around, pleasure. This ghettoization, this identification, this procedure of exclusion and so on—all of these have, as well, produced their countereffects. I dare not use the word *dialectics*—but this comes rather close to it.

Q: You write that power is not just a negative force but a productive one; that power is always there; that where there is power, there is resistance and that resistance is never in a position of externality vis-à-vis power. If this is so, then how do we come to any other conclusion than that we are always trapped inside that relationship—that we can't somehow break out of it.

MF: Well I don't think the work *trapped* is a correct one. It is a struggle, but what I mean by power relations is the fact that we are in a strategic situation towards each other. For instance, being homosexuals we are in a struggle with the government, and the government is in a struggle with us. When we deal with the government, the struggle, of course, is not symmetrical, the power situation is not the same, but we are in this struggle, and the continuation of this situation can influence the behavior or nonbehavior of the other. So we are not trapped. We are always in this kind of situation. It means that we always have possibilities, there are always possibilities of changing the situation. We cannot jump *outside* the situation, and there is no point where you are free from all power relations. But you can always change it. So what I've said does not mean that we are always trapped, but that we are always free. Well anyway, that there is always the possibility of changing.

Q: So resistance comes from within that dynamic?

MF: Yes. You see, if there was no resistance, there would be no power relations. Because it would simply be a matter of obedience. You have to use power relations to refer to the situation where you're not doing what you want. So resistance comes first, and resistance remains superior to the forces of the process; power relations are obliged to change with the resistance. So I think that *resistance* is the main word, *the key word*, in this dynamic.

Q: Politically speaking, probably the most important part of looking at power is that according to previous conceptions, "to resist" was simply to say no. Resistance was conceptualized only in terms of negation. Within your understanding, however, to resist is not simply a negation, but a creative process; to create and recreate, to change the situation, actually to be an active member of that process.

MF: Yes, that is the way I would put it. To say no is the minimum form of resistance. But of course, at times that is very important. You have to say no as a decisive form of resistance.

Q: This raises the question of in what way, and to what degree, can a dominated subject (or subjectivity) actually create its own discourse. In traditional power analysis, the omnipresent feature of analysis is the dominant discourse and only as a subsidiary are there reactions to, or within, that discourse. However, if what we mean by resistance in power relations is more than negation, then aren't some practices like, say, lesbian S/M, actually ways for dominated subjects to formulate their own languages?

MF: Well, you see, I think that resistance is a part of this strategic relationship of which power consists. Resistance really always relies upon the situation against which it struggles. For instance, in the gay movement the medical definition of homosexuality was a very important tool against the oppression of homosexuality in the last part of the 19th century and in the early 20th century. This medicalization, which was a means of oppression, has always been a means of resistance as well—since people could say, "If we are sick, then why do you condemn us, why do you despise us?" and so on. Of course, this discourse now sounds rather naïve to us, but at the time it was very important.

I should say, also, that I think that in the lesbian movement, the fact that women have been, for centuries and centuries, isolated in society, frustrated, despised in many ways and so on, has given them the real possibility of constituting a society, of creating a kind of social relation between themselves, outside the social world that was dominated by males. Lillian Faderman's book, *Surpassing the Love of Men,* is very interesting in this regard. It raises the question: what kind of emotional experience, what kind of relationships, were possible in a world where women in society had no social, no legal and no political power? And she argues that women used that isolation and lack of power.

Q: If resistance is a process of breaking out of discursive practices, it would seem that the case that has a prima facie claim to be truly oppositional might be something like lesbian S/M. To what degree can such practices and identities be seen as challenging the dominant discourse?

MF: What I think is interesting now in relation to lesbian S/M is that they can get rid of certain stereotypes of femininity that have been used in the lesbian movement; a strategy that the movement has erected from the past. This strategy has been based on their oppression. But now, maybe, these tools, these weapons are obsolete. We can see that lesbian S/M tried to get rid of all those old stereotypes of femininity, of antimale attitude and so on.

Q: What do you think we can learn about power, and for that matter about pleasure from the practice of S/M—that is, the explicit eroticization of power?

MF: One can say that S/M is the eroticization of power, the eroticization of strategic relations. What strikes me with regard to S/M is how it differs from social power. What characterized power is the fact that it is a strategic relation that has been stabilized through institutions. So the mobility in power relations is limited, and there are strongholds that are very, very difficult to suppress because they have been institutionalized and are now very pervasive in courts, codes and so on. All that means that the strategic relations of people are made rigid.

On this point, the S/M game is very interesting because it is a strategic relation, but it is always fluid. Of course, there are roles but everybody knows very well that those roles can be reversed. Sometimes the scene begins with the master and slave, and at the end the slave has become the master. Or, even when the roles are stabilized, you know very well that it is always a game. Either the rules are transgressed, or there is an agreement, either explicit or tacit, that makes them aware of certain boundaries. This strategic game as a source of bodily pleasure is very interesting. But I wouldn't say that it is a reproduction, inside the erotic relationship, of the structures of power. It is an acting out of power structures by a strategic game that is able to give sexual pleasure or bodily pleasure.

Q: How does this strategic relation in sex differ for that in power relations?

MF: The practice of S/M is the creation of pleasure, and there is an identity with that creation. And that's why S/M is really a subculture. It's a process of invention. S/M is *the use* of a strategic relationship as a source of pleasure (physical pleasure). It is not the first time that people have used strategic relations as a source of pleasure. For instance, in the Middle Ages there was the institution of "courtly love," the troubadour, the institutions of the love relationships between the lady and the lover, and so on. That as well was a strategic game. You even find this between boys and girls when they are dancing on Saturday night. They are acting out strategic relations. What is interesting is that in this heterosexual life those strategic relations come before sex. It's a strategic relation in order to obtain sex. And in S/M those strategic relations are inside sex, as a convention of pleasure within a particular situation.

In the one case the strategic relations are purely social relations, and it is your social being that is involved; while, in the other case, it is your body that is involved. And it is this transfer of strategic relations from the court(ship) to sex that is very interesting.

Q: You mentioned in an interview in *Gai pied* a year or two ago that what upsets people most about gay relations is not so much sexual acts per se but the potential for affectional relationships that are carried on outside the normative patterns. These friendships and networks are unforeseen. Do you think what frightens people is the unknown potential of gay relations, or would you suggest that these relations are seen as posing a direct threat to social institutions?

MF: One thing that interests me now is the problem of friendship. For centuries after antiquity, friendship was a very important kind of social relation: a social relation within which people had a certain freedom, certain kind of choice (limited of course), as well as very intense emotional relations. There were also economic and social implications to these relationships—they were obliged to help their friends, and so on. I think that in the 16th and 17th centuries we see these kinds of friendships disappearing, at least in the male society. And friendship begins to become something other than that. You can find, from the 16th century on, texts that explicitly criticize friendship as something dangerous.

The army, bureaucracy, administration, universities, schools etc.—in the modern senses of these words—cannot function with such intense friendships. I think there can be seen a very strong attempt in all these institutions to diminish, or minimize, the affectional relations. I think this is particularly important in schools. When they started grade schools with hundreds of young boys, one of the problems was how to prevent them, not only from having sex of course, but also from developing friendships. For instance, you could study the strategy of Jesuit institutions about this theme of friendship, since the Jesuits knew very well that it was impossible for them to suppress this. Rather, they tried to use the role of sex, of love, of friendship, and at the same time to limit it. I think now, after studying the history of sex, we should try to understand the history of friendship, or friendships. That history is very, very important.

And one of my hypotheses, which I am sure would be borne out if we did this, is that homosexuality became a problem—that is, sex between men became a problem—in the 18th century. We see the rise of it as a problem with the police, within the justice system, and so on. I think the reason it appears as a problem, as a social issue, at this time is that friendship had disappeared. As long as friendship was something important, was socially accepted, nobody realized men had sex together. You couldn't say that men *didn't* have sex together— it just didn't matter. It had no social implication, it was culturally accepted. Whether they fucked together or kissed had no importance. Absolutely no importance. Once friendship disappeared as a culturally accepted relation, the issue arose, "What is going on between men?" And that's when the problem appears. And if men fuck together, or have sex together, that now appears as a problem. Well, I'm sure I'm right, that the disappearance of friendship as a social relation, and the declaration of homosexuality as a social/political/medical problem, are the same process.

Q: If the important thing now is to explore anew the possibilities of friendships, we should note that, to a large degree, all the social institutions are designed for heterosexual friendships and structures, and the denial of homosexual ones. Isn't the real task to set up new social relations, new value structures, familial structures and so on? One of the things gay people don't have is easy access to all the structures and institutions that go along with monogamy and the nuclear family. What kinds of institutions do we need to begin to establish, in order not only to defend ourselves but also to create new social forms that are really going to be alternative?

MF: Institutions. I have no precise idea. I think, of course, that to use the model of family life, or the institutions of the family, for this purpose and this kind of friendship would be quite contradictory. But it is quite true that since some of the relationships in society are protected forms of family life, an effect of this is that the variations that are not protected are, at the same time, often much richer, more interesting and creative, than the others. But of course, they are much more fragile and vulnerable. The question of what kinds of institutions we need to create is an important and crucial issue, but one that I cannot give an answer to. I think that we have to try to build a solution.

Q: To what degree do we want, or need, the project of gay liberation today to be one that refuses to chart a course and instead insists on opening up new venues? In other words, does your approach to sexual politics deny the need for a program and insist on experimentation with new kind of relations?

MF: I think that one of the great experiences we've had since the last war is that all those social and political programs have been a great failure. We have come to realize things never happen as we expect from a political program; and that a political program has always, or nearly always, led to abuse or political domination from a bloc, be it from technicians or bureaucrats or other people. But one of the development of the '60s and '70s that I think has been a good thing is that certain institutional models have been experimented with without a program. Without a program does not mean blindness—to be blind to thought. For instance, in France there has been a lot of criticism recently about the fact that there are no programs in the various political movements about sex, about prisons, about ecology and so on. But in my opinion, being without a program can be very useful and very original and creative, if it does not mean without proper reflection about what is going on, or without very careful attention to what's possible.

Since the 19th century great political institutions and great political parties have confiscated the process of political creation; that is, they have tried to give to political creation the form of a political program in order to take over power. I think what happened in the '60s and early '70s is something to be preserved. One of the things that I think should be preserved, however, is the fact that there has been political innovation, political creation and political experimentation outside the great political parties, and outside the normal or ordinary program. It's a fact that people's everyday lives have changed from the early '60s to now, and certainly within my own life. And surely, that is not due to political parties but is the result of many movements. These social movements have really changed our whole lives, our mentality, our attitudes and the attitudes and mentality of other people—people who do not belong to these movements. And that is something very important and positive. I repeat, it is not the normal and old traditional political organizations that have led to this examination.

47

THE CULTURAL INSULARITY OF CONTEMPORARY MUSIC

MICHEL FOUCAULT: It is often said that contemporary music has gotten "off track"; that it had a singular destiny; that it reached a degree of complexity that renders it inaccessible; that its techniques have dragged it along paths that separate it more and more. However, what strikes me, on the contrary, is the multiplicity of links and relationships between music and all the other elements of culture. This appears in many ways. On one hand, music has been much more sensitive to technological transformations, much more tightly linked to them than most of the other arts (with the exception of cinema, without a doubt). On the other hand, the evolution of these musics since Debussy or Stravinsky presents remarkable correlations with that of painting. And then, the theoretical problems that music itself raised, the way it reflected on its language, its structures, its material, come from an investigation that, I believe, has traversed the entire 20th century: an investigation into "form" which was that of Cezanne or of the cubists, Schonberg's and also of the Russian formalists or the School of Prague. I do not believe that one has to wonder: since music has gone so far off, how can we retrieve it or repatriate it? But rather: since it is so close, so consubstantial to our entire culture, how it is that we feel as if it were projected far away and situated at an almost unattainable distance?

PIERRE BOULEZ: Is the "circuit" of contemporary music so different from the various "circuits" used by symphonic music, chamber, opera, baroque music, all circuits that are so very partitioned off, specialized to the point that one can wonder if there really exists something called general culture? Knowledge gained through records should, in principle, break down these barriers whose economic necessity we can understand, but we observe, on the contrary, that records corroborate both the public's and interpreters' sense of specialization. Even in the organization of a concert or a performance, the forces different types of music call in more or less exclude a common organization, even a polyvalence. Whoever says classical or romantic repertoire implies a standardized education which has a tendency to only include exceptions to this rule if the economy of the whole is not perturbed. Whoever says baroque music necessarily implies not only a restricted group, but instruments in reference with the music played, musicians who have acquired a specialized knowledge in terms of interpretation, based on the study of texts and theoretical works of the past. Whoever says contemporary music implies an approach involving new instrumental techniques, new notations, an aptitude to adapt oneself to new interpretive situations. This enumeration might be continued to show the difficulties to overcome in moving from one area to another: organizational difficulties, personal problems of fitting in, without mentioning the problem of adapting spaces to one sort of performance or another. So, there is a tendency for a larger or smaller society to take shape according to each category of music, and to establish a dangerously closed circuit between this society, its music, its musicians. Contemporary music does not escape this condition; even if the statistics of public attendance are proportionately low, it does not escape the weaknesses of musical society in general: it has its places, its meetings, its stars, snobisms, rivalries, its privileges; just like any other society, it has its stocks and bonds, its values, quotes and statistics. The various music circles, even if they do not belong to Dante, are still not any less revelatory of a prison system in which the majority is comfortable and of which some, on the contrary, feel the pain of constraint.

MF: One must account for the fact that for a very long time, music was linked to and unified by social rites: religious music, chamber music; in the 19th century, the connection between music and theatrical representation in opera (not to mention the political or cultural significations that this could have had in Germany or Italy) was also a factor of integration. I think that we cannot speak of the "cultural isolation" of contemporary music without immediately rectifying what is said about it, by thinking of other circuits of music. With rock, for example, we have the exact opposite phenomenon. Not only rock music (much more than jazz in the past) is an integral part of the life of many people, but it is an inductor of culture: to like rock, to like this type of rock music more than another type, is also a way of life, a way of reacting; it is a whole group of tastes and attitudes. Rock offers the possibility of an intense relationship, strong, lively, "dramatic" (in the sense that it constitutes a show, that listening is an event and that it is staged), with music that is in itself poor, but through which the audience asserts itself; and yet, there is a frail, chilly, distant, problematic rapport with learned music from which the cultivated audience feels excluded. One cannot speak of *a* relationship between contemporary culture and music, but rather of a more or less generous tolerance with respect to a plurality of musics. Each is given the "right" to exist; and this right is perceived as of equal value. Each is worth as much as the group that practices or recognizes it.

PB: Can the point be resolved by speaking about musics and displaying an eclectic ecumenicalism? It seems that, on the contrary, we are dodging the issue—in synch with the advocates of advanced liberal society. All musics are good, all musics are kind. Ah! pluralism! nothing like pluralism to remedy incomprehension. Therefore, let's love each other, each on your own and you will all love each other. Be liberal, be generous about the tastes of others, and they'll reciprocate. Everything is good, nothing is bad; there are no values, only pleasure. This speech, as liberating as it may be, reinforces, on the contrary, the ghettos, comforts one's good conscience to be in a ghetto especially if, from time to time, one engages in the voyeurism of exploring other peoples' ghettos. The economy is there to remind us, in case we get lost in this insipid utopia, that there are kinds of music that cost money whose purpose has nothing to do with profit. No liberalism will erase this difference.

MF: I have a feeling that many elements which aim at giving greater access to music end up impoverishing the relationship one has with it. There is a quantitative mechanism which is activated. A certain rarity of the relationship to music could preserve a freedom to listen, and a sort of flexibility of listening. But the more frequent this relationship (the radio, records, cassettes), the more familiarities are created; habits are crystallized; the most frequent becomes the most acceptable, and in a short time, the only receivable. A "fraying" is produced, as neurologists would say. Clearly market laws can easily be applied to this simple mechanism. The public listens to what is made available. And what the audience happens to listens to, since it is what is being offered, reinforces certain tastes, defines the limits of a well-defined capacity for listening, and determines more and more a listening pattern. It will be necessary to satisfy this expectation, etc. Thus, commercial production, critics, concerts, everything that multiplies the public's contact with music risks making it more difficult to perceive anything new. Of course, this is not a univocal process. And it is also clear that the growing familiarity with music increases the capacity for listening and gives access to possible differentiations, but this phenomenon mostly occurs in the margins; it can, in any case, remain secondary in terms of the great reinforcement of what is already acquired, if there is not an all-out effort to unsettle familiarities.

PB: We must observe not only a polarization in terms of the past, but even a polarization in terms of the past of the past, as far as the musician or interpreter are concerned. And this is how one reaches ecstasy, of course, in hearing the interpretation of a given classical work by a long-deceased musician; but the ecstasy reaches orgasmic heights when one can refer to the performance given on the 20th of July, 1947 or December 30th, 1938. We see a pseudo-culture of the document taking shape where everything is based on the exquisite hour and the lost moment in time, that reminds us of both the interpreter's fragility and perenniality, immortalized, competing therefore with the immortality of the masterwork. All the mysteries of the shroud of Turin, all the powers of modern magic, what more would you like as an alibi for reproduction confronted with present production? Modernity is the technical superiority we possess over the ancient centuries to be able to recreate the event. Ah! if we only had the first performance of the *Ninth* even — especially — with all its faults, or if we could tell the delectable difference between the Prague version and the

Vienna version of *Don Giovanni* by Mozart himself...This historicizing cara-
pace suffocates those who don it and compresses them into an asphixiating
rigidity; the mephitic air they breathe permanently weakens their organism in
terms of the current adventure. I imagine Fidelio thrilled to remain in his dungeon, or I think of Plato's cave: the civilization of shadow and shadows.

MF: Certainly listening to music becomes more difficult as its writing
relinquishes all kinds of patterns, signals, perceptible references to a repetitive
structure. In classical music, there is a certain transparency between writing and
listening. And even if pieces of Bach's or Beethoven's music are not identified
by most listeners, there are always others, and major ones, which are accessible.
So, contemporary music, inasmuch as it tends to turn each of its elements into a
singular event, makes any grasp or recognition by the auditor a problem .

PB: Is it only that the listener is indifferent or doesn't pay attention to
contemporary music? Are the complaints that are heard and so often formulated
only due to laziness, inertia and the happiness of remaining on familiar territory?
Berg wrote, half a century ago, a text entitled: "Why is Schonberg's music so
difficult to understand?" The difficulties that he was describing are approximately the same as those we hear about today. Has it always been the same?
Probably, each new thing shakes up sensibilities which are not accustomed to it.
But there is reason to believe that, today, communication between the work and
an audience presents specific difficulties. In classical or romantic music, which
constitute the main source of familiar repertoire, there are required patterns, that
can be followed independently of the work itself, or rather that the work is
required to manifest. The movements of a symphony are defined in form and in
character, in their very rhythmic life; they are distinct from one another, most of
the time actually separated by a cut, sometimes linked by a transition that can be
located. The vocabulary itself is based on the "classified" chords, which well
deserve their names: you do not need to analyze them to know what they are and
what function they have, they have the efficiency and security of signals; they
are found again and again from one piece to another, and always assume the
same appearance and the same functions. Progressively, these reassuring elements have disappeared from "serious" music; it has evolved into an always
more radical renewal of both the form and language of works. Works have
tended to become singular events which certainly have their antecedents, but
cannot be reduced to any guiding scheme, *a priori,* accepted by all. This certainly creates a handicap for immediate comprehension. Listeners are asked to
familiarize themselves with the course of the work, to do that, they have to listen
to it a number of times. Once the course becomes familiar, the comprehension of
the work, the perception of what is expressed can find a propitious ground for
their fulfillment. There are fewer and fewer chances that the first encounter can
illuminate perception and comprehension. There can be spontaneous attachment,
thanks to the force of the message, the quality of the composition, the beauty of
the sounds, the readability of the cues, but deep comprehension can only come

from repeated reading — this repetition taking the place of the accepted diagram, as it was practiced in the past. The diagrams (*schemas*)—of vocabulary, of form—that have been evacuated from serious (what was called in the past "learned") music can now be found in some forms of popular music, in objects of musical consumption. There, one still creates according to *genres,* according to accepted typologies. Conservatism is not necessarily always found where we expect it. It is undeniable that a certain conservatism of form and language is found as the basis for all commercial productions adopted with great enthusiasm by generations who consider themselves anything but conservative. It is a paradox of our times that played and sung protest are transmitted through a vocabulary which is eminently recuperable, and is bound to be coopted; commercial success dissipates protest.

MF: And, on this point, perhaps 20th century music and painting diverge in terms of their evolution. Painting has had the tendency, since Cezanne, to make itself transparent to the act of painting; this act became visible, insistent, definitively present in the painting, either through the use of elementary signs or through traces of its own dynamics. Instead, contemporary music only offers the external side of its writing to the listener. From this follows something difficult, imperious in listening to this music. From this, the fact that each performance is given as an event the listener attends, and must accept. He has no points of reference which tell him what to expect of it or how to recognize it. He listens to it being produced. And this is a very difficult kind of attention, which is in contradiction with the familiarities bred by the repeated listening of classical music. Cultural insularity in music today is not simply the consequence of a deficient pedagogy or lack of information. It would be too easy to moan about conservatories or complain about record companies. Things are more serious. This situation is unique, contemporary music owes it to its own writing. In that respect, it is intentional. It is not music that would try to become familiar; it is there to keep its edge. One can very well rehearse it; it is not reiterated. In this way, one cannot come back to it, like an object. It always erupts on the borders.

PB: Since it wants to be this way, in a perpetual situation of discovery—new areas of sensibilities, experimentation with new materials—is contemporary music condemned to remain a Kamtchatka (Baudelaire, Sainte-Beuve, you remember?) reserved for the intrepid curiosity of rare explorers? It is remarkable that the most reticent listeners are those who acquired their musical culture exclusively in the stores of the past, a certain past, and that the most open-minded—only because the most ignorant?—prove to be the listeners who feel a sustained interest for other means of expression: plastic arts in particular. The most receptive "foreigners"? Dangerous connections which would tend to prove that present-day music would detach itself from "true" musical culture to join a more vast and vague domain where amateurism would be preponderant, in both judgment and in terms of composition. Don't call that "music" any more, and we'll let you have your toy; this is another kind of appreciation which has nothing to do with what we reserve exclusively for real music, for the masters. This argument was proferred, and in its arrogant naivete it comes close to an undeniable truth. Judgment and taste are prisoners of categories, of pre-established diagrams to which one keeps referring, come what may. Not, as some would have us believe, that the distinction rests between an aristocracy of feelings, a nobility of expression and a chancy artistry based on experimenta-tion: thought against tool. It is rather the question of an ear that cannot be modulated, adapted to the different ways of inventing music. I will certainly not preach the ecumenicism of musics which seems to me just a supermarket aesthetics, demagogy that does not dare call itself by its righfful name, full of good intentions to better camouflage the misery of its compromises. I also do not refuse the demand for quality of sound and composition: aggressivity and provocation, do-it-yourself work and powder in the eyes are only lean and innocent palliatives; I know perfectly well—multiple experiences and the most direct kind possible— that beyond a certain complexity, perception is disoriented in an inextricable chaos, that it gets bored and tunes out. It is enough to say that I can preserve my critical reactions and that my support does not automatically go to sheer "contemporariness." Some modulations of listening are already produced, rather badly, in fact, beyond certain historical limits. One does not listen to Baroque music—especially the minor kind—as one listens to Wagner or Strauss; one does not listen to the polyphony of *Ars Nova* as one listens to Debussy or Ravel. But in this last case, how many listeners are ready to vary their "mode of being," musically speaking? And nevertheless for musical culture, all musical culture, to be assimilated, it is enough to adapt to the criteria, to the conventions to which the invention is submitted at a given moment in history. This wide respiration of centuries is placed at the extreme opposite of the asthmatic coughing that fanatics of ghostly reflections of the past in a tarnished mirror have us hear. A culture is forged, continued and transmitted in a two-faced adventure: sometimes brutality, protest, tumult, sometimes meditation, non-violence, silence. Whatever the form of the adventure—the most surprising is not always the noisiest, but the noisiest is not necessarily the most superficial—it is vain to ignore it, and even more vain to hide it. We can hardly say that there are probably key periods where the coincidence is felt more uncomfortably, where each aspect of invention seems to absolutely break away with what we can tolerate or "reasonably" absorb; that there exist other periods where repercussions of a more immediately accessible order are produced. The relationships among all these phenomena, individual and collective, are so complex that it is impossible to apply parallels or rigorous groupings. One would be more tempted to say: Gentlemen, place your bets and have faith, for the rest, here's to *l'air du temps!* But, by God, play! play! play! Without that what infinite secretions of boredom!

                                                            Translated by Lysa Hochroth.

48

ARCHAEOLOGY OF A PASSION

MF: I wrote this study of Raymond Roussel when I was quite young. It happened completely by chance, and I want to stress this element of chance because I have to admit that I had never heard of Roussel until the year 1957. I can recall how I discovered his work: it was during a period when I was living abroad in Sweden and returned to France for the summer. I went to the Libraire Jose Corli to buy I can't recall what book. Can you visualize that huge bookstore across from the Luxembourg Gardens? José Corti, publisher and bookseller, was there behind his enormous desk, a distinguished old man. He was busy speaking to a friend, and obviously he is not the kind of bookseller that you can interrupt with a "Could you find me such and such a book?" You have to wait politely until the conversation is over before making a request. Thus, while waiting, I found my attention drawn to a series of books of that faded yellow color used by publishing firms of the late nineteenth, early twentieth centuries; in short, books the likes of which aren't made anymore. I examined them and saw "Librairie Lemerre" on the cover. I was puzzled to find these old volumes from a publishing firm as fallen now in reputation as that of Alphonse Lemerre. I selected a book out of curiosity to see what José Corti was selling from the stock of the Lemerre firm, and that's how I came upon the work of someone I had never heard of named Raymond Roussel, and the book was entitled *La Vue*. Well, from the first time I was completely taken by the beauty of the style, so strange and so strangely close to that of Robbe-Grillet, who was just beginning to publish his work. I could see a relationship between *La Vue* and Robbe-Grillet's work in general, but Le Voeur in particular. At that point Jose Corti's conversation came to an end, I requested the book I needed, and asked timidly who was Raymond Roussel, because in addition to *La Vue,* his other works were on the shelf. Corti looked at me with a generous sort of pity and said, "But, after all, Roussel..." I immediately understood that I should have known about Raymond Roussel, and with equal timidity I asked if I could buy the book since he was selling it. I was surprised or rather disappointed to find that it was expensive. José Corti probably told me that day I should read *How I Wrote Certain of My Books*. Raymond Roussel's work immediately absorbed me: I was taken by the prose style even before learning what was behind it—the process, the machines, the mechanisms—and no doubt when I discovered his

process and his techniques, the obsessional side of me was seduced a second time
by the shock of learning of the disparity between this methodically-applied
process, which was slightly naive, and the resulting intense poetry. Slowly and
systematically I began to buy all of his works. I developed an affection for his
work, which remained secret, since I didn't discuss it.

The strange thing is thal I met Robbe-Grillet for the first time in
Hamburg in 1960 and we became friends and went to the Hamburg Fair
together, going through the fun house maze of mirrors. It's the starting point of
his novel *In the Labyrinth*. By a mental lapse that can't have been entirely innocent on my part, I never spoke of Roussel with him, nor asked about his relationship to Roussel. That's how things stood for several years until one day during
vacation I decided to write a small article on Roussel, but by then I was so
absorbed by Roussel and his work thal I isolated myself for two months and in
fact wrote what turned out to be this book.

Q: If you began with the idea for an article, did other ideas that had to
be explored come to you in the course of your work?

MF: My intention was to write an article on Roussel for *Critique* magazine. But after a few days I knew that it would be longer than an article, and I
wrote without any thought of where I would publish it or how. I had discussed
my work with friends who were critics, and, as a result, one day I received a
telephone call from an editor asking me what I was working on.

"Oh, I'm working on a book about Raymond Roussel."

"Would you let me read it when you've completed it? Will it take you a
long time?"

For once in my life I, who take such a long time with my books, could
answer proudly, "I'll be finished with it very soon."

"When?" he asked.

I answered, "In eleven or twelve minutes," an answer that was completely justified by the fact that I had started typing the last page. That's the story
of this book.

As for Robbe-Grillet and my lapse into silence, it was after the publication of the book that I learned that his novel *Le Voyeur* was originally entitled *La
Vue* as a tribute to Raymond Roussel. It was his editor who, for completely justifiable commercial considerations, thought the title made the novel unsalable, and
finally they agreed on *Le Voyeur.*

Q: At that time Roussel was part of your interest in the whole movement of the *nouveau roman.*

MF: Yes, I encountered *La Vue* by chance, and I believe I can honestly say
that if I hadn't been preconditioned by the reading of Robbe-Grillet, Butor, and
Barthes I would not have been capable on my own of experiencing this shock of
recognition while reading *La Vue.* The chance was greater of my being interested by

How I Wrote Certain of My Books, or by *Impressions d'Afrique,* or by any other sort of novelty than *La Vue.* I really believe that this previous conditioning was necessary.

To state things in another way: I belong to that generation who as students had before their eyes, and were limited by, a horizon consisting of Marxism, phenomenology, and existenlialism. Interesting and stimulating as these might be, naturally they produced in the students completely immersed in them a feeling of being stifled, and the urge to look elsewhere. I was like all other students of philosophy at that time, and for me the break was first Beckett's *Waiting for Godot,* a breathtaking performance; then reading the works of Blanchot, Bataille, and Robbe-Grillet, especially his novels *The Erasers, Jealousy,* and *The Voyeur;* Michel Butor, Barthes' *Mythologies;* and Lévi-Strauss. There's an enormous difference between Bataille, Lévi-Strauss, Blanchot, and Robbe-Grillet, and I don't want to make them seem similar. For my generation they represented the break with a perspective dominated by Marxism, phenomenology, and existentialism. Having had enough of this French university culture, I left the country to go to Sweden. Had I remained within that limited horizon of my student days, under the system of classes, and that sense of the world, the end of history, it seems likely that I could have opened Roussel's book and slammed it shut with a good laugh.

Q: But for you the break was made with your historical study of madness. You had formulated your ideas and you were committed to a direction even before discovering Roussel.

MF: In fact, I was reading Roussel at the time I was working on my book about the history of madness. I was divided between existential psychology and phenomenology, and my research was an attempt to discover the extent these could be defined in historical terms. That's when I first understood that the subject would have to be defined in other terms than Marxism or phenomenology.

Q: I was interested by the fact that Roussel was a contemporary of Marcel Proust. If Proust's work represents the final elaboration of nineteenth-century fiction, the novelistic conventions taken to extremes, then what is Roussel's position? Cocteau called Roussel "the Proust of dreams." To me Roussel's work is the "implosion" of all novelistic conventions; he is the artist who disappears behind his work; he is hidden by the"ready-made," by the "found" convention of language that he uses to create his work.

MF: Yes, I think my answer will startle you because you have become "Rousselian." I have to admit that I would not dare to compare Roussel to Proust. You are right in the historical scheme of things. But I would remain very cautious about Roussel's historical place. His was an extremely interesting experiment; it wasn't only. a linguistic experiment, but an experiment with the nature of language, and it's more than the experimentation of someone obsessed. He truly created, or, in any case, broke through, embodied, and created a form of beauty, a lovely curiosity, which is in fact a literary work. But I wouldn't say that Roussel is comparable to Proust.

Q: In the similarity to the work of Robbe-Grillet, was it his breaking with the literary conventions of his day that aroused your interest?

MF: There are several aspects I would comment on. First, it must be noted that Roussel belongs to a series of writers who exist in English, exist in German, exist in all languages. They are writers who have literally been obsessed with the problem of language, for whom literary construction and the "interplay of language" are directly related. I couldn't say that was a tradition because, in fact, it's a tradition that disappears with each writer as if it were so individual to each writer that it could not be transmitted but is rediscovered every time. And sometimes there are similarities that reappear. Roussel is part of that series. Of course, in the period when he was working, around 1925, he worked alone and was isolated, and, I believe, he could not be understood. There has been interest in his work only in two contexts: first, that of surrealism, with the problem of automatic writing; second, that of the nouveau roman in the years 1950 to 1960, a period when the problem of the relationship of literature and linguistic structure was not only a topic of theoretical speculation but also loomed large on the literary horizon.

Q: You had just finished your historical study of madness. Was it Roussel's psychological problems which drew your interest and made you decide to write about him at that time?

MF: Not at all. Once I had discovered Roussel and I learned that he had been a patient of Dr. Pierre Janet, and that his case had been written up in two pages that he quoted, I was delighted and tried to discover if anything else had been written about him in the medical literature of the day. But I could find nothing. I have to admit that my research was not extensive precisely because it was not his psychology that interested me. I don't think that I make extensive references to his psychopathology in my study.

Q: I assumed that your work on the history of madness would make you susceptible to Roussel.

MF: It's possible, but then I would say that I wasn't conscious of my interest. It wasn't because of the cultural, medical, scientific, institutional problems of madness that I became interested in Roussel. No doubt what could be said is that perhaps the same reasons which in my perverseness [laughs] and in my own psychopathological makeup made me pursue my interest in madness, on the one hand, made me pursue my interest in Roussel on the other.

Q: In your study you analyze the problem of "found" or "ready-made" language: When you referred to the surrealists' interest in automatic writing I immediately thought of their use of found objects, which has entered the mainstream of experimentation in the visual arts as well as writing. Were you challenged by the problem of how to define "found language"?

MF: Well, it is the interest I have in modes of discourse, that is to say, not so much in the linguistic structure which makes such a series of utterances possible, but rather the fact that we live in a world in which things have been said. These spoken words in reality are not, as people tend to think, a wind that passes without leaving a trace, but in fact, diverse as are the traces, they do remain. We live in a world completely marked by, all laced with, discourse, that is to say, utterances which have been spoken, of things said, of affirmations, interrogations, of discourses which have already occurred. To that extent, the historical world in which we live cannot be dissociated from all the elements of discourse which have inhabited this world and continue to live in it as the economic process, the demographic, et cetera, et cetera. Thus spoken language, as a language that is already present, in one way or another determines what can be said afterward either independent of or within the general framework of language. In certain of Roussel's works nothing is given at the beginning except the possibility of encountering the "already said," and with this "found language" to construct, according to his rules, a certain number of things, but on the condition that they always refer back to the "already said"—that at first delighted me, and seemed to be the interplay of literary creation starting from a cultural and historical fact. It also seemed to me that it was worth questioning.

Q: But the question remains, what is the relationship of the artist who will use, or starts with, a "ready-made" element in his work?

MF: Yes, if you wish, it's interesting to see how he distorts the fact. For example, as original as a novel might be, even if it is a *Ulysses* or a *Remembrance of Things Past,* it takes its place in a novelistic tradition and thus in the "already said" of the novel. The interesting thing about Roussel is that he doesn't use the generic matrix of the novelistic genre as the principle of development or construction. He starts with the "already said," and this "already said" can be a sentence found by chance, read in an advertisement, found in a book, or something practical....

Q: It's his point of departure. But after writing the novels, Roussel turned to the theater with the intention of communicating more easily with the public. You would think that the theater would lend itself to the use of a "found language," since it is the genre of the world of speech and conversation.

MF: Well, the use of an already spoken language in the theater usually has the function of establishing a sense of verisimilitude for what is seen on stage. The familiar language placed in the mouths of the actors makes the viewer forget the arbitrariness of the situation. What Roussel did was to take a completely banal sentence, heard every day, taken from songs, read on walls, and with it he constructed the most absurd things, the most improbable situations, without any possible relationship to reality. Starting from the "already said," it's a perverse play on the usual function it exercises in the theater.

Q: I wanted to point out that in the novels *Impressions d'Afrique* and *Locus Solus* the fantastic beings and situations he has created are very similar to nineteenth-century games and toys. Some scenes could be descriptions of the action of those exquisite and complex automatons such as the doll who can paint Napoleon's portrait, play the piano, or write a letter. You mentioned the naive or primitive aspect of his process. Without wanting to negate the complexity of Roussel's work, I wondered if this fundamentally private imagination was not a return to childhood, or rather a return to pure fantasy.

MF: It's absolutely true that there is an implicit and sometimes explicit reference to children's games, these automatons, rabbits playing drums and such, if they are taken to extremes. Only then could one say that this core of childlike imagination, the child which generally appears in all writers and is acclimated within the writing by a whole labor of elaboration, is pushed or taken toward another level of the fantastic. Roussel keeps them on their own level, in a way, and starting from the rabbit beating drums, makes the machine increasingly complex, but always remaining the same without ever passing to another register or level. There are constructions which are so intensely poetic that I don't think they are childish in themselves, but are a way of elaborating this core of childlike imagination.

Q: This is the aspect you analyzed in your study of his machines for the transformation of language and the hollowness, the emptiness within words. You quote Dumarsais' description of the "tropological" shift in the meaning of words as the basis of his creation. Beneath the text a secondary language is repeated, echoing within the text. Do you read Roussel listening for that second, dead-and-buried language?

MF: Yes, that's an interesting problem, and one of the things about Roussel that has remained completely enigmatic. It must be remembered that he didn't always use the process. In *La Vue* there is no process structuring the work. What I tried to accomplish in the book is to come to an understanding of what was the essential matrix that would take into account the texts without the process, and the texts with the process, those which obeyed the rules of the process and those which don't. I don't know if I accomplished what I set out to do, but that was my goal. The process poses a problem which is all the more interesting to me because I have a student who is completely bilingual— French-German—who is interested in Roussel, and who is trying to write texts with a linguistic process all the more complicated because he has to coordinate the use of two registers: French and German. The problem with the texts he has shown me is knowing if the interest, the complexity, the refinement are enough to confer literary merit on the texts produced. Working with him, reading his texts, I couldn't help thinking of what Roussel said: "Still, one needs to know how to use it. For just as one can use rhymes to compose good or bad verses, so one can use this method to produce good or bad works." Nevertheless Roussel's work gives the distinct impression of an aesthetic control of imaginative standards. It seemed to me that these aesthetic criteria, considering all the possible outcomes available to him, were inseparable from the nature of the process itself.

In the extreme, what if we didn't have *How I Wrote Certain of My Books* I believe it would be absolutely impossible to reconstruct his process. I'm not referring to *Nouvelles Impressions d'Afrique,* because there the process is typographical, thus evident on the page. But in *Impressions d'Afrique* and in *La Poussière de Soleils,* could one be unaware of a linguistic process? There's no doubt one can ignore it. Does it diminish the quality of the work? How would Roussel be perceived by a reader who was unaware of the process? For example, what of the American reader, or the Japanese reader, since he has been translated into Japanese? Can they become interested in Roussel or see the beauty of his work without knowing that there is a process, or even knowing that there is a process, not being able to perceive it since the original matrix of language is not available?

Q: Roussel's process incorporates word play and double-entendre which are considered trivial by us, but are basic aspects of Japanese poetics. Translations of classical Japanese poetry have footnotes giving the second reading of the poem. Reading Roussel in English translation, one knows there is another aspect which is not delivered, but the surface quality of language and imagination is strikingly original and delightful.

MF: There is a quality of imagination which makes the work, even without knowing about the process, stand on its own. But the knowledge that there is a process throws the reader into a state of being uncertain, and even while knowing that there is no way of rediscovering the process, and even if one enjoys simply reading the text, the fact that there is a secret transforms the experience of reading into one of deciphering, a game, a more complex undertaking, more disturbing, more anxious than when one reads a simple text for the pure pleasure of it. I believe it matters to some extent knowing what was the original text that produced such and such an incident. With hard work certain sentences that served as points of departure can be clarified. A whole team of people working for years could discover the sentences that served as matrixes for each episode in Roussel's novels. But I'm not certain that it would be interesting, because it seems that aside from the beauty of the text that is pleasing in itself, the consciousness of there being a process gives the act of reading a certain tension. I'm not convinced that a knowledge of the actual text from which it starts is at all necessary.

Q: Were you interested in his relationship to the surrealists? He seems to have influenced artists especially.

MF: No, but I learned that Michel Leiris knew Roussel. I was interested in his relationship because Leiris' novel *Biffures* has a number of things reminiscent of Roussel. I discussed it with Leiris, but everything he had to say about Roussel is contained in his articles.

Q: Marcel Duchamp and other artists discuss Roussel only incidentally; there is no attempt to come to grips with his work.

MF: I believe that the relationship between Roussel and the surrealists was only incidental, as opposed to Leiris, who knew him. I believe the surrealists were aroused and entertained by him; they saw him as a sort of Douanier Rousseau, a primitive of literature. But I don't believe the surrealists did more than orchestrate the character of Roussel, and the demonstrations defending the performances of his plays.

Q: How do you interpret his turning to theater to obtain popular success?

MF: But, you know, for him writing was that! There's a beautiful passage in which he said that after his first book he expected that the next morning there would be rays of light streaming from his person and that everyone on the street would be able to see that he had written a book. That's the obscure desire of a person who writes. It is true that the first text one writes is neither written for others, nor for who one is: one writes to become someone other than who one is. Finally there is an attempt at modifying one's way of being through the act of writing. It is this transformation of his way of being that he observed, he believed in, he sought after, and for which he suffered horribly.

Q: After twenty years, can you see the place of this study in the perspective of your work and the development of your thinking?

MF: Those things that matter to me in a personal way, or which are impotant to me just as they are, I don't feel any inclination to analyze.

Q: From the little that is known about Roussel's life, such as his use of drugs, was opium the drug of his day?

MF: Oh yes, but you know the use of cocaine was already fairly widespread. It's a subject which interests me greatly, but one which I've had to put aside the study of the culture of drugs or drugs as culture in the West from the beginning of the nineteenth century. No doubt it started much earlier, but it would come up to the present, it's so closely tied to the artistic life of the West.

Q: Roussel was hospitalized for drugs rather than emotional problems.

MF: The first time that he was treated by Dr. Janet, a great Parisian psychologist of the day, Roussel was quite young, seventeen or eighteen, and it was due to causes that were considered pathological, not because of his use of drugs.

Q: Yet in the end when he wanted to take the cure, it was for detoxification.

MF: I know that when he commited suicide in Palermo he had reserved rooms at the hospital in Kreuzlingen.

Q: The phenomenon of an artist obscured by his own work—do you think that it is related to his sexual identity?

MF: Between cryptography and sexuality as a secret, there is certainly a direct relationship. Let's take three examples: When Cocteau wrote his works, people said, "It's not surprising that he haunts his sexuality and his sexual preferences with such ostentation since he is a homosexual." Then Proust, and about Proust they said, "It's not surprising that he hides and reveals his sexuality, that he lets it appear clearly while also hiding it in his work, sihce he is a homoscxual." And it could also be said about Roussel, "It's not surprising that he hides it completely since he is a homosexual." In other words, of the three possible modes of behavior—hiding it entirely, hiding it while revealing it, or flaunting it—all can appear as a result of sexuality, but I would say that it is related to a way of living. It's a choice in relation to what one is as a sexual being and also as a writer. It's the choice made in the relationship between the style of sexual life and the work. On reflection it should be said that because he is homosexual, he hid his sexuality in his work, or else it's because he hid his sexuality in his life that he also hid it in his work. Therefore, I believe that it is better to try to understand that someone who is a writer is not simply doing his work in his books, in what he publishes, but that his major work is, in the end, himself in the process of writing his books. The private life of an individual, his sexual preference, and his work are interrelated not because his work translates his sexual life, but because the work includes the whole life as well as the text. The work is more than the work: the subject who is writing is part of the work.

Q: Did your study of Roussel not lead you to other subjects that continued the pursuit of your interest?

MF: No, I have kept my love of Roussel as something gratuitous and I prefer it that way. I'm not a literary critic nor a literary historian, and to the extent that Roussel was unknown, except by a few people, when I wrote about him, he was not part of the great literary patrimony. Perhaps those are the reasons I had no scruples about studying him. I did not do it for Mallarme or for Proust. I wrote about Roussel because he was neglected, hibernating on the shelves of José Corti's bookshop. I enjoyed doing it, but I am glad I never continued that work. I would have felt, not now, but in those days, that I was betraying Roussel, normalizing him, by treating him as an author like others if after writing about him I had started another study of another writer. Thus he remained unique.

Q: In this book there's a flight of style, a rhetorical play from chapter to chapter. Was this book different both in subject and in your approach to writing?

MF: Yes, it is by far the book I wrote most easily, with the greatest pleasure, and most rapidly; because I usually write very slowly, I have to rewrite endlessly, and finally there are countless corrections. I imagine it must be a complex work to read, because I belong to that category of people who, when they write spontaneously, write in a slightly convoluted manner and are obliged to simplify and clarify. In my other books I tried to use a certain type of analysis, and to write in a particular way—in short, much more deliberate, more focused. My relationship to my book on Roussel, and to Roussel's work, is something very personal, which I remember as a happy period. I would go so far as to say that it doesn't have a place in the sequence of my books. No one has tried to. explain that I wrote it because I had already written a study of madness and that I would write on the history of sexuality. No one has paid much attention to this book, and I'm glad; it's my secret affair. You know, he was my love for several summers... no one knew it.

Q: You've said you don't want to analyze your personal reactions.

MF: It is not a question that what I have to say can illuminate Roussel's text, but that it will eventually reveal the type of interest that a Frenchman of the 1960s could bring to these texts.

Q: I wanted to ask you about Roland Barthes' desire at the end of his life to create a synthesis of his ideas in a work of art. He began speaking about his diaries. I wondered how you understood this change in him.

MF: In the *Fragments of a Lover's Discourse* he revealed himself well enough. He never discussed it directly with me. What I can tell you is that the rumors that when he died he was in a crisis, and that he wanted to die, are completely false. It happens that I was with him at the moment of the accident, and I was at the hospital where they brought him and I spoke with his doctors—the rumors are completely false.

I also happened to see him a week before his accident, and watching him with his students at the university, I thought, He is in his element, he's acquired the distinguished bearing of a man who is mature, serene, completely developed. I remember thinking, He'll live to be ninety years old; he is one of those men whose most important work will be written between the ages of sixty and ninety. I do believe that in his eyes, his critical works, his essays, were the preliminary sketches of something which would have been very important and interesting.

Translated by Charles Ruas

49

What Our Present Is

Q: It would be interesting to me if you would tell us how you made your way through a series of problematics, a series of issues. Why you got interested in the history of psychiatry, the history of medicine, in prisons and now in the history of sexuality. Why, today, you seem to be interested in the history of law. What has been your itinerary? What was the driving force of your reflection, if it is possible to answer such a question?

MF: You are asking me a difficult question. First because the driving line cannot be determined until one is at the end of the road, and then, you know, I absolutely do not consider myself either a writer or a prophet. I work, it is true, for the most part in response to a set of circumstances, outside requests, various situations. I have no intention whatsoever of laying down the law and it seems to me that if there is a certain coherence in what I do, it is perhaps linked to a situation in which we all find ourselves, far more than a basic intuition or a systematic thinking. This has been true since Kant asked the question *"Was ist Aufklärung?"* that is, what is our own actuality, what is happening around us, what is our present. It seems to me that philosophy acquired a new dimension here. Moreover, it opened up a certain task that philosophy had ignored or didn't know even existed beforehand, and that is to tell us who we are, what our present is, what that is, today. It is obviously a question which would have had no meaning for Descartes. It is a question which begins to mean something for Kant, when he wonders what the *Aufklärung* is; it is, in a sense, Nietzsche's question. I also think that among the different functions that philosophy can and must have, there is also this one, asking oneself about who we are today, in our present actuality. I will say that it is around this that I raise the question and in this respect that I am Nietzschean or Hegelian or Kantian, from that very angle.

Well, how did I come to raise this type of question? Briefly, one can say the following about the history of our intellectual life in post-war Western Europe: first, during the 1950s, we had access to a perspective of analysis very deeply inspired by phenomenology which was, in a sense, at that time, the dominant philosophy. I say dominant without any pejorative in the word, for one cannot say that there was a dictatorship or despotism in this way of thinking; but in Western Europe, particularly in France, phenomenology was a general style of analysis. A style of analysis that claimed to analyze concrete things as one of its fundamental tasks. It is quite certain that from this point of view, one could have remained a bit dissatisfied in that the kind of concrete phenomenology referred to was a bit academic and university-oriented. You had privileged objects of phenomenological description, lived experiences or the perception of a tree through an office window...

I am a little harsh but the object field that phenomenology explored was somewhat predetermined by an academic philosophical tradition that was perhaps worth opening up.

Secondly, another important form of dominant thought was clearly Marxism. Marxism referred to a whole domain of historical analysis which, in a way, it left untouched. Reading Marx's texts and the analysis of Marx's concepts was an important task, but the content of historical knowledge to which these concepts had to refer, for which they had to be operational, these historical domains were a bit neglected. In any case, Marxism, or concrete Marxist history, at least in France, was not highly developed.

Then there was a third current which was especially developed and this was the history of sciences, with people like Bachelard, Canguilhem, etc...and Cavaillès. The problem was to know the following: is there a historicity of reason and can one devise the history of truth.

If you like, I would say that I situated myself at the intersection of these different currents and different problems. In relation to phenomenology, rather than making a somewhat internal description of lived experience, shouldn't one, couldn't one instead analyze a number of collective and social experiences?

As Binswanger showed, it is important to describe the conscience of the insane. And after all, is there not a cultural and social structuring of the experience of madness? And shouldn't that be analyzed?

This led me to a historical problem which was that of knowing: if one wants to describe the social, collective composition of an experience such as that of madness, what is the social field, what is the group of institutions and practices that must be historically analyzed and for which Marxist analyses are a bit like poorly tailored clothing.

And, thirdly, through the analysis of historical, collective and social experiences, linked to precise historical contexts, how can one define the history of knowledge, the history of what we know and how new objects are able to enter a domain of knowledge and can then be presented as objects to be known. So, if you like, concretely, that raises the following questions: is there an experience of madness which is characteristic of a given society, or not? How was this experience of madness able to constitute itself? How did it manage to emerge? And, through this experience of madness, how was madness presented as an object of knowledge for a kind of medicine which identified itself as mental medicine? Through which historical transformation, which institutional modification, was the experience of madness constituted with both the subjective pole of the experience of madness and the objective pole of mental illness?

Here is, if not the itinerary, at least the starting point. And, to return to the question you asked: why having chosen those objects? I will say that it seemed to me—and that was perhaps the fourth current, the fourth point of reference of my approach or of my attempts—that more literary texts existed, which were less integrated in a philosophical tradition. I am thinking about writers like Blanchot, Artaud, Bataille, who were very important for people of my generation. At bottom, they posed the problem of experiences on the edge, these forms of experiences that instead of being considered central, of being positively valued in a society, are deemed to be borderline experiences which put into question what is usually considered acceptable. Proceeding, in a sense, from the history of madness to a questioning of our system of reason.

Q: Madness as a borderline experience...

MF: That's it. For example, what is the relationship between medical thought, knowledge about illness and life? What is it in relation to the experience of death and how has the problem of death been integrated into this knowledge? Or how has this knowledge been indexed at this point in time, this absolute point of death? Same thing for crime in relation to the law. You interrogate the law itself, and what is the foundation of the law: taking crime as the point of rupture in relation to the system and adopting this point of view to raise the question: "Then what is the law?" Taking the prison as that which should enlighten us about what the penal system is, rather than taking the penal system for granted, interrogate it first from within, find out how it came about, how it was established and justified and only then, deduce what it was.

Q: You have presented contemporary philosophy in its actuality since Kant by asking a question which, basically, I think, interests us all and allows humans to question themselves about their position in history, in the world, in society. It seems to me that throughout all you have written from *Madness and Civilization* to *The History of Sexuality,* there is a perception of this reality that seems to especially concern you and which relates to everything one could call the techniques of containment, surveillance, control, in short, the way in which an individual in our society has been progressively controlled. Do you think that it is truly a question there of a classical element in our history, something essential to an understanding of modernity?

MF: Yes, it's true. It is not, if you like, a problem I wondered about in the beginning. While studying a number of things, namely, psychiatry, medicine, the penal system, little by little all these mechanisms of containment, exclusion, surveillance and individual control appeared to be very interesting, very important. I will say that I started raising these questions in a somewhat crude fashion when I realized that they were important ones. I believe that it is necessary to define what it is about and what kind of problem one can ask about all this. It seems to me that in most analyses, either properly philosophical or more political, if not with Marxist analyses, the question of power had been relatively marginalized or, in any case, simplified. Either it was a question of knowing the juridical bases which could legitimize a political power, or of defining power as a function of a simple conservation-reproduction in the relations of production. Then it was a matter of dealing with the philosophical question of the foundation of historical analysis of the superstructure. To me, this seemed insufficient or more exactly it was insufficient for a number of reasons. First because I believe—and many things in the concrete domains I have tried to analyze confirm it—that relations of power are much more deeply implanted than at the simple level of superstructures. Secondly, the question of the foundations of power is important but, forgive me, power isn't dependent on its foundation. There are powers which are unfounded but function very well and powers which tried to establish themselves, which actually managed to do so and which finally have no function. Therefore, if you like, my problem was to tell myself: but can't one study the way in which power really functions? So when I say "power," it is absolutely not a question of locating an instance or a kind of power that would be there, visible or hidden, it doesn't matter, and which would spread its deleterious beams across the social body or which would fatally extend its network. It is not power for something that would be the power to throw a tighter and tighter net strangling society and the people under its administration. It is certainly not about all that. Power is relations; power is not a thing, it is a relationship between two individuals, a relationship which is such that one can direct the behaviour of another or determine the behaviour of another. Voluntarily determining it in terms of a number of objectives which are also one's own. In other words, when one sees what power is, it is the exercise of something that one could call *government* in a very wide sense of the term. One can govern a society, one can govern a group, a community, a family; one can govern a person. When I say "govern someone," it is simply in the sense that one can determine one's behaviour in terms of a strategy by resorting to a number of tactics. Therefore, if you like, it is *governmentality* in the wide sense of the term, as the group of relations of power and techniques which allow these relations of power to be exercised, that is what I studied. How the mentally ill were governed; how the problem of governing the sick (once again, I put the word to govern in quotation marks, giving it both a rich and wide meaning); how the patients were governed, what one did with them, what status they were given, where they were placed, in what type of treatment, what kind of surveillance, also acts of kindness, philanthropy, economic field, care to be given to the ill: it is all that, I think, that one must try to see. So it is certain that this governmentality did not end, from one perspective, it became even more strict with the passing of time. The powers in a political system like those that existed in the Middle Ages, these powers understood in the sense of government of some by others, these were, in the end, rather loose. The problem was to extract taxes, which was necessary, useful. What people did with respect to their daily behaviour was not very important for the exercise of political power. It was very important, doubtless, in the ecclesiastical clergy whose power was a political power.

It is true that the number of objects that become objects of governmentality reflected inside political frameworks, even liberal ones, has increased a great deal. But I still do not think that one should consider that this governmentality necessarily takes on the tone of containment, surveillance and control. Through a whole series of subtle fabulations, one often actually ends up directing the behaviour of people or of acting in such a way that others' behaviour can have no negative effect on us later. And this is the field of governmentality that I wanted to study.

Q: And to study this object or the different objects that you studied, you used an historical method. But really what everyone sees today, and moreover, what for the most part makes for the originality of your analyses, not from the point of view of content but from the methodological point of view, is that you have operated a sort of displacement in historical method. That is, it is no longer the history of science, no longer an epistemology, no longer the history of ideologies, it is not even the history of institutions; one has the impression that it is all that at once but that in order to think about what psychiatry does, for example, or what criminologists do today—since criminologists called you here today—or in order to think about institutions such as prisons, asylums, etc..., you had to profoundly transform the way in which one conceived of history.

Does, for example, the opposition between knowledge and science that appears in your work and mainly in a number of your more methodological writings, seem to you more important from the perspective of the kind of history you are proposing to us?

MF: Well, I think, really, that the type of history I do carries a number of marks or handicaps, if you will. First, the thing that I would like to say is that the question I start off with is: what are we and what are we today? What is this instant that is ours? Therefore, if you like, it is a history that starts off from this present day actuality. The second thing is that in trying to raise concrete problems, what concerned me was to choose a field containing a number of points that are particularly fragile or sensitive at the present time. I would hardly conceive of a properly speculative history without the field being determined by something happening right now. So, the entire concern is not, of course, to follow what is happening and keep up with what is called fashion. Thus, for example, once one has written ten books, ten very good books, for that matter, on death, one doesn't have to write an eleventh one. One is not going to write an eleventh one, using as a pretext that it's a present day issue. The game is to try to detect those things which have not yet been talked about, those things that, at the present time, introduce, show, give some more or less vague indications of the fragility of our system of thought, in our way of reflecting, in our practices. Around 1955 when I was working in psychiatric hospitals, there was a kind of latent crisis, one felt very clearly that something was peeling off about which little had been said to date. It was, however, being experienced rather intensely. The best proof that this was being felt is that next door, in England, without ever having had any relationship with each other, people like Laing and Cooper were battling the very same problems. It is therefore a history which always refers to an actuality. As for the problem of medicine, it is true that the problem of medical power—in any case of the institutional field within which medical knowledge operates—was a question that was beginning to be asked, and was in fact widely discussed in the 1960s and which did not enter the public arena until after 1968. It is therefore history of actuality in the process of taking shape.

Q: Yes, but in terms of this actuality, the manner in which you tell its story seems original to me. It seems to be regulated by the very object you are analyzing. It is because of these key problems of our society that you are led to re-do history in a specific way.

MF: Fine. So, in terms of the objectives I set forth in this history, people often judge what I have done to be a sort of complicated, rather excessive analysis which leads to this result that finally we are imprisoned in our own system. The chords which bind us are numerous and the knots history has tied around us are oh so difficult to untie. In fact, I do just the opposite when I studied something like madness or prisons... Take the example of the prison: when we were discussing the reform of the penal system, a few years ago, say in the beginning of the 1970s, one thing that struck me in particular was that we could ask the theoretical question about the right to administer punishment or, on the other hand, we could deal with the problem of the re-organization of the penitentiary regime; but the kind of obvious fact that depriving people of their liberty is really the simplest, most logical, most reasonable, most equitable form of punishing someone for an infraction of the law, this was not very much discussed. So what I wanted to do was to show how much finally this equivalence—which for us is clear and simple—between punishment and depriving people of their liberty is in reality something relatively recent. It's a technical invention whose origins are distant but which was truly integrated into the penal system and became part of penal rationality by the end of the 18th century. And I have since then tried to find out the reasons why the prison then became a sort of obvious part of our penal system. It is a matter of making things more fragile through this historical analysis, or rather of showing both why and how things were able to establish themselves as such, and showing at the same time that they were established through a precise history. It is therefore necessary to place strategic logic inside the things from whence they were produced, to show that nonetheless, these are only strategies and therefore, by changing a certain number of things, by changing strategies, taking things differently, finally what appears obvious to us is not at all so obvious. Our relationship to madness is an historically established relationship, and from the second that it is historically constituted, it can be politically destroyed. I say politically in the very wide sense of the term, in any case, there are possibilities for action because it is through many actions, reactions, etc... through many battles, many conflicts to respond to a certain number of problems, that specific solutions are chosen. I wanted to reintegrate a lot of obvious facts of our practices in the historicity of some of these practices and thereby rob them of their evidentiary status, in order to give them back the mobility that they had and that they should always have.

Q: Yes, in one of your present lectures, you use the term "veridiction" which refers to telling the truth and which touches on the problem of truth in the method. In what you just said concerning both your interest in actuality and the manner in which you envision history and its very constitution at the heart of this actuality, you question what one might consider the bases of one practice or another. About power, you said that power does not really function from its basis but that there are always justifications or philosophical reflections that aim at founding power. Your historical method, which is a method which performs a kind of archeology or genealogy according to the objects or the very development of your thought, aims at showing that finally, there are no bases for the practices of power. Would you agree in saying that from the philosophical perspective and in the entirety of your development, that what you aim at is also deconstructing any enterprise which would aim at giving power a basis?

MF: But I think that the activity of giving a basis to power is an activity that is made up of investigating what founds the powers I use or what can found the power that is used over me. I think that this question is important, essential. I would even say that this is the fundamental question. But the basis one gives in response to this question is part of the historical field within which it has a very relative place, that is to say, one does not find the foundation. It is very important that in a culture such as ours—as to whether or not one can find it in another culture I have no idea—since not only for centuries but for millenia, a number of things, like the exercise of political power, interrogate themselves or are interrogated by people who ask the question: but what are they doing?...There is critical work there.

Q: But what you find important is precisely the critical work of this question that keeps coming back.

MF: The basis of political power has been investigated for the last two millenia. When I say two millenia, I mean two millenia and a half. And it is this interrogation which is fundamental.

Q: And really the type of history you have done is very much an analysis of strategies, but also an analysis of the way in which a number of practices sought out their own basis.

MF: Absolutely. I am going to use a barbarous word but words are only barbarous when they do not clearly say what they mean; it is known that many familiar words are barbarous because they say many things at once or say nothing at all, but, on the other hand, certain technical words which are bizarre in their construction are not barbarous because they say fairly clearly what they mean. I will say that it's the history of *problematizations,* that is, the history of the way in which things become a problem. How, why and in what exact way, does madness become a problem in the modern world, and why has it become an important one? It is such an important problem that a number of things, for example, psychoanalysis (and God knows how much it is spread throughout our entire culture), take off from a problem which is absolutely contained within the relationships that one could have with madness. No, you know, it's the history of these problems. In what new way did illness become a problem; illness which was obviously always a problem. But, it seems to me, that there is a new way of problematizing illness starting with the 18th and 19th centuries.

So, it is not, in fact, the history of theories or the history of ideologies or even the history of mentalities that interests me, but the history of problems, moreover, if you like, it is the genealogy of problems that concerns me. Why a problem and why such a kind of problem, why a certain way of problematizing appears at a given point in time. For example, in the area of sexuality, it took me a very long time to perceive how one could answer that one: what the new problem was. You see, in terms of sexuality, it is not enough to indefinitely repeat the question: was it Christianity or was it industrialization that led to sexual repression? Repression of sexuality is only interesting where on one hand, it makes many people suffer, even today, and on the other hand, it has always taken on different forms but has always existed. What seems to me to be an important element to elucidate is how and why this relationship to sexuality, or this relationship with our sexual behaviours became a problem and what forms of it became a problem since it was always a problem. But it is certain that it was not the same kind of problem for the Greeks in the 4th century B.C. as it was for the Christians in the 3rd and 4th centuries, or in the 16th, 17th, etc...You know, this history of problematizations in human practices, there is a point where in some way the certainties all mix together, the lights go out, night falls, people begin to realize that they act blindly and that consequently a new light is necessary, new lighting and new rules of behaviour are needed. So, there it is, an object appears, an object that appears as a problem, voilà...

Q: I would like to ask you one last question. You were invited here by the Law School and you are now particularly interested in law and the juridical phenomenon. Can you briefly explain where this interest comes from and what you hope to get out of it?

MF: Listen, I have always been interested in the law, as a "layman"; I am not a specialist in rights, I am not a lawyer or jurist. But just as with madness, crime and prisons, I encountered the problem of rights, the law and the question that I always asked was how the technology or technologies of government, how these relations of power understood in the sense we discussed before, how all this could take shape within a society that pretends to function according to law and which, partly at least, functions by the law. So, these are connections, relationships of cause and effect, conflicts, too, and oppositions, irreducibilities between this functioning of the law and this technology of power, that is what I would like to study. It seems to me that it can be of interest to investigate juridical institutions, the discourse and practice of law from these technologies of power—not at all in the sense that this would totally shake up history and the theory of law, but rather that this could illuminate some rather important aspects of judicial practices and theories. Thus, to interrogate the modern penal system starting with corrective practices, starting with all these technologies that had to be modeled, modified, etc...the criminal individual, it seems to me that this allows many things to appear clearly. Therefore, if you like, I never stop getting into the issue of law and rights without taking it as a particular object. And if God grants me life, after madness, illness, crime, sexuality, the last thing that I would like to study would be the problem of war and the institution of war in what one could call the military dimension of society. There again I would have to cross into the problem of law, the rights of people and international law, etc...as well as the question of military justice: what makes a Nation entitled to ask someone to die for it.

Q: Indeed we hope that God will grant you life, so that we can read your histories, these multiple histories that have so enriched us. I thank you.

Translated by Lysa Hochroth

50

PROBLEMATICS

Q: Both Max Weber and Jürgen Habermas locate their analysis of modern domination against the background of increasing rationalization of productive forces in society. You locate the conditions for economic rationality within a much broader array of social practices, and speak about local strategies of power. Would you say, nonetheless, that capitalist modes of production are the major generative force of modern domination?

MF: I am a little hesitant to use the word *domination* because domination, as far as I understand it, refers to a certain type of society in which a certain class or group exercises power over others. Certainly those forms of domination exist, in our society and in other societies. But I don't think that we have to analyse all power relations as a consequence of the dominance situation. Domination is a particular case within the different possibilities of power relations. You can have a power relation without this type of domination. But what makes me uncomfortable with these analyses—at least those by Habermas—is the fact that when he speaks about power, he always understands it as domination. And he translates "power" by "domination." Well, in our society there are production-relations, communications-relations and power-relations. By themselves neither production-relations, nor communications-relations, nor power-relations are bad or good. They exist, and you cannot live in any kind of society without these three different kinds of relations. They are not independent of one another, since we cannot have any kind of production-relations without communications-relations and without power-relations. But it is important to note that if they are not independent of one another, neither are they isomorphic. They have their own form, their own shape, and their own rules.

What I have tried to summarize are the kinds of power–relations which exist in our society, the ways in which they are related to other systems of relations, and the extent to which power–relations are embedded in our habits, behaviors, institutions, rules, political systems, and the extent to which these relations conform to the goals and values which these institutions, practices and habits take as their justification.

Take the problem of madness, for example. There are medical institutions which have as their goal the cure of mental illness. They imply, as the final value, mental health. And they propose technical and institutional ways to bring forth this value and obtain the goal of curing the mentally ill. And so for the past two centuries the mental hospital has been considered mandatory.

Are the power relations which are embedded in mental institutions, or even in the personal relations between the psychiatrist and his patient, in conformity with these goals? There are far too many power–relations, far too many dominations, in these institutions regarding their goals and their values. I would consider domination to be any kind of power-relation which, regarding its goals and values, can be judged from a rational point of view as efficient.

Q: One of the things that both interests and troubles people about your work is the question of capitalism. Clearly, for you capitalism is not the broadest grid of interpretation available to the understanding of society. One thinks immediately of Weber's idea of rationalization as a grid of intelligibility which is broader than capitalism, and one finds these processes in socialist societies and presumably in post–capitalist societies as well.

MF: These days we are more and more aware that capitalism was not at the root of every political or cultural institution that has produced changes in our society, first, because capitalism is an economic process which can take place in very different societies. There was a capitalism in Chinese society, and you find a kind of capitalism in Roman society, and so on. And on the other hand, one can say that some of the great institutions, and some of the great political and social structures in our society were developed before capitalism, and were, in fact, a condition of the development of capitalism.

Can we really consider that the political form which we call the State was an effect of capitalism, or on the contrary, that it was a condition of the development of capitalism? In speaking about our capitalism, it is very difficult to attribute all of the various institutions in the political field to capitalism as its main cause. There is a nexus of reciprocal relations, and our histories are very particular. We can refer everything in our society to capitalism if we consider that capitalism is not the economical root or principle of everything, but if we consider modern capitalism as an historical figure or field with its own identity. My second point is a generalization from this: I don't think that it is very interesting or very useful to use such categories as "capitalism" or "feudalism" in order to analyze any society. These are very specific formations, and it is the historians' task to analyse them in their specificity.

Q: One of the dramatic shifts in your recent work has been from a view of power as reductive and constraining, to one in which a number of different routes—metaphorically, activities of production, creation, expression, proliferation, and so on—demarcate power-relations.

MF: Yes. I would like to disconnect the notion of power from the notion of domination. Domination is only one form of power–relation. I should also note that power has to be de–connected from the notion of repression. There are a lot of power–relations which have repression–effects, but there are also a lot of power–relations which have something else entirely as their consequence.

Q: This is a question about mental institutions and reform. How do you respond to statements like "there are people out there who are suffering, what is to be done about it?"

MF: Sometimes people have read my book about madness as if I had written that madness does not exist, or that madness was either a myth in medical and psychiatric discourse, or that it was a consequence of mental institutions. I have never said that madness does not exist, or that it is only a consequence of these institutions. That people are suffering, that people make trouble in society or in families, that is a reality. What I have tried to analyse are the ways these conditions, and the context in which this kind of suffering—delirium, persecution, etc—are problematized as an illness, a mental illness, something which has to be cured inside such institutions and by such institutions.

It is not a critical history which has as its aim to demonstrate that behind this so–called knowledge there is only mythology, or perhaps nothing at all. My analysis is about the problematization of something which is real, but that problematization is something which is dependent on our knowledge, ideas, theories, techniques, social relations and economical processes. What I have tried to do is to analyze this kind of problematisation as it conforms to the objectives which it presupposes.

Q: What does the analysis of how mental illness has been problematized do for individuals to relieve their suffering?

MF: That's exactly the question I asked. Since there is this suffering, and since there are these practices and this kind of knowledge and these kinds of institutions that are supposed to effect a cure, are they really doing something? In many cases the sequestration of the patient is seen as the key, or the means, to suppress their sufferings. There are even cases in which the separation of the patient from his or her suffering would be a good thing.

There is also the question about intentions. In spite of what Laurence Stone has written,[1] I have never said that there were plots or conspiracies by doctors and physicians in the 19th century, or today, to take power in our society.

Q: There are studies that indicate that very few people are cured as a result of analysis, and that even those who are cured are controlled, and there is no increase in their pleasure or well being. To what do you attribute this failure of psychoanalysis?

MF: I have never said that there was a "failure of psychoanalysis." But I think that Freud was never the target of this criticism. The European Freud—the Austrian Freud—was much more worried about anxiety. His problem concerned the increase of anxiety, not the increase of pleasure. His problem was how to get people to get rid of their anxiety, and not to help people to get more pleasure than they have.

Q: There is also a question of motives. In *Discipline and Punish* you note that during the Enlightenment there were two dimensions of the heritage of Rome. One was the welfare state, taking care of the welfare of the citizen and the associated liberties that go along with that, and the other was the discipline of the Roman army camps. One of the contradictions in the way power has worked in the modern world is that this discourse about freedom, individualism, and liberty has proceeded along with the spread of discipline and disciplinary organizations, and that this is no accident. If there is not a causal relationship here, at least there is some complicity.

MF: During the 18th century there were different ways of considering the problem of political society. One of these was juridical: what are the rules, the problems, and the justifications for the existence of the sovereign, or of sovereignty in political society? Who is entitled to exercise power? We find that in Hobbes, for example. The historians and theoreticians of political thought have focused on this side of the problem, but there was also another problem which was quite different. It wasn't a problem of foundations or justification, of rules and of sovereignty, it was a technical problem: how can power be exercized in the best and most efficient way in society. This kind of technical problem, of how to use power, of which rational principles to follow, through which techniques, was also of great importance.

In Locke, at the beginning of the 17th century, we find both a reflection on the foundations of sovereignty, and on the practice of power. You find similar reflections about sovereignty in many of the important authors throughout the eighteenth century, in the Physiocrats, for instance. They were considered to be the first economists, the first theoreticians of economics, since they sought to analyse economic processes in society, how wealth comes about and circulates. Their economic analyses were a critique of the way societies were governed in those great states such as France and Austria, in order to propose another kind of government, and different types of power–relations in society. They were both theoreticians of economy and of power. If you read Adam Smith, it's the same. I think that you can read a lot writers in the eighteenth century as theoreticians of this aspect of the political problem. In this framework or field of analysis of power–relations the problem was the equilibrium between what is free, what has to be free, and what has to be regulated. In the economical framework, the problem was very clear: how far should the State actually control family life, sexuality, marriage, rates of birth, health and so on. Health is an interesting problem. Health, of course, is a public problem, since the strength of the State depends for a large part on the health of people. So, to what extent does the State become involved in public health? The relation of freedom and regulation are again a kind of problematization. First, you must give people a much larger degree of freedom in order to let them act as they want in the economic field. At the same time you must exert more and more control over them in their private, moral behavior. All of the interventions of the State, of royal power and royal administration in the field of clinical activity, perform this task.

You can see that on a small scale with the problem of crime. At first the penal system was much too heavy, the punishments were much too severe for very small crimes. At the same time they were conscious that this severe penal system was completely inefficient. And there were a lot of new crimes in our system. So people had to be controlled much more precisely, to both allow more freedom and to aspire to a much more efficient system of control. I think that you cannot understand the program of liberation from the pure point of view of political theory and the foundation of control. The question that has to be raised is how necessary this system of strict control is for our freedom.

Take, for example, the sex–life. In the 1950s one could read, in good Marxist books, that it was impossible for socialist societies to develop and to exist without a very strong, very strict, very repressive family life. If we now compare—25 or 30 years later—what's going on in our society with the situation in socialist countries you can see that capitalist states are not at all compromised or in danger from sexual freedom. But in socialist countries the relation is different, and the socialist control of private life seems much stronger than in the capitalist countries.

Q: What about the relationship between responsibility and freedom on the social level?

MF: Most of those social controls have been justified by invoking the idea of responsibility. For instance, if you read these incredibly boring books about masturbation and eroticism from the beginning of the 19th century, you can see the explanations given to children about the dangers of masturbation –if you masturbate you won't be able to have normal children, and you are responsible towards your family, your city, your country and towards mankind in general.

Q: You have been talking about a "history of problematics." What do you mean by this?

MF: For a long time I have been trying to see if it would be possible to describe the history of thought as distinct from both the history of ideas—by which I mean the analysis of systems of representation—and from the history of mentalities—by which I mean the analysis of attitudes and types of action and behavior. It seems to me that there was one element that was capable of describing the history of thought: this was what one would call the element of problems, or more precisely, problematisations. What distinguishes thought is that it is something quite different from the set of representations that underlies a certain behavior; it is also something quite different from the domain of attitudes that can determine this behavior. Thought is not what inhabits a certain conduct and gives it its meaning; rather, it is what allows one to step back from this way of acting or reacting, to present it to oneself as an object of thought and to question it as to its meaning, its conditions and its goals. Thought is freedom in relation to what one does, the motion by which one detaches oneself from it, establishes it as an object, and reflects on it as a problem.

To say that the study of thought is the analysis of a freedom does not mean one is dealing with a formal system that has reference only to itself. Actually, for a field of action, a behavior, to enter the domain of thought, it is necessary for a certain number of factors to have made it uncertain, to have made it lose its familiarity, or to have provoked a certain number of difficulties around it. These elements result from social, economic or political processes. But here their only role is that of instigation. They can exist and perform their action for a very long time, before there is effective problematisation by thought. And when thought intervenes, it doesn't assume a unique form that is the direct result or the necessary expression of these difficulties; it is an original or specific response—often taking many forms, sometimes even contradictory in its different aspects—to these difficulties, which are defined for it by a situation or a context and which hold true as a possible question.

To one single set of difficulties, several responses can be made. And most of the time different responses are actually proposed. But what has to be understood is what makes them simultaneously possible: it is the point in which their simultaneity is rooted; it is the soil that can nourish them in all their diversity and sometimes in spite of their contradictions. To the different difficulties encountered by the practice regarding mental illness in the 18th century, diverse solutions were proposed: Tuke's and Pinel's are examples; in the same way, a whole group of solutions was proposed for the difficulties encountered in the second half of the 18th century by the penal practice; or again, to take a very remote example, the diverse schools of philosophy of the Hellenistic period proposed different solutions to the difficulties of traditional sexual ethics.

But the work of a history of thought would be to rediscover at the root of these diverse solutions the general form of problematisation that has made them possible—even in their very opposition; or what has made possible the transformations of the difficulties and obstacles of a practice into a general problem for which one proposes diverse practical solutions. It is problematisation that responds to these difficulties, but by doing something quite other than expressing them or manifesting them: in connection with them it develops the conditions in which possible responses can be given; it defines the elements that will constitute what the different solutions attempt to respond to. This development of a given into a question, this transformation of a group of obstacles and difficulties into problems to which the diverse solutions will attempt to produce a response, this is what constitutes the point of problematisation and the specific work of thought.

It is clear how far one is from an analysis in terms of deconstruction Rather, it is a question of a movement of critical analysis in which one tries to see how the different solutions to a problem have been constructed; but also how these different solutions result from a specific form of problematisation.

---

[1] Laurence Stone, "Madness," *New York Review of Books,* December 16, 1982, 36 ff; see also the subsequent "Exchange" between Foucault and Stone, *New York Review of Books*, March 31, 1983, pp 42–44.

51

WHAT CALLS FOR PUNISHMENT?

Q: Your book *Discipline and Punish,* published in 1974, fell like a meteor onto the domain of criminology and penal studies. Proposing an analysis of the penal system in the perspective of political tactics and the technology of power, this work collided with traditional conceptions of delinquency and the social function of punishment. It has troubled repressive judges, at least those who examine the meaning of their work; it has shaken up a number of criminologists who hardly enjoyed having their discourse described as idle chatter. Increasingly rare today are books on criminology that don't refer to *Discipline and Punish* as an incontrovertible work. However, the penal system doesn't change and the "idle chatter" of criminologists continues invariably, as if one rendered homage to the theoretician of juridico-penal epistemology without being able to learn from his teachings, as if a totally airtight barrier existed between theory and practice. No doubt your intention was not to be a reformer, but can one imagine a politics of criminology that would take support from your analysis and try to draw from it certain lessons?

MF: Perhaps I first ought to explain precisely what I intended to do in this book. I didn't want to write a directly critical work, if one means by "critical" the denunciation of the drawbacks of today's penal system. Nor did I want to write an historical work about the institution, in the sense that I did not want to recount how the penal and carceral institution functioned in the course of the 19th century. I tried to raise another problem: to discover the system of thought, the form of rationality, which since the end of the 18th century has underlain the idea that the prison, in sum, is the best means, one of the most efficient and most rational, to punish infractions in a society. It is clear that in doing this I had certain preoccupations concerning what one could do now. Indeed, it often appeared to me that in opposing society as one usually did through reformism and revolution, one did not give oneself the means to think what could yield to a real, profound and radical transformation. It seems to me that very often in the reforms of the penal system one accepted implicitly and sometimes even explicitly the system of rationality that had been defined and put into place a long time ago, and that one tried simply to know what the institutions and the practices would be that would permit realization of the project and attainment of its ends. By isolating the system of rationality underlying punitive practices, I wanted to indicate what postulates of thought it was necessary to reexamine if one wanted to transform the penal system.

I do not say that one had necessarily to free oneself from them; but I believe that it is very important when one wants to do a work of transformation to know not only what are the institutions and their real effects, but equally what is the type of thought that sustains them: what can one still accept of this system of rationality? What part, on the contrary, deserves to be set aside, transformed, or abandoned? I had tried to do the same thing in regard to the history of psychiatric institutions. And it's true that I have been somewhat surprised and fairly disappointed to realize that so little resulted from reflection and thought that could have managed to assemble around the same problem, very different people: judges, theoreticians of penal law, employees of penitentiary institutions, lawyers, social workers, and people with prison experience. It's true, no doubt for social and cultural reasons, that the 1970s have been extremely disappointing. Many criticisms have been launched in every direction; often these ideas have had some influence, but rarely have questions, collectively raised, crystallized, to determine enough what transformations are to be made. In any case, for my part and despite my desire, I have never had the possibility of a working contact with any professor of penal law, any judge, or any political party—that's obvious. Thus the Socialist Party, founded in 1972, which for nine years was able to prepare its assumption to power and which to a certain point echoed in its discourse several themes developed in the course of the 1960s and 1970s, never made a serious attempt to define in advance what its real practice would be when it came to power. It seems institutions, groups and political parties that might have been able to promote this kind of reflection did nothing...

Q: One gives the impression that the conceptual system hasn't evolved at all. Although jurists and psychiatrists recognize the pertinence and the novelty of your analyses, they stumble, it would seem, on the impossibility of translating into practice and into research what is ambiguously called "a politics of criminality."

MF: You are raising a problem that indeed is very important and difficult. You know that I belong to a generation of people that has seen most of the utopias framed in the 19th century and at the beginning of the 20th century collapse in succession, and likewise the perverse and sometimes disastrous effects that follow from projects most generous in their intentions. I have always resisted playing the role of the intellectual prophet who tells people in advance what they must do and prescribes the frameworks of thought, the objectives and the means—all drawn from his own brain while working in an office among his books. It has seemed to me that the work of an intellectual, what I call a "specific intellectual," is to try to isolate, in their power of constraint but also in the contingency of their historical formation, the systems of thought that have now become familiar to us, that appear evident to us, and that have become part of our perceptions, attitudes and behavior. Next, it is necessary to work in common with practitioners, not only to modify institutions and practices but to elaborate forms of thought.

Q: What you have called the "idle chatter of criminologists," which has been poorly understood, is it precisely the fact that this system of thought in which all these analyses have been carried out for a century and a half has not been challenged?

MF: Yes, that's it. Perhaps that phrase was a little too off-hand. Let's take it back then. But I have the impression that the difficulties and contradictions that penal practice has experienced over the last two centuries have never been deeply re-examined. And now, one hundred and fifty years later, the same notions, the same themes, the same reproaches, the same criticisms, the same demands are being repeated, as if nothing had changed, and in a sense, indeed nothing has. From the moment when an institution presents so many drawbacks, arouses so much criticism, and can only give rise to the indefinite repetition of the same discourse, "idle chatter" is a serious symptom.

Q: In *Discipline and Punish,* you analyze this "strategy" which consists in transforming some illegalisms into delinquency, making a success out of this apparent failure of the prison. It's as if a "group" more or less consciously used this means to arrive at certain effects which would not be announced. One has the impression, perhaps false, that it's a ruse of power that subverts the projects and undermines the discourse of humanist reformers. From this point of view, there would be some similarity between your analysis and the model of Marxist interpretation of history (I am thinking of the paper in which you show that a certain type of illegalism is singled out for expression whereas others are tolerated). But one does not see clearly, in contrast with Marxism, what "group" or what "class" or what interests are at work in this strategy.

MF: Different things must be distinguished in the analysis of an institution. First, what one could call its rationality or its end, that is to say the objectives that it proposes and the means it has of reaching these objectives; in short, the program of the institution as it has been defined; for example, Bentham's conception of the prison. Secondly, there is the question of effect. Obviously the effects only rarely coincide with the ends; thus the objective of the corrective prison, of the means of rehabilitating the individual, has not been met; the effect has been rather the reverse, and the prison has dealt rather with the behavior of delinquency. But when the effect does not coincide with the end there are several possibilities: either one reforms or one utilizes these effects for something that wasn't foreseen at the beginning but which can well have a meaning and a use. This is what one could call the usage: the prison, unable to rehabilitate, has served rather as a mechanism of elimination. The fourth level of the analysis is what one could call the "strategic configurations"—in other words, beginning from these usages in some new and unforeseen way, one can construct new rational behaviors, different from the initial program but which fulfil their objective, and in which play between different social groups can take place.

Q: Effects that are themselves transformed into ends.

MF: That's right. They are effects that are taken up in different usages and these usages are rationalized, organized in any case by means of new ends.

Q: But that's obviously not premeditated. There's no occult Machiavellian project at the base.

MF: Not at all. There's no person or group, no titular head of this strategy; but a number of strategies are formed from effects which differ from their initial ends and from the capacity to utilize these effects.

Q: Strategies whose finality partly escapes in its turn those who conceive them.

MF: Yes. Sometimes these strategies are completely conscious: one can say that the way in which the police use the prison is almost conscious. These strategies are simply not formulated, in contrast to the program. The institution's first program, its initial finality is on the contrary displayed and used as justification, while the strategic configurations are not often clear in the very eyes of those who occupy a place and play a role there. But this play is perfectly capable of solidifying an institution, and the prison has been solidified, despite all the criticisms that have been made, because several strategies of different groups have come to intersect at this particular place.

Q: You explain very clearly how from the beginning of the 20th century the penalty of imprisonment was denounced as the great failure of penal justice, and in the same terms as is done today. There is no penal expert who is not convinced that the prison does not attain the ends it was given: the rate of criminality doesn't diminish; far from "socializing," the prison produces delinquents. It increases the recidivism; it doesn't guarantee security. Yet the penitentiary establishments are always full, and one sees no initiation of a change, in this regard, under the socialist government in France.

But at the same time you have turned around the question. Rather than searching for the reasons for a perennial failure, you are asking what this problematic failure serves, and who profits from it. You discover that the prison is an instrument of differential management and the control of illegalisms. In this sense, far from constituting a failure the prison on the contrary has succeeded perfectly in specifying a certain delinquency, that of the popular classes, in producing a determined category of delinquents, and in circumscribing them better to disassociate them from other categories of lawbreakers coming notably from the bourgeoisie.

Finally, you observe that the carceral system succeeds in rendering legitimate the legal power to punish, which it "naturalizes." This idea is linked to the old question of the legitimacy and the foundation of punishment, for the exercise of disciplinary power does not exhaust the power of punishment, even if that's its major function, as you have shown.

MF: Let's set aside, if you like, several misunderstandings. First, in this book on the prison it is clear that I did not want to raise the question of the foundations of the right to punish. What I wanted to show is the fact that, starting from a certain conception of the basis of the right to punish, one can find in the work of penal experts and philosophers of the 18th century that different means of punishment were perfectly conceivable. Indeed, in the reform movement of the second half of the 18th century, one finds a whole spectrum of means to punish that are suggested, and finally it happens that the prison was in some way the privileged one. It has not been the only means, but it became nonetheless one of the principle ones. My problem was to know why this means was chosen. And how this means of punishing reoriented not only judicial practice but even a number of rather fundamental problems in penal law. Thus the importance given to the psychological aspects or the psychopathology of the criminal personality, which is affirmed all along in the 19th century, and which was to a certain degree extrapolated from a punitive practice that took rehabilitation as its end and encountered only the impossibility of rehabilitating. I therefore left the problem of the basis of the right to punish to the side, in order to make another problem appear, which was I believe more often neglected by historians: the means of punishment and their rationality. But that does not mean that the question of the foundations of punishment is not important. On this point I believe that one must be radical and moderate at the same time, and recall what Nietzsche said over a century ago, to wit, that in our contemporary societies we no longer know what we are doing when we punish and what principle, at bottom, can justify punishment. Everything happens as if we carry out a punishment by allowing a number of heterogeneous ideas, at different layers of sedimentation and stemming from different histories, distinct movements and divergent rationalities, to prevail.

I have not spoken about the foundations for the right to punish it's not because I consider it to be unimportant: I think that one of the most fundamental tasks would be to rethink the meaning that one can give to legal punishment today, in its articulation with law, morality and the institution.

Q: The problem of defining punishment is all the more complex because not only do we not know exactly what it is to punish but it seems that we are loathe to do it. Indeed, judges more and more refrain from punishing; they intend to care for, treat, re-educate, and cure, as if they were trying to exculpate themselves from exercising repression. In *Discipline and Punish,* moreover, you write that "penal and psychiatric discourse blur their boundaries." And, "Thus is established, with the multiplicity of scientific discourses, a difficult and infinite relationship, which penal justice today is not ready to control.

The maker of justice is no longer the master of truth." Today resorting to psychiatry, to psychology and to social welfare is routine judiciary fact, as much penal as civil. You analyze phenomena that no doubt indicate an epistemological change in the juridico-penal sphere. The meaning of penal justice seems to have changed. The judge applies the penal code to a lawbreaker less and less; and more and more treats pathologies and disturbances of the personality.

MF: I think you're right. Why has penal justice established these relationships with psychiatry, which ought to greatly hinder it? For obviously, between the problematics of psychiatry and what is requested by the very practice of penal law concerning responsibility, I would not say there is contradiction but heterogeneity. They are two forms of thought that are not on the same level, and consequently one doesn't see by what rule one could utilize the other, yet it is certain—and it's a striking thing since the 19th century—that penal justice, which one would have expected to distrust psychiatric, psychological and medical thought enormously, instead seems to have been fascinated by it.

Of course there were resistances and conflicts; I wouldn't underestimate them. But finally, if one takes a longer period of time, a century and a half, it seems that penal justice has been very accommodating, and increasingly so to these forms of thought. It is reasonable that the psychiatric problematics have sometimes hampered penal justice. It seems that today it facilitates it by allowing it to leave in a state of equivocation the question of knowing what we do when we punish.

Q: You observe in the last pages of *Discipline and Punish* that the disciplinary technique has become one of the major functions of our society, that power attains its highest degree of intensity in the penitential institution. You say on the other hand that the prison does not remain necessarily indispensable to a society like ours, for it can lose much of its raison d'être, in a setting where mechanisms of normalization are more and more numerous. Could one therefore conceive of a society without prisons? This utopia begins to be taken rather seriously by certain criminologists. For example, Louk Hulsman, a professor of penal law at the University of Rotterdam and an expert on the United Nations, defends a theory of the abolition of the penal system. The reasoning that founds this theory brings together some of your analyses: the penal system creates the delinquent; it ends up being fundamentally incapable of realizing the social finalities that it allegedly pursues; every reform is illusory; the only coherent solution is its abolition. Louk Hulsman notes that a majority of offenses escape the penal system without endangering society. That being the case, he proposes to de-criminalize systematically the major part of the acts and behaviors that the law establishes as a crime offense, and to substitute for the concept of crime that of the "problem-situation." Instead of punishing and stigmatizing, try to regulate conflicts through procedures of arbitration and nonjudicial conciliation. Look at infractions as social risks, the essential being the indemnification of the victims. The intervention of the judicial apparatus would be reserved for serious matters, or as the last recourse in the case of failure in attempts of reconciliation or solutions by civil law. Louk Hulsman's theory is one of those that assumes a cultural revolution. What do you think of this idea of abolition that I have schematically summarized? Can possible extensions of *Discipline and Punish* be seen there?

MF: I think Hulsman's thesis is enormously interesting, even if it only challenges the foundation of the right to punish by asserting that there is no longer any reason to do so. I also find very interesting the fact that he raises this question in terms of the means by which one responds to what is considered an infraction. In other words, the question of means is not simply a consequence of what might be raised concerning the foundations of the right to punish; for him the reflection on these foundation and the way one reacts to an infraction must be part of the same thing. All that appears to be very stimulating and important. Perhaps I am not sufficiently familiar with his work, but I would ask about the following points. Is the notion of problem-situations not going to lead to a psychologizing of both the question and the reaction? Doesn't a practice like this one risk—even if it's not what he wants—leading to a kind of dissociation between on the one hand, the social, collective and institutional reactions to the crime thereby considered an accident and regulated in the same way, and then, on the other hand, a hyper-psychologizing of the criminal himself casting him as the object of psychiatric or medical interventions with a therapeutic intent?

Q: But won't this conception of the crime lead to the abolition of notions of responsibility and guilt? To the extent to which evil exists in our society, does not the consciousness of guilt, which according to Ricoeur was born with the Greeks, fill a necessary social function? Can one conceive of a society exonerated from every feeling of guilt?

MF: I don't think that the question is to know if a society can function without guilt but if a society can make guilt function as an organizing principle and foundation of a law. And that's where the question becomes difficult.

Paul Ricoeur is perfectly right to raise the problem of moral conscience, and he does it as a philosopher or historian of philosophy. It is perfectly legitimate to say that guilt exists, and that it has existed since a given time. One can discuss whether the feeling of guilt comes from the Greeks or has another origin. In any case, guilt exists and one doesn't see how a society like ours, still so strongly rooted in a tradition which is also that of the Greeks, could dispense with it. It has been possible for a very long time to consider whether or not one could directly articulate a system of law and a judicial institution onto a notion like that of guilt. For us, on the contrary, the question is open.

Q: Today, when an individual appears before one or another instance of penal justice, he must account not only for the forbidden act he has committed but also for his very life.

MF: It's true. In the United States, for example, indeterminate penalties have been much discussed. Almost everywhere, I believe, one has abandoned the practice, but it implied a certain tendency, a certain project that appears to me not to have disappeared; the tendency to make the penal judgement bear much more on a somehow quantitative level characterizing an existence and a manière d'être than on a specific act. There is also the measure passed recently in France concerning the implementation of punishments. One wanted to reinforce—and the intention is a good one—the power and control of the judiciary apparatus on the process of punishment. Which is good, because it diminishes the independence of the penitentiary institution. Only this is what it boils down to: there will now be a tribunal, three judges I think, who will decide whether or not conditional fredom can be accorded to a prisoner; and this decision will be made by taking into account elements in which there will be first the initial infraction, which will be revived in some way, since the civil party and the representatives of the victim will be present and will be able to intervene. And then one will integrate with that the elements of the individual's conduct in prison, such as have been observed, appreciated, interpreted, and judged by the guards, administrators, psychologists and doctors. It's this jumble of heterogeneous elements that will contribute to a judicial decision. Even if it is juridically acceptable, it is necessary to know what factual consequences all that will entail. And at the same time, what dangerous model that might present for penal justice in its current usage, if, in effect, a penal decision is usually dependent on good or bad conduct.

Q: The medicalization of justice leads little by little to a removal of the penal right of judiciary practices. The subject of law gives way to the neurotic or psychopath, more or less irresponsible, whose behavior would be determined by psycho-biological factors. In reaction against this conception, some penal experts envisage a return to the concept of punishment more susceptible to reconciliation with the respect of freedom and the dignity of the individual. It's not a question of returning to a system of brutal and mechanical punishment that would make an abstraction of the socio-economic regime in which it functions, and be ignorant of the social and political dimension of justice, but of recovering a conceptual coherence and of distinguishing between what stems from law and what from medicine. One thinks of Hegel's formula: "By considering that the penalty contains its law, one honors the criminal as a rational being."

MF: I believe that indeed the penal law is part of the social fabric in a society like ours, and that there's no reason to mask it. That means that individuals who are part of this society have to recognize each other as subjects of the law who as such are susceptible of being punished and chastised if they infringe upon some rule. There is nothing scandalous about that, I don't think. But it's the duty of society to act in such a way that concrete individuals can actually recognize each other as subjects of law. Which is difficult when the penal system used is archaic, arbitrary, and inadequate to the real problems that are posed to a society. Take for example the single domain of economic delinquency. The true a priori work is not to inject more and more medicine and psychiatry in order to modulate the system and make it more acceptable; it is necessary to rethink the penal system itself. I don't mean: let's return to the severity of the 1810 penal code; I mean let's return to the serious idea of a penal law that would clearly define what in a society like ours can be considered as necessary to punish, and what not; let's return to the very thought of a system defining the rules of social activity. I am suspicious of those who want to return to the system of 1810 under the pretext that medicine and psychiatry destroy the meaning of penal justice; but I am equally suspicious of those people who basically accept the system of 1810, simply by adjusting it, ameliorating it, and attenuating it through psychiatric and psychological modifications.

Translated by John Johnston

52

THE ETHICS OF THE CONCERN FOR SELF AS A PRACTICE OF FREEDOM

Q: First of all I would like to ask what is the focus of your current thinking. Having followed the latest developments in your thought, particularly your lectures at the Collège de France in 1981-82 on the hermeneutics of the subject, I would like to know if your current philosophical approach is still determined by the poles of subjectivity and truth.

MF: In actual fact, I have always been interested in this problem, even if I framed it somewhat differently. I have tried to find out how the human subject fits into certain games of truth, whether they were truth games that take the form of a science or refer to a scientific model, or truth games such as those one may encounter in institutions or practices of control. This is the theme of my book *The Order of Things,* in which I attempted to see how, in scientific discourses, the human subject defines itself as a speaking, living, working individual. In my courses at the Collège de France, I brought out the general outlines of this problematic.

Q: Isn't there a "break" between your former problematic and that of subjectivity/truth, particularly starting with the concept of the "care of the self"?

MF: Up to that point I had conceived the problem of the relationship between the subject and games of truth in terms either of coercive practices— such as those of psychiatry and the prison system—or of theoretical or scientific games—such as the analysis of the richness of language and of living beings. In my lectures at the Collège de France, I tried to grasp it in terms of what may be called a practice of the self; although this phenomenon has not been studied very much, I believe it has been fairly important in our societies ever since the Greco-Roman period. In the Greek and Roman civilizations, such practices of the self were much more important and especially more autonomous than they were later after they were taken over to a certain extent by religious, pedagogical, medical or psychiatric institutions.

Q: Thus there has been a sort of shift: these games of truth no longer involve a coercive practice, but a practice of self-formation of the subject.

MF: That's right. It is what one could call an ascetic practice, taking asceticism in a very general sense, in other words, not in the sense of a morality of renunciation but as an exercise of the self on the self, by which one attempts to develop and transform oneself, and to attain to a certain mode of being. Here I am taking asceticism in a more general sense than that attributed to it by Max Weber, for example, but along the same lines.

Q: A work of the self on the self that may be understood as a certain liberation, as a process of liberation?

MF: I would be more careful on that score. I have always been some-what suspicious of the notion of liberation, because if it is not treated with pre-cautions and within certain limits, one runs the risk of falling back on the idea that there exists a human nature or base that, as a consequence of certain histori-cal, economic and social processes, has been concealed, alienated or imprisoned in and by mechanisms of repression. According to this hypothesis, all that is required is to break these repressive deadlocks and man will be reconciled with himself, rediscover his nature or regain contact with his origin, and reestablish a full and positive relationship with himself. I think this idea should not be accepted without scrutiny. I am not trying to say that liberation as such, or this or that form of liberation, does not exist: when a colonized people attempts to liber-ate itself from its colonizers, this is indeed a practice of liberation in the strict sense. But we know very well, and moreover in this specific case, that this prac-tice of liberation is not in itself sufficient to define the practices of freedom that will still be needed if this people, this society and these individuals, are to be able to define admissible and acceptable forms of existence or political society. This is why I emphasize practices of freedom over processes of liberation; again, the latter indeed have their place but they do not seem to me to be capable by themselves of defining all the practical forms of freedom. This is precisely the problem I encountered with regard to sexuality: does it make any sense to say, "Let's liberate our sexuality"? Isn't the problem rather that of defining the practices of freedom by which one could define what is sexual pleasure and erotic, amorous and passionate relationships with others? This ethical problem of the definition of practices of freedom, it seems to me, is much more important than the rather repetitive affirmation that sexuality or desire must be liberated.

Q: But doesn't the exercise of practices of freedom require a certain degree of liberation?

MF: Yes, absolutely. And this is where we must introduce the concept of domination. The analyses that I am trying to make bear essentially on relations of power. By this I mean something different from states of domination. Power relations are extremely widespread in human relationships. Now this does not mean that political power is everywhere, but that there is in human relationships a whole range of power relations that may come into play among individuals, within families, in pedagogical relationships, political life, etc. The analysis of power relations is an extremely complex area; one sometimes encounters what may be called situations or states of domination in which the power relations, instead of being mobile, allowing the various participants to adopt strategies modifying them, remain blocked, frozen. When an individual or social group succeeds in blocking a field of power relations, immobilizing them and preventing any reversibility of movement by economic, political or military means, one is faced with what may be called a state of domination. In such a state, it is certain that practices of freedom do not exist or exist only unilaterally or are extremely constrained and limited. Thus I agree with you that liberation is sometimes the political or historical condition for a practice of freedom. Taking sexuality as an example, it is clear that a number of liberations were required vis-à-vis male power, that liberation was necessary from an oppressive morality concerning heterosexuality as well as homosexuality. But this liberation does not give rise to the happy human being imbued with a sexuality to which the subject could achieve a complete and satisfying relationship. Liberation paves the way for new power relationships, which must be controlled by practices of freedom.

Q: Can't liberation itself be a mode or form of practice of freedom?

MF: Yes, in some cases. You have situations where liberation and the struggle for liberation are indispensable for the practice of freedom. With respect to sexuality, for example—and I am not indulging in polemics, because I don't like polemics, I think they are usually futile—there is a Reichian model derived from a certain reading of Freud. Now, in Reich's view the problem was entirely one of liberation. To put it somewhat schematically, according to him there is desire, drive, prohibition, repression, internalization, and it is by getting rid of these prohibitions, in other words, by liberating oneself, that the problem gets resolved. I think—and I know I am vastly oversimplifying much more interesting and refined positions of many authors—this completely misses the ethical problem of the practice of freedom: how can one practice freedom? With regard to sexuality, it is obvious that it is by liberating our desire that we will learn to conduct ourselves ethically in pleasure relationships with others.

Q: You say that freedom must be practiced ethically...

MF: Yes, for what is ethics if not the practice of freedom, the conscious practice of freedom?

Q: In other words, you understand freedom as a reality that is already ethical in itself.

MF: Freedom is the ontological condition of ethics. But ethics is the form that freedom takes when it is informed by reflection.

Q: Ethics is what is achieved in the search for or the care of the self?

MF: In the Greco-Roman world, the care of the self was the mode in which individual freedom—or civic liberty, up to a point—was reflected as an ethics. If you take a whole series of texts going from the first Platonic dialogues up to the major texts of late Stoicism—Epictetus, Marcus Aurelius, etc.—you will see that the theme of the care of the self thoroughly permeated moral reflection. It is interesting to see that, in our societies on the other hand, at a time which is very difficult to pinpoint, the care of the self became somewhat suspect. Starting at a certain point, being concerned with oneself was readily denounced as a form of self-love, a form of selfishness or self-interest in contradiction with the interest to be shown in others or the self-sacrifice required. All this happened during Christianity; however, I am not simply saying that Christianity is responsible for it. The question is much more complex, for, with Christianity, achieving one's salvation is also a way of caring for oneself. But in Christianity salvation is attained through the renunciation of self. There is a paradox in the care of the self in Christianity—but that is another problem. To come back to the question you were talking about, I believe that among the Greeks and Romans—especially the Greeks—concern with the self and care of the self were required for right conduct and the proper practice of freedom, in order to know oneself—the familiar aspect of the *Gnothi seauton*—as well as to form oneself, to surpass oneself, to master the appetites that threaten to overwhelm one. Individual freedom was very important for the Greeks— contrary to the commonplace derived more or less from Hegel that sees it as being of no importance when placed against the imposing totality of the city. Not to be a slave (of another city, of the people around you, of those governing you, of your own passions) was an absolutely fundamental theme. The concern with freedom was an essential and permanent problem for eight full centuries of ancient culture. What we have here is an entire ethics revolving around the care of the self; this is what gives ancient ethics its particular form. I am not saying that ethics is synonymous with the care of the self, but that, in Antiquity, ethics as the conscious practice of freedom has revolved around this fundamental imperative: "Take care of yourself."

Q: An imperative that implies the assimilation of the *Logoi*, truths.

MF: Certainly. Taking care of oneself requires knowing oneself. Care of the self is, of course, knowledge of the self—this is the Socratic-Platonic aspect—but also knowledge of a number of rules of acceptable conduct or of principles that are both truths and prescriptions. To take care of the self is to equip oneself with these truths: this is where ethics is linked to the game of truth.

Q: You are saying that it involves making this truth that is learned, memorized, and progressively applied into a quasi-subject that reigns supreme in yourself. What is the status of this quasi-subject?

MF: In the Platonic current of thought, at least at the end of the *Alcibiades,* the problem for the subject or the individual soul is to turn its gaze upon itself, to recognize itself in what it is and, recognizing itself in what it is, to recall the truths that issue from it and that it has been able to contemplate; on the other hand, in the current of thinking we can broadly call Stoicism, the problem is to learn through the teaching of a number of truths and doctrines, some of which are fundamental principles while others are rules of conduct. You must proceed in such a way that these principles tell you in each situation and, as it were, spontaneously, how to conduct yourself. It is here that one encounters a metaphor that comes not from the Stoics, but from Plutarch: "You must learn the principles in such a constant way that, whenever your desires, appetites and fears awake like barking dogs, the *Logos* will speak like the voice of the master who silences his dogs with a single cry." Here we have the idea of a *Logos* functioning, as it were, without any intervention on your part; you have become the *Logos,* or the *Logos* has become you.

Q: I would like to come back to the question of the relationship between freedom and ethics. When you say that ethics is the reflective part of freedom, does that mean that freedom can become aware of itself as ethical practice? Is it first and always a freedom that is, so to speak, "moralized," or must one work on oneself to discover the ethical dimension of freedom?

MF: The Greeks problematized their freedom, and the freedom of the individual, as an ethical problem. But ethical in the sense in which the Greeks understood it: *ethos* was a way of being and of behavior. It was a mode of being for the subject, along with a certain way of acting, a way visible to others. A person's *ethos* was evident in his clothing, appearance, gait, in the calm with which he responded to every event, etc. For the Greeks this was the concrete form of freedom; this was the way they problematized their freedom. A man possessed of a splendid *ethos,* who could be admired and put forward as an example, was someone who practiced freedom in a certain way. I don't think that a shift is needed for freedom to be conceived as *ethos;* it is immediately problematized as *ethos.* But extensive work by the self on the self is required for this practice of freedom to take shape in an *ethos* that is good, beautiful, honorable, estimable, memorable and exemplary.

Q: Is this where you situate the analysis of power?

MF: I think that, insofar as freedom for the Greeks signifies non-slavery—which is quite a different definition of freedom from our own—the problem is already entirely political. It is political in that non-slavery to others is a condition: a slave has no ethics. Freedom is thus inherently political. And it also has a political model insofar as being free means not being a slave to oneself and one's appetites, which means that with respect to oneself one establishes a certain relationship of domination, of mastery, which was called *archè,* or power, command.

Q: As you have stated, care of the self is in a certain sense care for others. In this sense, the care of the self is also always ethical, and ethical in itself.

MF: What makes it ethical for the Greeks is not that it is care for others. The care of the self is ethical in itself; but it implies complex relationships with others insofar as this *ethos* of freedom is also a way of caring for others. This is why it is important for a free man who conducts himself as he should, to be able to govern his wife, his children, his household; it is also the art of governing. *Ethos* also implies a relationship with others, insofar as the care of the self enables one to occupy his rightful position in the city, the community or interpersonal relationships, whether as a magistrate or a friend. And the care of the self also implies a relationship with the other insofar as proper care of the self requires listening to the lessons of a master. One needs a guide, a counselor, a friend, someone who will be truthful with you. Thus the problem of relationships with others is present throughout the development of the care of the self.

Q: The care of the self always aims for the well-being of others; it aims to manage the space of power that exists in all relationships, but to manage it in a non-authoritarian manner. What role could a philosopher play in this context, as a person who is concerned with care for others?

MF: Let's take Socrates as an example. He would greet people in the street or adolescents in the gymnasium with the question: Are you taking care of yourself? For he has been entrusted with this mission by a god and he will not abandon it even when threatened with death. He is the man who cares about the care of others; this is the particular position of the philosopher. But let me simply say that in the case of the free man, I think the postulate of this whole morality was that a person who took proper care of himself would, by the same token, be able to conduct himself properly in relation to others and for others. A city in which everybody took proper care of himself would be a city that functioned well and found in this the ethical principle of its permanence. But I don't think we can say that the Greek who cares for himself must first care for others. To my mind, this view only came later. Care for others should not be put before the care of oneself. The care of the self is ethically prior in that the relationship with oneself is ontologically prior.

Q: Can this care of the self, which possesses a positive ethical meaning, be understood as a sort of conversion of power?

MF: A conversion, yes. In fact, it is a way of limiting and controlling power. For if it is true that slavery is the great risk that Greek freedom resists, there is also another danger which initially appears to be the opposite of slavery: the abuse of power. In the abuse of power, one exceeds the legitimate exercise of one's power and imposes one's fantasies, appetites and desires on others. Here we have the image of the tyrant, or simply of the rich and powerful man who uses his wealth and power to abuse others, to impose an unwarranted power on them. But one can see—in any case, this is what the Greek philosophers say— that such a man is the slave of his appetites. And the good ruler is precisely the one who exercises his power as it ought to be exercised, that is, simultaneously exercising his power over himself. And it is the power over oneself that thus regulates one's power over others.

Q: Doesn't the care of the self, when separated from care for others, run the risk of becoming an absolute. And couldn't this "absolutization" of the care of the self become a way of exercising power over others, in the sense of dominating others?

MF: No, because the risk of dominating others and exercising a tyrannical power over them arises precisely only when one has not taken care of the self and has become the slave of one's desires. But if you take proper care of yourself, that is, if you know ontologically what you are, if you know what you are capable of, if you know what it means for you to be a citizen of a city, to be the master of a household in an *oikos,* if you know what things you should and should not fear, if you know what you can reasonably hope for and on the other hand what things should not matter to you, if you know, finally, that you should not be afraid of death—if you know all this, you cannot abuse your power over others. Thus there is no danger. That idea will appear much later, when love of self becomes suspect and comes to be perceived as one of the roots of various moral offenses. In this new context, renunciation of self will be the prime form of care of the self. All this is evident in Gregory of Nyssa's *Treatise on Virginity,* which defines the care of the self, the *epimeleia heautoun,* as the renunciation of all earthly attachments. It is the renunciation of all that may be love of self, of attachment to an earthly self. But I think that in Greek and Roman thought the care of the self cannot in itself tend toward so exaggerated a form of self-love as to neglect others or, worse still, to abuse one's power over them.

Q: Thus it is a care of the self that, in thinking of itself, thinks of others?

MF: Yes, absolutely. He who takes care of himself to the point of knowing exactly what duties he has as master of a household and as a husband and father will find that he enjoys a proper relationship with his wife and children.

Q: But doesn't the human condition, in terms of its finitude, play a very important role here? You have talked about death: if you are not afraid of death, then you cannot abuse your power over others. It seems to me that this problem of finitude is very important; the fear of death, of finitude, of being hurt, is at the heart of the care of the self.

MF: Of course. And this is where Christianity, by presenting salvation as occurring beyond life, in a way upsets or at least disturbs the balance of the care of the self. Although, let me say it again, to seek one's salvation definitely means to take care of oneself. But the condition required for attaining salvation is precisely renunciation. Among the Greeks and Romans, however, given that one takes care of oneself in one's own life and that the reputation one leaves behind is the only afterlife one can expect, the care of the self can be centered entirely on oneself, on what one does, on the place one occupies among others. It can be centered totally on the acceptance of death—this will become quite evident in late Stoicism—and can even, up to a point, become almost a desire for death. At the same time it can be, if not a care for others, at least a care of the self that will be beneficial to others. In Seneca, for example, it is interesting to note the importance of the theme, let us hurry and get old, let us hasten toward the end, so that we may thereby come back to ourselves. This type of moment before death, when nothing more can happen, is different from the desire for death one finds among the Christians, who expect salvation through death. It is like a movement to rush through life to the point where there is no longer anything ahead but the possibility of death.

Q: I would now like to turn to another topic. In your lectures at the Collège de France you spoke about the relationship between power and knowledge. Now you are talking about the relationship between subject and truth. Are these pairs of concepts—power/knowledge and subject/truth—complementary in some way?

MF: As I said when we started, I have always been interested in the problem of the relationship between subject and truth. I mean, how does the subject fit into a certain game of truth? The first problem I examined was why was madness problematized, starting at a certain time and following certain processes, as an illness falling under a certain model of medicine? How was the mad subject placed in this game of truth defined by a medical model or body of knowledge? And it was while working on this analysis that I realized that, contrary to what was rather common practice at that time (around the early 1960s), this phenomenon could not be properly accounted for simply by talking about ideology. In fact, there were practices—essentially the widespread use of incarceration that had been developed starting at the beginning of the 17th century and that had been the condition for the insertion of the mad subject in this type of truth game—that sent me back to the problem of institutions of power much more than to the problem of ideology. This is what led me to pose the problem of knowledge and power, which for me is not the fundamental problem but an instrument that makes it possible to analyze the problem of the relationship between subject and truth in what seems to me the most precise way.

Foucault Live

Q: But you have always "forbidden" people to talk to you about the subject in general?

MF: No, I have not "forbidden" them. Perhaps I did not explain myself adequately. What I rejected was the idea of starting out with a theory of the subject—as is done, for example, in phenomenology or existentialism—and, on the basis of this theory, asking how a given form of knowledge was possible. What I wanted to try to show was how the subject constituted itself, in one specific form or another, as a mad or a healthy subject, as a delinquent or non-delinquent subject, through certain practices that were also games of truth, practices of power, etc. I had to reject a priori theories of the subject in order to analyze the relationships that may exist between the constitution of the subject or different forms of the subject and games of truth, practices of power, etc.

Q: That means that the subject is not a substance.

MF: It is not a substance. It is a form, and this form is not primarily or always identical to itself. You do not have the same type of relationship to yourself when you constitute yourself as a political subject who goes to vote or speaks at a meeting and when you are seeking to fulfill your desires in a sexual relationship. Undoubtedly there are relationships and interferences between these different forms of the subject; but we are not dealing with the same type of subject. In each case, one plays, one establishes a different type of relationship to oneself. And it is precisely the historical constitution of these various forms of the subject in relation to the games of truth that interests me.

Q: But the mad, the ill, the delinquent subject—and perhaps even the sexual subject—was a subject that was the object of a theoretical discourse, let us say a "passive" subject, while the subject you have been speaking about over the past two years in your lectures at the College de France is an "active," a politically active subject. The care of the self concerns all the problems of political practice and government, and so on. It would seem, then, that there has been a change for you, a change not of perspective but of problematic.

MF: If it is indeed true that the constitution of the mad subject may be considered the consequence of a system of coercion—this is the passive subject—you know very well that the mad subject is not an unfree subject and that the mentally ill person is constituted as a mad subject precisely in relation to and over against the one who declares him mad. Hysteria, which was so important in the history of psychiatry and in the asylums of the 19th century, seems to me to be the very picture of how the subject is constituted as a mad subject. And it is certainly no accident that the major phenomena of hysteria were observed precisely in those situations where there was a maximum of coercion to force individuals to constitute themselves as mad. On the other hand, I would say that if I am now interested in how the subject constitutes itself in an active fashion through practices of the self, these practices are nevertheless not something invented by the individual himself. They are models that he finds in his culture and that are proposed, suggested, imposed upon him by his culture, his society and his social group.

Q: It would seem that there is something of a deficiency in your problematic, namely, in the notion of resistance against power. Which presupposes a very active subject, very concerned with the care of itself and of others and therefore competent politically and philosophically.

MF: This brings us back to the problem of what I mean by power. I scarcely use the word "power," and if I use it on occasion it is simply as shorthand for the expression I generally use: "relations of power." But there are ready-made models: when one speaks of "power," people immediately think of a political structure, a government, a dominant social class, the master and the slave, and so on. I am not thinking of this at all when I speak of "relations of power." I mean that in human relationships, whether they involve verbal communication such as we are engaged in at this moment or amorous, institutional or economic relationships, power is always present: I mean a relationship in which one person tries to control the conduct of the other. So I am speaking of relations that exist at different levels, in different forms; these power relations are mobile, they can be modified, they are not fixed once and for all. For example, the fact that I may be older than you and that you may initially have been intimidated may be turned around during the course of our conversation, and I may end up being intimidated before someone precisely because he is younger than I am. These power relations are thus mobile, reversible and unstable. It should also be noted that power relations are possible only insofar as the subjects are free. If one of them were completely at the other's disposal and became his thing, an object on which he could wreak boundless and limitless violence, there wouldn't be any relations of power. Thus, in order for power relations to come into play, there must be at least a certain degree of freedom on both sides. Even when the power relation is completely out of balance, when it can truly be claimed that one side has "total power" over the other, a power can be exercised over the other only insofar as the other still has the option of killing himself, of leaping out the window or of killing the other person. This means that in power relations there is necessarily the possibility of resistance because if there were no possibility of resistance (of violent resistance, flight, deception, strategies capable of reversing the situation) there would be no power relations at all. This being the general form, I refuse to reply to the question I am sometimes asked: "But if power is everywhere, there is no freedom." I answer that if there are relations of power in every social field, this is because there is freedom everywhere. Of course, states of domination do indeed exist. In a great many cases power relations are fixed in such a way that they are perpetually asymmetrical and allow an extremely limited margin of freedom. To take what is undoubtedly a very simplified example, one cannot say that it was only men who wielded power in the conventional marital structure of the 18th and 19th centuries; women had quite a few options: they could deceive their husbands, pilfer money from them, refuse them sex. Yet they were still in a state of domination insofar as these options were ultimately only stratagems that never succeeded in reversing the situation. In such cases of domination, be they economic, social, institutional or sexual, the problem is knowing where resistance will develop. For example, in a working class that will resist domination, will this be in unions or political parties; and what form will it take—a strike, a general strike, revolution or parliamentary opposition? In such a situation of domination, all of these questions demand specific answers that take account of the kind and precise form of domination in question. But the claim that "you see power everywhere, thus there is no room for freedom" seems to me absolutely inadequate. The idea that power is a system of domination that controls everything and leaves no room for freedom cannot be attributed to me.

Q: You were talking before about the free man and the philosopher as two different modes of the care of the self. The care of the self of the philosopher would have a specificity that cannot be confused with that of the free man.

MF: I would say that these figures represent two different places in the care of the self, rather than two forms of care of the self. I believe that the form of such care remains the same, but in terms of intensity, in the degree of zeal for the self and, consequently, also for others, the place of the philosopher is not that of just any free man.

Q: Is there a fundamental link we can make at this point between philosophy and politics?

MF: Yes, certainly. I believe that the relationship between philosophy and politics is permanent and fundamental. It is certain that if one takes the history of the care of the self in Greek philosophy, the relationship with politics is obvious. And it takes a very complex form: on the one hand you have, for example, Socrates as well as Plato in the *Alcibiades* and Xenophon in the Memorabilia—greeting young men, saying to them: "You want to become a politician, to govern a city, to care for others, and you haven't even taken care of yourself. If you do not care for yourself you will make a poor ruler." From this perspective, the care of the self appears a pedagogical, ethical and also ontological condition for the development of a good ruler. To constitute oneself as a governing subject implies that one has constituted oneself as a subject who cares for oneself. Yet on the other hand we have Socrates saying in the *Apology* that he approaches everyone, because everyone has to take care of himself. But he also adds, "In doing so, I am performing the highest service for the city, and instead of punishing me, you should reward me even more than you reward a winner in the Olympic Games." Thus we see a very strong connection between philosophy and politics, which was to develop further when the philosopher would care not only for the soul of the citizen, but for that of the prince. The philosopher becomes the prince's counselor, teacher and spiritual advisor.

Q: Could the problematic of the care of the self be at the heart of a new way of thinking about politics, of a form of politics different from what we know today?

MF: I admit that I have not got very far in this direction, and I would very much like to come back to more contemporary questions to try to see what can be made of all this in the context of the current political problematic. But I have the impression that in the political thought of the 19th century—and perhaps one should go back even further, to Rousseau and Hobbes—the political subject was conceived of essentially as a subject of law, whether natural or positive. On the other hand, it seems to me that contemporary political thought allows very little room for the question of the ethical subject. I don't like to reply to questions I haven't studied. However, I would very much like to come back to the questions I examined through ancient culture.

Q: What is the relationship between the path of philosophy, which leads to knowledge of the self, and the path of spirituality?

MF: By spirituality I mean—but I'm not sure this definition can hold for very long—the subject's attainment of a certain mode of being and the transformations that the subject must carry out on itself to attain this mode of being. I believe that spirituality and philosophy were identical or nearly identical in ancient spirituality. In any case, philosophy's most important preoccupation centered around the self, with knowledge of the world coming after and serving, most often, to support the care of the self. Reading Descartes, it is remarkable to find in the *Meditations* this same spiritual concern with the attainment of a mode of being where doubt was no longer possible, and where one could finally know. But by thus defining the mode of being which philosophy gives access to, one realizes that this mode of being is defined entirely in terms of knowledge and that philosophy in turn is defined in terms of the development of the knowing subject, or of what qualifies the subject as such. From this perspective, it seems to me that philosophy superimposes the functions of spirituality upon the ideal of a grounding for scientific knowledge.

Q: Should the concept of the care of the self in the classical sense be updated to confront this modern thought?

MF: Absolutely, but I would certainly not do so just to say, "We have unfortunately forgotten about the care of the self; so here, here it is, the key to everything." Nothing is more foreign to me than the idea that, at a certain moment, philosophy went astray and forgot something, that somewhere in its history there is a principle, a foundation that must be rediscovered. I feel that all such forms of analysis, whether they take a radical form and claim that philosophy has from the outset been a forgetting, or whether they take a much more historical viewpoint and say, "Such and such a philosopher forgot something"— neither of these approaches is particularly interesting or useful. Which does not mean that contact with such and such a philosopher may not produce something, but it must be emphasized that it would be something new.

Q: This leads me to ask: Why should one have access to the truth today, to *truth* in the political sense, in other words, in the sense of a political strategy directed against the various "blockages" of power in the system of relations?

MF: This is indeed a problem. After all, why truth? Why are we concerned with truth, and more so than with the care of the self? And why must the care of the self occur only through the concern for truth? I think we are touching on a fundamental question here, what I would call *the* question for the West: How did it come about that all of Western culture began to revolve around this obligation of truth that has taken a lot of different forms? Things being as they are, nothing so far has shown that it is possible to define a strategy outside of this concern. It is within the field of the obligation of truth that it is possible to move about in one way or another, sometimes against effects of domination that may be linked to structures of truth or institutions entrusted with truth. To greatly simplify matters, there are numerous examples: there has been a whole so-called "ecological" movement—a very ancient one, by the way, that did not just start in the 20th century—that was often in opposition, as it were, to a science or, at least, to a technology underwritten by claims to truth. But this same ecology articulated its own discourse of truth: criticism was authorized in the name of a knowledge of nature, the balance of life processes, and so on. Thus one escaped from a domination of truth not by playing a game that was totally different from the game of truth, but by playing the same game differently or playing another game, another hand, with other trump cards. I believe that the same holds true in the order of politics; here one can criticize on the basis, for example, of the consequences of the state of domination caused by an unjustified political situation, but one can only do so by playing a certain game of truth, by showing its consequences, by pointing out that there are other reasonable options, by teaching people what they don't know about their own situation, their working conditions and their exploitation.

Q: With regard to the question of games of truth and games of power, don't you think that there can be found in history evidence of a particular kind of these games of truth, one that has a particular status in relation to all other possible games of truth and power and that is marked by its essential openness, its opposition to all blockages of power—power here meaning domination/subjugation?

MF: Yes, absolutely. But when I talk about power relations and games of truth, I am absolutely not saying that games of truth are just concealed power relations—that would be a horrible exaggeration. My problem, as I have already said, is in understanding how truth games are set up and how they are connected with power relations. One can show, for example, that the medicalization of madness, in other words, the organization of medical knowledge around individuals designated as mad, was connected with a whole series of social and economic processes at a given time, but also with institutions and practices of power. This fact in no way impugns the scientific validity or the therapeutic effectiveness of psychiatry: it does not endorse psychiatry, but neither does it invalidate it. It is also true that mathematics, for example, is linked, albeit in a completely different manner than psychiatry, to power structures, if only in the way it is taught, the way in which consensus among mathematicians is organized, functions in a closed circuit, has its values, determines what is good (true) or bad (false) in mathematics. This in no way means that mathematics is only a game of power, but that the game of truth of mathematics is linked in a certain way—without thereby being invalidated in any way—to games and institutions of power. It is clear than in some cases these connections are such that one could write the entire history of mathematics without taking them into account, although this problematic is always interesting and even historians of mathematics are now beginning to study the history of their institutions. Finally, it is clear that the connection that may exist between power relations and games of truth in mathematics is totally different from what it is in psychiatry; in any case, one simply cannot say that games of truth are nothing but games of power.

Q: This question takes us back to the problem of the subject because with games of truth it is a question of knowing *who is* speaking the truth, how he speaks it, and why he speaks it. For in games of truth one can play at speaking the truth: there is a game, one plays at truth or truth is a game.

MF: The word "game" can lead you astray: when I say "game," I mean a set of rules by which truth is produced. It is not a game in the sense of an amusement; it is a set of procedures that lead to a certain result, which, on the basis of its principles and rules of procedure, may be considered valid or invalid, winning or losing.

Q: There remains the problem of "who": is it a group, a body?

MF: It may be a group or an individual. Indeed there is a problem here. With regard to these multiple games of truth, one can see that ever since the age of the Greeks our society has been marked by the lack of a precise and imperative definition of the games of truth that are permitted to the exclusion of all others. In a given game of truth it is always possible to discover something different and to more or less modify this or that rule, and sometimes even the entire game of truth. This has undoubtedly given the West possibilities for development not found in other societies. Who speaks the truth? Free individuals who establish a certain consensus and who find themselves within a certain network of practices of power and constraining institutions.

Q: So truth is not a construction?

MF: That depends. There are games of truth in which truth is a construction and others in which it is not. One can have, for example, a game of truth that consists of describing things in such and such a way: a person giving an anthropological description of a society does not supply a construction but a description, which itself has a certain number of historically changing rules, so that one can say that it is to a certain extent a construction with respect to another description. This does not mean that there's just a void, that everything is a figment of the imagination. On the basis of what can be said, for example, about this transformation of games of truth, some people conclude that I have said that nothing exists—I have been seen as saying that madness does not exist, whereas the problem is absolutely the converse: it was a question of knowing how madness, under the various definitions that have been given, was at a particular time integrated into an institutional field that constituted it as a mental illness occupying a specific place alongside other illnesses.

Q: At the heart of the problem of truth there is ultimately a problem of communication, of the transparency of the words of a discourse. The person that has the capacity to formulate truths also has a power, the power of being able to speak the truth and to express it in the way he wants.

MF: Yes, and yet this does not mean that what the person says is not true, which is what most people believe. When you tell people that there may be a relationship between truth and power, they say: "So it isn't truth after all!"

Q: This is tied up with the problem of communication because, in a society where communication has reached a high level of transparency, game of truths are perhaps more independent of structures of power.

MF: This is indeed an important problem; I imagine you are thinking a little about Habermas when you say that. I am quite interested in his work, although I know he completely disagrees with my views. While I, for my part, tend to be a little more in agreement with what he says, I have always had a problem with the importance he attributes to communication relationships, particularly a function that I would call utopian. The idea that there could exist a state of communication that would allow games of truth to circulate freely, without any constraints or coercive effects, seems utopian to me. This is precisely a failure to see that power relations are not something that is bad in itself, that we have to break free of. I do not think that a society can exist without power relations, if by that one means the strategies by which individuals try to direct and control the conduct of others. The problem, then, is not to try to dissolve them in the utopia of completely transparent communication, but to acquire the rules of law, the management techniques, and also the morality, the *ethos,* the practice of the self, that will allow us to play these games of power with as little domination as possible.

Q: You are very far from Sartre, who told us power is evil.

MF: Yes, and that idea, which is very far from my way of thinking, has often been attributed to me. Power is not evil. Power is games of strategy. We all know that power is not evil! For example, let us take sexual or amorous relationships: to wield power over the other in a sort of open-ended strategic game where the situation may be reversed is not evil; it's a part of love, of passion and sexual pleasure. And let us take, as another example, something that has often been rightly criticized: the pedagogical institution. I see nothing wrong in the practice of a person who, knowing more than others in a specific game of truth, tells those others what to do, teaches them and transmits knowledge and techniques to them. The problem in such practices where power—which is not in itself a bad thing—must inevitably come into play is knowing how to avoid the kind of domination effects where a kid is subjected to the arbitrary and unnecessary authority of a teacher, or a student put under the thumb of a professor who abuses his authority. I believe that this problem must be framed in terms of rules of law, rational techniques of government and *ethos,* practices of the self and of freedom.

Q: Are we to take what you have just said as the fundamental criteria of what you have called a new ethics? It is a question of playing with as little domination as possible...

MF: I believe that this is in fact the hinge point of ethical concerns and the political struggle for respect for rights, of critical thought against abusive techniques of government and research in ethics that seeks to ground individual freedom.

Q: When Sartre speaks of power as the supreme evil, he seems to be alluding to the reality of power as domination. On this point you are probably in agreement with Sartre.

MF: Yes, I believe that all these concepts have been ill defined, so that one hardly knows what one is talking about. I am not even sure if I made myself clear, or used the right words, when I first became interested in the problem of power. Now I have a clearer sense of the problem. It seems to me that we must distinguish between power relations understood as strategic games between liberties—in which some try to control the conduct of others, who in turn try to avoid allowing their conduct to be controlled or try to control the conduct of the others—and the states of domination that people ordinarily call "power." And between the two, between games of power and states of domination, you have technologies of government—understood, of course, in a very broad sense that includes not only the way institutions are governed but also the way one governs one's wife and children. The analysis of these techniques is necessary because it is very often through such techniques that states of domination are established and maintained. There are three levels to my analysis of power: strategic relations, techniques of government and states of domination.

Q: In your lectures on the *Hermeneutics of the Subject* there is a passage in which you say that the first and only useful point of resistance to political power is in the relationship of the self to the self.

MF: I do not believe that the only possible point of resistance to political power—understood, of course, as a state of domination—lies in the relationship of the self to the self. I am saying that "governmentality" implies the relationship of the self to itself, and I intend this concept of "governmentality" to cover the whole range of practices which constitute, define, organize and instrumentalize the strategies individuals in their freedom can use in dealing with each other. Those who try to control, determine and limit the freedom of others are themselves free individuals who have at their disposal certain instruments that they can use to govern others. Thus the basis for all this is freedom, the relationship of the self to itself and the relationship to the other. Whereas if you try to analyze power not on the basis of freedom, strategies and governmentality, but on the basis of the political institution, you can only conceive of the subject as a subject of law. One then has a subject who has or does not have rights, who has had these rights either granted or removed by the institution of political society; and all this brings us back to a legal concept of the subject. On the other hand, I believe that the concept of governmentality makes it possible to bring out the freedom of the subject and its relationship to others—which constitutes the very stuff of ethics.

Q: Do you think that philosophy has anything to say about why there is this tendency to try to control the conduct of others?

MF: The way the conduct of others is controlled takes very different forms and arouses desires and appetites that vary greatly in intensity depending on the society. I don't know anything about anthropology, but I can well imagine societies in which the control of the conduct of others is so well regulated in advance that in a sense the game is already over. On the other hand, in a society like our own, games can be very numerous and the desire to control the conduct of others is all the greater—as we see in family relationships, for example, or emotional or sexual relationships. However, the freer people are with respect to each other, the more they want to control each others' conduct. The more open the game, the more appealing and fascinating it becomes.

Q: Do you think the role of philosophy is to warn of the dangers of power?

MF: This has always been an important function of philosophy. In its critical aspect—and I mean critical in a broad sense—philosophy is that which calls into question domination at every level and in every form in which it exists, whether political, economic, sexual, institutional, etc. To a certain extent this critical function of philosophy derives from the Socratic injunction "Take care of yourself," in other words, "Make freedom your foundation, through the mastery of yourself."

Translated by Phillis Aranov and Dan McGrawth

53

AN AESTHETICS OF EXISTENCE

Q: Seven years have passed since *A History of Sexuality* appeared. I know that your last books created problems for you and that you have encountered difficulties. Would you talk a little about these difficulties and this excursion to the Greco-Roman world, a world that was if not unknown at least foreign to you?

MF: The difficulties arose from the project itself, which was intended to avoid them. I planned my work in several volumes according to a program established in advance, telling myself that now the time had come when I could write them without difficulty simply by spinning out what was in my head, confirming what was there with the work of empirical research. But I almost died of boredom writing these books; they were too much like their precedents. For some authors, to write a book is always to risk something; for example, to fail to finish it. When one knows in advance where one wants to go, a dimension of the experience is lacking, which consists precisely in running the risk of not going to the end. Therefore I changed the general project: instead of studying sexuality at the confines of knowledge (savoir) and power, I tried to investigate at a deeper level how the experience of sexuality as desire had been constituted for the subject himself. In order to disengage this problematic, I was led to look very closely at very old Latin and Greek texts, which required much preparation and effort and which left me, until the end, with a good number of uncertainties and hesitations.

Q: There is always a certain "intentionality" in your works, which has often escaped your readers. *Madness and Civilization* was at bottom the history of the constitution of this knowledge that we call psychology; *The Order of Things* was the archeology of the human sciences; in *Discipline and Punish* you positioned the disciplines of the body and the soul. It seems that what is at the center of your last books is what you call the "game of truth."

MF: I don't think there is a great difference between these books and their precedents. When one writes books like these recent ones one wants very much to modify completely what one thinks and to find oneself at the end completely other than what one was at the start. Then one perceives that really one has changed very little. One has perhaps changed perspectives, one has turned the problem around, but it's always the same problem: that is, the relations between the subject, the truth and the constitution of experience. I have sought to analyze how fields like madness, sexuality and delinquence could enter into a certain game of the truth, and how on the other hand, through this insertion of human practice and behavior into the game of truth, the subject himself is effected. That was the problem of the history of madness, and of sexuality.

Q: Isn't it basically a question of a new genealogy of morals?

MF: If not for the solemnity of the title and the imposing mark that Nietzsche left on it, I would say yes.

Q: In a piece published in *Débat* (November, 1983), you speak in regard to Antiquity of a morality turned towards ethics and a morality turned towards a code. Is that the division between Greco-Roman morality and the one born of Christianity?

MF: With Christianity we see a slow progressive change brought about in relation to ancient morality, which was essentially a practice, a style of liberty. Naturally there were also certain norms of behavior that regulated the conduct of each person. But in Antiquity the will to be a moral subject, the search for an ethics of existence, was principally an effort to affirm one's liberty and to give to one's own life a certain form in which one could recognize oneself, be recognized by others, and in which even posterity could find an example.

This elaboration of one's own life as a personal work of art, even if it obeyed collective canons, was at the center, it seems to me, of moral experience, of the moral will, in Antiquity; whereas in Christianity, with the religion of the text, the idea of God's will and the principle of obedience, morality took much more the form of a code of rules. Only certain ascetic practices were more closely linked to the exercise of a personal liberty.

From Antiquity to Christianity one passes from a morality that was essentially a search for a personal ethics to a morality as obedience to a system of rules. And if I have taken an interest in Antiquity, it is because, for a whole series of reasons, the idea of a morality as obedience to a code of rules is now disappearing, has already disappeared. To this absence of a morality, one responds, or must respond, with an investigation which is that of an aesthetics of existence.

Q: Has all the knowledge of the body, sexuality and training that has accumulated in the last years improved our relationship with others and our being in the world?

MF: I can't help from thinking that the whole series of issues raised around some forms of existence, rules of behavior, etc., even independently of political choices, have been profoundly beneficial in relations with the body, between men and women, and with sexuality.

Q: So this knowledge has helped us to live better?

MF: There was not simply a change in our preoccupations, but in philosophical, critical, and theoretical discourse: in most of the analyses carried out one did not suggest what people ought to be, what they ought to do, what they ought to think and believe. It was a matter rather of showing how social mechanisms up to the present have been able to work, how forms of repression and constraint have acted, and then, starting from there, it seems to me, one left to the people themselves, knowing all the above, the possibility of self-determination and the choice of their own existence.

Q: Five years ago one began to read, in your seminar at the Collège de France, Hayek and Von Mises.[1] It was then said that, through a reflection on liberalism, Foucault is going to give us a book on politics. Liberalism seemed to be a detour taken to discover the individual beyond the mechanisms of power. Your dispute with the phenomenological subject, and the psychological subject is well-known. At that period, one began to speak of a subject of practices, and the rereading of liberalism took place somewhat in that context. It's no secret to anyone that, as was often said, there is no subject in Foucault's work. Subjects are always subjugated: they are the point of application of techniques, normative disciplines, but they are never sovereign subjects.

MF: We have to make distinctions. In the first place, I don't think there is actually a sovereign, founding subject, a universal form of subject that one could find everywhere. I am very skeptical and very hostile toward this conception of the subject. I think on the contrary that the subject is constituted through practices of subjection, or, in a more anonymous way, through practices of liberation, of freedom, as in Antiquity, starting of course from a number of rules, styles and conventions that are found in the culture.

Q: That leads us to the present political scene. These are difficult times: on the international level there's the blackmail of Yalta and the confrontation of blocks; on the national level there's the spectre of crisis. In relation to all this it seems that between the Left and the Right there is no longer anything but a difference of style. How can one achieve a self-determination then, taking at face value this reality and its dictates, which appear to offer no possible alternative?

MF: Your question seems to me both just and a little too compressed. One would have to break it into two kinds of questions: in the first place, is it necessary to accept or refute the present situation? Secondly, if one doesn't accept it, what can one do? To the first question one must respond without any ambiguity: it is not necessary to accept either the residues of the war and the prolongation of a strategic situation in Europe, or the fact that half of Europe is enslaved.

Next, the other question is posed: What can one do against a power like the Soviet Union, in relation to our own government and with the people on both sides of the iron curtain who intend to put into question the division such as it has been established? In relation to the Soviet Union there is not much to do, except to help as effectively as possible those who are fighting it on their own ground. As for the two other targets, there is a great deal to do: the bread is on the shelf?

Q: Therefore, one doesn't have to assume an Hegelian attitude, so to speak, by accepting reality such as it is and as it is presented to us. There remains a last question: Does "a truth in politics" exist?

MF: I believe too much in the truth not to assume that there are different truths and different ways of saying it. To be sure, one cannot expect a government to speak the truth, the whole truth, nothing but the truth. On the other hand, it is possible to expect from governments a certain truth in relation to final aims, to the general choice of its tactics, and to a number of specific points of its program: that is the *parrhesia* (free speech) of the governed, who, because they are citizens, can and must summon the government to answer for what it does, for the meaning of its actions, and the decisions that it has taken, in the name of their own knowledge and their experience.

Nevertheless, we must avoid a trap into which governments would want intellectuals to fall (and often they do): "Put yourself in our place and tell us what you would do." This is not a question to which one has to answer. To make a decision on any matter requires a knowledge of the facts refused us, an analysis of the situation we aren't allowed to make. There's the trap. Yet as governed we still have the perfect right to pose questions about the truth: "What are you doing, for example, when you are hostile to Euromissiles, or when, on the contrary, you re-structure the steel industry, or when you open the debates on free teaching?"

Q: In this descent into hell that involves a long meditation and research—a descent in search of the truth—what type of reader would you like to encounter and to whom could you recount this truth? While there still may be good authors, it's a fact that there are fewer and fewer good readers.

MF: I would say some readers. It's true that one is no longer read. The first book that one writes is read, because one is not known, because people don't know who we are, and it is read in disorder and confusion, which is fine with me. There is no reason for the writing of a book, nor is there a law of the book. The only law is that there are all manner of possible readings. I don't see any major inconvenience if a book, being read, is read in different ways. What is serious is that, as one continues to write one is no longer read at all; some readers, reading the new books on the backs of the earlier ones, and from one distortion to another, arrive at an absolutely grotesque image of the book.

Here we have a real problem: should one enter the fray and respond to each of these distortions, and, consequently, give the law to readers, which I am loath to do, or allow the book to be distorted into a caricature of itself, which I am equally loath to do?

There would be one solution: the only law for book publication, the only law concerning the book that I would like to see passed, would be to prohibit the use of the author's name more than once, with the additional right to anonymity and the use of pseudonyms, in order that each book might be read for itself. There are books for which recognition of the author provides the key to their intelligibility. But outside of a few great authors, this knowledge of the author's name has no real use. It serves only as a screen. For someone like me, who is not a great author but only someone who writes books, books ought to be read for themselves, with their imperfections and their possible good qualities.

Translated by John Johnston

---

[1] Friedrich A. Hayek, *Individualism and Economic Order* (Chicago: University of Chicago Press, 1948); Ludwig von Mises, *The Anti-Capitalist Mentality* (Libertarian Press, 1981).

54

THE CONCERN FOR TRUTH

Q: *The Archeology of Knowledge* announced a forthcoming *History of Sexuality*. The next volume appeared eight years later and according to a plan completely different.

MF: I changed my mind. A work, when it's not at the same time an attempt to modify what one thinks and even what one is, is not much fun. I had begun to write two books in accordance with my original plan; but very quickly I got bored. It was unwise on my part and contrary to my habits.

Q: Then why did you do it?

MF: Out of laziness. I dreamed that a day would come when I would know in advance what I meant and would only have to say it. That was a reflection of old age. I imagined I had finally reached the age when one only has to reel out what's in one's head. It was both a form of presumption and an abandonment of restraint. Yet to work is to undertake to think something other than what one has thought before.

Q: The reader thought so too.

MF: With respect to the reader, I feel at the same time certain qualms and a fair amount of confidence. The reader is like an auditor of a course. He can easily tell when one has worked and when one merely talks off the top of one's head. He may be disappointed, but not by the fact that I have said nothing else but what I was already saying.

Q: Your two new books, *The Use of Pleasure* and *The Concern for Self,* are offered foremost as the work of a practical historian, a systematizing of the sexual morals of Antiquity. Is it really about that?

MF: It's the work of an historian, but, to be more precise, these books like the others are a work on the history of thought. The history of thought—that means not simply a history of ideas or of representations, but also the attempt to respond to this question: how is it that thought, insofar as it has a relationship with the truth, can also have a history? That is the question posed. I try to respond to a specific problem: the birth of a morality, of a morality that is a reflection on sexuality, desire, pleasure.

Let it be clearly understood that I am not making a history of mores, of behavior, a social history of sexual practice, but a history of the manner in which pleasure, desires and sexual behaviors have been problematized, reflected upon and thought about in Antiquity in relation to a certain art of living. It is obvious that this art of living was practiced only by a small group of people. It would be ridiculous to think that what Seneca, Epictetus or Musonius Rufus can say about sexual behavior represented in one way or another the general practice of the Greeks and the Romans. But I maintain that the fact that these things have been said about sexuality, that they have constituted a tradition that one finds again, transposed, metamorphosed and profoundly modified in Christianity, constitutes a historical fact. Thought equally has a history; it is an historic fact, even if it has many other dimensions. In this respect, these books are completely similar to those that I wrote on madness or punishment. In *Discipline and Punish* I didn't want to do a history of the prison as an institution, which would have required different material and a different kind of analysis. Instead, I asked myself how thought about punishment has had, at the end of the 18th century and the beginning of the 19th, a certain history. What I tried to do was a history of the relationships that thought maintains with the truth, the history of thought insofar as it is thought about the truth. All those who say that for me the truth doesn't exist are simple-minded.

Q: In *The Use of Pleasure* and *The Concern for Self,* nevertheless, the truth takes a very different form from the one it had in your previous books, the painful form of subjection and objectification.

MF: What serves as a form common to the work I've done since *Madness and Civilization* is the notion of problematization, though I had not yet sufficiently isolated this notion. But one always moves backwards toward the essential; the most general things appear last. It's the price and recompense of all work whose theoretical stakes are elaborated from a certain empirical domain. In *Madness and Civilization* the question was to know how and why madness, at a given moment, had been problematized through a certain institutional practice and a certain apparatus of knowledge. Similarly, in *Discipline and Punish,* it was a question of analyzing changes in the problematization of relationships between delinquency and punishment through penal practices and institutions at the end of the 18th century and the beginning of the 19th. Now it's how sexual activity is problematized.

Problematization doesn't mean the representation of a pre-existent object, nor the creation through discourse of an object that doesn't exist. It's the set of discursive or nondiscursive practices that makes something enter into the play of the true and false, and constitutes it as an object for thought (whether under the form of moral reflection, scientific knowledge, political analysis, etc.).

Q: No doubt *The Use of Pleasures* and *The Concern for Self* emerge from the same problematic. Nevertheless, they appear to be very different from the preceding works.

MF: Indeed, I reversed tack. For the study of madness, I started from the "problem" that it could constitute in a certain social, political and epistemological context: the problem that madness posed to others. Here I started from the problem that sexual conduct could pose to individuals themselves (or at least to men in Antiquity). Then it was a matter of knowing how one "governed" the mad; now it is how one "governs" oneself. But I would quickly add that in the case of madness, I tried to go back to the constitution of the experience of the self itself as mad, within the framework of mental illness, the practice of psychiatry and the asylum. Here I would like to show how the government of self is integrated with the government of others. These are, in short, two inverse ways of access to the same question: how is an "experience" formed where the relationship to self and to others is linked?

Q: It seems to me that the reader will experience a double strangeness, the first in relation to you, and to what he expects of you...

MF: Perfect. I entirely assume this difference. That's the name of the game.

Q: The second strangeness concerns sexuality, and the relation between what you describe and our own experience of sexuality.

MF: In regard to the strangeness, we must not exaggerate. It's true that there's a certain doxa concerning Antiquity and that the ancient morality is represented as "tolerant." But just the same, many people know that in Antiquity there was an austere and rigorous morality. It's well known the Stoics were in favor of marriage and conjugal fidelity. In emphasizing this "severity" of moral philosophical morality, I'm not saying anything extraordinary.

Q: I was thinking of strangeness in relation to the themes that are familiar to us in the analysis of sexuality: those of the law, prohibitions, etc.

MF: It's a matter of a paradox which even surprised me, although I had already suspected it in *The History of Sexuality* when I posed the hypothesis that it wasn't simply by starting from the mechanisms of repression that one could analyze the constitution of a knowledge about sexuality. What struck me about Antiquity is that the points around which reflection is most active regarding sexual pleasure are not at all the points which represented the traditionally received forms of prohibition. On the contrary, it was where sexuality was the least restricted that the moralists of antiquity questioned themselves with the most intensity and where they succeeded in formulating the most rigorous doctrines. The simplest example: the status of married women prohibited them from having any sexual relationships outside of marriage; but on this "monopoly" one hardly finds any philosophical reflection or theoretical preoccupation. On the other hand, love with boys was free (within certain limits), and yet it's on this subject that a whole conception of restraint, abstinence and of a non-sexual relationship was elaborated. Thus it's not the prohibition that permits one to account for the forms of problematization.

Q: It seems you go much further, opposing to categories of the "law" and of "prohibition" those of the "art of living," "techniques of self" and "stylization of existence."

MF: I could have said, using rather current methods and schemes of thought, that certain prohibitions were effectively posed as such, and that others, more diffuse, were expressed in the form of morality. It seems to me that it was more appropriate to the domains I was treating and to the documents I had at my disposal to think this morality in the same form in which its contemporaries had reflected upon it, to wit, in the form of an art of existence, or rather let's say a technique of life. It was a matter of knowing how to govern one's own life in order to give it the most beautiful form possible (in the eyes of others, of oneself, and of the future generations for whom one could serve as an example). That's what I tried to reconstitute: the formation and development of a practice of self whose objective was to constitute oneself as the worker of the beauty of one's own life.

Q: As categories, the "art of living" and "techniques of self" do not have as their only valid domain the sexual experience of the Greeks and the Romans.

MF: I don't think there is a morality without a certain number of practices of the self. Sometimes these practices are associated with numerous, systematic, and restrictive kinds of codings. Sometimes they even lose almost all definition, to the profit of a set of rules which then appears as the essential of a morality. But it can also happen that they constitute the most important and the most active source of the morality, and that it is around them that reflection develops. The practices of the self thus take the form of an art of the self, relatively independent of any moral legislation. In its moral reflection Christianity has certainly reinforced the principle of the law and the structure of the code, even if its ascetic practices have retained a great importance.

Q: Our modern experience of sexuality begins then with Christianity?

MF: Early Christianity brought several important modifications to ancient asceticism: it intensified the form of the law, but it also re-oriented the practices of the self in the direction of a hermeneutic of self and a deciphering of self as subject of desire. The articulation of law and desire appear to be rather characteristic of Christianity.

Q: The descriptions of the disciplines in *Discipline and Punish* got us used to the most minute prescriptions. It's remarkable that the prescriptions of sexual morality in Antiquity are no different in this regard.

MF: One must go into the details. In Antiquity people were at the same time very attentive to elements of behavior and wanted each person to pay attention to them. But the modes of attention were not the same as the ones we have known subsequently. Thus the sexual act itself, its morphology, the way in which one sought or obtained one's pleasure and the "object" of desire hardly seem to have been a very important theoretical problem in Antiquity. On the other hand, what was the object of preoccupation was the intensity of the sexual activity, its rhythm, the moment chosen, and also the role—active or passive— that one assumed in the relationship. Thus one will find thousands of details on sexual acts in relation to the seasons, the hours of the day, the moment of rest or of exercise, or again on the manner in which a boy should behave in order to have a good reputation, but none of these catalogues of permitted and prohibited acts that will be so important in the Christian pastoral.

Q: The different practices you describe, in relation to the body, woman, boys—each appears to be considered for itself, without being linked together in a rigorous system. It's another difference in relation to your preceding works.

MF: I learned, reading one book, that I had summed up the whole experience of madness in the classic period in the practice of internment. Yet *Madness and Civilization* is built on the thesis that there were at least two distinctly different experiences of madness: one was that of internment, while the other was a medical practice with very distant origins. That one can have different experiences (simultaneous as well as successive) which have a unique reference is in itself nothing extraordinary.

Q: The architecture of your last books recalls somewhat the Table of Contents of Aristotle's *Nichomachean Ethics*. You examine each practice, one after another. What links together the relationships with the body, the home and wife, and with boys?

MF: A certain style of morality that is a self-mastery. The sexual activity is perceived and represented as a violence and thus problematized from the point of view of the difficulty in controlling it. Hubris is fundamental. In this ethics the rules of behavior must be constituted in order that one can be assured of this self-mastery, which itself can be ordered according to three distinct principles: (1) the relationship to the body and the problem of health; (2) the relationship to women, or rather to the woman who as wife to her husband is part of

the same household; (3) the relationship to particular individuals who are adolescents and who one day may become free citizens. In these three domains self-
mastery will take three different forms; there is not, as will be the case with the
flesh and sexuality, a single domain that would unify them all. Among the great
transformations that Christianity will bring will be an ethics of the flesh that will
hold in the same way for both men and women. On the contrary, in ancient
morality, self-mastery is a problem only for the individual who must be the master of himself and master of others and not for those who must obey others. It's
for this reason that this ethics only concerns men and that it doesn't take exactly
the same form in relation to one's own body or with one's wife or with boys.

Q: With these works the question of sexual liberation appears devoid of sense.

MF: One can say that in Antiquity one was concerned with willpower
in relation to rule and form, and with a search for austerity. How was this
willpower formed? Is this will-to-austerity nothing else but the expression of a
fundamental prohibition, or on the contrary was it not the original matrix from
which certain general forms of prohibition were derived?

Q: You are proposing then a complete reversal of the traditional manner
of viewing the relationships between sexuality and prohibition?

MF: In Greece there were fundamental prohibitions, incest for example.
But they were only of slight concern to philosophers and moralists compared to
the great care given to self-mastery. When Xenophon sets out the reasons for the
prohibition of incest, he explains that if one marries one's mother the difference in
age would be such that the children could be neither beautiful nor of good bearing.

Q: Sophocles however seems to have said otherwise.

MF: The interesting thing is that this prohibition, so serious and important, could be at the heart of a tragedy. Nevertheless, it was not at the center of
moral reflection.

Q: Why investigate these periods that some would say are very far away?

MF: I start with a problem as if it were posed in contemporary terms
and try to make a genealogy of it. A genealogy means that I conduct the analysis
beginning with a current question.

Q: What is that question here?

MF: For a long time some people have thought that the rigor of sexual
codes, in the form that we have experienced them, was indispensable to so-
called "capitalist" societies. Yet, the lifting of the codes and the dislocation of

the prohibitions have no doubt occurred more easily than one would have thought possible (which seems to indicate that their reason for being was not what one believed). And so the problem of an ethics as a form to be given to one's conduct and to one's life has again been raised. In short, we were mistaken when we believed that all morality was in prohibitions and that the lifting of the latter alone would resolve the question of ethics.

Q: Have you written these books for the liberation movements?

MF: Not for, but as a function of the situation today.

Q: You have said, in regard to *Discipline and Punish,* that it was your "foremost book." Can the expression be used even more appropriately on the occasion of the publication of *The Use of Pleasure* and *The Concern for Self?*

MF: To write a book is in a certain way to abolish the preceding one. Finally one perceives that what one has done is—both comfort and deception— rather close to what one has already written.

Q: You speak of "detaching yourself from yourself." Why a will power so singular?

MF: What can the ethics of an intellectual be—I reclaim the term "intellectual" which, at the present moment, seems to nauseate some—if not that: to render oneself permanently capable of self-detachment (which is the opposite of the attitude of conversion)? If I had wanted to be exclusively an academic, no doubt it would have been wiser to choose a single domain in which to deploy my activities, accepting a given problematic and trying either to put it to work or to modify it at certain points. I would then have been able to write books like the ones I planned for the six-volume *History of Sexuality,* knowing in advance what I wanted to do and where I wanted to go. To be at the same time an academic and an intellectual is to try to engage a type of knowledge and analysis that is taught and received in the university in a way so as to modify not only the thought of others but one's own as well. This work of modifying one's own thought and that of others seems to me to be the intellectual's reason for being.

Q: Sartre, for example, gave the impression of being an intellectual who spent his life developing a fundamental intuition. This will to "detach yourself from yourself" seems very much to singularize you.

MF: I couldn't say that there was anything singular there. But I insist that this change take the form neither of a sudden illumination that makes "the scales fall from the eyes" nor of an openness to every movement of the time. I would like it to be an elaboration of the self by the self, a studious transformation, a slow and arduous transformation through a constant care for the truth.

Q: Your preceding works have given you the image of a thinker of enclosures and subjugated subjects who are constrained and disciplined. *The Use of Pleasure* and *The Concern for Self* offer us a completely different image of free subjects. It seems that this is an important modification in your own thought.

MF: We will have to return to the relationships between knowledge and power. I think that in the public's eye I am the one who has said that knowledge has become indistinguishable from power, that it was only a thin mask thrown over the structures of domination and that the latter were always oppression and enclosure, etc. On the first point I will respond with a burst of laughter. If I had said, or wanted to say, that knowledge was power I would have said it, and having said it, I would no longer have anything to say, since in identifying them I would have had no reason to try to show their different relationships. I directed my attention specifically to see how certain forms of power which were of the same type could yield to forms of knowledge extremely different in their object and structure. Let's take the problem of the hospital's structure: it yielded to a psychiatric type of enclosure to which corresponded the formation of a psychiatric knowledge whose epistemological structure could remain rather special. But in another book, *The Birth of the Clinic,* I tried to show how this same hospital structure had developed an anatomic-pathological knowledge which was the foundation of a medicine with a completely different scientific fecundity. Thus one has structures of power, two neighboring institutional forms—psychiatric enclosure, medical hospitalization—to which different forms of knowledge are linked, between which one can establish relationships, conditional connections, but not of cause and effect, nor a fortiori of identity. Those who say that for me knowledge is the mask of power don't seem to have the capacity to understand. There's hardly any point in responding to them.

Q: Which you judge useful to do right now however.

MF: Which I find important to do now.

Q: Your last two works mark a passage from politics to ethics. On this occasion you will certainly be expected to answer the question: what must we do, what must we want?

MF: The role of an intellectual is not to tell others what they must do. By what right would he do so? And remember all the prophecies, promises, injunctions and plans intellectuals have been able to formulate in the course of the last two centuries and of which we have seen the effects. The work of an intellectual is not to mold the political will of others; it is, through the analyses that he does in his own field, to re-examine evidence and assumptions, to shake up habitual ways of working and thinking, to dissipate conventional familiarities, to re-evaluate rules and institutions and starting from this re-problematization (where he occupies his specific profession as an intellectual) to participate in the formation of a political will (where he has his role as citizen to play).

Q: Recently, intellectuals have been very much reproached for their silence.

MF: Even inopportunely, there is no need to enter into this controversy, whose point of departure was a lie. On the other hand, the campaign itself doesn't lack a certain interest. We must wonder why the socialists and the government have launched it or taken it up again, giving the appearance of a divorce between themselves and all leftist opinion which doesn't serve them. On the surface, in some places, to be sure, there was the constant outward display of the injunction to "shut up," meaning "since we don't want to hear you, shut up." But more seriously, in this reproach there was a demand and a complaint: "Tell us then a little of what we so much need to hear. During the whole period when we were managing with such difficulty our electoral alliance with the communists, it was obvious that we didn't want our 'socialist' discourse to be even slightly unacceptable to them. There were enough subjects of disagreement between us for us not to want to add that one. Thus, during this period, you only had to shut up and let us treat you, or the needs of our alliance, as the 'little Left,' as the 'American' or 'California' Left. But once we were in the government we needed you to speak. And that you furnish us with a discourse having a double function: it would show the solidity of Leftist opinion around us (at best it would be one of fidelity, although we would be content with one of toadyism): but it would also have to address the economic and political reality that we formerly took care to keep in the background of our own discourse. We needed others on our side to maintain a discourse of governmental nationality that would be neither the false one of our alliance nor the naked one of our adversaries to the right (the one we hold today). We wanted to bring you into the game; but you gave us enough rope to get midway across the river while you are still sitting on the banks." To which intellectuals could respond: "When you were pressing us to change our discourse you condemned us in the name of the most worn-out slogans. Now that you are changing front under the pressure of a reality that you weren't capable of perceiving, you demand that we furnish you, not with the thought that would permit you to confront it, but with a discourse that would mask your change. The evil doesn't come, as has been said, from the fact that intellectuals have ceased to be Marxists the moment the communists have come to power, but from the fact that the scruples of your alliance have prevented you when the time was right from doing the work with intellectuals that would have rendered you capable of governing. Of governing differently than with old catchwords and the badly rejuvenated techniques of others."

Q: Is there a common stance in the different interventions that you have been able to make in politics and in regard to Poland in particular?

MF: To try to pose several questions in terms of truth and error. When the Minister of Foreign Affairs said that Jaruzelski's coup was only a matter of concern for Poland, was it true? Is it true that Europe is such a trifling thing and that its division and the communist domination present there beyond an arbitrary line does not concern us? Is it true that the refusal of elementary labor-union liberties in a socialist country is a matter without importance in a country governed by socialists and communists? If it is true that the presence of communists in the government has no influence on major decisions of foreign policy, what can one think of this government and of the alliance on which it is based? These questions certainly don't define a politics; but they are questions to which those who do define a politics ought to respond.

Q: Would the role that you assume in politics correspond to this principle of "free speech" that has been the theme of your courses in recent years?

MF: Nothing is more inconsistent than a political regime that is indifferent to the truth; but nothing is more dangerous than a political system that claims to prescribe the truth. The function of "free speech" doesn't have to take legal form, just as it would be vain to believe that it resides by right in spontaneous exchanges of communication. The task of speaking the truth is an infinite labor: to respect it in its complexity is an obligation that no power can afford to shortchange, unless it would impose the silence of slavery.

Translated by John Johnston

55

THE RETURN OF MORALITY

Q: What strikes the reader of your last books is the writing—clear, pure, smooth, and very different from your habitual style. Why this change?

MF: I am currently rereading the manuscripts that I wrote for this history of morality and that concern the beginning of Christianity (these books—this is one reason for their tardiness—are presented in the inverse order of their composition). In rereading these manuscripts abandoned some time ago I find again the same refusal of style evident in *The Order of Things, Madness and Civilization* or *Raymond Roussel.* I should say that it's a problem for me because this break did not occur progressively. Very abruptly, in 1975-76, I completely gave up this style, for I had it in mind to do a history of the subject, which is not that of an event that would be produced one day and of which it would be necessary to recount the genesis and the outcome.

Q: In ridding yourself of a certain style, didn't you become more philosophical than you were before?

MF: In admitting—and I admit it!—that with *The Order of Things, Madness and Civilization,* even with *Discipline and Punish,* I put into practice a philosophical study essentially founded on a certain use of vocabulary, of play, of philosophical experience to which I adhered completely, you can be sure that now I'm trying to disengage myself from that form of philosophy. But I do this in order to make it serve as a field of experience to be studied, laid out and organized; so that this period, which some will see as one of radical non-philosophy, is at the same time a way of thinking more radically the philosophical experience.

Q: It seems that you are making explicit what could only be read between the lines in your preceding works?

MF: I must say that I don't see it that way. It seems to me that in *Madness and Civilization,* in *The Order of Things,* and also in *Discipline and Punish,* many things that are implicit could not be made explicit because of the way I posed the problems. I tried to mark out three types of problems: that of the truth, that of power, and that of individual conduct. These three domains of experience can be understood only in relation to each other and only with each other. What hampered me in the preceding books was to have considered the first two experiences without taking into account the third. By bringing this last experience to light, I had a guiding thread which didn't need to be justified by resorting to rhetorical methods by which one could avoid one of the three fundamental domains of experience.

Q: The question of style also involves the one of existence. But how can one make the style of life into a great philosophical problem?

MF: A difficult question, which I'm not sure I can answer. Actually I believe that the question of style is central in ancient experience: there's the stylization of one's relationship to oneself, the style of conduct, and the stylization of one's relationship with others. Antiquity never stopped asking if it were possible to define a style common to these different domains of conduct. Actually, the discovery of this style would no doubt have led to a definition of the subject. The unity of a "morality of style" only began to be thought under the Roman Empire, in the 2nd and 3rd centuries, and immediately in terms of a code and the truth.

Q: A style of existence—that's admirable. These Greeks, did you find them admirable?

MF: No.

Q: What did you think of them?

MF: Not very much. They were stymied right away by what seems to me to be the point of contradiction of ancient morality: between on the one hand this obstinate search for a certain style of existence and, on the other, the effort to make it common to everyone, a style that they approached more or less obscurely with Seneca and Epictetus but which would find the possibility of realization only within a religious style. All of Antiquity appears to me to have been a "profound error." (Laughter)

Q: You are not the only one to introduce the notion of style into history. Peter Brown does it in his book *The Making of Late Antiquity.* [1]

MF: The use I make of "style" is largely borrowed from Peter Brown. But what I'm going to say now, and which is not related to what he has written, doesn't involve him in any way. This notion of style seems to me very important in the history of ancient morality. I spoke badly of this morality a minute ago; now I can try to speak well of it. At first, ancient morality was addressed to only a small number of individuals; it did not demand that everyone obey the same scheme of behavior. It concerned only a very small minority among the people and even among those who were free. There were several forms of liberty: the liberty of the chief of state or of the army had nothing to do with that of the sage. Then this morality spread further. In the period of Seneca, and even more so in that of Marcus Aurelius, it might possibly apply to everyone; but it was never made an obligation for anyone. It was a matter of choice for individuals; each one could come to share in this morality. So much so that it is nevertheless very difficult to know who participated in this morality in Antiquity and under the Empire. We are thus very far from the moral conformities schematized by the sociologists and historians who study an assumed average population. What Peter Brown and I try to do permits us to isolate, by looking at their singularities, the individuals who have played a role in ancient morality or Christianity. We are at the early stage of these studies on style and it would be interesting to see how this notion was transmitted from the 4th century B.C. to the 1st century of our era.

Q: One can't study the morality of a philosopher of antiquity without taking into account, at the same time, all of his philosophy; and in particular when one thinks of the Stoics. It is said that precisely because Marcus Aurelius had neither a physics nor a logic, his morality tended toward what you call the Code, rather than toward what you call Ethics.

MF: You make, if I understand rightly, this long evolution the result of a loss. You would see in the works of Plato, Aristotle and the first Stoics a philosophy balanced particularly between conceptions of truth, politics, and private life. Little by little, from the 3rd century B.C. to the 2nd century of our era, questions about truth and political power would have been dropped, and people would have pondered over questions of morality. But in fact, from Socrates to Aristotle, philosophical reflection in general constituted the matrix of a theory of knowledge, of politics, and of individual conduct. And then political theory entered a period of regression because the ancient city disappeared and was replaced by the great monarchies that succeeded Alexander. The conception of the truth, for more complicated reasons, but of the same order it seems, entered equally into regression. Finally, it came down to this: in the 1st century, people said: philosophy doesn't have to concern itself with the truth in general, but with useful truths: politics, and above all, morality. You have there the great scene of ancient philosophy: Seneca begins to do philosophy at exactly the time when he has taken leave of political activity. He has been exiled, he has returned to power, he has exercised it, then he is sent back into a semi-exile and he dies in total exile. It is during those periods that philosophic discourse assumes all its meaning for him. This very important, essential phenomenon is, if you like, the misfortune of ancient philosophy, or, in any case, the historic starting point from which it yielded to a form of thought that was going to be found in Christianity.

Q: On several occasions you seem to make of writing a privileged practice of the self. Is writing at the center of the "culture of the self"?

MF: It's true that the question of the self and the writing of the self has been not central but always very important in the formation of the self. Take Plato for example, leaving aside Socrates, whom we know only through Plato. Plato is someone about whom the least one can say is that he has not cultivated the practice of the self as a written practice, as a practice of memory or as practice of the composition of self starting from his memories. If he has written a considerable amount on a number of political, moral and metaphysical problems, the texts that bear witness to the relationship to the self, in the Platonic debate, seem relatively restrained. This is equally the case in Aristotle.

In contrast, beginning in the 1st century of our era, one sees numerous writings which follow the model of writing as a relationship to the self (recommendations, advice, opinions given to disciples, etc.). Under the Empire young people were taught to behave in a correct manner from lessons which were given to them; they were then taught, but only subsequently, how to formulate their questions, then how to give their opinion, and to formulate these opinions in the form of lessons and finally in a didactic form. We have evidence of this in the texts of Seneca, Epictetus, and Marcus Aurelius. I would not be ready to say that ancient morality was a morality of attention to the self all along its history; but it became one at a certain moment. Christianity introduced perversions, and rather considerable modifications, when it organized extremely wide penitential functions which implied that one take account of the self, that one talk about oneself with another without anything being written. On the other hand, Christianity developed at the same period, or a little afterwards, a spiritual movement linking individual experiences—through the diary, for example—which allowed it to judge or in any case to appraise the reactions of each person.

Q: Between modern practices of the self and Greek practices of the self there are, it seems, enormous differences. Do they have anything to do with each other?

MF: Anything? Yes and no. From a strictly philosophical point of view, the morality of Greek antiquity and contemporary morality have nothing in common. On the other hand, if you take them for what they prescribe, intimate and advise, they are extraordinarily close. It's the proximity and the difference that we must bring to light and, through their interplay, we must show how the same advice given by the ancient morality can work differently in the style of contemporary morality.

Q: It would seem that we have an experience of sexuality very different from the one you attribute to the Greeks. Is there a place among them, as there is among us, for the lover's delirium, the loss of self? Does their eroticism communicate with what is strange or alien?

MF: I don't want to answer in general. I will answer you in relation to philosophy, that is to say, as I have learned it from texts which are philosophical. It seems to me that in the texts dating from the 4th century B.C. to the 2nd century A.D. there is hardly any conception of love receiving validation for having represented the experiences you're talking about: madness or the great passion of a lover.

Q: Not even in Plato's *Phaedrus?*

MF: Oh no! I don't think so! One would have to look closer, but it seems to me that in the *Phaedrus* there are characters who, following a lover's experience, neglect the current and unbroken tradition of their period which founded the erotic on a manner of "paying court," in order to arrive at a type of knowledge that would permit them on the one hand to love each other and on the other hand to have the appropriate attitude in regard to the law and the obligations imposed on citizens. One begins to see the emergence of the lover's delirium in Ovid at the moment when you have the possibility and the opening of an experience in which the individual completely loses his head in some way, no longer knows who he is, is unaware of his identity and lives his lover's experience as a perpetual forgetting of self. Now that's a late experience that in no way corresponds to that of Plato or Aristotle.

Q: Up till now we have been accustomed to finding you in the historical space that extends from the classical age to the end of the 19th century, but here you are where no one expected you: in Antiquity! Is there today a return to the Greeks?

MF: We have to be cautious. It's true, there is a return to a certain form of Greek experience. This return is a return to morality. We must not forget that this Greek morality has its origin in the 5th century B.C. and that Greek philosophy little by little transformed itself into a morality in which we now recognize ourselves. But there we forget, it must be said, what was its fundamental accompaniment in the 4th century: political philosophy and philosophy itself.

Q: But isn't the return to the Greeks the symptom of a crisis of thought, as in the case of the Renaissance, with its religious schism, and then later after the Revolution?

MF: It's very likely. Christianity has long represented a certain form of philosophy. Then periodically there have been efforts to rediscover in Antiquity a form of thought not contaminated by Christianity. In this regularly repeated return to the Greeks there is definitely a sort of nostalgia, an attempt to recuperate an original form of thought and to conceive the Greek world apart from Christian phenomena. In the 16th century it was a matter of re-discovering through Christianity a philosophy in some way Greco-Christian. Beginning with Hegel and Schelling this attempt took the form of a recuperation of the Greeks outside of Christianity, an attempt that one finds again in Nietzsche. To try to rethink the Greeks today consists not in valorizing Greek morality as the domain of morality par excellence which one would need for self-reflection, but in seeing to it that European thought can get started again on Greek thought as an experience given once and in regard to which one can be totally free.

Q: Hegel's and Nietzsche's returns to the Greeks put into play the relations between history and philosophy. For Hegel, it was a matter of founding historical thought on philosophical knowledge. For you and for Nietzsche, on the contrary, between history and philosophy there is a genealogy and a manner of alienating oneself. Does your return to the Greeks participate in a shaking up of the ground on which we think and live? What have you wanted to destroy?

MF: I haven't wanted to destroy anything! But I believe that in this "fishing around" that one undertakes with the Greeks it is absolutely necessary not to fix the limits nor to establish in advance a sort of program that would permit one to say: this part of the Greeks I accept, that other part I reject. The whole Greek experience can be taken up again in nearly the same way by taking into account each time the differences of context and by indicating the part of this experience that one can perhaps save and the part that one can on the contrary abandon.

Q: In what you describe you have found a meeting point between an experience of freedom and truth. There is at least one philosopher for whom the relationship between freedom and truth was the point of departure for Western thought: it is Heidegger who from this point founds the possibility of an ahistorical discourse. If you had Hegel and Marx in your line of sight before, don't you now have Heidegger?

MF: Of course. Heidegger has always been for me the essential philosopher. I started by reading Hegel, then Marx, and I began to read Heidegger in 1951 or 1952; then in 1952 or 1953, I no longer remember, I read Nietzsche. I still have the notes I took while reading Heidegger—I have tons of them!—and they are far more important than the ones I took on Hegel or Marx. My whole philosophical development was determined by my reading of Heidegger. But I recognize that Nietzsche prevailed over him. I don't know Heidegger well enough: I practically don't know *Being and Time* nor the things recently published. My knowledge of Nietzsche is much greater. Nevertheless, these were my two fundamental experiences. I probably wouldn't have read Nietzsche if I hadn't read Heidegger. I tried to read Nietzsche in the 1950s, but Nietzsche by himself said nothing to me. Whereas Nietzsche and Heidegger— that was the philosophical shock! But I've never written anything on Heidegger and only a very short article on Nietzsche. Yet these are the two authors whom I've read the most. I think it's important to have a small number of authors with whom one thinks, with whom one works, but on whom one doesn't write. Perhaps someday I'll write about them, but at that point they will no longer be instruments of thought for me. Finally, for me there are three categories of philosophers: those I don't know; those I know and discuss; and those I know and don't discuss.

Q: Isn't that precisely the source of the misunderstandings which surround your work?

MF: Do you mean that at the origin of these different misunderstandings lies my fundamental Nietzscheanism? There you are asking me an embarrassing question, for of those to whom it could be posed I'm in the most awkward position. It's addressed to those who are themselves asking the questions. I can only respond by saying: I am simply a Nietzschean, and I try as far as possible, on a certain number of issues, to see with the help of Nietzsche's texts—but also with anti-Nietzschean theses (which are nevertheless Nietzschean!)—what can be done in this or that domain. I attempt nothing else, but that I try to do well.

Q: Your books say something different from what their titles announce? Don't you play a double game with the reader, of surprise and deception?

MF: It's very likely that the works I write don't correspond exactly to the titles I've given them. It's a clumsiness on my part, but when I choose a title I keep it. I write a book, I revise it, I discover new problematics, but the title remains. There is also another reason. In the books I write, I try to pinpoint a type of problem that hasn't been discerned before. Consequently, and necessarily under these conditions, I must bring to light at the end of the work a certain type of problem that can't be rewritten into the title. That's why there is this sort of "play" between the title and the work. Clearly one ought either to tell me that these works don't reflect their titles at all and that I really must change the titles, or that there's a kind of gap that opens up between the title and the book's content, and that this discrepancy is to be understood as the distance I have taken myself in writing the book.

Q: To accomplish your Nietzschean project of genealogies you have had to jump across disciplines and take knowledge out of the institutions that control it. But is the power of the institution so intimidating that you insist on saying that you have done "studies of history" and not those of an "historian" and that you are neither a "Hellenist" nor a "Latinist"?

MF: Yes, I repeat it because it will be said in any case by someone—I can even tell you by whom! I'm not a Hellenist; I'm not a Latinist. I have some knowledge of Latin, and some of Greek, but I know it less well. I studied them again over the last years in order to pose some questions which, on the one hand, could be recognized by Hellenists and Latinists and which, on the other hand, figure as truly philosophical problems.

Q: You repeat: I have changed; I haven't done what I said I was going to do. But why announce it?

MF: When I wrote the first volume of *The History of Sexuality* some seven or eight years ago, I intended absolutely to write historical studies on sexuality starting from the 16th century and to analyze the development of this knowledge up to the 19th century. But while doing this work I realized that it wouldn't work. An important problem remained: why have we made of sexuality a moral experience? So I shut myself in, abandoned the work I had done on the 17th century and began to go back: first to the 5th century in order to see the beginnings of the Christian experience; then to the immediately preceding period, the end of Antiquity. Finally, three years ago, I completed a study of sexuality in the 5th and 4th centuries B.C. You will say to me: Was it a lapse of attention on your part, at the beginning, or a secret desire that you have hidden and would have revealed at the end? I don't really know. I admit that I don't even want to know. My experience, as it now appears to me, is that I could only do this History of Sexuality properly by taking up again what happened in Antiquity in order to see how sexuality has been manipulated, lived, and modified by a certain number of participants.

Q: In the introduction to *The Use of Pleasure* you present the fundamental problem of your history of sexuality: how are subjects constituted as subjects of desire and pleasure? This question of the subject is, you say, what deflected your study in a new direction. Yet your preceding books appear to ruin the sovereignty of the subject. Isn't this a return to an interminable question which for you will be the crucible of an infinite labor?

MF: An infinite labor?—that's for sure. It's exactly what I collided with and what I wanted to do, since my problem was not to define the moment from which something like the subject appeared but rather the set of processes through which the subject exists with his different problems and obstacles and through forms that are far from being exhausted. It was a matter therefore of reintroducing the problem of the subject that I had more or less left aside in my first studies and of trying to follow the progress and the difficulties through its whole history. Perhaps there is some guile in saying things this way, but in fact what I really wanted to do was to show how the problem of the subject has not ceased to exist throughout this question of sexuality, which in its diversity never ceases to encounter and multiply it.

Q: In your work is this subject the condition of possibility of an experience?

MF: Absolutely not. The experience is the rationalization of a process, itself provisional, which results in a subject, or rather in subjects. I would call subjectivization the process through which results the constitution of a subject, or more exactly, of a subjectivity which is obviously only one of the given possibilities of organizing a consciousness of self.

Q: Reading your books one has the impression that there was no theory of the subject for the Greeks. Could they have had one which was lost with the advent of Christianity?

MF: I don't think one should reconstitute an experience of the subject where it hasn't been formulated. I'm much closer to things than that. And, since no Greek thinker ever found a definition of the subject, never looked for one, I would simply say that there was no subject. Which doesn't mean that the Greeks didn't strive to define the conditions of an experience, but it wasn't an experience of the subject; rather, it was of the individual, insofar as he sought to constitute himself through self-mastery. Classical antiquity never problematized the constitution of the self as subject; inversely, beginning with Christianity, there is an appropriation of morality through the theory of the subject. Yet a moral experience centered essentially on the subject no longer seems to me satisfactory today. For that very reason a number of questions are raised for us in the very same terms in which they were posed in Antiquity. The search for styles of existence as different as possible from each other appears to me to be one of the points around which contemporary research could be initiated in particular groups in the past. The search for a form of morality that would be acceptable to everyone—in the sense that everyone would have to submit to it—strikes me as catastrophic.

But it would be senseless to want to found a modern morality on ancient morality without considering Christian morality. If I have undertaken such a long study, it's so that I can try to uncover how what we call Christian morality was embedded in European morality, and not since the beginnings of the Christian world, but since the morality of Antiquity.

Q: Insofar as you don't affirm any universal truth but raise paradoxes in thought and make of philosophy a permanent question, are you a skeptic?

MF: Absolutely. The only thing that I will not accept in the program of the skeptics is the attempt made to arrive at a certain number of results in a given order—for skepticism has never been total! It tried to raise problems in a given domain and then to valorize in other domains certain notions considered to be useful; secondly, it seems to me that for the skeptics, the ideal was to be optimistic, knowing relatively few things but knowing them in a sure and irrevocable way, whereas I would like to use philosophy in a way that would permit me to limit the domains of knowledge.

Translated by John Johnston

[1] Peter Brown, *The Making of Late Antiquity* (Boston: Harvard University Press, 1978).

BIBLIOGRAPHY & ACKNOWLEDGEMENTS

"Madness Only Exists in Society" was conducted by Jean-Paul Weber and first published in *Le Monde,* July 22, 1961 as "La folie n'existe que dans une société." Translated by Lysa Hochroth.

"André Breton: a Literature of Knowledge" was conducted by Claude Bonnefoy. First published in *Arts-Loisirs* 54, October 5, 1966 as "C'était un nageur entre les mots." Translated by John Johnston.

"The Order of Things" was conducted by Raymond Bellour and first published in *Les Lettres Françaises,* March 31, 1966. Reprinted in Bellour's *Le Livre des autres* (Paris: UGE, 1978). Translated by John Johnston.

"The Discourse of History" was conducted by Raymond Bellour. First published in *Les Lettres Françaises,* June 15, 1967. Reprinted in Bellour's *Le Livre des autres* (Paris: UGE, 1978). Translated by John Johnston.

"History, Discourse and Discontinuity" was published in *Esprit,* 371, May 1968 as "Réponse à une question." First published in English by *Salmagundi,* 20, Summer-Fall 1972. Translated by Anthony Nazzaro.

"Foucault Responds to Sartre," a radio interview conducted by Jean-Pierre El Kabbach, was published—unedited—in *La Quinzaine Littéraire* 46, March 1-15, 1969. Translated by John Johnston.

"The Archaeology of Knowledge" was conducted by Jean-Jacques Brochier. First published in *La Quinzaine Littéraire* in April-May, 1969. Translated by John Johnston.

"The Birth of a World" was conducted by Jean-Michel Palmier. First published in *Le Monde des Livres,* May 3, 1969. Translated by John Johnston.

"Rituals of Exclusion" was conducted by John K. Simon. First published in *Partisan Review,* 38, 2, 1971 as "A Conversation with Michel Foucault."

"Intellectuals and Power," a discussion between Michel Foucault and Gilles Deleuze, was recorded on March 4, 1972. It was published in a special issue of *L'Arc,* no. 49 on Deleuze. First published in *Language, Counter-Memory, Practice: Selected Essays and Interviews.* Ed. by Donald Bouchard. (Ithaca: Cornell University Press, 1977). Translated by Donald Bouchard and Sherry Simon.

"Confining Societies," a panel with Jean-Marie Domenach, Jacques Donzelot, Jacques Juilliard, Phillippe Meyer, René Pechen, Jean-Pierre Treanton and Paul Virilio, was first published as "Table-Ronde" in *Esprit* 413, April-May 1972. Edited version. Translated by Jeanine Herman.

"An Historian of Culture," a debate with Giulio Preti, was first published as "Un Dibatto Foucault-Preti" in *Il Bimestre* 22-23, September-December 1972. Edited by Michele Dziedusszycki. Translated from the Italian by Jared Becker and James Cascaito.

"The Equipments of Power," a discussion with Gilles Deleuze and Félix Guattari, was conducted by Francois Fourquet. First published in *Recherches* 13, December 1973. Special issue on "The Genealogy of the Capital." Translated by Lysa Hochroth.

"On Attica" was conducted by John Simon. First published in *Telos* 19, Spring 1974.

"Film and Popular Memory" was conducted by Pascal Bonitzer and Serge Toubiana. First published in *Cahiers du Cinéma* 251-52, July-August 1974 as "Anti-Rétro." First appeared in English in *Radical Philosophy*, 11, Summer 1975 [UK]. Translated by Martin Jordin.

"Talk Show," a radio-interview conducted by Jacques Chancel, was broadcast by Radio-France on October 3, 1975, with the title "Radioscopy of Michel Foucault." This is an unedited transcript. Translated by Phillis Aronov and Dan McGrawth.

"From Torture to Cellblock" was conducted by Roger-Paul Droit. First published in *Le Monde*, Feb 21, 1975. Translated by John Johnston.

"On Literature" was conducted by Roger-Paul Droit on June 20, 1975. First published in *Le Monde Sans Visa*, September 6, 1986 as "Foucault, passe-frontières de la philosophie." Translated by John Johnston.

"Infantile Sexuality" is the text of the (yet unpublished) paper given by Michel Foucault at the "Schizo-Culture" Conference organized by Semiotext(e) at Columbia University in 1975. Some two thousand people attended the various workshops, lectures, discussions on psychiatry, madness, political repression, Portugal, etc. This was Foucault's first appearance in the United States together with Gilles Deleuze, Félix Guattari and Jean-François Lyotard—the first encounter between post-'68 French theorists and the American "radical" academic constituency. Also present were Ti-Grace Atkinson, William Burroughs, John Cage and Richard Foreman. This paper is an early draft of Foucault's *History of Sexuality*. His lecture (read in English) was interrupted by an agent provocateur, presumably from Larouche's Labor Committee, who accused Foucault of belonging to the CIA. Foucault, very upset, denied the accusation.

"Schizo-Culture: On Prison and Psychiatry," a panel conducted by Sylvère Lotringer with Michel Foucault, Ronald D. Laing, Howie Harp and Judy Clark, was held during the "Schizo-Culture" Conference the morning after Foucault's presentation. It was, once again, interrupted by an "agitator" who publicly accused both Ronald D. Laing and Michel Foucault of being CIA agents. Foucault, who hadn't slept all night, by then had an answer ready: "Yes," he replied in English, "I belong to the CIA, Lotringer belongs to the CIA, everyone in this room belongs to the CIA—except you, who belong to the KGB!" The whole room cracked up, including the provocateur, and that was that.

Judy Clark, who represented the ex-cons at the Conference, was subsequently arrested during what Dhoruba Bin Wahad called the "Brinks expropriation operation" in New York in 1982. She is presently incarcerated at the Bedford Correctional Facility in Bedford, NY.

"Paul's Story," a discussion with René Feret, was first published in *Cahiers du Cinéma*, 262-3, January 1976. Translated by Lysa Hochroth.

"Sade: Sargent of Sex" was conducted by Gérard Dupont. First published in *Cinématographe*, 16, December 75-January 76. Translated by John Johnston.

"The Politics of Soviet Crime" was conducted by K.S. Karol. First published in *Le Nouvel Observateur*, 585, January 26, 1976 as "Crimes et chatiments en U.R.S.S. et ailleurs." First appeared in *Partisan Review*, 43, 3, 1976. Translated by Mollie Horwitz.

"The Social Extension of the Norm" was conducted by P. Werner. First published in *Politique Hebdo* 212, March 1976. Translated by Lysa Hochroth.

"Sorcery and Madness" was conducted by Roland Jaccard. First published in *Le Monde*, April 23, 1976. Translated by John Johnston.

"I, Pierre Rivière" was conducted by Pascal Kane. First published in *Cahiers du Cinéma*, November 1976 as "Entretien avec Michel Foucault." Translated by John Johnston.

"Power Affects the Body" was conducted by Lucette Finas. First published in *La Quinzaine Littéraire* 247, January 1-15, 1977 as "Les rapports de pouvoir passent à l'intérieur des corps." Translated by Jeanine Herman.

"The End of the Monarchy of Sex" was conducted by Bernard-Henry Lévy. First published in *Le Nouvel Observateur*, March 12, 1977. Translated by Dudley M. Marchi.

"The Eye of Power" was conducted by Jean-Pierre Barou and Michelle Perrot. First published in Jeremy Bentham, *Le Panoptique*. (Paris: Pierre Belfont, 1977). First appeared in English in *Semiotext(e)'s* "Schizo-Culture" issue, III, 2, 1978. Translated by Mark S. Seem. Modified translation.

"The Anxiety of Judging," a debate with Jean Laplanche and Robert Badinter, was first published in *Le Nouvel Observateur*, 655, May 30, 1977. Edited version. Translated by John Johnston.

"Clarifications on the Question of Power" was conducted by Pasquale Pasquino in February 1978. First published in *Aut Aut*, 167-68, 1978. Translated from the Italian by James Cascaito.

"The Danger of Child Sexuality," a dialogue with Guy Hocquenghem and Jean Danet, was produced by Roger Pillaudin and broadcast by France Culture on April 4, 1978. It was published as "La Loi de la pudeur" in *Recherches* 37, April 1979. An edited version of this discussion was first published in English in *Semiotext(e)'s* "Loving Boys/Loving Children" issue, Summer 1980 in a translation by Daniel Moshenberg. This is the complete version, published in Michel Foucault, *Politics, Philosophy, Culture*. Ed. by Lawrence D. Kritzman. (New York: Routledge, 1988). Translated by Alan Sheridan with the title "Sexual Morality and the Law."

"The Impossible Prison," a panel discussion with French historians, was held on May 20, 1978. First published in Michelle Perrot, ed., *L'Impossible prison.* (Paris: Editions du Seuil, 1980). Translated by Colin Gordon as "Questions of Method," *Ideology and Consciousness,* no. 8, Spring 1981.

"White Magic and Black Gown" was first published in *Actes, cahiers d'action juridique, Annexe* 5, as "Table ronde sur l'expertise psychiatrique." Reprinted in *Délinquances et ordre. (*Maspero, Paris: 1978). Edited version. Translated by Lysa Hochroth.

"Paris-Berlin" was first published in *Spiegel,* 44, October 30, 1978. On the "Paris-Berlin" exhibition held at the Centre Pompidou in Paris in 1978. First appeared in English in *New German Critique,* 16, Winter 1979 as "Spiegel Interview with Michel Foucault on 'Paris-Berlin.'" Translated from the German by J.D. Steakley.

"The Simplest of Pleasures" was first published in *Le Gai Pied* 1, April 1979. First published in English in *Fag Rag* 29, 1979. Translated by Mike Riegle and Gilles Barbedette.

"Truth is in the Future" was conducted by M. Dillon and first published in *Three Penny Review,* Vol. 1, No. 1, 1980 as "Conversation with Michel Foucault."

"The Masked Philosopher" was conducted by Christian Delacampagne. First published in *Le Monde,* April 6, 1980. Foucault's identity was not divulged. Translated by John Johnston.

"Friendship as a Way of Life" was conducted by René de Coccatty, Jean Danet and Jean Le Bitoux. First published in *Le Gai Pied* 25, April 1981. Translated by John Johnston.

"Passion According to Werner Schroeter," a discussion with Werner Schroeter, was recorded by Gérard Courant in Paris on Dec 3, 1981. First published as "A Conversation" in Gérard Courant, *Werner Schroeter.* (Paris: Cinémathèque Francaise et Goethe Institute, 1982). Translated by John Johnston.

"Sexual Choice, Sexual Act" was conducted by James O'Higgins in March 1982. First published in *Salmagundi,* 58-59, Fall-Winter 1982. Translated by James O'Higgins.

"Space, Knowledge and Power" was conducted by Paul Rabinow. First published in *Skyline, the Architecture and Design Review,* March 1982. Reprinted in P. Rabinow, ed., *Foucault Reader.* (New York: Pantheon Books, 1984).

"How Much Does it Cost to Tell the Truth" was conducted by Gerard Raulet. First published in *Spuren,* 1 & 2, May & June 1983. Translated from the German by Mia Foret and Marion Martius.

"History and Homosexuality" was conducted by J.P. Joecker, M. Ouerd and A. Sanzio. First published in *Masques,* 13, Spring 1982 as "L'Homosexualité dans l'antiquité." Translated by John Johnston.

"An Ethics of Pleasure" was conducted in English by Stephen Riggins on June 22, 1982 in Toronto. First published in *Ethos,* Volume I, 2, Autumn 1983 as "Michel Foucault: An Interview by Stephen Riggins."

"Sex, Power and the Politics of Identity" was conducted by Bob Gallagher and Alexander Wilson in Toronto in June, 1982. First published in *The Advocate,* No. 400, August 7, 1984.

"The Cultural Insularity of Contemporary Music," a discussion with Pierre Boulez, was first published in *CNAC,* May-June 1983 as "Foucault/Boulez: La Musique contemporaine et le public." Translated by Lysa Hochroth.

"Archeology of a Passion" was conducted by Charles Ruas in Paris on September 15, 1983. First published in *Le Magazine Littéraire* 221, July-August, 1985 as "Archéologie d'une passion." First appeared in English as a Postscript to Michel Foucault, *Death and the Labyrinth: The World of Raymond Roussel.* (New York: Doubleday & Co, 1986.) Translated by Charles Ruas as "An Interview with Michel Foucault."

"What Our Present Is" was conducted by André Berten at the School of Criminology of the University of Louvain, Belgium, in 1983. First published in *Cahiers du GRIFFE,* No. 37-38, 1988. Translated by Lysa Hochroth.

"Problematics" was conducted by Thomas Zummer on November 1983. First published in *Crash: nostalgia for the absence of cyberspace,* Robert Reynolds & Thomas Zummer, eds. (New York: Thread Waxing Space, 1994.)

"What Calls for Punishment?" was conducted by Foulek Ringelheim in December 1983 and corrected by Foucault on February 14, 1984. First published in *Revue de l'Université de Bruxelles,* 1984, with the title "Punir mon bon souci, Pour une raison pénale." Translated by John Johnston.

"The Ethics of the Concern for Self" was conducted by Raul Fornet-Betancourt, Helmut Becker and Alfredo Gomez-Muller on January 20, 1984. First published in *Concordia,* 6, 1984 [Valencia, Spain]. Translated by Phillis Aronov and Dan McGrawth.

"An Aesthetics of Existence" was conducted by Alessandro Fontana on April 15-16, 1984. First published in *Le Monde Aujourd'hui,* July 15-16, 1984. Translated by John Johnston.

"The Concern for Truth" was conducted by François Ewald. First published in *Magazine Littéraire,* May 1984. Translated by John Johnston.

"The Return of Morality" was conducted by Gilles Barbedette and Andre Scala on May 29, 1984. First published in *Les Nouvelles,* June 28-July 5, 1984. Translated by John Johnston. It is, reportedly, the last interview Foucault gave before his death on June 25, 1984.

T.A.Z. THE TEMPORARY AUTONOMOUS ZONE, ONTOLOGICAL ANARCHY, POETIC TERRORISM   Hakim Bey
THIS IS YOUR FINAL WARNING!   Thom Metzger
CASSETTE MYTHOS   THE NEW MUSIC UNDERGROUND   Robin James, ed.
FRIENDLY FIRE   Bob Black
THE DAUGHTER   Roberta Allen
THE LIZARD CLUB   Steve Abbott
MAGPIE REVERIES   The Iconographic Mandalas of James Koehnline
FIRST & LAST EMPERORS   THE ABSOLUTE STATE & THE BODY OF THE DESPOT   Kenneth Dean & Brian Massumi
INVISIBLE GOVERNANCE   THE ART OF AFRICAN MICROPOLITICS   David Hecht & Maliqalim Simone
ON ANARCHY & SCHIZOANALYSIS   Rolando Perez
GOD & PLASTIC SURGERY   MARX, NIETZSCHE, FREUD & THE OBVIOUS   Jeremy Barris
MARX BEYOND MARX   LESSONS ON THE GRUNDRISSE   Antonio Negri
THE NARRATIVE BODY   Eldon Garnet
MODEL CHILDREN   INSIDE THE REPUBLIC OF RED SCARVES   Paul Thorez
ABOUT FACE   RACE IN POSTMODERN AMERICA   Maliqalim Simone
COLUMBUS & OTHER CANNIBALS   THE WĒTIKO DISEASE & THE WHITE MAN   Jack Forbes
METATRON   Sol Yurick
SCANDAL   ESSAYS IN ISLAMIC HERESY   Peter Lamborn Wilson
CLIPPED COINS   JOHN LOCKE'S PHILOSOPHY OF MONEY   Constantine G. Caffentzis
HORSEXE   ESSAY ON TRANSSEXUALITY   Catherine Millot
THE TOUCH   Michael Brownstein
ARCANE OF REPRODUCTION   HOUSEWORK, PROSTITUTION, LABOR & CAPITAL   Leopoldina Fortunati
TROTSKYISM & MAOISM   A. Belden Fields
FILM & POLITICS IN THE THIRD WORLD   John Downing, ed.
ENRAGÉS & SITUATIONISTS IN THE OCCUPATION MOVEMENT   René Viénet
ZEROWORK   THE ANTI-WORK ANTHOLOGY   Bob Black & Tad Kepley, eds.
MIDNIGHT OIL   WORK, ENERGY, WAR, 1973 – 1992   Midnight Notes
PURE WAR   Paul Virilio & Sylvère Lotringer
WALKING THROUGH CLEAR WATER IN A POOL PAINTED BLACK   Cookie Mueller
STILL BLACK, STILL STRONG   Dhoruba bin Wahad, Mumia Abu-Jamal, Assata Shakur
HANNIBAL LECTER, MY FATHER   Kathy Acker
HOW I BECAME ONE OF THE INVISIBLE   David Rattray
GONE TO CROATAN   ORIGINS OF NORTH AMERICAN DROPOUT CULTURE   Ron Sakolsky & James Koehnline, eds.
SEMIOTEXT(E) ARCHITECTURE   Hraztan Zeitlian, ed.
SEMIOTEXT(E) USA   Jim Fleming & Peter Lamborn Wilson, eds.
OASIS   Maliqalim Simone, et al., eds.
POLYSEXUALITY   François Peraldi, ed.
THE ARCHEOLOGY OF VIOLENCE   Pierre Clastres
FATAL STRATEGIES   Jean Baudrillard
THE LOST DIMENSION   Paul Virilio
THE AESTHETICS OF DISAPPEARANCE   Paul Virilio
NOT ME   Eileen Myles
SICK BURN CUT   Deran Ludd
NEW FUCK YOU   ADVENTURES IN LESBIAN READING   Eileen Myles & Liz Kotz, eds.
THE CUTMOUTH LADY   Romy Ashby
READING BROOKE SHIELDS   Eldon Garnet
69 WAYS TO PLAY THE BLUES   Jürg Laederach
POPULAR DEFENSE & ECOLOGICAL STRUGGLES   Paul Virilio
CRACKING THE MOVEMENT   SQUATTING BEYOND THE MEDIA   Foundation for the Advancement of Illegal Knowledge

SEMIOTEXT(E) SF   Rudy Rucker, Robert Anton Wilson & Peter Lamborn Wilson, eds.
BOLO'BOLO   P.M.
SIMULATIONS   Jean Baudrillard
GERMANIA   Heiner Müller
COMMUNISTS LIKE US   Félix Guattari & Toni Negri
THE ECSTASY OF COMMUNICATION   Jean Baudrillard
IN THE SHADOW OF THE SILENT MAJORITIES   Jean Baudrillard
FORGET FOUCAULT   Jean Baudrillard
CHAOSOPHY   Félix Guattari
MICROPOLITICS OF DESIRE   Félix Guattari
CHAOS AND COMPLEXITY   Félix Guattari
FOUCAULT LIVE   Michel Foucault
LOOKING BACK ON THE END OF THE WORLD   Baudrillard, Virilio, et al.
REMARKS ON MARX   Michel Foucault
IF YOU'RE A GIRL   Ann Rower
SPEED AND POLITICS   Paul Virilio
NOMADOLOGY: THE WAR MACHINE   Gilles Deleuze & Félix Guattari
ON THE LINE   Gilles Deleuze & Félix Guattari
DRIFTWORKS   Jean-François Lyotard
THE MADAME REALISM COMPLEX   Lynne Tillman
THE DAMNED UNIVERSE OF CHARLES FORT   Louis Kaplan
RADIOTEXT(E)   Neil Strauss, Dave Mandl, et al, eds.
¡ZAPATISTAS! Documents of the New Mexican Revolution   Zapatistas
SEMIOTEXT(E) CANADAS   Jordan Zinovich, et al , eds.
DRUNKEN BOAT Art, Anarchy, Rebellion   Max Blechman, ed.
WIGGLING WISHBONE Stories of Patasexual Speculation   Bart Plantenga
THE ROOT IS MAN   Dwight Macdonald
THIS WORLD WE MUST LEAVE   Jacques Camatte
FORMAT & ANXIETY Paul Goodman Critiques the Media   Paul Goodman
FUTURE PRIMITIVE   John Zerzan
WHORE CARNIVAL   Shannon Bell
THE ELECTRONIC DISTURBANCE   Critical Art Ensemble
ELECTRONIC CIVIL DISOBEDIENCE   Critical Art Ensemble
THE UNHOLY BIBLE Hebrew Literature of the Kingdom Period   Jacob Rabinowitz
WILD CHILDREN   Mandl & Wilson, eds.
CALIBAN & THE WITCHES   Silvia Federici
ASSASSINATION RHAPSODY   Derek Pell
X—TEXTS   Derek Pell
BLOOD & VOLTS Edison, Tesla & the Electric Chair   Th. Metzger
DAY IN THE LIFE Tales from the Lower East Side   Moore & Gosciak, eds.
FILE UNDER POPULAR Critical Writing on Music   Chris Cutler
GULLIVER   Michael Ryan
SOUNDING OFF   Music as Subversion, Resistance, Revolution   Sakolsky and Ho, eds.
UNBEARABLES   The Unbearables
SPECTACULAR TIMES   Larry Law
CRIMES OF CULTURE   Richard Kostelanetz
BAMN: BY ANY MEANS NECESSARY Outlaw Manifestoes & Ephemera, 1965—1970   Stansill & Mairowitz, eds.
SOCIAL OVERLOAD   Henri-Pierre Jeudy
PIRATE UTOPIAS Moorish Corsairs & European Renegadoes   Peter Lamborn Wilson